Online Instruments, Data Collection, and Electronic Measurements:

Organizational Advancements

Mihai C. Bocarnea
Regent University, USA

Rodney A. Reynolds
California Lutheran University, USA

Jason D. Baker
Regent University, USA

Managing Director:	Lindsay Johnston
Book Production Manager:	Jennifer Romanchak
Publishing Systems Analyst:	Adrienne Freeland
Managing Editor:	Joel Gamon
Development Editor:	Myla Merkel
Assistant Acquisitions Editor:	Kayla Wolfe
Typesetter:	Henry Ulrich
Cover Design:	Nick Newcomer

Published in the United States of America by
Information Science Reference (an imprint of IGI Global)
701 E. Chocolate Avenue
Hershey PA 17033
Tel: 717-533-8845
Fax: 717-533-8661
E-mail: cust@igi-global.com
Web site: http://www.igi-global.com

Library of Congress Cataloging-in-Publication Data

Online instruments, data collection, and electronic measurements: organizational advancements / Mihai C. Bocarnea, Rodney A. Reynolds, and Jason D. Baker, editors.
      pages cm
  Includes bibliographical references and index.
  Summary: "This book aims to assist researchers in both understanding and utilizing online data collection by providing methodological knowledge related to online research, and by presenting information about the empirical quality, the availability, and the location of specific online instruments"-- Provided by publisher.
  ISBN 978-1-4666-2172-5 (hardcover) -- ISBN 978-1-4666-2174-9 (print & perpetual access) -- ISBN (invalid) 978-1-4666-2173-2 (ebook) 1. Social sciences--Statistical methods--Computer programs. 2. Surveys--Methodology--Computer programs. 3. Internet questionnaires. 4. Automatic data collection systems. I. Bocarnea, Mihai C., 1960- II. Reynolds, Rodney A. III. Baker, Jason D.
  HA32.O55 2013
  001.4'33--dc23
                                  2012019423

British Cataloguing in Publication Data
A Cataloguing in Publication record for this book is available from the British Library.

All work contributed to this book is new, previously-unpublished material. The views expressed in this book are those of the authors, but not necessarily of the publisher.

Editorial Advisory Board

Table of Contents

Section 3
New Measurements

Section 4
Uses and Comparisons

Detailed Table of Contents

Section 1
Methodological Issues

Chapter 1
Yael Brender-Ilan, Ariel University Center of Samaria, Israel
Gideon Vinitzky, Ariel University Center of Samaria, Israel

In recent years, there has been an increase in academic studies that examine the advantages and disadvantages of using e-questionnaires in organizations, but these studies have tended to ignore the potential differences between human resource (HR) managers and HR consultants with regards to using this tool. This chapter examines the use of e-questionnaires from the point of view of both types of practitioners. The study includes a qualitative exploratory survey, as well as a quantitative survey. T-tests, cluster analysis, and principal component analysis are performed and results support the three propositions that are presented. Specifically, it was found that (a) HR consultants and HR managers differ in the ranking of factors they think are important when deciding whether to use e-questionnaires; (b) preference differences exist between HR managers and HR consultants - managers are more directed by organizational constraints than consultants; and (c) the groupings for e-questionnaire preferences, compared to paper-and-pencil questionnaires, are consistent with Caldwell's four roles of HR managers. The chapter concludes with implications and suggestions for future research.

Chapter 2
Philip Salem, Texas State University, USA

Most organizational research employs either quantitative or qualitative methods. Furthermore, users of one methodology often dismiss those who use another. The purpose of this report was to describe how researchers could use mixed methods, especially online. Researchers often begin investigations with paradigmatic assumptions or multiple constructs that should lead to mixed methods. However, quantitative methodological assumptions may seem to contradict qualitative methodological assumptions, and scholars have found it easier and quicker to deliver results adopting only one methodology. Additionally, researchers may be resistant because making high quality inferences from mixed methods might seem too demanding. This chapter describes how one researcher grappled with these challenges when using mixed methods off-line. Online technologies contribute to resolving some difficulties more easily.

Chapter 3

Benjamin J. Bates, The University of Tennessee, USA
Ben Birch, The University of Tennessee, USA

The development of digital computing and the growth of the Internet have opened up new opportunities to engage in online research. These online research practices involving human subjects, often involving relatively new technologies, can create tension between the online investigator and the Institutional Review Boards (IRBs) who are required to review and approve such research prior to data collection. This chapter aims to reduce this tension by discussing the associated ethics issues and applicable federal regulations, identifying specific concerns from the perspective of IRBs, and offering suggestions as to how best to address these concerns in applications in a way that can hopefully serve both the researcher and the review board.

Section 2
Analysis of Established Measures

Chapter 4

Audrey Barrett, University of San Diego, USA
Fred Galloway, University of San Diego, USA

The Nonprofit Ethics Survey serves as the only empirically supported survey instrument specifically designed for nonprofit organizations to assess their ethical culture. Development of the instrument occurred through the use of principal components analysis conducted on a sample of 530 nonprofit affiliates. The results of the analysis yielded six parsimonious scales integral to assessing nonprofit ethics. To evaluate the internal reliability of each scale a measure of Cronbach's Alpha was also calculated. The alpha coefficients ranged from 0.86 - 0.94, indicating the survey provides a reliable means of measuring the constructs integral to assessing organizational ethics in nonprofit agencies. The creation of a statistically sound instrument designed for use with nonprofit organizations ensures that nonprofit leaders have the needed tools to accurately self-assess.

Chapter 5

Dan Lawson, Ashland University, USA

The Life Styles Inventory, developed by J. Clayton Lafferty, uses a combination of respected psychological and managerial theories to help individuals identify their beliefs, values, behaviors, and assumptions. This instrument presents twenty statements for each of the twelve life styles believed to influence the way we think and behave. The LSI 1 instrument is a self-assessment whereas the LSI 2 uses the same format and life styles to assess an individual through input from five or more other people. When used in combination, the two instruments use consensual validity to identify strengths and weaknesses for the development of a self-improvement plan. This chapter discussed the theoretical background of the Life Styles Inventory, as well as instrument validity and reliability. A description of the results upon taking the instrument is included, along with commentary on the instrument's utility. Web address, cost, terms, and definitions appear at the end of the chapter.

This chapter focuses on the most widely used and known leadership instrument: The Leadership Behavior Description Questionnaire (LBDQ). The LBDQ, and its sibling the LBDQ-XII, have been around for more than 50 years and are still being used today. As a result, the purpose of this chapter is to examine the instrument by summarizing its background, and giving a perspective on the instrument's reliability and validity. This was accomplished by looking at the LBDQ and LBDQ-XII's long history, how it has been applied over the years, while focusing on the scales main factors of Consideration and Initiation of Structure. Additionally, many analyses of the instruments (LBDQ and LBDQ-XII) were reviewed to support the instruments robust reliability and validity. Lastly, the location and cost of the instruments were revealed in order for the reader to utilize the instrument under study.

Chapter 7

Self-monitoring represents individual ability to control expressive behavior and self-presentation. This chapter offers insight into the development, test, and uses of the self-monitoring instrument. A central focus is on the research on the relationship between self-monitoring and impression management, leader emergence, career success, and citizenship behaviors.

Chapter 8

In this chapter, fatalism is conceptualized as a set of health beliefs that encompass the dimensions of predetermination, luck, and pessimism. It is argued that such fatalistic beliefs can be extended from health issues to organizational context as well. A recently developed fatalism scale is assessed, as well as other existing instruments using three criteria: (a) item content, (b) associations among the items, and (c) associations between the items and external variables. Available empirical evidence shows that the new scale is uni-dimensional, and demonstrates good construct validity as well as scale reliability. Implications for procrastination are discussed.

Section 3
New Measurements

Chapter 9

This chapter presents items comprising three scales that measure servant leadership using three key dimensions: service, humility, and vision. The instrument was used to measure servant leadership behaviors experienced by followers in the United States and Ghana. Reliability and validity evidence is included from two research studies. A discussion of the relationship of servant leadership behaviors with employee outcomes assessed in these studies concludes the chapter.

This study presents seven scales for the seven beatitudes found in Matthew 5: 3-10. Separate scales were created rather than a conceptual instrument with seven factors since the 'concept' of 'Beatitude' does not exist and since the seven beatitudes are related in various ways making them highly correlated. The seven scales were reduced to five items each. The resultant Chronbach alpha scores were .86, .95, .89, .92, .93, .93, .92 for each of the scales. The value of the seven scales lies in their ability to assist researchers to compare leadership effectiveness with the seven representative values and, in time after normative data is developed, to offer a measure to help with leadership selection.

Chapter 11

The Inventory of Leader Sternness (ILS) is a new leadership construct designed to measure sternness in an adult self-directed leader. Sternness, as a leadership construct, is derived from the writings of Sun Tzu in The Art of War. The author of this chapter developed the ILS to measure three co-occurring behavioral intentions of sternness: (a) a willingness to establish obedience through rewards and punishments within limits, (b) consistency in actions to ensure good behavior through rituals and respect, and (c) a determination to do the difficult tasks of leadership. The ILS is a valid and reliable instrument for use in the assessment of sternness in an adult self-directed leader.

Because shepherding is one of the oldest occupations of humanity, the metaphor of the shepherd as leader dates back thousands of years and is a universal image. Therefore, the shepherd leader metaphor is an ideal vehicle through which to study leadership. The Shepherd Leadership Inventory (SLI) measures the degree to which individual leaders are leading as shepherd leadership in the workplace. Through the initial study of the shepherd leader metaphor beginning with the Scriptures and continuing through modern authors, it was determined shepherd leaders are leaders who insure the wellbeing of their followers through the three primary leader behaviors of guiding, providing, and protecting. The Shepherd Leadership Inventory (SLI) incorporates items to assess these behaviors and was validated through the use of principal component factor analysis. This chapter discusses the background and development of the SLI including reporting on the reliability and validity of the instrument. The results of the inventory are discussed along with commentary on the SLI's relevance to researchers and practitioners. Information regarding cost and location, as well as additional reading recommendations, is included.

Chapter 13

The purpose of this research is to develop a direct and concise perceived leader integrity instrument that is posed from a positive perspective. The integrity construct in this study is developed from the tradition of moral philosophy and virtue ethics. The integrity construct in this study incorporates two aspects of integrity found in the literature, namely value-behavior congruence and a requirement that this congruence be grounded in morality. The moral philosophy used in this study to ground the integrity construct is virtue ethics as proposed by ancient philosophy and later maintained by Christian virtue ethics in the middle ages. An expert panel was used to establish content validity and construct validity/reliability was established via analysis of three samples of Air Force personnel associated with the U-2 pilot community. Overall, the Leader Integrity Assessment 15 was found valid and reliable and the integrity construct was found unidimensional as hypothesized.

Chapter 14

The focus in this chapter is a proposal for a measure of followership with three dimensions: resistant follower, compliant follower, and mature follower. The chapter contains an internet link to specific items and a format for the measure. The rationale centers on various theoretic views about followership. The chapter provides suggestions for using of the measure within organizations. The conclusion centers on a program for future research.

The Discernment Practices Indicator (DPI) reports three-factors: (a) Courage, (b) Intuition, and (c) Faith with Cronbach alpha values of (a) .85, (b) .89, and (c) .85, respectively. The Courage factor addresses the leader's mental and moral courage; willingness to accept uncertainty; use of common sense; ability to seek new ways to look at old things; see a future full of possibilities, believing in the equality of all people; and to be firm, but loving, in addressing issues. The Intuition factor addresses the leader's understanding of his or her emotions; willingness to make decisions, based on a hunch; as well as paying attention to body cues or thoughts that may flash across the mind. The Faith factor addresses the leader's use of quiet time (to include prayer and meditation) to reflect and find meaning; use of principles of faith as guidance; as well as incorporating religious beliefs in professional undertakings.

The Inventory of Learner Persistence (ILP) was designed to assess persistence in learning and specifically within the context of autonomous learning. Autonomous learning is defined as the manifestation of persistence along with desire, resourcefulness, and initiative in learning; learner autonomy is defined as the characteristic or personal attribute of the individual to exhibit agency or intentional behavior. Thus, persistence in learning is the exhibition of volition, goal directedness and self-regulation. The development of items for the ILP provides a theoretical framework for defining persistence from a cognitive and psychological perspective and provides a mechanism for understanding persistence from other than a post hoc behavioral standpoint. The implications of such assessments can provide an analysis of where a learner may be in terms of their development and readiness for learning that will require persistent skills for success.

Section 4
Uses and Comparisons

The present book chapter focuses on e-leadership, reviewing and discussing the latest developments in new (e-)leadership conceptions, such as transformational leadership and others. Alongside personality tests and group process development units that were built from the Existential Mapping Process, the tool contains modules that help leaders and team members to identify their Ohio State leadership styles. The VTT relates the results of the self- and other-questionnaires regarding team structure, development, and modifications and improvement of leadership skills.

The instrument described in this chapter is designed for instructors of e-learning, for the purpose of giving faculty an opportunity to identify, express, and suggest features in a Course Management System (CMS) that they feel are pedagogically important. Appropriate for use in universities or corporations, this survey can provide instructors with a greater voice in the CMS decision making process, thereby giving pedagogy a greater influence on the practice of technology implementation in the learning environment. This chapter describes the construction of the survey, its psychometric properties, and preliminary data gathered at a private university in New York State. The findings differentiate among CMS' features that faculty consider important, not important, or feel neutral about. Further, the results underscore the differences between previous users and non-users of CMSs in assigning importance to types of features. The author discusses the implications of using the survey in both educational and corporate settings with the purpose of helping institutions that utilize e-learning to meet the educational standard set by current best practices.

Chapter 19

Jason D. Baker, Regent University, USA

The commonality among online instruments – regardless of discipline – is the use of online tools to administer the electronic measurements, collect participant responses, and aggregate the results for data analysis. Under the heading of software as a service (SaaS) or cloud computing, online survey software makes it possible for individuals and organizations to easily develop and administer online instruments. This chapter provides a background into SaaS and cloud computing, profiles three leading online survey software tools – SurveyMonkey, Qualtrics, and LimeSurvey – along with the PollEverywhere online and mobile polling tool. The chapter concludes with the corresponding cost and links to these online survey tools along with relevant terms and resources.

Foreword

This is an exciting and unprecedented time for organizational scholars and practitioners who utilize surveys and established measures. The growth of the Internet and developments surrounding digital computing have greatly expanded opportunities for survey research with online tools designed to administer electronic measures, collect participant responses, and aggregate the results for data analysis.

Technological advances in computer hardware and software have enabled researchers and practitioners to create complex questionnaires, responses to which can be stored, analyzed, and compared at multiple points in time. Surveys of organizational members' attitudes, morale, training needs, learning, and traits can be conducted electronically -- rather than with paper questionnaires -- for reasons of ease, efficiency, speed, wider reach, accuracy in data entry, and lower costs. Nonetheless, challenges with low(er) response rate, errors in comprehension, and respondents' difficulties with the electronic interface among others must be confronted.

Readers will find the chapters in this much-needed publication to be invaluable in managing these opportunities and challenges while collecting information from organizational members and stakeholders.

Some chapters in this exciting volume offer *new measures* for organizational researchers and practitioners: a survey designed for nonprofit organizations to assess their ethical culture, and several inventories to help individuals identify their assumptions, beliefs, values, behaviors associated with life styles, discernment, and fatalism. Two chapters provide major reviews of research utilizing the Self-Monitoring Scale and the Leadership Behavior Description Questionnaire.

Several chapters introduce highly original *leadership inventories*, including measures of leader sternness, leader shepherding, perceived leader integrity, servant leadership, and followership. A related chapter reviews the Virtual Team Trainer, an online tool that enables respondents to assess team leader and team member behaviors and – through embedded modules – to improve their skills. This is an intriguing example of the ways in which information technology systems influence and are influenced by new leadership behaviors, processes, and outcomes.

Two *mixed methods studies* are reported in other chapters. One includes how researchers might use online technologies to resolve difficulties associated with mixed methods designs in off-line investigations. The other finds differences between human resource (HR) managers and HR consultants with regard to using e-questionnaires in organizations. In a complementary third chapter, suggestions are offered for addressing *Institutional Review Board* ethical concerns as well as federal and state regulations related to online research including human subjects. Another chapter profiles prominent *online survey software tools* (e.g., SurveyMonkey, Qualtrics, and LimeSurvey) as well as the PollEverywhere online and mobile polling tool.

Two chapters offer measures that are useful resources for providing or assessing organizational members' *learning*. One instrument enables e-learning instructors (in universities, corporations, and government agencies) to propose features in a Course Management System (CMS) that they feel are pedagogically important. The other instrument is designed to assess persistence in learning and specifically within the context of autonomous learning.

Online Instruments, Data Collection, and Electronic Measurements: Organizational Advancements is an important resource. It conjoins practical information about online research with profiles of specific new measures, thus making this volume indispensable to at least three audiences. First, organizational scholars and practitioners will learn much in these chapters that will help them understand and manage the advantages and challenges of online survey data collection. Second, organizational researchers who gather data via online surveys will find a wealth of new tools here as well as sage advice on matters ranging from study design, use of online tools, and data analysis techniques. Finally, the nascent state of several of these measures sets an agenda for continued validation of the instruments by organizational researchers in many disciplines.

David R. Seibold
University of California, Santa Barbara, USA

David R. Seibold joined the Department of Communication as a Professor in 1990, and served as Department Chair from 1998-2004. Since 2000 he also has been Director of UCSB's interdisciplinary Graduate Program in Management Practice, a part of the Technology Management Program in the College of Engineering. Formerly he was a faculty member at Purdue University (1975-1976) and the University of Illinois at Urbana-Champaign (1976-1990), having earned a B.A. at Iona College (Summa Cum Laude), an M.A. at the University of Michigan, and a Ph.D. at Michigan State University. He also has been a distinguished visiting professor and lectured at more than two dozen universities worldwide, and he has received several teaching honors including campus teaching excellence and professional society teaching awards. Dave has published more than 125 scholarly works -- books, journal articles, chapters, and delivered more than 200 conference papers and scholarly presentations, in four areas that represent his continuing research interests: communication and interpersonal influence (persuasion, compliance-gaining, motivation); group communication(structuration of decision making, argument and influence processes, facilitation of meetings, problem-solving techniques); organizational communication(participation structures and processes, temporality in workgroups, innovation and organizational change, management and strategic communication); and applied communication(bridging theory and practice, organizational training and development, evaluation of communication programs). Recipient of more than a dozen "top paper" awards at scholarly conferences, his published research also has been recognized by the National Communication Association with Golden Anniversary Monograph Awards in 1976, 1981, and 1986, and the Charles Woolbert Research Award in 1989 for research that has stood the test of time. In 2000 and 2008 he received the Dennis S. Gouran Research Award from the NCA Group Communication Division for the best article published in the preceding year by a division member. He also was the 1999 recipient of the Gerald M. Phillips Award for Distinguished Applied Communication Scholarship. In 2004 Dave was named a Distinguished Scholar by the National Communication Association, its highest award for a lifetime of scholarly achievement. In 2009, he also was elected an ICA Fellow, the International Communication Association's highest honor for career contributions to the study of human communication. A past editor of the Journal of Applied Communication Research (1997-1999), Dave has been member of the editorial boards of 13 communication journals (under 24 different editors) since 1978, has he reviewed for numerous other journals including Administrative Science Quarterly, Journal of Language and Social Psychology, Human Relations, and Academy of Management Review, for Stanford University Press, and for numerous commercial publishers.

Preface

Organizational advancement is no longer defined by charismatic leaders guiding via intuition. The near-ubiquity of the Internet and a growing willingness among individuals to self-report all manner of behavior has combined with an increased interest in accountability to prompt a new type of organizational leadership. Evidence-based management, and its educational counterpart data-driven decision-making, seeks to incorporate relevant and timely analysis of behavioral information to guide organizational decisions.

In *Digital Natives, Digital Immigrants*, Marc Prensky distinguished between the native speakers of the digital language of the Internet and the immigrants who have learned the Internet as a second language. For those of us who can remember life before the Internet, we're mere immigrants who still enter the digital environment with an accent. Yet the digital natives abandoned email years ago because it was too slow, reveal more details in Facebook and Twitter posts than at the dinner table, and expect that companies and organizations will customize their products and experiences to personal preferences and desires.

Consider the average user accessing the Internet from a computer or smartphone. The odds are quite high that during activities as simple as checking email or reading news headlines, this person will be offered at least one opportunity to participate in an online survey. Perhaps it's an online questionnaire about how to improve the look of a particular web site, or a political survey seeking feedback on a candidate's position, or questions gauging the effectiveness of an online marketing campaign. Academics have also capitalized on the benefits of online surveys by using the Internet for online course evaluations, faculty benefit surveys, and data collection for dissertation and article research. Similarly, organizations have sought to use psychometric instruments and online feedback systems to assess their own effectiveness, steer employees into leadership positions, and determine customer preferences and satisfaction. Even individuals are including short polls and quizzes on their personal blogs and social media pages for fun and insight.

If we've indeed transitioned into an evidence-based or data-driven world, it behooves us to understand not only what's available in the realm of online instruments but how to effectively use the Internet for data collection and electronic measurement. What are the challenges associated with using the Internet for online research? What programs are available to create and administer online questionnaires? Are there existing instruments online that I can use in my research? Can I improve my organization by having employees participate in online surveys and tests? How do I know whether such instruments are valid and reliable?

Online Instruments, Data Collection, and Electronic Measurements: Organizational Advancements provides answers to these and many other questions. This book is a valuable resource for organizational leaders and academics alike who are interested in the use of the Internet for data collection and a source-book for those interested in finding available online instruments for their use. The focus on organizational leadership instruments combined with practical and ethical issues associated with online data collection makes this a unique contribution to the field.

The seventeen chapters in this book are divided into four major sections. The first section on methodological issues contains three chapters that address particular issues about methods for the use of electronic measurements in organizational settings. The second section features five chapters analyzing and reviewing established measurements that can be employed within organizational contexts to support leadership, ethics, and self-monitoring. The third section of the handbook contains eight chapters discussing the development, testing, and application of relatively new measurements for use within organizations. The majority of these relate to various aspects of leadership with others measure follow-ership, discernment, and persistence. The fourth and final section contains three chapters about online survey and data collection software issues.

The first section contains three chapters on methodological issues related to online instruments and data collection. In "The Use of E-Questionnaires in Organizational Surveys," the late Yael Brender-Ilan and Gideon Vinitzky present a study which consider how human resource managers and human resource consultants use electronic questionnaires and find significant differences between these two groups which reveal issues of motivation and vision that should be considered when employing online survey research. Philip Salem's "The Use of Mixed Methods in Organizational Communication Research" describes how researchers can and should use both qualitative and quantitative research methods. He offers recommendations about how online surveys can be used to improve the overall research results. In "Online Research and Obtaining Human Subjects/IRB Approvals," Benjamin J. Bates and Ben Birch consider ethical issues associated with online data collection. They identify applicable federal regulations and offer guidance concerning how to work with an Institutional Review Board to protect human subjects while conducting data online.

The second section features five chapters analyzing and reviewing more established measurements that can be used online. Audrey Barrett and Fred Galloway present "The Nonprofit Ethics Survey: Assessing Organizational Culture and Climate," which can be used to assess the ethical culture of nonprofit organizations. Dan Lawson's "Analysis and Use of the Life Styles Inventory 1 and 2 by Human Synergistics International" discusses the background, validity, and reliability of this tool, which draws from psychological and managerial theories to help identify the beliefs, values, behaviors, and assumptions of individuals. Rody Rodriguez presents "Leadership Behavior Description Questionnaire (LBDQ & LBDQ-XII)," a standard assessment of leadership for fifty years, which can be used to identify dimensions of leadership. In their "Self-Monitoring Scale" chapter, Sharon E. Norris and Tracy H. Porter present a self-monitoring instrument which examines the relationship between self-monitoring and impression management, leader emergence, career success, and citizenship behaviors. Finally, Lijiang Shen and Celeste M. Condit conceptualize fatalism as a set of health beliefs encompassing the dimensions of predetermination, luck, and pessimism and assess a fatalism scale that can be used within an organizational context.

The third section of the book contains eight chapters profiling relatively recent measurements including information about the development of these measures and their application. In "A Cross-cultural Measure of Servant Leadership Behaviors," Jeff R. Hale and Dail Fields consider a measure of servant-leadership using the dimensions of service, humility, and vision and report on the results of international testing and application of the measure. "Seven Scales to Measure the Seven Beatitudes in Leaders" reports on the development and testing of measures of the leadership characteristics of humility, concern for others, discipline, justice, mercy, focus, and peacemaking by John Kilroy, Corné L. Bekker, Mihai C. Bocarnea, and Bruce E. Winston. Continuing with leadership-oriented measures, W. David Winner and Rushton S. Ricketson present the "Inventory of Leader Sternness (ILS)" which is a measure of establishing obedience, ensuring good behavior through rituals and respect, and the determination to do difficult tasks associated with leadership. Jamie Swalm discusses "The Shepherd Leadership Inventory (SLI)" which is an assessment of leader behaviors that guide, provide, and protect to ensure the wellbeing of followers. J. Alan Marshall shares the "Development of the Leader Integrity Assessment" and focuses on the scale development and testing of a perceived leader integrity instrument that is posed from a positive perspective. Paul Kaak, Rodney A. Reynolds, and Michael Whyte discuss "Measuring Followership" with a measurement of followership with three dimensions: resistant follower, compliant follower, and mature follower. In "An Online Measure of Discernment," Hazel C. V. Traüffer, Corné L. Bekker, Mihai C. Bocarnea, and Bruce E. Winston highlight the Discernment Practices Indicator (DPI), a measure with the three-factors of courage, intuition, and faith. Finally, M. Gail Derrick's "The Inventory of Learner Persistence" offers a measure of persistence in learning that contains the exhibition of volition, goal directedness, and self-regulation.

The fourth section highlights issues related to online survey and data collection software. In "The Mutual Influence of Technology and Leadership Behaviors," Tobias Heilmann and Ulf-Dietrich Reips bring together a number of e-leadership conceptions and measures into a proposed online leadership tool and website. Orly Calderon's "Preferred Features of Course Management Systems in Post Secondary and Corporate On-Line Learning" considers the role of course management systems in organizational education, development, and survey data collection. Finally, Jason D. Baker profiles various cloud-computing survey applications in "Online Survey Software" and also discusses mobile polling.

The editors of *Online Instruments, Data Collection, and Electronic Measurements: Organizational Advancements* believe that the chapters assembled here provide a valuable framework for academics and leaders to select and implement online measurements for organizational improvement. The instruments profiled in the middle sections of this handbook have a distinct focus on organizational leadership, followership, and learning, while the chapters in the first and last sections provide the support structure necessary for the implementation of online data collection. Such resources will promote effective evidence-based management and data-driven decision-making and will accrue to the benefit of many.

Mihai C. Bocarnea
Regent University, USA

Rodney A. Reynolds
California Lutheran University, USA

Jason D. Baker
Regent University, USA

Section 1
Methodological Issues

Chapter 1
The Use of E-Questionnaires in Organizational Surveys

Yael Brender-Ilan
Ariel University Center of Samaria, Israel

Gideon Vinitzky
Ariel University Center of Samaria, Israel

ABSTRACT

In recent years, there has been an increase in academic studies that examine the advantages and disadvantages of using e-questionnaires in organizations, but these studies have tended to ignore the potential differences between human resource (HR) managers and HR consultants with regards to using this tool. This chapter examines the use of e-questionnaires from the point of view of both types of practitioners. The study includes a qualitative exploratory survey, as well as a quantitative survey. T-tests, cluster analysis, and principal component analysis are performed and results support the three propositions that are presented. Specifically, it was found that (a) HR consultants and HR managers differ in the ranking of factors they think are important when deciding whether to use e-questionnaires; (b) preference differences exist between HR managers and HR consultants - managers are more directed by organizational constraints than consultants; and (c) the groupings for e-questionnaire preferences, compared to paper-and-pencil questionnaires, are consistent with Caldwell's (2003) four roles of HR managers. The chapter concludes with implications and suggestions for future research.

INTRODUCTION

Surveys conducted by human resource (HR) managers and HR consultants were traditionally performed using paper-and-pencil questionnaires. These surveys were mainly used to appraise employee attitude and morale, but they also allowed the firm to develop and assess its strategic objectives. The logic of this process was based on the idea that employees are in an optimal position to report information, given their place in the firm, and this was shown to be very valuable

DOI: 10.4018/978-1-4666-2172-5.ch001

to the organization (Schneider, Ashworth, Higgs & Carr, 1996).

While this process is still carried out, nowadays many people are already familiar with the electronic interface; thus, major firms use electronic data collection instead of traditional paper questionnaires (Thompson, Surface, Martin & Sanders, 2003). In both methods, surveyors need and rely upon employee collaboration within the organization. The electronic questionnaire (e-questionnaire) is a computer program that guides respondents through the interview process and checks their answers on the spot. The development of computer hardware and software has made it possible to formulate very large and complex e-questionnaires. Electronic data procurement makes it possible to build a database that can be used and compared at several points in time. This is beneficial for academic researchers, as well as for relevant practicing managers and consultants.

Researchers suggest that electronic surveys are less expensive than traditional pencil-and-paper surveys, and that they increase the efficiency of collecting large organizational data sets. Moreover, the electronic survey is a more appropriate data collection method for measuring sensitive issues, such as negative employee attitudes and counterproductive behaviors (Stanton, 1998; Smith & Leigh, 1997; Krantz & Dalal, 2000; Eaton and Struthers, 2002). Although the internet provides opportunities to conduct surveys more efficiently and effectively than traditional means (Zhang, 2000), it also involves methodological issues and concerns (Andrews, Nonnecke & Preece, 2003; Cho & LaRose, 1999; Cook, Heath & Thompson, 2000; Vehovar et al., 2001). Researchers are concerned with employees' reactions to the shift towards electronic surveys, which were found to be mixed. While there is some evidence that employees are comfortable with this method of surveying (Thompson, Martin & Sanders, 2003), evidence has shown that, as this method becomes more prevalent, there are some concerns as well (Thompson & Surface, 2007).

HR Managers and HR Consultants as Surveyors

There are two types of human resource (HR) practitioners who may want to use e-questionnaires: HR managers and HR consultants.

HR managers are employees who work in the firm's human resources department. The HR manager plans, organizes and directs human resource programs for the organization; provides administrative staff assistance to the general director; and performs other related work as required. HR consultants are usually professionals who work as freelancers and are external to the organization. They are responsible for assisting clients (the hiring firm) with the strategic integration of effective HR processes, programs and practices in their daily operations. In addition, they are responsible for maximizing the client's performance in regard to human resources by introducing or marketing "best practice" products or services, as well as for providing periodic feedback to clients regarding their performance related to annual management objectives. Both HR managers and HR consultants need to gather information regarding the operation of the firm as carried out and perceived by its employees. To accomplish this, they need to perform needs assessments or audits and require the cooperation of the organization's employees.

A-priori, HR managers are different from HR consultants in several ways. Because managers are employees of the organization and consultants are external agents (Glasser, 2002), we hypothesize the existence of disparate loyalties, responsibilities, emphases and concerns. The HR manager has hands-on experience with the organization and is usually very familiar with its day-to-day operations and concerns. The HR consultant has the privilege of being supposedly neutral and familiar with similar organizations, allowing a broader outlook for comparison and diagnosis unavailable to HR mangers (Turner, 1982). As externals, consultants look at the client's situation with a fresh perspective (Kuber, 1996), since their job includes the element of being objective (Greiner and Metzger, 1983). Turner (1982) proposed a hierarchy of eight task categories that consulting should focus on:

1. Providing information to a client
2. Solving a client's problem
3. Making a diagnosis which may necessitate redefinition of the problem
4. Making recommendations based on the diagnosis
5. Assisting with implementation of recommended actions
6. Building a consensus and commitment around a corrective action
7. Facilitating client learning
8. Permanently improving organizational effectiveness

The HR consultant has a different frame of reference than that of the HR manager (Church, 1997). Being external to the organization, consultants are different from managers in several ways: consultants are emotionally, administratively, politically and financially independent from the organization (Kubr, 1996); managers as part of the organizational staff have direct clout in the organization, while consultants do not (Appelbaum and Steed, 2005); consultants and managers have a different grasp and appreciation of the organization's true goals (Gabble, 1996); consultants have little or no formal authority in the work situation (Glasser, 2002); the consultant has little control and is assigned limited responsibilities (McLachlin, 1999); consultants engage in a dynamic dialectical relationship with the organization; and they must enter an ambiguous power-control situation in order to perform their task (Glasser, 2002). Four major qualities, which are obviously expected from managers, but are critically required from consultants, are: credibility, effectiveness (Glasser, 2002) integrity (McLachlin, 1999) and trust (Glasser, 2002; Edverdsson, 1998).

The external position of the consultant may lead to some tension between HR managers and HR consultants. For instance, HR consultants are commercial entities with a strong focus on revenues, which often affects their suggestions in regards to best solutions. In addition, HR consultants are less restricted by budget than HR managers(Poulfelt, 1997).

Proposition 1: HR consultants and HR managers will differ in the ranking of factors they think are important when making a decision regarding the use or non-use of e-questionnaires.

This chapter examines the use of e-questionnaires from the point of view of human resource (HR) managers and HR consultants. Based on the discussions of e-questionnaires in the literature, and on the differences in the characteristics and concerns of HR managers and consultants, we raise several propositions regarding their view on e-questionnaires and examine them using data collected from a sample of Israeli HR practitioners of both types. The chapter is arranged as follows: First, we define and discuss the study's two target groups (HR managers and HR practitioners). Next, we talk about general concerns raised in the literature in regard to using electronic surveys, after which we describe the method used in the study, which included two stages – qualitative and quantitative. We describe the data analysis of the results, which includes both cluster and factor analyses. These analyses enable us to identify distinct groups which hold different opinions about e-questionnaires. Finally, a discussion summarizes and analyzes the study's findings.

Concerns Related to using Electronic Surveys

Various studies conducted in recent years have supported the claim that web surveys are equivalent to paper-and-pencil surveys. Moreover, the fact that support for this claim was found in studies conducted in organizations operating both on the domestic level (Stanton, 1998; Buchanan & Smith, 1999) and on the international level (Beuckelaer & Lievens, 2009; Cole, Bedeian & Field, 2006), encourages organizational managers and consultants alike to expand the use of web surveys versus paper-and-pencil surveys. Managers and consultants required to perform surveys within the organization need to take various aspects related to their decisions into consideration, to ensure effective performance of the survey.

Various studies state that electronic surveys have several advantages over paper-and-pencil surveys (Yun & Trumbo, 2000): They are the least expensive type of survey to conduct (Dillman, 2000; Kraut & Saari, 1999; Schaffer & Dillman, 1998; Sproull, 1986; Yun & Trumbo, 2000; Schmidt, 1997), and they enable more flexibility in planning and design (Dillman, 2000), including the possibility of reducing the order effect of question presentation (Bowling, 2005). The research shows that electronic surveys enable rapid data collection (Schaffer & Dillman, 1998; Sproull, 1986), support varied response formats (Simsek & Veigha, 2001), ensure less missing data (Stanton, 1998), and minimize typos (Cook, Health, Thompson & Thompson, 2001; Roberts, Konczak & Macan, 2004). In addition, the high accessibility of the internet enables data collection in a wider geographical radius (Epstein, Klinkenberg, Wiley & McKinley, 2001). Another advantage is reducing the possible bias of data collectors, an advantage achieved because information is entered into the system by respondent employees rather than by mediators (Birnbaum, 2001; Reips, 2000).

Alongside the obvious advantages of conducting electronic surveys, organizational managers and consultants must also be aware of their disadvantages. Studies indicate various limitations involved in the use of electronic surveys. While paper-and-pencil surveys are administered to employees in a centralized manner, and it is possible to ensure high response rates, electronic surveys suffer from a relatively low response rate (Schaffer & Dillman, 1998; Sproull, 1986). In addition, when employees respond to an electronic survey at home or at work, they may answer incorrectly, due to inadequate comprehension of the survey's purpose or even dishonest or inaccurate responses (Booth-Kewley, Edwards & Rosenfeld, 1992; Lautenschlager & Flaherty, 1990). Moreover, there is a risk of duplicate responses by the same people (Reips, 2000).

Researchers further suggest that web surveys require attention to the technology involved in implementing the survey. First, it is necessary to relate to possible problems resulting from the use of technological means (Kraut & Saari, 1999) and to the various levels of accessibility of computerized means enabling survey response in organizations (Bowling, 2005; Stanton & Rogelberg, 2001). This is particularly relevant in the case of international organizations maintaining units located in geographical areas with less accessibility to computers (Beuckelaer & Lievens, 2009). Kraut et al. (2004) state various possible effects of these difficulties in the case of psychological studies, which may influence the performance of organizational surveys. An example of these influences is *sample bias* – which stems from diversity within the selected research population, as well as the process of self-selection and desertion.

The research review cited above offers a list of the organizational advantages and disadvantages of conducting web surveys, in general. Beuckelaer and Lievens (2009) intuitively state that the considerations guiding organizations in the performance of electronic surveys rather than paper-and-pencil ones are:

(a) increasing the efficiency of data collection, (b) reducing human errors involved in the encoding process, and (c) reducing costs. However, there seems to be a lack of information in prior studies regarding the differences between the characteristic motivations of human resource managers who decide to perform electronic surveys versus those of organizational consultants - an important issue, given the significant and changing role of HR consultants in organizations.

The role of the HR manager has changed over the past two decades (Heneman et al., 1998; Caldwell, 2003). Most of these changes have been attributed to transformations in the workplace. The role of HR managers has become more complex and multifaceted, while competing role-demands continue and involve ever-increasing expectations in regard to managerial performance and new professional challenges. At the same time, consultants "roam" the organizational environment, searching for a place to make their mark and share their expertise. HR management members are often advised by experts to hire consultants in order to better utilize processes in their organization (Manewitz, 1997; Turner, 1982). Based on the literature review above, there is reason to believe that differences exist between managers and consultants in the way they think and behave. It is beyond the scope of this chapter to answer the question of whether consults are better or more 'right for the organization' than in-house staff, namely – the HR managers. However, we can still appreciate the fact that the two are not identical. In-house managers and consultants will always have a different type of clout in an organization (Appelbaum and Steed, 2005).

Proposition 2: There will be differences in preferences between HR managers and HR consultants; thus, managers will be more directed by organizational constraints than consultants.

Previous studies distinguish between four different roles of HR managers (Caldwell, 2003). In these roles, managers need to perform various activities that also require the use of surveys. In this study, we will attempt to identify a match between these roles and managers and consultants' various approaches to the research tools. The four roles of HR managers proposed by Caldwell (2003) are:

1. Advisors or internal consultants who actively offer senior management and line managers HR advice and expertise
2. Service providers who are called in by line managers to provide specific HR assistance and support as required
3. Regulators who formulate, promulgate, and monitor the observance of personnel or HR policy and practices
4. Change agents who actively advance culture change and organizational transformation processes

Theoretically, we suggest that HR managers and consultants' opinions regarding the use of e-questionnaires will vary and can be organized and explained in light of the different roles they play. Since these roles are discussed by Caldwell with regard to managers only, and are not necessarily suitable for consultants; and since this is an exploratory study, at this stage we will use this categorization and test it only in regard to managers.

Proposition 3: The preferences for e-questionnaires compared to paper-and-pencil questionnaires can be grouped and characterized according to Caldwell's four roles of HR managers.

Method

Our survey was transmitted on the web to two types of HR practitioners: HR managers and HR consultants. The questionnaire was designed in two stages. First, a questionnaire consisting of open-ended questions was sent to a group of HR practitioners as a pilot study. Each group (managers and consultants) consisted of twenty respondents. In the second stage, based on the responses of the pilot, we designed our research questionnaire (see Appendix A). Specifics regarding the questionnaire are detailed in the Qualitative section below. The first stage, involving open-ended questions, also attempted to achieve a better match between the questionnaire and the target sample, in order to improve respondents' compliance with the questionnaire.

FIRST STAGE: QUALITATIVE ANALYSIS

The initial exploratory pilot study had three main purposes. The first was to investigate whether managers and consultants use the same set of considerations in their decision of whether to perform electronic surveys; the second was to try and identify different priorities regarding these considerations; and the third was to construct a tool for developing the research questionnaire. Ten HR managers and ten organizational consultants with a minimum of five years' experience in large organizations participated in the pilot study. After a preliminary conversation with each of the participants, they received an electronic form with seven open-ended questions adapted to their role (either managers or consultants). Of

the twenty participants, responses were received from seventeen: nine consultants and eight HR managers. The questions examined managers and consultants' attitudes towards electronic and paper-and-pencil questionnaires, their reasons for choosing a certain format, and factors barring use of the digital format (Table 1 summarizes the main answers to each question by managers and organizational consultants). The following analysis presents the main points mentioned by participants in response to each question and compares the various roles examined.

The first question asked was: *In your opinion, what are the advantages of electronic questionnaires versus traditional paper-and-pencil questionnaires?*

Responses demonstrate that, according to HR managers, the main advantage of electronic surveys is efficient performance. In addition, they emphasized dimensions related to the time required to complete the survey, cost efficiency, and high efficacy of the survey process. For example, one of the managers said: "Cost efficiency,

Table 1. Main findings of pilot study on attitudes towards electronic and paper-and-pencil surveys among HR managers and organizational consultants

	Managers	Consultants
Advantages of electronic format	Efficiency and cost	Highly functional; accessible from a distance; efficiency; cost; accuracy; promotes image
Disadvantages of electronic format	The large majority stated no technological difficulties Reliance on external factors Concerns related to potential deceit	Technological difficulties – need for adaptation; concern that respondents will be exposed; concern of social influence; reliance on external factors; low response rate; advanced preparation necessary
Situations in which e-questionnaires have priority	Information gathering; particularly in large groups; wide geographical dispersal; when the information required is of a quantitative nature; limited supervision required	Wide geographical dispersal Time restrictions Supervision of the process
Use of paper-and-pencil	When qualitative information is required; performance appraisal surveys; in a small group of employees	Depends on the survey's cost Employee proficiency
Barriers to use of electronic questionnaires	Technology Costs Difficulty controlling surroundings	Information security; technology; disparity between existing and required skills for completing electronic surveys; reliance on a third factor; cost
Barriers to use by others	None	Compromising anonymity; reliance on external or internal factors; technology; adaptation of the organization

ability to process data rapidly, and accessibility to the entire population".

In contrast to managers, organizational consultants stated a wider range of advantages regarding e-questionnaires: user convenience, employee's convenience, supports employee accessibility in remote locations, rapid implementation, cheap, more accurate and more efficient, and augments the organization's image. An example is provided by one of the consultants: "Analysis is performed automatically (avoiding the need for typing, typos, enabling observation of results at each stage, etc.). It is easy to distribute the survey – it can be sent to a very large number of respondents simultaneously. Significant reduction of time needed to administer and analyze the survey. Easier to transfer (no need for complicated "logistics" – facsimiles, printing, travel…). The survey's response rate increases due to the instrument's attractiveness and accessibility. The organization conveys its innovativeness and progress."

These disparate answers may attest to the wider perspective of organizational consultants, the need to receive reliable and objective information in order to reach decisions; and in contrast, a lack of managerial experience which may have demanded attention to the operative aspects of collecting information.

The second question answered by managers and consultants was: *In your opinion, what are the disadvantages of electronic questionnaires versus traditional paper-and-pencil questionnaires?* An analysis of managers' answers demonstrates two different trends.

The first group consists of managers who had no problem with the use of electronic questionnaires. The second consists of managers who stressed problems related to successful administration of surveys and the need to rely on external factors. This includes the need to have computers available for employees, fear of deceit, and employee concerns of being exposed, affecting the quality of the information they could provide. Thus, for example, one manager suggests that

potential problems are related to "reluctance to complete electronic forms, for fear of exposure through an IP address; computer accessibility. It is impossible to know whether employees have completed more than one questionnaire. Costs and reliance on external factors."

In contrast to managers, consultants recognized disadvantages in the need for respondents' technical skills, concerns that participant's identity might be exposed, and social bias. In addition, consultants identified as a disadvantage the need for participants to have the technical abilities required to complete the questionnaire, concerns related to social influence, dependence on computerized means, and the fact that, unlike paper-and-pencil questionnaires, employees cannot be brought together physically for the purpose of supervising the process. Moreover, they also mentioned the need for organizations to prepare themselves in advance by creating a distribution list.

One of the respondents provided this example: "It is difficult to maintain anonymity; thus, results will probably be biased due to social desirability. With traditional questionnaires, it is possible to gather a large group of employees and reserve time for them to complete the survey: tasks noted on their schedule will probably be performed. Sometimes when people see others completing (a survey), they will do so as well." Another consultant focuses on the cultural effects of the internet and states that some are worried that survey participants will have a superficial approach. This consultant wrote: "The culture of the internet is an instant culture: This culture might have an impact on completion of electronic questionnaires. People might be concerned that information will "trickle" out through the web."

It is interesting that the majority of managers mentioned no disadvantages. This finding is compatible with the narrow concept of managers in their responses to the first question. However, both the managers who recognized problems and consultants suggest that the need for technological adaptation, reliance on external factors, and concern over intentionally biased results are disadvantages of electronic surveys. In addition, both managers and organizational consultants are aware of problems related to maintaining employee privacy and concern over deceit issues.

The third question examined under what circumstances one would choose to use an electronic questionnaire. Several managers stated inclusively that they would prefer to use electronic surveys whenever they are required to gather information. Others stated that they would use an internet format when it is necessary to gather information from a large decentralized group of employees, when employee proficiency is compatible with the electronic format, when there is no need for eye contact and constant supervision of employees during data collection, and when the collected information is of a quantitative, rather than qualitative, nature. One of the managers gave the following examples: (a) When the population is decentralized, (b) when it is necessary to process data (numerical results, closed-ended questions), and (c) when the target population has good computer skills.

Unlike managers, consultants mentioned three factors facilitating the use of electronic questionnaires: (a) a wide geographical distribution of the firm's employees, (b) time restrictions, and (c) control of survey execution. For example, one of the consultants mentioned the following difficulties: "Surveying a geographically dispersed population, which would find it difficult to gather in one place. When the survey must "run" over time and reach a long list of participants. When there is a prepared distribution list. When it is important to receive reports at various stages of the survey (for example response rates, intermediate results, etc.), and when it is necessary to reduce the time devoted to analysis of results."

Results indicate that both managers and consultants are aware of the benefits of holding electronic surveys in an organization consisting of a large group of widely-dispersed employees. In addition, both managers and consultants are aware of the need to adapt the questionnaire

format to the employees' capabilities. However, managers believe that electronic questionnaires are less capable of developing impressions formerly reached in the field through personal qualitative conversations, and that survey characteristics do not enable sufficient oversight of the qualitative aspect of employee responses.

The fourth question examined under which circumstances one would choose to use a paper-and-pencil questionnaire. Analysis of the results shows that in response to this question, managers indicated surveys requiring qualitative information or surveys which, if performed electronically, would be inefficient. In this context, managers mentioned performance appraisal surveys and small-group surveys. Examples of situations in which managers would prefer paper-and-pencil questionnaires are: "When there is a need for a great deal of free expression" and "when there is a variety of open-ended questions, a local population, and a small number of employees."

In contrast, in answer to this question consultants said that use of paper-and-pencil questionnaires would be preferable if it is less expensive or if employee skills are incompatible with the electronic format. An example of such cases was given in one consultant's response: "If some of the research/survey population does not have easy access to a computer. When it is easy to gather the survey population and administer a paper-and-pencil survey (for example, after a convention or meeting). When there is no prepared distribution list. When surveys must be administered to a small number of participants. When the cost of designing the survey and conducting it on the internet significantly raises the cost of its administration."

These results show certain differences regarding concerns affecting the selection of survey formats: managers perceive paper-and-pencil questionnaires as a mature and fitting instrument for gathering qualitative information, while consultants do not mention this. This difference may be explained by consultants' perception of electronic questionnaires as a capable and fitting instrument for the gathering of qualitative information, while managers - who probably conduct performance appraisal processes more than consultants - find that the instrument is unsuitable for this purpose.

The fifth question examined factors perceived as barriers in the use of electronic questionnaires among other HR managers/consultants (colleagues). Managers state several entry barriers which focus on technological entry barriers, costs, and difficulties in neutralizing the effects of one's surroundings. For example, one of the managers reported the following: "Control of the process and maintaining discretion during questionnaire completion; difficulties involving the neutralizing of one's surroundings; accessibility of existing applications and; (d) cost of applications for conducting electronic surveys."

In contrast, consultants state the need for information security, fear of technology, concern that employees will not be able to handle questionnaires in a digital format, the wish to avoid being dependent on a third factor, and the price element, which raises the cost of consultation services. For example, one of the consultants wrote: "The only possibility that I can envision is if respondents are concerned due to issues of confidentiality or information security. There are problems with conveying information online without knowing for sure where it will end up. In addition, when it is necessary to arouse respondents' motivation to participate, the act of physically handing a questionnaire to someone you know, increases the chance of receiving a response, compared to an electronic questionnaire which can be ignored." These differences emphasize consultants' external position in relation to the organization. Consultants also mention the price element, which increases consultation costs, reliance on external factors, and concerns of unsuccessful survey administration, as a result of lack of control over employees.

The final question examined which factors are perceived as barriers to the use of electronic questionnaires by the other target population studied. Thus, managers/consultants were asked about

barriers in the use of electronic questionnaires among organizational consultants/managers. Interestingly, managers were unaware of possible barriers among organizational consultants, and did not state any significant barriers. In contrast, organizational consultants realized that managers would avoid performing electronic surveys for fear of compromising anonymity, and due to reliance on external or internal factors and a lack of technical support. In addition, consultants mentioned that managers would avoid performing electronic surveys if some of the employees had no access to computerized systems. For example, one of the consultants emphasized the following issues: "Technological phobia on the part of respondents or problems connected to the lack of technical support when necessary, reliance on external factors, and cost issues."

These differences between managers and consultants may stem from existing disparities in the perceived commitment of managers and organizational consultants. Managers do not mention factors that may impact consultants' decisions, while consultants are aware of the many concerns of managers. We believe this is because one of the roles of a consultant is to diagnose the organization and its managers (Edvardsson, 1989), something which managers don't necessarily do with regards to their consultants.

SECOND STAGE: QUANTITATIVE ANALYSIS

Research Questionnaire

The qualitative study confirmed that considerations assessed by managers and consultants for performing electronic surveys are similar or identical to those mentioned in the literature reviewed above. In addition, differences were found between managers and consultants in their emphases on various decision components. To examine the significance of these differences, a questionnaire was developed using the responses to the pilot. The questionnaire used for this study is composed of three main parts.

The first part of the questionnaire consists of a rating scale regarding the different weights accorded to decision components referring to electronic surveys. Specifically, participants were asked to rank each of the following components from 1 to 7: speed of execution, control of the process, quality of information gathered, anonymity of respondents, organization compatibility with the survey format, response rate, and image. This scale is intended to identify disparities between managers and consultants.

Based on the qualitative analysis reported above, the second part focused on the various perceived advantages of conducting electronic surveys versus paper-and-pencil questionnaires. Study participants were asked to mark on a scale of 1 (definitely not) to 7 (definitely yes) to what degree they agree with statements representing electronic surveys' preference or inferiority versus paper-and-pencil surveys in regard to 11 different factors. Specifically, the qualitative analysis discovers different factors which may have an affect on the perceived advantages of holding electronic surveys versus paper-and-pencil questionnaires. Managers and consultants based their attitudes on the following factors: efficient performance (i.e. time, control, cost and amount of data collection - questions number 12, 8, 13 and 17 in the questionnaire), process convenience (i.e. high accessibility – questions number 10 and 14), privacy and deceit issues (questions number 11, 18 and 15 in the questionnaire), dependency on external factors (question number 16), and image contribution (question number 9). One example of an item in the questionnaire is: "Compared to paper-and-pencil questionnaires, electronic surveys afford better control of the process" (for a detailed description of the questionnaire, see Appendix). Finally, subjects were asked to provide information regarding their job, such as: position, size of the organization, as well as demographic details: age, gender, tenure and education.

Sample

The sample, consisting of 113 participants, included two types of HR practitioners: 47 HR managers and 66 HR consultants. Almost all of these consultants (64) indicated that they were independent consultants and two indicated that they were employees of a consulting firm. The sample was random using a list of HR manages from medium to large size organizations. Respondents consisted of 36 men and 77 women, with a mean age of 45. Mean tenure in the HR field is 12 years, with a minimum of 1 and a maximum of 30 years. Mean seniority for HR managers is 9 years and for HR consultants 14. Mean experience with web-surveys for both groups is 18 months. The education level of HR managers varied. One manager had a high school degree, three had completed certification studies, seventeen had a Bachelor's degree, and twenty-six managers had post-graduate degrees. The education level of HR consultants was homogeneous and all had post-graduate degrees. Forty-two participants indicated that they did not have experience with electronic surveying and 71 indicated that they did.

Results

The first part of the questionnaire asked respondents to rank, in order of importance, 7 factors that influence their decision to use e-questionnaires. The means and standard deviations of these factors are shown in Table 2. In this analysis, we included only respondents who used the exact rating rule (i.e. in a list of seven variables only one factor received a rating of 7, one factor received a rating of 6, etc.).

We used cluster analysis in order to examine our first proposition, which stated that managers and consultants will differ in ranking the importance of decision factors. The questionnaire began by asking respondents to rate factors affecting decisions to use e-questionnaires in terms of importance. A K-means cluster analysis was conducted[1] in order to explore whether respondents

Table 2. Means and standard deviations of decision factors

Decision factor	Mean rank	*SD*
Speed of use	4.81	1.86
Control over process	4.45	1.71
Quality of data obtained	4.78	1.86
Anonymity of participants	3.53	1.95
Match between questionnaire type and organization	4.45	1.86
Response rate	3.83	1.86
Image of organization when using e-questionnaire	2.16	1.54

hold different patterns of decision governance regarding use of electronic surveying. Since the k-mean procedure requires an a-priori specification for the number of clusters, we repeated the analysis several times, selecting a different number of clusters each time. After inspecting the two-, three- and four-cluster solutions, we decided that the three-cluster solution was best suited for our purposes. This clustering, although it has one variable (response rate) which does not differ across the three clusters (with a rating of '4' across clusters), shows significant differences in all other characteristics and has an appropriate number of participants in each of the clusters (23, 35 and 36, respectively) (see Figure 1 below). The 2-cluster solution did not demonstrate significant differences in two of the variables, while the 4-cluster solution did not show significant differences in two of the variables, and included two clusters with an unsatisfactory sample size (15 and 18).

Mean scores and standard deviations for each of the clusters are presented in Table 3.

Clusters 1 and 2 did not differ in demographics, but did differ in substance. As is shown in Figure 1 above, Cluster 1 is characterized by a high score on matching the type of questionnaire to the organization, anonymity of respondents, and quality of data obtained. Compared to Cluster 3, it has significantly more consultants than managers, $t(78)=1.86$, $p= .07$. It appears that members of this cluster tend to prefer decision

variables that emphasize the tendency to focus on the needs of the organization and the employees. We termed this cluster: 'The attention to needs Cluster'.

Cluster 2 is characterized by a high score on speed of use and on matching the type of questionnaire to the organization. Compared to Cluster 3, this cluster also has significantly more consultants than managers, $t(78)= 2.03$, $p< .05$, and also significantly older participants, $t(78)= -1.91$, $p= .06$. It appears that members of this cluster tend to prefer decision variables that emphasize the process, and we termed it: 'The operation Cluster'.

Cluster 3 is characterized by a high score on speed of use, control of process, and quality of data obtained. Compared to Clusters 1 and 2, this cluster has significantly more managers than consultants. This cluster shows some differences in the way participants perceive e-questionnaires. Members of this cluster believe that there is more control over data collection when using this type of questionnaire, compared to members of Cluster 1. When asked whether co-workers have a greater effect on employees' participation in surveys with e-questionnaires they disagreed more than members of Clusters 1 and 2. Moreover, compared to members of Cluster 2, they believed that e-questionnaires do not restrict data collection. We termed this cluster: "The efficiency Cluster". It is important to note that no demographic differences were found. We also checked the differences between the two consultant groups.

Figure 1. The three clusters

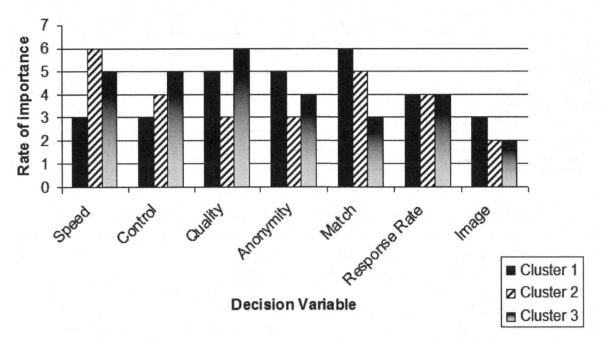

In addition to cluster analysis, a rank test was conducted with regards to the ranking of the decision factors to use e-questionnaires. No differences were found between the rank of consultants and the rank of managers, except for the variable 'match' (the match between questionnaire type and organization). The details of this analysis are as follows: The data was analyzed separately for each of the seven ranked decision variables. Each variable was tested using an independence test and the 'match' variable showed a significant difference in ranking between consultants and managers (see Table 4).

For this variable only, an exploratory system of data-mining algorithm was used, in order to determine the most suitable model. A polarity test

Table 3. Mean and standard deviation of clusters

Decision Variable	Cluster 1 (n=23)		Cluster 2 (n=35)		Cluster 3 (n=36)			
	M	*SD*	*M*	*SD*	*M*	*SD*	*F*	*p*
Speed of use	2.57	1.20	6.03	1.25	5.06	1.39	50.73	.00
Control over process	3.04	1.19	4.43	1.91	5.36	1.10	17.34	.00
Quality of data obtained	5.43	1.53	3.20	1.47	5.89	1.26	35.6	.00
Anonymity of participants	4.57	1.85	2.74	1.70	3.64	1.94	6.94	.00
Match between questionnaire type and organization	5.70	1.36	5.40	1.33	2.72	1.14	54.27	.00
Response rate	4.04	2.16	3.94	1.73	3.58	1.79	0.53	.59
Image of organization when using e-questionnaire	2.65	1.90	2.26	1.38	1.75	1.36	2.6	.08

Table 4. Results of independence test-Difference between decision factors' ranking of consultants and managers

Variable name	p-value
Speed of use	0.35
Control over process	0.94
Quality of data obtained	0.40
Anonymity of participants	0.97
Match between questionnaire type and organization	0.04
Response rate	0.34
Image of organization when using e-questionnaire	0.94

was chosen as the appropriate model and was used on the data. Table 5 shows the results of the polarity test separately for managers and consultants. Figure 2 illustrates the polarity test results graphically. For consultants, more than half think that 'match' is an unimportant variable in the decision of whether to use e-questionnaires (a polarity index of 1.33), while for managers the contrary is true. More than half think that 'match' is an important decision factor (a polarity index of 14.5).

The second part of our questionnaire was designed to examine possible characteristics of e-questionnaires which differ from those of paper-and-pencil ones. Respondents were asked to consider eleven characteristics and answer whether they perceive a difference in these characteristics between the two types of questionnaires.

Table 6 shows the means and standard deviations of the answers to our research questions regarding e-questionnaires compared to paper-and pencil questionnaires.

Managers and consultants differ in their perception of three items concerning characteristics of e-questionnaires (see Table 6). Consultants perceive this technique as more accessible to employees, but are also more concerned (than managers) with the likelihood of deceit during data collection and with other restrictions and limitations of this method. We also found that HR practitioners who had prior experience with e-questionnaires, and those who have more seniority in the field of HR, think that when using e-questionnaires one has more control over the data collection process, $(t(111)=2.18, p<.05; t(111)=2.09, p<.05$ (respectively). Comparing men

Table 5. Variables' distribution and polarity rate of the decision factor 'match' for managers and consultants

Decision variable	Managers	Consultants
1	0.02	0.06
2	0.09	0.28
3	0.14	0.22
4	0.14	0.14
5	0.21	0.14
6	0.12	0.08
7	0.29	0.08
Polarity	14.50	1.33

1=anonymity, 2=control, 3=image, 4=response rate, 5=quality, 6=speed, 7=match

Figure 2. Histograms of the importance of decision variables shown separately for managers and consultants

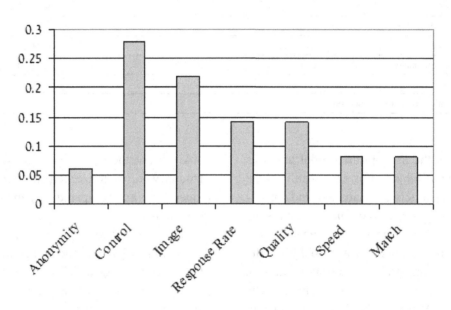

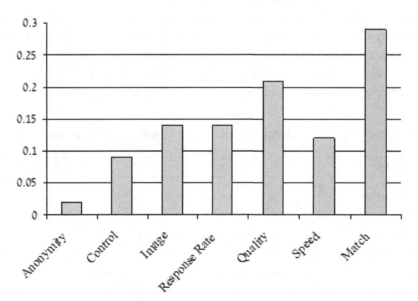

Table 6. Means and standard deviations of answers to questions concerning e-questionnaire character-istics and differences between managers and consultants

Question	Full sample (n=113) M (SD)	Managers (n= 46) M (SD)	Consultants (n= 66) M (SD)	t(p)
E-questionnaires allow for better control over the surveying process	4.84 (2.08)	5.04 (2.11)	4.67 (2.09)	1.05 (.29)
E-questionnaires give a better image to the organization	4.34 (1.68)	4.40 (1.71)	4.24 (1.68)	.63 (.53)
E-questionnaires allow for increased employee accessibility	4.63 (1.85)	4.24 (1.93)	4.89 (1.71)	-1.96 (.05)
E-questionnaires allow for increased anonymity	4.10 (2.13)	3.89 (2.23)	4.23 (2.05)	-.86 (.39)
E-questionnaires are more time-efficient	6.12 (1.16)	6.16 (1.04)	6.08 (1.26)	.44 (.66)
E-questionnaire are more costly	3.42 (1.90)	3.53 (1.98)	3.38 (1.88)	.30 (.76)
E-questionnaires provide a higher percentage of participation	4.42 (1.55)	4.53 (1.74)	4.33 (1.45)	.65 (.51)
With e-questionnaires, I am more concerned about employees' deceit	2.94 (1.60)	2.51 (1.42)	3.18 1.64)	-1.9 (.06)
With e-questionnaires, I am more dependent on internal or external factors	4.01 (1.74)	3.91 (1.78)	4.09 (1.76)	-.59 (.56)
E-questionnaires pose more restrictions on data collection	2.88 (1.80)	2.40 (1.48)	3.29 (1.91)	-2.97 (.00)
With e-questionnaires, coworkers affect participation in survey	3.68 (1.70)	3.44 (1.59)	3.88 (1.76)	-1.28 (.19)

practitioners to women practitioners, men believe that e-questionnaires allow better respondent anonymity, $t(111) = -1.99, p<.05$), but when using them one needs to be more concerned about deceit, $t(111) = -1.99, p<.05$). Younger practitioners think so as well, $t(111) = -2.21, p<.05$. Finally, practitioners with prior questionnaire experience think that they are more time-efficient compared to those with no such experience, $t(111)=1.96, p<.05$.

A factor analysis was performed on these eleven answers and results showed four distinct factors (see Table 7). We called Factor 1 "bias" and it includes the characteristics of 'constraints', 'deceit' and 'influence of others'. Factor 2 was called "conduct" and included the characteristics of 'accessibility', 'response rate' and 'anonymity'. Factor 3 was called "dependency" and included

the characteristics of 'cost', 'reliance on intrinsic and extrinsic factors' and 'image'. Finally, Factor 4 was called "operation" and it included the characteristics of 'control' and 'efficiency'.

Proposition 2 suggested that there would be differences between managers and consultants in their preferences for using electronic questionnaires over paper-and-pencil questionnaires. A t-test was performed for each factor, separately (see Table 8). The results demonstrated that organizational consultants are more concerned than managers in regard to possible bias in results produced by electronic surveys, $t(111)=2.74$, $p<.01$. In addition, a marginally significant difference ($p= 0.1$) was found in the perception of electronic surveys as more suitable for the organization's needs in regard to their operation. Thus,

Table 7. Principal component analysis results

Questions	Components			
	1	**2**	**3**	**4**
18 In e-surveys, coworkers influence participation in surveys	.78	-.17	.13	.19
17 E-surveys pose more restrictions on data collection	.68	.08	.03	-.25
15 In e-surveys, I am more concerned about employee deceit	.58	.09	.34	-.15
10 E-surveys allow for increased employee accessibility	-.05	.78	.01	-.02
11 E-surveys allow for increased anonymity	.29	.74	-.06	-.08
14 E-surveys have a higher percentage of participation	-.14	.68	.09	.16
13 E-surveys are more costly	.16	-.04	.69	-.01
16 In e-surveys, I am more dependent on internal or external factors	.27	-.04	.67	-.21
9 E-surveys give the organization a better image	-.14	.23	.64	.36
8 E-surveys allow for better control over the survey process	-.25	-.07	.08	.78
12 E-surveys are more time-efficient	.38	.27	-.32	.60

managers perceive electronic surveys as more efficient and controllable than organizational consultants. These findings support the research proposition that managers and organizational consultants have different motivations, as reflected in their emphases regarding the performance of electronic surveys. This information was not found to be influenced by either the personality variables of research participants or by the characteristics of respondents' organizations.

Proposition 3 suggested that there would be a match between grouped preferences and the four roles of HR managers, as delineated by Caldwell (2003). We used principal component analysis to group the preferences and matched them with HR manager roles (see Table 9) as follows: The Regulator role requires the professional to con- centrate on process, rules and policy. In this role, any diversion from the norm or restriction of standard practice will be noticed and attempts will be made to deal with it. Therefore, we perceived this role as the most suitable for members of Factor 1- *bias*, which deals with constraints, deceit and the influence of others.

The second role, Advisor, was found by Caldwell (2003) to be the most common role of HR managers. The advisor offers expertise or advice on ways to achieve goals. Therefore, this role type would be most fitting for members of Factor 2 - *conduct*, which deals with characteristics related to the most suitable way of conducting the survey: accessibility, response rate and anonymity.

Table 8. Means and SD of preferences for managers and consultants by factors

Factors	Managers (n=47)		Consultants (n=66)			
	M	*SD*	*M*	*SD*	*t*	*p*
Factor 1: Bias	.24	.91	.19	1.02	2.74	.01
Factor 2: Conduct	-.11	1.07	.06	.93	-.93	.30
Factor 3: Dependency	.02	.98	-.15	1.02	.91	.85
Factor 4: Operation	.17	.85	-.13	1.08	1.56	.10

Table 9. Matching factors with roles

Factor	HR manager role
1 - Bias	Regulator
2 - Conduct	Advisor
3 - Dependency	Change agent
4 - Operation	Service provider

The third role, Change Agent, found by Caldwell (2003) to be the second most important role of HR managers, is characterized by realism and fatalistic acceptance. Thus, it is a good match with our Factor 3 - *dependency*, a group emphasizing characteristics that are beyond the practitioner's control and which are affected by other forces. This factor deals with cost, reliance on intrinsic and extrinsic factors, and the image of the organization.

Finally, the fourth role, Service Provider, is the role that emphasizes serving the needs of the system. In this sense, this role type would be most fitting for members of Factor 4 - *operation*, which deals with the characteristics of control and efficiency.

DISCUSSION

Our goal in this chapter was to examine beneficial and detrimental characteristics of e-questionnaires for the purpose of HR surveys. We were specifically interested in two types of HR practitioners – HR managers and HR consultants, and in potential differences between their perceptions of e-questionnaires. Since this study is exploratory, it was done in two stages. The first stage was a qualitative analysis in which we identified differences between managers and consultants. We found that managers and consultants use different judgments regarding the decision to use e-questionnaires. The managers' point of view is wider and includes a larger variety of considerations. An interesting observation that came out

of the qualitative analysis was the a-symmetry of the ability of managers and consultants to assess the other group's considerations in using e-questionnaires: managers had difficulties envisioning the consultants' hesitations in using e-questionnaires, while the consultants could point out many considerations that managers should take into account when deciding to use such a surveying technique.

The quantitative analysis of the data indicates that in three cases there are statistically significant differences between managers and consultants in their perception of e-questionnaires. Specifically, consultants perceive this technique as more accessible to employees, but are also more concerned (than managers) with the likelihood of deceit during data collection and with other restrictions and limitations related to this method. Therefore, similar to the qualitative findings, it seems that consultants' position regarding e-questionnaires is more complex than that of managers and that they are more aware of the range of advantages and disadvantages of this method.

In our main statistical analysis, we made use of three statistical procedures – rank test analysis, factor analysis and cluster analysis. The rank test analysis indicated one clear difference between managers and consultants in the importance they attribute to decision factors about whether to use e-questionnaires. Out of seven decision factors, only the decision factor of 'Matching the method to the organization' was ranked differently by the two groups. While managers find the match between the e-questionnaire method and the organization an important factor in the decision of whether to use the method or not, consultants do not consider it an important factor in the decision. This result is not surprising. It is expected that managers will anticipate the long-term effect of choosing a method for the organization, since they are the ones who will have to continue the process in the future. Consultants, on the other hand, are less concerned with matching the method to the organization, since they will not necessarily stay in the organization long enough to deal with a method that may or may not be a good match.

The factor analysis portrayed four groups of variables, each emphasizing different characteristics of e-questionnaires and showing a resemblance to the common roles of HR practitioners mentioned in the literature. The results demonstrated dissimilarity between managers and consultants, in regard to two main factors affecting the choice of electronic versus paper-and-pencil questionnaires. It was found (though with marginal significance) that in comparison to consultants, managers find that e-questionnaires are faster and more efficient and allow more control than paper-and-pencil questionnaires. Furthermore, they are less concerned about the possible biases that can take place when using the web for surveying. This is especially important, since data collection in organizations is often managed internally by the HR department and, as such, a lack of awareness to such biases can harm the reliability of the survey without the prospect of external monitoring and adjustment.

Our cluster analysis results indicated three distinct groups which perceive e-questionnaires differently. In two of them, we found more consultants and in one, more managers. These three groups differed in their perceptions of e-questionnaires and in the variables that influence their decision to use them. Based on the variables they indicated, we characterized the two consultant-dominant groups as the "attention to needs" group and the "operation" group. We characterized the manager-dominant group as the "efficiency" group. The two consultant-dominant

groups did not vary demographically. We found the emphases of these two groups of consultants not surprising, since they are more typical of consultants who are judged, among other things, by their ability to provide good service to the organization (stressing the "attention to needs" variable) and by the importance they attribute to sound operation. The manager-dominant group perceived e-questionnaires differently. When comparing e-questionnaires to paper-and-pencil questionnaires, they believed that when using the former, practitioners have better control over the process, that this type of questionnaire poses less restrictions on data collection, and that when using it, other employees have less influence on their co-workers' participation. This group focused on the efficiency of the process and thought more as internal members of the organization – as managers would – compared to external members of the organization – as consultants would. Despite the differences we found between managers and consultants, there were factors that they agreed on, such as those related to external influences and procedure. *Image* was the one variable that was rated equally by all three groups as having moderate importance. All participants answered that when considering the use of e-questionnaires, the image of the organization (as one that uses the web for survey purposes) has a moderate effect on their decision. Hence, although not a top consideration of HR practitioners, image is certainly a variable that influences the decision to use e-questionnaires in HR surveying. It is important to point out that our results were almost entirely unaffected by organization size, managers or consultants' tenure, experience, age or gender. This indicates that the job-holder himself/herself is the most dominant factor in survey technique preferences. It is important to mention the fact that we could not perform a regression analysis due to the small sample size.

The simplicity of using e-questionnaires contributes to its widespread and ever-increasing use. However, not all practitioners and managers adopt it or agree on it use. It is not uncommon for an organization to hire an external HR consultant, and it is not uncommon for HR managers to disagree with the consultant (who may have different work patterns preferences). Therefore, we expect the two groups to differ in their attitudes towards e-questionnaires. The differences in approach to surveys, as shown here, may add to the tension between the two and increase the likelihood of conflict. Awareness of the possible differences could help ease these relationships.

This study is exploratory in nature and, as such, does not intend to fully describe the gap between the opinions of HR managers and HR consultants regarding web surveys, but rather to simply point out their existence. We assumed that the differences between the two stem from existing differences in the role itself. Our preliminary results show that this issue is worth further research and calls for additional work with a larger sample that will allow multi-variate analysis. It could be beneficial to examine the following: when, and in regard to which issues, the two types of practitioners reach an agreement; and whether this process is one of persuasion or coercion - when either the consultant tries to please the manager, i.e. the client, or the manager submits to the consultant because of top management commands.

REFERENCES

Andrews, D., Nonnecke, B., & Preece, J. (2003). Electronic survey methodology: A case study in reaching hard-to-involve Internet users. *International Journal of Human-Computer Interaction, 16*(2), 185–210. doi:10.1207/S153275901-JHC1602_04

Appelbaum, S. H., & Steed, A. J. (2005). The critical factors in the client-consulting relationship. *Journal of Management, 24*(1), 68–93.

Birnbaum, M. H. (2001). *Introduction to behavioral research on the internet.* Upper Saddle River, NJ: Prentice-Hall.

Boothkewley, S., Edwards, J. E., & Rosenfeld, P. (1992). Impression management, social desirability, and computer administration of attitude questionnaires - Does the computer make a difference? *The Journal of Applied Psychology, 77*(4), 562–566. doi:10.1037/0021-9010.77.4.562

Bowling, A. (2005). Mode of questionnaire administration can have serious effects on data quality. *Journal of Public Health, 27*(3), 281–291. doi:10.1093/pubmed/fdi031

Buchanan, T., & Smith, J. L. (1999). Using the Internet for psychological research: Personality testing on the World Wide Web. *The British Journal of Psychology, 90*, 125–144. doi:10.1348/000712699161189

Caldwell, R. (2003). The changing roles of personnel managers: Old ambiguities, new uncertainties. *Journal of Management Studies, 40*(4), 983–1004. doi:10.1111/1467-6486.00367

Cho, H., & LaRose, R. (1999). Privacy issues in internet surveys. *Social Science Computer Review, 17*(4), 421–434. doi:10.1177/089443939901700402

Church, A. (1997). Do you see what I see? An exploration of congruence in ratings from multiple perspectives. *Journal of Applied Social Psychology, 27*(11), 983–1020. doi:10.1111/j.1559-1816.1997.tb00283.x

Cole, M. S., Bedeian, A. G., & Feild, H. S. (2006). The measurement equivalence of Web-based and paper-and-pencil measures of transformational leadership - A multinational test. *Organizational Research Methods, 9*(3), 339–368. doi:10.1177/1094428106287434

Cook, C., Heath, F., & Thompson, R. L. (2000). A meta-analysis of response rates in Web- or internet-based surveys. *Educational and Psychological Measurement, 60*(6), 821–836. doi:10.1177/00131640021970934

Cook, C., Heath, F., Thompson, R. L., & Thompson, B. (2001). Score reliability in Web- or Internet-based surveys: Unnumbered graphic rating scales versus Likert-type scales. *Educational and Psychological Measurement, 61*(4), 697–706. doi:10.1177/00131640121971356

De Beuckelaer, A., & Lievens, F. (2009). Measurement equivalence of paper-and-pencil and internet organisational surveys: A large scale examination in 16 countries. *Psychologie Appliquee-Revue Internationale, 58*(2), 336–361. doi:10.1111/j.1464-0597.2008.00350.x

Dillman, D. A. (2000). *Mail and internet surveys: The tailored design method* (2nd ed.). New York, NY: John Wiley & Sons.

Eaton, J., & Struthers, C. W. (2002). Using the Internet for organizational research: A study of cynicism in the workplace. *Cyberpsychology & Behavior, 5*(4), 305–313. doi:10.1089/109493102760275563

Edvardsson, B. (1990). Management consulting: Towards a successful relationship. *International Journal of Service Industry Management, 1*(3), 4–19. doi:10.1108/09564239010136902

Epstein, J., Klinkenberg, W. D., Wiley, D., & McKinley, L. (2001). Insuring sample equivalence across internet and paper-and-pencil assessments. *Computers in Human Behavior, 17*(3), 339–346. doi:10.1016/S0747-5632(01)00002-4

Glasser, J. K. (2002). Factors related to consultant credibility. *Consulting Psychology Journal: Practice and Research, 54*(1), 28–42. doi:10.1037/1061-4087.54.1.28

Greiner, L., & Metzger, R. (1983). *Consulting to management.* Englewood Cliffs, NJ: Prentice Hall.

Heneman, H. G. III, Metzler, C. A., Roosevelt Thomas Jr, R., Donohue, T. J., & Frantzreb, R. B. (1998). Future challenges and opportunities for the HR profession. *HRMagazine, 43*(3), 68–72.

Krantz, J. H., & Dalal, R. (2000). Validity of Web-based psychological research. In Birnbaum, M. H. (Ed.), *Psychological experiments on the internet.* San Diego, CA: Academic Press. doi:10.1016/B978-012099980-4/50003-4

Kraut, A. I., & Saari, L. M. (1999). Organizational surveys: Coming of age for a new era. In Kraut, A. I., & Korman, A. K. (Eds.), *Evolving practices in human resource management* (pp. 302–327). San Francisco, CA: Jossey-Bass.

Kubr, M. (1996). *Management consulting: A guide to the profession* (3rd ed.). Geneva, Switzerland: International Labour Office.

Lautenschlager, G. J., & Flaherty, V. L. (1990). Computer administration of questions - More desirable or more social desirability. *The Journal of Applied Psychology, 75*(3), 310–314. doi:10.1037/0021-9010.75.3.310

Manewitz, M. (1997). When should you call a consultant? *HRMagazine, 42*, 84–88.

McLachlin, D. R. (1999). Factors for consulting engagement success. *Management Decision,* 394–402. doi:10.1108/00251749910274162

Poulfelt, F. (1997). Ethics for management consultants. *Business Ethics (Oxford, England), 6*(2), 65–70. doi:10.1111/1467-8608.00050

Reips, U. D. (2000). The web experiment method: Advantages, disadvantages and solutions. In Birnbaum, M. H. (Ed.), *Psychological experiments on the internet* (pp. 89–117). San Diego, CA: Academic Press. doi:10.1016/B978-012099980-4/50005-8

Roberts, L. L., Konczak, L. J., & Macan, T. H. (2004). Effects of data collection method on organizational climate survey results. *Applied H.R.M. Research, 9*(1), 13–26.

Schaefer, D. R., & Dillman, D. A. (1998). Development of a standard E-mail methodology - Results of an experiment. *Public Opinion Quarterly, 62*(3), 378–397. doi:10.1086/297851

Schmidt, W. C. (1997). World-Wide Web survey research: Benefits, potential problems, and solutions. *Behavior Research Methods, Instruments, & Computers, 29*(2), 274–279. doi:10.3758/BF03204826

Schneider, B., Ashworth, S. D., Higgs, A. C., & Carr, L. (1996). Design, validity, and use of strategically focused employee attitude surveys. *Personnel Psychology, 49*(3), 695–705. doi:10.1111/j.1744-6570.1996.tb01591.x

Simsek, Z., & Veiga, J. F. (2001). A primer on Internet organizational surveys. *Organizational Research Methods, 4*(3), 218–235. doi:10.1177/109442810143003

Smith, M. A., & Leigh, B. (1997). Virtual subjects: Using the Internet as an alternative source of subjects and research environment. *Behavior Research Methods, Instruments, & Computers, 29*(4), 496–505. doi:10.3758/BF03210601

Sproull, L. S. (1986). Using electronic mail for data-collection in organizational research. *Academy of Management Journal, 29*(1), 159–169. doi:10.2307/255867

Stanton, J. M. (1998). An empirical assessment of data collection using the Internet. *Personnel Psychology, 51*(3), 709–725. doi:10.1111/j.1744-6570.1998.tb00259.x

Stanton, J. M., & Rogelberg, S. G. (2001). Using Internet/intranet web pages to collect organizational research data. *Organizational Research Methods, 4*(3), 200–217. doi:10.1177/109442810143002

Thompson, L. F., & Surface, E. A. (2007). Employee surveys administered online - Attitudes toward the medium, nonresponse, and data representativeness. *Organizational Research Methods, 10*(2), 241–261. doi:10.1177/1094428106/294696

Thompson, L. F., Surface, E. A., Martin, D. L., & Sanders, M. G. (2003). From paper to pixels: Moving personnel surveys to the Web. *Personnel Psychology, 56*(1), 197–227. doi:10.1111/j.1744-6570.2003.tb00149.x

Turner, A. N. (1982). Consulting is more than giving advice. *Harvard Business Review, 60*(5), 120–129.

Vehovar, V., Manfreda, K. L., & Batagelj, Z. (2001). Sensitivity of electronic commerce measurement to the survey instrument. *International Journal of Electronic Commerce, 6*(1), 31–51.

Yun, G. W., & Trumbo, C. W. (2000). Comparative response to a survey executed by post, e-mail, & web form. *Journal of Computer-Mediated Communication, 6*(1).

Zhang, Y. (2000). Using the Internet for survey research: A case study. *Journal of the American Society for Information Science American Society for Information Science, 51*(1), 57–68. doi:10.1002/(SICI)1097-4571(2000)51:1<57::AID-ASI9>3.0.CO;2-W

KEY TERMS AND DEFINITIONS

Decision Factor: Reasons for choosing a course of action.

E-Questionnaire: A digital questionnaire administered via computer.

HR Consultant: An outside practitioner advising organizations in matters of human resource.

HR Manager: An organizational employee in a managing position practicing human resource work.

Online Surveys: Data colleted via internet.

Organization Surveys: Data collection and assessment concerning issues of interest to the organization.

Paper-and-Pencil Questionnaires: A questionnaire administered in a hardcopy form.

ENDNOTE

[1] This type of analysis was chosen in place of a multiple discriminant analysis because of the sample size.

APPENDIX

Questionnaire for HR managers/HR consultants

The following are ranking questions.

Below is a list of 7 different factors, which may affect your decision regarding whether to perform organizational feedback with an internet survey. Please rank the factors affecting selection of electronic survey instruments from 1 to 7, in order of importance. Please give each factor a separate ranking, even if you think that different factors have a similar or almost identical level of importance in the decision to select a certain type of feedback.

1. Speed of execution
2. Control of the process
3. Quality of information collected
4. Respondent anonymity
5. Compatibility of the organization with this type of internet questionnaire
6. Response rate
7. Image

State your opinion regarding the use of electronic (computer/internet) surveys versus traditional paper-and-pencil surveys (1 – completely disagree; 7 – completely agree).

8. Compared to paper-and-pencil questionnaires, computerized surveys afford more control over the process.
9. Compared to paper-and-pencil questionnaires, computerized surveys have a more positive effect on the company's image as perceived by employees.
10. Compared to paper-and-pencil questionnaires, computerized surveys are more easily accessible to the entire population of employees.
11. Compared to paper-and-pencil questionnaires, computerized surveys maintain better respondent anonymity.
12. Compared to paper-and-pencil questionnaires, computerized surveys are more economical, save time, and enable more rapid implementation.
13. Compared to paper-and-pencil questionnaires, computerized surveys are more costly.
14. Compared to paper-and-pencil questionnaires, computerized surveys facilitate a higher response rate / participation rate of employees.
15. Compared to paper-and-pencil questionnaires, computerized surveys arouse more concern about possible employee deceit.
16. Compared to paper-and-pencil questionnaires, when using computerized surveys, I am more dependent on internal or external factors.
17. Compared to paper-and-pencil questionnaires, computerized surveys have limitations regarding the ability to gather information.
18. Compared to paper-and-pencil questionnaires, when using computerized surveys, colleagues have a greater effect on the participation process (participation, per se, as well as content of responses).

Finally, several general and demographic questions were asked:

Type of consulting: 1. Internal consultant; 2. Employee in a consulting firm; 3. Independent consultant; 4. Academician (appeared only in the consultants' questionnaire)

Number of employees in the company you work for: _____ (appeared only in the managers' question-naire).

Your tenure in the field of HR (in years): _____

Do you have experience with the use of e-surveys? 1. Yes 2. No

Gender: 1. Male 2. Female

Age: _____

Formal education: 1. Primary; 2. Secondary; 3. Certification studies; 4. Bachelors Degree (BA); 5. Masters Degree (MA) or higher

Chapter 2
The Use of Mixed Methods in Organizational Communication Research

Philip Salem
Texas State University, USA

ABSTRACT

Most organizational research employs either quantitative or qualitative methods. Furthermore, users of one methodology often dismiss those who use another. The purpose of this report was to describe how researchers could use mixed methods, especially online. Researchers often begin investigations with paradigmatic assumptions or multiple constructs that should lead to mixed methods. However, quantitative methodological assumptions may seem to contradict qualitative methodological assumptions, and scholars have found it easier and quicker to deliver results adopting only one methodology. Additionally, researchers may be resistant because making high quality inferences from mixed methods might seem too demanding. This chapter describes how one researcher grappled with these challenges when using mixed methods off-line. Online technologies contribute to resolving some difficulties more easily.

INTRODUCTION

Although organizational researchers have always used a variety of research methods, a single type of methodology appeared to influence the research published during any given era. For example,

quantitative methods dominated organizational communication research by the 1970's (Salem, 1999). Although a few communication scholars had been employing qualitative methods in the 1970's (e.g., Browning, 1978), there is little doubt that the special issue of the *Western Journal Speech*

DOI: 10.4018/978-1-4666-2172-5.ch002

Communication in Spring, 1982 (volume 46, no. 2) stimulated the greater use of such methods. Today, organizational communication researchers have a greater choice of methods, but most choose methods consistent with one methodology. Generally, organizational research is mono method, either quantitative or qualitative.

From the earliest times, it appears that those who use one methodology have sought to discredit the other. One researcher noted the following in 1969:

Even though case studies have a richness of detail, they have at least four drawbacks: they are (a) situation specific, (b) ahistorical, (c) tacitly prescriptive, and (4) one-sided. (p. 18)

And then he made the following argument:

The experimental method, whether applied in field experiments . . . controlled naturalistic observation . . . contrived laboratory experiments . . . or simulated environments . . . is the principal tactic by which more durable data and useful data can be obtained. (p. 21)

Ironically, the same researcher wrote the following in 1979:

. . . there is not an underlying "reality" waiting to be discovered. Rather, organizations are viewed as the inventions superimposed on flows of experience and momentarily imposing some order on those streams. (pp. 11-12)

And later in the same the work, he explained how researchers make sense of data.

In the process of embellishing, reworking and contemplating each prior example, we begin to identify some elements associated with organizing. In each example, some portions of the stream of experience was bracketed, and efforts were made to turn the stream into information and then to do something about the information that had been constructed. (p. 12)

These are striking differences between Karl Weick's comments about research methods in the first edition of *The Social Psychology of Organizing* (1969), when he espoused quantitative methods, and his comments in the second edition (1979), when he advocated qualitative methods.

From the 1960's to the present, academicians and consultants developed an alternative body of methodological literature (Tashakkori & Teddlie, 1998). Researchers documented the systematic and planned use of quantitative and qualitative methods in the same study. This led to the development of mixed models of phenomena that included both quantitative and qualitative methodological assumptions. Today, there are several approaches that include both methods and represent a separate methodology (Tashakkori & Teddlie, 2003a).

The purpose of this essay is to explain the use of mixed methods in organizational research. By reporting on the use of mixed methods, this chapter may provide a deeper appreciation of both methodologies and an understanding of the strengths and challenges of using mixed methods. Online technology may make it more likely to employ mixed designs.

FROM MULTIPLE METHODS TO MIXED MODELS

Developing Alternatives

Methods are only one level of knowing, and they are tied to broader concerns such as methodologies and paradigms. For purposes of this essay, *paradigms* are sets of assumptions scholars employ to highlight features of phenomena and to suggest ways of developing and demonstrating theory. A *research method* is a particular and specific approach to developing and demonstrating theory, and a *methodology* is a system of methods, a collection of methods along with rules for their use. Behavioral science researchers generally value alignment of these levels of knowing with specific paradigms suggesting specific methodologies and methods but also excluding others.

There have been noteworthy calls to employ several methods *within* a methodology. Campbell often argued for a multi-trait multi-method approach to improve the veracity of theoretical claims (Campbell & Fiske, 1959). Cook and Campbell (1979) contended that when researchers measured a construct using only one method, it would be difficult to differentiate the construct from its particular and single operational definition. The International Communication Association Organizational Communication Audit procedures (Goldhaber & Rogers, 1979) involved six different methods as part of a design to triangulate results, but all methods led to some quantification, and few clients chose to contract for all six methods. Similarly, Lincoln and Guba (1985) have urged qualitative researchers to improve the trustworthiness of their research by using multiple sources of data and by keeping accurate and extensive records, but few qualitative reports contain detailed sections on research methods. Scholars might have wanted to include and report on multiple methods even within methodologies, but editors and page limitations have led to less reporting of the confirmatory phases of research in journals, and clients did not want their reports cluttered with too many methodological concerns. Mixed designs compound the problems.

Mixed methods developed in atheoretical projects seeking data to investigate some "problem." Paradigmatic and methodological differences were less important than developing answers. The "dictatorship of the research question" is an expression that captures this perspective (Teddlie & Tashakkori, 2003). Mixed methods advocates often employed American pragmatism to link the methods to some philosophical base (Maxcy, 2003). They adopted the position that all research involves interpretation, that researchers' values will always be part of that interpretation, and that the ultimate "truths" in a project emerge from what works.

There are several ways to "mix methods" (Teddlie & Tashakkori, 2003). Utilizing *multiple methods* refers to a researcher employing different methods within a methodology. When a researcher includes questions in an online survey about the extent to which individuals receive needed information through e-mail and also counts e-mail inquiries about received messages as an alternative indicator, the researcher is using multiple methods. Using *mixed methods* refers to exploiting methods from differing methodologies. The most obvious example is to use some quantitative and some qualitative methods, but the methods may be differing approaches to the same or similar constructs. A *mixed design* is the precise description of the ways researchers used mixed methods. A *mixed model* is a theoretical perspective with different constructs suggesting differing methods or methodologies. Both the set of research questions and the theoretical framework lead to mixed methods when starting with a mixed model.

The Implications of a Mixed Model

I employed a mixed model for a five-year study of communication and organizational change in a Texas state government organization (GOV). During the first year, GOV employees had experienced a change of reporting lines within the government bureaucracy, a reexamination of the internal structure of the unit and the structure of the jobs within GOV, a change of leadership, and a physical move to a new building. I began the project in 1997-1998, and I directed five research teams until 2002, a period of relative stability for GOV.

The GOV changes were purposeful attempts at organizational change, and the common expression to reference these attempts is "strategic initiatives." The traditional view is that management can create these initiatives to accomplish a lasting or transformational change (Fredig & Ludema, 2005; Nadler, Shaw, & Walton, 1995). Alternative expressions for transformational change are discontinuous and episodic change (Weick & Quinn, 1999), second order change (Watzlawick, Weakland, & Fisch, 1994), and double loop learning (Argyris, 1992).

The vast majority of these change initiatives fail to demonstrate meaningful changes in performance or organizational outcomes (Robbins & Finely, 1996). Cameron and Quinn (1999) reviewed the most popular initiatives of the last decade and concluded that enduring improvement is impossible without a change of culture (p. 9). Their results were consistent with a study of the hospital industry that found lasting change occurred only 30% of the time (Meyer, Goes, & Brooks, 1995). Strategic initiatives whose purpose was to change the organization's culture succeed less than 20% of the time (Smith, 2002). What this suggests is that most established cultures are robust and resistant to strategic initiatives. What management intends to be lasting change may be integrated into the organization as simple adaptations.

The GOV study employed a model of organizations as a complex adaptive system in which change and communication happened analogous to the processes described by complexity theory (Salem, 2009; Stacy, 2001, 2003). One aspect of my approach was to distinguish culture from climate. Culture refers to those relatively enduring distinctive perceptions and behaviors shared by individuals identifying themselves as members of that organization (adapted from Agar, 1994). Cultural perceptions, values, and rules act as passive constraints emerging from the communication enacted by individual agents (Salem, 2009). The ideas that cultural relationships, social relationships, and self emerge concomitant with communication and that the emergence of these psycho-social factors could limit communication are old ideas going back to Mead (Salem, 2004a).

Structuration theory (Giddens, 1984) is a logical extension of this type of thinking, and the ideas about the emergence of culture and communication lend themselves to complexity theory (Salem, 2009; Stacey, 2001, 2003).

Climate refers to perceptions of characteristic social and work conditions such as autonomy, warmth and consideration, formalization and structure, and equity of rewards (Litwin & Stringer, 1968). Climate is about perceptions of organizational life, and culture is about the norms and values that prompt those events and perceptions (Verbeke, Volgering, & Hessels, 1998; Schneider, 1990). Communication behavior constitutes the culture and creates the climate. That is, communication behavior is between cultural perceptions and climate.

Strategic initiatives often lead to organizational climate changes, but transformational change requires a change in culture, and cultural change is rare. Changes in climate would be more rapid than changes in culture, and quantitative methods would be more sensitive to the more immediate changes while qualitative methods would capture the depth of more lasting change. This approach was consistent with the work of many organizational researchers, but some researchers have employed models suggesting only one methodology for both culture and climate (Cameron & Quinn, 1999; Schneider, 1990; Verbeke, Volgering, & Hessells, 1998).

The assumptions in the entire model led to two research questions. (a) How do organizational members communicate during a time of turbulence? (b) What features of this communication suggest the potential for or resistance to transformative change? In order to answer the first question, a researcher needs to gather data at different points of time to discover what communicative features are unique to the period of turbulence. Furthermore, the researcher would need to employ mixed methods in order to separate those features that penetrated the culture from those temporary features that altered climate.

I have described and applied the portions the model distinguishing culture and climate (Salem, 1994), described the full model and reported the qualitative results (Salem, Barclay, & Hoffman, 2003), and reported the quantitative results (Salem, 2004b). I have integrated all my results with those of other change studies to reveal a general pattern (Salem, 2008). What is important to this essay is that I began with a mixed model suggesting mixed methods, and I will describe my experiences with mixed methods as examples.

The primary qualitative method was face-to-face ethnographic interviews to indicate something about culture and about the current climate during the changes. These interviews included questions directly about the more enduring communication practices such as routines, rituals and rites, stories, documents, vocabulary, and other symbolic artifacts that are part of culture (Bantz, 1993; Trice & Beyer, 1993) and about current communication and organizational activity during the time of change. Qualitative interviews may begin with some structure such as an interview guide, but the primary advantage of this approach is that it encourages open-ended answers and stories (Kvale, 1996; Rubin & Rubin, 1995; Spradley, 1979). This allows for more expansive answers that could explore aspects of cultural perceptions such as paradigms (Pfeffer, 1982), premises (Perrow, 1979), theories of action (Argyris, 1992), ideology (Alvesson, 1987), and values (Quinn & Rohrbaugh, 1983). These interviews also hold the promise of indicating something about members' organizational identification (Scott & Lane, 2000). It is possible to conduct online interviews through e-mail and chat, but any online method is asynchronous, slower, and less spontaneous. A researcher should treat online data as unique and separate from face-to-face data.

Other qualitative methods were observation of meetings, thematic analysis of documents, and focus groups. This would be similar to lurking, being just an observer to online chat, and analyses of blogs or web pages. One recent study analyzed nearly 2,000 messages posted on a company message board (Bates, 2006). Our extra efforts were attempts to support interview data and to look for themes contradicting the interview data. We used the entire qualitative package twice – once at the beginning of the period and once at the end of the five years.

The primary quantitative method was a survey. The initial survey contained ninety-two items we used to construct eighteen scales. These scales were about aspects of communication climate such as information adequacy, communication skills, the effectiveness of communication technology, as well as the more traditional aspects of relational and organizational climate. This was a typical package of scales for climate (Falcione, Sussman, & Herden, 1987; Putnam & Cheney, 1985), but I believed the interviews suggested the specific scales in this package. We administered the survey during staff meetings and requested returns within the week. We used the survey every other year beginning in 1998 to look for changes in climate and current communication practices.

MIXED METHODS DESIGNS

There have been many attempts to develop design typologies, but designs are evolving, and no one typology appears to capture all the potential ways to use mixed methods. Differing designs could also function differently, and so I will begin this section by describing the functions of mixed methods. I will conclude this section by describing some fundamental considerations related to designing a mixed method project.

Functions

Greene, Caracelli, and Graham (1989) identified five purposes for using mixed methods. A researcher could direct a multi-method design to accomplish one or two purposes, but using a mixed model often leads to accomplishing all five purposes. Purposes become functions in a design investigating a mixed model, and the design is likely to accomplish many functions. The GOV study accomplished all five functions.

The most obvious use of mixed methods is *triangulation*, seeking a convergence of results. I intended the multiple qualitative methods to triangulate to each other, but some patterns in that data should also find their way into the quantitative data. Using mixed methods in my investigation was advantageous because it produced triangulation across methods. Some qualitative data described communication and suggested climate outcomes during the turbulent period, and the climate data confirmed the likelihood of these trends.

A researcher can use mixed methods *developmentally*, using one method to inform another. Qualitative methods informed quantitative ones at the start of the GOV project. The qualitative methods suggested communication practices I represented in the survey scales. My model assumed organizational culture and the organizational changes prompted the behaviors that are the basis for climate perceptions, and so an analysis of qualitative data should inform the investigation of climate.

Methods are *complementary* when results from different methods reveal different facets of phenomena, and methods allow *expansion* when mixed methods add scope and breadth to a study. One normally associates complementarity and expansion with designs in which the qualitative portion either accompanies or follows the quantitative portion. This pattern was reversed in the GOV study. Interview themes suggested problems with information adequacy, a defensive climate, minimal skills, etc., and I designed the climate survey to investigate these problems in greater detail.

Normally, one thinks of the qualitative portion supplying complementarity and expansion because of the richness of the data. However, qualitative methods typically identify the presence or absence of something while quantitative methods involve investigating the degree to which a feature is present (Kirk & Miller, 1986). Furthermore, quantitative methods can test for relationships between interval level variables. An advantage of mixed methods is the potential for various methods to be mutually complementary and expansive.

One important theme in the GOV initial qualitative data involved conflict. Quantitative data complemented and expanded our understanding of conflict. The first administration of the survey contained a small scale indicating the use of conflict tactics: avoidance, competition, and cooperation. Our statistical analysis suggested avoidance was critical to explaining the other outcome variables. This analysis led to revising and expanding the conflict scales in two later administrations, and so each use of quantitative methods led to greater complementarity and expansion of the next use of those methods. Another reason for revisions was to develop more reliable and valid scales with greater detail. Finally, the analysis of the last survey data led to probing the relationship within the quantitative conflict data by asking about this relationship in the final round of qualitative interviews. The GOV study exemplifies how quantitative data can complement and expand qualitative data, how methods within a methodology can complement and expand data, and how qualitative data can complement and expand quantitative data.

Initiation, the final function, occurs when mixed methods reveal contradictions or perspectives unavailable to a single method. GOV organizational members complained about members avoiding confrontations in the first round of qualitative interviews. When I correlated conflict avoidance items with outcome variables, avoidance was positively correlated to seven of the eight outcome variables. That is, more avoidance was associated with more positive outcomes. I expanded the investigation of conflict, but the contradiction still persisted. Revealing contradictions and unexpected perspectives are definitely advantages of using mixed methods.

Design Considerations

There are several alternatives for the design of research using mixed methods (Teddlie & Tashakkori, 2003). Morse (1991) used a notation system that provided an easy way to understand the choices for the simplest design, and that notation system has become a common method for describing designs. Several analyses of advanced designs often simply relabeled constructs, but they highlighted what to consider when creating a design (Cresswell, Plano Clark, Gutmann, & Hanson, 2003; Tashakkori & Teddlie &, 2003b). I will review four of those considerations below.

The first consideration in a project is *the place of theory*. The project may be one aimed at developing theory, and so, theoretical perspectives may be implicit. That is, the study may be exploratory in nature, more inductive than deductive, and the researcher might embed theoretical considerations in the construction of quantitative instruments or in the interpretation of qualitative data. A common approach in reporting qualitative research is to describe theoretical frames one might bring to data, and any literature review will reveal implicit theory. Exploratory pieces often end with a more explicit statement of theory or a description of a model. Mixed methods are popular in exploratory studies (Cresswell, Plano Clark, Gutmann, & Hanson, 2003; Morse, 1991; Tashakkori & Teddlie, 2003b).

By contrast, theory may be explicit, and the project may be a more direct test of hypotheses. The approach may be one of confirming theory, more deductive than inductive, and the report of such research often begins with a detailed explanation of a theory or paradigmatic perspective. Researchers often use mixed methods to triangulate results and for complementarity and expansion when theory is explicit (Cresswell,

Plano Clark, Gutmann, & Hanson, 2003; Morse, 1991; Tashakkori & Teddlie, 2003b).

Although the GOV study employed an explicit mixed model, I detailed the model to explain the theoretical frame for creating methods and interpreting data. Although I had a model of organizational change, I did not know how the subjects made sense of change or communicated about it. Although the model linked organizational culture to climate, I did not know what features of culture might be important or what features of climate should be on a survey until after the first interviews. Furthermore, although I maintained the same survey format over three time periods, I did change some items and scales and the final interview guide to reflect patterns in earlier data. The mixed model provided some direction, but the GOV study was considerably more exploratory than confirmatory.

A second consideration is *the dominance or priority of one method over another*. Organizational researchers and consultants often use one method to develop a second, and the second method dominates the report. Another common design expands or complements results from one method with results from another method, but the first method is the dominant one. An additional pattern is using a second method to confirm the results of the first, and the first method dominates. Morse (1991) indicated a method's dominance with capital letters and the secondary method in lower case letters. A qual-QUANT design would be one in which the qualitative data supported the quantitative data.

I gave no priority to one method over another in the GOV study because I did not intentionally use two methodologies for one construct. Interview data indicated conflict avoidance was a cultural norm, climate survey analyses demonstrated subjects' associated conflict avoidance with positive outcomes, and the survey analyses led us to explore the avoidance norm in the final interviews. I should note that most climate data varied across the five-year period, consistent with the assumptions about climate. My assumptions about change assumed there might be few, but meaningful changes in culture by the end of the period. There were no significant changes in the culture.

The third consideration is *sequence or order of gathering data.* Morse (1991) used "+" to indicate the researcher used methods simultaneously and "→" to indicate one method following another. One could display a common design in which a researcher conducted a dominating survey and did triangulating or expansive interviews as QUAN→qual.

One might think the availability of online material would make "+" more likely, but a potential difficulty will be the analysis and interpretation of qualitative data. Qualitative research proceeds through three phases: (a) description, (b) analysis, and (c) explanation and interpretation (Kirk & Miller, 1986). *Description* involves gathering data and coding it according to themes within the data, *analysis* may combine themes or recode categories into theoretical constructs, but *explanation and interpretation* involve linking data to theory. Analysis and interpretation will take longer than description, and the researcher needs to expect this. If a researcher intended a complementary QUAL+quan, interpreting qualitative data may take longer than anticipated, and constructing a survey to represent qualitative data may not be possible until one or two months later.

However, time is relative to the theoretical framework of the project. If a researcher conducted a quantitative survey of culture and also conducted triangulating qualitative culture interviews at the same time, then "+" seems obvious. What about one, two or three months between methods? How much time between methods leads to "→" when the construct is culture?

The GOV project exemplified these sequencing challenges. I had intended the project to begin as QUAL+QUAN with QUAL discovering something about culture and QUAN discovering something about climate. Qualitative interviews

would also suggest the aspects of climate for the survey. We completed interviews in early 1998 and identified descriptive themes within a few weeks of final interviews. I then began using the themes to suggest scales for the survey. I concluded the preliminary qualitative analysis pointed to the importance of superior-subordinate relationships and co-worker relationships as part of climate, and I included scales for each of these relational climates in the survey. We administered the survey in early March. Later, I realized my selection of these scales and the corresponding variables an artificially reinforcing qualitative analysis and a de facto connection to constructs. When we completed our analysis of the qualitative data later, I realized trust and identification were the critical aspects during change. What should have happened is that I should have created separate scales on identification and trust as a part of the relational climate material or, even better, as stand alone portions of the survey. What I lost was triangulation, complementarity, expansion, and initiation about identification and trust. One disadvantage of using mixed methods is that the researcher may rush to develop one method from another prematurely. I would have allowed more time to complete the qualitative analysis if I had thought of the design as more sequential and developmental, rather than simultaneous and complementary.

Using online methods would have helped with some of these challenges. It would be easier to download and format online data for analysis than to transcribe and then format similar face-to-face data for use in a software program. However, the time for analysis and interpretation would be similar, and the theoretical nuances would still exist.

My original design for the GOV project began with QUAL+QUAN because of the model of how culture related to climate. Culture should not change much over a few months, and climate results should clarify which aspects of the interviews were about culture and which communication was unique to the period of change.

Also, the Texas legislature meets in the spring of odd numbered years, and most state agencies spend most of that time dealing with legislators. The full design for the entire project was QUAL+QUAN$_{1998}$→QUAN$_{2000}$→QUAN+QUAL$_{2002}$. I waited until the more stable period of 2002 to gather more qualitative data because I wanted to compare a period of stability to one of turbulence. The 2002 quantitative data suggested relative stability. I could have used online interviews to check some aspects of culture in 2000. I did not, and this was one weakness of the project.

A final consideration is *integration. When* does one actually mix the methods? There are four possibilities (Cresswell et al, 2003): (a) collection and description of data, (b) analysis of data, (c) interpretation of data or results, and (d) some combination of the above. When to mix methods depends on the theory, dominance, and sequence decisions made earlier.

Researchers could reduce one type of data into another or treat each set of data as complementary in some way. Reduction is possible because of similarities between methodologies. Researchers begin describing qualitative data by coding, and analysis extends coding into theoretical constructs. At either point, the researcher could train coders, test for inter-rater reliability, and treat the data as quantitative. Categorizing qualitative data with theoretical constructs is similar to labeling factors with a quantitative study. Interpretation of qualitative data can lead to constructing visual representations (Strauss & Corbin, 1998), and these models often resemble path or other causal models.

I treated each set of data as complementary in the GOV project because of theoretical considerations. All data contributed to an overall interpretation of communication during periods of organizational change. I mixed results, instead of data or preliminary analysis, from two differing methodologies. Mixing methods before interpretation could challenge the integrity of the data or the veracity of the inferences drawn from that data.

INFERENCE QUALITY

Inference quality is the extent to which a researcher has accurately drawn both inductive and deductive conclusions from a study (Teddlie & Tashakkori, 2003). From the perspective of argument, inference quality is about the relationships between the evidence and the claims. Empirical researchers connect inferences to data, and so *inference quality* is about how well data and data analysis support claims.

Inference quality may be low because data are suspect. These are data gathering or measurement issues. Quality may be low because procedures used to confirm or induce inferences may be flawed or inappropriate. In some fashion or another, these are design issues. Furthermore, quality may be low because the researcher made inferences beyond the results. Inferences may not logically fit the results, and the researcher could improve the quality by changing the claim to conform to the limits of sound data and analysis. Several researchers have argued there are comparable terms in quantitative and qualitative research for these issues (Miles & Huberman, 1994; Teddlie & Tashakkori, 2003). Taken together, these terms and the procedures become a catalog of ways to demonstrate inference quality when using mixed methods.

Some qualitative or interpretive researchers would reject the notions that inferences might vary in their quality or that researchers could or should judge the quality of other researchers' inferences. However, the mixed methods researcher has the task of maintaining the integrity of different methodologies and demonstrating the quality of inferences from one methodology to researchers who might be from another methodology and to researchers who might be suspicious of mixing methodologies. Table 1 displays comparable terms from quantitative and qualitative research with explanations below adapted from an analysis by Lincoln and Guba (1985). Instead of explaining every aspect of the table, I will describe how I

Table 1. A comparison of ways to improve inference quality

QUAN Concern	Demonstrated by	QUAL Concern	Demonstrated by
External Validity	Sampling method; comparing population to sample statistics	Transferability	Comparisons to theory and past studies; thick descriptions
Operational Validity	Manipulation checks; panel reviews; factor analysis	Confirmability	Prolonged engagement; persistent observation; triangulation; audits; member checks
Reliability	Statistical tests of raters, items, scales	Dependability	Multiple researchers; audits
Internal Validity	Random assignment; matching subjects to conditions; statistical methods	Credibility	Prolonged engagement; persistent observation; triangulation; member checks; negative cases

tried to demonstrate inference quality in the GOV project.

External validity and *transferability* are both about generalizing results. I attempted comprehensive samples of GOV with each administration of the survey, and I am confident I can generalize the results to the entire organization. We administered the survey three times over five years, and samples ranged from 86% to 91% of the population. Our own analysis of the demographic data in the survey showed we only missed some part-time employees and a few full-time employees who were traveling during the administration period. An online administration might have helped with traveling employees, but the return rate need not have been higher to make inferences about the GOV employees.

I made no attempt to generalize our quantitative findings to organizations or organizational members beyond GOV. Some scales had norms because I adapted them from audit type surveys, but I was interested in comparing the organizational communication during turbulent and stable periods. The more important comparisons were of the organization to itself at different times. Organizational studies do not employ a random sample of employees beyond those identified within a few organizations, a sector, or region.

Lincoln and Guba (1985) argued that the researcher has a responsibility to provide a thick enough description of a case to enhance the potential for connecting one case to another. Our teams tried to develop such detailed material, and our

first report was such a report (Salem, Barclay, & Hoffman, 2003), but providing very much detail in a publication is difficult. Researchers can achieve minimal levels of transferability when they link data to theory, but this connection could only happen at the interpretation or analysis stages. Our initial report did easily connect our results to the theoretical literature about communication and organizational culture, and the latest report of the project (Salem, 2008) was part of connecting our results to the results of others.

Reliability and *dependability* are both about data consistency and variability. I checked the inter-item reliability of the scales with the usual statistical procedures. The survey yielded 18 scales, we administered the survey three times, and nearly all scales had Cronbach alphas of .70 or better with the noted exception being the conflict items. We kept extensive records of our qualitative data in anticipation of data audits. We also reviewed data weekly, providing an opportunity to note and account for variability. Finally, constant comparative coding, the method used to identify themes, reviews past data and coding to check for inconsistencies (Strauss & Corbin, 1998). Our quantitative data and scales were reliable, and our qualitative data and descriptive inferences were dependable.

Operational or measurement validity involves checking how well indicators represent constructs in a faithful manner. Nearly all items in the survey were adapted from other instruments, and reliability checks and confirmatory factor analysis of the first quantitative study supported the validity of the measures except for the scale involving conflict. This led to revisions of this operationalization in later quantitative efforts. I was confident in the face or content validity and the predictive validity of the quantitative measures, and the construct validity of all the measures except the conflict one.

A qualitative study is *confirmable* if the researcher can support coding. We were confident of our own descriptive coding for three reasons. First, we used constant comparative coding to check our labeling and the potential for other labels. This is a form of persistent observation checking for the depth of data. Second, we continued to gather data when data merely repeated themes. For example, after the first fourteen initial interviews, the data began to saturate, but we continued to interview more than twenty employees. This type of prolonged engagement checks the breadth of data - that data have indeed saturated and that we did not miss a theme. Finally, the documents and observations served to triangulate with interview data.

We were also confident we could demonstrate the soundness of our coding if clients, other researchers, or reviewers would audit our data. We employed expressions from the subjects as labels for our initial coding, a process called *in vivo* coding (Strauss & Corbin, 1998). I also connected the descriptive labels directly to the theoretical ones in an orthogonal manner so that others could see the labeling easily. Online data would be easier to enter into analytical software because the researcher only needs to do a little editing and formatting instead of transcribing and editing. Coding may take the same amount of time, but the latest software holds all the data in a project folder, and researchers can obtain all examples of a coding in an instant.

The previous ideas in this section were about the soundness of data gathering and the extent to which data and methods connect to constructs. *Internal validity and credibility* are about the extent to which data and methods support the

way researchers connected constructs – the support for relational inferences. In experimental research, there are checks on the representation of the assumed causal variable and various ways of controlling for intervening variables. Most applied research is quasi-experimental or pre-experimental ex post facto research (Campbell & Stanley, 1963). One supports inferences by using the proper statistical methods and accounting for data gathering errors in those methods. The GOV design explored three different periods of time seeking to identify unique features of the first time period, the period of maximum organizational change. I used tests of difference – t-tests and analysis of variance, and I also displayed various correlational results for the three periods, attenuating for any questionable scale reliabilities when appropriate. Still, I did not control the manipulation or potential intervening variables. I can describe differences, but the quantitative methods cannot directly support a causal inference.

Demonstrating credibility involves procedures similar to demonstrating confirmability. One additional powerful procedure we employed in 1998 and 2002 is member checks. For example, in January 1998, we presented our preliminary results to two focus groups to confirm our coding and preliminary *in vivo* inferences. The members of both focus groups were so confident in our themes that upper management considered ending the project because they were not certain a quantitative effort later in the spring would provide any greater insight. A second procedure is the use of a negative case – the equivalent of contradictory data or a control group. We did look for negative cases in 1998 and 2002, but the only instances were when an interviewee provided data consistent with some themes but not all. The 2002 data were from a time of relative stability, and so the two sets of data acted as comparison groups, with the 2002 data acting as a control on data from the earlier turbulent period. Online data collection and using software to compare data would assist the search for such negative cases. Finally, the integration of results from various studies in 2008 was similar to the experience of looking for negative cases within data sets in one study. I was confident our data was credible.

CONCLUSION

Most organizational communication research uses either quantitative or qualitative methods. Furthermore, the users of one methodology often dismiss those who use a different one. The purpose of this report was to describe how mixed methods could be used in organizational communication research.

Paradigmatic assumptions lead to a choice of research questions and ultimately to a choice of methods. I described some features of a five-year project investigating organizational communication and change. Most organizational strategic initiatives do not succeed in achieving lasting change. Temporary change can be detected as a change in organizational climate, and investigating climate typically involves quantitative methods. More lasting change appears to require a change in culture, and investigating culture typically involves qualitative methods. Therefore, mixed methods seemed best to understand how lasting organizational change occurs or fails. This paper used descriptions of this effort to highlight advantages and disadvantages of using mixed methods.

Mixed methods can function in many ways. Most are familiar with using multiple methods to triangulate or confirm data, but one method can lead to the development of the other. Mixed methods can also complement and expand each other, and they can lead to discovering and exploring inconsistencies between types of data.

There are many forms of mixed designs, and a researcher develops a particular design by considering many design features. Researchers might use mixed methods deductively to confirm theory or inductively to develop theory. Some researchers might want to use one method to support another, and some might want to use methods

simultaneously while others prefer to use them sequentially. Also, researchers may plan to mix methods at the initial point of data collection or wait until later, sometimes waiting until the final interpretation of results.

Researchers are faced with the challenge of making high quality inferences. Both quantitative and qualitative researchers have employed various procedures to support the inferences they make from data. A mixed methods researcher should be familiar with these comparable practices.

Online data collection is more efficient than traditional face-to-face methods, and researchers can easily format and analyze both quantitative and qualitative online data. The availability of online data collection could help lead to better designs, and researchers could demonstrate inference quality more easily.

Hopefully, this description of mixed methods will lead to an appreciation of both quantitative and qualitative methods – an appreciation of the strengths and weaknesses of each. Many research questions suggest one or the other method, but using mixed methods may lead to richer results and a greater understanding of organizations. Furthermore, using mixed methods can lead researchers to consider different and more complex aspects of organizational life.

REFERENCES

Agar, M. (1994). *Language shock: Understanding the culture of conversation*. New York, NY: William Morrow and Company, Inc.

Alvesson, M. (1987). Organizations, culture and ideology. *International Studies of Management and Organizations, 3*, 4–18.

Argyris, C. (1992). *On organizational learning*. Cambridge, MA: Blackwell.

Bantz, C. R. (1993). *Understanding organizations: Interpreting organizational communication culture*. Columbia, SC: University of South Carolina Press.

Bates, C. M. (2006, February). *Identity, identification, and the organization: A Burkean approach to understanding the use of electronic message boards to discourage organizational identification*. Paper resented at the convention of the Western States Communication Association meeting in Palm Spring, CA.

Browning, L. D. (1978). A grounded theory of organizational communication. *Communication Monographs*, *45*, 93–109. doi:10.1080/03637757809375957

Cameron, K. S., & Quinn, R. E. (1999). *Diagnosing changing organizational culture: Based on the competing values framework*. Reading, MA: Addison-Wesley.

Campbell, D. T., & Fiske, D. W. (1959). Convergent and discriminant validation by the multitrait multimethod matrix. *Psychological Bulletin*, *56*, 81–105. doi:10.1037/h0046016

Campbell, D. T., & Russo, M. J. (2001). *Social measurement*. Thousand Oaks, CA: Sage.

Campbell, D. T., & Stanley, J. C. (1963). *Experimental and quasi-experimental designs for research*. Chicago, IL: Rand McNally & Company.

Cook, T. D., & Campbell, D. T. (1979). *Quasiexperimentation: Design and analysis issues for field settings*. Boston, MA: Houghton Mifflin.

Cresswell, J. W., Plano Clark, V. L., Gutmann, M. L., & Hanson, W. E. (2003). Advanced mixed methods research designs. In Tashakkori, A., & Teddlie, C. (Eds.), *The handbook of mixed methods in social and behavioral research* (pp. 209–240). Thousand Oaks, CA: Sage.

Falcione, R. L., Sussman, L., & Herden, R. P. (1987). Communication climate in organizations. In Jablin, F. M., Putnam, L. L., Roberts, K. H., & Porter, L. W. (Eds.), *Handbook of organizational communication: An interdisciplinary perspective* (pp. 195–204). Beverly Hills, CA: Sage.

Ferdig, M. A., & Ludema, J. D. (2005). Transformative interactions: Qualities of conversations that heighten the vitality of self-organizing change. In W. A., Pasmore, & R. W. Woodman (Eds.), *Research in organizational change and development: Vol. 15* (pp. 169-205). Stamford, CT: JAI Press.

Giddens, A. (1984). *The constitution of society*. Berkley, CA: University of California Press.

Goldhaber, G. M., & Rogers, D. P. (1979). *Auditing organizational communication systems: The ICA Communication Audit*. Dubuque, IA: Kendall/Hunt.

Greene, J. C., Caracelli, V. J., & Graham, W. F. (1989). Toward a conceptual framework for mixed-method evaluation designs. *Educational Evaluation and Policy Analysis*, *11*(3), 255–274.

Kirk, J., & Miller, M. L. (1986). *Reliability and validity in qualitative research*. Beverly Hills, CA: Sage.

Kvale, S. (1996). *Interviews: An introduction to qualitative research interviewing*. Thousand Oaks, CA: Sage.

Lincoln, Y. S., & Guba, E. G. (1985). *Naturalistic inquiry*. Newbury Park, CA: Sage.

Litwin, G., & Stringer, R. (1968). *Motivation and organizational climate*. Cambridge, MA: Harvard University Press.

Maxcy, S. J. (2003). Pragmatic threads in mixed methods research in the social sciences: The search for multiple methods of inquiry and the end of the philosophy of formalism. In Tashakkori, A., & Teddlie, C. (Eds.), *The handbook of mixed methods in social and behavioral research* (pp. 51–89). Thousand Oaks, CA: Sage.

Meyer, A. D., Goes, J. B., & Brooks, G. R. (1995). Organizations reacting to hyperturbulence. In Huber, G. P., & Van de Ven, A. H. (Eds.), *Longitudinal field research methods: Studying processes in organizational change* (pp. 66–111). Thousand Oaks, CA: Sage.

Miles, M. B., & Huberman, A. M. (1994). *Qualitative data analysis: An expanded sourcebook* (2nd ed.). Thousand Oaks, CA: Sage.

Morse, J. M. (1991). Approaches to qualitative-quantitative methodological triangulation. *Nursing Research*, *40*(2), 120–123. doi:10.1097/00006199-199103000-00014

Nadler, D. A., Shaw, R. B., & Walton, A. E. (1995). *Discontinuous change: Leading organizational transformation*. San Francisco, CA: Jossey-Bass.

Pacanowsky, M. E., & O'Donnell-Trujillo. (1982). Communication and organizational cultures. *Western Journal of Speech Communication*, *46*, 115–130. doi:10.1080/10570318209374072

Perrow, C. (1979). *Complex organizations: A critical essay*. New York, NY: Random House.

Pfeffer, J. (1982). *Organizations and organization theory*. Boston, MA: Pittman.

Putnam, L. L., & Cheney, G. (1985). Organizational communication: Historical developments and future directions. In Benson, T. W. (Ed.), *Speech communication in the twentieth century* (pp. 130–156). Carbondale, IL: Southern Illinois University Press.

Quinn, R. E., & Rohrbaugh, J. (1983). A spatial model of effectiveness criteria: Towards a competing values approach to organizational analysis. *Management Science*, *29*, 363–377. doi:10.1287/mnsc.29.3.363

Robbins, H., & Finely, M. (1996). *Why change doesn't work: Why initiatives go wrong and how to try again – and succeed*. Princeton, NJ: Peterson's.

Rubin, H. J., & Rubin, I. S. (1995). *Qualitative interviewing*. Thousand Oaks, CA: Sage.

Salem, P. (1999). The changes and challenges for organizational communication in the next century. In Salem, P. (Ed.), *Organizational communication and change* (pp. 3–27). Cresskill, NJ: Hampton Press.

Salem, P. J. (1994). Learning to learn: The challenges in Russia. *Intercultural Communication Studies*, *4*(2), 17–41.

Salem, P. J. (2004a). Mead on management. *Review of Communication*, *4*(1), 97–105. doi:10.1080/1535859042000250344

Salem, P. J. (2004b, May). *A longitudinal study of organizational communicational communication climate*. Paper presented at the Annual Meeting of the International Communication Association meeting in New Orleans, LA.

Salem, P. J. (2008). The seven communication reasons organizations do not change. *Corporate Communications*, *13*(3), 333–348. doi:10.1108/13563280810893698

Salem, P. J. (2009). *The complexity of human communication*. Cresskill, NJ: Hampton Press.

Salem, P. J., Barclay, F., & Hoffman, M. (2003, May). *Organizational culture at the edge: A case study of organizational change*. Paper presented at the Annual Meeting of the International Communication Association meeting in San Diego, CA.

Schneider, B. (Ed.). (1990). *Organizational climate and culture*. San Francisco, CA: Jossey-Bass.

Scott, S. G., & Lane, V. R. (2000). A stakeholder approach to organizational identity. *Academy of Management Review*, *25*(1), 46–62.

Smith, M. E. (2002). Success rates for different types of organizational change. *Performance Improvement*, *41*(1), 26–33. doi:10.1002/pfi.4140410107

Spradley, J. (1979). *The ethnographic interview.* New York, NY: Holt, Rinehart & Winston.

Stacey, R. D. (2001). *Complex responsive processes in organizations: Learning and knowledge creation.* London, UK: Routledge.

Stacey, R. D. (2003). *Strategic management and organizational dynamics: The challenge of complexity.* New York, NY: Prentice-Hall/Financial Times.

Strauss, A., & Corbin, J. (1998). *Basics of qualitative research: Techniques and procedures for developing grounded theory* (2nd ed.). Thousand Oaks, CA: Sage.

Tashakkori, A., & Teddlie, C. (1998). *Mixed methodology: Combining quantitative and qualitative approaches.* Thousand Oaks, CA: Sage.

Tashakkori, A., & Teddlie, C. (Eds.). (2003a). *The handbook of mixed methods in social and behavioral research.* Thousand Oaks, CA: Sage.

Tashakkori, A., & Teddlie, C. (2003b). The past and future of mixed methods research: From data triangulation to mixed model designs. In Tashakkori, A., & Teddlie, C. (Eds.), *The handbook of mixed methods in social and behavioral research* (pp. 671–701). Thousand Oaks, CA: Sage.

Teddlie, C., & Tashakkori, A. (2003). Major issues and controversies in the use of mixed methods in the social and behavioral sciences. In Tashakkori, A., & Teddlie, C. (Eds.), *The handbook of mixed methods in social and behavioral research* (pp. 3–50). Thousand Oaks, CA: Sage.

Trice, H. M., & Beyer, J. M. (1993). *The cultures of work organizations.* Englewood Cliffs, NJ: Prentice Hall.

Verbeke, W., Volgering, M., & Hessells, M. (1998). Exploring the conceptual expansion within the field of organizational behavior: Organizational culture and organizational climate. *Journal of Management Studies, 35*(3), 303–330. doi:10.1111/1467-6486.00095

Watzlawick, P., Weakland, J., & Fisch, R. (1974). *Change: Principles of problem formation and problem resolution.* New York, NY: Norton.

Weick, K. E. (1969). *The social psychology of organizing.* Reading, MA: Addison-Wesley.

Weick, K. E. (1979). *The social psychology of organizing* (2nd ed.). Reading, MA: Addison-Wesley.

Weick, K. E., & Quinn, R. E. (1999). Organizational change and development. *Annual Review of Psychology, 50,* 361–386. doi:10.1146/annurev.psych.50.1.361

KEY TERMS AND DEFINITIONS

Design Considerations: A set of issues a researcher considers when creating and arranging mixed methods for a particular research project. These issues include (a) the place of theory, (b) methodological dominance, (c) sequencing of methods, and (d) methodological integration.

Functions or Purposes of Mixed Methods: What can be accomplished by using mixed methods including (a) triangulation, (b) development, (c) complementarity, (d) expansion, and (e) initiation.

Inference Quality: The extent to which the researcher can demonstrate the data supports the claims. These challenges include demonstrating external validity, operational validity, internal validity and reliability in quantitative research and demonstrating transferability, confirmability, dependability, and credibility in qualitative researcher.

Methodological Data Reduction: Gathering data using multiple methodologies but analyzing them within only one methodology. For example, a researcher might begin with an online survey, a quantitative method, and online ethnographic interviews, a qualitative method, but train coders to quantify interview data.

Methodology: A system of research methods, a collection of methods along with the rules for use. Most organizational research employs either a quantitative or qualitative methodology.

Methods: Particular and specific approaches to developing and demonstrating theory including surveys, interviews, case studies, and textual analysis.

Mixed Methods: Using methods from two differing methodologies in the same project, using both quantitative and qualitative methods in the same project.

Mixed Models: A theoretical approach to a project with some constructs suggesting quantitative methods and other constructs suggesting qualitative methods.

Multiple Methods: The use of more than one method *within* one methodology in the same project such as using content analysis of online documents and an online survey in a quantitative project.

Chapter 3
Online Research and Obtaining Human Subjects/IRB Approvals

Benjamin J. Bates
The University of Tennessee, USA

Ben Birch
The University of Tennessee, USA

ABSTRACT

The development of digital computing and the growth of the Internet have opened up new opportunities to engage in online research. These online research practices involving human subjects, often involving relatively new technologies, can create tension between the online investigator and the Institutional Review Boards (IRBs) who are required to review and approve such research prior to data collection. This chapter aims to reduce this tension by discussing the associated ethics issues and applicable federal regulations, identifying specific concerns from the perspective of IRBs, and offering suggestions as to how best to address these concerns in applications in a way that can hopefully serve both the researcher and the review board.

PASSING REVIEW: ONLINE RESEARCH AND OBTAINING HUMAN SUBJECTS/IRB APPROVALS

Research ethics became a major concern in the middle of the 20th century, largely in response to growing awareness of the potential risks and harms faced by some participants epitomized by several scandals (Baker & McCullough, 2008).

As a result, research involving human subjects is not merely required to be conducted in an ethical manor but often formally reviewed by an Institutional Review Board (IRB) prior to data collection. Such review boards are required for federally funded research but also are used by research organizations inside and outside of the United States in order to ensure that research is conducted in such a way as to protect the rights of the participants.

DOI: 10.4018/978-1-4666-2172-5.ch003

IRBs are guided by a series of ethical concerns, and Federal and (sometime) state regulations designed to protect the rights of human subjects. New methods and procedures can become particularly problematic, as both researchers and IRBs seek to determine appropriate policies and standards while maintaining and protecting the rights of the populations under study. The rise of online research has been a recent example of old boards being faced with the challenge of reviewing new methods.

The Internet has opened the gates to a wealth of potential research observations and data collection methods. It has arguably allowed researchers access to much wider populations and large amounts of content and communication created by people. The nature of the Internet has also raised some troubling issues, related to its "public nature." One aspect of that nature is the fact that most communication, content, and traffic on the Internet are public; moreover, the process of Internet communications includes address tags, which can be linked to sites and potentially individuals. This raises inherent questions about the potential for anonymity and confidentiality in online data collection. In addition, there is another "public" issue that arose very early in online research: for years, observations of normal public behaviors and content analysis (the observation and coding of published content) have been considered to not require IRB review. The problem has been that some researchers consider material public if they can find it on the Internet, but the participants may have thought that some level and expectation of privacy applied in private lists or discussion areas. The debate over whether certain materials are truly public or private has raged since some of the earliest online research, and forms one of the fundamental debates with IRBs.

The concern about ethics in online research is hardly new. A number of scholars have identified some of the emerging issues and problems (Jones, 1994; Frankel & Siang, 1999; Walther, 2002; Ess & Jones, 2004; Jones et al., 2004; Ess, 2007), and

groups like the Association of Internet Researchers made developing their own ethics guidelines one of the first official acts of the association (Ess & Jones, 2004). Much more has been written in recent years about specific issues and problems. While many, starting with Jones (1994), found a certain tension between traditional research guidelines and online research practices, few addressed the issue of how to reduce the tension and accomplish online research within the existing legal framework.

The tension may be compounded by the fact that both researcher and IRB members may lack familiarity with the specifics of Internet operations. The members of IRBs are representative of many disciplines, and also tend to be more senior scholars. Many may lack familiarity with the technical implications and nature of the Internet and various online research methods. This can lead to some confusion and a tendency to overprotect human subjects.

This chapter will try to help reduce the tension by taking a practical approach, with the hope of informing both researchers and IRBs about some of the human research ethics issues raised by online research methods, identifying the more specific concerns from the perspective of IRBs, and offering suggestions as to how to best address those issues and pass IRB review. While the concerns and issues associated with ethical research are global, this chapter will focus on the specifics of the U.S. regulations and IRB review process.

FEDERAL REGULATIONS REGARDING HUMAN RESEARCH

Institutional IRBs are given oversight over all research involving human subjects conducted under their auspices, or by their faculty or employees.[1] While the potential range and scope of human research is near boundless, there are three general classifications of data collection activities from an IRB perspective. First, there are research methods and activities that do not involve the collection of "research data from human subjects", and thus are outside the review process. Second, there is research that is considered "exempt" from review, although one must realize that this exemption is only from full formal review (IRBs must still review such research proposals to validate that they are exempt). Finally, everything else is required to be reviewed, although the regulations allow for some types of research to go through an "expedited" review process.

What falls outside the scope of federal human subjects regulations? The answer to that question is tied to the definition of two key terms "human subjects" and "research". If your research does not collect data from or about people (human subjects), then it clearly isn't covered by human subjects research regulations.[2] However, this is not as clear as it may seem, particularly with online research, where you may not be interacting with people directly, but can still be collecting information about people, their attitudes and behaviors. In general terms, only information that does not come from people, or is not about people or their behaviors, can be clearly seen as falling outside Federal regulations and IRB review. There are some minor exceptions, which will be talked about later. A major exception involves how "research" is defined, and permits the collection of information from people, but not for research purposes. Examples are information that an organization might collect for internal records or evaluations, coursework, and comments left on websites. However, this also means that the information collected for non-research purposes cannot later be used for research without having to undergo an IRB review. The way the regulations are written, data that should be reviewed but is collected without approval (or validation of "exempt" status) cannot be used for research purposes without penalty, so if it's not absolutely clear that your research falls "outside review", you might want to check with your institution's Human Research Compliance Officer

What research and data collection qualifies as "exempt" is clearly spelled out in 45 CFR 46.101(b). This section outlines six general categories for exemption that can generally be described as methods and studies that have little or no potential risk for participants (while still including an adequate informed consent process). While the label of "exempt" may suggest that there is no need for IRB review and approval, these studies still need to be submitted, and reviewed, in order to validate their status as qualifying for the exemption. Applications for exemption use a simpler application form (Form A) and generally can be handled more quickly, as they only address the issue of whether or not the proposed research qualifies under one or more of the enumerated exemptions. The specific exemptions, and their application to online research, are discussed in more detail in the following section.

All other research involving human subjects must go through a more complete review process, often involving several levels of review. In general, these studies have the potential for some degree of risk to participants, and the IRB's role is to judge whether the researchers have taken steps to minimize any risk, have justified that the potential benefits of the research outweigh the potential risks, that potential subjects are informed of these risks, and that they can freely decide whether or not they want to assume the risk before any data is collected that will end up in the research. As such, these applications request and require more information about the methods of collecting and storing information, about potential benefits and risks from the study, and how researchers plan to address any legal and ethical issues their research may raise (using "Form B").

Over time, regulations have mandated that certain types of studies, types of information collection methods, certain potential subject groups, and certain topics must follow this more formal review process (under the assumption that there are specific identifiable risks to be addressed). Given the nature of bureaucracies, it's not surprising that the list of items triggering full review gets longer each year. The Federal regulations allow for "expedited review", however, when the potential risk is generally minimal, falls into one or more of several well-recognized categories, and where the researcher incorporates procedures to minimize potential risk.

It is the "full review" that generally creates most of the controversy over the IRB review process, in large part because the full institutional IRB tends to deal with more controversial research issues. That, and applications needing full review can take months to gain approval, and often require one or more revisions and resubmissions before the research proposal is approved. In some cases, where risks are recognized, addressed, but still potentially serious, the need for a full review is recognized by researchers. In other cases, applications may end up going through "full review" because the principal investigators have failed to recognize and address potential sources of risk (or the IRB members are unsure of what risks there might be, or whether they are adequately addressed). Such situations may occur more frequently for online research, as many of the online methods and approaches are relatively new, the research contexts may not be well understood, and the sources of potential risk may not be well recognized.

This chapter hopes to help this process by identifying many of the sources of potential risk in various online research methods, indicating what the concerns of the IRB are, and making some suggestions as to how to address those concerns in applications in a way that can hopefully anticipate IRB concerns and obtain a speedier review and approval. Please note that some institutions may expand what kinds of research is covered by their IRB procedures (i.e., beyond the Federal regulations), and so it is always best to get to know your local IRB representatives, procedures, and requirements. .

INTERNET RESEARCH AND DATA OUTSIDE OF IRB REVIEW PROCESS

Since IRBs are concerned with protecting the rights of human subjects during the research process, the key exceptions to going through any IRB review process involves research where your data is not collected from humans, or where what you are doing isn't considered "research". One advantage of using the Internet for research purposes is that in its operation and oversight, it generates a large amount of data directly and more or less independently of specific human involvement (tracking message flows, network linkages, etc.). If you want to collect information that does derive from human activity, things get a bit trickier; the keys are whether your online data collection involves "human subjects" and "research." The regulations define the research on human subjects as collecting information that comes directly or indirectly as responses from people, or include personal or identifiable information for research purposes. That leaves two areas that fall "outside" of IRB review, and one that may be more problematic.

The first is collection of information for "non-research purposes." This is actually a very wide exception. This exception covers things like data collected for educational purposes (say for a project in a research methods course), responses collected for administrative purposes (say, peer evaluations), or materials and responses collected for other non-research purposes (for instance, an oral history project). Here, it is not the methodology that is key, it is the intent; if the collected materials are labeled as "research" or are analyzed and presented publicly as research, then that study falls under the regulations. If you want to use and report the results of your class project outside of the classroom, say, in a conference paper or publication (or even report it in the school newspaper), then it's research. If you want to record oral histories, or collect stories or creative work, but use that information for your dissertation, then it's research. Thus, this exception is not one that researchers tend to be very interested in, as the result of making this argument is that you can't use any data collected in this manner for research (then or later). The regulations are written in such a way that they do not permit the use of information collected for non-research purposes for research, without going through IRB review. Thus, it's not a useful back door that you can use to avoid IRB review. Still, knowing about this exception can be useful in teaching or learning about online research methods, since it allows you to practice and collect information as long as it is not presented publically as "research."

The second exception is for collecting information derived from observations of public behaviors, as long as the researcher is not soliciting or prompting the behaviors. Historically, published materials have fallen into this category, allowing content analysis and the secondary analysis of pre-existing datasets to be largely exempt from IRB review. The nature of the Internet allows for a lot of indirect collection of information by, from, and about people, as it acts as a repository for an immense amount of human interaction, records of human activities, and human-produced content.

Some of this online material consists of data collected by other researchers that is being made publicly available. In general, the secondary analysis of data (derived online or not) is considered to fall outside of IRB review, as it is presumed that the data was originally collected after being reviewed and approved. There are two possible exceptions to this that you might want to check with your local IRB about – first, foreign data may not be subject to U.S. rules, and you need to consider whether or not the data contains "personally identifying information." The second case would be if you want to add new cases or data to the existing data set (in which case it becomes a new data set and new research).

What about collecting information "published" on the Internet? Some scholars have argued that since the Internet is public, that any information and content they can find fits the definition of "public behavior." They argue that IRB review isn't needed for information collected from or on pre-existing online sites, since you aren't collecting this information directly from people (and thus aren't interacting with them), that it's been "published" on the Internet, and that the Internet is a public place; however that is not always the case. Here we need to refer to how the regulations[3] define research on "human subjects" as a guide for what types of "indirect" human research and data collection fall outside review. The regulations define research on human subjects as collection of data from living individuals (1) through intervention or interaction with the individual, or (2) collection of identifiable private information. (Historians are in luck – if your information is about dead people, you're safe from IRB review.)

One key consideration here is hidden in how the regulations define identifiable private information. The definition of identifiable private information in Federal regulations limits what can be considered public, by focusing on the perception of the subject rather than the accessibility to the researcher. The regulation defines identifiable private information as resulting from a setting where participants have a reasonable expectation of privacy, or can reasonably expect that no observation is taking place. An example of this kind of situation may occur if you want to use already existing responses gathered from a "private" chat room or listserv or website with restricted access, where it may be reasonable to expect a degree of privacy. Some online communities identify themselves as "safe" or private places to share thoughts within a narrow community; in those cases, there may be a clear expectation of a degree of privacy, even if it doesn't technically exist. The issue of whether or not researchers should respect the privacy of such sites was one of the earliest ethical debates in online research methods. If there is any doubt about whether or not the source of materials is truly "public", you should check with your institution's compliance officer.

The problem here is with researchers trying to avoid the IRB process by claiming that their data collection falls outside the IRB review process when it may not. If there is a question over the "public" nature of the materials, or if the materials include "identifiable personal information," you may be able to make a case that the data being collected does not require review. On the other hand, if there is any doubt, or if you want to make sure you are in compliance, and not putting your research or your institution at risk, for your collection of information from "public" online data sources, you probably should check with your institutions research compliance officer.

Further, there is a way to proceed with the use of such materials that may not require full review. One of the categories for "exempt" research is for the collection of existing materials, if those are publicly available, or if the researcher records the data in a way that specific individuals cannot be identified.[4] That is, if you remove identifiers that are linkable to people (like screen names or email addresses), and clean the information to remove any other identifying information as you record the data, you may qualify for exempt status. And while you still have to submit an IRB application, this avoids the often problematic debate over whether the source of the data is "public" or whether the personal information being collected is identifiable, by indicating that you will take reasonable steps to make sure that the final research data is recorded in a way that does not include identifiable information.

To give you an indication of how this may be done, consider the case of using student comments on a course site in a study of pedagogical approaches. Simply taking the raw comments (including student identifiers), as your data set would pose privacy and anonymity concerns, potentially placing those students at risk (assuming that you

didn't think to get their informed consent at the start of the class). If you were to insist on using that set of responses, you'd probably be asked to do a full review, and likely turned down, as one fundamental rule is that you can't use information generated in the absence of informed consent. However, if you indicate on your IRB application that instead of using the raw data, you will strip it of IDs and other identifying information, and/or replace them with generic subject IDs or other identifiers before analysis (making the cleaned information your research data), then you can use the specific "exemption" and most likely get quick approval of your IRB application for exemption.[5]

What about the collection of new, current, or ongoing online information? Here, the key is whether the researcher is interacting in any way with the people providing the materials or information. If you directly interact with individuals, for example soliciting people to take an online survey or to offer comments, you are interacting with them and what you are doing is considered human subjects research. Also, if you participate in that online chat, or even if you set up the separate chat room, listserv, or other location where people provide information you wish to use, then you can be considered to be intervening in the context in which the information is generated. In other words, if your research is actively involved in the situation that generates the information you want to use for research purposes, then you are likely covered by the regulations and will need to go through some IRB process. To not be considered "human subjects research" you should avoid any direct or indirect interaction or intervention with people.

Thus, there can be a lot of online research that falls outside of the "human subjects research" review process. There is much online that's not about "human subjects." Still, there's also a lot of interesting information online that comes from people, directly and indirectly. In general, if you're doing research and you're using information from, by, or about people, then it's safest to go through IRB review unless it's clear that you're collecting information exclusively from sources that you had no role in creating (or influence on) and are clearly public. In many cases, online research can be conducted, and information recorded, in a way that minimizes risk, and the level of researcher involvement in the IRB process. It can be well worth the initial effort for online researchers to be proactive in addressing research ethics and IRB concerns and procedures, educating both yourself and your institution's IRB on the issues and developing guidelines.

EXEMPT RESEARCH

Federal regulations identify six basic categories of human research that may qualify as "exempt." While the regulations use the term exempt, their meaning is that these forms of research and data collection are "exempt" from the full review process. Researchers still have to apply to their institutional IRB to have that status recognized and approved. So what kind of research and data collection qualifies as "exempt"?

As a general rule, if you're collecting information with little or no risk to participants, with their informed consent, and using standard and recognized research methods, it may qualify as exempt if it fits within one of the enumerated categories. Most online research that qualifies as exempt will fall under two categories of eligibility for exemption. The other four categories involve narrowly defined circumstances.

Category (2) covers research using surveys, educational tests, interviews, or direct observations of public behavior, but only if the information is recorded in a way that cannot be linked, directly or indirectly, to individuals and that the information collected is considered harmless. Most data collected directly from people online is done in one or more of the four methods outlined. The key to this exemption is thus what kind of information is collected and how is it recorded.

Collecting information that may place the individual at risk can disqualify the study for exempt status and require going through a formal IRB review. The problem researchers face lies in knowing what kinds of information can pose a potential risk. Some of it is fairly obvious, such as asking about illegal activities; however the regulation phrases it more broadly - anything that could expose subjects to criminal or civil liability, or possibly damage their financial standing, employability, or reputation.[6] Asking for information that might be embarrassing if revealed may qualify. To qualify, you need to make the case that the information you seek is clearly harmless (and be ready for the chance that your IRB may not agree with you). Just asserting that there is no risk is usually not enough to pass review for exempt status – you need to indicate what kinds of information is being collected, and you may need to make a case for collecting anything considered personal, private, or dealing with risky behaviors. If the information has a reasonable potential for risk, you cannot qualify as exempt under this category.

The first part of the qualifying conditions is often thought of as happening when the data is collected anonymously.[7] Truly anonymous data collection from participants is problematic online due to the basic nature and structure of the Internet. Online interviews, surveys, education tests all involve information being transmitted over the Internet, and every Internet transmission includes potentially identifiable information. Among the more obvious are things like IP addresses, email addresses, user names, and screen names, which are typically linked to specific individuals or computers. Furthermore, every packet of information sent over the Internet contains routing information, even those sent through secure sites, providing possible linking information in the form of Internet addresses. Observation of even "public" behaviors online often involves identifiers (although some are indirect).

However, to qualify under this category, it is not strictly necessary to collect the data in such a way as to preclude any and all potentially identifying information (which would be virtually impossible given the aforementioned computer addressing schema), just as long as it is recorded in a way that does not link responses to an identifiable participant. To qualify for exemption, the IRB needs to know that you acknowledge the presence of these inherent identifiers, and clearly indicate in the application that either you will not collect such information, or will remove it in the process of recording it. For example, if you want to collect some very basic non-risky information by online survey, you have to be clear that when you record the data, you will not also record the corresponding IP addresses or other potentially identifying information along with the responses.

Some online interview and online survey methods can pose the risk of breach of confidentiality, due to the public nature of the Internet and the way it operates. Information sent over the Internet is tagged with address information for both the sender and receiver in each data packet. Also, in the process of transmission, copies of packets are made and can be copied at various points. Some degree of privacy can be obtained by encrypting packets, but even then privacy is not absolute.[8] The use of email is particularly problematic for two reasons: first, each exchange clearly has an identifier (email address); also, emails are not private - even if you promise to remove the email address, the data you collected exists in a form where the identifier remains, and thus the responses can be traced back to the individual subject. It probably also exists in back-up records of mail servers, and may be legally accessible to the organization providing the email service. Many IRBs will only approve the use of email for data collection if the subjects are made aware of these limitations.[9]

Data collection using online survey servers can offer an acceptable degree of privacy and anonymity under the following conditions, and

the application should note them. First, that the server hosting the online survey is a secure server, using an encryption system to protect the privacy of the information during transmission.[10] Second, make sure that the survey service records responses in a separate data file from the addressing log files, rather than recording the full exchange of information together. You also need to assure that any address or identifying information is either not collected or recorded during the survey, made generic, or removed by the researcher prior to its examination and use for research purposes. Finally, that access to the raw data during collection is restricted to the researcher. Most institutional and professional online survey systems qualify, but to qualify for the exemption, you need to indicate how you will ensure that no identifiable information is recorded. If the person reviewing your application is not familiar with the particular online survey service, you may need to provide assurances that the above conditions apply.

Another advantage of using an online survey system is in the collection of written consent. Collecting written consent can be problematic for online research, as the preferred standard is to collect signed written consent from participants prior to data collection. Collecting online signatures can be difficult, and asking for, and collecting, informed consent in person or by mail is burdensome. However, for low-risk research of the sort that would qualify for "exempt" status, the regulations permit the use of what is called an informed consent statement. Informed consent statements need to contain essentially the same information, but allow respondents to indicate their willingness to participate by taking some affirmative action prior to their providing any research responses.

Please note, though, that the researcher cannot assume consent is given by the fact that responses are provided; there must be an affirmative positive action to indicate that consent has been given. It is relatively easy to put an informed consent statement as the gateway to the survey, and if participants can't enter the survey without reading and affirmatively agreeing to the statement, then one can demonstrate the informed consent prior to data collection.

Observation of "public" activities online is somewhat less problematic, since it is the observed activities that are transmitted over the Internet, not the collected information. In this case, you only need to make it clear that what you observe will not include identifiers that can link observations to individuals. If some identifiers are needed, indicating that you will use generic identifiers or pseudonyms will generally suffice. If anonymity is a concern, that can be addressed somewhat by having the removal of personal identifiers, or their replacement with more generic indicators, done by somebody other than the researcher (with that outside person signing a confidentiality pledge). In that case, the researcher can make a case that they do not know who provided which information.

Category (4) covers research involving the study or collection of existing materials (such as online content) under two conditions. Either the materials must be clearly "public", or the data must be recorded in a way that specific sources or respondents cannot be identified. A good working definition of public for this purpose is material that is intentionally presented to the general public without restriction. If it's not clear that the existing materials you wish to use qualify, then you can still seek exemption under the second condition - essentially that you'll treat the data as confidential by not recording it in an identifiable manner. If you need identifiers in your data, indicate that you will use pseudonyms or generic identifiers. To provide an additional precautionary level of protection, have someone other than the researcher substitute generic identifiers for participants before making the data available to the researcher.

The four other exemptions focus on either specific research topics or subject pools, so there are no distinctive issues for online researchers. Category (1) basically covers research on educational practices, involving normal practices in accepted or established educational settings. Category (3) covers research where your subjects are public officials or candidates for public office (apparently they have no rights as research subjects). Category (5) covers research evaluating public benefit or service programs. Category (6) involves research on food taste and quality, as long as the food is safe and wholesome.

It should be noted that even if your research would otherwise qualify for exemption, there are several research contexts that require formal IRB review, normally because there is thought to be an inherent level of risk. Among these are the uses of protected populations[11] among your research participants, the use of audio or video recording devices[12], research that is Federally funded, and methods that might pose physical or other risks for participants.[13]

RESEARCH REQUIRING FORMAL REVIEW

Any "human subjects research" that doesn't qualify as exempt must go through a formal IRB review and approval process. While the formal review process does ask for more information from the researchers, and generally takes longer to review and approve, the process can be expedited under certain conditions. In general, the key points in passing formal IRB review is to acknowledge potential risk, ensure adequate informed consent, and make a case that the research is worth the risk.

Informed consent is where these all tie together. The informed consent language must outline what you are asking participants to do, clearly identify potential risks and benefits, indicate what protections are being offered, and obtain free and willing legal consent. Which, of course, requires that the researcher be aware and address the potential for risk so that it can be identified for the participants. Risk can go beyond the actual physical, emotional, or psychological harm that might arise from the activities you are asking participants to undertake. In particular, there is risk of breach of confidentiality, of participants being linked to the data that is collected from them.

As discussed in the "exempt" section above, collecting data online does create potential breach of confidentiality issues, due to the public nature of the Internet. In addition, placing data or research materials on the Internet can create significant long-term privacy and confidentiality issues. Once materials are placed on the Internet, the researcher may lose effective control over them. Internet sites are routinely scanned and archived by a number of users, who can archive and redistribute the information and content. And the researcher has little or no ability to limit access or guarantee their removal.

Researchers collecting or posting collected research information online have to be very careful in terms of how they promise confidentiality, particularly if the information collected may be harmful. This is where clarity and precision in informed consent can become important. Rather than simply promising confidentiality or privacy, the researcher collecting information online may only promise that they will not divulge information in a way that can be linked to respondents.

Another particular risk that may come from online data collection is the possibility that your data collection procedures may cause some harm to the participant's computer or terminal. Thus, when sending materials online to participants, it is important to ensure that those are virus-free, and that any online data-collection procedure does not install programs (or cookies) on respondent machines without their knowledge and approval. It also helps to minimize risk to ensure that the materials are removed afterward.

The use of recording systems in collecting responses is one of the specific criteria that mandate formal IRB review. This is due largely to the fact that audio and video recordings do provide a means to identify participants and link them to their comments and actions. It is possible to record online data collection without using regular audio or video recording devices. Computers can record audio and video chat sessions, which are clearly analogous to more typical recordings of interview or focus groups. But computers can also record other interactions (such as IM flows, capture keystrokes, track sessions, capture search strategies, etc.). If their research employs such technology, the researcher needs to consider whether or not the type and content of the recordings makes the respondent identifiable. If so, the online researcher needs to address the same basic issues as those taping or recording research sessions. These include minimizing access to raw recordings, how information is extracted and recorded, and what will be done with the recordings afterwards.

One major protected population that requires formal approvals is kids, due to issues in obtaining legal informed consent. Younger kids may not be able to fully understand the normal consent form. More fundamental, however, is the issue that kids (generally anyone under age 18 in the U.S.) are considered unable to provide legal consent. Thus, researchers have to obtain legal consent from parents or other legal guardians first, and then also obtain the assent of the child. Getting legally recognized agreement online can be problematic enough, but there is also concern over identity.[14] To assure the proper consent process, the researcher will need to develop a means for validating parental consent, and restricting access to data collection only to those whose parents have provided consent. This may require some additional protections and procedures to control both access and privacy during both data collection and in the treatment of collected data.

Exposing participants to potential risk while doing online research can also pose some additional concerns. Online data collection is often asynchronous, so that the researcher may not be aware if the data collection is creating a negative reaction in the respondent. If there is a real risk of such, the researcher may need to think about how they will provide help or assistance. For example, if they would provide a list of available counseling if they collected the same information during personal interviews, they may need to consider how they will provide a similar list to online participants. If the risk is high enough, they may want to indicate that they will regularly monitor responses so that they may respond in a timely manner.

As noted in the previous section, maintaining privacy while engaged in online research is generally problematic, given its public nature. Thus, one can generally assume the potential for breach of confidentiality in any online research involving human subjects. There are two components to this risk. The first is the likelihood of a breach occurring. Here the researcher can indicate what steps they can and will take to minimize that potential. The second is the degree of potential harm. The greater the potential harm, the more important it becomes to not only minimize the potential of breach of confidentiality, but to also try to minimize the impact of any breach. The IRB application needs to identify what steps the researcher plans to take to minimize risks. For online, this can mean using encrypted means to collect and store information, and to keep raw data offline and in secure locations. Of course, there is also the option of not promising privacy or confidentiality, and still gaining informed consent. In that case, the researcher needs to be clear in the informed consent that responses may become public, and indicate the risks involved.

In sum, researchers need to identify risks and discuss how they will be handled in their IRB applications. Online researchers, in particular, need to demonstrate that they are aware of the particular risks posed by their chosen online research methods, and how those will be addressed in their proposed research designs. This may involve developing distinctively online approaches in some cases; in others, it may only be a case of acknowledging risks or limiting anonymity or confidentiality promises made to participants. Online research may pose new challenges in re-

search ethics and the protection of human subjects, but addressing them will help develop consensus and hopefully also help improve online research methodologies.

SUMMARY

The development of digital computing and the rise of the Internet have opened up new opportunities to engage in online research. Collecting research materials and data online can be fast, inexpensive, and expand both the scale and scope of data collection. As online research methods have developed and diffused throughout research communities, there are some attributes and types of online research and data collection that have created new ethical concerns, and created difficulties in getting research approved by IRBs.

Many of these issues relate to the concept of what is considered to be "public" online, and the ways that online research methods may differ from, or have different implications than, traditional research methodologies. The concern of the Federal regulations and the IRB process is the protection of human subjects, in large part by ensuring that potential participants are adequately informed of what is being asked of them, and the potential risks, if any, that participation may bring. Their purpose is not to limit or hinder research, or to dictate methodologies, although that may be the way that some researchers see it. But online research methods may pose different risks than more traditional methods, either by opening up new areas for study and data collection (areas where the notion of what is public and what is private are still being developed), or new ways of collecting, storing, and using information that, again, might be more public, and less private and secure, than traditional methods.

Part of the problem is that, as with any new methodology, both online researchers and IRBs are still discovering what particular risks are associated with various online research methods, and where to draw the line between public (published) information and private information and behaviors. The IRBs, in their duty to protect potential human research subjects, are likely to be more conservative in the drawing of boundaries, and see greater potential risk, than the researcher. And over time, as online research methods mature, and IRBs and researchers both educate themselves as to the underlying risks, the differences in perceptions should shrink as a consensus develops as to how to handle online research through the IRB process.

REFERENCES

Baker, R. B., & McCullough, L. B. (Eds.). (2008). *The Cambridge world history of medical ethics*. New York, NY: Cambridge University Press. doi:10.1017/CHOL9780521888790

Ess, C. (2007). Internet research ethics. In Johnson, A. N., & McKenna, K. (Eds.), *The Oxford handbook of internet psychology*. New York, NY: Oxford University Press.

Ess, C., & Jones, S. (2004). Ethical decision-making and internet research: Recommendations from the AoIR ethics working committee. In Buchanan, E. A. (Ed.), *Readings in virtual research ethics: Issues and controversies*. Reading, PA: Information Science Publishing. doi:10.4018/978-1-59140-152-0.ch002

Frankel, M. S., & Siang, S. (1999). *Ethical and legal aspects of human subjects research on the internet: A report of a workshop June 10-11, 1999*. Retrieved from http://www.aaas.org/spp/dspp/sfrl/projects/intres/report.pdf

Jones, M. D., Chen, S.-L. S., & Hall, G. J. (Eds.). (2004). *Online social research: Methods, issues & ethics*. New York, NY: Peter Lang.

Jones, R. A. (1994). The ethics of research in cyberspace. *Internet Research*, *4*(3), 30–35. doi:10.1108/10662249410798894

Walther, J. P. (2002). Research ethics in internet-enabled research: Human subjects issues and methodological myopia. *Ethics and Information Technology*, *4*(3), 205–216. doi:10.1023/A:1021368426115

ADDITIONAL READING

Amdur, R. J., & Bankert, E. A. (2007). *Institutional review board member handbook*. Sudbury, MA: Jones and Bartlett.

Amdur, R. J., & Biddle, C. (1997). Institutional review board approval and publication of human research results. *Journal of the American Medical Association*, *277*, 909–914. doi:10.1001/jama.1997.03540350059034

Bankert, E. A., & Amdur, R. J. (Eds.). (2006). *Institutional review board: Management and function*. Sudbury, MA: Jones and Bartlett.

Berry, D. M. (2004). Internet research: Privacy, ethics and alienation: An open source approach. *Internet Research*, *14*, 323–332. doi:10.1108/10662240410555333

Boser, S. (2007). Power, ethics and the IRB: Dissonance over human participant review of participatory research. *Qualitative Inquiry*, *13*, 1060–1074. doi:10.1177/1077800407308220

Buchanan, E. A. (Ed.). (2003). *Readings in virtual research ethics: Issues and controversies*. Reading, PA: Information Science Publishing. doi:10.4018/978-1-59140-152-0

Buchanan, E. A., & Ess, C. (2008). Internet research ethics: The field and its critical issues. In Himma, K. E., & Tavani, H. T. (Eds.), *The handbook of information and computer ethics* (pp. 273–292). Hoboken, NJ: John Wiley. doi:10.1002/9780470281819.ch11

Burke, G. S. (2005). Looking into the institutional review board: Observations from both sides of the table. *The Journal of Nutrition, 135*, 921–924.

Byers, J. F. (2004). Protecting patients during clinical research. *Critical Care Nurse, 24*(1), 53–59.

Chiasson, M. A., Parsons, J. T., Tesoriero, J. M., Carballo-Dieguez, A., Hirshfield, S., & Remien, R. H. (2006). HIV behavioral research online. *Journal of Urban Health, 83*(1), 73–85. doi:10.1007/s11524-005-9008-3

Childress, J. F., Meslin, E. M., & Shipiro, H. T. (Eds.). (2005). *Belmont revisited: Ethical principles for research with human subjects.* Washington, DC: Georgetown University Press.

Chung, G., & Grimes, S. M. (2005). Data mining the kids: Surveillance and market research strategies in children's online games. *Canadian Journal of Communication, 30*, 527–548.

Emanuel, E. J., Crouch, R. A., Arras, J. D., Moreno, J. D., & Grady, C. (Eds.). (2003). *Ethical and regulatory aspects of clinical research: Readings and commentary.* Baltimore, MD: The Johns Hopkins University Press.

Ess, C. (2006). Ethical pluralism and global information ethics. *Ethics and Information Technology, 8*, 215–226. doi:10.1007/s10676-006-9113-3

Faden, R. R., & Beauchamp, T. L. (1986). *A history and theory of informed consent.* New York, NY: Oxford University Press.

Gunsulus, C. K. (2007). The Illinois white paper: Counteracting IRB mission creep. *Qualitative Inquiry, 13*(5), 617–649. doi:10.1177/1077800407300785

Hilton, E., & Hall, D. (Eds.). (2005). *Working effectively with and within IRBs: A practical guide for investigators, sponsors, and IRB members.* Hagerstown, MD: University Publishing Group.

Homan, R. (1991). *The ethics of social research.* New York, NY: Longman.

Hookway, N. (2008). 'Entering the blogosphere': Some strategies for using blogs in social research. *Qualitative Research, 8*(1), 91–113. doi:10.1177/1468794107085298

Hudson, J. M., & Bruckman, A. (2004). "Go away": Participant objections to being studied and the ethics of chat room research. *The Information Society, 20*, 127–139. doi:10.1080/01972240490423030

Hudson, J. M., & Bruckman, A. (2006). Using empirical data to reason about Internet research ethics. In H. Gellersen et al. (Eds.), *ECSCW 2005: Proceedings of the Ninth European Conference on Computer-Supported Cooperative Work,* 18-22 September 2005, Paris, France, (pp. 287-306).

Kanuka, H., & Anderson, T. (2007). Ethical issues in qualitative e-learning research. *International Journal of Qualitative Methods, 6*(2), Article 2.

Kitchin, H. A. (2008). *Research ethics and the internet: Negotiating Canada's tri-council policy Statement.* Fernwood Publishing.

Markham, A. N. (2008). The methods, politics, and ethics of representation in online ethnography. In Denzin, N. K., & Lincoln, Y. (Eds.), *Collecting and interpreting qualitative materials* (pp. 247–284). Thousand Oaks, CA: Sage.

Mazur, D. J. (2007). *Evaluating the science and ethics of research on humans: A guide for IRB members.* Baltimore, MD: The Johns Hopkins University Press.

Mazur, D. J. (2008). Consent and informed consent: Their ongoing evolutions in clinical care and research on humans. *Social Compass, 2*(1), 253–267. doi:10.1111/j.1751-9020.2007.00059.x

McKee, H. A., & Porter, J. E. (2009). *The ethics of Internet research: A rhetorical, case-based process.* New York, NY: Peter Lang.

Patchin, J. W., & Hinduja, S. (2006). Bullies move beyond the schoolyard: A preliminary look at cyberbullying. *Youth Violence and Juvenile Justice*, *4*(2), 148–169. doi:10.1177/1541204006286288

Pitts, V. (2004). Illness and Internet empowerment: Writing and reading breast cancer in cyberspace. *Health*, *8*(1), 33–59. doi:10.1177/1363459304038794

Rier, D. A. (2007). Internet social support groups as moral agents: The ethical dynamics of HIV+ status disclosure. *Sociology of Health & Illness*, *29*, 1043–1058. doi:10.1111/j.1467-9566.2007.01023.x

Sales, B. D., & Folkman, S. (Eds.). (2000). *Ethics in research with human participants*. Washington, DC: American Psychological Association.

Tackett-Gibson, M. (2008). Constructions of risk and harm in online discussions of ketamine use. *Addiction Research and Theory*, *16*(8), 245–257. doi:10.1080/16066350801983699

KEY TERMS AND DEFINITIONS

Chat Room: A Web site, typically one dedicated to a particular topic, where a number of users can communicate in real time by typing messages onscreen which makes them appear to scroll by as a conversation develops with other visitors to the site.

Cookie: A cookie is a small piece of text stored on a user's computer by a web browser. A cookie consists of bits of information such as user preferences, shopping cart contents, the identifier for a server-based session, or other data used by websites.

Encryption: The reversible transformation of data from the original (the plaintext) to a difficult-to-interpret format (the ciphertext) as a mechanism for protecting its confidentiality, integrity, and sometimes its authenticity. Encryption uses an encryption algorithm and one or more encryption keys.

Focus Group: A small group selected from a wider population and sampled, as by open discussion, for its members' opinions about or emotional response to a particular subject or area, used especially in market research or political analysis.

Header: Supplemental data placed at the beginning of a block of data being stored or transmitted. A packet (see definition) includes a header with to and from addresses, relation to other packets (sequencing), and error checking information.

Human Research Compliance Officer: The person designated by an institution as having overall responsibility for ensuring that the institution is in compliance with all applicable federal and state laws/regulations regarding research involving human subjects.

IM: Instant messaging (IM) is a form of real-time communication between two or more people based on typed text. The text is conveyed via devices connected over a network such as the Internet.

Informed Consent: The voluntary consent given by an individual to participate in a research study. The participant must be informed of the study's purpose, procedures, benefits, risks, compensation, confidentiality, and duration.

Institutional Review Board (IRB): An IRB is the group or committee that is given the responsibility by an institution to review that institution's research projects involving human subjects. The primary purpose of the IRB review is to assure the protection of the safety, rights, and welfare of the human subjects.

IP Address: An Internet Protocol (IP) address is a unique number identifying all devices connected to the Internet. This number is usually shown as four numbers from 0 to 255, separated by periods, for example 207.46.230.218.

Listserve: A list of email addresses of people with common interests who have subscribed to the list. Software enables people who belong to the list to send messages to the group without typing a series of addresses into the message header.

Oral History: Historical information, usually tape-recorded or videotaped, obtained in interviews with persons having firsthand knowledge.

Packets: Under packet switching protocols, messages are divided into pieces called packets before they are sent. Each packet is then transmitted individually and can even follow different routes to its destination. Once all the packets arrive at the destination, they are recompiled into the original message.

Principal Investigator: The scientist or scholar with primary responsibility for the design and conduct of a research project.

Screen Names: A screen name is the name a user chooses to use when communicating with others online. A screen name can be a person's real name, a variation of the person's real name, or it can be a pseudonym.

Server: A server is a computer that, using the client/server model, handles requests for data, email, file transfers, and other network services from other computers (clients).

Virus: A computer program that is designed to replicate itself by copying itself into the other programs stored in a computer. It may be benign or have a negative effect, such as causing a program to operate incorrectly or corrupting a computer's memory.

ENDNOTES

[1] Protections for human subjects are required under Department of Health and Human Services (HHS) regulations at *45 CFR 46*, under authority granted by *5 U.S.C. 301; 42 U.S.C. 289(a)*. These regulations constitute the *Federal Policy (Common Rule) for the Protection of Human Subjects*, which has been adopted by an additional 16 Executive Branch Departments and Agencies. Institutions receiving Federal research funds are required to comply with these regulations.

[2] It may still be covered by other Federal research regulations, which cover (among others) animals, radiation, genetic materials (and genetically engineered materials), medical samples, food and drugs, etc.

[3] 45 CFR 46.102(f)(1),(2)

[4] 45 CFR 46.101(b)(4)

[5] Although you might need to remind your IRB reviewer that the data doesn't have to be collected anonymously, only recorded anonymously.

[6] 45 CFR 46.101(b)(2). One example of the breadth of what information may pose a potential risk is that Federal guidelines recently identified collecting information about smoking behaviors as "risky," since it may impact on employability or insurability.

[7] The regulations define anonymous data collection as occurring when no one, not even the researcher, can know or determine who provided which set of information or responses. Just as collecting information from a personal interview cannot possibly be anonymous, neither can collecting responses by email. (since names and addresses are part of the email.)

[8] Virtually any encryption system can be overcome, given sufficient time and resources. Also, some countries, including the U.S., require that electronic communications be interceptable by authorities under certain conditions. Thus, no Internet communication can be considered absolutely secure and private.

[9] If you want, you can promise them that you will not report any information in a way that can be linked to them - you just can't promise that no one can link responses to individuals.

[10] One can identify a secure server because its IP address uses the https:// prefix rather than http://.

[11] The primary protected populations are children and prisoners. In general, this can cover any group where it is not clear that individuals may freely give legal consent. This may include those with diminished mental capacity, pregnant women and fetuses, and situations where there may be pressure to consent.

[12] It is presumed that individuals are identifiable through the recording.

[13] Most of these involve risk of physical harm, such as invasive medical procedures, the use of radiation, exposure to viruses and diseases, genetically engineered materials, etc.

[14] The basic concern can be phrased as how can you be sure you have both parental consent and participant assent for the respondent prior to collecting information. This may involve how you try to link the three, as well as how do you assure that the appropriate parties are providing the consent/assent.

Section 2
Analysis of Established Measures

Chapter 4
The Nonprofit Ethics Survey:
Assessing Organizational Culture and Climate

Audrey Barrett
University of San Diego, USA

Fred Galloway
University of San Diego, USA

ABSTRACT

The Nonprofit Ethics Survey serves as the only empirically supported survey instrument specifically designed for nonprofit organizations to assess their ethical culture. Development of the instrument occurred through the use of principal components analysis conducted on a sample of 530 nonprofit affiliates. The results of the analysis yielded six parsimonious scales integral to assessing nonprofit ethics. To evaluate the internal reliability of each scale a measure of Cronbach's Alpha was also calculated. The alpha coefficients ranged from 0.86 - 0.94, indicating the survey provides a reliable means of measuring the constructs integral to assessing organizational ethics in nonprofit agencies. The creation of a statistically sound instrument designed for use with nonprofit organizations ensures that nonprofit leaders have the needed tools to accurately self-assess.

BACKGROUND

Introduction

The Nonprofit Ethics Survey serves as the only empirically supported survey instrument developed exclusively for nonprofit organizations to conduct an assessment of their ethical culture. The survey provides an organizational-level evaluation yielding a three-hundred sixty degree view capable of identifying disparities between the ethical practices of members at different levels of the organization (e.g., between board members and line staff). The benefit of the Nonprofit Ethics Survey to nonprofit leaders cannot be overemphasized as ethics and the perception of having an

DOI: 10.4018/978-1-4666-2172-5.ch004

ethical organization are intricately linked to the viability of nonprofit agencies (Gregorian, 2004). This linkage has long been intuitively known; however, the recent sector-wide meltdown in donor giving precipitated by the ethical lapses of a few large nonprofits provides a potent reminder (Light, 2006).

The significance of having a valid and reliable instrument designed specifically for use with nonprofit organizations serves as an additional point needing to be underscored. For example, while the majority of existing work on nonprofit ethics focuses on compliance and resides in the practitioner literature, the introduction of the Nonprofit Ethics Survey will help solve a number of important contemporary assessment problems, including the alignment problem that exists when instruments from the for-profit or governmental sectors are inappropriately used in assessing the ethical health of non-profits (Hansmann, 1980 as cited in Steinberg, 2006; and Steinberg, 2006). While this practice has become increasingly common, a growing body of evidence suggests that the tools and best practices effective in other sectors do not directly translate to the third sector (Lohmann, 2007; Mulligan, 2007; Prewitt, 2006), and more importantly, may cause real harm to the nonprofit and its ability to fulfill its mission. For these varied reasons the presence of an empirically supported instrument in the nonprofit literature serves to fill a long unmet need.

The design of the Nonprofit Ethics Survey as an *organizational-level* assessment tool facilitates the instruments ability to provide users with a comprehensive picture of ethical health. This serves as critical given that research clearly demonstrates that culture wields a stronger effect over peoples' actions than policy (Brown & Trevino, 2006; Milgram, 1963, 1974; Hemmelgarn, Glissen, and James, 2006; Seligson & Choi, 2006; Trevino et al., 1998; Zimbardo, 2007), and that the culture of an organization starts with its leadership (Ethics Resource Center, 2008). Thus by making the entire organization the unit of analysis, not solely the senior management or board of directors, a measure of intended culture (the tone the board and senior management intends to set) can be compared to actual culture (the perceptions of ethics at all levels of the organization), illuminating the strengths and weaknesses in ethical culture and current practices.

Overview of the Instrument

The Nonprofit Ethics Survey employs mostly five-point, Likert-style, questions rated from "strongly agree" to "strongly disagree" to assess six empirically supported constructs relevant to assessing nonprofit ethics. A neutral point of "neither agree nor disagree" in addition to options to select "don't know" and "decline to answer" serve to clarify responses to the survey. The five points from "strongly agree" to "strongly disagree" have corresponding numerical values assigned of five, four, three, two, and one. The two additional response options of "don't know" and "decline to answer" each receive a numerical weight of zero.

Five of the constructs assessed by the Nonprofit Ethics Survey are assessed at each level of the organization: line staff; middle management; senior management; and board members. These five empirically supported constructs are: Daily-Ethics Behaviors; Accountability; Organizational Transparency; Open Communication; and Decision Making. Governance serves as the sixth construct and it is only assessed at one level of the organization. The questions about governance are asked solely of survey respondents who identify as voting members of the organizations board of directors as they are the only affiliates expected to have complete knowledge of governance issues.

In addition to eighty-seven Likert-style questions, the survey employs two demographic questions, three dichotomous variables to facilitate the skip logic, and three overall rating questions. The demographic questions inquire regarding the participant's position within the organization and length of time with the organization.

Following the two demographic questions, one of the dichotomous variables inquires whether a participant serves as a voting member of the board of directors. This question comes after participants have completed the first portion of the survey which assesses the first five constructs. When a respondent indicates they are a voting member of the board, the survey directs them to respond to an additional twenty-eight questions about organizational governance. If a respondent indicates they are not a voting member of the board, the survey navigates to an open-ended question providing the opportunity to share any additional information regarding ethics in their organization. Thus, the survey ends after fifty-nine questions if a participant is not a voting member of the board and eighty-seven questions if the participant is a voting board member.

In addition to the questions on the survey designed to assess the six identified constructs, additional questions contained in a section called *ethical context* gather supplemental information about contextual elements of the organization related to ethics. This section was crafted out of questions contained on the original survey instrument that only received a moderate level of statistical support through factor analysis, but that received strong anecdotal support from the leaders of the nonprofit organizations who participated in the testing of the survey.

Taken together, the Nonprofit Ethics survey provides nonprofit organizations with a statistically supported, user-friendly means for gathering critical information about their organizational culture and how it either facilitates strong ethical health or the opportunity for ethical lapses. Used longitudinally, the survey also provides an opportunity to measure the organization over time or in response to particular events (e.g., ethics trainings, a publicized ethical breech, or a change in leadership). The position of the Nonprofit Ethics Survey as the only empirically supported survey instrument designed specifically to assess nonprofit ethics at the organizational-level

serves as significant and has resulted in the survey obtaining an overwhelmingly positive response from the nonprofit community.

Developing the Instrument

The creation of the Nonprofit Ethics Survey utilized a mixed methodological approach. Extensive qualitative work to identify constructs relevant to nonprofit organizational ethics, followed by a comprehensive literature review including work in the fields of business, philanthropy, sociology, anthropology, public service, ethics, psychology, and leadership, was conducted. In total the qualitative research and literature review identified seven constructs. Questions were then crafted and a draft was reviewed extensively. All necessary revisions were completed prior to the preparation of a beta version of the Nonprofit Ethics Survey for online testing.

Subject Recruitment

Subjects identified for testing the survey instrument included individuals in two categories: (1) individuals associated with a wide variety of nonprofit organizations taking the survey out of interest in developing an instrument for the sector; and (2) individuals affiliated with a one of seven particular nonprofit organizations participating in the study, at the request of their executive director. The identification of individuals for recruitment, for both categories of participants, occurred as a result of the individuals' information existing on a database maintained by the Institute for Nonprofit Education and Research at the University of San Diego.

The individuals recruited in category one represented a diverse cross section of nonprofit agencies as defined by budget size, employee number, and mission. Approximately 300 individuals comprised the category one recruitment and of these potential participants, 142 individuals clicked the electronic link and completed the informed consent to participate in the study. One hundred and eight of these 142 individuals completed one or more of the survey questions after completing the consent. The organizations recruited for category two again represented a broad spectrum of potential organizations based on employee number, budget size, stability, and willingness to participate within the time frame of the study. Twelve organizations were recruited and seven agreed to participate. These seven organizations provided a pool of 955 potential participants, and 422 of these 955 nonprofit affiliates clicked the electronic link, completed the informed consent to participate in the study, and answered one or more of the survey questions after completing the consent.

Sample Characteristics

Survey results incorporated into the database for analysis of the Nonprofit Ethics Survey came from a sample obtained by combining the participants from both categories of recruitment. As shown in Table 1, combining the groups yielded a sample of 530 subjects with the following characteristics:

seventy-two participants identified as a board member, 59 as a senior staff member, 123 as a middle manager, 230 as a line staff member, and 46 participants did not provide a response to the question. Regarding length of time with the organization, 90 individuals identified as having less than one year, 218 had one to five years, 94 had six to ten years, 39 had eleven to fifteen years, 17 had 16-20 years, 21 had 21 or more years, and 51 participants did not provide a response to the question. In the combined sample 78 participants identified as a voting board member.

Usage and Scoring of the Instrument

Usage

Nonprofit organizations interested in assessing the perceptions of ethics held by their affiliates represent the end-user of the Nonprofit Ethics Survey. Thus, the statistically-supported and theoretically-grounded instrument serves to provide nonprofit organizations and their leadership with a parsimonious, user-friendly method for comprehensive ethics assessment at the organi-

Table 1. Characteristics of the combined sample N = 530

	Positional Status	**Length of Time**	**Voting Board Member**
Board Member	72 (14%		
Senior Staff	58 (11%)		
Middle Management	123 (23%)		
Line Staff	230 (43%)		
No Response	46 (9%)		
Less than 1 yr		90 (17%)	
1-5 years		218 (41%)	
6-10		94 (18%)	
11-15		39 (7%)	
16-20		17 (3%)	
20 or more yrs		21 (4%)	
Yes			78 (15%)
No			402 (76%)
No Response			50 (9%)

zational level. Organizations choosing to use the survey access it electronically. A representative of the nonprofit typically serves as the survey administrator for their organization and completes an online request for using the survey with their agency. The creation of this request establishes an account for the administrator and they receive two e-mails: (1) containing a username and password for accessing survey results and reports and, (2) sample e-mail text for inviting members of their organization to participate in the survey and a weblink to access the unique survey for that organization. This allows organizations to independently administer the survey to their organizations. An informational brochure and help guide can be found on the website along with the online survey request form. Additionally, assistance can be sought by contacting the Institute for Nonprofit Education and Research.

Scoring

The scoring of the survey presents as straightforward. As described previously, each point on the Likert-style scale has a numerical value ranging from five (strongly agree) to one (strongly disagree); moreover, since all items are written from the same perspective no items need to be reverse-scored. Thus each question that a respondent answers by selecting one of the five options between "strongly agree" and "strongly disagree" gets included in calculating a mean score for that survey item. Responses of "don't know" and "decline to answer" have a numerical value of zero recorded and solely a frequency report of these responses is generated.

Confidentiality

To protect the confidentiality of survey respondents, results will only be accessible to the survey administrator after a minimum of five respondents from any one positional category (e.g., board member, senior management, line staff) have completed the survey. This prevents the accidental identification of respondents and also helps organizations recognize if they are large enough to utilize the survey (see the following section for more information).

Organizations Not Well-Suited for the Survey

Nonprofit scholar Preston (2007) notes that the third sector constitutes a sector with tremendous diversity as organizations with different service missions, budgets, and number of employees all receive the same Internal Revenue Service classification, 501(c)(3) nonprofit organization. Further, some nonprofit organizations exist largely to give or distribute funds (e.g., most types of foundations) while others primarily exist to secure funding and provide direct services. Adding to the complexity, additional variation in developmental levels across organizations within the sector and within individual silos of the sector, further contribute to the sector's heterogeneity.

The variation within the sector serves as important in determining the appropriateness of individual organizations for using and benefiting from the Nonprofit Ethics Survey. Organizations that have achieved a higher developmental level typically have more resources, experience, and ability to focus on issues such as ethics. While organizations functioning at an earlier developmental level may only possess the resources needed to focus on basic issues, such as organizational viability. As such, we recommend that organizations have a minimum of three years of functioning as an active nonprofit, without significant concern for future viability, before using the Nonprofit Ethics Survey to assess the perceptions of ethics within their organization.

In addition, we urge caution for those nonprofit organizations with a small number of affiliates because the design of the Nonprofit Ethics Survey intends that all members of the organization participate. Achieving significant participation within the organization contributes to the survey results in two ways: (a) it provides an accurate picture of the perceptions of ethics within the organization at all levels and, (b) ensures confidentiality for participants by reporting results in aggregate form. For these reasons, nonprofit organizations using the survey must ensure they have several members at each level of the organization; of course, smaller organizations may collapse respondents into just two categories, board member and staff, while larger organizations may use the full range of positional options including middle management and senior staff. No limitation exists for use of the survey as number of organizational affiliates increases, and for any organizational size the higher the percentage of respondents the more reliable the survey results (Hinkle, Wiersma, & Jurs, 2003).

Organizations that have not achieved a certain level of homeostasis represent another organizational type for which the Nonprofit Ethics Survey is not recommended. Specifically, organizations experiencing significant transition, such as if more than half of their employees or board members have less than six months of experience with the organization. Until this transitional period has passed, the Nonprofit Ethics Survey may not yield valid results for two reasons: (a) the extreme change may actually alter the ethical context of the organization through the influx of new affiliates and, (b) the socialization of affiliates into a particular organization's social context occurs over time, thus, new affiliates may not have enough experience with the organizations to have learned or understood the ethical context of the organization. As such, we urge organizations to pay close attention to the transitional status of their employees in assessing whether or not the use of the survey at a particular point in time is warranted.

One other source of variation concerns the extent to which particular industries are in the professional ethics spotlight; for example, health care organizations have a greater emphasis on ethics due to dual regulatory demands within the medical services sector at both the institutional level (where organizations may require ethics trainings or allegiance to ethics codes to maintain a license as a health care facility) and at the individual level (where physicians, nurses, and social workers are required to maintain a license within their area of specialty). Thus, legislative and licensing requirements likely account for additional variation regarding levels of ethical awareness across the sector.

As a result, the survey results for an organization with both professional and organizational emphases on ethics will likely follow one of two outcomes. The first is that there may be there is an overall feeling of ethical behavior, consideration, and health in the organization; in this case, even with high overall scores the survey responses can still point out areas within the organization that need additional work. The second pattern that may occur is that ethically sophisticated organizations may actually report lower scores than anticipated since their increased knowledge of how things *should be* in the organization may cause greater dissatisfaction with how things *actually are*, resulting in lower scores. Clearly, context matters in interpreting survey responses.

VALIDITY

Empirical testing of the Nonprofit Ethics Survey indicates that it provides a valid measure of the ethical culture in nonprofit organizations. This section will discuss the principal components analyses conducted during the development of the survey, including a brief discussion about data preparation and best practices in using principal components analysis. For the purposes of this study, we used principal components analysis to identify which survey items grouped together to measure the same underlying construct, as well as to eliminate any duplicative survey items as well as those that did not group with any other survey items. However, since the 24 questions that comprised the Governance construct had a significantly smaller number of respondents than did the other questions and constructs (because they were only asked of the 78 individuals who identified themselves as voting members of an organization's board of directors versus the 530 respondents that responded to all the other questions), we decided to conduct separate factor analyses. Taken together, however, the analyses conducted on the survey data resulted in markedly little revision to the original survey and yielded six empirically supported scales and strong support for a seventh construct.

The Basic Principal Components Analysis

In this section, we begin with the factor analysis conducted on all the survey questions -- with the exception of the 24 questions involving Governance. To assess the appropriateness of this data set for conducting principal components analysis, we first obtained a measure of the Kaiser-Meyer-Olkin (KMO) score to assess the sampling adequacy of the data set, and then completed Bartlett's test of sphericity to ensure that the underlying matrix did not represent an identity matrix (Rossi, Wright, & Anderson, 1983; Field, 2005; Mertler & Vannatta, 2005; Meyers, Gamst, and Guarino, 2006). In both cases we found the data supportive of the proposed analysis; our KMO score was 0.93 which is considered "superb" by Hutcheson and Sofroniou (1999), and Bartlett's test was also highly significant (p=.00), proving that the underlying matrix was not an identity matrix (Field, 2005).

After this important determination, we turned to the problem of missing data, a challenge faced by all empirical researchers. Since there are three traditional methods for dealing with missing data – list-wise deletion, pairwise deletion, and replacement of missing values with the mean score – we investigated all three methods and found that both the KMO score and p-value

for Bartlett's test were invariant with respect to method; more importantly, we found that applying all three methods for managing missing data to the sample provided no notable variation in the general results, meaning that the same questions loaded on the same components in all three methods. Ultimately, as the pairwise method appears in the literature as the most common method for managing missing data when conducting principal components analysis, the results reported are from the pairwise sample (Field, 2005). As a result of this decision, our final sample size ranged from 485 to 530 – considered "very good" by Comrey and Lee (as cited in Meyers et al., 2006).

With these issues resolved, we then selected the popular Varimax rotation technique for our first factor analysis, comforted by the work of Meyers et al. (2006) that showed little difference in the results of various analyses based on which rotational technique a researcher selects (e.g., Oblique, Equimax, or Varimax). The results of our principal components analysis yielded six factors with four or more items that loaded at a level of 0.60 or higher. Additionally, two groups of three questions each loaded together on factors other than one through six. These two, three-question groups, were determined to add value to the survey even though they did not achieve the four question requirement. Three of them appear on Table 2 below with ** beside them and the other three are not represented in Table 2. The six factors identified through the principal components analysis, inclusive of the six additional questions, accounted for approximately 61% of the total variance in this model. Table 2 reports the factor loads for the rotated component matrix for each of the six factors, and Table 3 reports the eigenvalues for each of the fourteen factors extracted by the analysis with an eigenvalue of one or greater.

As noted, the principal components analysis did not include the 24 questions within the Governance construct due to sample size concerns; however, the next section discusses a preliminary assessment of the Governance construct

Table 2. Rotated component matrix with factor loads per variable

Question	Factor 1	Factor 2	Factor 3	Factor 4	Factor 5	Factor 6
T 6	.78					
T 5	.76					
T 2	.75					
T 7	.73					
T 1	.70					
T4	.68					
T 10	.65					
T11	.64					
DEB 5		.85				
DEB 4		.84				
DEB 1		.81				
DEB 3		.80				
DEB 2		.80				
OC 5			.82			
OC 1			.81			
OC 2			.80			
OC 3			.69			
OC 6			.59			
OC 4			.59			
OC 9			.52			
OC 8			.52			
OC 7			.43			
DEB 10				.80		
DEB 9				.80		
DEB 6				.79		
DEB 7				.76		
DEB 8				.69		
DM 8					.89	
DM 7					.88	
DM 6					.79	
DM 3					.74**	
DM 4					.71**	
DM 1					.61**	
DEB 17						.81
DEB 16						.79
DEB 15						.72
DEB 18						.68
DEB 14						.64

* Items loading at < 0.60.

** Items regarding decision making loaded in two clusters of three questions each.

Note: Three additional questions retained during the survey revisions do not appear on this table.

Table 3. Eigenvalues for factors with an Eigenvalue of one or greater after extraction

Factor	Eigenvalue	% of Variance	Cumulative % of Variance
1	21.25	30.36	30.36
2	5.58	7.98	38.34
3	3.53	5.04	43.38
4	2.76	3.95	47.32
5	2.48	3.47	50.79
6	2.15	3.02	53.82
7	1.91	2.73	56.54
--------------------------	--------------------------	--------------------------	--------------------------
8*	1.88	2.68	59.22
9*	1.56	2.23	6.45
10	1.32	1.88	63.33
11	1.23	1.76	65.09
12	1.12	1.61	66.70
13	1.05	1.49	68.19
14	1.04	1.48	69.67

---- The hashed line demarks factors with four or more variables loading at ≥ 0.60 with the exception of factor six which had three variables loading at ≥0.60.

*Some questions that loaded on these factors were included in the final survey.

The Governance Construct Principle Component Analysis

Nonprofit organizations typically have a board of directors consisting of five to twenty-five members. This remains true even for very large nonprofits. Thus, it serves as logical that within a sample of 530 nonprofit affiliates only about 15% of them or 78 participants identified themselves as board members. This presented a challenge to the analysis of the Nonprofit Ethics Survey as the 24 questions composing the Governance construct only had a sample size of 78 participants. Fortunately, when a small sample must be considered for use with principal components analysis, methods exist for assessing their appropriateness without compromising the quality of results. In addition to assessing the KMO and Bartlett's test results, checking the communality values for each variable after extraction provides an extra measure of assessment. The value should be 0.50 or higher

without exceeding 0.90 for each variable. Variables not within this tolerance range should be removed prior to completing the analysis (Field, 2005).

To assess whether a sample of 78 participants was appropriate to conduct a principal components analysis for the 24, five-point, Likert-style questions composing the Governance construct that were not included in the principal components analysis described previously, an extra measure of assessment was used. The results of this testing indicated that the data set, although small, was adequate for principal components analysis. The KMO score registered at 0.76 which achieves the "good rating" per Hutcheson and Sofroniou (1999), the Bartlett's test of sphericity demonstrated that the underlying matrix did not represent an identity matrix (p=.00), and a review of the communality coefficients indicated all were within the boundaries of 0.50 and 0.90 for each of the 24 questions.

As a result of these statistical tests, a principal components analysis was conducted on those 78 survey participants who identified as a voting member of the board of directors and who completed one or more of the questions regarding governance. To manage missing data in this sample we again used pairwise deletion which yielded between 73 and 78 total cases. We also used the Varimax rotation technique which ultimately yielded a total of six components. Of these six components, one contained nine items that loaded at 0.60 or higher with additional items loading between 0.59 and 0.50, and one contained three items that loaded at 0.60 or

higher with two additional items between 0.59 and 0.50. Table 4 below reports the factor loads for the rotated component matrix for each of the six factors and includes variables that registered at a lenient guideline of 0.50 or higher. Table 5 reports the eigenvalues for each of the 6 factors with an eigenvalue of one or greater.

The results of the analysis conducted on the survey questions composing the Governance construct yielded support for one sixteen item factor and a second five item factor. Revisions to the survey based on the information from this second principal components analysis are discussed in the section that follows.

Table 4. Rotated component matrix with factor loads per variable for the secondary analysis

Original Name	Factor 1	Factor 2	Factor 3	Factor 4	Factor 5	Factor 6
G 13	.80					
G 12	.78					
G 11	.77					
G 3	.72					
G 18	.68					
G 17	.66					
G 4	.65					
G 9	.62					
G 7	.61					
G 6	.58					
G 21	.56	.51				
G 16	.55					
G 8	.55					
G 14	.54	.58				
G 10	.54					
G 19	.54					
G 24		.79				
G 23		.66				
G 22		.63				
G 5			.54			
G 20				.51		
					N/A	
G 1						.52

* Loaded at < 0.60.

Note: Some variables loaded on more than one component at a level ≥ 0.50. Further testing with a larger sample size will determine which variables should be eliminated from the survey.

Table 5. Eigenvalues for factors with an eigenvalue of one or greater after extraction

Factor	Eigenvalue	% of Variance	Cumulative % of Variance
1	7.88	32.83	32.83
-----------------------------	-----------------------------	---------------------------	---------------------------
2	3.12	13.01	45.84
3	2.26	9.42	55.26
4	1.60	6.66	61.92
5	1.37	5.70	67.62
6	1.08	4.50	72.12

---- The hashed line demarks factors with four or more variables loading at ≥ 0.60.

Interpretation of the Two Analyses

Ultimately, a total of 70 survey items composed the variables in the first principal components analysis, and it was conducted using a sample size of 530. Twenty-four survey items composed the variables in the second principal components analysis, and it was conducted using a sample size of 78. The results of these analyses provide strong support for the validity of the Nonprofit Ethics Survey, and two key indicators support its strong theoretical grounding. First, all of the identified constructs had high factor loads and corresponding eigenvalues; as reported in Table 2, factor loads ranged from 0.61 to 0.89 with a majority of variables loading at 0.70 or higher. Second, the statistical support provided by the principal components analysis for the existence of five of the seven original constructs further evinces the surveys solid theoretical underpinnings. This means that valid constructs were identified, with no questions crossing over to different constructs during the principal components analysis. Specifically, eight of the original 13 questions that composed the construct of Transparency remain in the final construct, as do six of the original questions for Open Communication, and all of the Daily-Ethics Behaviors questions – despite this construct being broken into three separate constructs.

Most of the question sets initially designed to measure specific constructs were identified by the analyses as being appropriately grouped with other questions designed to measure that specific construct. This stability suggests that the multiple questions crafted to measure each construct, at a minimum represent questions that measure the same concept, and at a maximum indicates that each scale actually measures the intended construct. Initial support for the claim of construct validity stemmed from the performance of the survey as anticipated (or at least based on theoretical predictions) and the results of the principal components analyses. However, as construct validity assumes two verified relationships: (1) between the survey questions and the theory and (2) between questions in each scale (Rossi et al., 1983), it remains important to note that a supported statement of construct validity will require multiple applications of the survey and additional analyses to determine with a degree of certainty.

Revising the Survey Based on Measures of Validity

Various recommendations exist in the literature for the amount of factor load required to include a question or variable in a factor. Stephens (as cited in Steele, 2007) has the most generous guidelines, identifying reliable factors as those that contain four or more variables with a factor load of 0.60 or greater, regardless of sample size. Additionally, Stephens identifies reliable factors as those composed of ten or more variables with a factor load of 0.40 when using a minimum sample size of least 150 (cited in Steele, 2007). Meyers et al. (2006) hesitantly provides support for Stephens' claim by endorsing the existence of a "lenient loading criterion of 0.40" (p.512) as a practice of some researchers. The hesitancy of supporting this practice is noted by their comment on this practice, "Ideally, you should have enough variables in the 0.70 range or higher to not worry about bringing in variables that are in the 0.40's" (p.512). Meyer's et al. overall endorses the use of 0.70 as a general inclusion criterion, and they state that typically researchers require the presence of four or more variables with a factor load at this level to compose a factor.

Meyers and colleagues (2006) also clearly note the art and science that co-occur when using principal components analysis. The science presents itself in the outputs of factor loads, scree plots, eigenvalues, and rotated component matrices. The art lies in the interpretation of the data by the researcher and the transformation of the theoretically-grounded, statically-supported instrument into a tool the end consumer can use; in this case nonprofit organizations and the third sector at large.

The results of the two principal components analyses guided the revision of the Nonprofit Ethics Survey, and provided support for its solid theoretical grounding. Of the original seven constructs generated and supported by theory, the analyses identified four of them as statistically valid, one as actually containing three distinct constructs, and two with questions that provide supportive information and or that complement the Governance scale. This validation met a criterion that constituted a hybrid-blend of Stephens (as cited in Steele, 2007) and Meyers et al. (2006) criteria. For this study, a factor was considered

to be statistically supported when four or more variables loaded on a single factor at a level of 0.60 or higher. Notably, most variables in the analysis loaded at a level of 0.70 or higher, thereby meeting the strictest set of criteria as expressed by Meyers and colleagues.

Transparency, Open Communication, and Decision Making constitute the three constructs that remained largely intact. Following the decision rule that a factor was statistically supported when four or more factors loaded on a single factor, these three constructs underwent a revision process that yielded scales containing five to eight questions per construct. As shown in Table 6, the Transparency construct was reduced from thirteen questions to eight, the Open Communication construct from eight questions to six, and the Decision-Making construct from ten questions to eight.

Although these three constructs stayed largely intact, the principal components analysis also revealed that the construct of Daily-Ethics Behaviors, which originally contained eighteen Likert-style questions, actually represented three distinct constructs about senior management, board members, and accountability. These new constructs, which contain five questions each, are referred to as the Daily-Ethics Behaviors of Senior Staff, the Daily-Ethics Behaviors of Board Members, and Accountability. Interestingly, the three questions that remained from the original Daily-Ethics Behaviors construct also clustered together; however, since there were only three of them and our decision-rule required at least four questions to constitute a construct, these three questions were not bundled into a construct, but were still included in the final survey because they provide a collateral source for assessing the information provided by participants when the survey asks them directly about ethical issues. For example, if when using this survey with a single organization, the affiliates' answers to direct questions about ethics vary from their answers to indirect questions about coworker ethics, this

Table 6. Comparison of Beta survey constructs to the final survey constructs

Original Construct	Number of Questions	New Construct Name	New Number of Questions
Transparency	13	Transparency	8
Open Communication	9	Open Communication	5
Decision Making	10	Decision Making	6
Daily Ethics Behaviors	18	Daily Ethics: Senior Management	5
		Daily Ethics: Board	5
		Daily Ethics: Account-ability	5
--------------------	--------------------	--------------------	--------------------
Governance	24	Governance	24/41%
++++++++++++++++	++++++++++++++++	++++++++++++++++	++++++++++++++++
Mission	10	N/A	N/A
Advocacy, Educational Opportunities & Training	10	N/A	N/A

--- Indicates two separate principal components analyses.
++ Indicates unsupported constructs.
* Indicates expanded Governance construct with 7 Mission questions and 10 AET questions.

suggests that a disparity exists within the organization.

From a leadership perspective, the existence of a disparity highlights an area that may warrant further attention in the form of training, education, policy, or other support. Specifically, the indirect assessment questions in the Nonprofit Ethics Survey work because when asked about a coworker, board members responding to the survey are reporting on *their* coworkers, which then provide a secondary assessment of board members. When questioning line staff members about *their* coworkers, the responses provide a secondary assessment of line staff. This dual assessment of perceptions provides additional opportunities to analyze the data on an individual organizational basis. Thus, the decision was made to include these questions in the revised survey – not as a construct, but as supportive questions in a section called ethical context, that provide valuable information to the individual organizations that will ultimately use the Nonprofit Ethics Survey.

Two of the remaining original constructs – Advocacy, Educational Opportunities, and Training, and Mission -- did not contain four or more questions with a factor load of 0.60 or higher on any one factor identified through the use of principal components analysis. As a result, these constructs were removed from the survey; however some of the questions have been retained; in particular, seventeen of them have been moved to the Governance construct for further testing, while three have been retained as supportive questions that provide valuable information to the organizations using the survey. Despite having a small sample of respondents, the remaining original construct, Governance, underwent a promising preliminary evaluation. As a result, all 24 questions remain at least temporarily in the survey and as discussed above, 17 more questions have been moved to this section for further empirical testing. Until then, the Governance construct will consist of 41 potential questions, although this number will certainly be reduced when the sample size becomes large enough for meaningful analysis.

As a result of this reduction process, the revised Nonprofit Ethics Survey contains six scales measuring the constructs of: Transparency; Daily-Ethics Behaviors; Accountability; Open Communication; Decision Making; and Governance. As noted earlier, Table 6 provides a summary of the original construct names, the number of questions per original construct, the revised construct names, and the number of questions in each revised construct.

Content Validity

Content validity often references the ability of an instrument or scale to measure what it claims to measure, and many scholars evince the content validity of the instruments they design by anchoring them in theory (Fink, 2003). Thus, the comprehensive literature review and qualitative process used to obtain input from members of the San Diego nonprofit community provide significant support for the content validity of the Nonprofit Ethics Survey. Theoretical underpinnings identified through the literature review and qualitative process served as a guide for both the question crafting and development of each construct. Thus, support for the constructs of the Nonprofit Ethics Survey through the use of principal components analysis provides assurance that the survey constitutes an instrument possessing content validity.

Face Validity

In contrast to content validity, a survey does not require theoretical grounding to possess face validity. Face validity largely assesses to what extent an instrument asks all the needed questions, and if the survey asks the questions at an appropriate level for its intended audience (Fink, 2003). Establishing that the Nonprofit Ethics Survey possesses face validity has occurred through multiple methods including: (1) review of the instrument by colleagues at the Caster Family Center for Nonprofit and Philanthropic Research,

(2) review of the instrument by peers in a doctoral class on survey methodology, (3) review of the instrument by my dissertation committee chair and, (4) review of the domain analysis by the members of the San Diego nonprofit community following the qualitative analysis process. The feedback provided from these sources assisted in developing the survey delivered to organizational participants in this study and indicated that the Nonprofit Ethics Survey successfully achieved face validity.

Additional information regarding the face validity of the Nonprofit Ethics Survey was obtained anecdotally while administering the instrument to the seven organizations involved in this study. Coordinating survey delivery often involved having the executive director, board chairperson or president, human resources personnel, and or members of administrative support staff review the instrument to determine if it represented a survey they would like to have their organizational affiliates complete. The overwhelmingly positive collective feedback provided from this process indicated that the survey provides a comprehensive measure of ethical perceptions and asks all needed questions at an appropriate level. Taken together, feedback from multiple sources appears to indicate that the Nonprofit Ethics Survey constitutes an instrument with face validity.

RELIABILITY

Cronbach's Alpha, which is commonly used as a measure of the internal consistency, or reliability of an instrument, was used in this study to describe how well various sets of statements measured our seven latent constructs. Operationally, this meant that for each construct we examined the extent to which each potential question in the Nonprofit Ethics Survey cohered with the other questions measuring that construct (DeVellis, 1991). Using the widely accepted standard of .70 as a minimum threshold to indicate reliable internal consistency

(Santos, 1999), we found that each one of the seven constructs measured by the Nonprofit Ethics Survey qualified as reliable; this information is shown in Table 7.

These strong measures of internal consistency, ranging from 0.86 to 0.94 for the seven constructs, provide further evidence that the Nonprofit Ethics Survey possesses a solid theoretical grounding, suggesting that the questions measuring each construct would produce similar results upon repeated administrations of the survey (Santos, 1999). In addition, the coefficients provide a reality check for the constructs created through the principal components analyses; taken together, the available empirical evidence strongly suggest that the questions comprising each construct actually cohere or hang together well (Santos, 1999).

RESULTS FROM SURVEY USE

Given that access to the survey is electronic and self-administered, in theory any nonprofit organization in the world with English speaking affiliates could choose to use the survey with their organization. After completion of the survey, an organization's survey administrator will receive a report describing the mean scores for each question on the survey as well as an overall score for the organization. Survey administrators can then use the report generated by the survey software or export results to another data management option such as *Microsoft Excel or Statistical Package for the Social Sciences (SPSS)*. This allows the organization to analyze results in the manner most helpful to them (e.g., grouped by positional status, provided as an overall organizational score, assessed via coworker questions); we envision that the information received from the survey will create a safe space to begin important conversations about ethics within their organization.

COST AND LOCATION

The survey can be accessed free of charge from the Institute for Nonprofit Education and research webpage at www.sandiego.edu/soles/npresearch. The survey is self-administered and generates a user-friendly report of results once a minimum number of surveys have been completed by members of the organization; this restriction is in place to protect the confidentiality of participants. To allow for more analysis on the Governance construct as well as to develop a database of ethical behavior among nonprofits, the institute

Table 7. Cronbach's Alpha score for each factor or construct in the nonprofit ethics survey

Factor Name & Number (Revised)	Number of Items in the Final Scale	Alpha Score
Transparency (1)	8	.91
Daily-Ethics: Board Members (2)	5	.94
Open Communication (3)	5	.89
Daily-Ethics: Senior Management (4)	5	.93
Decision Making*** (6)	6	.86
Daily-Ethics: Accountability (7)	5	.88
------------------------------------	------------------------------------	------------------------------
Governance (1A)	24	.90

* Includes all 24 Likert-Style questions in the original survey construct

** Three of the Decision Making questions loaded together at a level ≥0.60 on Factor six and three loaded together at ≥ 0.60 on Factor eight.

--- Denotes division of results from the first and second principal components analysis.

hosting the survey requests permission to use the data generated by survey respondents; however, organizations are free to decline this request and still use the survey with their organization.

Commentary

The impact of having an instrument such as the Nonprofit Ethics Survey creates new opportunities for the leadership of nonprofit organizations and for the third sector at large. From a compliance standpoint use of the survey, and an increased focus on ethics, will likely increase preparedness for pending governmental regulation and accountability measures. From an operations standpoint, use of the survey by nonprofit organizations to engage in comprehensive self-assessment will likely improve their performance in their stewardship of public monies and trust (Barrett, 2008). And from a macro perspective, the existence of the Nonprofit Ethics Survey as the first empirically supported tool designed specifically for assessing nonprofit organizations serves as an important starting point for future research and discussion.

Additionally, the creation of the Nonprofit Ethics Survey as an online instrument, versus a paper and pencil document, provides numerous advantages. Commencing with distribution, the survey can easily be administered to all affiliates of the organization with a valid email address eliminating printing costs and the environmental impact of using a paper survey. Survey respondents also can complete and return the survey at their convenience avoiding the risk of unnecessary missing data due to individuals who may complete a paper survey, but then never turn it in to be scored. The benefits continue with the ease of gathering and analyzing survey results. With an online survey the need for manual data entry is eliminated (again reducing the risk of errors, and decreasing the amount of organizational resources required to use the survey) and all survey data is immediately available for analysis. Finally, given the survey exists as an online tool nonprofit orga-

nizations with affiliates in multiple locations can easily distribute the survey and utilize the data; a task that would be significantly more challenging, and require additional resources, to complete with a paper instrument.

Returning for a moment to the benefits individual organizations using the survey may experience, Bruckmaster (1999) and Kaptein, Huberts, Avelino, and Lasthuizen (2005) have shown that organizations whose practices include self-assessment, such as the Nonprofit Ethics Survey affords, adopt more practices identified as characteristic of *learning organizations,* including the use of best practices. Since Argyris (1977) and Senge (1990) describe learning organizations as those that identify and remove barriers to knowledge and learning, self-assessment and other methods of evaluation provide a means for organizations to actively identify potential barriers and to shift organizations from single-loop to double-loop learning. The advantage afforded to organizations that make this shift can be summarized as movement from reactive practices to proactive prevention. Nonprofit organizations and the third sector at large typically embody a reactive or single-loop approach to ethics accountability and the requirements of governmental regulation. A lack of financial resources and well-intended commitment to serving the organization's mission statement may account for the inability of nonprofit managers to get and stay ahead of legislative and accountability issues. However, root-cause aside, reactivity leads to a crisis form of operation.

Bruckmaster (1999) and Kaptein et al., (2005) also note that the use of evaluation and best practices in an organization represent positively correlated variables. The use of best practices in the areas assessed by the Nonprofit Ethics Survey clearly contribute to positive ethical health in organizations, and to the creation of an ethically strong culture as described by the Ethics Resource Center (2008). Taken together, these contributions provide important support for using the Nonprofit Ethics Survey with philanthropic organizations since the survey allows organizations to obtain an accurate picture of the perceptions of ethics held by their affiliates. This data-based perspective provides critical information regarding areas in need of change as well as areas of ethical vulnerability so that organizations can move out of crisis mode and strengthen their ethical culture.

REFERENCES

Argyris, C. (1977, September-October). Double-loop learning in organizations. *Harvard Business Review*, 115–125.

Barrett, A. (2008). *The nonprofit ethics survey: A contextual approach.* Doctoral dissertation, The University of San Diego.

Brown, M. E., & Trevino, L. K. (2006). Ethical leadership: A review and future directions. *The Leadership Quarterly, 17*, 595–616. doi:10.1016/j.leaqua.2006.10.004

Buckmaster, N. (1999). Associations between outcome measurement, accountability and learning for non-profit organisations. *International Journal of Public Sector Management, 12*(2), 186–197. doi:10.1108/09513559910263499

DeVellis, R. F. (1991). *Scale development: Theory and applications.* Newbury Park, CA: Sage Publications.

Ethics Resource Center. (2008). *National nonprofit ethics survey: An inside view on nonprofit sector ethics.*

Field, A. (2005). *Factor analysis using SPSS.* Retrieved on March, 3, 2008, from www.sussex.ac.uk/Users/andyf/factor.pdf

Fink, A. (2003). *The survey handbook* (2nd ed.). Thousand Oaks, CA: Sage.

Gregorian, V. (2004, April). Philanthropy should have glass pockets. *The Chronicle of Philanthropy*, 43 – 44.

Hemmelgarn, A. L., Glisson, C., & James, L. R. (2006, Spring). Organizational culture and climate: Implications for services and interventions research. *Clinical Psychology: Science and Practice, 13*(1), 73–89. doi:10.1111/j.1468-2850.2006.00008.x

Hinkle, D. E., Wiersma, W., & Jurs, S. G. (2003). *Applied statistics for the behavioral sciences* (5th ed.). Boston, MA: Houghton Mifflin.

Hutcheson, G., & Sofroniou, N. (1999). *The multivariate social scientist: Introductory statistics using generalized liner models.* Thousand Oaks, CA: Sage.

Kaptein, M., Huberts, L., Avelino, S., & Lasthuizen, K. (2005, Fall). Demonstrating ethical leadership by measuring ethics: A survey of U.S. public servants. *Public Integrity, 7*(4), 299–311.

Lohmann, R. A. (2007, May/June). Charity, philanthropy, public service, or enterprise: What are the big questions of nonprofit management today? *Public Administration Review, 67*(3), 437–444. doi:10.1111/j.1540-6210.2007.00727.x

Mertler, C. A., & Vannatta, R. A. (2005). *Advanced and multivariate statistical methods: Practical application and interpretation* (3rd ed.). Glendale, CA: Pyrczak.

Meyers, L. S., Gamst, G., & Guarino, A. J. (2006). *Applied multivariate research: Design and interpretation.* Thousand Oaks, CA: Sage.

Milgram, S. (1974). *The individual in a social world: Essays and experiments.* New York, NY: McGraw Hill.

Mulligan, L. N. (2007, June). What's good for the goose is not good for the gander: Sarbanes-Oxley-style nonprofit reforms. *Michigan Law Review, 105*(8), 1981–1999.

Preston, C. (2007). Nonprofit leaders' debate: Whether or not all philanthropy is equal? *The Chronicle of Philanthropy, 20*(2), Prewitt, K. (2006). Foundations. In Powell, W., & Steinberg, R. (Eds.), *The nonprofit sector: A research handbook* (1st ed., pp. 355–377). New Haven, CT: Yale University Press.

Rossi, P. H., Wright, J. D., & Anderson, A. B. (Eds.). (1983). *Handbook of survey research*. San Diego, CA: Academic Press.

Santos, J. R. (1999, April). Cronbach's alpha: A tool for assessing the reliability of scales. *Journal of Extension, 37*(2), 1–5.

Seligson, A. L., & Choi, L. (2006). *Critical elements of an organizational ethical culture*. Washington, DC: Ethics Resource Center.

Senge, P. M. (1990). *The fifth discipline: The art and practice of the learning organization*. New York, NY: Doubleday Currency. doi:10.1002/pfi.4170300510

Steinberg, R. (2006). Economic theories of nonprofit organizations. In Powell, W., & Steinberg, R. (Eds.), *The nonprofit sector: A research handbook* (1st ed., pp. 117–139). New Haven, CT: Yale University Press.

Trevino, L. K., Butterfield, K. D., & McCabe, D. L. (1998). The ethical context in organizations: Influences on employee attitudes and behaviors. *Business Ethics Quarterly, 8*(3), 447–476. doi:10.2307/3857431

Zimbardo, P. (2007). *The Lucifer effect: Understanding how good people turn evil*. New York, NY: Random House.

ADDITIONAL READING

Panel on the Nonprofit Sector. (2007, October). *Principles for good governance and ethical practice: A guide for charities and foundations*. Published by The Panel on the Nonprofit Sector: Convened by Independent Sector.

Vidaver-Cohen, D. (1998, August). Moral climate in business firms: A conceptual framework for analysis and change. *Journal of Business Ethics, 17*(11), 1211–1226. doi:10.1023/A:1005763713265

KEY TERMS AND DEFINITIONS

Double-Loop Learning: Organizational learning that not only resolves a problem, but seeks to determine the root cause and make systemic changes to proactively prevent the problem from recurring.

Learning Organization: Any organization that works to identify and remove barriers to acquiring knowledge and learning.

Nonprofit Affiliate: Any individual associated with a particular nonprofit agency including board members, senior or executive staff members, middle management, line staff, volunteers, major donors, or other key individuals.

Organizational Level Assessment: An assessment conducted using the organization as the unit of analysis. Ideally, all members or affiliates of the organization participate in an organizational-level analysis to ensure comprehensive data collection.

Single-Loop Learning: Organizational learning that solves problems as they arise, but takes no action to determine the root cause of the problem to prevent it from recurring.

Social context: An emerging concept in the literature that combines the often conflicting notions of organizational climate and organizational culture into a cohesive construct. Ethical context is one component of social context.

Third Sector: The economic sector comprised of nonprofit or charitable organizations. Most scholars agree that there are three economic sectors 1) private, business, or the for-profit sector; 2) government or the civil service sector; and 3) the nonprofit or third sector.

Chapter 5
Analysis and Use of the Life Styles Inventory 1 and 2 by Human Synergistics International

Dan Lawson
Ashland University, USA

ABSTRACT

The Life Styles Inventory, developed by J. Clayton Lafferty, uses a combination of respected psychological and managerial theories to help individuals identify their beliefs, values, behaviors, and assumptions. This instrument presents twenty statements for each of the twelve life styles believed to influence the way we think and behave. The LSI 1 instrument is a self-assessment whereas the LSI 2 uses the same format and life styles to assess an individual through input from five or more other people. When used in combination, the two instruments use consensual validity to identify strengths and weaknesses for the development of a self-improvement plan. This chapter discussed the theoretical background of the Life Styles Inventory, as well as instrument validity and reliability. A description of the results upon taking the instrument is included, along with commentary on the instrument's utility. Web address, cost, terms, and definitions appear at the end of the chapter.

ANALYSIS OF THE INSTRUMENT

Introduction

In recent history, self-assessment has become a basic component in management assessment and leadership development. A large number of self-assessment surveys and instruments are now available to help individuals understand and modify their personal behavior and thinking patterns. However, self-assessment is only as effective as the assessed individual's truthfulness. Often the assessed individual will respond with answers he or she thinks are the correct response rather than give a truthful response that may reveal a perceived weakness. Self-deception is an all too common practice that negates the validity and reliability of many self-assessment instruments. As human beings, we have a great capacity to deceive ourselves into thinking we are a better leader than we are in reality.

DOI: 10.4018/978-1-4666-2172-5.ch005

By adding consensual validity to the assessment process, the results of an individual's analysis can be much more effective. Consensual validity is the measure of agreement between self-assessment and assessment by others (Cooke, Rousseau, & Lafferty, 1987). This form of assessment is particularly important when the assessment is focused upon leaders and managers whose effectiveness depends upon interaction with subordinates, co-workers, and clients. The *Life Styles Inventory*™ (LSI; Lafferty, 1973)[1] makes use of both self-assessment and assessment by others to identify the degree of consensual validity and provide structured feedback for the assessed individual. This chapter offers an evaluation of the theoretical background, validity, and reliability of the LSI 1 (self-report) and the LSI 2 (description by others) instruments. In addition, the web location and cost associated with the LSI instrument appears at the end of the chapter, followed by a list of the twelve life styles and their definitions. A suggested reading list also appears at the end of the chapter.

Background

Leaders and managers often confuse perception of self with how they think they should act (Sullivan, 1953). An often subconscious process occurs with many leaders and managers wherein they attempt to match their leadership and management style to the perceived expectations of others. This creates a complex process of psychological self-deception and self-delusion, the result of which is an inaccurate self-appraisal of an individual's leadership abilities. Therefore, it is unlikely that self-assessment alone will lead to effective insights and behavior modification, particularly those insights that some individuals are not willing to accept or acknowledge about themselves (Horney, 1945). However, constructive feedback from trusted others can provide valuable insight for the assessed individual, thereby prompting the adoption of suggested changes to make improvements to his/her behavior. Well-structured feedback on

an individual's communication styles, personal orientation, behaviors, and values can provide a benchmark for change, growth, and development. For this reason, Human Synergistics International (HSI) offers the *Life Styles Inventory* 1 and 2. *Life Styles Inventory* 1 (LSI 1) is a self-assessment instrument, while *Life Styles Inventory* 2 (LSI 2) uses the exact same questions and life styles to conduct assessment by others. Although the LSI 1 can be used as a standalone assessment, the two assessments (LSI 1 and 2), when used together, provide consensual validity, a comparison of agreement between assessment by self and assessment by others. This process is deeply revealing and highly effective in the examination of an individual's thinking and behavior styles.

The theoretical basis for the *Life Styles Inventory*, created by Lafferty (1973), comes largely from Maslow's (1954) hierarchy of human needs. Maslow postulated a rank order of needs from strongest to weakest. He ranked physiological needs as the strongest among human needs, followed by safety needs, acceptance/belonging needs, self-esteem/self-importance needs, and finally fully developed personality needs (Cangemi, 2009). Lafferty supplements his approach to leadership and management behavior with material from other need theorists, management theorists, and personality psychologists (Nediger & Chelladurai, 1989) in order to develop a more well rounded instrument.

While Lafferty, founder of Human Synergistics International, developed the *Life Styles Inventory* as a general assessment to help individuals understand and modify their behavior and thinking styles, this assessment has been especially useful in manager and leader development. He writes, "Because it measures what drives your behavior (your thoughts and self-concept), the inventory is your tool for self-discovery" (*Life Styles Inventory Self-Development Guide*, 1973/2004, p. 5). Lafferty delineates twelve life styles on the *Life Styles Inventory*, which he originally placed within four broad categories[2]. His twelve life styles are Humanistic/Helpful (later changed to Humanistic-Encouraging), Affiliative, Approval, Conventional, Dependent, Avoidance, Oppositional, Power, Competitive, Competence (later changed to Perfectionistic), Achievement, and Self-Actualizing. He arranged these life styles in a circumplex (see Figure 1) and postulated contiguous styles would have high correlation. Likewise, those styles that are noncontiguous will have less correlation. In fact, he posited the further the life styles are from one another on the circumplex, the greater the degree of non-correlation. When conducting ongoing research on Lafferty's LSI 1 instrument, Cooke and Rousseau (1983) discuss the correlation of the life styles on the *Life Styles Inventory*. They wrote, "Life styles near each other *(on the circumplex)* (e.g., styles 1 and 2 or styles 4 and 5) are predicted to be more highly and positively correlated than life styles further apart (e.g., styles 1 and 6 or 3 and 9)" (p. 451).

Lafferty also expected life styles 12 and 1 to have a positive correlation, which causes the continuum to fall into a circumplex.

Lafferty credits Timothy Leary (1955) with developing the original idea of a circumplex. Leary (1957) developed a diagnostic instrument called the Interpersonal Check List, which used a circumplex structure, originally called the Leary Circumplex or the Leary Circle. Leary's circumplex was defined by two orthogonal axes, a vertical axis that identified degrees of status, power, and control, and a horizontal axis that identified degrees of solidarity, friendliness, and warmth. Based upon Leary's work, Lafferty initially divided his life styles circumplex using a vertical and horizontal axis, which created four broad categories (quadrants) (see Figure 1) labeled (a) Concern for People and Satisfaction; (b) Concern for People and Security; (c) Concern for Task and Satisfaction; and (d) Concern for Task and Secu-

Figure 1. The original circumplex for the Level 1: Life Styles Inventory as first conceived by J.C. Lafferty. From Life Styles Inventory Self-Development Guide. (© 1980, Plymouth, MI: Human Synergistics. Used with permission.)

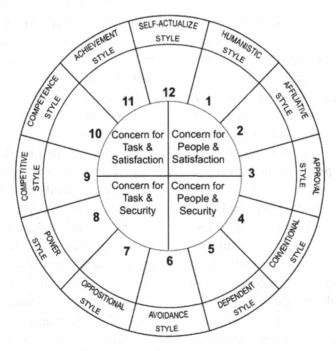

rity (Cooke & Lafferty, 1981). His conceptual model revealed two bipolar dimensions to reflect his distinction between security needs versus satisfaction needs and an orientation of task versus people. Half of the life styles in the security/ satisfaction dimension are associated with Maslow's (1954) lower-order needs and half are associated with Maslow's higher-order needs (Cooke & Rousseau). When divided along the bipolar dimension task/people, half of the life styles are associated with task orientation, similar to those defined by Stogdill's (1963) initiating structure, Blake and Mouton's (1964) concern for production, or Katz, Maccoby, and Morse's (1959) production-centered behavior. The other half of the life styles were associated with a people orientation, "similar to consideration, concern for people, and employee centered behavior" (Cooke & Rousseau, p. 450).

Following a series of studies to validate the instrument statistically (discussed later in this chapter) Lafferty revised the four broad categories down to three interpretable factors (Nediger & Chelladurai, 1989). This revision was heavily based upon the factors empirically identified by Cooke and Rousseau (1983) and the clusters proposed by Robert A. Cooke for the prototype of the *Organizational Culture Inventory* ® (1983)[3]. Subsequently, those three categories were labeled by Cooke and Lafferty as Constructive styles, Passive/Defensive styles, and Aggressive/Defensive styles. (see Figure 2)

Reliability

The results of any one study may not be enough to argue for instrument reliability. Reliability of an instrument means the instrument repeatedly comes up with the same measurement (deVaus, 2001). Specialists argue repeated replication of statistical research provides for a real substantive argument in favor of instrument reliability. Cattell (1978) wrote, "… firm replication of a given factor simply as an empirical pattern at a sheer

descriptive level . . . is the most needed achievement" (p. 496). He argued effective research places no confidence in a single factor analysis due to the imperfect nature of assigning statistical significance. Illustrating factorial invariance through repeated investigation, designed to replicate previous findings, is necessary to assess the real effectiveness of an instrument. Furthermore, Nunnally (1978) argued, "most measures must be kept under constant surveillance to see if they are behaving as they should" (p. 87). In other words, if a researcher can replicate earlier research results for instrument reliability in a different study, a different culture, or a different context, then the generalizability of the concept and the applicability of the instrument are stronger and the instrument becomes more reliable. This analysis of the *Life Styles Inventory* has revealed several studies conducted independently, in different settings, and different cultures that confirm the statistical reliability of the *Life Styles Inventory*.

Twenty items for each of the twelve life styles compile the 240 words and phrases used in the *Life Styles Inventory* instrument. Assessed individuals take the *LSI* 1 and respond to the 240 items by marking a three point Likert-like scale ranging from "like you most of the time" to "essentially unlike you." Cooke and Lafferty (1981), the first to report on the psychometric properties of the LSI, found statistical results that indicated the twelve scales had acceptable reliability with Cronbach's Alpha values ranging from .80 to .88. Cooke and Rousseau (1983) used the same data set to confirm these finding and identify the three factors mentioned earlier.

When looking only at the results of a factor analysis with a three-factor solution, Ware, Leak, and Perry (1985) found "Cronbach's *alpha* estimates of internal consistency for the factor scores, based on normalized variables and the factor score coefficient matrix, yielded reliability coefficients of .79, .67, and .75 for Factors 1, 2, and 3 respectively" (p. 967). As a result, they found remarkable similarity with previous studies.

Figure 2. The Life Styles Inventory™ (LSI) circumplex. (© 1973-2009, Research and Development by J. Clayton Lafferty, Ph.D., Human Synergistics International. Used with permission.)

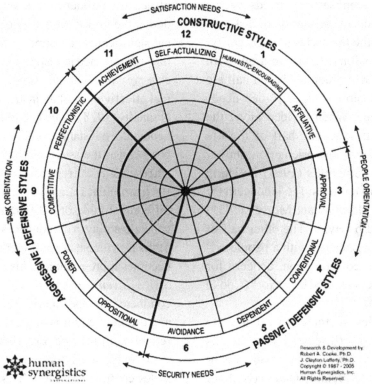

Furthermore, when they applied a calculation of Tucker's (1951) congruence coefficient (r_e) they found numerical indices of pattern matching. In all three of their comparison studies, they found r_e values greater than .98 ($p < .05$). In Tucker's 1951 study, he accepts coefficients ranging from 0.99998 to 0.9398 as an indication of acceptable congruence. These results in Ware, Leak, and Perry's (1985) study provided strong support for the generality of the factor structure. They wrote, "This finding is remarkable because there are differences across researches in population of subjects, methods of factor extraction, and size of samples, all of which influence the nature of the factor solution obtained" (Ware, Leak, & Perry, 1985, p. 967).

Nediger and Chelladurai (1989) also attempted to replicate the findings of previous studies, but added three issues not mentioned in the previous

studies; a Canadian context, as opposed to the United States, gender groupings, and Lafferty's proposition that the twelve styles would fall on a circumplex. Regarding internal consistency, Nediger and Chelladurai found Cronbach's alpha coefficients ranging from .78 to .88 ($M = .85$) for data in the female subgroup and .76 to .87 ($M = .84$) for data in the male subgroup. The range was .79 to .88 ($M = .85$) in the total sample. They found these results to be sufficiently high and acceptable.

When used together, Cooke, Rousseau, and Lafferty (1987) found the LSI 1, (self-assessment), and the LSI 2, (assessment by others), provides consensual validity. To determine inter-rater reliability, they reported correlations among same-style different-rater ranging from .16 to .32 with an average of .24. They wrote, "For about half of the 12 styles, the same-style different-rater correlation coefficients are larger than any relevant different-style different-rater coefficients" (p. 820).

In their study of the correlation among sub-scales, Nediger and Chelladurai (1989) found 55 of the 66 correlations to be statistically significant. They found strong correlations between the styles that appear next to each other on the circumplex. Correlations decreased or turned negative as distance between the life styles increased. They did find exceptions in this pattern; however, when their research revealed a weak correlation between the contiguous styles Affiliative and Approval. They also found that the neighboring styles on each side of these two contiguous styles correlated highly with both of these styles at the same time. When they analyzed the male and female subgroups separately, they found similar results. Because of these findings, they did not support consistent evidence that the twelve life styles form a closed circumplex.

Each of these studies, conducted independent of the others, found extraordinarily similar results regarding the reliability of the *Life Styles Inventory*. These findings substantiate Cattell's (1978) insistence that independent replication is the most needed achievement to support the statistical reliability of an instrument.

Validity

To determine the validity of an instrument, the researcher must ask, Does the instrument do what it claims to do (de Vaus, 2001)? A study by Cooke and Lafferty (1981) was the first to address this question with the *Life Styles Inventory*. They were also the first to report on the psychometric properties of the *Life Style Inventory*. Their study assessed,

...construct validity inferred from the pattern of intercorrelations and cluster analysis for the twelve styles; convergent and discriminant validity evidenced by the item-to-total correlation of the 240 items; and criterion related validity suggested by the relationship of the twelve styles to behavior of the employee, such as tendency to

cooperate and perform tasks effectively. (Nediger & Chelladurai, 1989, p. 902)

Cooke and Lafferty (1981) found support for instrument validity; however, subsequent factor analysis indicates the items of the instrument load on only three factors rather than the four first posited by Lafferty.

Two other studies by Cooke and Rousseau (1983) and Ware, Leak and Perry (1985) studied the dimensionality of the twelve styles, both finding items loading on only three factors rather than the four that Lafferty first posited. This factor loading explained approximately 70% of the common variance in thinking/behavior styles. Cooke, Rousseau, and Lafferty (1987) report the three factors reflect personal satisfaction, people security, and task security.

In their study, Ware, Leak, and Perry (1985) took a slightly different approach. They used principal-axis factor analysis to generate the factor matrix followed by varimax (Camrey, 1973) and oblique rotation. Varimax rotation tries to minimize the number of variables that load highly on a factor. Oblique rotation relaxes the assumption that the factors must be orthogonal, or at right angles to one another (Rummel, 1970). Ware, Leak, and Perry first sought to emphasize the factorial invariance of responses to the inventory by following Gorsuch's (1983) argument. They wrote, "If a highly similar factor pattern emerged when varying both population of participants and methods of extraction, then greater confidence could be placed in the generality of the factor structure of the inventory" (Ware, Leak, & Perry, 1985, p. 966). They also argued that the principal-axis technique was much more appropriate than principal components because principal-axis techniques do not assume error-free measurement and they produce loadings that are more conservative (Gorsuch, 1983). Furthermore, principal-axis analysis does not mix common and unique variance, thereby making "hybrid" factors less likely (Ware, et. al., 1985).

Using Kaiser criterion, the results of Ware, Leak, and Perry's (1985) factor analysis also produced three factors, similar to the studies mentioned earlier. However, four clear factors were evident when they used Cattell's (1966) scree test. Some evidence has emerged that indicates the Kaiser criterion "occasionally underestimates the correct number of factors" (Ware, Leak, and Perry, 1985, p. 966) (Gorsuch, 1983). Cattell (1978) argued that the Kaiser criterion "... is wrong, in principle, and erratic in practice ..." (p. 162). In fact, the Kaiser criterion is in error five times more often than the scree test (Ware, Leak, and Perry, 1985). Child (1973) suggested the Kaiser criterion is appropriate with factors that ranged between 20 and 50; however, he argued that it is prone to underextraction with less than 20 variables. For this reason, Ware, Leak, and Perry (1985) found support for a four-factor solution with statistical significance ($p < .10$). They write, "By contrast, the three-factor solution of Cooke and Rousseau (1983) was nonsignificant" (p. 966). However, Ware, Leak, and Perry went on to argue in favor of a three-factor rather than a four-factor solution for two reasons. First, the four-factor solution was "without psychological importance" (p. 966) and accounted for only 5% of the common variance with no loadings greater than .40. This made factor interpretation on samples of 100 or less unnecessarily risky. Second, the purpose of their study was for comparison of other research findings. Therefore, they suggest a common basis for comparison was necessary.

The results of Nediger and Chelladurai's (1989) factor analysis were similar to previous studies in that they also found the twelve styles to load on three factors. In their conclusion, Nediger and Chelladurai (1989) wrote,

... our results support the stability of the subscale structure of the Life Styles Inventory in the Canadian context. Its subscales were found to be internally consistent. The item-to-total correlations yield acceptable estimates of convergent and

discriminant validity. The pattern of correlation among the twelve styles also indicated construct validity. Therefore, the Life Styles Inventory can be profitably used as a research and/or diagnostic tool. (p. 908)

At this point, there has been more than three decades of research as well as practical experience with the *Life Styles Inventory*. Lafferty developed the *Life Styles Inventory* within a framework of content validity (Ware, Leak, & Perry, 1985). Evidence of the instrument's construct validity rests primarily upon the instrument's internal structure, as indicated above. Empirical investigation of the LSI repeatedly has confirmed the presence of three underlying dimensions, thus providing support for construct validity (Skenes & Honig, 2004; Cooke & Rousseau, 1983; Gratzinger, Warren, & Cooke, 1990; Masi, & Cooke, 2000; Ware, Leak, & Perry, 1985). Cooke and Lafferty (1981) also suggested evidence for criterion validity as well, based upon the relationship of the twelve Life Styles to the "promotability" of employees supported by employee propensity to cooperate with others and perform tasks and duties effectively. In addition, Cooke, Rousseau, and Lafferty (1987) argue for support of consensual validity based upon the degree of agreement between self-assessment and assessment by others.

The assessments of the LSI 1 and LSI 2 conducted to date have found sufficient agreement as to warrant both reliability and validity of the instrument in its current form. The subscales have repeatedly proven to be internally consistent. The item-to-total correlations in various studies have yielded acceptable estimates of convergence and discriminant validity and the pattern of correlation among the twelve life styles has repeatedly indicated construct validity. Each of the studies researched for this analysis have found the *Life Styles Inventory* to be an effective diagnostic and/or research tool, with the exception of Nediger and Chelladurai who could neither prove nor deny a circular continuum, or circumplex of the twelve styles.

RESULTS

The *Life Style Inventory* consists of 240 words and phrases to which the respondent evaluates him/herself on a three point scale as being "like you most of the time," "like you quite often," or "essentially unlike you" (Lafferty, 1989, p. 4). The *Life Styles Inventory* 2 (LSI 2) is completed in a similar format by at least five others who know the assessed individual quite well. It is recommended that, if possible, one or more of the five others who complete the LSI 2 on behalf of the assessed individual be someone who has one of the following relationships with the assessed person; a boss, a direct report, a coworker, peer, and/or a friend. The assessed individual can decide who he or she would like to complete the LSI 2 on his or her behalf.

Individuals who complete the *Life Styles Inventory* (LSI 1) self-assessment receive raw scores in each of the twelve styles. The raw score is compared to a general population norming sample of over 9000 individuals, compiled by Human Synergistics International, and a percentile score is provided. Human Synergistics has recently released a 40th anniversary edition of the instrument with a new norming sample of 14,000 individuals. They continue to offer percentile scores against the original 9,000 individuals in the norming sample for those who are conducting a reassessment with the instrument where the first assessment made use of the original 9,000. This allows assessed individuals to measure progress against the same sample group. Each of the two norming samples were taken from North America, specifically the United States and Canada. The percentile scores, rather than the raw scores, are primarily used in the feedback and development process. The percentile score generalizes the results into a low, medium, or high range for each of the twelve styles. In other words, the assed individual is ranked in comparison to a low percentage of the norming sample, a medium percentage of the norming sample, or a high percentage of the norming sample. For the

LSI 2 assessment by others, the report gives a score in each style calculated as a composite from the results of the five surveys completed by others. In a similar fashion to the LSI 1, the average scores from the LSI 2 receive a generalized rating ranging from low, medium, to high when compared to the norming sample. Once again, the percentile scores, rather than the averaged raw scores, are primarily used in the feedback and development process. The low range includes the zero to the twenty-fifth percentile of the norming sample. The medium range includes the twenty-fifth percentile to the seventy-fifth percentile. The high range is above the seventy-fifth percentile.

The assessed individual receives an outcome report, called a profile summary, with the results from the LSI 1. As a supplement to the profile summary, which comes as an addition to the profile summary at an added expense, Human Synergistics International (HSI) provides a series of 36 small cards. There are three cards for each of the twelve styles. Each card provides a brief summary description for individuals scoring in the low, medium, or high range for each life style.

In order to provide quick, effective feedback at a glance, HSI provides for the arrangement of the 36 cards placed into a profile folder sectioned according to the three categories; Constructive styles, Passive/Defensive styles, and Aggressive/Defensive styles. The card with the individual's percentile score, low, medium, or high, is place on top and in the corresponding life style pocket for display. This allows the assessed individual to see at a glance their percentile scores in each of the three categories as well as each individual style. A brief description on each card provides them with additional supplemental information.

To aid in the interpretation of the LSI 1 results, HSI offers a *Self-Development Guide* (1973/2004) that provides detailed explanations for each of the twelve life styles, along with strengths and weakness for each style, as well as a description of the management style consistent with each life style. For example, someone scoring high in the

Humanistic – Encouraging style would read the following about his or her management skills:

Humanistic-Encouraging managers inspire their subordinated to think, grow and take responsibility for themselves. They do this by demonstrating belief in what their staff members can accomplish. These managers build problem-solving skills and confidence by asking insightful questions designed to help subordinates arrive at their own solutions.

Humanistic-Encouraging managers consistently show faith in their subordinates' ability to improve themselves, and actively support their efforts. As a management style, Humanistic-Encouraging is highly effective at obtaining measurable, bottom-line results; subordinates easily develop respect for these managers, and are motivated to achieve and sustain peak performance. (Life Styles Inventory Self Development Guide, 1973/2004, p. 13. Used by permission.)

The *Self-Development Guide* also provides descriptions for the assessed individual who scored in the low range, as well as the medium, or high range in each of the twelve styles. Likewise, a very helpful section appears at the end of each style that describes how the particular style relates to other styles. In addition, the *Self-Development Guide* provides suggestions for self-development and improvement in each of the twelve life styles.

As mentioned earlier in this chapter, a strength of the *Life Styles Inventory* is the consensual validity, or comparison of agreement between the self-assessment and assessment by others. Therefore, when the two instruments, LSI 1 self-assessment and LSI 2 assessment by others, are completed and scored, the outcome results of the two instruments appear in a side-by-side comparison called a Profile Supplement. The Profile Supplement simply displays the circumplexes (see figure 2) from the LSI 1and LSI 2 assessments. As mentioned above, the report of the LSI 2 assessment by others is an average of the results from the five

people who completed the assessment on behalf of the assessed individual.

Plotting the results on the circumplex (see figure 2) is an excellent way for the assessed individual to see instantly the scores from all twelve styles in one place. The side-by-side comparison provided in the Profile Supplement allows the assessed individual to instantly see the consensus, or lack thereof, between the self-assessment and the assessment by others. In other words, the assessed individual can quickly see the degree of agreement or differences between the way he or she views him or herself and the way others view his or her thinking and behavior as defined by the twelve life styles. This allows the assessed individual to consider if he or she has an accurate or inaccurate view of him/herself.

In addition to providing feedback in the form of the Profile Supplement for side-by-side comparison of the assessment by self circumplex and the assessment by others circumplex, HSI offers the *Description by Others Self-Development Guide* (1990/2004) for those who have had others complete the LSI 2 assessment on their behalf. The purpose of the *Description by Others Self-Development Guide* is to help the assessed individual understand how others view their behavioral and thinking styles. The authors write, "We all wonder 'how we're doing' in terms of our professional performance. Yet as we work to become better leaders and managers, one of the most serious difficulties is our lack of information about how others see us" (*Life Styles Inventory LSI 2: Description by Others Self-Development Guide*, 1990/2004, Introduction).

The *Description by Others Self-Development Guide* provides summary information of each of the twelve styles quite similar to the *Life Styles Inventory Self-Development Guide* (1973/2004) for the LSI 1 self-assessment. The assessed individual is able to read general style characteristics as well as management-related characteristics for each of the twelve styles. One difference between the two Self-Development Guides is that the *De-*

scription by Others Self-Development Guide offers "Thought Starters" in a workbook, fill in the blank format aimed at helping the assessed individual to begin thinking about his or her strengths and weaknesses and how he or she might develop a plan for improvement.

In similar format to the *Self-Development Guide* for the LSI 1 self-assessment, the *Description by Others Self-Development Guide* provides information on the relationship of each style to other styles. This is helpful in the process of identifying patterns of behavior in key areas and the process of understanding how improvement in one style may simultaneously create improvement in another related style.

A highly beneficial component of the *Description by Others Self-Development Guide* is the comparison graph that plots the raw score of the LSI 1 self-assessment against the (averaged) raw score of the LSI 2 assessment by others in each of the twelve styles. The point of comparison graph for the positively worded Constructive styles is a mirror image of the point of comparison graph for the more negatively worded Defensive styles (see figure 3).

HSI divides the point of comparison graph into nine sections. "Each section designates one of the nine possible *relationships* between your

LSI 1 and LSI 2 scores" (*Description by Others Self-Development Guide*, 1990/2004, p. 9). The objective is simply to plot the point where the two scores intersect by drawing a line vertically and diagonally from the respective raw scores on the X and Y axis. HSI calls this point of intersection the "point of comparison," the location of which reveals a specific meaning.

The "point of comparison" identifies the consensual validity of the two instruments. If both the LSI 1 self-assessment and the LSI 2 assessment by others agree, the "point of comparison" falls within an area on the comparison graph identified as a "Confirmed Strength." If the assessed individual scores him/herself lower in a Constructive style than the assessment by others, or higher in a Defensive style than the assessment by others, the "point of comparison falls within an area identified as an "Unrecognized Strength." That is to say, others recognize an area of strength in the assessed individual that he or she did not recognize in him/herself. If the raw scores from the LSI 1 self-assessment agree with the scores from the LSI 2 assessment by others and both scores are low in a Constructive style or high in a Defensive style, the "point of comparison" falls within an area on the comparison graph identifies as a "Stumbling Block." This suggests that both

Figure 3. Side-by-side comparison of the LSI 1 profile and LSI 2 profile. (© 1973-2009, Research and Development by J. Clayton Lafferty, Ph.D., Human Synergistics International. Used with permission.)

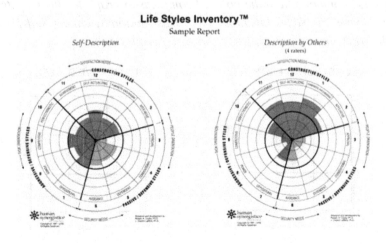

the assessed individual and the assessment by others recognize and agree upon an area of weakness that may cause potential problems to arise in the leadership and management style of the assessed individual. Finally, if the assessed individual's raw scores are higher in a Constructive style than the raw scores from the assessment by others, or the LSI 1 self-assessment raw scores are lower than the raw scores in the assessment by others for a Defensive style, the "point of comparison" falls within an area of the comparison graph that is identified as a "Blind Spot." This suggests the assessed individual is unaware of weaknesses in his or her leadership style that others have observed and identified. Figure 4 illustrates a "point of comparison" on the Humanistic-Encouraging style that suggests a Blind Spot for the assessed individual.

When the "point of comparison" falls within an Unrecognized Strength, a Stumbling Block, or a Blind Spot, the results indicate an opportunity for the assessed individual to develop a self-improvement plan. The *Description by Others Self-Development Guide* (1990/2004) provides excellent commentary and suggestions for a self-improvement plan. The *Description by Others Self-Development Guide* has a "Self-Development Thought Starter" section, along with a section entitled "Improving your Performance: Change Suggestions" and a "Self-Development Plan"

section wherein the assessed individual can write his or her observations, ideas, and plans for growth and change.

COMMENTARY

The *Life Styles Inventory* is an outstanding assessment tool for identifying key strengths and weaknesses in one's leadership and management thinking and behavioral styles. Research to date suggests strong agreement about the statistical validity and reliability of the instrument. In addition, the consensual validity revealed by the side-by-side comparison of the assessment by self and the assessment by others provides a strong onus for the assessed individual to overcome the self-deception that may occur through self-assessment alone. As discussed earlier in the chapter, many times an individual may not have a clear self-assessment of his or her personal styles. Regardless of the strengths of this instrument, however, like any other assessment tool, this instrument has a few areas in which it lacks utility.

The *Life Styles Inventory* was initially developed for the general population to assess thinking and behavioral styles. Therefore, the norming samples used to provide the percentile scores were taken from the general population. Those using this instrument as a part of a leadership or man-

Figure 4. A side-by-side comparison of the point of comparison graph for the Constructive Styles and the Defensive Styles. From Life Styles Inventory LSI 2 Description by Others Self-Development Guide. (© 2008, Plymouth, MI: Human Synergistics. Used with permission.)

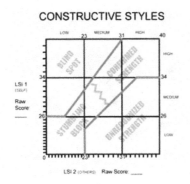

Figure 5. An example of an individual with an LSI 1 raw score of 36 and an LSI 2 raw score of 24 on the Humanistic Encouraging style. The point of comparison falls into a Blind Spot for the assessed individual. From Life Styles Inventory LSI 2 Description by Others Self-Development Guide. (© 2008, Plymouth, MI: Human Synergistics. Used with permission.)

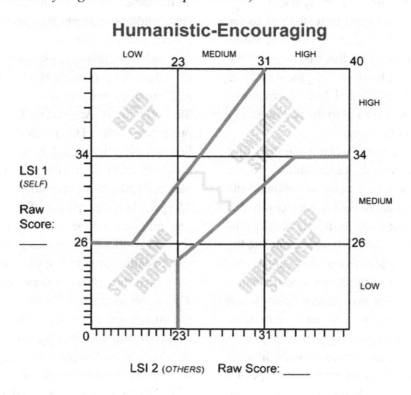

agement assessment should recognize the fact that the percentile scores are compared to the general population and not specific to a sample group of leaders or managers. HSI recognizes this fact about the *Life Styles Inventory* and offers the *Acumen Leadership WorkStyles* ™ (LWS)[4] instrument for managers, executives, project managers, and others in leadership positions. The results of the LWS are compared to a specific norming sample of leaders rather than the general population. At the time of this writing, HSI reported they are in the process of updating their norming samples for the LSI to include sampling from a general population all around the world. The original samples were only gathered from North America, specifically the United States and Canada.

A supplement to the feedback for the *Life Styles Inventory* LSI 1 self-assessment comes in the form

of 36 cards, three for each of the twelve styles. The assessed individual or assessment facilitator is to select the one card from each of the twelve styles that matches the raw score's range of low, medium, or high. The assessed individual or facilitator places the selected cards in designated slots in the Profile Summary folder that allocates the twelve styles into the three categories mentioned earlier; Constructive styles, Passive/Defensive styles, and Aggressive/Defensive styles. This method of feedback is bulky and cumbersome. The information on the cards is redundant when compared to the information in the *Self-Development Guide* (1972/2004). It is just as easy, and perhaps more effective to study the results as they appear on the circumplex, along with the information provided in the Self-Development Guide. In addition, there is the question of what to do with the unused cards. Should you throw them away or should they remain in the possession of the assessed individual for further study? Many assessment facilitators simply acknowledge the supplemental cards and provide them to the assessed individual for further personal study. The primary method of feedback is the use of the circumplex along with *Self-Development Guide* to explain the results of the LSI 1 self-assessment, which raises the question as to the real necessity for the Profile Summary cards.

A difficulty that arises when using the LSI 2 assessment by others is the dependability of those selected. There may be a delay in obtaining the results of the assessment because one or more of those selected to complete the assessment by others simply does not take the time to complete the instrument. HSI suggests that it takes only twenty to thirty minutes to complete the questionnaire, yet some may delay or procrastinate completing the instrument because they do not have the time or they are avoiding what they perceive to be an unpleasant task. This forces the assessed individual or the assessment facilitator to make repeated contact with those completing the assessment by others to ensure that the assessment is eventually completed. This problem is not specific to the *Life Styles Inventory*, but rather it applies to all 360-degree assessment instruments that depend on assessment by others.

Another problem with the LSI 2 assessment by others, which is also common among all 360-degree assessment tools, is the potential for one or more of those completing the assessment on behalf of the assessed individual to skew the results. HSI only requires five people to complete the LSI 2 assessment by others. However, they can generate a feedback report with as little as three completed assessments by others. If one or more or those completing the assessment should have a personal grudge or vendetta, which causes them to think poorly of the assessed individual, those poor responses may skew the results by giving abnormally low scores in the Constructive

styles or abnormally high scores in the Defensive styles. This could distort the average of the five scores and ultimately the raw score reported as an outcome. This problem could be lessened by simply adding more people who complete the LSI 2 assessment by others.

In addition, this author has personally observed an interesting phenomenon wherein women and minority individuals score slightly above the norm in the Aggressive Defensive, or self-projection styles. This phenomenon has not yet been statistically studied or validated. It is simply an observation made after administering several hundred LSI 1 and 2 instruments over a period of 15 years. It is the opinion of this author that this phenomenon may be due to a perceived need on the part of these individuals to be more aggressive in calling attention to themselves in order to gain what they consider to be equal recognition. This is not to suggest a weakness on the part of the instrument, but rather a possible recognition of human behavior among underrepresented individuals in contemporary society.

Finally, even after recognizing the strength of the instrument's consensual validity, the effectiveness of the instrument is dependent upon those whom the assessed individual selects to complete the LSI 2 assessment by others. It is possible that some people will select, knowingly or subconsciously, those whom they perceive to be like them or share their thinking and behavior patterns. As a result, if they are like-minded, those who complete the LSI 2 assessment by others may not give a fair and accurate assessment of the assessed individual's leadership and management thinking and behavioral styles. In other words, the results of the side-by-side comparison of the LSI 1 (self-assessment) and the LSI 2 (assessment by others) could be a product of a phenomenon similar to groupthink (Janis, 1972; Janis, 1982). Those experiencing or participating in groupthink do not consider all alternatives and they often desire unanimity at the expense of quality decisions. In defense of the LSI instrument, groupthink occurs in group decisions and the LSI 2 (assessment by others) is not completed in a group, but rather by individuals alone. However the potential remains for a restriction of range wherein like-minded people provide similar results.

Costs

Both the LSI 1 self-assessment and the LSI 2 assessment by others are available for administration in the traditional paper and pencil format, or through Internet Data Collection. HSI has also created a Web-based method for administering, scoring, and reporting the results of the *Life Styles Inventory* LSI 1 self-assessment. Prices may vary slightly from this report due to inflationary adjustments.

The traditional paper and pencil version of the *Life Styles Inventory* allows the assessed individual to hand score and interpret his or her own results for the LSI 1 self-assessment. This is useful when the assessment is only for those completing the LSI 1 self-assessment and situation calls for administering and scoring the instrument onsite during a class, conference or seminar. After the assessed individual completes and scores the instrument, the facilitator should provide each assessed person with the paper version of the *Self-Development Guide* for the LSI 1 self-assessment, published by Human Synergistics International (HSI), along with structured feedback to help interpret the results.

The *Life Styles Inventory* LSI 2 assessment by others is also available in paper form. This obviously requires distributing the five LSI 2 Descriptions by Others Inventories, collecting the completed surveys, and hand scoring the results. The results are recorded on the Scorer's Worksheet and the scores are averaged to arrive at the raw score for each of the twelve styles. As with any of the delivery methods, a trained facilitator should provide the assessed individual with a paper copy of the *Description by Others Self-Development Guide*, published by HSI, along with structured

feedback to help the assessed individual understand and interpret the results. This is most valuable when the assessed individual is receiving feedback from both the LSI 1 self-assessment and the LSI 2 assessment by others, particularly when there is divergent agreement between the assessment by self and assessment by others.

HSI offers paper versions of the LSI 1 Basic Kit, which includes the Self-Description Inventory and the LSI 1 *Self-Development Guide* for $25. The LSI 1 Full Kit, which includes the same elements of the Basic Kit plus the Profile Summary Cards, is available for $34. The Profile Summary Cards with folder is available separately for a cost of $10.

A paper version of the LSI 2 Kit, which includes five LSI 2 Inventories, an LSI 2 *Self-Development Guide*, a Scorer's worksheet, and a Profile Supplement, is available for $55. The LSI 2 Descriptions by Others Inventory is available for a cost of $8 each. A combination of the LSI 1 and 2 Basic Kit is available for $65 and the LSI 1 and 2 Full Kit, which includes all of the material from the LSI 1 Full Kit and the LSI 2 Full Kit, is available for $75. These costs do not include time and labor for scoring the instruments and compiling the results. Scoring services are available from HSI at a cost of $6 for the LSI 1 self-assessment and $35 for the five surveys included in the LSI 2 assessment by others.

Facilitator materials are also available from HSI. The *LSI Leader's Guide* is $75. A set of LSI Mastery Cards are $25. A set of twenty LSI Transparencies are available for $50. The LSI Comparative Profiles, a set of twelve, is available for $50 and the LSI Flipchart pad is available for $35.

The Internet Data Collection format of the *Life Styles Inventory* is obviously an electronic version of the material discussed above. It is useful in large-scale applications when there are several individuals to assess. HSI will email an invitation to each participant complete with a web address, user name and password. Participants are able to complete the instrument at their convenience.

This is true for those who are completing the self-assessment as well as those who are completing the assessment by others. HSI provides the facilitator conducting the assessment with a feedback profile on the assessed individual. These profiles arrive within seven to ten business days after all surveys are complete. At the time of this writing, HSI reported that they were beta testing new software that will allow their scoring department to produce the feedback profile within three to five business days. It should be noted that HSI is unable to generate the most beneficial assessment profile until all LSI 1 participants have completed their self-assessment surveys. However, as a part of the cost for this service, HSI will track those who have completed the instrument and inform the facilitator regarding the status of completed and not completed surveys. It should be noted that, for the sake of privacy (confidentiality), HSI does not disclose the names of those who have not completed the instrument. They simply inform the facilitator of the number of surveys that are still outstanding. Once the facilitator has received the profile results, he or she provides the results to the assessed individual along with a paper copy of the *Self-Development Guide* and the *Description by Others Self-Development Guide*. As mentioned above, a trained facilitator should provide structured feedback and assist in the interpretation of the results.

The cost of the Internet Data Collection format of the *Life Styles Inventory* is very similar to the paper costs. Obviously the paper form of the *Self-Development Guide* and the *Description by Others Self-Development Guide* is the same as that mentioned above, as is the cost of the scoring fees. However, with the paper version of the LSI 1 and 2, the facilitator can choose to hand score each completed survey, thereby avoiding the added expense of the scoring fee. With the Internet Data Collection format, the scoring fees cannot be waived because the responses for each survey are transmitted electronically to Human Synergistics International, who then score the results and send the feedback profile to the facilitator.

The Internet Data Collection version of the LSI 1 and 2 also requires an administration fee. For the complete 360-degree process of LSI 1 and five LSI 2 surveys the fee is $30. However if you wish to use only the LSI 1 the fee is $10 for each self-assessment and if you wish to use only the LSI 2 surveys the fee is $30 for 5 surveys. This administration fee covers the expense of distributing email invitations, reminders and updates throughout the project.

Finally, the Internet Data Collection format also requires a $100 "build fee" to prepare the electronic surveys, create the usernames and passwords, and to send that information to each assessed individual and each person completing the assessment by others. The build fee for the Internet Data Collection format can be waived if the facilitator is completing assessments for 10 or more assessed individuals.

The most versatile version of the *Life Styles Inventory* is the new Web-based format recently developed by HSI. The Web-based version is only available for the LSI 1 self-assessment. At this time the LSI 2 assessment by others is not available in the Web-based format. The Web-based format is very similar to Internet Data Collection format in that respondents for the LSI 1 self-assessment are assigned a user name and password. They simply log into a secure web site to complete the survey using the assigned user name and password. HSI provides the facilitator conducting the assessment with an account wherein he or she can set up the user names and passwords for each participant completing a self-assessment. Facilitators can pre-purchase credits, which can be used at a later date as the need arises. This bypasses the necessity to purchase each assessment one at a time. The cost of each Web-based LSI 1 self-assessment is $25.

Aside from the fact that the Web-Based version is only available for the LSI 1 self-assessment, the main difference between the Web-based format and the Internet Data Collection format is the fact that the Web-based format provides real-time results. You no longer have to wait seven to ten business days to get the assessment profile. The real-time results of the Web-based format of the Life Styles Inventory LSI 1 self-assessment can be provided in three different ways.

In the first delivery method, the feedback profile is provided immediately to the facilitator who then provides the assessed individual with the feedback profile along with a paper version of the *Self-Development Guide*. The well trained facilitator will provide structured feedback and help the assessed individual interpret the profile.

The second delivery method of the Web-based version of the *Life Styles Inventory* provides the feedback profile immediately to both the assessed individual and the facilitator. In this situation the well trained facilitator will have provided a paper copy of the Self-Development Guide in advance and made arrangements to provide structured feedback to help the assessed individual interpret the feedback profile.

The third delivery method of the Web-based version of the *Life Styles Inventory* provides a totally web-based kit to the assessed individual wherein he or she receives the results along with an interactive, electronic version of the Self-Development Guide customized to the feedback profile of the assessed individual emphasizing his or her strongest styles. As with the other delivery methods, it will be prudent for a well-trained facilitator to help the assessed individual interpret the feedback profile.

All prices mentioned within this section are current as of the time of this writing and are subject to change. HSI provides a 30 day notice prior to price revisions. HSI also provides an educational discount as well as a volume discount. Contact Human Synergistics International for specific quotes.

Location

The web address for Human Synergistics International is www.humansynergistics.com. This site contains information about HSI as well as all of the products available. You can navigate to the information on the *Life Styles Inventory* by clicking on the word "Assessments" under the Products / Individual Development heading. A link to the *Life Styles Inventory* page is available on the Individual Assessments page. The direct link to the Life Styles Inventory page is http://humansynergistics.com/products/lsi.aspx.

REFERENCES

Blake, R. R., & Mouton, J. S. (1964). *The managerial grid*. Houston, TX: Gulf Publishing.

Camrey, A. L. (1973). *A first course in factor analysis*. New York, NY: Academic Press.

Cangemi, J. (2009). Analysis of an adversarial labor/management situation in a Latin American industrial setting. *Organization Development Journal*, *27*(1), 37–47.

Cattell, R. B. (1966). The screen test for the number of factors. *Multivariate Behavioral Research*, *1*, 140–161. doi:10.1207/s15327906mbr0102_10

Cattell, R. B. (1978). *The scientific use of factor analysis in the behavioral and life sciences*. New York, NY: Plenum. doi:10.1007/978-1-4684-2262-7

Child, D. (1973). *The essentials of factor analysis*. New York, NY: Holt.

Cooke, R. A. (1983). *Organizational culture inventory*. Plymouth, MI: Human Synergistics International.

Cooke, R. A., & Lafferty, J. C. (1981). *Level I: Life style inventory - An instrument for assessing and changing the self-concept of organizational members*. Plymouth, MI: Human Synergistics, Inc.

Cooke, R. A., & Rousseau, D. M. (1983). The factor structure of Level I: Life styles inventory. *Educational and Psychological Measurement*, *43*, 449–457. doi:10.1177/001316448304300214

Cooke, R. A., Rousseau, D. M., & Lafferty, J. C. (1987). Thinking and behavioral styles: Consistency between self-descriptions and descriptions by others. *Educational and Psychological Measurement, 47*, 815–823. doi:10.1177/001316448704700336

deVaus, D. A. (2001). *Research designs in social research*. Thousand Oaks, CA: SAGE Publications.

Gorsuch, R. I. (1983). *Factor analysis* (2nd ed.). Hillsdale, NJ: Erlbaum.

Gratzinger, P. D., Warren, R. A., & Cooke, R. A. (1990). Psychological orientation and leadership: Thinking styles that differentiate between effective and ineffective managers. In Clark, K. E., & Clark, M. B. (Eds.), *Measures of leadership* (pp. 239–247). West Orange, NJ: Leadership Library of America.

Horney, K. (1945). *Our inner conflicts*. New York, NY: W. W. Norton & Co.

Janis, I. (1972). *Victims of groupthink*. Boston, MA: Houghton Mifflin.

Janis, I. (1982). *Groupthink: Psychological studies of policy decisions and fiascos* (2nd ed.). Boston, MA: Houghton Mifflin. doi:10.1177/000271627340700115

Katz, D., Maccoby, N., & Morse, N. C. (1959). *Productivity, supervision, and morale in an office situation*. Ann Arbor, MI: Institute for Social Research, The University of Michigan.

Lafferty, J. C. (1973). *Level I: Life styles inventory (self description)*. Plymouth, MI: Human Synergistics, Inc.

Lafferty, J. C. (1989). *Life styles inventory LSI 1: Inventory*. Plymouth, MI: Human Synergistics, Inc.

Leary, T. (1955). The theory and measurement of interpersonal communication. *Psychiatry, 18*, 147–161.

Leary, T. (1957). *Interpersonal diagnosis of personality*. New York, NY: Ronald Press.

(2004). *Life Styles Inventory LSI 1 Self-Development Guide*. Plymouth, MI: Human Synergistics, Inc. (Original work published 1973)

(2004). *Life Styles Inventory LSI 2: Description by Others Self-Development Guide*. Plymouth, MI: Human Synergistics, Inc. (Original work published 1990)

Masi, R. J., & Cooke, R. A. (2000). Effects of transformational leadership on subordinate motivation, empowering norms, and organizational productivity. *The International Journal of Organizational Analysis, 8*(1), 16–47. doi:10.1108/eb028909

Maslow, A. H. (1954). *Motivation and personality*. New York, NY: Harper and Row.

Nediger, W. G., & Chelladurai, P. (1989). Life Styles Inventory: Its application in the Canadian context. *Educational and Psychological Measurement, 49*, 901–909. doi:10.1177/001316448904900413

Nunnally, J. C. (1978). *Psychometric theory*. New York, NY: McGraw-Hill Book Company.

Rummel, R. J. (1970). *Applied factor analysis*. Evanston, IL: Northwestern University Press.

Skenes, R. E., & Honig, C. A. (2004). Pretest/posttest use of the life styles inventory for outcomes assessment of a professional master's in managerial leadership program. *Group & Organization Management, 29*(2), 171–200. doi:10.1177/1059601103262043

Stogdill, R. M. (1963). *Manual for the leader behavior description questionnaire - Form XII*. Columbus, OH: Bureau of Business Research, Ohio State University.

Sullivan, H. S. (1953). *The interpersonal theory of psychiatry*. New York, NY: Norton.

Tucker, L. R. (1951). *A method of synthesis of factor analysis studies*. Princeton, NJ: ETS.

Ware, M. E., Leak, G. K., & Perry, N. W. (1985). Life styles inventory: Evidence for its factorial validity. *Psychological Reports, 56*, 963–968. doi:10.2466/pr0.1985.56.3.963

ADDITIONAL READING

A Cross-Cultural Perspective. (2005). (Original work published 1987). Retrieved from http://humansynergistics.com/news/CaseStudies.aspx

Bass, B. M. (1990). *Bass & Stogsdill's handbook of leadership: Theory research and managerial applications* (3rd ed.). New York, NY: Free Press.

Blake, R. R., & Mouton, J. S. (1964). *The managerial grid*. Houston, TX: Gulf Publishing.

Boglarsky, C. A., & Kwantes, C. T. (2005, Summer). *Conflict perceptions and their role in manager's choice of resolution style*. Paper presented at the Fourth Biennial Conference on Intercultural Research, Kent, OH.

Boglarsky, C. A., & Kwantes, C. T. (2005, Summer). *Who is happy and why? Subjective well-being and associated thinking styles of US and Canadian students*. Paper presented at the 17th Annual Convention of the American Psychological Society, Los Angeles.

Cooke, R. A., Rousseau, D. M., & Lafferty, J. C. (1987). Thinking and behavioral styles: Consistency between self-descriptions and descriptions by others. *Educational and Psychological Measurement, 47*, 815–823. doi:10.1177/001316448704700336

Creating a Customer-Driven Culture Using Project Teams in the Insurance Industry. (2005). (Original work published 1987). Retrieved from http://humansynergistics.com/news/CaseStudies.aspx

Elliot, M., & Meltsner, S. (1993). *The perfectionist predicament: How to stop driving yourself and others crazy*. New York, NY: Berkley Books.

Finance Industry— Leadership development. (2005). (Original work published 1987). Retrieved from http://humansynergistics.com/news/CaseStudies.aspx

Gratzinger, P. D., Warren, R. A., & Cooke, R. A. (1990). Psychological orientations and leadership: Thinking styles that differentiate between effective and ineffective managers. In Clark, K. E., & Clark, M. B. (Eds.), *Measures of leadership*. Greensboro, NC: Center for Creative Leadership.

Hendlin, S. J. (1992). *When good enough is never enough: Escaping the perfection trap*. New York, NY: Putnam.

Human Synergistics. (1986). *Improving store management effectiveness*. Atlanta, GA: Coca Cola Retailing Research Council.

Johns, E. F. (1989). *The reliability of the life styles inventory (LSI 1)*. Plymouth, MI: Human Synergistics, Inc.

Lafferty, J. C. (1980). *Item frequency and distribution – Level 1 life styles inventory*. Plymouth, MI: Human Synergistics, Inc.

Leary, T. (1955). The theory and measurement of interpersonal communication. *Psychiatry, 18*, 147–161.

Leslie, J. B., & Fleenor, J. W. (1998). *Feedback to managers: A review and comparison of multirater instruments for management development* (3rd ed.). Greensboro, NC: Center for Creative Leadership.

Masi, R. J. (1993). *Impact of the transformational leader style, empowering culture, and individual empowerment on productivity and commitment to quality: An empirical investigation of the behavioral aspects of these two outcomes.* Unpublished doctoral dissertation, University of Illinois at Chicago, Chicago.

Masi, R. J., & Cooke, R. A. (2000). Effects of transformational leadership on subordinate motivation, empowering norms, and organizational productivity. *The International Journal of Organizational Analysis, 8*(1), 16–47. doi:10.1108/eb028909

McClellan, D. C. (1985). *Human motivation.* Glenview, IL: Scott, Foresman.

Moving toward franchising in the retail industry: Building a strong sales culture. (2005). (Original work published 1987). Retrieved from http://humansynergistics.com/news/CaseStudies.aspx

Nediger, W. G., & Chelladurai, P. (1989). Life Styles Inventory: Its application in the Canadian context. *Educational and Psychological Measurement, 49*, 901–909. doi:10.1177/001316448904900413

Olympic Gold — Achievement or Competitive? (2005). (Original work published 1987). Retrieved from http://humansynergistics.com/news/CaseStudies.aspx

Perry, N. W., & Ware, M. E. (1987). Facilitating growth in a personal development course. *Psychological Reports, 60*, 491–500. doi:10.2466/pr0.1987.60.2.491

Peters, T. J., & Waterman, R. A. Jr. (1982). *In search of excellence: Lessons from America's best-run companies.* New York, NY: Warner Books.

Skenes, R. E., & Honing, C. A. (2004). Pretest/posttest use of the life styles inventory for outcomes assessment of a professional master's in managerial leadership program. *Group & Organization Management, 29*(2), 171–200. doi:10.1177/1059601103262043

Stoddard, A. (1995). *The art of possible: The path from perfectionism to balance and freedom.* New York, NY: William Morrow.

Szumal, J. L., & Cooke, R. A. (2004). Increasing personal success and effectiveness: Thinking and behavioral styles at work. In Silberman, M., & Philips, P. (Eds.), *The 2004 training and performance sourcebook.* Princeton, NJ: Active Training.

Ware, M. E., Leak, G. K., & Perry, N. W. (1985). Life styles inventory: Evidence for its factorial validity. *Psychological Reports, 56*, 963–968. doi:10.2466/pr0.1985.56.3.963

ENDNOTES

[1] *Life Styles Inventory*™ is a trademark of Human Synergistics International. Used with permission.

[2] All LSI terminology, style names and descriptions: From *Life Styles Inventory*™ by J.C. Lafferty, Human Synergistics International. Copyright 2009 by Human Synergistics. Adapted by permission

[3] *Organizational Culture Inventory* is a registered trademark of Human Synergistics International Copyright © 2009 Human Synergistics International.

[4] *Acumen Leadership WorkStyles*™ is a trademark of Human Synergistics International. Used with permission.

APPENDIX

The following are descriptions of the twelve Life Styles provided by Human Synergistics International.

Life Styles Inventory™

Style Descriptions

- **Constructive**

    1:00 The *Humanistic-Encouraging* style reflects an interest in the growth and development of people, a high positive regard for them, and sensitivity to their needs. People with this style devote energy to counseling and coaching others, interact with others in a thoughtful and considerate way, and provide them with support and encouragement. *(encourages others, willing to take time with people)*

    2:00 The *Affiliative* style reflects an interest in developing and sustaining pleasant relationships with others. People with this style share their thoughts and feelings with others, are friendly and cooperative, and make others feel like they are part of the team. *(cooperative, likes to include others in activities)*

    11:00 The *Achievement* style is based on the need to attain high quality results on challenging projects, the belief that outcomes are linked to one's effort rather than chance, and the tendency to personally set challenging yet realistic goals. People exhibiting this style think ahead and plan, explore alternatives before acting, and learn from their mistakes. *(enjoys a challenge, sets own goals)*

    12:00 The *Self-Actualizing* style is based on needs for personal growth, self-fulfillment, and the realization of one's potential. People exhibiting this style demonstrate a strong desire to learn and experience things, creative yet realistic thinking, and a balanced concern for people and tasks. (*optimistic & realistic, high personal integrity*)

- **Passive/Defensive**

    3:00 The *Approval* style reflects a need to be accepted and a tendency to tie one's self-worth to being liked by others. People with this style try very hard to please others, make a good impression, and be agreeable or obedient. (*generous to a fault, agrees with everyone*)

    4:00 The *Conventional* style reflects a preoccupation with conforming and "blending in" with the environment to avoid calling attention to oneself. People with this style tend to rely on established routines and procedures, prefer to maintain the status quo, and desire a secure and predictable work environment. (*thinks rules more important than ideas, conforming*)

    5:00 The *Dependent* style reflects a need for self-protection coupled with the belief that one has little direct or personal control over important events. People who exhibit this style (possibly as a result of recent changes in their personal or work lives) allow others to make decisions for them, depend on others for help, and willingly obey orders. (*obeys too willingly, very respectful to superiors*)

    6:00 The *Avoidance* style reflects apprehension, a strong need for self-protection, and a propensity to withdraw from threatening situations. People with this style "play it safe" and minimize risks, shy away from group activities and conversations, and react to situations in an indecisive or non-committal way. (*evasive, leaves decisions to others*)

- **Aggressive/Defensive**

  7:00 The *Oppositional* style reflects a need for security that manifests itself in a questioning, critical and even cynical manner. Though people exhibiting this style ask tough questions that can lead to better ideas, they might also emphasize even minor flaws, use criticism to gain attention, and blame others for their own mistakes. (*slow to forgive a wrong, opposes new ideas*)

  8:00 The *Power* style reflects needs for prestige and influence and the tendency to equate self-worth with controlling others. People with strong tendencies along this style dictate (rather than guide) the actions of others, try to run everything themselves, and treat others in aggressive and forceful ways—which, ironically, limits their true influence. (*runs things by self, abrupt*)

  9:00 The *Competitive* style is based on a need to protect one's status by comparing oneself to others, outperforming them, and never appearing to lose. People with this style seek recognition and praise from others, view even non-competitive situations as a contest or challenge to "prove" themselves, and try to maintain a sense of superiority. (*overestimates ability, gets upset over losing*)

  10:00 The *Perfectionistic* style is based on the need to attain flawless results, avoid failure, and involves the tendency to equate self-worth with the attainment of unreasonably high standards. People who exhibit this style are preoccupied with details, place excessive demands on themselves and others, and tend to show impatience, frustration, and indifference to the needs of others. (*de-emphasizes feelings, impatient with own errors*)

Chapter 6

Leadership Behavior Description Questionnaire (LBDQ & LBDQ–XII)

Rody Rodriguez
University of Utah, USA

ABSTRACT

This chapter focuses on the most widely used and known leadership instrument: The Leadership Behavior Description Questionnaire (LBDQ). The LBDQ, and its sibling the LBDQ-XII, have been around for more than 50 years and are still being used today. As a result, the purpose of this chapter is to examine the instrument by summarizing its background, and giving a perspective on the instrument's reliability and validity. This was accomplished by looking at the LBDQ and LBDQ-XII's long history, how it has been applied over the years, while focusing on the scales main factors of Consideration and Initiation of Structure. Additionally, many analyses of the instruments (LBDQ and LBDQ-XII) were reviewed to support the instruments robust reliability and validity. Lastly, the location and cost of the instruments were revealed in order for the reader to utilize the instrument under study.

BACKGROUND

Leadership has been a major facet for researchers for many years (Bass, 1990; Chang & Lin, 2008; Halpin, 1954; Hills, 1963; Inderlied & Powell, 1979; Katerberg & Hom, 1981; Kenis, 1978; Littrell, 2002; Sashkin, 1979; Schriesheim, 1982; Schriesheim & Kerr, 1974; Stogdill, 1963; Tracy,

1987). From government institutions (such as the military) to industry, to gender, to the clergy, as well as to athletes, the questions as to what makes an person an effective leader, what behaviors do skilled leaders exhibit, and how a person's natural abilities can be fostered to become a leader have been aspects that researchers have sought to answer. As a result, several measurements have

DOI: 10.4018/978-1-4666-2172-5.ch006

been developed and used to address this inquiry, but none more regarded and widely used as the Leadership Behavior Description Questionnaire (LBDQ) (Chang & Lin, 2008; Halpin, 1957; Hills, 1963; Katerberg & Hom, 1981; Kenis, 1978; Judge, Piccolo, & Ilies, 2004; Littrell, 2002; Littrell & Nkomo, 2005; Littrell & Valentin, 2005; Schriesheim, 1982; Stogdill, 1963, 1974; Sashkin, 1979; Tracy, 1987).

Before the LBDQ was devised, researchers desired to determine the characteristics of a leader. One group of researchers sought to answer this very issue. The Ohio State University Studies (OSUS) was founded in 1945 by Shartle to address this query (Bass, 1990; Stogdill, 1974). During this time, there were no satisfactory leadership theories or way of determining leadership characteristics. At first, these researchers assumed that a person was born with leadership abilities. For this reason, they sought to identify traits possessed by leaders (Bass, 1990; Stogdill, 1974). However, this led to a dead end. Analysis of the prior research conducted by the group revealed:

(1) [T]hat little success had been attainted in attempts to select leaders in terms of traits, (2) that numerous traits differentiated leaders from followers, (3) that traits demanded in a leader varied from one situation to another, and (4) that the trait approach ignored the interaction between the leader and his group. (Stogdill, 1974, p. 128)

The OSUS researchers then decided that rather than trying to isolate specific traits associated with leaders, it would be much more efficient to determine the behaviors connected with leadership. Specifically, the researchers wanted "to describe individuals' behavior while they acted as leaders of groups or organizations" (Bass, 1990, p. 511). Thus, traits took a back seat to while behaviors came to the forefront of determining what makes a person an influential leader.

The turn away from analyzing traits to behavior was mainly because of the work Hemphill (Bass, 1990; Stogdill, 1974). Hemphill himself had begun looking at behaviors as opposed to traits while he was at the University of Maryland. His work thus reinforced what the OSUS team had begun to observe in their studies. Later Hemphill himself joined the OSUS to further his work in understand leadership behavior. As a result, he and his colleagues set out to examine leadership and assess what behaviors leaders' encompass. To accomplish this, they created a list of 1,800 statements describing various characteristics of the behaviors exhibited by leaders (Bass, 1990). This was broken down into 150 statements that could all be assigned to one subscale. These statements were consequently used to create the first form of the LBDQ. However, as the subscales totals were interrelated, two factors were produced. These were *Consideration* and *Initiation of Structure in Interaction* (Bass, 1990; Chang & Lin, 2008; Halpin, 1957; Judge et al., 2004; Katerberg & Hom, 1981; Sashkin, 1979; Seltzer & Bass, 1990; Schriesheim, 1982; Schriesheim & Kerr, 1974; Stogdill, 1963, 1974; Tracy, 1987).

Consideration refers to how much a leader shows concerns for the interests of the members of the group. As Bass (1990) remarked:

The considerate leader expresses appreciation for good work, stresses the importance of job satisfaction, maintains and strengthens the self-esteem of subordinates by treating then as equals, makes special efforts to help subordinates' suggestions into operation, and obtains subordinates' approval on important matters before going ahead. (p. 511)

In short, Consideration is centered toward relationships the leader has with the other members of the group. The more positive the relationship, the more a leader's behavior is viewed as constructive for group members. On the contrary, a leader who is considered inconsiderate exhibits behavior such as criticizing subordinates in public, not considering a group member's feelings, causes a member to feel insecure, rejects any suggestions, or even explains his or her decisions.

Initiation of Structure (also referred to as Initiating Structure) on the other hand denotes a "leader's behavior in delineating the relationship between himself and the members of his group, and in endeavoring to establish well-defined patterns of organization, channels of communication, and ways of getting the job done" (Halpin, 1957, p. 1). The leader also is always oriented to the task and he or she acts promptly without consulting the group. In contrast, a leader that displays low Initiation of Structure is portrayed as cautious regarding undertaking initiatives, fails to take needed actions, formulates suggestions only when group members ask, and allows the members to do the work by method they believe is most appropriate.

Consequently, because of Consideration and Initiation of Structure, an instrument was developed for measuring these two factors of leadership behavior, which their research determined to be the most important behaviors an effective leader possesses. This instrument was aptly named the "Ideal LBDQ" by Hemphill, Seigel, and Westie; thus the LBDQ was born (Bass, 1990; Chang & Lin, 2008; Halpin, 1957; Judge et al., 2004; Sashkin, 1979; Schriesheim, 1982; Stogdill, 1963, 1974; Tracy, 1987). The LBDQ consists of 40 statements to measure the two factors. There are 15 statements for both Consideration and Initiation of Structure, while 10 statements are not scored concerning each factor. Each item is rated on a five-point Likert-type scale indicated by the frequency of committing the described behavior. The scale is broken down as follows: 1) *Always*; 2) *Often*; 3) *Occasionally*; 4) *Seldom*; and 5) *Never*. Examples of statements are "He does personal favors for group members" (Halpin, 1957, p. 4), "He makes his attitudes clear to the group" (p. 6), and "He lets group members know what is expected of them" (p. 6).

When LBDQ was created, it was made in an era where research on leadership was scarce (Stogdill, 1974). Therefore, when Consideration

and Initiation of Structure became the sole factors in describing leadership behavior, researchers began to argue for additional criteria that could help further describe leadership behavior. For example, Halpin and Croft (as cited in Bass, 1990) were not satisfied with leadership behavior being described by only two factors. They felt that the two factors did not adequately describe all the complexities of a leader's behavior. Through their research regarding leader behavior of school principles, they argued that four additional factors could be used alongside the two main factors to help clarify leadership behaviors.

Influenced by studies such as the one presented by Halpin and Croft (as cited in Bass, 1990), other OSUS researchers started to develop their own modified versions, as well as completely new ones, based on the original LBDQ (Bass, 1990; Stogdill, 1974). Such instruments were the Supervisory Behavior Description Questionnaire (SBDQ) and the Leadership Opinion Questionnaire (LOQ) (Bass, 1990). These scales were built on the foundations of the LBDQ and its two factors. However, unlike the LBDQ for instance, the SBDQ was made to study an industrial supervisor's leadership behavior rather than being able to be adapted to other areas of leadership study.

Nevertheless, in spite of these modified and new leadership instruments, there were none more favored than the newly developed instrument by Stogdill (Bass, 1990; Stogdill, 1974). Over time, Stogdill began to also feel that that the two original constructs were not enough. He, through his theoretical work on factors involved in differentiation of group roles and reexaminations of the data on Consideration and Initiation of Structure, determined that additional factors could be used to give a better idea on a leader's behavior (Bass, 1990; Stogdill, 1963; 1974). Thus, in his research he established 10 additional factors in order to tackle all observable variance in leadership to go along with Consideration and Initiation of Structure. Stogdill as a result created LBDQ Form XII, also known as LBDQ-XII (which it will be hereafter referred to as), utilizing 12-dimensions. These include:

1. **Representation**: Speaks and acts as the representative of the group. (5 items)
2. **Demand Reconciliation:** Reconciles conflicting demands and reduces disorder to system. (5 items)
3. **Tolerance of Uncertainty:** Able to tolerate uncertainty and postponement without anxiety or upset. (10 items)
4. **Persuasiveness:** Uses persuasion and argument effectively; exhibits strong convictions. (10 items)
5. **Initiation of Structure:** Clearly defines own role, and lets followers know what is expected. (10 items)
6. **Tolerance of Freedom:** Allows followers scope for initiative, decision and action. (10 items)
7. **Role Assumption** [also referred to as Role Retention]: Actively exercises the leadership role rather that surrendering leadership to others. (10 items)
8. **Consideration:** Regards the comfort, well being, status, and contributions of followers. (10 items)
9. **Production Emphasis:** Applies pressure for productive output. (10 items)
10. **Predictive Accuracy**: Exhibits foresight and ability to predict outcome accurately. (5 items)
11. **Integration**: Maintains a closely-knit organization; resolves intermember conflicts. (5 items)
12. **Superior Orientation** [also referred to as Influence with Superiors]: Maintains cordial relations with superiors; has influence with them; is striving for higher status. (10 items) (Stogdill, 1963, p. 3)

Each item utilizes the same five-point Likert-type scale employed by the original LBDQ.

At this time, researchers were finding the development of the LBDQ and the LBDQ-XII to be profound in the area of understanding leadership. Researchers found these instruments to be a valuable tool. Many studies from various areas began to employ them as a means of analyzing leadership behavior (Andreescu & Vito, 2010; Ayman & Chemers, 1983; Appleton & Stanwyck, 1996; Bass, 1990; Boatwright, Lopez, Sauer, VanDer-Wege, & Huber, 2010; Canales, Tejeda-Delgado, & Slate, 2008; Christner & Hemphill, 1955; de Vries, 2008; DeCaro & Bowen-Thompson, 2010; Hackman et al., 1999; Halpin, 1954, 1957; Hemphill, 1963; Keller, 2006; Littrell, 2002; Littrell & Nkomo, 2005; Littrell & Valentin, 2005; Putti, 1985; Putti & Tong, 1992; Streufert, Streufert, & Castore, 1968; Stogdill, 1963, 1965; 1974). Numerous studies also detailed the reliability and validity of the instruments (Bass, 1990; de Vries, 2008; Derue, Nahrgang, Wellman, & Humphrey, 2011; Greene, 1975; Halpin, 1954, 1957; Hemphill, 1963; Judge et al., 2004; Katerberg & Hom, 1981; Littrell & Nkomo, 2005; Sashkin, 1979; Schriesheim & Kerr, 1974; Stogdill, 1963, 1974; Tracy, 1987). The studies assessed the psychometric properties of the instruments and found them to be consistent as well as valid. Thus, for a time the instruments had become quintessential in understanding leadership.

Even though LBDQ had been widely used for many years and for many different studies (such as military, education, gender, cultural, and industrial areas), the questionnaire and its factors (mainly Consideration and Initiation of Structure) were for at this time seen as obsolete. Consequently, Judge et al. (2004), in their meta-analysis of Consideration and Initiation of Structure's relationship with leadership, feared that "[t]hese behaviors seem to be in danger of being viewed as historical artifacts in leadership research – important artifacts – but artifacts of little contemporary relevance nonetheless. This denouncement for the Ohio State leadership behaviors, however, may be premature" (pp. 43-44). They believed that contemporary researchers might bypass the LBDQ because of a perception of it being a dinosaur in the world of leadership study. This, to them, would be a disservice to not only to the researchers, but also to the field itself. They hence conducted a meta-analysis to determine its relevance in contemporary research, and after supporting its reliability and construct validity, they argued for the LBDQ and LBDQ-XII's resurrection from the depths of leadership studies. Thus, they concluded:

What we are arguing is that it is inadvisable, at this point, to abandon Consideration and Initiating Structure in leadership research. Some of the more prominent organizational psychologists in the history of the field – Stogdill, Shartle, and Fleishman, among others – spent the better part of their careers researching these concepts. It appears their investigations were more productive than previously thought, and that the fruit born of these investigations could prove useful once again in leadership research. (p. 47)

With the help from researchers such as Judge et al. (2004), the instrument has been making a comeback as researchers seem to be revisiting the importance of the measure and its factors in studying leadership behavior in recent studies (Andreescu & Vito, 2010; Boatwright et al., 2010; Canales et al., 2008; Chang & Lin, 2008; de Vries, 2008; DeCaro & Bowen-Thompson, 2010; Judge et al., 2004; Keller, 2006; Littrell, 2002; Littrell & Nkomo, 2005; Littrell & Valentin, 2005). Today, more than 50 years after the initial LBDQ was conceived, when analyzing leadership behavior one does not have to go far before he or she encounters the LBDQ. It is one of the most used, if not the most used, questionnaire researchers use when they want to peer into the internal aspects of leadership, so much so that it "is perhaps the best established and most widely used instrument among those focusing on the internal aspects of the leadership problem" (Hills, 1963, p. 90). The LBDQ for this reason would be a valuable instrument for anyone desiring to understand the behaviors of leaders.

RELIABILITY

Correlation analyses of the 40 items of the LBDQ and the 100 items of the LBDQ-XII have shown a strong level of reliability (Judge et al., 2004; Halpin, Keller, 2006; 1957; Stogdill, 1963). Also, there have been shown a high level of correlation for the LBDQ two factors Consideration and Initiation of Structure and the scales of each of the other 10 factors of the LBDQ-XII. Halpin (1957), in the original manual for the LBDQ, found the reliability for Consideration at .92 and for Initiation of Structure at .83. The F ratios were all found at the .01 level.

Bass (1990) noted that the LBDQ had a reliability of .93 for Consideration and .81 for Initiation of Structure. He also noted that the LBDQ-XII had a reliability of .90 for Consideration and .78. Seltzer and Bass (1990) moreover recorded a reliability of .69 for Consideration and .42 for Initiation of Structure. In Schriesheim and Kerr (1974) assessment of the psychometric properties of the OSUS scales, the found high internal consistency with the instruments. In other words, the items correlated specifically with the factors they were made to associate with.

Stogdill (1963) himself observed the reliabilities of his LBDQ-XII, using a modified Kuder-Richardson formula. He found reliabilities correlated for Representation of Group ranged from .55-.85; Demand Reconciliation ranged from .58-.81; Tolerance Uncertainty ranged from .58-.85; Persuasiveness ranged from .69-.85; Initiation of Structure ranged from .70-.80; Tolerance Freedom ranged from .58-.86; Role Assumption ranged from .57-.86; Consideration ranged from .38-.87; Production Emphasis ranged from .59-.79; Predictive Accuracy ranged from .62-.91; Integration ranged from .73-.79; and Superior Orientation ranged from .60-.81 (see p. 10).

VALIDITY

The LBDQ and the LBDQ-XII has more than a half-a-century worth of studies outlining their use and analysis as instruments. For more than 50 years, these instruments have been employed across fields in order to determine and understand leadership behavior. For this reason, there are many studies in the literature validating both LBDQ and LBDQ-XII, and therefore, show the consistency and genuine dependability of the instruments.

Possibly the most useful examination of the validity of both the LBDQ and the LBDQ-XII was the comprehensive analysis of Consideration and Initialization of Structure by Judge et al. (2004). In their meta-analysis of nearly every study regarding Consideration and Initiation of Structure's relationship with leadership, they examined the four leadership instruments created by the Ohio State University researchers (LBDQ, LBDQ-XII, SBDQ, and the LOQ). They found that LBDQ and LBDQ-XII displayed sufficient construct validity. In general, they determined that all the instruments together had an overall correlation of .48 Consideration and Initiation of Structure was observed at .29. Nevertheless, the researchers found that the LBDQ and LBDQ-XII by themselves displayed strong validity as it pertained to these two factors. The LBDQ displayed validities at .34 for Consideration and .29 for Initiation of Structure while LBDQ-XII validated at .54 for Consideration and .32 for Initiation of Structure. They argued that the LBDQ and the LBDQ-XII "had the highest validities averaged across Consideration and [Initiation of] Structure" (p. 44) when compared to the SBDQ and the LOQ – the two other leadership behavioral instruments examined. They further argued:

The meta-analysis results, on the basis of 163 correlations for Consideration and 159 correlations for Initiating Structure, revealed that both Consideration and [Initiation of] Structure evince nonzero correlations across the leadership criteria. Specifically, because the 90% confidence intervals excluded zero, we can be confident that the mean Consideration correlation and the mean Initiating Structure correlation are nonzero. Furthermore, because the 80% credibility intervals exclude zero, more than 90% of the individual correlations for Consideration and [Initiation of] Structure are greater than zero (a maximum of 10% lie at or beyond the upper bond of the interval). (p. 39)

What this means is that because the total correlations are sound and the credibility intervals exclude zero, "the overall validities for Consideration and Initiation of Structure are interpretable" (p. 40). Thus, the validities for the instruments can be determined and argued for because of the nonzero interval.

Furthermore, in a recent study in which its authors undertook the goal of formulating a definitive theory of leadership, Derue et al. (2011) conducted a meta-analysis of leadership as it pertains to both behavior and recent trait studies. The authors noted the affects of leadership behaviors on leadership effectiveness. With that, they observed the role Consideration and Initiation of Structure played in identifying leader effectiveness. They discovered, "The most important leader behavior for predicting group performance is initiation of structure" (p. 30). They found that Consideration also helped to predict worker satisfaction with the leader. As a result of their study, they supported previous researchers' assertion that "leader behaviors had a greater impact on leadership effectiveness criteria than did leadership traits" (p. 37).

Taylor, Cook, and Dropkin (1961), in their attempt to understand emerging behavior of individuals in small leaderless groups using the LBDQ, noted the instruments dependability when it came to Consideration and Initiation of Structure. What they observed, consequently, was that the instrument was consistently reliable and valid. They noticed, "The present instrument seems to satisfy the criteria for content validity, rater reliability, and overall reliability" (p. 17). Furthermore, Katerberg and Hom (1981) observed how well the instrument operated. When looking at LBDQ for Consideration and Initiation of Structure, they found that "Each individual LBDQ scale significantly predicted all criteria. High consideration and high initiation of structure were associated with higher satisfaction with leadership, co-workers, and the organization itself and with higher role clarity and lower role conflict" (p. 220). Lowin, Hrapchak, and Kavanagh (1969) likewise took noticed as to the validations of Consideration and Initiation of Structure. They stated:

The manipulations seem to have been effective in that those subjects subjected to the high consideration supervisor reported their supervisor higher on consideration that those subject to low consideration, and those subjugated to supervisors with high initiation of structure reported their supervisor higher on initiation of structure that those subjugated to low initiation of structure. The effects were significant at p < .01 by analyses variance. (p. 245)

Greene (1975) as well noted the significance of high Consideration and high Initiation of Structure with leader satisfaction. The study suggested that Consideration did cause workers to be satisfied with the leader. With that, Greene found validations of the two over a one-month period yielded correlations ranging from .68-.78 for Consideration and .58-.73 for Initiation of Structure. Therefore, in summary, leaders demonstrating high levels Consideration were reported on the LBDQ as being high on Consideration while leaders demonstrating high levels of Initiation of Structure were reported on the LBDQ as being high on Initiation of Structure.

Consideration and Initiation of Structure have been suggested to correlate with one another (Bass, 1990; Greene, 1975; Judge et al., 2004; Schriesheim, House, & Kerr, 1976; Schriesheim & Kerr, 1974; Schriesheim & Murphy, 1976).

Theoretically, the two factors should be independent from one another. However, a number of studies have shown that this may not be the case. For example, Schriesheim and Kerr (1974) suggested that the out of 48 studies, 37 the two factors intercorrelated with each other. Another study conducted by Schriesheim et al. (1976) found that out of 13 studies, 11 reported positive correlations between them, and for the LBDQ-XII, in 10 studies the median correlation was .52 between Consideration and Initiation of Structure. Greene (1975) in his study of worker satisfaction with high Consideration and high Initiation of Structure further found that the two are connected. He found that Consideration moderated Initiation of Structure's relationship with worker satisfaction. In other words, he observed that Consideration correlated between itself and Initiation of Structure, thus showing that high levels of Consideration and Initiation of Structure lead to higher levels of worker satisfaction. Also, Schriesheim and Murphy (1976) noted strong intercorrelations between Consideration and Initiation of Structure. Their study addressed the possible moderators of the relationships between subordinate satisfaction and performance and leader behavior. Using LBDQ-XII, the two researchers found an intercorrelation of .74 between the two factors. They argued that Consideration might moderate worker reactions to leader Initiation of Structure. Thus, the two were found to be interconnected. Even so, despite these studies suggestions, the implied correlations appear not to influence the results of the scale. Judge et al. (2004) commented, "...Consideration and Initiating Structure intercorrelations are quite small, and our results confirm this observation. The correlations between the LBDQ and LBDQ-XII Consideration and Initiating Structure scales were appreciably larger, but not so large as to render the two concepts redundant" (p. 44). As a result, the results led them to conclude:

There appears to be a trade-off in that the most valid measures across both factors (LBDQ,

LBDQ-XII) also have the strongest intercorrelations between the two factors. It seems that the higher overall validity of the LBDQ and LBDQ-XII measures of Consideration and Structure is paid in the coin of higher intercorrelations between the measures. (p. 46)

In sum, despite studies suggesting strong intercorrelations between the two main factors of the LBDQ and LBDQ-XII, the instruments were determined to be the most valid when compared to the other OSUS leadership behavioral instruments. Thus, some studies have found that the intercorrelations may be present, but research has suggested that this does not appear to alter the overall results.

One study conducted by Rush, Phillips, and Lord (1981) examined whether temporal delay would influence the results of the LBDQ. They purported that temporal delay would affect the workers, what they aptly named the General Leadership Impressions (GLI). Rush et al. only partially supported their hypothesis and found that even though there were some affects of temporal delays in their population, "there was absolutely no *decrease* [italics added] in the proportion of variance associated with behavior as a function of the temporal delay" (p. 447). Nevertheless, they concluded that the influence of temporal delay were a result of the participants using the behavior to form a simplified GLI.

The LBDQ-XII has been shown by itself to be a valid instrument. In an analysis of Consideration and Initiation of Structure, Tracy (1987) noted that the LBDQ-XII displayed "support for the construct validity of the C [Consideration] and IS [Initiation of Structure]" (p. 30). Schriesheim and Kerr (1974) moreover analyzed the four versions of leadership as designed by the researchers at OSUS for validity and reliability. Although critical of the instruments' scales under study, they fancied the LBDQ-XII because of its history of reliability and validity as an instrument. They deduced:

One optimistic note is that the LBDQ Form XII, which is coming into greater use as a measure of leader behavior, apparently does not suffer from some of the more serious shortcomings which plague the other versions. Its contents appear reasonably valid, it has been subjected to experimental validation with successful results, and it does not confound frequency of behavior with magnitude. (p. 764)

Similarly, Sashkin (1979), in a review of Stogdill's LBDQ-XII, concluded, "The extensive research base and amply demonstrated validity make the LBDQ-XII a more desirable instrument for use in organizational studies than any of the many commercially available leadership-style measures" (p. 250). Lastly, Sashkin in his analysis of LBDQ-XII argued that there were a "great number of research studies that have repeatedly demonstrated that C [Consideration] and IS [Initiation of Structure] do represent leader behaviors and that these two scales are reliable and valid measures of such behavior" (p. 248).

Furthermore, the LBDQ-XII's 10 other factors, i.e. the factors that are not Consideration and Initiation of Structure, have also been tested for their validity. For one, Stogdill (1969) himself tested his new version of the LBDQ, the LBDQ-XII. In order to determine its validity, he used experienced actors to play the roles of supervisors as well as workers. Two different actors performed each individual role while at the same time each actor played the two different roles. Observers watching the recorded performances used the LBDQ-XII to explain the supervisor's behavior. Stogdill determined that there were no differences between the two different actors when playing the same role. As a result, he reasoned that the instrument was validated based on these results. Furthermore, Stogdill, Goode, and Day (1962, 1963a, 1963b, 1964) used four studies of senators, corporation presidents, presidents of labor unions, and collegiate presidents to validate the scales with each factor of the LBDQ-XII. They found through their studies that the factors correlated to the scales for Representation of Group ranged from .80-.94; Demand Reconciliation ranged from .63-.83; Tolerance Uncertainty ranged from .93-.95; Persuasiveness ranged from .74-.95; Initiation of Structure ranged from .67-.82; Tolerance Freedom ranged from .89-.97; Role Assumption ranged from .57-.86; Consideration ranged from .38-.87; Production Emphasis ranged from .59-.79; Predictive Accuracy ranged from .62-.91; Integration ranged from .73-.79; and Superior Orientation ranged from .60-.81.

Along with studies on the psychometric properties of the scales, there have been numerous studies that support the validity of the instruments. Take the many studies centered on examining military (e.g. aircrews) and in managerial leadership (Andreescu & Vito, 2010; Ayman & Chemers, 1983; Bass, 1990; Boatwright et al., 2010; Christner & Hemphill, 1955; Greene, 1975; Halpin, 1954, 1957; House, Filley, & Kerr, 1971; Katerberg & Hom, 1981; Kenis, 1978; Schriesheim & Murphy, 1976; Stogdill, 1963, 1965, 1974). For instance, Halpin (1954) examined leadership behaviors of combat pilots. He noted that superiors were inclined to assess aircrew commanders who were found to be high in Consideration and Initiation of Structure in a positive manner. Furthermore, he found differences of leader assessment between training and actual combat. Training crews displayed positive Consideration (.48) but negative Initiation of Structure (-.17). However, in combat, Consideration and Initiation of Structure were both positively rated with the same crew surveyed. Correlations in combat were .64 for Consideration and .35 for Initiation of Structure. He also found reliability ratios of .94 for Consideration and .76 for Initiation of Structure. Between the 353 members of the 52 B-29 aircrew, he found correlations of .54 for Consideration and .36 for Initiation of Structure. Halpin even discovered a correlation score of .45 at the .01 level between the two factors. Another example was a similar study done by Christner and Hemphill (1955) regarding

Air Force personnel crewmembers. They found that changes in behavior of the crewmembers with each other were directly linked with the leadership behavior of the crew's commander. When the crewmembers viewed the commander as being high in Consideration, their satisfaction with their leader was also found to be high. Lastly, the LBDQ has been used for industrial studies (Ayman & Chemers, 1983; Greene, 1975; House et al., 1971; Kenis, 1978; Schriesheim & Murphy, 1976). Schriesheim and Murphy (1976), case in point, looked at leader behavior and worker satisfaction and performance. They suggested that "in low-stress jobs consideration enhances satisfaction" (p. 634) while in high stress jobs, Initiation of Structure was seen as helpful to the workers. Boatwright et al. (2010), in their recent study of adult attachment styles on preferences and a leader's relational behavior, using the LBDQ-XII found that "the alpha coefficients for the relationship-oriented and task-oriented subscales were .73 and .78, respectively" (p. 7). Another quite recent study observed leadership behavior of American police managers (Andreescu & Vito, 2010). Also utilizing the LBDQ-XII, they found correlations for the 12-subscales ranging from .63 to .82. Furthermore, their study found that gender and race played a role in leadership preferences for the police officers.

The LBDQ has also been used to address leadership in education as well as in analyzing team performance (Appleton & Stanwyck, 1996; Canales, Tejada-Delgado, & Slate, 2008; Hemphill, 1955; 1963; 1977; Keller, 2006; Streufert, Streufert, & Castore, 1968). Hemphill (1955), in a study of the relationship between leadership behavior and a college department's reputation for administrative competence, determined correlations of .36 for Consideration and .48 for Initiation of Structure. Canales et al. (2008) further examined the affects of leadership in education. In their study of superintendent and principles leadership behaviors, they used the LBDQ-XII to determine what behaviors were most effective.

In order to ensure the reliability of the LBDQ-XII, they decided to pilot test the instrument by distributing it two groups. They found the first group to have a reliability of .67 and the second group was determined to correlate to ".95, which is considered to be a high degree of reliability" (p. 2). They concluded that Tolerance of Freedom, Representation, and Consideration were found to be the most important leadership behavior amongst the superintendents and principles examined in the study. Lastly, Keller (2006) used the LBDQ in a five year study to test transformational leadership, Initiation of Structure, and substitutes for leadership by measuring team performance in research and development teams. He utilized the LBDQ-XII specifically to measure Initiation of Structure in evaluating a team's performance under the leader. Keller found that Initiation of Structure correlated with all five performance measures used for the study. Furthermore, because Initiation of Structure's effectiveness in the study, Keller argued that, "Because initiating structure predicted unique variance in all five of the performance measures, the results suggest it is time to bring initiating structure back into models of leadership for teams" (p. 209). He believed that using Initiation of Structure helped in determining team performance and concluded that it should be revisited for measuring leadership behavior in the same fashion as Judge et al. (2004) argued.

The LBDQ has additionally been employed to look at how gender is represented (Inderlied & Powel, 1979; Lee & Alvares, 1977). Lee and Alvares (1977) looked at the effect of gender when it came to subordinates and supervisors. They used undergraduate students to portray men and women in various roles as either subordinates or supervisors. The researchers found that for the most part there were no differences in the gender of the supervisors. They did notice, however, that supervisory style was dissimilar between males and females. For instance, males who were portrayed as lower in Initiation of Structure than their female counterparts. Female subordinates moreover noted

that male supervisors higher in Consideration than did male subordinates. Another study regarding gender focused on sex-role identification and leadership style (Inderlied & Powell, 1979). Using the LBDQ, Inderlied and Powel found that their sample had a stronger preference for masculine characteristics and Initiation of Structure behavior of a masculine leader. They also determined that there was little support between femininity and Consideration.

Several authors have used the LBDQ-XII to measure leadership behavior as it pertains to culture. These studies include how leadership is affected by different cultures, how leadership is affected interculturally by examining co-cultures in business, as well as cross-culturally (Anderson, 1966; Ayman & Chemers, 1983; Chang & Lin, 2008; de Vries, 2008; DeCaro & Bowen-Thompson, 2010; Hackman et al., 1999; Kenis, 1977; Littrell, 2002; Littrell & Nkomo, 2005; Littrell & Valentin, 2005; Putti, 1985; Putti & Tong, 1992). For example, in a study of leadership in the Netherlands, the Dutch version of the LBDQ demonstrated high reliabilities with Consideration at .92 and Initiation of Structure at .81 (de Vries, 2008). An additional example is Putti and Tong's (1992) study of leader behavior in Civil Service Administration in Asia. Using LBDQ-XII, they found "positive and significant correlations between leadership styles and subordinate satisfaction with supervision" (p. 61). The LBDQ also has been used intercultural studies such as in a research study regarding minority business entrepreneurs (DeCaro & Bowen-Thompson, 2010). The researchers used the LBDQ-XII in order to determine what behaviors successful minority business entrepreneurs utilized. Initiation of Structure and Consideration were measured against task ambiguity. They concluded that Initiation of Structure significantly moderate minority business owners who won contracts while Consideration moderated task ambiguity. However, Initiation of Structure was found to be more significant for minority business owners who were successful at gaining contracts than through utilizing Consideration. The instruments have also been used cross-culturally. A study conducted by Kenis (1977) examined the differences between American and Turkish supervisors. Kenis found that Americans and Turkish supervisors responded well to Consideration. Correlations between satisfaction with supervisors and Consideration were high for both the American sample (.74) and the Turkish sample (.63). However, Initiation of Structure showed differences between the two cultures. Correlations for the American sample were positive (.32), but low for the Turkish sample (-.0028).

Even though the there is not sufficient evidence that the instrument can adequately compare leadership skills culturally, research has suggested that although "[t]he data is as yet sparse, . . . analysis indicates that LBDQ XII [*sic*] does discriminate between cross-cultures samples, and provides consistent geographic (regional and national) differences in preferences for the behavior of managerial leaders" (Littrell & Valentin, 2005, p. 422). Chang and Lin (2008) additionally supported this view in their study of cross-cultural leadership. They stated, "LBDQ form XII and PVQ were proved effectively when they were used separately in cross-cultural research" (p. 76). In other words, the LBDQ *did* note accurate and useful results when examining leadership behaviors cross-culturally. Also, Littrell and Nkomo (2005) determined that the majority of the factors across cultures ranged between .60-.90. Similarly, Hackman et al. (1999) studied leadership communication in three cultural groups (United States, New Zealand, and the former Soviet Republic of Kyrgzstan) to determine if Self-Construal was a factor in Consideration and Initiation of Structure as well as to validate scales analyzing this factor. Using Cronbach's alpha to determine the scales reliability within each culture, they found that the 15 items of Consideration were correlated overall at .88 with .89 for the United States, .90 for New Zealand, and .78 for Kyrgyzstan. The 15 items

for Initiation of Structure were correlated overall at .79 with .80 for the United States, .83 for New Zealand, and .70 for Kyrgyzstan.

In spite of the attractiveness of the LBDQ and the LBDQ-XII, from its inception critics began to question the instrument's construct validity (in other words whether the instrument measures what it is supposed to measure), whether Consideration and Initiation of Structure truly represent fundamental dimensions of leadership behavior, or whether it truly distinguishes between different degrees of leadership behavior (Bass, 1990; Derue et al., 2011; Lowin et al., 1969; Hills, 1963; Schriesheim, 1982; Schriesheim & Kerr, 1974; Tracy, 1987; Witta & Gupton, 1999). For one, it has been suggested by researchers that there are faults in the psychometric properties of the instrument (Bass, 1990; Lowin et al., 1969; Schriesheim & Kerr, 1974). In other words, researchers argued that the consistency of the instruments were not truly valid. In Schriesheim and Kerr's (1974) study of the psychometric properties of the four OSUS major leadership behavioral instruments, which included the LBDQ and LBDQ-XII as well as the SBDQ and the LOQ, they claimed the instruments required extra evidence of their constructive validity before they can be argued to measure what they are believed to measure. They also argued that the instruments experience scaling problems. They maintained the LBDQ did not "contain a sufficient number of reflected [Initiation of] Structure items, making it possible that an agreement response tendency is distorting respondent scores" (p. 764). Schriesheim and Kerr's further surmised that there was evidence indicating that the "response intervals used in the four versions of the scales produced ordinal data only, rather than interval data as is often assumed" (p.764).

An additional limitation in the psychometric properties of the LBDQ and the LBDQ-XII has been the assertion that the LBDQ suffers from leniency effects, specifically halo effects (Bass, 1990; Hills, 1963; Schriesheim & Kerr, 1974;

Schriesheim, Kinicki, & Schriesheim, 1979). Halo effects "refers to the inability of raters to differentiate individual dimensions from an overall impression or evaluation" (Schriesheim & Kerr, 1974, p. 761). Halo effects remove descriptive details and as such affects the general quality of the instrument. This occurs because the higher the halo effect, the higher the correlation will be between the dimensions or factors. In other words, if the rater already feels that the person under evaluations is good in one category, then it will likely lead them to feel that they are good in another category. In the case of the LBDQ and its two factors, Schriesheim and Kerr explained, "for high intercorrelations and lack of independence between leader behavior description dimensions is that leaders cannot behave independently on the two dimensions" (pp. 761-762). According to these researchers, there was only one attempt to address and eliminate any halo effects in the OSUS scales, which was administered during the conception of the OSUS instruments, but according to Schriesheim and Kerr these effects still exist. Furthermore, in another study, Schriesheim et al. (1979) analyzed the LBDQ and argued that it had leniency issues, mainly when it came to Consideration (Initiation of Structure did not suffer from such effects). They argued that raters had a tendency to describe others in a positive light rather than in more accurate terms. They believed that Consideration items were not politically correct and prone to leniency issues, Consideration displayed no causal leniency problem when applied to a field setting, and leniency justified most or all of the variance in Consideration.

A handful researchers have also contended that leader's with high Consideration and high Initiation of Structure do not correlate with one another (Bass, 1990; Lowin et al., 1969; Schriesheim, 1982). In other words, high Consideration has been suggested not to lead to high Initiation of Structure or that because a leader has high Consideration and high Initiation of Structure it does not lead to a higher worker satisfaction. For instance, Schriesheim (1982) in his study argued that high Consideration and high Initiation of Structure are not an *a priori* to worker satisfaction by examining the notion that high Consideration and high Initiation of Structure leadership style have a higher standard of satisfied workers that with any other leadership combinations. He used SBDQ and the LBDQ-XII to determine whether the two correlated. He concluded, "The results reported . . . support the assertion that the superiority of high-Consideration [*sic*] and high-Initiating Structure [*sic*] leadership style is indeed an American myth" (p. 226). In addition, in spite of Lowin et al. (1969) reporting that high Consideration and high Consideration led to better worker satisfaction, they argued that the two did not show a correlation between each other. In other words, even though high Consideration and high Initiation of Structure by themselves led to higher worker satisfaction, the two together did not necessarily lead to greater worker satisfaction. For this reason, they decided to reflect back to the literature in order to see how often the two were found to correlate with one another. They found in the literature the correlations ranging from .70 to -.57. Thus, they concluded that together Consideration and Initiation of Structure are not factors that determine positive, i.e. satisfactory, leadership behavior.

Lastly, it has been suggested that the LBDQ does not differentiate between different levels of leadership behavior and its effectiveness. In Derue et al.'s (2011) recent meta-analysis of leadership behavior and trait studies, they argued that the existing leadership measurements, specifically the LBDQ and the Multifactor Leadership Questionnaire, "are limited in their ability to distinguish between different categories of leader behaviors" (pp. 38, 40). In other words, the measurements do not truly scale the degree to which leadership behaviors vary from each other, and as a result, cannot provide precise results.

In spite of these criticisms of the instrument and its factors, it would be too easy to quickly right off the LBDQ. For instance, Judge et al. (2004) findings, in their meta-analysis of Consideration and Initiation of Structure, led them concluded that the more than 50 years of history with the instrument demonstrates that Consideration and Initiation of Structure are capable of determining a leader's behavior. They argued:

The results of the present quantitative review revealed that both Consideration and Initiating Structure have important main effects on numerous criteria that most would argue are fundamental indicators of effective leadership. It is striking how the validities for each behavior generalized – across criteria, across measures, and even over time and across sources. Of course, these behaviors are not all there is to solving the mysteries of leadership effectiveness. However, just as surely, the results do suggest that these behaviors – Consideration and Initiating Structure – are important pieces in the leadership puzzle. (p. 44)

Hence, Consideration and Initiating Structure appear to be important aspects in the leadership study, and therefore, should continue to be considered and used in future research.

ITEM DESCRIPTION AND RESULTS

The LBDQ is available online as a workable measurement while both the LBDQ and LBDQ-XII are also available online as PDF files, which allows anyone to have access to the forms. While the LBDQ online version does all the calculations, one could opt for the PDF version for convenience – as well as to utilize the LBDQ-XII and its 10 additional factors. These PDF files contain manuals for both instruments as well as the forms themselves. However, a person using the instrument will have to print out the instrument in order to complete it manually. The person or a moderator can distribute the questionnaire to the subordinates either individually or as a group. The researcher begins by

having the subordinates answer the questionnaire whether online or in paper form, however unlike the online form he or she afterwards will have to tabulate the results. Next, the researcher compares the data with other studies to determine the level of leadership behavior exhibited.

The LBDQ can be found on the Web as a questionnaire. Below are descriptions of its items, and the method of scoring and interpreting the results. The LBDQ consists of 40 Likert-type scaled items. Each question utilizes four responses (*Always, Often, Occasionally, Seldom,* and *Never*) that denote the level of leadership behavior. The corresponding items of Consideration and Initiation of Structure factors for the LBDQ are as follows:

1. **Consideration:** 1, 3, 6, 8, 12, 13, 18, 20, 21, 23, 26, 28, 31, 34, and 38
2. **Initiation of Structure:** 2, 4, 7, 9, 11, 14, 16, 17, 22, 24, 27, 29, 32, 35, and 39
3. **Items not scored for either:** 5, 10, 15, 19, 25, 30, 33, 36, 37, and 40

The LBDQ is scored by adding the values corresponding to the answer selected for each question. For questions 1, 3, 6, 8, 13, 21, 23, 26, 28, 31, 34, and 38 pertaining to Consideration, traditionally the answer are given the following values: *Always* is given a value of 4, *Often* is given a value of 3, *Occasionally* is given a value of 2, *Seldom* is given a value of 1, and *Never* is given a value of 0. For questions 12, 18, and 20, the values are reversed. For questions 2, 4, 7, 9, 11, 14, 16, 17, 22, 24, 27, 29, 32, 35, and 39 for Initiation of Structure, the answers are given the same values as Consideration. However, unlike the questions for Consideration, there are no reversed values. (Please note that the online version gives values similar to the LBDQ-XII version, i.e. it gives a value of 5 to *Always*. 4 to *Often*, and so on while not having a zero value for *Never*.) After administering the test, the scores are then added up for each question to produce a raw score. A researcher can also calculate a mean and standard deviation (or have it calculated through the online version) for each factor if researching a sample or population. Instead of the questionnaire providing a scale for differentiating types of leaders, the numbers themselves are compared with three different studies used as "a rough guide" (Halpin, 1957, p. 3) in interpreting scores for Consideration and Initiation of Structure. Other, more current studies can also be used to compare the data as well as to clarify the extent of leadership behavior. For the online version, to ascertain the results, one has to provide his or her e-mail. The results will then be sent to the recipients e-mail and from there the researcher can determine the significance of the findings. Note, make sure that the participants use the researcher's e-mail or the researcher will fail to receive the results.

In addition, the LBDQ-XII could also be used to determine leadership behavior, albeit it will have to be calculated manually. The LBDQ-XII consists of 100 Likert-type scaled items. The corresponding items of the 12 factors for the LBDQ-XII are as follows:

1. **Representation:** 1, 11, 21, 31, and 41
2. **Demand Reconciliation:** 51, 61, 71, 81, and 91
3. **Tolerance of Uncertainty:** 2, 12, 22, 32, 42, 52. 62, 72, 82, and 92
4. **Persuasiveness:** 3, 13, 23, 43, 53, 63, 73, 83, and 93
5. **Initiation of Structure:** 4, 14, 24, 34, 44, 54, 64, 74, 84, and 94
6. **Tolerance and Freedom:** 5, 15, 25, 35, 45, 55, 65, 75, 85, and 95
7. **Role Assumption:** 6, 16, 26, 36, 46, 56, 66, 76, 86, and 96
8. **Consideration:** 7, 17, 27, 37, 47, 57, 67, 77, 87, and 97
9. **Production Emphasis:** 8, 18, 28, 38, 48, 58, 68, 78, 88, and 98
10. **Predictive Accuracy:** 9, 29, 49, 59, and 89
11. **Integration:** 19, 39, 69, 79, and 99
12. **Superior Orientation:** 10, 20, 30, 40, 50, 60, 70, 80, 90, and 100

The LBDQ-XII is scored by adding the value represented by letter circled for each item. The letters are given the following values similar to the original LBDQ: "A" (which represents *Always*) is given a value of 5, "B" (which represents *Often*) is given a value of 4, "C" (which represents *Occasionally*) is given a value of 3, "D" (which represents *Seldom*) is given a value of 2, and E (which represents *Never*) is given a value of 1. With that, the 20-starred items in the questionnaire are reversed scored. In the same vein as the original LBDQ, after tallying all the scores the researcher uses sample studies as a means of interpreting the data, and like previously stated, recent studies can also be used to interpret results.

LBDQ and the LBDQ-XII (both only found in the PDF version) both come with a self-evaluation form. A supervisor, or in fact any person of leadership, could also take the self-evaluation in order to determine his or her leadership behavior in addition to or as a supplement to the standard forms. Also, because of the instruments flexibility, the person can merely make changes to the original forms to evaluate his or her own leadership behavior.

COMMENTARY

It has been the goal of this chapter to illustrate the LBDQ and the LBDQ-XII, and how the reader may benefit from using the instruments under spotlight by showcasing the many areas the instruments have been used. This was accomplished by demonstrating the background of the instruments, their reliabilities, the instruments' construct validities, items of the questionnaire and scoring method, and by explaining where instrument can be ascertained on the Internet in order to utilize them. Therefore, this section will give a summary of the chapter as well as observations as to why the instruments are valuable to any contemporary researcher desiring to understand leadership behavior.

The LBDQ and LBDQ-XII have had a lengthy history spanning more than 50 years. This lengthy timeframe has created an extensive and deep literature that has given the instruments breadth and significance. So much so that they have been widely used to understand leadership behavior in many different facets; stemming from industrial studies, to military, to education, to gender, to law enforcement, and even in cross-cultural research (see Andreescu & Vito, 2010; Ayman & Chemers, 1983; Appleton & Stanwyck, 1996; Bass, 1990; Boatwright, Lopez, Sauer, VanDerWege, & Huber, 2010; Canales, Tejada-Delgado, & Slate, 2008; Christner & Hemphill, 1955; de Vries, 2008; DeCaro & Bowen-Thompson, 2010; Hackman et al., 1999; Halpin, 1954, 1957; Hemphill, 1963; Keller, 2006; Littrell, 2002; Littrell & Nkomo, 2005; Littrell & Valentin, 2005; Putti, 1985; Putti & Tong, 1992; Streufert et al., 1968; Stogdill, 1963, 1965; 1974). This long history has given the instruments a strong understanding as to its capabilities and its breadth in understanding leadership. As a result, the instruments presented here have been shown to be a valuable and useful instrument in understanding a leader's behavior and how his or her workers are receiving him or her.

With that, and because of the half-a-century of its use, these two instruments have been shown to display results that are consistently valid and reliable (Bass, 1990; de Vries, 2008; Derue et al., 2011; Greene, 1975; Halpin, 1954, 1957; Hemphill, 1963; Judge et al., 2004; Katerberg & Hom, 1981; Littrell & Nkomo, 2005; Sashkin, 1979; Schriesheim & Kerr, 1974; Stogdill, 1963, 1974; Tracy, 1987). For one, many studies have shown that both instruments are consistent internally (Bass, 1990; Halpin, 1954, Judge et al., 2004; 1957; Stogdill, 1963, 1974). The instruments have displayed reliability coefficients that allow them to register accurate results repeatedly. The LBDQ and LBDQ-XII also has been shown to be valid (Bass, 1990; de Vries, 2008; Canales et al. 2008; Greene, 1975; Halpin, 1954, 1957; Hemphill, 1963; Judge et al., 2004; Katerberg & Hom, 1981; Littrell & Nkomo, 2005; Sashkin, 1979; Schriesheim & Kerr, 1974; Stogdill, 1963, 1974; Tracy, 1987). The construct validity has

been examined by researchers and has shown to be applicable to examining leadership behavior. The instruments appear to observe what it is supposed to observe. This is especially noticeable when compared to other leadership behavioral instruments, such as the additional instruments created by the OSUS team (Judge et al., 2004). The LBDQ and LBDQ-XII revealed better overall validations than the SBDQ and the LOQ when comparing Consideration and Initiation of Structure, and as such, seen as a much better alternative to the two.

There have been limitations to the instruments as identified by various researchers. These limitations include criticism of the instruments construct validity, whether Consideration and Initiation of Structure represent fundamental dimensions of leadership behavior, whether it distinguishes between different degrees of leadership behavior, as well as concerns of latency issues and halo effects (Bass, 1990; Derue et al., 2011; Lowin et al., 1969; Hills, 1963; Schriesheim, 1982; Schriesheim & Kerr, 1974; Tracy, 1987; Witta & Gupton, 1999). However, in spite of these criticisms, the instrument has been widely used with consistent results. This consistency suggests that the instrument is still capable today. Like Judge et al. (2004) argued, it would be unwise to abandon these instruments merely because of any inadequacies or age of the instruments, and because of the validities shown and recent studies utilizing the instruments, it appears that they would help in research more than to adhere in understanding leadership. Therefore, even with these criticisms, the instruments are still applicable to contemporary research.

Researchers should not overlook the LBDQ and the LBDQ-XII. The instruments have been shown that, despite their age, they are still applicable in contemporary research. The instruments are also reliable and valid covering many different areas of research, thus allowing the researcher an adequate instrument for understanding leadership behavior in most facets. It may not give exact understandings of leadership behavior, such as degrees to which one is a leader or cross-culturally, but it can give the researcher an opportunity to identify any differences or similarities. For this reason and others presented in this chapter, researchers should continue to make the most of the LBDQ and LBDQ-XII. Thus, these instruments should not be put to pasture, but instead find new life for many years to come.

Cost

The online version of the original LBDQ (which uses 5 to 1 scoring method like the LBDQ-XII) can be found on the Internet free of charge. Any researcher can input the information of the leader understudy and determine to what effect the person is considered a leader. The Web site will ask for the researcher's email address in order to send him or her the results (note that if the researcher fails to receive the e-mail, he or she can check the spam as the researcher's e-mail may considered it spam; thus the researcher needs to be aware of his of her spam-filter).

Additionally, both the LBDQ and the LBDQ-XII are offered as PDF files on the Internet and available for anyone to use at no cost (which as noted before include the documents needed to conduct the questionnaire as well as the manual for its application). Also, as documented on the Web site, there is no need to request permission to use any of the LBDQ forms made available as long as it is used specifically for research purposes. However, if the forms are not used for nonprofit research purposes but instead used for monetary gain, then permission needs to be approved by the license holders for their use.

Location

The online version of the LBDQ can be found on the University of Purdue's The Center for Educational Leadership Web site at http://cel.calumet. purdue.edu/content/lbdq.html.

Paper versions of both the LBDQ and the LBDQ-XII are located on the Ohio State University's Fisher College of Business Web site at http://fisher.osu.edu/research/lbdq/.

REFERENCES

Anderson, L. R. (1966). Leader behavior, member attitude, and task performance of intercultural discussion groups. *The Journal of Social Psychology*, *69*(2), 305–319. doi:10.1080/0022454 5.1966.9919730

Andreescu, V., & Vito, G. F. (2010). An exploratory study of ideal leadership behaviour: The opinions of American police managers. *International Journal of Police Science and Management*, *12*(4), 567–583. doi:10.1350/ijps.2010.12.4.207

Appleton, B. A., & Stanwyck, D. (1996). Teacher personality, pupil control ideology, and leadership style. *Individual Psychology*, *52*(2), 119–129.

Ayman, R., & Chemers, M. M. (1983). Relationship of supervisory behavior ratings to work group effectiveness and subordinate satisfaction among Iranian managers. *The Journal of Applied Psychology*, *68*(2), 338–341. doi:10.1037/0021-9010.68.2.338

Bass, B. M. (1990). *Handbook of leadership: Theory, research, and managerial applications* (3rd ed.). New York, NY: The Free Press.

Boatwright, K. J., Lopez, F. G., Sauer, E. M., VanDerWege, A., & Huber, D. M. (2010). The influence of adult attachment styles on workers' preferences for relational leadership behaviors. *The Psychologist Manager Journal*, *13*(1), 1–14. doi:10.1080/10887150903316271

Brown, S. E., & Sikes, J. V. (1978). Morale of directors of curriculum and instruction as related to perceptions of leader behavior. *Education*, *99*(2), 121–126.

Canales, M. T., Tejeda-Delgado, C., & Slate, J. R. (2008). Leadership behaviors of superintendent/principles in small, rural school districts in Texas. *Rural Educator*, *29*(3), 1–7.

Chang, H. W., & Lin, G. (2008). Effect of personal values transformation on leadership behavior. *Total Quality Management*, *19*(1-2), 67–77. doi:10.1080/14783360701601967

Christner, C. A., & Hemphill, J. K. (1955). Leader behavior of B-29 commanders and changes in crew members' attitudes toward the crew. *Sociometry, 18*(1), 82–87. doi:10.2307/2785831

de Vries, R. E. (2008). What are we measuring? Convergence of leadership with interpersonal and non-interpersonal personality. *Leadership, 4*(4), 403–417. doi:10.1177/1742715008095188

DeCaro, N., & Bowen-Thompson, F. O. (2010). An examination of leadership styles of minority business entrepreneurs: A case study of public contracts. *The Journal of Business and Economic Studies, 16*(2), 72–79.

Derue, D. S., Nahrgang, J. D., Wellman, N., & Humphrey, S. E. (2011). Trait and behavioral theories of leadership: An integration and meta-analytic test of their relative validity. *Personnel Psychology, 64*(1), 7–52. doi:10.1111/j.1744-6570.2010.01201.x

Greene, C. N. (1975). The reciprocal nature of influence between leader and subordinate. *The Journal of Applied Psychology, 60*(2), 187–193. doi:10.1037/h0076552

Hackman, M. Z., Ellis, K., Johnson, C. E., & Staley, C. (1999). Self-construal orientation: Validation of an instrument and a study of the relationship to leadership communication style. *Communication Quarterly, 47*(2), 183–195. doi:10.1080/01463379909370133

Halpin, A. W. (1954). The leadership behavior and combat performance of airplane commanders. *Journal of Abnormal Psychology, 49*(1), 19–22. doi:10.1037/h0055910

Halpin, A. W. (1957). *Manual for the leadership behavior description questionnaire*. Ohio State University, Fisher College of Business. Retrieved March 22, 2009, from http://fisher.osu.edu/offices/fiscal/lbdq

Hemphill, J. K. (1955). Leadership behavior associated with the administrative reputation of college departments. *Journal of Educational Psychology, 46*(7), 385–401. doi:10.1037/h0041808

Hills, R. J. (1963). The representative function: Neglected dimensions of leadership behavior. *Administrative Science Quarterly, 8*(1), 83–101. doi:10.2307/2390888

House, R. J., Filley, A. C., & Kerr, S. (1971). Relation of leader consideration and initiating structure to R and D subordinates' satisfaction. *Administrative Science Quarterly, 16*(1), 19–30. doi:10.2307/2391283

Inderlied, S. D., & Powell, G. (1979). Sex-role identity and leadership style: Different labels of the same concept? *Sex Roles, 5*(5), 613–625. doi:10.1007/BF00287664

Judge, T. A., Piccolo, R. F., & Ilies, R. (2004). The forgotten ones? The validity of consideration and initiating structure in leadership research. *The Journal of Applied Psychology, 89*(1), 36–51. doi:10.1037/0021-9010.89.1.36

Katerber, R., & Hom, P. W. (1981). Effects of within-group and between-groups variation in leadership. *The Journal of Applied Psychology, 66*(2), 218–223. doi:10.1037/0021-9010.66.2.218

Keller, R. T. (2006). Transformational leadership, initiating structure, and substitutes for leadership: A longitudinal study of research and development project team performance. *The Journal of Applied Psychology, 91*(1), 202–210. doi:10.1037/0021-9010.91.1.202

Kenis, I. (1977). A cross-cultural study of personality and leadership. *Group & Organization Studies, 2*(1), 49–60. doi:10.1177/105960117700200107

Kenis, I. (1978). Leadership behavior, subordinate personality, and satisfaction with supervision. *The Journal of Psychology, 98*(1), 99–107. doi:10.1080/00223980.1978.9915952

Littrell, R. F. (2002). Desirable leadership behaviors of multi-cultural managers in China. *Journal of Management Development, 21*(1), 5–74. doi:10.1108/02621710210413190

Littrell, R. F., & Nkomo, S. M. (2005). Gender and race differences in leader behavior preferences in South Africa. *Women in Management Review, 20*(8), 562–580. doi:10.1108/09649420510635204

Littrell, R. F., & Valentin, L. N. (2005). Preferred leadership behaviors: Exploratory results from Romania, Germany, and the UK. *Journal of Management Development, 24*(5), 421–442. doi:10.1108/02621710510598445

Lowin, A., Hrapchak, W. J., & Kavanagh, M. J. (1969). Consideration and initiation of structure: An experimental investigation of leadership traits. *Administrative Science Quarterly, 14*(2), 238–253. doi:10.2307/2391102

Putti, J. M. (1985). Leader behavior and group characteristics in work improvement teams – The Asian context. *Public Personnel Management, 14*(3), 301–306.

Putti, J. M., & Tong, A. C. (1992). Effects of leader behavior on subordinate satisfaction in a civil service-Asian context. *Public Personnel Management, 21*(1), 53–63.

Rush, M. C., Phillips, J. S., & Lord, R. G. (1981). Effects of a temporal delay in rating on leader behavior descriptions: A laboratory investigation. *The Journal of Applied Psychology, 66*(4), 442–450. doi:10.1037/0021-9010.66.4.442

Sashkin, M. (1979). Instrumentation: A review of Ralph M. Stogdill's leadership behavior description questionnaire – Form XII. *Group & Organizational Studies (pre-1986), 4*(2), 247-250.

Schriesheim, C. A. (1982). The great high consideration – High initiation on structure leadership myth: Evidence on its generalizability. *The Journal of Social Psychology, 116*, 221–228. doi:10.1080/00224545.1982.9922774

Schriesheim, C. A., House, R. J., & Kerr, S. (1976). Leader initiating structure: A reconciliation of discrepant research results and some empirical tests. *Organizational Behavior and Human Performance, 15*(2), 297–321. doi:10.1016/0030-5073(76)90043-X

Schriesheim, C. A., & Kerr, S. (1974). Psychometric properties of the Ohio State leadership scales. *Psychological Bulletin, 81*(11), 756–765. doi:10.1037/h0037277

Schriesheim, C. A., Kinicki, A. J., & Schriesheim, J. F. (1979). The effect of leniency on leader behavior descriptions. *Organizational Behavior and Human Performance, 23*(1), 1–29. doi:10.1016/0030-5073(79)90042-4

Schriesheim, C. A., & Murphy, C. J. (1976). Relationships between leader behavior and subordinate satisfaction and performance: A test of some situational moderators. *The Journal of Applied Psychology, 61*(5), 634–641. doi:10.1037/0021-9010.61.5.634

Seltzer, J., & Bass, B. M. (1990). Transformational leadership: Beyond initiation and consideration. *Journal of Management, 16*(4), 693–703. doi:10.1177/014920639001600403

Stogdill, R. M. (1963). *Manual for the leadership behavior description questionnaire – Form XII.* Ohio State University, Fisher College of Business. Retrieved March 22, 2009, from http://fisher.osu.edu/offices/fiscal/lbdq

Stogdill, R. M. (1965). *Managers, employees, organizations.* Columbus, OH: Ohio State University, Bureau of Business Research.

Stogdill, R. M. (1969). Validity of leader behavior descriptions. *Personnel Psychology, 22*(2), 153–158. doi:10.1111/j.1744-6570.1969.tb02298.x

Stogdill, R. M. (1974). *Handbook of leadership: A survey of theory and research.* New York, NY: The Free Press.

Stogdill, R. M., Goode, O. S., & Day, D. R. (1962). New leader behavior description subscales. *Journal of Psychology: Interdisciplinary and Applied, 54*(2), 259–269. doi:10.1080/0022 3980.1962.9713117

Stogdill, R. M., Goode, O. S., & Day, D. R. (1963a). The leader behavior of corporation presidents. *Personnel Psychology, 16*(2), 127–132. doi:10.1111/j.1744-6570.1963.tb01261.x

Stogdill, R. M., Goode, O. S., & Day, D. R. (1963b). The leader behavior of United States Senators. *Journal of Psychology: Interdisciplinary and Applied, 56*(1), 3–8. doi:10.1080/00223 980.1963.9923691

Stogdill, R. M., Goode, O. S., & Day, D. R. (1964). The leader behavior of labor unions. *Personnel Psychology, 17*(1), 49–57. doi:10.1111/j.1744-6570.1964.tb00050.x

Streufert, S., Streufert, S., & Castore, C. H. (1968). Leadership in negotiations and the complexity of conceptual structure. *The Journal of Applied Psychology, 52*(3), 218–223. doi:10.1037/h0025852

Taylor, M., Crook, R., & Dropkin, S. (1961). Assessing emerging leadership behavior in small discussion groups. *Journal of Educational Psychology, 52*(1), 12–18. doi:10.1037/h0045144

Tracy, L. (1987). Consideration and initiating structure: Are they basic dimensions of leader behavior? *Social Behavior and Personality, 15*(1), 21–33. doi:10.2224/sbp.1987.15.1.21

Witta, E. L., & Gupton, S. L. (1999). *Crossvalidation and confirmatory factor analysis of the 30-item leadership behavior description questionnaire: Implications for use by graduate students.* Paper presented at the Annual Meeting of the American Educational Research Association 1999 Conference, 19-23 April, 1999.

ADDITIONAL READING

Bass, B. M. (1999). Two decades of research and development in transformational leadership. *European Journal of Work and Organizational Psychology, 8*(1), 9–32. doi:10.1080/135943299398410

Bernardin, H. J. (1987). Effect of reciprocal leniency on the relation between Consideration scores from the leader behavior description questionnaire and performance ratings. *Psychological Reports, 60*(2), 479–487. doi:10.2466/pr0.1987.60.2.479

Brown, A. F. (1967). Reactions to leadership. *Educational Administration Quarterly, 3*(1), 62–73. doi:10.1177/0013161X6700300107

Chemers, M. M. (1997). *An integrative theory of leadership.* Mahwah, NJ: Lawrence Erlbaum Publishers.

Day, D. R. (1968). *Descriptions of male and female leader behavior by male and female subordinates.* Urbana, IL: University of Illinois.

Day, D. R., & Stogdill, R. M. (1972). Leader behavior of male and female supervisors: A comparative study. *Personnel Psychology, 25*(2), 353–360. doi:10.1111/j.1744-6570.1972.tb01110.x

Fleishman, E. A. (1995). Consideration and structure: Another look at their role in leadership research. In Dansereau, F., & Yammarino, F. J. (Eds.), *Leadership: The multiple-level approaches* (pp. 51–60). Stamford, CT: JAI Press.

Halpin, A. W. (1955). The leadership ideology of aircraft commanders. *The Journal of Applied Psychology, 39*(2), 82–84. doi:10.1037/h0047338

Halpin, A. W., & Croft, D. B. (1962). *The organization climate of schools*. St. Louis, MO: Washington University Press.

Hunt, J. G., Sekaran, U., & Schriesheim, C. A. (Eds.). (1981). *Leadership: Beyond establishment views*. Carbondale, IL: Southern Illinois University.

Kavanagh, M. J., & Weissenberg, P. (1973). *The relationship between psychological differentiation and perceptions of supervisory behavior*. Paper presented at the Annual Meeting of the American Psychological Association 1973 Conference, 27-31 August, 1973.

Korman, A. K. (1966). "Consideration," "initiation structure," and organizational criteria: A review. *Personnel Psychology, 19*(4), 349–361. doi:10.1111/j.1744-6570.1966.tb00310.x

Rambo, W. W. (1958). The construction and analysis of a leadership behavior rating form. *The Journal of Applied Psychology, 42*(6), 409–415. doi:10.1037/h0040118

Schriesheim, C. A., & Bird, B. (1979). Contributions of the Ohio State Studies to the field of leadership. *Journal of Management, 5*(2), 135–145. doi:10.1177/014920637900500204

Schriesheim, C. A., Murphy, C. J., & Stogdill, R. M. (1974). Toward a contingency theory of leadership based upon the consideration and initiating structure literature. *Organizational Behavior and Human Performance, 12*(1), 62–82. doi:10.1016/0030-5073(74)90037-3

Schriesheim, C. A., & Stogdill, R. M. (1975). Differences in factor structure across three versions of the Ohio State leadership scales. *Personnel Psychology, 28*(2), 189–206. doi:10.1111/j.1744-6570.1975.tb01380.x

Schriesheim, J. F. (1980). The social context of leader-subordinate relations: An investigation of the effects of group cohesiveness. *The Journal of Applied Psychology, 65*(2), 183–194. doi:10.1037/0021-9010.65.2.183

Shapiro, M. I. (1971). Initiating structure and consideration: A situationist's view of the efficacy of two styles of leadership. *Dissertation Abstracts International, 31*(7-B), 4382-4383.

Sheridan, J. E., & Vredenburgh, D. J. (1978). Predicting leadership behavior in a hospital organization. *Academy of Management Journal, 21*(4), 679–689. doi:10.2307/255708

Sheridan, J. E., & Vredenburgh, D. J. (1978). Usefulness of leadership behavior and social power variables in predicting job tension, performance, and turnover of nursing employees. *The Journal of Applied Psychology, 63*(1), 89–95. doi:10.1037/0021-9010.63.1.89

Stogdill, R. M. (1965). *Manual for job satisfactions and expectation scales*. Columbus, OH: Ohio State University, Bureau of Business Research.

Stogdill, R. M. (1968). *Leadership: A survey of the literature. I. Selected topics*. Greensboro, NC: Smith Richardson Foundation.

Stogdill, R. M., & Coons, A. E. (1957). *Leader behavior: Its description and measurement*. Columbus, OH: Ohio State University, Bureau of Business Research.

Stogdill, R. M., & Shartle, C. L. (1948). Methods for determining patterns of leadership behavior in relation to organization structure and objectives. *The Journal of Applied Psychology, 32*(2), 286–291. doi:10.1037/h0057264

Stogdill, R. M., & Shartle, C. L. (1956). *Methods in the study of administrative leadership (Research Monographs 80)*. Columbus, OH: Ohio State University, Bureau of Business Research.

Weissenberg, P., & Kavanagh, M. J. (1972). The independence of initiating structure and consideration: A review of the evidence. *Personnel Psychology, 25*(1), 119–130. doi:10.1111/j.1744-6570.1972.tb01095.x

Yukl, G. (1998). *Leadership in organizations.* Upper Saddle River, NJ: Prentice Hall.

KEY TERMS AND DEFINITIONS

Consideration: Refers to how much a leader displays concerns for the interests of the members of the group through his or her expressing. Examples of considerate behavior are appreciation for work, emphasis on job satisfaction, and sustaining and reinforcing worker and leader equality.

Cronbach's Alpha: A statistical formula that calculates the internal consistency of psychometric instruments with both dichotomous and non-dichotomous (continuous) choices.

Halo Effects: The perception of one trait that influences the perception of the subsequent interpretations.

Initiation of Structure: Refers to the leader's behavior in outlining the relationship between leader and the members of the group by creating good channels of communication and ways of getting the job done.

Kuder-Richardson Formula: A statistical formula that addresses internal consistency of instruments with dichotomous choices.

Leadership Behavior: Actions and manners deemed to exhibit leadership qualities.

Leniency Effects: Refers to rating error in which ratings are distorted so that the average rating is given a substantially higher rating than the median of the rating scale.

Psychometric Properties: The field of study that address theory and technique of educational and psychological instruments.

Chapter 7
Self–Monitoring Scale

Sharon E. Norris
Spring Arbor University, USA

Tracy H. Porter
Cleveland State University, USA

ABSTRACT

Self-monitoring represents a social psychological construct of expressive behavior and self-presentation. The original 25-item Self-Monitoring Scale was developed by Snyder (1974) to measure the extent to which individuals differ in their use of social cues to guide behavior. High self-monitors tailor their behavior to fit the social context and make a good impression (Snyder, 1979). Low self-monitors are less responsive to situational and interpersonal cues (Snyder & Cantor, 1980). Social psychologists were the earliest users of the Self-Monitoring Scale, but its use has expanded to include researchers studying organizational behavior, group and organizational management, consumer marketing, and human relations. Researchers report a relationship between self-monitoring and impression management, leader emergence, career success, and citizenship behaviors.

INTRODUCTION

Self-monitoring is a social psychological construct of expressive behavior and self-presentation (Snyder 1974, 1979). In organizational life, people portray images of themselves that they believe will make a good impression on others. High self-monitors are characterized as individuals who pay close attention to social cues and modify their behavior to fit the situation whereas low self-monitors do not vary their behavior much across different situations (Baumeister & Twenge, 2003). The original Self-Monitoring Scale is a set of 25 true-false statements that were developed by Snyder (1974) to measure the extent to which individuals differ in their use of social cues to monitor and regulate their expressive behavior and self-presentation (Snyder, 1979).

In this chapter, we highlight self-monitoring as an important individual difference character-

DOI: 10.4018/978-1-4666-2172-5.ch007

istic for researchers and consultants to consider when studying people in organizations. First, we examine the background of the self-monitoring construct and the development of the original 25-item Self-Monitoring Scale (Snyder, 1974). We discuss some of the reasons why people engage in self-monitoring behaviors, how high and low self-monitors differ, the way researchers can measure self-monitoring, and how to use the scale. We also share what the critics have to say about the original Self-Monitoring Scale, and how self-monitoring behaviors influence factors associated with organizational settings. Next, we provide information on the reliability and validity of the Self-Monitoring Scale, results, commentary, costs, location, additional readings, and key terms.

We present self-monitoring as a relevant construct in organizational research because self-monitoring behaviors influence the way individuals differ when they are engaged in a variety of situations in organizational life. While there are a growing number of studies that have examined the influence of self-monitoring on organizational variables, we believe more empirical research on self-monitoring will help researchers and consultants gain a better understanding of how self-monitoring behaviors influence the way people interact and influence organizational outcomes.

BACKGROUND

Is Life a Theater, the Entire World a Stage, and People Merely Players?

James (1890) asserted that people show a different side of themselves to different groups of people, and Goffman (1955, 1959, 1963, 1967) compared social interactions to theatrical performances where people take the stage and act out their lives in the presence of others. When people interact, they attempt to present themselves in a manner that others expect and approve. The social life as

a stage metaphor portrays life as a theater where there are differences between public appearance and private reality (Snyder, 1979).

The extent to which people monitor social context cues and tailor their behavior to fit the social environment explains self-monitoring behaviors (Jawahar, 2001; Snyder, 1979). When individuals self-monitor their behaviors, they attempt to control the impressions that they make on others through their social interactions (Snyder, 1979). Self-monitors use social cues to guide their selection of and judgment regarding the appropriateness of expressive behaviors. As social roles and expectations become salient, their self-presentations shift from situation to situation (Gordon & Gergen, 1968; Snyder, 1979). Self-monitored behaviors are intentionally selected to convey a favorable social identity in each social setting or interpersonal context (Alexander & Knight, 1971; Alexander & Lauderdale, 1977; Alexander & Sagatun, 1973; Snyder, 1979).

In order to create a desired image in the eyes of beholders during social interactions, self-monitors also attempt to manage or control their verbal and nonverbal self-presentations (Snyder, 1979). Effective social and interpersonal functioning requires that people possess some ability to manage and control their expressive behaviors (Snyder, 1974). Expressive behaviors include both verbal and nonlanguage behaviors and communication. Nonlanguage behaviors include but are not limited to "voice quality, body motion, touch, and the use of personal space" (Snyder, 1974, p. 526). Nonverbal communication includes voluntarily expressed behaviors as well as uncensored behaviors. Uncensored behaviors represent involuntary expressions whereas the behaviors that are purposefully selected and controlled represent deliberate and self-managed expressions. Ekman (2003) explained, "if we try to control what we do and say, it will be a struggle between our deliberate voluntary efforts and our involuntary emotional behavior" (p. 53).

Why do People Monitor Expressive Behaviors?

Self-monitoring has been defined as a process of "self-observation and self-control guided by situational cues to social appropriateness" (Snyder, 1974, p. 526). Individuals differ in the extent to which they will monitor their "self-presentation, expressive behavior, and nonverbal affective displays" (Snyder, 1974, pp. 526-527). Through social interactions, people learn that expressive behaviors can result in either social approval or disapproval. Because others may interpret certain behaviors as inappropriate, high self-monitors will manage and control their expressive presentation (Snyder, 1974). Social cognitive theory explains that human functioning is influenced by the triadic reciprocal interaction of influences that are personal, behavioral, and environmental (Bandura, 1986). The expressive behaviors of low self-monitors are primarily controlled from within by affective states whereas the expressive behaviors of high self-monitors are also influenced by cognitive appraisals (Snyder, 1974).

How do High Self-Monitors and Low Self-Monitors Differ?

Based on Snyder's (1974, 1979) research and writing, Bass and Stogdill (1990) explained, "individuals differ in the extent to which they monitor and control the presentation of themselves in social situations" (p. 132). High self-monitors are sensitive to the way other people respond to them, and they act in response by modifying and controlling their behavior to achieve social approval (Snyder, 1979). Snyder and Gangestad (1982) stated, "high self-monitoring individuals chronically strive to appear to be the type of person called for by each situation in which they find themselves" (p. 124). Kilduff and Day (1994) reported, "high self-monitors strive to maintain flexibility and make little emotional investment in relationships" (p. 1049).

Low self-monitoring individuals are less attentive to social information, and their self-presentation skills are not as well developed as high self-monitors (Snyder, 1979). Low self-monitors "strive to display their own personal dispositions and attitudes in each situation in which they find themselves" (Snyder & Gangestad, 1982, p. 124). Kilduff and Day (1994) explained that low self-monitors "insist on being themselves despite social expectations" (p. 1048). Snyder (1974) referred to this type of individual as a "non-self-monitoring person" (p. 536) whose "presentation and expression appear to be controlled from within" (p. 536). Low self-monitors are described as committed and principled, and they invest emotionally in relationships (Kilduff & Day, 1994).

Snyder and Cantor (1980) explained that "high self-monitoring individuals are relatively situationally guided; low self-monitoring individuals are relatively dispositionally guided" (pp. 222-223). Miller and Thayer (1989) stated:

People who are high self-monitors are oriented toward external matters and concerns for the normative appropriateness of their behavior, whereas those who are low self-monitors are more oriented toward internal concerns and are motivated to behave in a manner consistent with their internal states and traits. (p. 143)

How do Researchers Measure Self-Monitoring Behaviors?

Capturing and measuring individual differences in self-monitoring behaviors led Snyder (1974) to the development of the original Self-Monitoring Scale. The original Self-Monitoring Scale measures individual responsiveness to social cues with 25 self-descriptive statements. According to Snyder (1979), the self-monitoring scale measures a) concern for social appropriateness; b) attention to social comparison information; c) ability to control and modify self-presentation; d) flexible use of self-monitoring ability in particular situations; and e) extent that expressive behaviors are tailored to specific social situations (pp. 89-90).

Self-monitoring instruments have been utilized for testing a variety of organizational phenomena, and some of the notable studies include self-monitoring and student integration in higher education (Zweigenhaft & Cody, 1993); self-monitoring and materialism (Browne & Kaldenberg, 1997); self-monitoring and fashion branding (Auty & Elliott, 1998); self-monitoring and the effects on impression management (Montagliani & Giacalone, 1998); self-monitoring and cheating behavior (Covey, Saladin, & Killen, 2001); self-monitoring and gender response to humorous advertising (Lammers, 1991); self-monitoring and future time orientation in romantic relationships (Oner, 2002); and self-monitoring and leader flexibility across multiple group situations (Zaccaro, Foti, & Kenny, 1991).

What do Critics Say about the Self-Monitoring Scale?

The original Self-Monitoring Scale developed by Snyder (1974), as well as the self-monitoring construct, has been "embroiled in controversy that derives largely from disagreement about what the scale measures" (Briggs & Cheek, 1988, p. 663). Briggs and Cheek (1988) explained that the scale is multidimensional and its components "seem at odds with one another" (p. 663). In an analysis of the scale, Briggs, Cheek, and Buss (1980) explained that the characteristics of high self-monitors include "concern for the appropriateness of social behavior, sensitivity to important cues, and self-regulation" (p. 679). Briggs et al. (1980) further pointed out, "there has been no analysis of the internal structure of the scale" (p. 679).

After analyzing the internal structure of the original Self-Monitoring Scale, Briggs et al. (1980) identified three distinct factors and labeled these factors extraversion, other-directedness, and acting. Briggs et al. explained that two of the factors, extraversion and other-directedness, were uncor-

related meaning that individuals scoring high on extraversion display behaviors that are distinct from other-directedness. Briggs et al. argued, "the Acting factor may be a better instrument for selecting actors than it is a measure of self-presentation in everyday life" (p. 684). Briggs et al. concluded "there may be a gap between the construct of self-monitoring and its operationalization in the Self-Monitoring Scale" (p. 686).

Snyder and Gangestad (1986) addressed the concerns posed by various authors (e.g., Briggs & Cheek, 1986; Lennox & Wolfe, 1984) regarding possible psychometric weaknesses of the original 25-item Self-Monitoring Scale (Snyder, 1974). Snyder and Gangestad (1986) proposed a new 18-item scale and reported, "this new measure is more factorially pure than the original measure" (p. 137).

Gangestad and Snyder (2000) acknowledged the multifactor nature of the scale. "Although there is widespread agreement about the multifactorial nature of the items of the Self-Monitoring Scale – an agreement in which we share – there exists diverging viewpoints on the proper interpretation of this state of affairs" (Gangestad & Snyder, 2000, p. 533). The controversy and confusion associated with the internal structure of the scale has raised questions regarding the existence and nature of self-monitoring (Gangestad & Snyder, 2000).

Even with all of the years of debate and controversy regarding the self-monitoring construct and the original Self-Monitoring Scale (Gangestad & Snyder, 2000), self-monitoring remains an individual difference characteristic that a wide range of researchers study. Between 1981 and 2000 there were over 200 empirical journal articles published on self-monitoring (Gangestad & Snyder, 2000). Approximately half of the empirical studies on self-monitoring that were reviewed by Gangestad and Snyder (2000) appeared in personality and social psychology journals such as the "*Journal of Personality and Social Psychology, Journal of Personality, Journal of Experimental Social Psychology,* and *Personality and Social Psychol-*

ogy Bulletin" (p. 538). The remaining articles that they examined were located in specialized journals and field journals such as the *Journal of Nonverbal Behavior, Journal of Applied Social Psychology, Communication Monographs*, and *Journal of Personal Selling and Sales Management* (Gangestad & Snyder, 2000).

Gangestad and Snyder (2000) also reported that "a large number of dissertations have used the Self-Monitoring Scale over the years" (p. 538). More recently, studies examining self-monitoring have been published in the *Journal of Project and Brand Management, Organizational Behavior and Human Decision Processes, Group and Organization Management, Journal of Occupational Health Psychology, Journal of Consumer Marketing, Journal of Organizational Behavior, Journal of Cross-Cultural Psychology, Academy of Management Journal,* and *Human Relations*. Briggs and Cheek (1988) acknowledged, "the Self-Monitoring Scale (Snyder, 1974) is one of the most popular measures of personality to be introduced in recent years" (p. 663). It is likely that researchers will continue to use the Self-Monitoring Scale until a better measure of self-presentation is developed (Briggs & Cheek, 1988).

How does Self-Monitoring Influence Factors Associated with Organizational Settings?

While the earliest studies measured the influence of self-monitoring behaviors on social outcomes, more recent studies have been conducted on the influence of self-monitoring styles on behaviors and outcomes associated with organizational settings and work environments. Snyder and Copeland (1989) stated, "organizational settings provide the backdrop for observing a myriad of strategic self-presentational activities" (p. 9). Snyder and Copeland further discussed the impact of self-monitoring on the job search process, interviewing,

job performance, promotion opportunities, and decisions to leave an organization.

Connections have also been made between self-monitoring and impression management. Turnley and Bolino (2001) explained, "researchers generally acknowledge that self-monitoring encompasses both the tendency to use impression management and the skill to successfully execute such behaviors" (p. 352). Self-monitoring ability helps individuals determine the appropriate impression management tactics necessary for creating a desired image (Sosik & Jung, 2010). High self-monitors are concerned about the impressions that they are making on other people whereas low self-monitors are generally concerned about living according to their internalized standards (Tetlock & Manstead, 1985). Tetlock and Manstead (1985) explained, "overall, the behavior of high self-monitors appears to be primarily under the control of impression management concerns; the behavior of low self-monitors primarily under the control of intra-psychic processes" (p. 70).

Speaking up in the workplace has been described as a willingness to voice concerns by "openly stating one's views or opinions about workplace matters" (Premeaux & Bedeian, 2003, p. 1538). Premeaux and Bedeian (2003) examined the moderating influence of self-monitoring on speaking up behaviors and reported that as trust in the supervisor increased, low self-monitors were more likely to speak up. In comparison, high self-monitors were less likely to speak up as trust in the supervisor increased (Premeaux & Bedeian, 2003). Premeaux and Bedeian explained that high self-monitors were aware of their audience and considered how their speaking up would affect their public appearance. They concluded that high and low self-monitors "are driven by different motives in speaking up" (Premeaux & Bedeian, p. 1560).

Flynn (2010) speculated that self-monitoring "might be a strong determinant of charismatic leadership" (p. 288). High self-monitors and charismatic individuals have been described as social actors (Gardner & Avolio, 1998). Prior research has also connected the high self-monitoring tactics of charismatic leaders with their development of vision statements (Sosik & Dinger, 2007). Sosik and Dinger (2007) posited, "charismatic leaders who are also high self-monitors will use an image-based approach to create vision statements with more inspirational themes" (p. 139).

How do Users or Researchers Score the Self-Monitoring Scale?

The true-false 25-item survey is available online. Individual users can print the survey from the website and complete the questionnaire, or researchers can obtain the survey and incorporate items statements into custom designed questionnaires. The survey can be accessed online free of charge and anyone can utilize the instrument; therefore, anyone can also score the 25 true-false self-descriptive statements. Items are scored 0 or 1 and summed. Scores range from 0 to 25. A score between 0 and 12 indicates the respondent is a relatively low self-monitor. A score range between 13 and 25 indicates the respondent is a relatively high self-monitor.

Another Self-Monitoring Scale can be accessed online that measures the 25 item-statements using a 5-point Likert Scale. Users can complete the survey online, and the scoring is computed automatically. Scores range from 0 to 100. A score below 40 indicates the respondent is a relatively low self-monitor. A score above 70 indicates a relatively high self-monitor.

RELIABILITY

The internal consistency reliability of the 25-item true-false version of the Self-Monitoring Scale can be measured using Kuder-Richardson Formula 20 (Kuder & Richardson, 1937). The 25-item true-false version of the Self-Monitoring Scale represents a test composed of items that are scored dichotomously as 0 and 1. Rajamanickam (2001) explained, "the Kuder-Richardson formula 20 is more suitable for tests in which items are scored with 'yes' or 'no' answers" (p. 201).

The Self-Monitoring Scale was originally constructed with 41 true-false self-descriptive item statements (Snyder, 1974). Snyder (1974) administered the scale to 192 Stanford University undergraduate students. "An item analysis was performed to select items to maximize the internal consistency" (Snyder, p. 529). Sixteen items were discarded, and the remaining 25 items had a Kuder-Richardson 20 reliability of .70. Snyder reported that the 25-item scale also had a test-retest reliability of .83 ($df = 51$, $p < .001$, one month interval). Snyder cross-validated the 25-item scale during scale construction with an independent sample of 146 undergraduate students from the University of Minnesota, and the cross-validation analysis yielded a Kuder-Richardson 20 reliability of .63.

Since the construction of the Self-Monitoring Scale, various researchers have reported reliability of the scale. Ajzen, Timko, and White (1982) conducted a study with "a total of 155 undergraduate students enrolled in psychology courses at the University of Massachusetts" (p. 428) using Snyder's (1974) 25-item true-false version of the Self-Monitoring Scale. Ajzen et al. (1982) reported that the internal consistency of the scale was .69.

Briggs and Cheek (1988) conducted a six-sample study ($N = 3,615$) using the 25-item Self-Monitoring Scale with six separate samples of students between 1978 and 1985. The psychometric properties of the 25-item scale were measured including the reliability coefficients. The fall 1978 and spring 1980 samples yielded a coefficient alpha of .64, but the reliability coefficients in the remaining samples yielded a range of coefficient alphas from .67 to .70 (Briggs & Cheek, 1988).

Briggs et al. (1980) conducted an analysis of Snyder's (1974) Self-Monitoring Scale with students taking introductory psychology courses at the University of Texas. "A sample of 140 students completed both the true-false forms and those with 5-point scales 45 days apart" (Briggs et al., 1980, p. 680). Briggs et al. reported the two tests yielded a correlation of .72 ($p < .001$) and were comparable to Snyder's (1974) test-retest correlation of .83 and Kuder-Richardson 20 of .70. In a study with 103 male introductory psychology students from Texas A&M University, the internal consistency reliability of the 25-item Self-Monitoring Scale measure was .73 (Graziano & Bryant, 1998). A recent study with 162 Korean business owners was conducted, and Oh and Kilduff (2008) reported an estimated Kuder-Richardson reliability as .73. Oner (2002) noted the reliability of a Turkish translation of Snyder's (1974) Self-Monitoring Scale as .82.

The 18-item version of the Self-Monitoring Scale has been utilized in a growing number of empirical research studies. The internal consistency for the 18-item version was reported as .70 by Gangestad and Snyder (1985). In a study of discrepant perceptions of leadership behavior, Becker, Ayman, and Korabik (2002) reported an internal consistency of .70 of the 18-item version of the scale with a sample of 49 Canadian leaders. Caligiuri and Day (2000) reported an internal consistency of .72 of the 18-item version of the Self-Monitoring Scale in their study with a sample of expatriate employees who participated in a cross-national work setting study examining the effects of self-monitoring on work performance ratings. In a cross-cultural study, Gudykunst et al. (1992) utilized an 18-item version of the Self-Monitoring Scale and reported, "reliability analyses yielded alphas of .70 in the U.S. sample, .67 in the Australian sample, .72 in the Japanese sample, and .74 in the Hong Kong sample" (p. 202).

VALIDITY

Snyder (1974) was the first scholar to report construct validity for the Self-Monitoring Scale in "a sociometric study of peer ratings" (Snyder, 1979, p. 90). Snyder (1979) explained that high self-monitors pay attention to what is socially appropriate, have self-control over their emotional expression, and "use this ability to create the impressions they want" (p. 90). According to Snyder (1979), high self-monitors are "vigilant and attentive to social comparison information" (p. 91).

Snyder (1974) evaluated the construct validity of the Self-Monitoring Scale by administering the survey to predetermined groups of people and predicted how they would score (Snyder, 1979). Snyder (1979) reported:

According to this strategy, groups of individuals known to be particularly skilled at controlling their expressive behavior (e.g., actors, mime artists, and politicians) ought to score higher on the Self-Monitoring Scale than an unselected comparison sample. Indeed, professional stage actors have substantially higher scores on the Self-Monitoring Scale than do comparison samples of university undergraduates (Snyder, 1974). (p. 90)

Snyder (1979) observed that high self-monitors are skilled at expressing a wide variety of emotions such as happiness, sadness, anger, fear, surprise, disgust, and remorse. Using expressive mannerisms, high self-monitors can convincingly portray themselves as reserved and introverted and with chameleon-like skill display outgoing and extraverted mannerisms (Lippa, 1976; Snyder, 1979). Additionally, people who score high on the Self-Monitoring Scale are more likely to vigilantly seek information from others and pay attention to the expressive behaviors of others (Snyder, 1974, 1979).

The discriminate validity of the Self-Monitoring Scale has been demonstrated as it correlates with "related but conceptually distinct individual differences measures" (Snyder, 1974, p. 530). In Snyder's (1974) construction of the Self-Monitoring Scale, measures were obtained from respondents on self-monitoring behaviors using the 25-item Self-Monitoring Scale, and measures were obtained from the same respondents on need for approval using the Marlowe-Crowne Social Desirability Scale (Crowne & Marlowe, 1964). Snyder (1974) reported, "there is a slight negative relationship (r = -.1874, df= 190, p < .01) between the SM and the Marlowe-Crowne Social Desirability Scale (M-C SDS, Crowne & Marlowe, 1964)" (p. 530). These results demonstrate that self-monitoring and need for approval represented related but conceptually distinct constructs (Snyder, 1974).

Snyder (1974) tested the discriminate validity of the Self-Monitoring Scale with the Minnesota Multiphasic Personality Inventory Psychopathic Deviate Scale and the *c* scales of the Performance Style tests. Snyder (1974) reported a "low negative relationship (r = -.2002, df = 190, p < .01) between the SM and the Minnesota Multiphasic Personality Inventory Psychopathic Deviate scale" (p. 530). Likewise, he stated there is "a small and nonsignificant negative relationship (r = -.25, df = 24, *ns*) between the SM and the *c* scale of the Performance Style tests (e.g., Ring & Wallston, 1968)" (Snyder, 1974, p. 530).

Day and Kilduff (2003) argued, "previous research has shown that self-monitoring has good discriminate validity with other personality constructs" (p. 208). Snyder (1987) reported that self-monitoring is not meaningfully correlated with locus of control, self-esteem, neuroticism, trait anxiety, or intelligence. Snyder (1974) reported that the original Self-Monitoring Scale was "unrelated to Christie and Geis (1970) Machiavellianism (r = .0931, df = 51, *ns*), Alpert-Haber (1960) Achievement Anxiety Test (r = .1437, df

= 51, *ns*), and Kassarjian's (1962) inner-other directedness (r = -.1944, df = 54, *ns*)" (p. 530).

Self-monitoring behaviors have been reported to play a pivotal role in shaping who succeeds in an organization and emerges into leadership (Day, Schleicher, Unckless, & Hiller, 2002; Ellis, 1988). Day et al. (2002) reported that self-monitoring "is significantly related to work-related outcomes associated with job performance and advancement, ability, leadership behavior and emergence" (p. 397).

Flynn, Reagans, Amanatullah, and Ames (2006) evaluated the correlation between self-monitoring behavior using the 25-item Self-Monitoring Scale and an 8-item need for social status scale that was developed specifically for the study. Testing 100 Columbia University undergraduate students, Flynn et al. (2006) noted, "positive and significant correlations between the participants' reported need for social status and their self-monitoring scores" (p. 1125).

Using the 18-item version of the Self-Monitoring Scale, the construct of self-monitoring has been used to gain a better understanding of self-monitoring and perceptions of leader behavior (Becker et al., 2002), self-monitoring and performance ratings (Caligiuri & Day, 2000), self-monitoring and in-group and out-group communication (Gudykunst et al., 1992), self-monitoring and turnover and intention to leave (Jenkins, 1993), and the effect of self-monitoring on managerial careers (Kilduff & Day, 1994).

RESULTS

In order to organize the true-false data that is collected using the 25-item Self-Monitoring Scale (Snyder, 1974), researchers may find it helpful to code high-self monitoring responses with a 1 and low self-monitoring responses with a 0. In a study conducted by Ajzen et al. (1982), the sample data were dichotomized at the median self-monitoring score. Scores obtained above the median were identified as high self-monitors, and scores below the median were identified as low self-monitors. Other researchers have categorized respondents with scores of 11 or greater as high self-monitors and 10 and below as low self-monitors based on Gangestad and Snyder's (1985) recommendation (e.g., Becker et al., 2002).

Typically, researchers will incorporate the Self-Monitoring Scale (Snyder, 1974) into a questionnaire that measures multiple variables specific to a research site or a particular research study. While the results obtained from the Self-Monitoring Scale will identify individuals as either high or low self-monitors, these data may be most useful when considered in combination with other variables. For instance, various researchers identify self-monitoring as a moderating variable (e.g., Premeaux & Bedeian, 2003).

COMMENTARY

Self-monitoring represents a self-regulation strategy that has been utilized as an assessment procedure for evaluating intervention effectiveness (Reid & Lienemann, 2006). Reid and Lienemann (2006) explained, "the act of self-monitoring a behavior caused changes in the behavior. This led to the use of self-monitoring as an intervention" (p. 72). Once this phenomenon was discovered, psychologists began using self-monitoring as an assessment methodology that subjects could use to systematically record self-observations of behavior (Rehm & Rokke, 1988). Used as such, "no claim is made that self-monitoring instruments are reliable, valid, or have other psychometric desiderata" (Cartwright & Weisz, 1984, p. 158).

In organizational science, researchers have explored the influence of self-monitoring on behaviors related to career success in corporate settings (Kilduff & Day, 1994). One particular role that has been explored relates to the boundary spanning function. Reeves (2010) defined boundary-spanners as "people who connect one

network to another" (p. 113). Snyder and Copeland (1989) stated, "boundary spanning roles seem particularly well-suited to the interpersonal styles of high self-monitors" (p. 13). Caldwell and O'Reilly (1982) conducted a study with 93 field representatives who acted as boundary spanners in a large franchise organization and examined the impact of self-monitoring on individual performance. Caldwell and O'Reilly concluded, "the boundary-spanning role places individuals in situations where they must be sensitive to the social cues of different groups if they are to perform the boundary-spanning function effectively" (p. 126).

Kilduff and Day (1994) conducted a study with 139 graduates from a nationally ranked MBA program and reported that "high self-monitors were more likely to achieve cross-company promotions ($p < .05$), change employers ($p < .001$), and make geographic moves ($p < .05$) than were low self-monitors" (p. 1053). While previous research has demonstrated that high self-monitors may be more likely to get ahead in organizational settings (Kilduff & Day, 1994), Blakely, Andrews, and Fuller (2003) questioned whether these chameleons represent good organizational citizens. Blakely et al. (2003) posited, "in organizations which foster a spirit of cooperativeness, high self-monitors may exhibit greater citizenship while in organizations which foster individual competitiveness high self-monitors may exhibit less citizenship" (p. 142).

High self-monitors will appraise a given situation and then choose the behavior that they believe will help them gain social approval. When individuals engage in high self-monitoring behaviors, they use "cues from the external environment to regulate their behavior" (Bono & Vey, 2007, p. 182). Various researchers have also studied the regulations of emotions at work (e.g., Brotheridge & Grandey, 2002; Diefendorff & Richard, 2003; Goffman, 1959; Rafaeli & Sutton, 1989). When individuals attempt to regulate their emotions at work, they may draw from two strategies: deep acting or surface acting (Bono & Vey, 2007;

Grandey, 2003). Bono and Vey (2007) explained, "employees who use *deep acting* attempt to modify their feelings or emotions to meet the demands of the situation" (p. 179). Grandey (2003) posited, "in *surface acting*, the alternative strategy, employees modify their displays without shaping their inner feelings" (p. 87). Surface acting "can create dissonance between their felt and expressed emotions" (Bono & Vey, p. 179). Based on the results of an empirical study on emotional performance, Bono and Vey reported, "self-monitors engage in deep acting and experience less stress" (p. 187).

Future researchers may be interested in examining the effects of self-monitoring on additional organizational behaviors and performance outcomes such as prosocial behaviors, organizational commitment, and motivation to lead. The development of a self-monitoring scale specifically designed for measuring self-presentation and expressive behaviors in organizational settings may also be beneficial for future researchers.

Costs

The 25-item Self-Monitoring Scale (Snyder, 1974) is available on the Internet and available for anyone to use.

Location

The 25-items Self-Monitoring Scale (Snyder, 1974) is located at two different locations on the Internet. The self-scoring true-false instrument is located at http://pubpages.unh.edu/~ckb/SELF-MON2.html. The electronic scoring Likert-scale instrument is located at http://www.outofservice.com/self-monitor-censor-test/.

REFERENCES

Ajzen, I., Timko, C., & White, J. B. (1982). Self-monitoring and the attitude-behavior relation. *Journal of Personality and Social Psychology*, *42*(3), 426–435. doi:10.1037/0022-3514.42.3.426

Alexander, C. N. Jr, & Knight, G. W. (1971). Situated identities and social psychological experimentation. *Sociometry*, *34*(1), 65–82. doi:10.2307/2786351

Alexander, C. N. Jr, & Lauderdale, P. (1977). Situated identities and social influence. *Sociometry*, *40*(3), 225–233. doi:10.2307/3033529

Alexander, C. N. Jr, & Sagatun, I. (1973). An attributional analysis of experimental norms. *Sociometry*, *36*(2), 127–142. doi:10.2307/2786562

Alpert, R., & Haber, R. N. (1960). Anxiety in academic achievement situations. *Journal of Abnormal and Social Psychology*, *61*(2), 207–215. doi:10.1037/h0045464

Auty, S., & Elliott, R. (1998). Fashion involvement, self-monitoring and the meaning of brands. *Journal of Project and Brand Management*, *7*(2), 109–123. doi:10.1108/10610429810216874

Bandura, A. (1986). *Social foundations of thought and action: A social cognitive theory*. Englewood Cliffs, NJ: Prentice-Hall.

Bass, B. M., & Stogdill, R. M. (1990). *Bass & Stogdill's handbook of leadership: Theory, research, & managerial applications*. New York, NY: The Free Press.

Baumeister, R. F., & Twenge, J. M. (2003). The social self. In Millon, T., Lerner, M. J., & Weiner, I. B. (Eds.), *Handbook of psychology: Personality and social psychology* (pp. 327–352). Hoboken, NJ: John Wiley & Sons.

Becker, J., Ayman, R., & Korabik, K. (2002). Discrepancies in self-subordinates' perceptions of leadership behavior: Leader's gender, organizational context, and leader's self-monitoring. *Group & Organization Management, 27*(2), 226–244. doi:10.1177/10501102027002004

Blakely, G. L., Andrews, M. C., & Fuller, J. (2003). Are chameleons good citizens? A longitudinal study of the relationship between self-monitoring and organizational citizenship behaviors. *Journal of Business and Psychology, 18*(2), 131–144. doi:10.1023/A:1027388729390

Bono, J. E., & Vey, M. A. (2007). Personality and emotional performance: Extraversion, neuroticism, and self-monitoring. *Journal of Occupational Health Psychology, 12*(2), 177–192. doi:10.1037/1076-8998.12.2.177

Briggs, S. R., & Cheek, J. M. (1986). The role of factor analysis in the development and evaluation of personality scales. *Journal of Personality, 54*(1), 106–148. doi:10.1111/j.1467-6494.1986.tb00391.x

Briggs, S. R., & Cheek, J. M. (1988). On the nature of self-monitoring: Problems with assessment, problems with validity. *Journal of Personality and Social Psychology, 54*(4), 663–678. doi:10.1037/0022-3514.54.4.663

Briggs, S. R., Cheek, J. M., & Buss, A. H. (1980). An analysis of the self-monitoring scale. *Journal of Personality and Social Psychology, 38*(4), 679–686. doi:10.1037/0022-3514.38.4.679

Brotheridge, C. M., & Grandey, A. A. (2002). Emotional labor and burnout: Comparing two perspectives of people work. *Journal of Vocational Behavior, 60*(1), 17–39. doi:10.1006/jvbe.2001.1815

Browne, B. A., & Kaldenberg, D. O. (1997). Conceptualizing self-monitoring: Links to materialism and product involvement. *Journal of Consumer Marketing, 14*(1), 31–44. doi:10.1108/07363769710155848

Caldwell, D. F., & O'Reilly, C. A. (1982). Boundary spanning and individual performance: The impact of self-monitoring. *The Journal of Applied Psychology, 67*(1), 124–127. doi:10.1037/0021-9010.67.1.124

Caligiuri, P. M., & Day, D. V. (2000). Effects of self-monitoring on technical, contextual, and assignment-specific performance: A study of cross-national work performance ratings. *Group & Organization Management, 25*(2), 154–174. doi:10.1177/1059601100252004

Cartwright, D., & Weisz, G. (1984). Self-report ratings and inventories. In Hersen, M., Michelson, L., & Bellack, A. S. (Eds.), *Issues in psychotherapy research* (pp. 133–170). New York, NY: Plenum Press.

Christie, R., & Geis, F. L. (1970). *Studies in Machiavellianism*. New York, NY: Academic Press.

Covey, M. K., Saladin, S., & Killen, P. J. (2001). Self-monitoring, surveillance, and incentive effects on cheating. *The Journal of Social Psychology, 129*(5), 673–679. doi:10.1080/00224545.1989.9713784

Crowne, D. P., & Marlowe, D. (1964). *The approval motive: Studies in evaluative dependence*. New York, NY: Wiley.

Day, D. V., & Kilduff, M. (2003). Self-monitoring personality and work relationships: Individual differences in social networks. In Barrick, M. R., & Ryan, A. M. (Eds.), *Personality and work: Reconsidering the role of personality in organizations* (pp. 205–228). San Francisco, CA: Jossey-Bass.

Day, D. V., Schleicher, D. J., Unckless, A. L., & Hiller, N. J. (2002). Self-monitoring personality at work: A meta-analytic investigation of construct validity. *The Journal of Applied Psychology, 87*(2), 390–401. doi:10.1037/0021-9010.87.2.390

Diefendorff, J. M., & Richard, E. M. (2003). Antecedents and consequences of emotional display rule perceptions. *The Journal of Applied Psychology, 88*(2), 284–294. doi:10.1037/0021-9010.88.2.284

Ekman, P. (2003). *Emotions revealed: Recognizing faces and feelings to improve communication and emotional life*. New York, NY: Owl Books.

Ellis, R. J. (1988). Self-monitoring and leadership emergence in groups. *Personality and Social Psychology Bulletin, 14*(4), 681–693. doi:10.1177/0146167288144004

Flynn, F. J. (2010). Power as charismatic leadership: A significant opportunity (and a modest proposal) for social psychology research. In Guinote, A., & Vescio, T. K. (Eds.), *The social psychology of power* (pp. 284–309). New York, NY: The Guilford Press.

Flynn, F. J., Reagans, R. E., Amanatullah, E. T., & Ames, D. R. (2006). Helping one's way to the top: Self-monitors achieve status by helping others and knowing who helps whom. *Journal of Personality and Social Psychology, 91*(6), 1123–1137. doi:10.1037/0022-3514.91.6.1123

Gangestad, S., & Snyder, M. (1985). To carve nature at its joints: On the existence of discrete classes in personality. *Psychological Review, 92*(3), 317–348. doi:10.1037/0033-295X.92.3.317

Gangestad, S. W., & Snyder, M. (2000). Self-monitoring: Appraisal and reappraisal. *Psychological Bulletin, 126*(4), 530–555. doi:10.1037/0033-2909.126.4.530

Gardner, W. L., & Avolio, B. J. (1998). The charismatic relationship: A dramaturgical perspective. *Academy of Management Review, 23*(1), 32–58.

Goffman, E. (1955). On face-work: An analysis of ritual elements in social interaction. *Psychiatry, 18*, 213–231.

Goffman, E. (1959). *The presentation of self in everyday life*. Garden City, NY: Doubleday-Anchor.

Goffman, E. (1963). *Stigma: Notes on the management of spoiled identity*. Englewood Cliffs, NJ: Prentice-Hall.

Goffman, E. (1967). *Interaction ritual: Essays on face-to-face behavior*. Garden City, NY: Doubleday-Anchor.

Gordon, C., & Gergen, K. J. (1968). *The self in social interaction*. New York, NY: Wiley.

Grandey, A. A. (2003). When 'the show must go on': Surface acting and deep acting as determinants of emotional exhaustion and peer-rated service delivery. *Academy of Management Journal, 46*(1), 86–96. doi:10.2307/30040678

Graziano, W. G., & Bryant, W. H. M. (1998). Self-monitoring and the self-attribution of positive emotions. *Journal of Personality and Social Psychology, 74*(1), 250–261. doi:10.1037/0022-3514.74.1.250

Gudykunst, W. B., Gao, G., Schmidt, K. L., Nishida, T., Bond, M. H., & Leung, K. (1992). The influence of individualism collectivism, self–monitoring and predicted-outcome value on communication in in-group and out-group relationships. *Journal of Cross-Cultural Psychology, 23*(2), 196–213. doi:10.1177/0022022192232005

James, W. (1890). *The principles of psychology*. New York, NY: Holt. doi:10.1037/11059-000

Jawahar, I. M. (2001). Attitudes, self-monitoring, and appraisal behavior. *The Journal of Applied Psychology, 86*(5), 875–883. doi:10.1037/0021-9010.86.5.875

Jenkins, J. M. (1993). Self-monitoring and turnover: The impact of personality on intent to leave. *Journal of Organizational Behavior, 14*(1), 83–91. doi:10.1002/job.4030140108

Kassarjian, W. M. (1962). A study of Riesman's theory of social character. *Sociometry, 25*(3), 213–230. doi:10.2307/2786125

Kilduff, M., & Day, D. V. (1994). Do chameleons get ahead? The effect of self-monitoring on managerial careers. *Academy of Management Journal, 37*(4), 1047–1060. doi:10.2307/256612

Kuder, G. F., & Richardson, M. W. (1937). The theory of estimation of test reliability. *Psychometrika, 2*(3), 151–160. doi:10.1007/BF02288391

Lammers, B. (1991). Moderating influence of self-monitoring and gender on responses to humorous advertising. *The Journal of Social Psychology, 131*(1), 57–69. doi:10.1080/00224545.1991.9713824

Lennox, R., & Wolfe, R. (1984). Revision of the self-monitoring scale. *Journal of Personality and Social Psychology, 46*(6), 1349–1364. doi:10.1037/0022-3514.46.6.1349

Lippa, R. (1976). Expressive control and the leakage of dispositional introversion-extraversion during role-played teaching. *Journal of Personality, 44*(4), 541–559. doi:10.1111/j.1467-6494.1976.tb00137.x

Miller, M. L., & Thayer, J. F. (1989). On the existence of discrete classes in personality: Is self-monitoring the correct joint to carve? *Journal of Personality and Social Psychology, 57*(1), 143–155. doi:10.1037/0022-3514.57.1.143

Montagliani, A., & Giacalone, R. A. (1998). Impression management and cross-cultural adaptation. *The Journal of Social Psychology, 138*(5), 598–608. doi:10.1080/00224549809600415

Oh, H., & Kilduff, M. (2008). The ripple effect of personality on social structure: Self-monitoring origins of network brokerage. *The Journal of Applied Psychology, 93*(5), 1155–1164. doi:10.1037/0021-9010.93.5.1155

Oner, B. (2002). Self-monitoring and future time orientation in romantic relationships. *The Journal of Psychology, 136*(4), 420–424. doi:10.1080/00223980209604168

Premeaux, S. F., & Bedeian, A. G. (2003). Breaking the silence: The moderating effect of self-monitoring in predicting speaking up in the workplace. *Journal of Management Studies, 40*(6), 1537–1562. doi:10.1111/1467-6486.00390

Rafaeli, A., & Sutton, R. I. (1989). The expression of emotion in organizational life. *Research in Organizational Behavior, 11*, 1–42.

Rajamanickam, M. (2001). *Statistical methods in psychological and educational research.* New Delhi, India: Concept Publishers.

Reeves, M. E. (2010). *Women in business: Theory, case studies, and legal challenges.* New York, NY: Routledge.

Rehm, L. P., & Rokke, P. D. (1988). Self-management therapies. In Dobson, K. S. (Ed.), *Handbook of cognitive-behavioral therapies* (pp. 136–166). New York, NY: Guilford Press.

Reid, R. C., & Lienemann, T. O. (2006). *Strategy instruction for students with learning disabilities.* New York, NY: Guilford Press.

Ring, K., & Wallston, K. (1968). A test to measure performance styles in interpersonal relations. *Psychological Reports, 22*(1), 147–154. doi:10.2466/pr0.1968.22.1.147

Snyder, M. (1974). Self-monitoring of expressive behavior. *Journal of Personality and Social Psychology, 30*(4), 526–537. doi:10.1037/h0037039

Snyder, M. (1979). Self-monitoring processes. In Berkowitz, L. (Ed.), *Advances in experimental social psychology* (*Vol. 12*, pp. 86–128). New York, NY: Academic Press.

Snyder, M. (1987). *Public appearances, private realities: The psychology of self-monitoring.* New York, NY: W.H. Freeman.

Snyder, M., & Cantor, N. (1980). Thinking about ourselves and others: Self-monitoring and social knowledge. *Journal of Personality and Social Psychology, 39*(2), 222–234. doi:10.1037/0022-3514.39.2.222

Snyder, M., & Copeland, J. (1989). Self-monitoring processes in organizational settings. In Giacalone, R. A., & Rosenfeld, R. (Eds.), *Impression management in the organization* (pp. 7–19). Hillsdale, NJ: Lawrence Erlbaum.

Snyder, M., & Gangestad, S. (1986). On the nature of self-monitoring: Matters of assessment, matters of validity. *Journal of Personality and Social Psychology, 51*(1), 125–139. doi:10.1037/0022-3514.51.1.125

Snyder, M. J., & Gangestad, S. (1982). Choosing social situations: Two investigations of self-monitoring processes. *Journal of Personality and Social Psychology, 43*(1), 123–135. doi:10.1037/0022-3514.43.1.123

Sosik, J. J., & Dinger, S. L. (2007). Relationships between leadership style and vision content: The moderating role of need for social approval, self-monitoring, and need for social power. *The Leadership Quarterly, 18*(2), 134–153. doi:10.1016/j.leaqua.2007.01.004

Sosik, J. J., & Jung, D. I. (2010). *Full range leadership development: Pathways for people, profit, and planet.* New York, NY: Psychology Press.

Tetlock, P. E., & Manstead, A. S. R. (1985). Impression management versus intrapsychic explanations in social psychology: A useful dichotomy? *Psychological Review, 92*(1), 59–77. doi:10.1037/0033-295X.92.1.59

Turnley, W. H., & Bolino, M. C. (2001). Achieving desired images while avoiding undesired images: Exploring the role of self-monitoring on impression management. *The Journal of Applied Psychology, 86*(2), 351–360. doi:10.1037/0021-9010.86.2.351

Zaccaro, S. J., Foti, R. J., & Kenny, D. A. (1991). Self-monitoring and trait-based variance in leadership: An investigation of leader flexibility across multiple group situations. *The Journal of Applied Psychology, 76*(2), 308–315. doi:10.1037/0021-9010.76.2.308

Zweigenhaft, R., & Cody, M. L. (1993). The self-monitoring of black students on a predominantly white campus. *The Journal of Social Psychology, 133*(1), 5–10. doi:10.1080/00224545.1993.9712113

ADDITIONAL READING

Anderson, L. R. (1987). Self-monitoring and performance in non-traditional occupations. *Basic and Applied Social Psychology, 8*(1/2), 85–96.

Anderson, N., Silvester, J., Cunningham–Snell, N., & Haddleton, E. (1999). Relationships between candidate self-monitoring, perceived personality, and selection interview outcomes. *Human Relations, 52*(9), 1115–1131. doi:10.1177/001872679905200901

Chen, C. M., & Chartrand, T. L. (2003). Self-monitoring without awareness: Using mimicry as a nonconscious affiliation strategy. *Journal of Personality and Social Psychology, 85*(6), 1170–1179. doi:10.1037/0022-3514.85.6.1170

Dabbs, J. M., Evans, M. S., Hopper, C. H., & Purvis, J. A. (1980). Self-monitors in conversation: What do they monitor? *Journal of Personality and Social Psychology, 39*(2), 278–284. doi:10.1037/0022-3514.39.2.278

Douglas, C., & Gardner, W. L. (2004). Transition to self-directed work teams: Implications of transition time and self-monitoring for managers' use of influence tactics. *Journal of Organizational Behavior, 25*(1), 47–65. doi:10.1002/job.244

Furnham, A., & Capon, M. (1983). Social skills and self-monitoring processes. *Personality and Individual Differences, 4*(2), 171–178. doi:10.1016/0191-8869(83)90017-X

Gabrenya, W. K., & Arkin, R. M. (1980). Self-monitoring scale: Factor structure and correlates. *Personality and Social Psychology Bulletin, 6*(1), 13–22. doi:10.1177/014616728061002

Garland, H., & Beard, J. F. (1979). The relationship between self-monitoring and leader emergence across two-task situations. *The Journal of Applied Psychology, 64*(1), 72–76. doi:10.1037/h0078045

Goodwin, R., & Soon, A. (1994). Self-monitoring and relationship adjustment: A cross-cultural analysis. *The Journal of Social Psychology, 134*(1), 35–39. doi:10.1080/00224545.1994.9710880

Gudykunst, W. B., Yang, S., & Nishida, T. (1987). Cultural differences in self-consciousness and self-monitoring. *Communication Research, 14*(1), 7–34. doi:10.1177/009365087014001002

Hogg, M. K., Cox, A. J., & Keeling, K. (2000). The impact of self-monitoring on image congruence and product/brand evaluation. *European Journal of Marketing, 34*(5/6), 641–667. doi:10.1108/03090560010321974

Hoyle, R. H., & Lennox, R. D. (1991). Latent structure of self-monitoring. *Multivariate Behavioral Research, 26*(3), 511–540. doi:10.1207/s15327906mbr2603_8

John, O. P., Cheek, J. M., & Klohnen, E. C. (1996). On the nature of self-monitoring: Construct explication with Q-sort ratings. *Journal of Personality and Social Psychology, 71*(4), 763–776. doi:10.1037/0022-3514.71.4.763

Krosnick, J. A., & Sedikides, C. (1990). Self-monitoring and self-protective biases in the use of consensus information to predict one's own behavior. *Journal of Personality and Social Psychology, 58*(4), 718–728. doi:10.1037/0022-3514.58.4.718

Lennox, R. (1988). The problem with self-monitoring: A two-sided scale and a one-sided theory. *Journal of Personality Assessment, 52*(1), 58–73. doi:10.1207/s15327752jpa5201_5

Miell, D., & Le Voi, M. (1985). Self-monitoring and control in dyadic interactions. *Journal of Personality and Social Psychology, 49*(6), 1652–1661. doi:10.1037/0022-3514.49.6.1652

Mill, J. (2006). High and low self-monitoring individuals: Their decoding skills and empathic expression. *Journal of Personality, 52*(4), 372–388. doi:10.1111/j.1467-6494.1984.tb00358.x

Miller, J. S., & Cardy, R. L. (2000). Self-monitoring and performance appraisals: Rating outcomes in project teams. *Journal of Organizational Behavior, 21*(6), 609–626. doi:10.1002/1099-1379(200009)21:6<609::AID-JOB42>3.0.CO;2-K

Norris, S. L., & Zweigenhaft, R. L. (1999). Self-monitoring, trust, and commitment in romantic relationships. *The Journal of Social Psychology, 139*(2), 215–220. doi:10.1080/00224549909598375

Nowack, W., & Kammer, D. (1987). Self-presentation: Social skills and inconsistency as independent facets of self-monitoring. *European Journal of Personality, 1*(2), 61–77. doi:10.1002/per.2410010202

Riggio, R. E., & Friedman, H. S. (1982). The interrelationships of self-monitoring factors, personality traits, and nonverbal social skills. *Journal of Nonverbal Behavior*, 7(1), 33–45. doi:10.1007/BF01001776

Rotenberg, K. J., Hewlett, M. G., & Siegwart, C. M. (1998). Principled moral reasoning and self-monitoring as predictors of jury functioning. *Basic and Applied Social Psychology*, 20(2), 167–173. doi:10.1207/s15324834basp2002_8

Schlenker, B. R., & Wowra, S. A. (2003). Carryover effects of feeling socially transparent or impenetrable on strategic self-presentation. *Journal of Personality and Social Psychology*, 85(5), 871–880. doi:10.1037/0022-3514.85.5.871

Slama, M. E., & Singley, R. B. (1996). Self-monitoring and value expressive vs. utilitarian ad effectiveness: Why the mixed findings? *Journal of Current Issues and Research in Advertising*, 18(2), 39–52. doi:10.1080/10641734.1996.10505050

Snyder, M., Gangestad, S., & Simpson, J. A. (1983). Choosing friends as activity partners: The role of self-monitoring. *Journal of Personality and Social Psychology*, 45(5), 1061–1072. doi:10.1037/0022-3514.45.5.1061

Tobey, E. L., & Tunnell, G. (1981). Predicting our impressions on others: Effects of public self-consciousness and acting, a self-monitoring subscale. *Personality and Social Psychology Bulletin*, 7(4), 661–669. doi:10.1177/014616728174024

Wayne, S. J., & Liden, R. C. (1995). Effects of impression management on performance ratings. A longitudinal study. *Academy of Management Journal*, 38(1), 232–260. doi:10.2307/256734

KEY TERMS AND DEFINITIONS

High Self-Monitors: High self-monitors are people who are sensitive and responsive to social expectations. They strive to meet social expectations and use cues from social interactions to guide behavior.

Impression Management: The behavioral tactics that people use in order to influence the way other people evaluate them. People use impression management tactics to influence the evaluative thinking of others so as to be viewed as socially desirable.

Low Self-Monitors: People who allow their personal attitudes and beliefs to guide and influence their behavior more so than cues from social interactions.

Machiavellianism: Manipulating others in order to achieve some end that benefits self.

Other-Directedness: People who are other-directed are willing to change their behavior in order to suit another person.

Self-Monitoring: Out of concern for social appropriateness, a person is sensitive to others in social situations and uses these cues as guidelines for monitoring his or her own self-presentation.

Self-Presentation: The way people present and express themselves in social interactions.

Chapter 8
On Measurement Instruments for Fatalism

Lijiang Shen
University of Georgia, USA

Celeste M. Condit
University of Georgia, USA

ABSTRACT

In this chapter, fatalism is conceptualized as a set of health beliefs that encompass the dimensions of predetermination, luck, and pessimism. It is argued that such fatalistic beliefs can be extended from health issues to organizational context as well. A recently developed fatalism scale is assessed, as well as other existing instruments using three criteria: (a) item content, (b) associations among the items, and (c) associations between the items and external variables. Available empirical evidence shows that the new scale is uni-dimensional, and demonstrates good construct validity as well as scale reliability. Implications for procrastination are discussed.

INTRODUCTION

Recent research has shown an increasing interest in the role of fatalism in health and other type of behaviors, both as an independent and dependent variable (Powe & Finnie, 2003). This interest has been generated by the fact that fatalistic attitudes are correlated with lower intentions to change behavior and with a variety of negative outcomes (Powe & Finnie, 2003). The interest is heightened by the identification of disproportionate fatalism among low income and minority populations who are impacted negatively by health disparities. In a broader sense, fatalism can also occur within organization settings, where individuals are not motivated to make any effort to obtain personal growth, or other desirable outcomes, due to such beliefs. Thus, reducing or eliminating one's fatalistic beliefs might help increase level of efficacy, motivation, and likelihood of behavior (change)

DOI: 10.4018/978-1-4666-2172-5.ch008

in various settings. But, before fatalism can be further studied and utilized, a valid and reliable means of measuring the construct is needed.

The goal of this chapter is to assess existing measurement instruments to measure the construct of fatalism and explore its utility in organizational settings. First, existing measurement instruments for fatalism will be reviewed and evaluated. Second, a recently developed scale will be introduced and empirical evidence for its validity and reliability presented. The new scale will also be compared vis-a-vis an existing scale. Implications for communication in organizational settings, on fatalism and procrastination in particular, will be discussed.

Conceptualization of Fatalism

The overwhelming majority of research on fatalism has been in health contexts. Fatalism has been defined in a range of ways from passively denying personal control (Neff & Hoppe, 1993) to the belief that death is inevitable when a serious disease (i.e., cancer) is present (Powe, Daniels, & Finnie, 2005). In existing literature, the nature of fatalism encompasses one, or some combination of the following dimensions: (a) the individual's perceived lack of (internal) control over external events in his or her life (e.g., Chavez, Hubbell, Mishra, & Valdez, 1997; Davison, Fankel, & Smith, 1992; Kohn & Schooler, 1983; Neff & Hoppe, 1993; Straughan & Seow, 1998; Wade, 1996), (b) notions of fate, luck, destiny and predestination of negative outcomes such as a disease or health condition (e.g. Cohen & Nisbett, 1998; Davison et al., 1992; Straughan & Seow, 1998; Vetter, Lewis, & Charny, 1991), and (c) perceptions of powerlessness, hopelessness, and meaninglessness due to expectations of negative consequences(e.g., Scheier & Bridges, 1995; Powe & Johnson, 1995). Despite the differences, these scholars tend to agree that fatalism is cognitive in nature. Also, this body of literature as a whole suggests that fatalism can be conceptualized as a set of beliefs that encompasses such dimensions as predestination, pessimism, and attribution of one's life events (health) to luck.

According to Miller and Nicholson (1976), from the content validity perspective, good operationalization should satisfy the following criteria: (a) It should tap or encompass as much of the richness of the conceptual definition as possible; (b) It should allow for standardization of terms through concreteness, i.e., it should say exactly what is observed; (c) It should be replicable; and (d) It should match the concept to a good numerical scale. In addition to content validity, assessment of measurement instruments should be based on internal consistency and external consistency (Hunter & Gerbing, 1982). Existing measurement instruments for fatalism will be assessed according to these criteria.

Evaluation of Existing Measurement Instruments

Quite a few scholars have developed scales to measure fatalism (e.g., Cohen & Nisbett, 1998; Cuellar, Arnold, & Gonzalez, 1995; Egede & Bonadonna, 2003; Kalichman, Kelly, Morgan, & Rompa, 1997; Neff & Hope, 1993; Straughan & Seow, 1998; Wade, 1996). A review of the existing fatalism scales is available in Powe and Finne (2003). The most widely used measurement instrument has been the 15-item Powe Fatalism Inventory (PFI, Powe, 1995). In most of the studies where the Powe Inventory was not applied, fatalism was not investigated as the key construct. The majority of the scales used in these studies capture one single dimension in the construct of fatalism, and to our knowledge, none of them has undergone a systematic development through rigid content assessment and psychometric development. In contrast, the PFI captures multiple dimensions and demonstrated good reliabilities. Recently, Shen, Condit and Wright (2009) developed and validated a 20-item new scale for fatalism, which contains with sub-dimensions: predetermination, luck and pessimism. The scale assessment and comparison will mainly focus on the Powe Inventory and the Shen et al. scale.

Content Validity

The Powe Inventory. Powe originally conceptualized and operationalized the PFI among African American samples based on four philosophical components: fear, predetermination, pessimism, and inevitable death (Powe, 1995). Such a conceptualization is considered as problematic in several ways. First, the meaning of fatalism might be unstable when it comes to other cultures. As Powe and Finnie (2003) noted, when working with other groups, especially of Chinese heritage, the PFI produced slightly different implications. Second, the four components of fatalism do not seem to reflect the construct well. As a set of beliefs, fatalism is cognitive in nature; hence, fear should not be a sub-dimension. Cognition and affect are distinct constructs, although there is evidence that the two are intertwined (Phelps, 2006) and controversy exists over the primacy of the two (see Lazarus, 1999). It is more appropriate to conceptualize fear as an immediate consequence of fatalism. The other three components also seem to overlap with each other (e.g., inevitable death and pessimism, inevitable death and predetermination), and might not be mutually exclusive. Additionally, other scholars have suggested the dimension of luck in fatalism (e.g., Cohen & Nisbett, 1998; Davison et al., 1992; Straughan & Seow, 1998; Vetter et al., 1991); however, it is not captured by the PFI.

A final content constraint of the PFI is that it is cancer-specific. The PFI was developed solely with regard to cancer, and the scale requires researchers to specific a single, specific disease (e.g., bowel cancer). The focus on death in the scale may be appropriate to cancer, but other diseases may have a wider range of potential outcomes of issue (e.g., disability). Recent efforts at bundling disease messages and the overlap between the causes of many common diseases and particular health behaviors related to them also make non-disease specific scales desirable for some applications (e.g., excessive caloric consumption contributes to both diabetes and heart disease risk). Although the PFI can be extended to other types of cancers by slightly revising the wording in the items, it encounters considerable difficulties to be extended to broader, non-cancer related contexts.

The Shen et al. Scale

The recently developed Shen et al. (2009) scale is no longer cancer specific and consists of three sub-dimensions of predetermination, luck, and pessimism. However, it is still confined to health conditions. We argue that the concept of fatalism can be extended to other contexts, including organizational settings as well. Particularly, it might be used to explain and predict the phenomenon of procrastination. The exact wording of the items in the scale; however, needs to be adjusted accordingly. Compared to PFI, the new scale encompasses the richness of the fatalism construct to a larger degree, and is more replicable across different contexts given its advantage regarding content validity.

Uni-Dimensionality

For a multi-item scale to be used as the measurement instrument for a single construct it must demonstrate the psychometric property of uni-dimensionality, that is, the multiple items are measuring the same latent construct. Uni-dimensionality is usually established via factor analysis, which can be exploratory or confirmatory. Exploratory factor analysis (EFA) could be described as orderly simplification of interrelated measurement items. EFA traditionally has been used to explore the possible underlying factor structure of a set of observed variables without imposing a preconceived structure on the outcome (Fabrigar, Wegener, MacCallum, & Strahan,

1999). By performing EFA, the underlying factor structure is identified. Confirmatory factor analysis (CFA) is a statistical technique used to verify the factor structure of a set of observed variables. CFA allows the researcher to test the hypothesis that a relationship between observed variables and their underlying latent constructs exists (see Thompson, 2004 for detailed discussion and a comparison between EFA and CFA).

Uni-dimensionality can be established on the first order if the multiple items in the scale are loaded on a single factor, demonstrating a simple structure, that is, their loadings on the factor are equal or similar. Except for the differences discussed in the preceding paragraph, both EFA and CFA can be used to establish uni-dimensionality on the first order. Uni-dimensionality can also be established on the second order when there exist more than one dimension on the first order. Only CFA is appropriate in such cases. Evidence for the uni-dimensionality should come from: (a) a first order oblique factor model should fit to the data and the correlations among the three factors should be similar (i.e., a simple factor structure), and (b) statistical equivalence has to be established between the first order multi-factor model and a second order single-factor model.

In addition, the scale should also demonstrate internal consistency (Hunter & Gerbing, 1982). Internal consistency refers to the degree to which each item in a scale relates independently to the rest of the items and how they are related overall. Equal or similar factor loadings for each item on the latent factor demonstrate internal consistency. Substantial differences among the factor loadings indicate otherwise.

The Powe Inventory

The criterion regarding associations among the items of the scale requires that the scale should demonstrate a simple factor structure. Powe (1997) reported unpublished factor analyses findings and claimed that the 15 items of PFI loaded on a single factor, except that two of them had low loadings. Powe did not provide much detail about her factor analysis. However, we suspect that the single factor could be the artifact of three of the four dimensions (i.e., inevitable death, pessimism, and predetermination) overlapping with each other and that the two items with low factor loadings were the fear dimension. Without further information, it was also impossible to assess if factor loadings demonstrated a simple structure.

In addition, obviously what Powe reported was from exploratory factor analyses. Although exploratory analysis is appropriate when there are no prior hypotheses concerning factor structure, the confirmatory approach provides a more meaningful test by requiring the researcher to specify the number of factors according to theoretical and substantive knowledge, then to constrain some of the factor loadings to zero (Bollen, 1989; DeVellis, 1991). Good reliabilities (e.g., Mayo, Ureda, & Parker, 2001; Powe, 1995, 1997, 2001; Powe & Weinrich, 1999) provided little support for the uni-dimensionality claim. Finally, the claim of first-order uni-dimensionality obviously contradicted her four components of fatalism, which suggest that the construct has four (first order) factors. The review of the existing literature on the PFI shows that the uni-dimensionality of the scale has not been established either on the first order, or on the second order.

The Shen et al. scale. Shen et al. (200) validated the new scale with a nationally representative sample in the United States (N=1145). The scale was submitted to confirmatory factor analyses. Because a factor model with three indicators is just-identified (i.e., d.f.=0), the second order single-factor model would have the same degrees of freedom and the exact model fit indices as the first order oblique three-factor model. To test the statistical equivalence of the two, three instrumental variables, namely genetic determinism, perceived benefits from lifestyle change, and intention to engage in healthy behaviors, were introduced such that the two models would differ in degrees of freedom. All three external variables were entered in the structural equation models together with the 20 fatalism items. The three instrumental variables gave six degrees of freedom between the first order three-factor model and the second-order single factor model.

The following fit indices were used to assess and compare model fit: (a) the Goodness of Fit Index (GFI) produces values ranging from 0 to 1 with values in excess of .90 indicating good fit; (b) the Comparative Fit Index (CFI) produces values ranging from 0 to 1 with values larger than .90 indicating good fit (Bentler, 1990; Hu & Bentler, 1999); (c) Browne and Cudeck (1993) contend that values of the Root Mean Square Error of Approximation (RMSEA) of .08 or lower indicate reasonable fit, though values of .06 or below should be preferred; and (d) the Bayesian Information Criterion (BIC) is constructed such that negative values provide evidence of model fit, while positive BIC values suggest problematic model fit. Differences in BIC of 2 are thought to provide some evidence favoring one model over another; 6 or more, strong evidence; and 10 or more, very strong evidence for the superiority of one model over another (Raftery, 1995).

The model fit indices were: For first order single factor model: chi square=3268.94, d.f.=227, RMSEA=.14, CFI=.85, GFI=.85, BIC=1670.14; for first order oblique three factor model: chi square=1064.68, d.f.=.218, RMSEA=.06, CFI=.96, GIF=.92, BIC=-470.73; for the second order single factor model: chi square=.1084.95, d.f.=224, RMSEA=.06, CFI=.96, GFI=.91, BIC=-492.72. The values for RMSEA, GFI, and CFI were the same for the second order single-factor model as the first order three-factor model. More importantly, the BIC difference was 21.99 and in favor of the second order uni-dimensional model. Although all fit indices have both proponents and detractors (cf. Bollen, 1989; Mulaik, et al., 1989), multiple fit indices combined give a clearer picture in model fit assessment and comparison. These

results from confirmatory factor analyses showed that (a) the 20-item scale was not uni-dimensional on the first order, (b) the first order three-factor model fits the data well, more importantly (c) a second order single-factor model also fits the data well with fit indices almost identical to those from the first order three-factor model. These results provided evidence that the second order single-factor model is adequate for the fatalism scale, and can be considered as statistically equivalent to the first order three-factor model. In other words, the (second order) uni-dimensionality of the scale was established.

Construct Validity

Construct validity of a measurement instrument refers to if a scale measures or correlates with another construct that is theorized. Construct validity is related to the theoretical ideas behind the construct under consideration. There are two types of construct validity. Convergent validity is the degree to which measures of constructs that theoretically should be related to each other are, in fact, observed to be related to each other (that is, you should be able to show a correspondence or convergence between similar constructs). Significant correlations as predicted between the scale and external constructs would be evidence of a convergent validity. In other words, convergent validity shows that the assessment is related to what expected theoretical relationships. Discriminant validity describes the degree measures of constructs that theoretically should not be related to each other are, in fact, observed to not be related to each other (that is, you should be able to discriminate between dissimilar constructs). Non-significant or near zero correlations between the scale and external variables as predicted demonstrates discriminant validity. A successful evaluation of discriminant validity also shows that a test of a concept is not highly correlated with other tests designed to measure theoretically different concepts. Campbell and Fiske (1959) stressed the importance of using both discriminant and convergent validity in assessing measurement instruments.

Criterion validity can also be used to assess measurement instruments. Criterion validity is the extent to which the measures are related to concrete criteria in the "real" world. There are also two types of criterion validity. Concurrent validity demonstrates relationship between the scale and an external variable that are assessed simultaneously. Predictive validity refers to the degree to which any measure can predict future concrete events.

In a word, the validity of a measurement instrument should be assessed in a nomological network, that is, within a system of theoretically related constructs, rather than with single constructs. Regarding construct and criterion validity, the scale should also demonstrate external consistency (Hunter & Gerbing, 1982). External consistency, also called parallelism, refers to the degree to which each item, or each first order factor, in a scale correlated with variables outside of the cluster. The general statement of parallelism is that items in a uni-dimensional scale should have similar patterns of correlations with items in other clusters, or other traits.

The Powe Inventory

Although there is evidence that the PFI is correlated with external variables such as demographics (e.g., Powe, 2001), spirituality (e.g., Powe, 1997) and screening behavior (e.g., Mayo et al., 2001; Powe, 1995), they provide little support for the scale's construct or criterion validity for the following three reasons: (a) The scale's uni-dimensionality has yet to be established in these studies. These correlations are suspect at the best; (b) selection of the external variables did not tend to be theory-based, and (c) in most cases, only single variables were used in each study. The validity of the scale has not been assessed in a nomological network.

The Shen et al. Scale

Three external variables, genetic determinism, perceived benefits of life style change, and intention to engage in healthy behaviors, were used to assess the construct validity of the Shen et al. (2009) scale. Genetic determinism is the belief that genes determine physical and behavioral phenotypes. It is usually taken to mean that the genes one was born with completely determine one's life events (including health) (Parrott, Silk, Weiner, Condit, Harris, & Bernhardt, 2004; Peters, 2002). Some argue that genetic determinism could be a cause of fatalism (e.g., Alper & Beckwith, 1993; Emery, 2001; Senior, Marteau, & Peters, 1998). Hence, it is predicted that fatalism is positively associated with genetic determinism. Perceived benefits of life style change refer to the subjective utility of the action recommended. In other words, it refers to how desirable a lifestyle change is for an individual. Researchers have argued that such subjective utility is a positive function of expectancy (likelihood of happening) and value, but a negative function of delay (in materialization of the outcome) (Steel & Konig, 2006). Intention to engage in healthy behavior refers to the degree to which the individual plans to enact certain behaviors that are beneficial to their health. More fatalistic individuals tend to be pessimistic about benefits of lifestyle change, and less likely to adopt health behaviors such as health lifestyles (e.g., Niederdeppe & Levy, 2007; Straughton & Seow, 1998). Therefore, it is predicted that fatalism is negatively associated with estimated benefits of lifestyle change and intention to engage in healthy behaviors.

Results showed that the three first order factors (predetermination, luck, and pessimism) had significant associations with genetic determinism, with similar magnitude (ranging from .17 to .19). There was a similar pattern regarding perceived benefits of lifestyle change (ranging from -.12 to -.19). The evidence for construct validity was mixed regarding the third external variable, intention to engage in healthy behaviors. The association between the first order factors and behavioral intention were positive and similar, but the direction was opposite to what was predicted. Overall, examination of the relationship between the scale and a nomological network of three external variables revealed that there was evidence for the construct validity and external consistency of the Shen et al. (2009) scale.

Scale Reliability

The Powe Inventory

Powe and her colleges reported good reliabilities for the PFI (alpha reliabilities above .80 in multiple studies). However, these reliabilities are suspect due to the lack of evidence for the scale's uni-dimensionality. If the scale is multi-dimensional, then it is more appropriate and meaningful to use the sub-dimensions, instead of the entire scale as a whole.

The Shen et al. Scale

Shen et al. (2009) also reported good reliabilities for the new scale. Among the three first order factors, the alpha reliabilities was .86 for predetermination, .80 for luck, and .82 for pessimism. The reliability for the whole scale was .88. Alpha if item deleted fell around .88 for each of the 20 items. These results provided evidence that the 20-items fatalism scale was reliable.

Summary

Following the criteria recommended by Miller and Nicholson (1976) and Hunter & Gerbing (1982), the Powe Fatalism Inventory and the Shen et al. (2009) scale were compared regarding content validity, uni-dimensionality, internal and external consistency. Results showed that the Shen et al. scale is superior, particularly regarding evidence for uni-dimensionality, internal and external con-

sistency. It should be noted that only convergent validity of the scale was assessed in Shen et al. (2009). Better evidence for the construct validity of the scale should come from future studies that assess both convergent and discriminant validity with more variables in a nomological network. Its advantage in content validity, however, is subject to public scrutiny of the research community.

FATALISM IN ORGANIZATION SETTING

The conceptual meaning in fatalism ranges from (a) perceived lack of (internal) control over external events in his or her life, (b) attribution one's outcomes to fate, luck, destiny and other types of predetermination, and (c) perceptions powerlessness, hopelessness, and meaninglessness due to expectations of negative consequences. Given such an explication, the application of the construct should be well beyond cancer and health domain, and can be extended to other contexts including organizational settings. In particular, fatalism might be a cause of procrastination, or individuals' justification for their procrastination.

Procrastination

Procrastination is a quintessential self-regulatory failure (Steel, 2007) and can be defined as voluntary and irrational delay of behavior, including beginning or completing an intended course of action despite the fact that the individual have the knowledge that they will be worse off for such delays (Akerlof, 1991; Beswick & Mann, 1994; Lay & Silverman, 1996; Milgram, 1991). There is evidence that procrastination is extremely prevalent among college students (e.g., Day, Mensink, & O'Sullivan, 2000; Onwuegbuzie, 2000; Steel, 2007), as well as among adults (e.g., Hammer & Ferrari, 2002), and across different cultures (e.g., Klassen et al., 2010). There is also evidence that procrastination negatively impacts an individual's performance (e.g., Steel, Brothen, & Wambach, 2001) and could lead to decreased (financial and physical) well-being for the individual (e.g., Bogg & Roberts, 2004; Tice & Baumeister, 1997), as well as for the organization they work for (e.g., Gersick, 1989; Holland, 2001).

Individuals might procrastinate due to situational factors, for example, task characteristics including timing of rewards and punishments (Loewenstein, 1992; O'Donoghue & Rabin, 1999) and task aversiveness (e.g., Harris & Sutton, 1983; Milgram, Sroloff, & Rosenbaum, 1988). Procrastination can also be caused by dispositional factors such as irrational beliefs (e.g., Beck, Koons, & Milgram, 2000), low self-efficacy and low self-esteem (e.g., Bandura, 1997; Judge & Bono, 2001), and self-handicapping (e.g., Brown & Marshall, 2001). Among the dispositional factors, irrational beliefs that are associated with procrastination include beliefs that oneself is inadequate and that the world is too difficult and demanding. Low self-esteem occurs if one has a low overall evaluation or appraisal of his or her own worth. One would have low level of self-efficacy when they do not perceive themselves capable of enacting a particular behavior. Self-handicapping refers to dysfunctional self-regulation driven by a desire to protect one's self-esteem by giving oneself an external reason if one fails. A close examination of these constructs reveals that they are very similar to the conceptualization of fatalism (i.e., predestination, pessimism, and attribution of one's life events to luck).

Steel's (2007) meta-analytic study provided empirical evidence that such beliefs are indeed correlated with procrastination: The association between irrational beliefs and procrastination was $r=.17$ ($K=71$); the association between self-efficacy and procrastination was $r=-.38$ ($K=39$); that impact of self-esteem on procrastination was $r=-.27$ ($K=33$). The effect of self-handicapping on procrastination was $r=.46$ ($K=56$). It should be noted, however, that these evidence is rather

indirect for the association between fatalism and procrastination.

Fatalism, Behavioral Intention, Behavior, and Procrastination

Recall that the association between fatalism and intention to engage in healthy behavior was significant and positive in Shen et al. (2009), which was opposite to what was predicted. The method employed in this study (i.e., probability sampling and a nationally representative sample with N=1218) suggested that sampling error was an unlikely cause of this positive association. And the fact that the effects of genetic determinism and perceived benefits of lifestyle change, and that of demographic variables were partialled out indicated that this positive association was probably not spurious. The relationship between behavioral intention and fatalism and its dimensions exhibited a parallel pattern, which also indicated non-spuriousness. On the other hand, both the conceptualization of fatalism and available empirical evidence (e.g., Niederdeppe & Levy, 2007; Straughton & Seow, 1998, see also Powe & Finnie, 2003 for a review) indicate that fatalism can function as a barrier to cancer prevention and screening behaviors. Several plausible explanations for this apparent inconsistency were offered in Shen et al. (2009), which are also relevant to the possible connection between fatalism and procrastination.

Intention-Behavior Gap

The first explanation lies in a possible disconnection between actual behavior and behavioral intention. Ajzen and Fishbein (1980) suggest that the association between intention and behavior is determined by the degree of correspondence in the measurement of the two constructs, specifically; the target, action, context, and time (see also Kim & Hunter, 1993). First, our measure of behavioral intention lacked specific contexts.

Behavioral intention with a particular situation is called implementation intention and is more predictive of future behavior (Warshaw & Davis, 1985). Fatalistic individuals might have a higher intention to engage in such healthy behaviors without specific situations, but less likely to act upon their intention when they anticipate negative outcomes (e.g., the potential results of cancer screening). Second, temporal stability is one property of behavioral intention (Sheeran, 2002). The theory of reasoned action (Ajzen & Fishbein, 1980) suggests that one's intention can fluctuate over time and does not necessarily provide accurate predictions of behavior. The measure for behavior in Shen et al. (2009) refers to long-term and repeated commitments, while behavior measures in the literature (e.g., Niederdeppe & Levy, 2007; Powe & Finnie, 2003; Straughton & Seow, 1998) tend to be short-term and require one-time commitment only. Therefore, the measurement correspondence between intention and behavior was rather low, which might have been the cause of the inconsistent findings.

According to Steel and Konig (2006), procrastination is a negative function of perceived utility of the action, which further is a negative function of delay in positive outcome. This leads to the conclusion that procrastination is a positive function of delay in positive outcomes resulting from healthy behavior. Consider the nature of healthy behaviors recommended in public health campaigns. Their outcomes are oftentimes not so visible and delayed, which means, individuals tend to procrastinate even though they might have formed strong intentions to engage in these actions. Steel's (2007) meta-analysis offered evidence for such a possibility. His study revealed that intention and procrastination are basically independent of each other (r=-.03, K=8). It seems that procrastinators' efforts to enact the desired behaviors tend to fall short, not that they do not have the intention to do so.

Efficacy

The second explanation takes the perspective of efficacy. Response-efficacy refers to the effectiveness of a behavior in preventing/reducing certain health risks. Self-efficacy can be defined as individuals' perceived ability to enact behaviors that might prevent/reduce health risks (Bandura, 1997; Rogers, 1983). The health belief model contends that enactment of health behaviors requires both response- and self-efficacy (Janz & Becker, 1984). Fatalistic individuals tend to be low in both: The dimension of pessimism suggests low response-efficacy and the notions of lack of control and predetermination indicate low self-efficacy. It is plausible that individuals are well aware of the right course of action and indeed intend to follow the various recommendations; however, their fatalistic beliefs lead to low levels of perceived response-efficacy, as reflected in the negative association between fatalism and perceived benefits of lifestyle change; and hence lack of behavior. In other words, low response-efficacy might be the main cause of inaction.

This offers an alternative explanation for procrastination. Procrastination has been attributed to low self-efficacy (and low self-esteem). This suggests that procrastination could occur even when self-efficacy is high, if response efficacy is low. This is particularly relevant in organization settings when individuals have the intention to engage in certain actions and they believe they can do it (i.e., self-efficacy), but the behavior never materialize due to the perception that they will not change anything (i.e., low or delayed utility).

Irrational Reasoning

The third explanation originates from irrational reasoning such as the optimistic bias (Weinstein, 1982) and egocentric thinking. Unrealistic optimism and egocentrism might lead to overestimates in likelihood of positive things and underestimate in likelihood of negative events happening to oneself, while the pattern would be reserved for others: Positive things are less likely, and negative things are more likely to happen. It is possible that individuals' fatalistic beliefs might concern others more than oneself -- they underestimate other people's control over and luck with one's health, but overestimate their own control over and luck with health and life events. The referents in the measures in Shen et al. (2009) suggested that this might be a possibility: The fatalism items concerned both unspecific members of the general public (i.e., "someone") as well as oneself. The measure of perceived benefits of lifestyle change focused on an unspecific other; and the benefit-fatalism relation was as predicted. The measure of behavioral intention referred to oneself, and the intention-fatalism association was inconsistent with the prediction.

Condit et al. (2009) suggest that there might exist a "two-track" model used by most people in accounting for health outcomes: Individuals have both a script for attributing a health outcome to genes and a script for attributing health to behavior. It is possible that individuals might use fatalism to make sense of the obvious discrepancy between the behavior track and their risky behaviors (or lack of healthy behavior). If this is the case, it means that individuals could be using such fatalistic and irrational reasoning to justify their procrastination. Fatalistic beliefs and procrastination then could form a malicious circle and both would be intensified in a spiral.

Summary

It would be premature to consider these results as challenging the empirical findings regarding negative association between fatalism and health behaviors, or as refuting the conclusion that fatalism might function as a potential inhibitor of healthy lifestyle/changes. These results do suggest, however, there might be more nuances in the construct of fatalism (i.e., fatalism about self vs. others, fatalism in general vs. fatalism

regarding a specific disease/health condition). More importantly, literature on procrastination suggests that irrational and voluntary delay of behavior might explain this discrepancy. In turn, individuals might also use fatalism to justify and make sense of their procrastinating. Fatalistic beliefs and procrastination could also mutually cause and intensify each other.

COMMENTARY

This chapter introduces the construct of fatalism, evaluates existing measurement instruments, and discusses its potential application in organization settings, regarding procrastination in particular. The most widely used PFI scale and a new scale (Shen et al., 2009) were evaluated with regard to content validity, uni-dimensionality, and construct validity (internal and external consistency). Following Miller and Nicholson's (1976) criteria, the PFI is problematic regarding content validity while the Shen et al. (2009) scale does a good job capturing the full range of meaning in fatalism with approximate degree of precision. According to Hunter and Gerbing's (1982) criteria, the PFI is also deemed problematic due to the fact that its uni-dimensionality has not been established, and that its construct validity has not been vigorously tested. On the other hand, Shen et al. (2009) reported empirical evidence for the scale's uni-dimensionality on the second order and construct validity using three external variables. The new scale also yielded good reliabilities.

The scale can also be used in a short form, instead of in its entirety. Shen, Wright, Flannery, Harris, & Condit (2009) used the short form of the fatalism scale in multiple studies, where the short form demonstrated a uni-dimensional factor structure and good reliabilities. There might be utility in adopting the short form instead of the entire scale since it offers more parsimony and could potentially reduce participant fatigue. The tradeoff is that the full version tends to have higher alpha reliability simply because there are more items in the scale, given the fact that Cronbach's alpha is a function of average inter-item correlation and number of items (Cronbach, 1951, 2004). Alpha scale reliability could lead to more statistical power, given the same effect size in the population (DeVellis, 1991). This means that less resource is required to achieve the same level of accuracy in survey research. Researchers and practitioners can choose which version of the sale to use upon their own discretion.

It is proposed that the utility of the fatalism construct and its measurement instrument can be extended to organizational settings and other non-health contexts as well. Minor revisions to the items might be necessary in such applications though. Two inherent issues with this extension are factor structure and construct validity because they do not necessarily translate to a different context or content domain, although the revision to the wording might be minor. Use of the fatalism scale in organization settings might be with caution before further validation of the scale in the new content domain and with revisions to the items.

Cost

The Powe Fatalism Inventory is available in Powe (1995) and Powe et al. (2005). The instrument is available in Shen et al. (2009). The items in each scale are also presented in the notes. The cost to revise the Shen et al. scale for the organization setting should also be minimal.

NOTES

The items for the PFI are: I think if someone is meant to have bowel cancer, it doesn't matter what kinds of food they eat, they will get bowel cancer anyway; I think if someone has bowel cancer, it is already too late to get treated for it; I think someone can eat fatty foods all their life, and if they are not meant to get bowel cancers,

they won't get it; I think if someone is meant to get bowel cancer, they will get it no matter what they do; I think if someone gets bowel cancer, it was meant to be; I think if someone gets bowel cancer, their time to die is soon; I think if someone gets bowel cancer, that's the way they were meant to die; I think getting checked for bowel cancer makes people scared that they may really have bowel cancer; I think if someone is meant to have bowel cancer, they will have bowel cancer; I think some people don't want to know if they have bowel cancer because they don't want to know they may be dying from it; I think if someone gets bowel cancer, it doesn't matter whether they find it early or late, they will still die from it; I think if someone has bowel cancer and gets treatment for it, they will probably still die from the bowel cancer; I think if someone was meant to have bowel cancer, it doesn't matter what doctors and nurses tell them to do, they will get bowel cancer anyway; I think if someone is meant to have bowel cancer, it doesn't matter if they eat healthy foods, they will still get bowel cancer; I think bowel cancer will kill you no matter when it is found and how it is treated.

The items for predetermination are: If someone is meant to get a serious disease, it doesn't matter what kinds of food they eat, they will get that disease anyway; If someone is meant to get a serious disease, they will get it no matter what they do; If someone gets a serious disease, that's the way they were meant to die; If someone is meant to have a serious disease, they will get that disease; If someone has a serious disease and gets treatment for it, they will probably still die from it; If someone was meant to have a serious disease, it doesn't matter what doctors and nurses tell them to do, they will get the disease anyway; How long I live is predetermined; I will die when I am fated to die; My health is determined by fate; My health is determined by something greater than myself. Items for luck are: I will get diseases if I am unlucky; My health is a matter of luck; How long I live is a matter of luck; I will stay healthy if I am lucky. Items for pessimism are: Everything that can go wrong for me does; I will have a lot of pain from illness; I will suffer a lot from bad health; I often feel helpless in dealing with the problems of life; Sometimes I feel that I'm being pushed around in life; There is really no way I can solve some of the problems I have.

REFERENCES

Ajzen, I., & Fishbein, M. (1980). *Understanding attitudes and predicting social behavior*. Englewood Cliffs, NJ: Prentice-Hall.

Akerlof, G. A. (1991). Procrastination and obedience. *The American Economic Review, 81*(2), 1–19.

Alper, J. S., & Beckwith, J. (1993). Genetic fatalism and social policy: The implications of behavior genetics research. *The Yale Journal of Biology and Medicine, 66,* 511–524.

Bandura, A. (1997). *Self-efficacy: The exercise of control*. New York, NY: Freeman.

Beck, B. L., Koons, S. R., & Milgram, D. L. (2000). Correlates and consequences of behavioral procrastination: The effects of academic procrastination, self-consciousness, self-esteem and self-handicapping. *Journal of Social Behavior and Personality, 15,* 3–13.

Bentler, P. M. (1990). Comparative fit indexes in structural models. *Psychological Bulletin, 107,* 238–246. doi:10.1037/0033-2909.107.2.238

Beswick, G., & Mann, L. (1994). State orientation and procrastination. In Kuhl, J., & Beckmann, J. (Eds.), *Volition and personality: Action versus state orientation* (pp. 391–396). Gottingen, Germany: Hogrefe & Huber.

Bogg, T., & Roberts, B. W. (2004). Conscientiousness and health-related behaviors: A meta-analysis of the leading behavioral contributors to mortality. *Psychological Bulletin, 130,* 887–919. doi:10.1037/0033-2909.130.6.887

Bollen, K. A. (1989). *Structural equations with latent variables*. New York, NY: Wiley.

Brown, J. D., & Marshall, M. A. (2001). Great expectations: Optimism and pessimism in achievement settings. In Chang, E. C. (Ed.), *Optimism and pessimism: Implications for theory, research, and practice* (pp. 239–255). Washington, DC: American Psychology Association. doi:10.1037/10385-011

Browne, M. W., & Cudeck, R. (1993). Alternative ways of assessing fit. In Bollen, K. A., & Long, J. S. (Eds.), *Testing structural equation models* (pp. 136–162). Newbury Park, CA: Sage.

Campbell, D. T., & Fiske, D. W. (1959). Convergent and discriminant validation by the multitrait-multimethod matrix. *Psychological Bulletin, 56,* 81–105. doi:10.1037/h0046016

Chavez, L. R., Hubbell, F. A., Mishra, S. I., & Valdez, R. B. (1997). The influence of fatalism on self-reported use of Papanicolaou smears. *American Journal of Preventive Medicine, 13,* 418–424.

Cohen, D., & Nisbett, R. (1998). Are there differences in fatalism between rural Southerners and Midwesterners? *Journal of Applied Social Psychology, 28,* 2181–2195. doi:10.1111/j.1559-1816.1998.tb01366.x

Condit, C. M., Gronnvoll, M., Landau, J., Shen, L., Wright, L., & Harris, T. (2009). *Believing in both genetic determinism and behavioral action: A materialist framework and implications*. Public Understanding of Science, iFirst.

Cronbach, L. (2004). My current thoughts on coefficient alpha and successor procedures. *Educational and Psychological Measurement, 64*(3), 391–418. doi:10.1177/0013164404266386

Cronbach, L. J. (1951). Coefficient alpha and the internal structure of tests. *Psychometrika, 16*(3), 297–334. doi:10.1007/BF02310555

Cuellar, I., Arnold, B., & Gonzalez, G. (1995). Cognitive referents of acculturation: Assessment of cultural constructs in Mexican Americans. *Journal of Community Psychology, 23,* 339–356. doi:10.1002/1520-6629(199510)23:4<339::AID-JCOP2290230406>3.0.CO;2-7

Davison, C., Frankel, S., & Smith, G. (1992). The limits of lifestyle: Re-assessing fatalism in the popular culture of illness prevention. *Social Science & Medicine, 34,* 675–685. doi:10.1016/0277-9536(92)90195-V

Day, V., Mensink, D., & O'Sullivan, M. (2000). Patterns of academic procrastination. *Journal of College Reading and Learning, 30,* 120–134.

DeVellis, R. F. (1991). *Scale development: Theory and applications.* Newbury Park, CA: Sage.

Egede, L. E., & Bonadonna, R. J. (2003). Diabetes self-management in African Americans: An exploration of the role of fatalism. *The Diabetes Educator, 29,* 105–115. doi:10.1177/014572170302900115

Emery, J. (2001). Is informed choice in genetic testing a different breed of information decision-making? A discussion paper. *Health Expectations, 4,* 81–86. doi:10.1046/j.1369-6513.2001.00124.x

Fabrigar, L. R., Wegener, D. T., MacCallum, R. C., & Strahan, E. J. (1999). Evaluating the use of exploratory factor analysis in psychological research. *Psychological Methods, 4*(3), 272–299. doi:10.1037/1082-989X.4.3.272

Gersick, C. J. G. (1989). Making time: Predictable transitions in task groups. *Academy of Management Journal, 33,* 274–309. doi:10.2307/256363

Hammer, C. A., & Ferrari, J. R. (2002). Differential incidence of procrastination between blue- and white-collar workers. *Current Psychology (New Brunswick, N.J.), 21,* 333–338. doi:10.1007/s12144-002-1022-y

Harris, N. N., & Sutton, R. I. (1983). Task procrastination in organizations: A framework for research. *Human Relations, 36,* 987–995. doi:10.1177/001872678303601102

Holland, T. (2001). The perils of procrastination. *Far Eastern Economic Review, 164,* 66-72.

Hu, L., & Bentler, P. M. (1999). Cutoff criteria for fit indexes in covariance structure analysis: Conventional criteria versus new alternatives. *Structural Equation Modeling, 6*(1), 1–55. doi:10.1080/10705519909540118

Hunter, J. E., & Gerbing, D. W. (1982). Unidimensional measurement, second order factor analysis, and causal models. In Staw, B. M., & Cummings, L. L. (Eds.), *Research in organizational behavior* (*Vol. 4*). Greenwich, CT: JAI Press.

Janz, N., & Becker, M. (1984). The health belief model: A decade later. *Health Education & Behavior, 11,* 1–47. doi:10.1177/109019818401100101

Judge, T. A., & Bono, J. E. (2001). Relationship of core self-evaluations traits self-esteem, generalized self-efficacy, locus of control, and emotional stability-with job satisfaction and job performance: A meta-analysis. *The Journal of Applied Psychology, 86,* 80–92. doi:10.1037/0021-9010.86.1.80

Kalichman, S., Kelly, J., Morgan, M., & Rompa, D. (1997). Fatalism, current life satisfaction, and risk for HIV infection among gay and bisexual men. *Journal of Consulting and Clinical Psychology, 65,* 542–546. doi:10.1037/0022-006X.65.4.542

Kim, M. S., & Hunter, J. E. (1993). Relationships among attitudes, behavioral intentions, and behavior: A meta-analysis of past research, Part 2. *Communication Research, 20,* 331–364. doi:10.1177/009365093020003001

Klassen, R. M., Ang, R. P., Chong, W. H., Krawchuk, L. L., Huan, V. S., Wong, I. Y. F., & Yeo, L. S. (2010). Academic procrastination in two settings: Motivation correlates, behavioural patterns, and negative impact of procrastination in Canada and Singapore. *Applied Psychology: An International Review, 59,* 1–19.

Kohn, M. L., & Schooler, C. (1983). *Work and personality: An inquiry into the impact of social stratification.* Norwood, NJ: Ablex Pub. Corp.

Lay, C. H., & Silverman, S. (1996). Trait procrastination, anxiety, and dilatory behavior. *Personality and Individual Differences, 21,* 61–67. doi:10.1016/0191-8869(96)00038-4

Loewenstein, G. (1992). The fall and rise of psychological explanations in the economics of intertemporal choice. In Loewenstein, G., & Elster, J. (Eds.), *Choice over time* (pp. 3–34). New York, NY: Russell Sage Foundation.

Mayo, R., Ureda, J., & Parker, V. (2001). Importance of fatalism in understanding mammography screening in rural elderly women. *Journal of Women & Aging, 13,* 57–72. doi:10.1300/J074v13n01_05

Milgram, N. A. (1991). Procrastination. In Dulbecco, R. (Ed.), *Encyclopaedia of human biology* (*Vol. 6,* pp. 149–155). New York, NY: Academic Press.

Milgram, N. A., Sroloff, B., & Rosenbaum, M. (1988). The procrastination of everyday life. *Journal of Research in Personality, 22,* 197–212. doi:10.1016/0092-6566(88)90015-3

Miller, G. R., & Nicholson, H. E. (1976). *Communication inquiry: A perspective on a process.* Reading, MA: Addison-Wesley.

Mulaik, S. A., James, L. R., Van Alstine, J., Bennett, N., Lind, S., & Stilwell, C. D. (1989). Evaluation of goodness-of-fit indices for structural equation models. *Psychological Bulletin, 105,* 430–445. doi:10.1037/0033-2909.105.3.430

Neff, J. A., & Hoppe, S. K. (1993). Race/ethnicity, acculturation, and psychological distress: Fatalism and religiosity as cultural resources. *Journal of Community Psychology, 21*(1), 3–20. doi:10.1002/1520-6629(199301)21:1<3::AID-JCOP2290210102>3.0.CO;2-9

Niederdeppe, J., & Levy, A. G. (2007). Fatalistic beliefs about cancer prevention and three preventive behaviors. *Cancer Epidemiology, Biomarkers & Prevention, 16,* 998–1003. doi:10.1158/1055-9965.EPI-06-0608

O'Donoghue, T., & Rabin, M. (1999). Incentives for procrastinators. *The Quarterly Journal of Economics, 114,* 769–816. doi:10.1162/003355399556142

Onwuegbuzie, A. J. (2000). Academic procrastinators and perfectionistic tendencies among graduate students. *Journal of Social Behavior and Personality, 15,* 103–109.

Parrott, R., Silk, K., Weiner, J., Condit, C., Harris, T., & Bernhardt, J. (2004). Deriving lay models of uncertainty about genes' role in illness causation to guide communication about human genetics. *The Journal of Communication, 54,* 105–122. doi:10.1111/j.1460-2466.2004.tb02616.x

Peters, T. (2002). *Playing God? Genetic determinism and human freedom.* New York, NY: Routledge.

Phelps, E. A. (2006). Emotion and cognition: Insights from studies of the human amygdala. *Annual Review of Psychology, 57,* 27–53. doi:10.1146/annurev.psych.56.091103.070234

Powe, B. D. (1995). Fatalism among elderly African Americans: Effects on colorectal screening. *Cancer Nursing, 18,* 385–392. doi:10.1097/00002820-199510000-00008

Powe, B. D. (1997). Cancer fatalism: Spiritual perspectives. *Journal of Religion and Health, 36,* 135–144. doi:10.1023/A:1027440520268

Powe, B. D. (2001). Cancer fatalism among elderly African American women: Predictors of the intensity of the perceptions. *Journal of Psychosocial Oncology, 19,* 85–96. doi:10.1300/J077v19n03_07

Powe, B. D., Daniels, E. C., & Finnie, R. (2005). Comparing perceptions of cancer fatalism among African American patients. *Journal of the American Academy of Nurse Practitioners, 17,* 318–324. doi:10.1111/j.1745-7599.2005.0049.x

Powe, B. D., & Finnie, R. (2003). Cancer fatalism: The state of the science. *Cancer Nursing, 26,* 454–465.

Powe, B. D., & Johnson, A. (1995). Fatalism as a barrier to cancer screening among African-Americans: Philosophical perspectives. *Journal of Religion and Health, 34*(2), 119–126. doi:10.1007/BF02248767

Powe, B. D., & Weinrich, S. (1999). An intervention to decrease cancer fatalism among rural elders. *Oncology Nursing Forum, 26,* 583–588.

Raftery, A. E. (1995). Bayesian model selection in social research. In Marsden, P. V. (Ed.), *Sociological methodology* (pp. 111–163). Cambridge, UK: Basil Blackwell.

Rogers, R. W. (1983). Cognitive and physiological processes in fear appeals and attitude change: A revised theory of protection motivation. In Cacioppo, J. T., & Petty, R. E. (Eds.), *Social psychophysiology: A source book* (pp. 153–176). New York, NY: The Guilford Press.

Scheier, M., & Bridges, M. (1995). Person variables and health: Personality predispositions and acute psychological states as shared determinants for disease. *Psychosomatic Medicine, 57,* 255–268.

Senior, V., Marteau, T., & Peters, T. J. (1998). Will genetic testing for predisposition for disease result in fatalism? A qualitative study of parents' responses to neonatal screening for familial hypercholesterolaemia. *Social Science & Medicine, 48,* 1857–1860. doi:10.1016/S0277-9536(99)00099-4

Sheeran, P. (2002). Intention-behavior relations: A conceptual and empirical review. *European Review of Social Psychology, 12,* 1–36. doi:10.1080/14792772143000003

Shen, L., Condit, C., & Wright, L. (2009). The psychometric property and validation of a fatalism scale. *Psychology & Health, 24,* 597–613. doi:10.1080/08870440801902535

Shen, L., Wright, L., Flannery, D., Harris, T., & Condit, C. (2009). *Teaching the concept of gene-environment interaction to the lay public: Challenges, rewards, and limitations.* Unpublished manuscript, The University of Georgia.

Steel, P. (2007). The nature of procrastination: A meta-analytic and theoretical review of quintessential self-regulatory failure. *Psychological Bulletin, 133,* 65–94. doi:10.1037/0033-2909.133.1.65

Steel, P., Brothen, T., & Wambach, C. (2001). Procrastination and personality, performance, and mood. *Personality and Individual Differences, 30,* 95–106. doi:10.1016/S0191-8869(00)00013-1

Steel, P., & Konig, C. J. (2006). Integrating theories of motivation. *Academy of Management Review*, *31*, 889–913. doi:10.5465/AMR.2006.22527462

Straughan, P. T., & Seow, A. (1998). Fatalism reconceptualized: A concept to predict health screening behavior. *Journal of Gender, Culture, and Health*, *3*, 85–100. doi:10.1023/A:1023278230797

Thompson, B. (2004). *Exploratory and confirmatory facto analysis: Understanding concepts and applications*. Washington, DC: Sage. doi:10.1037/10694-000

Tice, D. M., & Baumeister, R. F. (1997). Longitudinal study of procrastination, performance, stress, and health: The cost and benefits of dawdling. *Psychological Science*, *8*, 454–458. doi:10.1111/j.1467-9280.1997.tb00460.x

Vetter, N., Lewis, P., & Charny, M. (1991). Health, fatalism, and age in relation to lifestyle. *Health Visitor*, *64*, 191–194.

Wade, T. J. (1996). An examination of locus of control/fatalism for black, whites, boys, and girls over a two year period of adolescence. *Social Behavior and Personality*, *24*, 239–248. doi:10.2224/sbp.1996.24.3.239

Warshaw, P. R., & Davis, F. D. (1985). Disentangling behavioral intention and behavioral expectation. *Journal of Experimental Social Psychology*, *21*, 213–218. doi:10.1016/0022-1031(85)90017-4

Weinstein, N. D. (1982). Unrealistic optimism about susceptibility to health problems. *Journal of Behavioral Medicine*, *5*, 441–460. doi:10.1007/BF00845372

KEY TERMS AND DEFINITIONS

Confirmatory Factor Analysis (CFA): Seeks to determine if the number of factors and the loadings of measured (indicator) variables on them conform to what is expected on the basis of pre-established theory. Indicator variables are selected on the basis of prior theory and factor analysis is used to see if they load as predicted on the expected number of factors. A minimum requirement of confirmatory factor analysis is that the researcher should hypothesize beforehand the number of factors in the model, but usually also the researcher will posit expectations about which variables will load on which factors.

Construct Validity: The degree to which a measure relates to other variables as expected within a system of theoretical relationships.

Content Validity: The degree to which a scale covers the range of meaning included within a concept.

Convergent Validity: The degree to which measures of constructs that theoretically should be related to each other are, in fact, observed to be related to each other.

Discriminant Validity: The degree measures of constructs that theoretically should not be related to each other are, in fact, observed to not be related to each other.

Exploratory Factor Analysis (EFA): Seeks to uncover the underlying structure of a relatively large set of variables. The researcher's α priori assumption is that any indicator may be associated with any factor. This is the most common form of factor analysis. There is no prior theory and one uses factor loadings to intuit the factor structure of the data.

External Consistency: Also called parallelism, refers to the degree to which each item in a scale correlated with variables outside of the cluster. The general statement of parallelism is that items in a unidimensional scale should have similar patterns of correlations with items in other clusters, or other traits.

Fatalism: A set of beliefs that encompasses such dimensions as predestination, pessimism, and attribution of one's prospect/well-being to luck.

Genetic Determinism: The belief that genes determine physical and behavioral phenotypes. It is usually taken to mean that the genes one was born with completely determine one's life events (including health).

Internal Consistency: The degree to which each item in a scale relates independently to the rest of the items and how they are related overall.

Nomological Network: A system of theoretically related constructs used to assess construct validity. It include the theoretical framework for what you are trying to measure, an empirical framework for how you are going to measure it, and specification of the linkages among and between these two frameworks.

Procrastination: Refers to irrational and voluntary delay of beginning or completing an intended course of action. It is essentially a quint-essential self-regulatory failure.

Section 3
New Measurements

Chapter 9
A Cross–Cultural Measure of Servant Leadership Behaviors

Jeff R. Hale
WellSpirit Consulting Group, Inc., USA

Dail Fields
Regent University, USA

ABSTRACT

This chapter presents items comprising three scales that measure servant leadership using three key dimensions: service, humility, and vision. The instrument was used to measure servant leadership behaviors experienced by followers in the United States and Ghana. Reliability and validity evidence is included from two research studies. A discussion of the relationship of servant leadership behaviors with employee outcomes assessed in these studies concludes the chapter.

BACKGROUND: THE NATURE OF SERVANT LEADERSHIP

An examination of the variety of concepts used to describe servant leadership could suggest that what appears to be a relatively straight-forward concept is either quite complicated or lends itself to elaboration with a wide variety of terms. For example, scholars (Barbuto & Wheeler, 2006; Dennis & Bocarnea, 2005; Farling, Stone, & Winston, 1999; Hale & Fields, 2007; Liden, Wayne, Zhao & Henderson, 2005; Page & Wong, 2000; Patterson, 2003; Sendjaya, 2003) describe servant leadership with behaviors or leader characteristics including:

- Humility
- Relational power
- Service orientation
- Follower development
- Encouragement of follower autonomy
- Altruistic calling
- Emotional healing
- Persuasive mapping

DOI: 10.4018/978-1-4666-2172-5.ch009

- Wisdom
- Organizational stewardship
- Moral love (also termed agape love)
- Altruism
- Vision
- Trust
- Service (behavior)
- Follower empowerment
- Influence
- Credibility
- Voluntary subordination
- Authentic self
- Covenantal relationship with followers
- Responsible morality
- Transcendental spirituality
- Transforming influence
- Creating value for the community
- Conceptual skills,
- Helping subordinates grow and succeed
- Putting subordinates first
- Behaving ethically

Despite the vast array of terms various formulations of servant leadership have employed, three major descriptors originally employed by Greenleaf (1977) consistently are cornerstones of servant leadership. These are:

- **Service:** To followers, an organization, and society. Based on the alternative descriptions of servant leadership noted above, this dimension may include service orientation, follower development, organizational stewardship, follower empowerment, covenantal relationship, responsible morality, helping followers grow, and putting followers first.
- **Humility:** Putting the success of followers ahead of the leader's personal gain. This dimension may include relational power, altruistic calling, emotional healing, moral love, altruism, credibility, voluntary subordination, authentic self, transcendental spirituality, emotional healing, and behav-

ing ethically from the various alternative servant leadership formulations above.

- **Vision:** Having foresight combined with the ability to communicate vision to and influence followers in developing a shared vision for an organization. This dimension includes wisdom, persuasive mapping, influence, transforming influence, credibility, creating value for the community, and conceptual skills from the various alternative servant leadership formulations above.

These three cornerstone concepts guided the selections and adaptation of eighteen items from forty-three statements used by Dennis (2004). The three resulting scales described the servant leadership behaviors of service to followers, humility in interactions with followers, and involvement of followers in establishing vision. Table 1 presents the scale items. The items employ a Likert-type response ranging from 1 to 7, where 1 = strongly disagree and 7 = strongly agree.

Two studies, one of which examines its nature across culture, tested the resultant relatively parsimonious measure of servant leadership.

RELIABILITY AND VALIDITY

In this section, we discuss the reliability and validity tests performed on the three proposed dimensions of servant leadership with two studies. In the first study, Hale and Fields (2007) used the three scales in research concerning working adults who were also studying in two Christian seminaries, one located in Ghana, and the other located in the mid-Atlantic region of the United States (Hale & Fields, 2007). The sub-sample from Ghana contained 60 people, 93% of which were male, with average age of 34.5 years. The Ghanaians in our sample had average work experience of 6.5 years. Sixty-five percent of the Ghanaian sub-sample worked in churches or other religious organizations, 18% worked in schools,

Table 1. Scale items used to measure service, humility, and vision

Please answer each statement by indicating the extent to which you agree that your leader behaves in the manner described.
Service items
1. Sees serving as a mission of responsibility to others.
2. Models service to inspire others.
3. Understands that serving others is most important.
4. Understands that service is the core of leadership.
5. Aspires not to be served but to serve others.
6. Models service in his or her behaviours, attitudes, or values.
Humility items
1. Talks more about employees' accomplishments than his or her own.
2. Does not overestimate her or his merits.
3. Is not interested in self-glorification.
4. Is humble enough to consult others in the organization when he or she may not have all the answers.
5. Does not center attention on his or her own accomplishments.
6. Exhibits a demeanor of humility.
Vision items
1. Has sought my vision regarding the organization's vision.
2. Has encouraged me to participate in determining and developing a shared vision.
3. He/she and I have written a clear and concise vision statement for our organization.
4. Has asked me what I think the future direction of our organization should be.
5. Has shown that he or she wants to include employees' vision into the organization's goals and objectives.
6. Seeks my commitment concerning the shared vision of our organization.

Response scale: 1 = strongly disagree; 2 = disagree; 3 = somewhat disagree; 4 = neither; 5 = somewhat agree; 6 = agree; 7 = strongly agree

and 17% worked in other types of organizations. The sub-sample from the USA consisted of 97 persons, 55% of which were male, with average age of 39 years. Members of the American sub-sample had average work experience of 13 years. Sixty-two percent of the USA sub-sample worked in churches, 5% in schools, and 33% in other types of organizations. The sub-samples were significantly different in mean age (t = 3.75,

p < .01) and gender composition (t = 2.64, p < .05). On average members of the US sub-sample were older and more likely to be female than the members of the Ghanaian sub-sample.

The sub-scale measuring service had reliability coefficient alpha of .94 in the USA sub-sample and .92 in the Ghanaian sub-sample. The sub-scale for humility had coefficient values of .95 in the USA sub-sample and .82 in the Ghanaian sub-sample. The sub-scale for vision had coefficient alpha values of .83 in the USA sub-sample and .91 in the Ghanaian sub-sample.

Persons in Ghana completed the survey in paper and pencil form. From 70 persons contacted, we received 61 completed surveys, 60 of which were usable in this study. Subjects in the USA completed a web-based version of the survey. From 110 persons contacted, we received 97 completed surveys that were usable in this study. Recent studies (Carlbring, Brunt, Bohman, Austin, Richards, Ost, & Andersson, 2005) comparing paper and internet based versions of psychological measures indicate that as long as item sequence and format are consistent, psychometric properties of measures administered through both media are equivalent. Based on this information, we anticipated that differences between our sub-samples in level and relative weighting of the items used to measure the constructs would more likely be attributable to differences in culture than differences in media used for collecting the data.

The instrument asked each respondent to think of a leader the respondent had worked for in the past 5 years. For Ghanaian respondents, the leader was described as a West African leader, defined in the survey form as one who (a) is ethnically West African, (b) has lived most of his or her life in Africa, and (c) the respondent's leader-follower relationship with this leader occurred in West Africa. For US respondents, a USA leader was defined is a person (a) born in the USA, (b) has lived the majority of his or her life in the USA, and (c) the respondent's leader-follower relationship with this leader occurred in the USA.

Hale and Fields (2007) tested for measurement equivalence of the constructs within the samples of Ghanaian and American respondents. Following Riordan and Vandenberg (1994), we first examined if the covariance matrices were identical. This test indicated that the covariance matrices were significantly different ($\Delta\chi^2 = 540.19$, d.f. = 24; p<.01). The second step was to examine the extent to which the factor loadings for each of the constructs were identical within the two sub-samples (Riordan & Vandenberg, 1994). Table 2 reports these results.

As this table shows, the fit of the models for service and humility improved significantly when the loadings relating the items to the latent constructs varied between the sub-samples. However, there was not a significant change in model fit when the loadings for leader effectiveness and vision were allowed to differ between the two sub-samples. Thus, the items seem to be related to the constructs of effectiveness and vision in the same way for both Ghanaian and US respondents. However, the loadings differ for the constructs of service and humility. Since the loadings relating the measurement items to the latent constructs for service and humility differed between the Ghanaian and American sub-samples, we next examined the extent to which the service and humility constructs were empirically distinct within each sub-sample. A model with two separate factors for service and humility fit the data better than a model combining the service and humility constructs in both the Ghanaian sub-sample ($\Delta\chi^2 = 19.57$, d.f.=1, p < .01) and the U.S. sub-sample ($\Delta\chi^2 = 59.28$, d.f.=1). Table 3 shows the loadings of the items for the service and humility constructs for the Ghanaian and U.S. sub-samples.

Hale and Fields (2007) tested the extent to which the outcome variable of leadership effectiveness was empirically distinct from the variables measuring the leader behaviors of service, humility, and vision. Examining the fit of alternative confirmatory factor models evaluated discriminant validity within the combined sample (Riordan & Vandenburg, 1994). We used the combined sample for this analysis to assure that the number of cases sufficiently exceeded the number of parameters estimated in the four factor confirmatory model. The model with four separate factors fit the data significantly better than alternative three factor models (a) combining perceived leader effectiveness with vision ($\Delta\chi^2 = 17.58$, d.f. = 3; p<.01), (b) combining leader effectiveness with humility ($\Delta\chi^2 = 12.49$, d.f. = 3; p<.01), and (c) combining leader effectiveness with service ($\Delta\chi^2 = 38.77$, d.f. = 3; p<.01). The four factor model also fit the data significantly better than a 2 factor model combining the dimensions of service humility, and vision together ($\Delta\chi^2 = 35.12$, d.f. = 7; p<.01). The four factor model also fit the data significantly better than a one-factor model combining all four key constructs together.

In a recent study, West (2009) examined the three dimensional measure of servant leadership in a sample of personnel working in the U.S.

Table 2. Tests of construct measurement equivalence between Ghana and USA sub-samples

Construct	Model fit-same loadings	Model Fit-same pattern	Change in model fit
Effectiveness	$\chi^2 = 65.51$, d.f.=23	$\chi^2 = 60.39$, d.f.=18	$\Delta\chi^2 = 5.12$, d.f.=5, n.s.
Service	$\chi^2 = 55.81$, d.f.=23	$\chi^2 = 30.40$, d.f.=18	$\Delta\chi^2 = 25.41$, d.f.=5 **p<.01**
Humility	$\chi^2 = 48.56$, d.f.=23	$\chi^2 = 22.16$, d.f.= 18	$\Delta\chi^2 = 26.40$, d.f.=5 p<.01
Vision	$\chi^2 = 40.38$, d.f.=23	$\chi^2 = 35.69$, d.f.=18	$\Delta\chi^2 = 4.69$, d.f.=5 n.s.

Table 3. Loadings of measurement items with service and humility constructs in Ghana and USA sub-samples

Items	Loading n USA sub-sample	Loading in Ghana sub-sample
Service Items		
1. Sees serving as a mission of responsibility to others.	1.00	1.00
2. Models service to inspire others.	.90	1.13
3. Understanding that serving others is most important.	1.02	1.30
4. Understands that service is the core of leadership	1.02	1.24
5. Aspires not to be served but to serve others	1.22	1.34
6. Models service in his or her behaviors, attitudes, or values.	.44	1.31
Humility Items		
1. Talks more about employees' accomplishments than his or her own.	.69	1.50
2. Does not overestimate her or his merits.	1.31	1.44
3. Is not interested in self-glorification	1.72	1.72
4. Is humble enough to consult others in the organizations when he or she may not have all the answers	1.19	1.43
5. Does not center attention on his or her own accomplishments.	1.26	1.55
6. Exhibits a demeanor of humility	.65	1.57

Navy. For this study, 302 members of the U. S. Navy participated. Participants' included: (a) 251 men and 51 women; (b) 256 officers and 46 enlisted; (c) community representation of 44 Air, 12 Submarine, 215 Surface, and 31 Other, including Medical, Supply Corps, Intelligence, Judge Advocate General, Civil Engineering, and others; and (d) 292 participants reported having greater than 6 years of tenure.

Using responses from this sample, West (2009) conducted a factor analysis on the eighteen item instrument. West first evaluated the data using the Kaiser-Meyer-Olkin measure of sampling adequacy. This test provides researchers with an indication of the amount of common variance among the items under investigation. The scores for this test can vary between 0 and 1, with 0 indicating that the items in question actually measure a common factor and 1 indicating that the items in question do not measure a common factor. This test resulted in a score of .96, indicating the existence of almost no common variance between the factors measured.

In the factor analysis, Component 1 displayed an Eigenvalue of 11.33 and it accounted for 62.94% of the initial variance. Component 2 displayed an Eigenvalue of 1.64 and it accounted for 9.14% of the initial variance. Component 3 displayed an Eigenvalue of 1.00 and it accounted for 5.55% of the initial variance. As noted in Table 4, Component 1 primarily represented the items associated with Humility; Component 2 represented the items associated with Shared Vision; and Component 3 primarily represented the items associated with Service. Using a Varimax rotation with Kaiser Normalization, all items loaded at > .50 on the appropriate components previously suggested, as expected, and as noted in Table 4.

The Varimax rotation method skews the position of the data, so as to cause the individual given factors to load highly on the fewest number of variables possible -- ideally on a singular variable. The items loading at > .50 in column 1 of table 4 relate to and represent the previously theorized humility factor and the resulting variable. The items loading at > .50 in column 2 relate to and represent the previously theorized shared vision factor and the resulting variable. The items loading at > .50 in column 3 relate to and represent the previously theorized service factor and the resulting variable. As also noted in Table 4, Service factor items 5 and 6, valued at .64 and .57, respectively, cross-loaded with the humility factor at .52 and .56, respectively. Therefore, West (2009) dropped those two items from further analyses.

The resultant scales for service, humility and shared vision had Cronbach's alpha values of .90, .95, and .93 respectively.

Relationship to Outcomes for Employees

Hale and Fields (2007) compared the levels of the three dimensions of servant leadership reported by Ghanaians and Americans in their sample controlling for social desirability in reporting, the extent of work experience, age, and the gender of each respondent. Table 5 reports the result of this comparison.

*p < .05; **p < .01

There was a significant multivariate difference in the levels of the servant leadership dimensions reported by Ghanaians and Americans (Wilks Lambda = .648, p < .001). In contrast to Ghanaians, North Americans reported experiencing each of the three servant leadership dimensions from their referent leaders more frequently than did Ghanaians.

Using multivariate regression models in which the three servant leadership dimensions are exogenous predictors of leadership effectiveness, Hale and Fields (2007) evaluated the extent to which Ghanaian and American followers perceive servant leadership dimensions as related to leadership effectiveness. In these models, we also controlled respondent social desirability in reporting, levels of work experience, age, and gender. We first assessed the fit of a model in which the path coefficients from the servant leadership dimensions to leader

effectiveness are required to be identical for both Ghanaians and Americans. We then assessed the fit of a model in which the path coefficients were free to vary between Ghanaians and Americans. The model in which the paths were free to differ between the two sub-samples fit the data significantly better than the model requiring the paths to be identical ($\Delta\chi^2 = 26.88$, d.f.=5, p < .01). The path coefficient estimates for each sub-sample are show in Figure 1.

As Figure 1 shows, the path coefficient relating vision to leadership effectiveness was significantly larger for Ghanaians than for Americans. The coefficients for the paths relating service and humility with leadership effectiveness were not significantly different between the two sub-samples. However, the Ghanaian sub-sample reported judgments concerning leadership effectiveness as significantly related to work experience and age. In the USA sub-sample, none of the control variables significantly related to judgments of leadership effectiveness.

West (2009) found that service, humility and shared vision all had positive statistically significant correlations with referent, coercive, expert, reward, and legitimate power and with two outcome variables of job satisfaction and affective organizational commitment. The three servant leadership dimensions were all significant predictors of job satisfaction and affective organizational commitment when used simultaneously in regression models estimated for these dependent variables. West (2009) also examined possible moderating effects of alternative sources of power. The study results indicated that service, humility, and shared vision exhibited stronger positive relationships with affective organizational commitment among subordinates who perceived higher rather than lower levels of leader expert, reward, referent, and legitimate power and lower rather than higher levels of leader coercive power. In addition, collectively, service, humility, and shared vision exhibited stronger positive relationships with job satisfaction among subordinates

Table 4. Rotated components matrix from West (2009)

Item	Component		
	1	2	3
Service 1	.18	.19	.80
Service 2	.47	.37	.67
Service 3	.42	.32	.72
Service 4	.34	.35	.75
Service 5	.52	.31	.64
Service 6	.56	.38	.57
Humility 1	.82	.29	.23
Humility 2	.82	.25	.35
Humility 3	.85	.26	.28
Humility 4	.64	.38	.37
Humility 5	.87	.27	.23
Humility 6	.72	.34	.39
Shared Vision 1	.30	.77	.24
Shared Vision 2	.28	.80	.26
Shared Vision 3	.21	.74	.20
Shared Vision 4	.21	.87	.16
Shared Vision 5	.34	.76	.30
Shared Vision 6	.24	.70	.32

who perceived higher, rather than lower, levels of leader displayed reward and legitimate power and lower, rather than higher, levels of leader displayed coercive, expert, and referent power.

COMMENTARY

In exploring the relationship of the three servant leadership dimensions with leadership effective-

ness, Hale and Fields (2007) found no significant differences in the effects of service and humility between the Ghanaian and American sub-samples. However, in this study vision had a significantly stronger relationship with leader effectiveness for Ghanaians. This result was consistent with expectations for vision, but inconsistent with expectation for service. Because Ghanaian culture exhibits higher power distance in current practices, followers may express greater expectations than

Table 5. Multivariate comparison of servant leadership dimensions

	Mean Levels (Controlling for social desirability, work experience, age, and gender)		
	Ghana	USA	F Value
Service[1]	4.21	6.80	49.11
Humility[1]	6.80	8.21	57.60
Vision	4.29	4.93	5.31

[1]Values computed using weights derived from analysis of measurement equivalence

Figure 1. Path coefficients and standard errors for relationships of servant leadership dimensions with leadership effectiveness

Ghana sub-sample

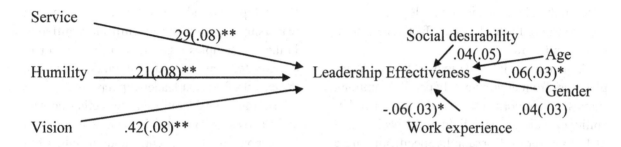

USA sub-sample

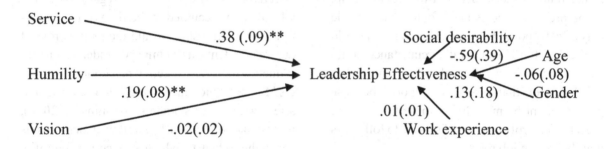

North Americans express that people in leadership roles will provide vision, foresight, and direction for followers. Followers in Ghanaian culture may view leaders who provide less vision as inadequate and ineffective. That is, Hofstede (2001) has suggested that members of higher power distance cultures tend to view leaders as people who are somehow different from followers. This increased social distance or distinction between followers and leaders may carry with it higher expectations for leaders to perform in order to be considered effective. Consequently, a leader's vision (or lack of it) and a leader's behaviors that facilitate follower success may be stronger determinants of judgments about overall leadership effectiveness than in a lower power distance culture like the USA. In North American culture, which has lower levels of power distance, followers may see

leaders as people who are similar in many respects to themselves. In this case, followers may not rely as much as Ghanaians may rely on the leader to provide vision and foresight. North American followers may not judge a leader who is less visionary as significantly less effective because the followers are more comfortable figuring out direction for themselves. Thus, the leader's vision and facilitation of follower performance have less effect on judgments about overall leadership effectiveness.

It may be useful to consider the Hale & Fields (2007) results in light of the estimates of cultural values for the two countries obtained in the GLOBE project (House, Hanges, Javidian, Dorfman, & Gupta, 2004).. In particular, West Africans, when asked about how things should be in society, place much greater emphasis on uncertainty avoidance than do Americans. It is possible that the value Ghanaians place on uncertainty avoidance manifests itself in a preference for leaders who provide vision. Consequently, Ghanaians may view vision as a hedge against uncertainty. Therefore, visionary leaders receive higher ratings for leadership effectiveness from Ghanaian followers.

Although the Hale and Fields (2007) sub-samples were from approximately parallel sampling frames, it is important to consider the generalizability of their results in light of the background of the followers in their sample. Specifically, more than half of the referent leaders used by respondents in both the Ghanaian and USA sub-samples were acting in the role of a Christian church pastor at the time of the leader-follower relationship. Some previous studies have found that job role may affect reports about leader behaviors (Herold & Fields, 2004). Thus, this circumstance could have affected the mean levels of servant leadership behaviors that respondents reported because pastors might be more likely to be humble and see a leader's role in terms of service to followers than leaders in job roles.

In post-hoc analysis, Hale and Fields (2007) tested for a 'pastor effect' in the levels of servant leadership reported in each sub-sample. In general, the respondents from both countries whose referent leaders were church pastors at the time of the leader-follower relationships reported higher levels of service, humility and vision compared to respondents whose referent leaders were in other job roles ($F = 3.48$, $p < .05$). It is noteworthy that the levels of servant leadership behaviors reported by respondents whose leaders were in non-pastor roles were still significantly higher for the USA compared to Ghanaian respondents. Still, it is unclear as to whether we might see the same types of differences in levels of servant leadership reported by respondents from Ghana and the USA if all referent leaders were in other job roles, such as managers expected to provide profitable results. It is worthwhile to observe that since the

proportion of referent leaders who were pastors in each sub-sample were nearly equal (60% for Ghanaian sub-sample and 54% for the USA sub-sample), the 'pastor effect' would seem to argue for smaller differences in the levels of servant leadership reported. Since the levels of servant leadership reported were significantly different in the sub-samples regardless of job role, there do seem to be meaningful cultural differences in the extent of servant leadership reported.

The other consideration in interpreting the Hale and Fields (2007) results is the extent to which the respondents, all currently studying either full or part time in Christian seminaries, would tend to increase the connection between servant leadership dimensions and judgments about leader effectiveness. In other words, regardless of the job role they occupied at the time of the leader-follower relationship, would the present role of our respondents as seminary students tend to influence their retrospective perceptions of leaders? Since his/her current job role is expected to affect a follower's identity (Collinson, 2006), it may also directly affect follower perceptions about the extent to which service and humility are key ingredients for effective leaders. Since Christian studies tend to emphasize the value of both service and humility as positive personal attributes, our respondents may have seen these as more important to leader effectiveness than might respondents currently working in a variety of other job roles.

It is notable that Hale and Fields (2007) did find that Ghanaians related vision differently to leadership effectiveness than did Americans. However, across both sub-samples the concepts of service and humility similarly related similarly to leadership effectiveness. Since the importance of vision for leadership effectiveness might not be subject to a 'seminary effect' as much as service and humility, this aspect of our results does raise some suspicions that some contextual effect may be tending to equalize the value placed on service and humility of leaders.

Cost of the Servant Leadership Scale

The scale is available free of charge.

Location

The scale is available in electronic form at: http://www.wellspiritconsulting.com/free-resources .

REFERENCES

Barbuto, J., & Wheeler, D. (2006). Scale development and construct clarification of servant leadership. *Group & Organization Management*, *31*(3), 300–326. doi:10.1177/1059601106287091

Carlbring, P., Brunt, S., Bohman, S., Austin, D., Richards, J., Ost, L., & Andersson, G. (2005). Internet vs. paper and pencil administration of questionnaires commonly used in panic/agoraphobia research. *Computers in Human Behavior*, *23*(3), 1421–1434. doi:10.1016/j.chb.2005.05.002

Collinson, D. (2006). Rethinking followership: A post-structuralist analysis of follower identities. *The Leadership Quarterly*, *17*, 179–189. doi:10.1016/j.leaqua.2005.12.005

Dennis, R. (2004). *Servant leadership theory: Development of the servant leadership assessment instrument.* Unpublished 3133544, Regent University, Virginia Beach.

Dennis, R. S., & Bocarnea, M. C. (2005). Development of the servant leadership assessment instrument. *Leadership and Organization Development Journal*, *26*(8), 600–615. doi:10.1108/01437730510633692

Farling, M. L., Stone, A. G., & Winston, B. E. (1999). Servant leadership: Setting the stage for empirical research. *The Journal of Leadership Studies*, *6*(1/2), 49–72. doi:10.1177/107179199900600104

Hale, J. R., & Fields, D. L. (2007). Exploring servant leadership across cultures: A study of followers in Ghana and the USA. *Leadership*, *3*(4), 397–417. doi:10.1177/1742715007082964

Herold, D., & Fields, D. (2004). Making sense of subordinate feedback for leadership development: Confounding effects of job role and organizational rewards. *Group & Organization Management*, *29*(6), 686–701. doi:10.1177/1059601103257503

Hofstede, G. (2001). *Culture's consequences: Comparing values, behaviors, institutions, and organizations across nations* (2nd ed.). London, UK: Sage Publications.

House, R. J., Hanges, P. J., Javidan, M., Dorfman, P. W., & Gupta, V. (Eds.). (2004). *Culture, leadership, and organizations: The GLOBE study of 62 cultures*. Thousand Oaks, CA: Sage Publications, Inc.

Liden, R. C., Wayne, S. J., Zhao, H., & Henderson, D. (2005, November). *Development of a multidimensional measure of servant leadership*. Paper presented at the Annual Meeting of the Southern Management Association, Charleston, SC.

Patterson, K. A. (2003). *Servant leadership: A theoretical model. Unpublished UMI 3082719*. Virginia Beach: Regent University.

Riordan, C., & Vandenberg, R. (1994). A central question in cross-cultural research: Do employees of different cultures interpret work-related measures in an equivalent manner? *Journal of Management*, *20*, 642–571.

Senjaya, S. (2003, August). *Development and validation of servant leadership behavior scale*. Paper presented at the Servant Leadership Research Roundtable, Regent University, Virginia Beach, VA.

West, G. R. B. (2009). *Expert, coercive, legitimate, referent, and reward power bases as moderating variables upon the relationships between service, humility, and shared vision with affective organizational commitment, and job satisfaction among members of the U.S. Navy.* Unpublished Doctoral dissertation, Regent University, Virginia Beach, VA.

ADDITIONAL READING

Akuchie, N. D. (1993). The servants and the superstars: An examination of servant leadership in light of Matthew 20: 20-28. *The Christian Education Journal, 16*, 39–43.

Avolio, B. J., & Locke, E. E. (2002). Philosophies of leader motivation: Altruism versus egoism. *The Leadership Quarterly, 13*, 169–191. doi:10.1016/S1048-9843(02)00094-2

Choi, Y., & Mai-Dalton, R. R. (1998). On the leadership function of self-sacrifice. *The Leadership Quarterly, 9*(4), 1–20. doi:10.1016/S1048-9843(98)90012-1

Collinson, D. (2006). Rethinking followership: A post-structuralist analysis of follower identities. *The Leadership Quarterly, 17*, 179–189. doi:10.1016/j.leaqua.2005.12.005

Davis, J. H., Schoorman, F. D., & Donaldson, L. (1997). Toward a stewardship theory of management. *Academy of Management Review, 22*, 20–47.

Ehrhart, M. G., & Klein, K. J. (2001). Predicting followers' preferences for charismatic leadership: The influence of follower values and personality. *The Leadership Quarterly, 12*, 155–179. doi:10.1016/S1048-9843(01)00074-1

Greenleaf, R. K. (1970). *The servant as a leader.* Indianapolis, IN: Greenleaf Center.

Greenleaf, R. K. (1972). *The institution as servant.* Indianapolis, IN: Greenleaf Center.

Greenleaf, R. K. (1974). *Trustees as servants.* Indianapolis, IN: Greenleaf Center.

Greenleaf, R. K. (1977). *Servant leadership: A journey into the nature of legitimate power and greatness.* Mahwah, NJ: Paulist Press.

Greenleaf, R. K. (1996). *On becoming a servant leader.* San Francisco, CA: Jossey-Bass.

Greenleaf, R. K. (2002). *Servant leadership: A journey into the nature of legitimate power and greatness* (25th anniversary ed.). Mahwah, NJ: Paulist Press.

Hawkinson, J. R., & Johnston, R. K. (1993). Servant leadership: *Vol. 2. Contemporary models and the emerging challenge.* Chicago, IL: Covenant.

Koshal, J. O. (2005, August). *Servant leadership theory: Application of the construct of service in the context of Kenyan leaders and managers.* Paper presented at the Servant Leadership Research Roundtable, Regent University, Virginia Beach, VA.

Laub, J. (2004, August). *Defining servant leadership: A recommended typology for servant leadership.* Paper presented at the Servant Leadership Research Roundtable, Regent University. Virginia Beach, Virginia.

Nelson, L. (2003). *An exploratory study of the application and acceptance of servant-leadership theory among black leaders in South Africa.* Unpublished 3086676, Regent University, Virginia Beach.

Peck, M. S. (1998). Servant-Leadership training and discipline in authentic community. In Spears, L. C. (Ed.), *Reflections on leadership* (pp. 87–98). New York, NY: John Wiley.

Rugege, S. (1994). *The institution of traditional leadership and its relation with the elected local government.* Retrieved April 6, 2004, from http://www.kas.org.za/Publications/SeminarReports/Constitution%20and%20Law%20iv/rugege.pdf

Sandbrook, R., & Oelbaum, J. (1997). Reforming dysfunctional institutions through democratization? Reflections on Ghana. *The Journal of Modern African Studies, 35*(4), 603–646. doi:10.1017/S0022278X97002565

Sendjaya, S., & Sarros, J. C. (2002). Servant leadership: Its origin, development, and application in organizations. *Journal of Leadership & Organizational Studies, 9,* 47–64. doi:10.1177/107179190200900205

Senjaya, S. (2003, August). *Development and validation of servant leadership behavior scale.* paper presented at the Servant Leadership Research Roundtable, Regent University, Virginia Beach, VA.

Smith, B. N., Montagno, R. V., & Kuzmenko, T. N. (2004). Transformational and servant leadership: Content and contextual comparisons. *Journal of Leadership & Organizational Studies, 10,* 80–91. doi:10.1177/107179190401000406

Snodgrass, K. R. (1993). Your slaves—An account of Jesus' servant leadership in the New Testament. In Hawkinson, J. R., & Johnstone, R. K. (Eds.), *Servant leadership* (*Vol. 1,* pp. 17–19). Chicago, IL: Covenant.

Spears, L. C. (Ed.). (1995). *Reflections on leadership: How Robert K. Greenleaf's theory of servant-leadership influenced today's top management thinkers.* New York, NY: John Wiley and Sons, Inc.

Spears, L. C. (2002). Introduction: Tracing the past, present and future of servant-leadership. In Spears, L. C. (Ed.), *Focus on leadership* (pp. 1–18). New York, NY: John Wiley.

KEY TERMS AND DEFINITIONS

Cross-Cultural: Comparing or dealing with two or more different cultures.

Humility: Putting the success of others ahead of the leader's personal gain.

Individualism Versus Collectivism: A dimension of national culture developed by Geert Hofstede. This dimension of culture considers how individuals are integrated into groups. In individualist societies, individuals are expected to look after her/himself and her/his immediate family. Conversely, collectivist societies are integrated into strong, cohesive in-groups, which are often extended families that provide ongoing protection in exchange for unquestioning loyalty.

Power Distance: A dimension of national culture developed by Geert Hofstede. This dimension of culture focuses the extent to which the less powerful members of society expect and accept that power is distributed unequally.

Service: Behaviors that that contribute to the well-being of followers, an organization, and society.

Servant Leadership: A concept encompassing a variety of leadership definitions and styles that, in general, attempt to maximize leader effectiveness through an emphasis on ethical behaviors that contribute to the well-being of the follower and the organization.

Vision: Combining leader foresight with the ability to influence followers in developing a shared vision (preferred future outcomes) for their organization.

Chapter 10
Seven Scales to Measure the Seven Beatitudes in Leaders

John Kilroy
Fresno Pacific University, USA

Corné L. Bekker
Regent University, USA

Mihai C. Bocarnea
Regent University, USA

Bruce E. Winston
Regent University, USA

ABSTRACT

This study presents seven scales for the seven beatitudes found in Matthew 5: 3-10. Separate scales were created rather than a conceptual instrument with seven factors since the 'concept' of 'Beatitude' does not exist and since the seven beatitudes are related in various ways making them highly correlated. The seven scales were reduced to five items each. The resultant Chronbach alpha scores were .86, .95, .89, .92, .93, .93, .92 for each of the scales. The value of the seven scales lies in their ability to assist researchers to compare leadership effectiveness with the seven representative values and, in time after normative data is developed, to offer a measure to help with leadership selection.

BACKGROUND

This study builds on Winston's (2002) conceptual work about the Beatitudes from Matthew 5: 3-10 being the values base of leadership. No valid scale development work has been done on Winston's conceptual propositions or, for that matter, on the beatitudes as related to leadership. A premise for this paper is that each beatitude of the seven found in Matthew 5: 3-10 is a separate concept and, as such, we developed a separate scale. As a corollary to this the authors posit that 'Beatitude' in general is not a single concept and as such neither attempted to, nor believe that there should be a single instrument to measure 'Beatitude' in which the intent would be to have seven scales within the single instrument. This study produced

DOI: 10.4018/978-1-4666-2172-5.ch010

seven instruments – one instrument for each of the seven Beatitudes.

The word "beatitude' does not exist in the Bible but is a term, according to Langan (1977), that means 'happiness'. Winston (2002) suggested that a leader's foundational values yield beliefs, beliefs yield intentions, and intentions yield behavior. Winston further posits that a leader's behavior forms the follower's attitude, and the follower's attitude affects the follower's behavior (p. IV). Bass and Steidlmeier (1999) noted, "with the renewed emphasis upon strategic leadership and ethics, the virtues and moral character of leaders have taken centered stage" (p.194). Winston's suggestion established a circular pattern of the leader's behavior influencing the formation of the followers' behavior, which, in turn influences or reinforces the leader's behavior. The concept of leader-follower influence is not new to leadership research and is incorporated in one's personal and group efficacy belief (Bandura, 1997). Nonetheless, Winston's concept is unique in its premise that *Agapao* love forms the basis of such leader-follower influence and it is foundational to effective leader behavior. Furthermore, Winston associated the above behaviors with the values Jesus articulated in the Beatitudes contained in the Sermon of the Mount and found in the gospel of Matthew 5:3-9. In these Beatitudes, Jesus exhorted his followers to (a) demonstrate humility and a willingness to learn, (b) have compassion for others, (c) exhibit controlled discipline, wisdom, and compassion, (d) be highly focused, and (e) be a peacemaker. These characteristics represent the "inward traits and principles that a godly person possesses" (p. 135). Winston's incorporation of *Agapao* love, which is a manifestation of one's spiritual principles, is the foundation of the values. This argument links spirituality and leadership a concept which is gaining popularity among researchers and leadership practitioners (Burke, 2006; Fry, 2003; Klenke, 2005; Kriger & Seng, 2005; Mitroff & Denton, 1999).

Values Research

The premise that a leader's behavior is reflective of his/her values and has an influence on both followers and the organization is not a new position, nor is it limited to a biblical perspective (Mitroff & Denton, 1999). Northouse (2007) believed leadership decisions were "informed and directed by their ethics" reflecting the virtuousness and motives of the individual (p. 342). Northouse further stated that virtue-based theories focus on "who the leader is as a person and that virtues and moral abilities can be acquired and learned through practice" (p. 345). Writing on leadership, Kriegbaum (1998) asserted that values control behaviors, which are based on one's belief, and whoever influences a group's core value is in fact the leader who has the responsibility to direct followers toward the right goals. Behr (1998) stipulated "those who practice value-centered leadership create the organizational integrity needed to compete in an ever-changing world" (p. 51). Northouse (2007) further stipulated that the values leaders promote influence organizational values. Northouse's position on values supports Winston's (2002) writings that identified the concept that a leader's behavior forms the followers' attitudes and the followers' attitude affects their behavior consequently forming the values displayed within an organization.

Kriger and Seng (2005) discussed the values and concepts of spiritual leadership within Buddhism, Christianity, Hinduism, Islam, and Judaism, which represent the five major religions and encompass 72% of the world's population. Their research of the various religions indicated that a leader's actions are based upon religious values and teachings, and as the leader practices their beliefs, followers eventually internalize the behavior thereby becoming part of the organizations values. However, Kriger and Seng suggested the knowledge of how values based upon ones religion can deepen the practice of leadership in organizations is under-discussed and under-researched even though a literature review of the religious teachings demonstrated a connection. Kriger and Seng wrote that spiritual leadership should be an extension to the Contingency Theory and hypothesized that a leader's values will shape the leader's behavior and have a direct effect on the subordinates' commitment, which in turn will impact the organizations performance. Kriger and Seng identified 17 characteristics emerging from literature on spirituality namely (a) forgiveness, (b) kindness, (c) integrity, (d) compassion/empathy, (e) honesty/truthfulness, (f) patience, (g) courage/inner strength, (h) trust, (i) humility, (j) loving kindness, (k) peacefulness, (l) thankfulness, (m) service to others, (n) guidance, (o) joy, (p) equanimity, and (q) stillness/inner peace. These characteristics also found in the five major religious of the world, correlate to the seven leadership values inspired by the Beatitudes as shown in Table 1.

The review of values and spirituality research demonstrates a connection of the leader's value to their behavior and its influence on followers and the organization. What forms the foundation of the value system? Winston (2002) suggested it is *Agapao* love.

Winston (2002) defined *Agapao* love as a kind of morality, whereby leaders "consider the human and spiritual aspects of their employees/followers" (p. 9). To further develop the definition, Winston suggested that leaders view their employees as "hired hearts considering their needs, wants, and desires" instead of as "hired hands" (p. 9). Winston's work with the Beatitudes defined seven basic core values and related behaviors for leaders who are attempting to operate within *Agapao* love (Tse, 2006; Winston, 2002). Several studies (Dennis, 2004; Dennis & Bocarnea, 2005; Patterson, 2003; Stone, Russell, & Patterson, 2004) have investigated the *Agapao* construct; however, to date it has not been measured.

According to Winston (2002), a leader's behavior is the outward demonstration reflecting embraced values and an approach toward life based upon a foundation of *Agapao* love.

Klenke (2005) believed that strong corporate cultures evolve when employees and managers share similar values which form the organization mission and values.

However, the use of the leadership values inspired by the Beatitudes is not an attempt to link spirituality to leadership any more than to infer that transformation leadership is linked to spirituality (Dent, Higgins, & Wharff, 2005). Blanchard and Hodges (2005) posited that "values are the non negotiable principles that define character in a leader" (p. 90). Bandura (1997) supported Blanchard and Hodges perspective when he stated that "efficacy beliefs are concerned not only with the exercise of control over action but also with the self-regulation of thought processes, motivation, and affective and physiological states" (p. 36). A leader's value system inspired by the Beatitudes is built upon a set of values linked in history to the beginnings of Christianity, Judaism, and Islam whose practice is globally forming the bases for governments and businesses. Winston's linkage of the Beatitudes to a set of values provides a foundational base of values and behaviors not limited to a Western World view providing a common definition linking values to behaviors which could advance the theory of value-based leadership.

Blanchard's (2007) position on beliefs is that they are the essence of the person forming one's purpose and values. Blanchard further stipulated that organizational values define leadership and the way employees act on a day-to-day basis while pursuing the organizations purpose and future. Blanchard suggested organizations work more effectively and avoid unethical situations if clear visions and values are established. Similarly, Fry (2003) proposed that a leader "should lead by values that drive out fear and abuse of the work place and engage the hearts and minds of the people" (p. 704). Blanchard and Fry complemented Northouse's (2007) position that leaders have an impact in the establishment and sharing of personal, team, and organizational values.

Table 1. Correlation of 17 spiritual characteristics and the Beatitudinal values

Spiritual characteristics	Leadership value	Beatitude
Forgiveness	Compassionate, Merciful	Blessed are the merciful for they will be shown mercy.
Kindness	Concern for others and Highly Focused	Blessed are those who mourn for they will be comforted. Blessed are the pure in heart for they will see God.
Integrity	Continually seeks what is right	Blessed are those who hunger and thirst for righteousness for they will be filled.
Compassion /empathy	Compassionate, merciful	Blessed are the merciful for they will be shown mercy.
Honesty /truthfulness	Righteousness	Blessed are those who hunger and thirst for righteousness for they will be filled.
Patience	Compassionate, merciful	Blessed are the merciful for they will be shown mercy.
Courage/inner strength	Peacemaker	Blessed are the peacemakers for they will be called sons of God.
Trust	Righteousness	Blessed are those who hunger and thirst for righteousness for they will be filled.
Humility	Humble	Blessed are the poor in Spirit for theirs is the kingdom of heaven.
Loving kindness	Concern for others	Blessed are those who mourn for they will be comforted.
Peacefulness	Peacemaker	Blessed are the peacemakers for they will be called sons of God.
Thankfulness	Humble	Blessed are the poor in Spirit for theirs is the kingdom of heaven.
Service to others	Focused and Concern for others	Blessed are the pure in heart for they will see God. Blessed are those who mourn for they will be comforted.
Guidance	Controlled discipline	Blessed are those who mourn for they will be comforted.
Joy	Peacemaker	Blessed are the peacemakers for they will be called sons of God.
Equanimity	Controlled discipline	Blessed are those who mourn for they will be comforted.
Stillness/inner peace	Humble and Peacemaker	Blessed are the poor in Spirit for theirs is the kingdom of heaven. Blessed are the peacemakers for they will be called sons of God.

Based on the above surveyed literature, the values of leadership are an important construct and should be considered, and the establishment of independent scales for each of the seven behaviors proposed by Winston (2002) could serve as an initial step in determining a foundation by which leadership who embrace the Beatitudes values operate.

VALIDITY

The leadership values inspired by the Beatitudes spoken by Jesus as recorded in the Gospel of Matthew 5:3-9, have been a source for teachings within Christian communities for centuries. The Beatitudes encourage the Christian leader to be

a) humble and teachable, b) show concern for others, c) demonstrate controlled discipline, d) display wisdom, compassion, e) be highly focused, and f) act as a peacemaker. Because the values of Christianity have been accepted around the world, the values inspired by the Beatitudes are not constrained to a western cultural perspective or application (Kolbell, 2003; Kriger & Seng, 2003). Kolbell strengthened the worldview concept of the Beatitudes by stating "We will not find one single statute, law, commandment, proverb, parable, or homily in the entire bible that is not in some way reflected in one of the verses" (p.13). The values inspired by the Beatitudes could be considered part of the Christian culture or from an organizational view, the espoused values, what Schein (1992) called "publicly announced principles and values that the group claims to be trying to achieve" (p. 9). Lord and Brown (2001) believed that values are "used in generating and evaluating behavior, cognition, and affect" and that "leadership works best when there is a match between the identity level of followers and the focus of the leader" (p. 136-137). Therefore, Winston's (2002) proposition that the Beatitudes inspire seven leadership values producing certain leadership behaviors are global in nature and not solely linked to a single religious perspective.

In each of the subsequent seven subsections each item referenced used a response scale from 1 to 7 with '1' labeled as 'Not at all like him/ her' and '7' labeled 'exactly like him/her'. The responses of 2 through 6 were not labeled thus allowing the participant to select the score along the continuum that best fits his/her opinion. A panel of three experts familiar with the Beatitudes and with Winston's work were asked to review the 12 items and determine if, in their opinion, there was face validity to the items. The three experts confirmed the face validity of the items and recommended minor changes to wording.

THE FIRST BEATITUDE: BLESSED ARE THE POOR IN SPIRIT

Winston's (2002) description of the first leadership value inspired by the Beatitudes stipulates that followers of a leader who values being humble and teachable would observe a humility and teachableness behavior (p. 22-27). Table 2 was derived from Winston's work:

THE SECOND BEATITUDE: BLESSED ARE THOSE WHO MOURN

The second leadership value, concern for others, is inspired by the second Beatitude; blessed are those who mourn for they will inherit the earth. The Greek word *pentheó* is translated into English as mourn meaning a great concern for others. Concern for others is demonstrated by a leader who understands the value of employees to rest, has compassion for employees, and seeks to right injustices (Kolbell, 2003; Winston, 2002).

Table 2. Items for the First Beatitude

Item Number	Item
1	My supervisor asks questions of us in order that she/he might learn about a problem or situation at work.
2	My supervisor is humble.
3	My supervisor shows a genuine interest in the work we do.
4	My supervisor's behavior implies that she/he does not know everything.
5	My supervisor teaches employees how to solve problems.
6	My supervisor shows respect for us in both her/his behavior and words.
7	When I have a concern about work, my supervisor listens to me and considers my opinions in her/his decisions.
8	If someone asked me for an example of a humble supervisor, I would willingly say that my supervisor is a great example.
9	My supervisor gives credit for success to the employees in the organization.
10	My supervisor openly admits her/his weakness.
11	My supervisor willingly admits when she/he doesn't know something.
12	My supervisor uses her/his emotions and honestly in working through conflict.

Table 3. Items for the Second Beatitude

Item Number	Item
1	My supervisor seeks to pay me adequately for the work that I do.
2	If I need time off for personal issues my supervisor does all that she/he can to accommodate me.
3	My supervisor's behavior shows that she/he is concerned about my well-being.
4	My supervisor makes decisions with my best interest in mind.
5	If I needed financial help my supervisor would do all that she/he could to help me.
6	My supervisor does all that she/he can to balance my workload so that I am not overworked.
7	After we finish a big project my supervisor gives time for all involved employees to pause and reflect on what we did.
8	My supervisor cares for me as a person.
9	My supervisor cares for other departments in the organization and seeks to do what is right for everyone in the organization rather than just for her/his department.
10	My supervisor puts the interests of others before her/his own interests.
11	My supervisor does all that she/he can to accommodate my needs in the workplace.
12	My supervisor is concerned about my emotional well-being.

The work of Dennis and Bocarnea (2005) as well as Patterson (2003), define the altruism construct of servant leader as a leader who demonstrated concern for the welfare of others. Fry (2003) posits a similar definition of altruistic love as a leader who shows "genuine care, concern, and appreciation for both self and others" (p. 695). If a leader values others then the leader's behavior would demonstrate his/her caring for others (Winston, 2002). (see Table 3)

THE THIRD BEATITUDE: BLESSED ARE THE MEEK

The third Beatitude, Mathew 5:5 is blessed are the meek for they will inherit the earth. The Greek term associated with meek is *praeis* which is translated as humility meaning the application of humility through demonstrated patience, calmness, and teaching of others (Winston, 2002). Winston associates the Hebrew term *anayv*, which means gentle in mind or circumstances to the leadership value of humility found in this Beatitude (p.42).

Howell (2006) notes the third Beatitude captures the inner attitude of the leader who never advances her/his own agenda but instead shows love and compassion. Leaders operating within this value seek to find the cause of problems and solutions verse over reacting or trying to place blame or persecuting employees. The above behaviors demonstrated by leaders instill a sense of trust in employees encouraging them to "take risks" (Winston & Patterson, 2006).

Leadership focused on finding the cause verse blame provides intrinsic motivation manifested through "autonomy, competence, and relatedness" (Fry, 2003, p.699). Through their demonstrated behavior of showing concern for followers, leaders influence followers to make a connection with the organizational goals and values thereby raising their level of effort and in turn the leaders. By removing a fear of blame or retribution from the workplace, leaders would be engaging the whole person toward organizational goals which Fry sees as representative of transformational leadership.

Therefore, if a leader values controlled discipline, the observable behavior would be her/

Table 4. Items for the Third Beatitude

Item Number	Item
1	When my supervisor gets angry it is for a just cause.
2	My supervisor uses necessary discipline to teach and train.
3	My supervisor controls her/his temper in the workplace.
4	My supervisor seeks to know why something went wrong before she/he reacts.
5	My supervisor uses her/his power in the organization wisely.
6	My supervisor seeks to have me learn from my mistakes.
7	If my supervisor has to terminate an employee she/he will seek to help the employee get another job.
8	My supervisor believes that most of the mistakes are caused by factors other than the employee.
9	My supervisor does not demean employees in her/his words or actions.
10	My supervisor does not punish employees as an example to others.
11	My supervisor welcomes disagreements from employees.
12	My supervisor uses her/his emotions wisely in working through conflict.

his patience, calmness, and willingness to teach. (see Table 4)

THE FOURTH BEATITUDE: BLESSED ARE THOSE WHO HUNGER AND THIRST FOR RIGHTEOUSNESS

Blessed are those who hunger and thirst for righteousness for they will be filled is the fourth Beatitude from which the values of wisdom (Hebrew *chockma*), understanding (Hebrew *biynah*), counsel (Hebrew *etzah*), and righteousness (Greek *dikaisunen*) are inspired. The leadership behavior demonstrated by this Beatitude is a leader who continually seeks what is right and just, and expresses his/herself in specific acts (Allen, 1953; Howell, 2006; Kolbell, 2003; Winston, 2002). Klenke (2005) writes that transformational leaders operate out of a deeply held personal value system which includes the values of justice and integrity. Kouzes and Posner (2001) emphasize that leaders should build relationships based on trust, respect, and caring.

The Greek terms translated as hunger and thirst are *pein* and *dipsao* meaning "famished or crave for and to thirst" (Winston, 2002, p.51). The Greek term translated as righteousness is *dikaisunen* translated "holy, just, right and equity" which Winston noted is the "unfolding of an ethical leader" from the Beatitudes" (p.54). A leader who values wisdom, understanding, counsel, and righteousness would demonstrate the value of the fourth Beatitude by continually seeking what is good, just, right, and equitable for employees and organizations through specific acts. (Winston, 2002). Howell (2006) noted such a leader would express this Beatitude through specific acts. The "presence of righteousness is obvious because of the mutual presence of the Spirit of wisdom (knowing what is right for the situation) and understanding (ability to put action to thoughts)" (Winston, p. 58). Recognition received by leadership is indicative of their focus on the organization and employees verse a focus on self-aggrandizing (Winston, 2006, Howell, 2006, Allen, 1953).

The knowledge of doing what is right is reflective in the ethical conduct of the leader and is a part of the leadership value stated in the fourth

Table 5. Items for the Fourth Beatitude

Item Number	Item
1	My supervisor seeks what is right for the organization.
2	My supervisor explains to employees what is right for the organization so that we can do the right things.
3	If a news crew showed up at my supervisor's office I would know they were there to find out about something good rather than something bad.
4	An investigative reporter would not be able to find anything un-ethical in my supervisor's conduct.
5	My supervisor does the right things even if it is detrimental to him/her personally.
6	When my supervisor asks me to do something I know it is for the right reason.
7	I trust my supervisor to make the right decision in the work place.
8	My supervisor acts ethically in all aspects of her/his life to the best of my knowledge.
9	My supervisor earns the respect of everyone in the organization.
10	People in the organization seek out my supervisor to ask her/his opinion about what they should do in difficult situations.
11	Rather than treating all people in the organization in the same manner, my supervisor treats everyone justly – providing to each person what that person needs.
12	My supervisor demonstrates wisdom in her/his decisions.

Beatitude. As Klenke (2005) noted, there is a linkage between the ethical behavior of the leader and effective leadership and that the company's moral health is a reflection of the values leaders' model. Lord and Brown (2001) drew a similar linkage as Klenke noting that a leaders values influence her/his behavior and the goals and behaviors of the followers and the organization culture.

Specific acts by a leader who value wisdom, understanding, counsel, and righteousness will continually extract what is good, just, right, and equitable by developing a relationship with followers "based on mutual respect and caring" which develops the follower and the leader (Kouzes & Posner, 2001, p.85). To Kouzes and Posner such actions demonstrate self-awareness and a willingness to be taught which exemplifies the previous Beatitudes contributing to Winston's (2002) concept that each Beatitudes draws upon the previous value and builds a linkage to the next.

Therefore, if a leader values wisdom and understanding, the observable behavior would be her/his continually seeking what is good, just, right, and equitable for employees and the organization through specific acts. (see Table 5)

THE FIFTH BEATITUDE: BLESSED ARE THE MERCIFUL

The fifth Beatitude, Mathew 5:7 is blessed are the merciful for they shall be shown mercy. The Greek word associated with merciful is *eleemon* meaning compassion or merciful displayed by a leader who shows compassionate or is merciful. A leader who embraces the value inspired by the fifth Beatitude would listen to followers displaying a compassion for their mistakes. By their actions leaders influence followers to show compassion and mercy to each other for mistakes resulting in a willingness by all followers to take calculated risks (Winston & Patterson, 2006, Winston, 2002). Howell (2006) writes that this is not just an inner attitude but also something you do toward others an act of listening with mercy. Allen (1953) writes that "If we are not merciful then we are blocking God's mercy out of our own lives" (p. 145) and for anyone "to not extend mercy is to know hate, revenge, and destruction" (p.148).

Leaders who look at the organization and social systems within which people operate understand better the influential forces at work developing

Table 6. Items for the Fifth Beatitude

Item Number	Item
1	My supervisor seeks to learn the heart of the employee when determining what to do in a situation in which the employee failed.
2	My supervisor is compassionate when dealing with employees.
3	My supervisor looks beyond the policies and deals with people mercifully.
4	My supervisor when discipling employees looks to the future and seeks long-term improvement rather than short-term punishment.
5	My supervisor forgives and forgets (must do both) rather than holds a grudge.
6	My supervisor's kindness makes it easier to tell him/her when I do something wrong.
7	Even when punishment is warranted my supervisor avoids using punishment except as a last resort.
8	When a problem occurs my supervisor seeks to understand the situational factors in order to determine if the employee was wrong or not.
9	Employees in other departments, other than my own, tell me that they think my supervisor is compassionate.
10	If an employee quits to take a perceived better job but came back after awhile because the employee made a bad decision and wanted her/his own job back (presuming it was available) my super-visor would welcome him/her back and not hold the employee's leaving against him/her.
11	If my supervisor makes a mistake that causes me problems and IF I show my supervisor that I don't hold this against her/him, my supervisor would show me that she/he values my forgiving behavior.
12	My supervisor's compassionate approach to problems makes it easier for employees to openly discuss problems.

the leaders "compassion and empathy" thereby undermining "attitudes of blame and guilt" (Senge, 1990, p.171). Kouzes and Posner (2006) when addressing the legacy of leaders expanded the concepts of Senge (1990) and Fry (2003) suggesting that within the complexity of organizational challenges, leadership demonstrating forgiveness and grace support the growth of their employees by extending to them the very grace and opportunity the leader received.

Therefore, if a leader values compassion and is merciful, the observable behavior would be her/his listening and showing of compassion. (see Table 6)

THE SIXTH BEATITUDE: BLESSED ARE THE PURE IN HEART

The sixth Beatitude, found in Mathew 5:8, is blessed are the pure in heart for they will see God. Winston (2002) notes there are two Greek terms

associated with pure in heart, *katharos* translated meaning "clear, clean, and pure" and *kardia* meaning "heart, thoughts, and feelings" (p.72). This value indicates someone who is highly focused, an intensity of purpose (Winston, 2002; Winston & Patterson, 2006). Howell (2006) believes such a leader is singular in mind focused on one goal. Leaders taking on this value, focus on the mission of the organization by aligning followers' values, commitments, and energy to accomplish the organizations objectives (Winston, 2002; Winston & Patterson 2006).

A leader transmits the value and importance of an organization's purpose through the support and encouragement provided to followers and how she/he personally faces difficult times. Through the visible focused behavior of the leader, followers develop trust and respect for leadership resulting in the follower's in-crease motivation and commitment (Yukl, 2002). Yukl's view of a transformational leader depicts the behavior of a leader who values being focused on the organiza-

Table 7. Items for the Sixth Beatitude

Item Number	Item
1	My supervisor is focused on her/his job.
2	My supervisor has integrity in that what she/he says aligns with what she/he does.
3	My supervisor keeps 'the main thing the main thing' and is not diverted from doing what needs to be done in the organization.
4	My supervisor's behavior makes it evident that she/he lives the organization's mission statement.
5	My supervisor reminds employees about the organization's mission at every meeting.
6	My supervisor is not distracted by 'good' ideas that might pull her/his attention away from the main purpose of the organization.
7	My supervisor means what she/he says.
8	My supervisor's motives are aligned with both her/his words and actions (must have both aligned).
9	My supervisor is truthful.
10	My supervisor would not try to cover up a mistake that she/he made.
11	My supervisor really believes in what the organization stands for.
12	My supervisor really is the person that she/he portrays.

tion mission. The value of being pure in heart or highly focused as noted in the sixth Beatitude.

Kouzes & Posner (2006) encapsulate the concepts expressed by Schein (1992), Winston, (2002) and Yukl (2002) and the value of the sixth Beatitude by noting leadership must be "flexible in style but firm on standards" which brings about a team of diverse individuals who are then demonstrating "a unison toward an ennobling future" (p. 48).

Therefore, if a leader values being highly focused, the observable behavior would be her/his intensity and focus on the organization objectives. (see Table 7)

THE SEVENTH BEATITUDE: BLESSED ARE THE PEACEMAKERS

The seventh Beatitude, Mathew 5:9 is blessed are the peacemakers for they will be called sons of God. Winston (2002) notes that the Greek term *eirenopoios* used in this Beatitude is translated peacemaker one who promotes peace, who causes peace and quietness. Winston explains that the

leader who values being a peacemaker is a leader actively pursuing peace and unity in the work environment. Howell (2006) contributes to this understanding by noting that the leader is aggressively engaging in making peace or reconciliation. To be a peacemaker at work the leader must first experience peace in her/his own life before attempting to instill in the organization (Winston). This requirement of first experiencing the value in their personal life is not a unique requirement for the seventh Beatitude but in fact is a foundational understanding and requirement for all seven values. Winston and Patterson (2006) suggest the seventh Beatitude requires "all prior six values to be in place and fully practiced" and by embracing peace a leader would demonstrate a "successful and intentional management of tension and the resolution of conflict" (p.32).

Howell (2006) noted such a leader is one who thrashes through issues, listening, learning, and testing out ideas, and understanding why others think as they do. Kolbell (2003) draws a similar image of a leader who attempts to "live peaceably with others under circumstances that are not always easy" she/he is a leader who is "reflexive,

Table 8. Items for the Seventh Beatitude

Item Number	Item
1	My supervisor seeks to build unity in the workplace.
2	My supervisor seeks to help resolve conflict in the workplace.
3	My supervisor has peace in her/his personal life, to the best of my knowledge.
4	My supervisor intervenes in employees' relationships as needed to reduce conflict.
5	My supervisor recognizes that peace is not the absence of conflict but the intentional resolution of conflict.
6	My supervisor uses conflict wisely to resolve problems in the organization.
7	My supervisor looks for alternative solutions to problems such that all parties are benefited by the solution.
8	My department is perceived as a peaceful place by people out-side the department.
9	My supervisor encourages open discussion of disagreement among employees on all workplace topics.
10	My supervisor respects the opinions of people who disagree with him/her.
11	My supervisor is not afraid to confront conflict and work to re-solve it.
12	My supervisor accepts solutions to problems when the solution did not come from her/him.

anticipate, prepare, and assume a disposition that allows for peace" (p. 116-117). The leader described by Howell and Kolbell above can be viewed in a global light as well when she/he uses conflict to cause, create, or maintain peace or when demonstrating consideration of the various cultures of followers to bring about or maintain a peaceful work environment (Winston & Patterson, 2006).

Kouzes and Posner (2006) suggest all leaders should learn from conflict and through the conflict process, the leader learns what is motivating others. Once the motivating values are understood from the perspective of all parties, then creativity and innovation is unleashed toward developing a unifying set of goals and objectives (Kouzes & Posner). It is through the process of conflict management that a leader has the opportunity to instill peace thereby demonstrating the leadership value of peacemaker inspired by the seventh Beatitude.

Therefore, if a leader embraces the value of peacemaker, the observable behavior would be her/his seeking to build and sustain unity in the workplace. (see Table 8)

RELIABILITY

This study used DeVellis (2003) "Guidelines in Scale Development" (pp.60-101) to develop the seven scales within the inventory for the leadership values. DeVellis guidelines for scale development consist of eight steps: (1) determine clearly what it is you want to measure, (2) generate an item pool, (3) determine the format for measurement, (4) have the initial item pool reviewed by experts, (5) consider inclusion of validation items, (6) administer items to development sample, (7) evaluate the items, and (8) optimize scale length.

The first and second steps of DeVellis sequence were provided for in the prior sections of this study in which the authors present the concept of a beatitude and the items generated from Winston's (2002) conceptual study.

Scale Development

Respondents for the scale study were requested to indicate their attitude toward their leader on a semantic differential scale with a quantitative seven-point response scale ranging from negative to positive (DeVellis, 2003; Gay & Airasian, 2003).

Data Collection

Sixty-one companies were contacted using two or more of the following methods; (a) direct mailing to the senior manager, (b) e-mail to the senior leader, (c) personal telephone conversations, or (d) personal meetings. Each contact with the company was provided an overview of the research, the cost, the value for participating, and requested participation of employees in a web survey, paper survey, or a combination of both methods. Companies were provided the option of inviting all their employees to participate or designating a single section or division within the organization if applicable based on the total size of the organization. The contacted organizations represented a cross section of businesses located in the United States and internationally consisting of universities, high school districts, churches, US government agency, state government agencies, local city and county agencies, aerospace companies, technology firms, financial organizations including; banks, credit unions, investment and wealth management firms, international missionary organizations, national charity organizations, radio companies, retail businesses, commercial businesses, national food chains, employment agencies, and professional service organizations.

Of the 61 companies contacted, eight (13%) agreed to participate in the data collection. The participating organizations comprised of a U.S. government outsourced call center, law enforcement organization, a South African wholesale distributor, a university, a high school, two international missionary organizations, and a wealth management firm. One hundred and forty-six participants or 12 respondents per item from the eight participating companies completed either the web-based survey, paper version, or a combination of both. The 12 respondents per item exceeded the desired objective of 5 respondents per item or 60 per section as recommended in the literature (DeVellis, 2003; Gay & Airasian, 2003; Hair, Anderson, Tatham & Black, 1998). Participation in the study was both voluntary and anonymous for the participants and the organizations.

Survey Participants' Profile

Table 10 shows the demographic information on the participants.

Data Analysis

A principal component analysis was performed for each of the seven instruments with the desired intent of reducing the number of items from the original twelve. The following seven subsections provide the results of the principal component analysis

The First Beatitude: Blessed are the Poor in Spirit

The initial analysis extracted two components, with Eigenvalues greater than 1.0. The findings as noted in Table 11 indicate two components that explained 67.12% of the variance, with the first component accounting for 57.4% of the variance while the second component consisting of one item and accounting for 9.7% of the variance. The second component was rejected since it consisted of only one item.

In order to create a parsimonious, yet reliable scale, the researchers selected the five highest loading items in the component for retention as a factor representing the scale for the first Beatitude – Blessed are the Poor in Spirit (DeVellis, 2003). The retained items are noted in Table 12.

The Chronbach Alpha reliability of the scale consisting of the retained items was .91. A positive correlation relationship (Pearson-correlation = .86 p=.01) existed between supervisor effectiveness and the first beatitude scale, which serves as a criterion validity check.

Table 10. Demographic profile of participants

Demographics ($N = 146$)	Number	Percentage
Ethnicity		
African-American	3	2.0
Asian-American	1	0.8
European-American	59	40.4
Hispanic-American	34	23.3
South African & Other	3	2.0
Undeclared	46	31.5
Years working for supervisor		
1 to 2 years	101	69.2
3 to 6 years	24	16.4
over 7 years	7	4.8
undeclared	14	9.6
Respondents level within the organization		
Front line service/production area	61	41.8
Mid-level supervisor	14	9.6
Administrative staff/support	26	17.8
Senior management level	16	10.9
Declared as other	29	19.9
Number of people reporting to supervisor		
3 to 10 direct reports	69	47.3
10 to 15 direct reports	42	28.8
16 to 30 direct reports	9	6.2
31 to 100 direct reports	4	2.7
Undeclared	22	15.0
Number of people the respondent supervises		
0-10 employees	114	78.1
11 to 25 employees	20	13.7
75 to 150 employees	2	1.4
undeclared	10	6.8
Total employee population		
Under 1000 employees	81	55.5
1000 to 4500 employees	18	12.3
5000 to 55000 employees	13	8.9
Undeclared	34	23.3
Gender		
Male	56	39.2
Female	87	59.6
Undeclared	3	1.2
Age		
Below 30	49	33.6
30-40 years	22	15.0
41 to 50 years	28	19.2
51 to 71	33	22.6
Undeclared	14	9.6
Religious Affiliation		
Atheist	2	1.4
Buddhism	3	2.0
Christianity	93	63.7
Other	48	32.9
Industry representation		
Profit	115	78.8
State Government	12	8.2
Not for profit	19	13.0

Table 11. First Beatitude—Component matrix

Question	Component	
	1	2
B1Q01	0.71	
B1Q02	0.80	
B1Q03	0.84	
B1Q04		0.80
B1Q05	0.79	
B1Q06	0.88	
B1Q07	0.86	
B1Q08	0.75	
B1Q09	0.80	
B1Q10	0.69	
B1Q11	0.77	
B1Q12	0.74	

Table 12. Retained items

Item Number	Item	Loading
B1Q02	My supervisor is humble.	.80
B1Q03	My supervisor shows a genuine interest in the work we do.	.84
B1Q06	My supervisor shows respect for us in both her/his behavior and words (must be both to qualify).	.88
B1Q07	When I have a concern about work, my supervisor listens to me and considers my opinions in her/his decisions.	.86
B1Q09	My supervisor willingly admits when she/he doesn't know something.	.80

The Second Beatitude: Blessed Are Those who Mourn

A principal component analysis was performed to measure the inter-relationships between the items with the desired intent of reducing the number of items from the original twelve. The initial analysis extracted one component, with an Eigenvalue of 7.61 explaining 64% of the variance. (see Table 13)

In order to create a parsimonious, yet reliable scale, the researchers selected the five highest loading items in the component for retention as a factor representing the scale for the Beatitude – Blessed are they that Mourn (DeVellis, 2003).

The retained items are noted in Table 14. The Chronbach Alpha for the retained items was .95. The Pearson-R correlation of the second beatitude score and the scale for leadership effectiveness was .77 that was significant at the .01 level for a two-tailed test.

The Third Beatitude: Blessed Are the Meek

A principal component analysis was performed to measure the inter-relationships between the items with the desired intent of reducing the number of items from the original twelve. The initial analysis

Table 13. Second Beatitude—Component matrix

Question	Component
	1
B2Q01	0.60
B2Q02	0.66
B2Q03	0.87
B2Q04	0.88
B2Q05	0.57
B2Q06	0.85
B2Q07	0.77
B2Q08	0.86
B2Q09	0.78
B2Q10	0.84
B2Q11	0.89
B2Q12	0.91

Table 14. Retained items

Item Number	Item	Loading
B2Q03	My supervisor's behavior shows that she/he is concerned about my well-being	.86
B2Q04	My supervisor makes decisions with my best interest in mind.	.88
B2Q08	My supervisor cares for me as a person.	.86
B2Q11	My supervisor does all that she/he can to accommodate my needs in the workplace.	.89
B2Q12	My supervisor is concerned about my emotional well-being.	.91

extracted three components, with Eigenvalues of: (a) 5.27 explaining 44% of the variance, (b) 1.27 explaining 10.6% of the variance, and (c) 1.16 explaining 9.6% of the variance respectfully.

Since question 2 loaded on two components it was dropped from consideration. Since questions 7 and 8 loaded on separate components they were dropped from consideration as well. In order to create a parsimonious, yet reliable scale, the researchers selected the five highest loading items in the resultant component for retention as a factor representing the scale 'Controlled discipline' (DeVellis, 2003). The retained items are noted in

Table 16. The Cronbach Alpha for the retained questions was .89.

The Fourth Beatitude: Blessed Are Those who Hunger and Thirst for Righteousness

A principal component analysis was performed to measure the inter-relationships between the items with the desired intent of reducing the number of items from the original twelve. The initial analysis extracted one component with an Eigenvalue of 7.28 explaining 61% of the variance.

Table 15. Third Beatitude—Component matrix

Question	Component		
	1	**2**	**3**
B3Q01	0.51		
B3Q02	0.65	-0.55	
B3Q03	0.75		
B3Q04	0.81		
B3Q05	0.79		
B3Q06	0.68		
B3Q07			0.84
B3Q08		0.56	
B3Q09	0.73		
B3Q10	0.64		
B3Q11	0.64		
B3Q12	0.82		

Table 16. Retained items

Item Number	Item	Loading
B3Q03	My supervisor controls her/his temper in the workplace.	.75
B3Q04	My supervisor seeks to know why something went wrong before she/he reacts.	.81
B3Q05	My supervisor uses her/his power in the organization wisely.	.79
B3Q09	My supervisor does not demean employees in her/his words or actions.	.73
B3Q12	My supervisor uses her/his emotions wisely in working through conflict.	.82

Table 17. Retained items

Item Number	Item	Loading
B4Q06	When my supervisor asks me to do something I know it is for the right reason.	.85
B4Q07	I trust my supervisor to make the right decision in the workplace.	.88
B4Q08	My supervisor acts ethically in all aspects of her/his life to the best of my knowledge.	.81
B4Q09	My supervisor earns the respect of everyone in the organization.	.83
B4Q12	My supervisor demonstrates wisdom in her/his decisions.	.88

Table 18. Fifth Beatitude—Component matrix

Question	Component	
	1	2
B5Q01	0.75	
B5Q02	0.85	
B5Q03	0.62	0.60
B5Q04	0.81	
B5Q05	0.81	
B5Q06	0.89	
B5Q07	0.56	0.53
B5Q08	0.83	
B5Q09	0.69	
B5Q10	0.73	
B5Q11	0.75	
B5Q12	0.88	

Table 19. Retained items

Item Number	Item	Loading
B5Q02	My supervisor is compassionate when dealing with employees.	.85
B5Q04	My supervisor, when discipling employees looks to the future and seeks long-term improvement rather than short-term punishment.	.81
B5Q06	My supervisor's kindness makes it easier to tell him/her when I do something wrong.	.89
B5Q08	When a problem occurs my supervisor seeks to understand the situational factors in order to determine if the employee was wrong or not.	.83
B5Q12	My supervisor's compassionate approach to problems makes it easier for employees to openly discuss problems.	.88

In order to create a parsimonious, yet reliable scale, the researchers selected the five highest loading items in the resultant component for retention as a factor representing the scale 'Controlled discipline' (DeVellis, 2003). The retained items are noted in Table 17. The Cronbach Alpha for the retained questions was .92.

The Fifth Beatitude: Blessed Are the Merciful

A principal component analysis was performed with the desired intent of reducing the number of items from the original twelve. The initial analysis extracted two components. The first component had an Eigenvalue of 7.1 explaining 59.6% of the variance. The second component had an Eigenvalue of 1.0 explaining 8.4% of the data. The two items comprising the second component were removed due to their cross-loading with component 1.

In order to create a parsimonious, yet reliable scale, the researchers selected the five highest loading items in the resultant component for retention as a factor representing the fifth beatitude (DeVellis, 2003). The retained items are noted in Table 19. The Chronbach Alpha for the retained questions was .93.

Table 20. Section 1—Component matrix

Question	Component	
	1	**2**
B6Q01	0.79	
B6Q02	0.88	
B6Q03	0.77	
B6Q04	0.83	
B6Q05	0.55	
B6Q06	0.54	0.73
B6Q07	0.82	
B6Q08	0.90	
B6Q09	0.87	
B6Q10	0.65	
B6Q11	0.81	
B6Q12	0.77	

Table 21. Retained items

Item Number	Item	Loading
B6Q02	My supervisor has integrity in that what she/he says aligns with what she/he does.	.88
B6Q04	My supervisor's behavior makes it evident that he/she lives the organization's mission statement.	.83
B6Q07	My supervisor means what she/he says.	.82
B6Q08	My supervisor's motives are aligned with both her/his words and actions (must have both aligned).	.90
B6Q09	My supervisor is truthful.	.87

The Sixth Beatitude: Blessed Are the Pure in Heart

A principal component analysis was performed with the desired intent of reducing the number of items from the original twelve. The initial analysis extracted two components that explained 68.6% of the variance, with the first component accounting for 60.0% of the variance while the second component consisting of one item and accounting for 8.6% of the variance. The second component was rejected since the one item cross-loaded with component 1

In order to create a parsimonious, yet reliable scale (DeVellis, 2003), the researchers selected the five highest loading items in the component

for retention as a factor representing the sixth beatitude – Blessed are the Pure in Heart. The retained items are noted in Table 21.

The Seventh Beatitude: Blessed Are the Peacemakers

A principal component analysis was performed with the desired intent of reducing the number of items from the original twelve. The initial analysis extracted one component with an Eigenvalue of 7.21 that explained 60.1% of the variance.

In order to create a parsimonious, yet reliable scale (DeVellis, 2003), the researchers selected the five highest loading items in the component for retention as a factor representing the seventh

Table 22. Seventh Beatitude—Component matrix

Question	Component 1
B7Q01	0.83
B7Q02	0.85
B7Q03	0.75
B7Q04	0.69
B7Q05	0.80
B7Q06	0.74
B7Q07	0.82
B7Q08	0.62
B7Q09	0.73
B7Q10	0.85
B7Q11	0.71
B7Q12	0.86

Table 23. Retained items

Item Number	Item	Loading
B7Q01	My supervisor seeks to build unity in the workplace.	.83
B7Q02	My supervisor seeks to help resolve conflict in the workplace.	.85
B7Q07	My supervisor looks for alternative solutions to problems such that all parties are benefited by the solution.	.82
B7Q10	My supervisor respects the opinions of people who disagree with him/her.	.85
B7Q12	My supervisor accepts solutions to problems when the solution did not come from him/her.	.86

beatitude – Blessed are the Peacemakers. The retained items are noted in Table 23.

The Chronbach Alpha reliability of the retained items was .92. A positive correlation relationship (Pearson-correlation = .78 p=.01) existed between supervisor effectiveness and the sixth beatitude scale, which serves as a criterion validity check.

RESULTS

The participant upon submitting the data for the seven scales receives a total score for each beatitude as shown in Figure 1.

The authors of the scales will provide normative data for participants after normative data is collected.

Commentary

In this section each of the seven instruments are addressed in sequence.

The First Beatitude: Blessed Are the Poor in Spirit

This scale to measure 'Poor in Spirit' can be used to measure the level of humility in leaders. Collins (2001) indicated that humility and fierce resolve were the two common characteristics of 'great' leaders. This scale may be useful as a before/after measure for leadership development. The findings suggest that a leader who is humble, interested in, and respectful of employees will be open to learn from them. Such openness to

Figure 1. Seven instruments to measure seven Beatitudes

Your scores for the seven Beatitudes are expressed as a total score for each Beatitude. The maximum score for each beatitude is 35.	
Beatitude	**Score**
Beatitude one: Blessed are the Poor in Spirit	30
Beatitude two: Blessed are the Meek	30
Beatitude three: Blessed are the Merciful	30
Beatitude four: Blessed are the Peacemakers	30
Beatitude five Blessed are Those Who Mourn	30
Beatitude six: Blessed are Those Who Hunger and Thirst for Righteousness	30
Beatitude seven: Blessed are the Pure in Heart	30
For information on each of the Beatitudes please see Winston's 'Be a Leader for God's Sake'.	

learning from others, especially subordinates, reveals one's vulnerability, and lends itself to the raising of each other's level of motivation, commitment, and effectiveness. The first behavior and value inspired by the Beatitudes is reflective of a servant leader according to Patterson (2003) who identified humility as a main characteristic of Servant Leadership. Klenke (2005) and Senge (1990) argued that a humble leader has an honest assessment of their strengths, weaknesses, and accomplishments and as a lifetime learner remains teachable and humble. Leaders who are humble and teachable will demonstrate this value through a behavior reflecting humility and teachableness (Winston, 2002) thereby, providing a positive influence on employees' commitment and effectiveness.

The Second Beatitude: Blessed Are Those who Mourn

If a leader embraced the second Beatitude and demonstrated 'concern for others', the observable behavior would be her/his caring for others. Based on the principal component analysis from Section 2, five questions were retained representing the second leadership behavior of caring for others with a Chronbach Alpha of .95.

The relationship between supervisor effectiveness and the second Beatitude was investigated using a Pearson product-moment correlation coefficient of .82 with a p value of .01 (2-tailed). This positive and significant finding is indicative of a strong relationship between the second Beatitude and supervisory effectiveness (Kilroy, 2008).

The Third Beatitude: Blessed Are the Meek

If a leader embraced the third Leadership Value of controlled discipline, the observable behavior would be her/his patience, calmness, and willingness to teach. Based on the principal component analysis from Section 3, five questions were retained representing the third Leadership Behavior of patience, calmness, and willingness to teach with a Cronbach Alpha of .89.

Inclusion of the six supervisor effectiveness questions (section 9) in the Leadership Values instrument was intended to demonstrate correlation or non-correlation between patience, calmness, and willingness to teach (third Leadership Behavior) and perceived supervisory effectiveness/satisfaction. The correlation between supervisor effectiveness and the third Beatitude was .77 with a p value of .02 (2-tailed). This positive and significant finding is indicative of a strong relationship between the third Beatitude and supervisory effectiveness (Kilroy, 2008).

The Fourth Beatitude: Blessed Are Those who Hunger and Thirst for Righteousness

If a leader embraced the fourth Beatitude the observable behavior would be her/his continually seeking what is good, just, right, and equitable for employees and the organization through specific acts. Based on the principal component analysis five questions were retained representing the fourth leadership behavior of continually seeking what is good, just, right, and equitable for employees and the organization through specific acts with a Chronbach Alpha of .92.

The Pearson-R correlation result of .73 with a p value of .01 (2-tailed) indicates a significant positive relationship between the fourth beatitude and leadership effectiveness (Kilroy, 2008).

The scale developed in this study may be useful in leadership selection as well as in leadership evaluation and development. The findings also draw attention to Bass and Steidlmeier (1999) position that the virtues and moral character of a leader are important and Kriegbaum's (1998) assertion that values control behaviors that are based on one's belief.

The Fifth Beatitude: Blessed Are the Merciful

If a leader embraced the fifth beatitude, the observable behavior would be her/his listening and showing of compassion. Based on the principal component analysis five questions were retained representing the fifth beatitude with a Chronbach Alpha of .925. A correlation analysis of the fifth beatitude and the summated score for the leadership effectiveness returned a Pearson-R value of .82 with a p-value of .01(Kilroy, 2008).

The scale developed in this study may be useful in leadership selection as well as in leadership evaluation and development. The findings also draw attention to Bass and Steidlmeier (1999) position that the virtues and moral character of a leader are important and Kriegbaum's (1998) assertion that values control behaviors that are based on one's belief.

The Sixth Beatitude: Blessed Are the Pure in Heart

If a leader embraced the sixth Leadership Value of being highly focused, the observable behavior would be her/his intensity and focus on the organization objectives. Based on the principal component analysis from Section 6, five questions were retained representing the sixth leadership behavior of intensity and focus on the organization objectives with a Cronbach Alpha of .93. The relationship between supervisor effectiveness and the sixth Beatitude was investigated using a Pearson product-moment correlation coefficient of .61 with a p value of .000 (2-tailed). This positive and significant finding is indicative of a strong relationship between the sixth Beatitude—Blessed are the Pure in Heart and supervisory effectiveness (Kilroy, 2008).

The Seventh Beatitude: Blessed Are the Peacemakers

If a leader embraced the seventh beatitude of peacemaker, the observable behavior would be her/his seeking to build and sustain unity in the workplace. Based on the principal component analysis five questions were retained representing the seventh leadership behavior of seeking to build and sustain unity in the workplace with a Chronbach Alpha of .920. The relationship between supervisor effectiveness and the seventh Leadership Behavior was investigated using a Pearson product-moment correlation coefficient of .78 with a p value of .000 (2-tailed). This positive and significant finding is indicative of a strong relationship between the seventh Leadership Behavior—seeking to build and sustain unity in the workplace and supervisory effectiveness (Kilroy, 2008).

COMMENTARY

Knowledge of one's personal values, coupled with knowledge of how the behavior is perceived by those being led, is important for a leader. Dent, Higgins, & Wharff, D (2005) wrote, "Organizational leaders who are more willing to use their personal spiritual values to make business decisions and transform organizations instill value that become the standard against which all organizational activities are measured" (p. 693). It is important for organizations as well to determine if the organization's leadership is demonstrating the articulated organizational values. In other words, are the leaders' observable behaviors, their walk, reflecting the organizational talk to its stakeholders?

If the premise that value-centered leadership creates organizational integrity (Behr, 1998) is embraced then through the use of the Beatitude instruments developed in this study, organizations could ascertain the values and behaviors of their leaders and the affect on the followers' commitment and effectiveness that represents the culture customers observe when interacting with the organization

The findings also draw attention to Bass and Steidlmeier (1999) position that the virtues and moral character of a leader are important and Kriegbaum's (1998) assertion that values control behaviors that are based on one's belief. The seven instruments developed in this study collectively or a customized combination may be useful to an organization in the selecting, evaluation, and development of leadership reflective of an organizations espoused values.

Cost

The instrument is free.

Location

The instrument is located at: http://www.bealeaderforgodssake.org/beatitudes.html

REFERENCES

Allen, C. L. (1953). *God's psychiatry*. New Jersey: Fleming H. Revell Company.

Bandura, A. (1997). *Self-efficacy: The exercise of control*. New York, NY: W.H. Freeman and Company.

Bass, B., & Steidlmeier, P. (1999). Ethics, character, and authentic transformational leadership behavior. *The Leadership Quarterly*, *10*(2), 181–218. doi:10.1016/S1048-9843(99)00016-8

Behr, E. T. (1998, March). Acting from the center: Your response to today's leadership challenges must be grounded in personal values. *Management Review*, *51*(5).

Blanchard, K. (2007). *Leading at a higher level*. Upper Saddle River, NJ: Pearson.

Blanchard, K., & Hodges, P. (2005). *Lead like Jesus: Lessons from the greatest leadership role model of all times*. Nashville, TN: W Publishing Group.

Burke, R. (2006). Leadership and spirituality. *Foresight*, *8*(6), 14–25. doi:10.1108/14636680610712504

Collins Business. (2001). *Good to great: Why some companies make the leap... and others don't*. New York, NY: Author.

Dennis, R. (2004). *Servant leadership theory: Development of the servant leadership assessment instrument*. Retrieved from Dissertations and Theses database AAT 3133544.

Dennis, R., & Bocarnea, M. (2005). Development of the servant leadership assessment instrument. *Leadership and Organization Development Journal*, *26*(8), 600–615. doi:10.1108/01437730510633692

Dent, E., Higgins, M., & Wharff, D. (2005). Spirituality and leadership: An empirical review of definitions, distinctions, and embedded assumptions. *The Leadership Quarterly, 16*, 625–653. doi:10.1016/j.leaqua.2005.07.002

DeVellis, R. F. (2003). *Scale development theory and application* (2nd ed.). Thousand Oaks, CA: Sage Publishing.

Fry, L. (2003). Toward a theory of spiritual leadership. *The Leadership Quarterly, 14*, 639–727. doi:10.1016/j.leaqua.2003.09.001

Gay, L. R., & Airasian, P. (2003). *Educational research competencies for analysis and applications* (7th ed.). Upper Saddle River, NJ: Merrill Prentice Hall.

Hair, J. F. Jr, Anderson, R. E., Tatham, R. L., & Black, W. C. (1998). *Multivariate data analysis* (5th ed.). Upper Saddle River, NJ: Prentice Hall International.

Howell, J. C. (2006). *The beatitudes for today.* Louisville, KY: Westminster John Knox Press.

Kilroy, J. J. (2008). *Development of seven leadership behavior scales based upon the seven leadership values inspired by the beatitudes* (Doctoral dissertation). Available from ProQuest Dissertation and Theses database, 149 pages; AAT 3340922. Retrieved from http://proquest.umi.com/pqdlink?did=1654488921&Fmt=7&clientId=79356&RQT=309&VName=PQD

Klenke, K. (2005). Corporate values as multi-level, multi-domain antecedents of leader behaviors. *International Journal of Management, 26*(1), 50–66.

Kolbell, E. (2003). *What Jesus meant: The beatitudes and a meaningful life.* Louisville, KY: Westminster John Knox Press.

Kouzes, J., & Posner, B. (2001). Bringing leadership lessons from the past into the future. In Bennis, W., Spreitzer, G., & Cummings, T. (Eds.), *The future of leadership* (pp. 81–90). San Francisco, CA: Josey-Bass.

Kouzes, J., & Posner, B. (2006). *A leader's legacy.* San Francisco, CA: Josey-Bass.

Kriegbaum, R. (1998). *Leadership prayers.* Wheaton, IL: Tyndale House Publishers.

Kriger, M., & Seng, Y. (2005). Leadership with inner meaning: a contingency theory of leadership based on the worldviews of five religions. *The Leadership Quarterly, 16*(5), 771–806. doi:10.1016/j.leaqua.2005.07.007

Langan, J. (1977). Beatitude and moral law in St Thomas. *The Journal of Religious Ethics, 5*, 183–195.

Lord, R., & Brown, D. (2001). Leadership, values, and subordinate self-concepts. *The Leadership Quarterly, 12*, 133–152. doi:10.1016/S1048-9843(01)00072-8

Mitroff, I., & Denton, E. (1999). *A spiritual audit of corporate America.* San Francisco, CA: Jossey-Bass.

Northouse, P. (2007). *Leadership theories and practice* (4th ed.). Thousand Oaks, CA: Sage Publishing.

Patterson, K. (2003). *Servant leadership: A theoretical model.* (Doctorial dissertation, Regent University, 2004). (UMI 3082719).

Patterson, K. A., Russell, R. F., & Stone, A. G. (2004). Transformational versus servant leadership - A difference in leader focus. *Leadership and Organization Development Journal, 25*(4).

Schein, E. H. (1992). *Organizational culture and leadership* (2nd ed.). San Francisco, CA: Jossey-Bass.

Senge, P. (1990). *The fifth discipline*. New York, NY: Currency Doubleday.

Stone, G., Russell, R., & Patterson, K. (2004). Transformational versus servant leadership: A difference in leader focus. *Leadership and Organization Development Journal, 25*(4), 349–361. Retrieved from www.emeraldinsight.com/0143-7739.htm doi:10.1108/01437730410538671

Tse, R. (2006). The leadership files: Dr. Bruce Winston of Regent University. *The Christian Post*. Retrieved July 2006, from http://www.christianpost.com/article/20060110/13937.htm

Winston, B. (2002). *Be a leader for god's sake*. Virginia Beach, VA: Regent University.

Winston, B., & Patterson, K. (2006). An integrative definition of leadership. *International Journal of Leadership Studies, 1*(2), 6–66.

Yukl, G. (2002). *Leadership in organizations* (5th ed.). New Jersey: Prentice Hall.

KEY TERMS AND DEFINITIONS

Beatitude: Happiness.

Blessed are the Meek for They Will Inherit the Earth: Leaders who have controlled discipline.

Blessed are the Merciful for They Shall Be Shown Mercy: Leaders who display compassion or mercy.

Blessed are the Peacemakers for They Will Be Called Sons of God: A leader who promotes peace, who causes peace and quietness.

Blessed are the Poor in Heart: Leaders who are highly focused, and have intensity of purpose.

Blessed are the Poor in Spirit: A leader who values being humble and teachable.

Blessed are those Who Hunger and Thirst for Righteousness for They Will Be Filled: The leadership behavior demonstrated by this Beatitude is a leader who continually seeks what is right and just, and expresses his/herself in specific acts.

Blessed are Those Who Mourn for They Will Inherit the Earth: Having great concern for others.

Chapter 11
Inventory of Leader Sternness (ILS)

W. David Winner
Regent University, USA

Rushton S. Ricketson
Luther Rice Seminary & University, USA

ABSTRACT

The Inventory of Leader Sternness (ILS) is a new leadership construct designed to measure sternness in an adult self-directed leader. Sternness, as a leadership construct, is derived from the writings of Sun Tzu in The Art of War as proposed by Carr, Coe, Derrick, and Ponton (2007). Winner (2008) developed the ILS to measure three co-occurring behavioral intentions of sternness: (a) a willingness to establish obedience through rewards and punishments within limits, (b) consistency in actions to ensure good behavior through rituals and respect, and (c) a determination to do the difficult tasks of leadership. The ILS is a valid and reliable instrument for use in the assessment of sternness in an adult self-directed leader.

BACKGROUND

The Inventory of Leader Sternness (ILS) is designed to measure sternness in an adult self-directed leader. Winner (2008) defines sternness as a behavioral syndrome described by the presence of co-occurring behaviors, (a) a willingness to establish obedience through rewards and punishments within limits, (b) consistency in actions to ensure good behavior through rituals and respect,

and (c) a determination to do the difficult tasks of leadership. Leader sternness is a new leadership construct derived from the writings of Sun Tzu, an ancient Chinese general who operationally defined leadership in The Art of War (Carr et at, 2007). Sun Tzu (as cited in Cleary, 2000) defined leadership as "a matter of intelligence, trustworthiness, humaneness, courage and sternness" (p. 44). Similarly, Gagliardi (2002) asserted:

DOI: 10.4018/978-1-4666-2172-5.ch011

For over two thousand years, people have pre-served and treasured Sun Tzu's famous treatise on war for one reason: its competitive methods work extremely well. As the first of the military classics, The Art of War offers a distinct, non-intuitive philosophy on how to discover a path. This philosophy works in any dynamic environment where people find themselves contesting with one another for a specific goal. (p. viii)

McNeilly (1996) reported the modern impact:

Today, Sun Tzu's appeal has extended beyond the military realm into the world of business. Because business by definition deals with competition, Sun Tzu's principles are ideally suited to competitive business situation. In the United States and Europe, The Art of War has been quoted in numerous books on strategy, organization and competition. Many of its more striking verses have been the lead-in for countless business articles. (p. 5)

Krause (2005) continued, "In the latter half of the twentieth century, *The Art of War* became a worldwide management phenomenon. Understanding and using Sun Tzu's principles is now a requirement for everyone who wants to succeed in business anywhere in the world" (p. 2). Wu, Chou, and Wu (2004) agreed, "We know that the principles of Sun Tzu's, *The Art of War*, can be applied in today's business operations" (p. 397). Li (2000) asserted, "Sun Tzu's work is a treatise *on* leadership--*by* one who aspires to be a leader in war management *for* the eyes of a leader in state governance" (p. 3).

Wu et al. (2004) performed research to test the relationships between the principles of Sun Tzu's *The Art of War* and the key success factors of an organization. The study concluded by stating, "The results of the canonical analysis indicate that Sun Tzu's principles of situation appraisal, strategy implementations and strategic control had significant influence on KSFs [key success factors]" (p. 406). The implication from this study is that principles of Sun Tzu have been found to

have manifest positive relationships with success factors when used in an organization. This supports the suggestion of Carr et al. (2007) that the five factors mentioned in Sun Tzu's definition of leadership (intelligence, trustworthiness, humaneness, courage, and sternness) are applicable to today's leaders.

Prior to the study by Winner (2008), no instrument existed to measure sternness in an adult self-directed leader. The ILS is based upon recent research identifying the characteristic behaviors of sternness (Adams, 1963; Ames, 2000; Bandura, 1986, 1997, 2006; Chen, 1994; Cleary, 1989, 2000; Gagliardi, 2004a, 2004b; McNeilly, 1996; Michaelson, 2001; Michaelson & Michaelson, 2003; Wong, Maher, & Lee, 1998). This literature review asserts that sternness is a behavioral syndrome described by the presence of co-occurring behaviors. The three behaviors are (a) a willingness to establish obedience through rewards and punishments within limits, (b) consistency in actions to ensure good behavior through rituals and respect, and (c) a determination to do the difficult tasks of leadership.

The ILS is the first instrument created to measure one of the five elements of leadership as defined by Sun Tzu. In fact, until the ILS, sternness was not even mentioned as a necessary leadership construct. Winston and Patterson (2005) reviewed 160 documents on leadership literature and identified "92 discrete dimensions" (p. 4). Sternness was not indentified as a leadership construct in their integrated definition of leadership. The ILS was created to fill this research gap by answering this research problem:

The problem to be addressed is the lack of a detailed theoretical construct, based upon current research into sternness contextually dependent upon the construct of leadership, which can be used to develop an instrument to measure this conative factor. Prior to this research, there was no instrument available to measure co-occurring behaviors of sternness. (Winner, 2008, p. 3)

The ILS is a valid and reliable instrument "that acts as a mechanism to understand more fully sternness within a self-directed leader" (Winner, p. 7).

Self-directed leadership is a new construct proposed by Carr, et al. (2007) as flowing out of the self-directed learning and autonomous learning literature and Sun Tzu's definition of a leader. Carr et al. (2007) suggested that self-directed leadership could be developed in the same way that Confessore created and validated the LAP. By following this model, the definition of leadership provided by Sun Tzu can be operationally defined, and instrumentation can be developed and validated independently which "may give rise to a new construct—Self-Directed Leadership" (p. 27).

Confessore (1992) offered a succinct definition of self-directed learning: "Very simply, self-directed learning manifests itself in people who feel a need to learn something" (p. 3). He proposed that people will assess their external resources and internal resources to decide what might be useful to reduce or fulfill that need. Confessore contended, "once that is done, self-directed learning, as with any human endeavor, becomes a matter of drive, initiative, resourcefulness and persistence to see ourselves through to some level of learning that is personally satisfying" (p. 3). Later, he changed drive to desire, as describing more succinctly what happens in the learner. Confessore concluded that these four conative factors constitute the construct of autonomous learning.

Ponton and Carr (1999) describe the relationship between self-directedness, self-directed learning and autonomous learning. Self-directedness is needed to engage in self-directed learning. "Learner self-directedness includes the internal characteristics of a person (cognition and affection) that create the motivation for subsequent behavioral intentions (conations) and behavior. The pedagogic process of self-directed learning includes the behavioral intentions, behaviors and the subsequent self-reflection" (Ponton & Carr, p. 5). This distinction is important because self-directedness precedes self-directed learning by

influencing the behavioral intentions of a person to engage in self-directed learning. Ponton and Carr suggest that autonomous learning is a subset of self-directed learning and self-directedness because autonomous learning exists within the realm of intentional behavior and conation.

Autonomous learning is defined as "an agentic learning process in which the conative factors of desire, initiative, resourcefulness and persistence are manifest" (Ponton, 1999, p. 15-16). These four dynamics, as outlined by Confessore, became the foundation for the research conducted by Carr (1999), Ponton (1999), Derrick (2001), and Meyer (2001). The resulting four instruments were used by Confessore to comprise the Learner Autonomy Profile (LAP). As Confessore and Park (2004) reported:

The LAP is structured around the assertion that learner autonomy must be understood in terms of conation or the learner's behavioral intentions. This assertion directs attention away from ex post facto assessment of learning in terms of behavioral outcomes and directs attention toward understanding the behavioral intentions of learners as predictors of learned behaviors. (p. 40-41)

The LAP is used to provide diagnostic information for the learner and facilitator in relation to autonomous learning.

Meyer (2001) studied desire as a precursor to autonomous learning. She declared, "Intentionality is essential to learner autonomy, and presupposes the ability to access and direct our power to become the masters of our own destinies" (p. 1). By focusing on emotions, Meyer believed learners could gain control of their emotions and harness them to develop intentional behavior, which leads to greater autonomous learning. She developed the Inventory of Learned Desire (ILD) with 57 items to "determine whether the individual is free to focus on their purpose, manage their power and develop skills to overcome life's distractions" (p. 52). The ILD is a self-reported instrument designed to measure perceptions of basic freedoms, management of power within relationships to others and material objects, and current skills (Meyer). Internal validity of the ILD was determined by a Cronbach's alpha of .90. Based on the study, Meyer found the ILD to be a sound measure of the precursors of intentionality. Confessore and Park (2004) conducted further validation studies and determined that 24 items could be removed to reduce the ILD to 33 items.

Carr (1999) researched the behaviors associated with resourcefulness. He described resourcefulness as four co-occurring behaviors:

The behaviors are (1) Prioritizing learning over other things, (2) making choices in favor of learning when in conflict with other activities, (3) looking to the future benefits of the learning undertaken now, and (4) solving problems (planning, evaluating alternatives, and anticipating consequences). (p. 5)

Carr developed the Inventory of Learner Resourcefulness (ILR) with 80 self-report items to measure these four co-occurring constructs of resourcefulness. Internal validity of the ILR was determined by a Cronbach's alpha of .96. Further validation studies reduced the ILR to 53 items (Confessore & Park, 2004).

Ponton (1999) explored the behaviors associated with personal initiative. He described initiative as set of co-occurring behaviors: "The five behaviors that constitute self-directed learner initiative are goal-directedness, action-orientation, persistence in overcoming obstacles, active-approach to problem solving, and self-startedness (Ponton & Confessore, 1998)" (p. 2). Ponton created the self-reported Inventory of Learner Initiative (ILI) with 55 items. Internal validity was determined by a Cronbach's alpha of .94. Confessore and Park (2004) conducted further validation studies and reduced the ILI to 44 items.

Derrick (2001) focused on the behaviors associated with persistence in learning. Her research

concluded that "the characteristic behaviors of intentions to persist in autonomous learning were identified through research that identifies persistence as a behavior syndrome described by the presence of co-occurring behaviors: volition, self-regulation, and goal-directedness" (p. 5). Derrick developed the Inventory of Learner Persistence (ILP), a self-assessment comprised of 52 items. Internal validity was determined by a Cronbach's alpha of .85. Confessore and Park (2004) conducted further validation studies and determined that all 52 items should be retained.

Confessore and Park (2004) continued research on the LAP by conducting validation studies on the original LAP. The results of these studies reduced the LAP to 164 items (version 3.0). They also determined the need for the creation of a short form LAP with 66 items as compared to the long form with 164 items. Confessore and Park described how they created the short form:

In order to increase the likelihood of high concurrent validity of Version 3.0 and the Short Form, it was decided that the Short Form should be extracted from the Version 3.0 by means of statistical analysis, rather than creation of new items. (p. 54)

The results of the study concluded that the short form "may be used to make an initial assessment of a respondents' Learner Autonomy Profile" (Confessore & Park, p. 55). However, it will not give a detailed assessment; thus, it should not be used in individual intervention plans.

Ponton, Carr, and Derrick (2004) conducted further research on the LAP by performing a path analysis on the four conative factors of desire, resourcefulness, initiative, and persistence.

The present analysis suggests that fostering resourcefulness should be a critical goal in effecting learning persistence. Initiative should be a focus in concert with resourcefulness, but not in isolation—resourcefulness triggers persistence with an effect size similar to the path with initiative as a mediator. (Ponton, Carr, & Derrick, p. 67)

Ponton, Carr and Derrick suggested that further research should include a motivation and self-efficacy instrument to be used with autonomous learning. Ponton, Derrick, Hall, Rhea, and Carr (2005) took up that challenge and created the Appraisal of Learner Autonomy (ALA). They conducted two pilot studies on the nine-item inventory and found it to be valid and internally reliable with a Cronbach's alpha of .86.

The work of Carr (1999), Ponton (1999), Derrick (2001), and Meyer (2001) further validated the work of autonomous learning with the creation of the LAP. The LAP has added to the literature of self-directed learning by focusing on the psychological dimension of self-directed learning. Long (1998) asserted that the psychological dimension is more important than the social and pedagogical dimension. Ponton (1999) explained the two aspects of the psychological dimension and its affect on learning: "One aspect of the psychological dimension consists of the learner identifying needs that serve as motivational inducements to cogitate learning goals. Another aspect of the dimension is the learner's personal attributes/characteristics" (p. 13). Vaill (1996) continued this theme by describing a version of self-directed learning:

In the phrase learning as a way of being, being refers to the whole person—to something that goes on all the time and that extends into all aspects of a person's life; it means all our levels of awareness and, indeed, must include our unconscious minds. (p. 43)

This psychological dimension parallels self-directed learning and self-directed leadership. Vaill (1996) suggested the term *leaderly learning* to describe the overlap of leadership and learning, "Is that managerial leadership is not learned; managerial leadership is learning. Permanent white water has made learning the preeminent requirement of all managerial leadership, beyond all characteristics and requisite competencies" (p.

126). Vaill further asserted that self-directed learning is essential to leadership when he posited, "The relevance of self-directed learning to leadership is this: the behavior we call leadership is, being it is anything else, an initiative from within oneself. Leadership has self-direction as its essence" (p. 61). This internal initiative is a key aspect of the psychological dimension within leadership, autonomous learning, and self-directed learning.

The concept of autonomy is one component of the personal attributes of a learner (Merriam & Caffarella, 1999). Chene (1983) defined autonomy within adult education as having two meanings: "one meaning of autonomy is psychological, another is related to a methodology which either assumes that the learner is autonomous or aims at achieving autonomy through training" (p. 40). Autonomy as a psychological dimension focuses on the internal decisions that go into deciding to be a self-directed learner.

Following on the work of self-directed learning, autonomous learning and autonomy, the ILS focuses on the intention to engage in the behavior of sternness. Fishbein and Ajzen (1975) contend there is a relationship between beliefs, attitudes, intention, and behaviors. This simple model describes the process where beliefs influence attitude, which influences intentions, and then influence a behavior. Therefore, one's attitude towards a behavior directly affects a set of beliefs held about that behavior, which influence the intentions to do the behavior. However, three aspects influence the level of relationship between intention and resulting behaviors: "the degree to which intention and behavior correspond in their levels of specificity: stability of the intention; and the degree to which carrying out the intention is completely under the person's volitional control" (Fishbein & Ajzen, p. 369). Therefore, in order for the intentional behaviors to correspond highly with a behavior, each of these three aspects must be present in sufficient degrees. Bandura (1986), while writing about social cognitive theory noted, "Intention plays a prominent role in the self-regulation of behavior. An intention is defined as the determination to perform certain activities or to bring about a certain future state of affairs" (p. 467).

To be an agent is to intentionally influence one's functioning and life circumstances through forethought. In this view, personal influence is part of a casual structure. People are self-organizing, proactive, self-regulating, and self-reflecting (Bandura, 2006). Bandura (1986) continued:

Social cognitive theory favors conception of interaction based on triadic reciprocality (Bandura, 1977a, 1978a). In this model of reciprocal determinism . . . behavior, cognitive and other personal factors, and environmental influences all operate interactively as determinants of each other. In this triadic reciprocal determinism, the term reciprocal refers to mutual action between causal factors. The term determinism is used here to signify the production of effects by certain factors, rather than in the doctrinal sense of actions being completely determined by a prior sequence of causes operating independently of the individual. (p. 23-24)

Bandura (1997) also insisted:

In social cognitive theory, human agency operates within an interdependent causal structure involving triadic reciprocal causation. In this transactional view of self and society, internal personal factors in the form of cognitive, affective, and biological events; behavior; and environmental events all operate as interacting determinants that influence one another bidirectionally. Human adaptation and change are rooted in social systems. Therefore, personal agency operates within a broad network of sociostructural influences. In agentic transactions, people are both producers and products of social structures. (p. 6)

This human agency operates within a triadic reciprocal causation between "Personal factors in the form of cognitive, affect and biological event;

behavior; and environmental events" (Bandura, 1997, p. 6). Alves, Manz, and Butterfield (2004) emphasized the importance of cognition by comparing western leadership and leadership in China. One conclusion focused on cognition, "In terms of cognition, Chinese place more emphasis on intuitive, sense-making and non-abstract processes than Westerners" (Alves et al., p. 13). Sun Tzu wrote from a cognitive perspective similar to that of the current, modern leadership of China. Social cognitive theory and agency is the backdrop in which sternness is being defined as a behavioral syndrome.

Based on these theoretical underpinnings, sternness is defined as a behavioral syndrome. The ILS is designed to assess an individual's intention to perform the behaviors associated with sternness within the context of self-directed leadership, thus the inventory is worded as a future intention as a precursor to a future behavior.

The definition of sternness used in the ILS derives from recent research identifying the characteristic behaviors of sternness based on the writings of Sun Tzu. Winner (2008) defined sternness as co-occurring behaviors including (a) a willingness to establish obedience through rewards and punishments within limits, (b) consistency in actions to ensure good behavior through rituals and respect, and (c) a determination to do the difficult tasks of leadership. Each of these three behaviors has a theoretical basis that guides the creation of the self-assessment items. Winner reported:

Each of the three behaviors associated with sternness has particular characteristics that can be used to separate the behavior from the remaining ones conceptually. The three behaviors with their subbehaviors are (a) a willingness to establish obedience through rewards (Adams, 1963; Bandura, 1986; Chen, 1994; Cleary, 2000) and punishments (Bandura, 1986, 1997; Chen, 1994; Cleary, 2000; Gagliardi, 2004a; McNeilly, 1996) within limits (Bandura, 1986; Cleary, 1998, 2000; Wong et al., 1998), (b) consistency in actions to ensure good behavior (Bandura, 1986; Cleary, 1989, 2000; Ji, 1989; Michaelson, 2001) through rituals and respect (Cleary, 2000; McNeilly; Michaelson & Michaelson, 2003; Wong et al.), and (c) a determination to do the difficult tasks of leadership (Ames, 2000; Chen, 1994; Gagliardi, 2004b). (p. 32-33)

The language used within the ILS comes directly from the literature. However, some of the language, like the word sternness, may have authoritative overtones. Winner (2008) has shown that, "sternness as used by Sun Tzu is a multidimensional construct which includes three specific co-occurring behaviors" (p. 76). The first co-occurring behavior is establishing obedience through rewards and punishments within limits. The concept of this first behavior subgroup is that a leader with sternness will be concerned with team obedience, unity, or discipline. Rewards and punishments are the means to achieve obedience but are not the focus of the sternness behavior. Sternness is concerned with the effort to establish obedience, unity, or discipline for a team or person. The focus should be on using rewards and punishments as an external motivation to increase a person's internal motivation.

The second co-occurring behavior is a consistency in actions to ensure good behavior through rituals and respect. The focus is on the actions of a leader with sternness, meaning whether his or her actions are consistent and dependable. This consistency is shown through the rituals he or she creates and whether he or she lives a life worthy of respect. The result of this consistency is to ensure good behavior of one's followers, which implies that a person will mirror the actions of a leader. Kouzes and Posner (2002) emphasized the importance of leaders modeling the way: "Leaders take every opportunity to show others by their own example that they're deeply committed to the values and aspirations they espouse. Leading by example is how leaders make visions and values tangible" (p. 77). A leader with sternness understands the

importance of a consistent lifestyle, which earns the respect of followers and adds to the leader's referent power (Northouse, 2010, p. 7).

The third co-occurring behavior is a determination to do fulfill the difficult tasks of leadership. A leader with sternness is determined to do what is just and right, even if the job is difficult. The determination is focused on a steel resolve of doing what is morally right even if it is difficult. Gagliardi (2004b) stated, "We must honor our agreements scrupulously" (p. 45). This includes facing problems head-on or confronting potential problems. It involves a higher level of differentiation of self. Walsh and McGraw (2002) explained this Bowenian concept:

Highly differentiated individuals have a more fully integrated, solid self (i.e., a concept of self that is nonnegotiable with others), and their behaviors are guided primarily by their intellect. Individuals with low levels of differentiation are guided predominately by their pseudo-self (i.e., a concept of self that is negotiable with others), and their behavior tends to be directed by their emotions. (p. 36)

A leader with sternness allows his or her own intellect to guide her or his behavior. He or she is not easily guided by emotions. This leader has a strong moral core, which helps interpret his or her emotions in light of the objectively right thing to do. Then, the leader chooses the right course of action even if it is difficult. As Michaelson and Michaelson (2003) emphasized, "The strength of moral influence is at the heart of Sun Tzu's ability to lead an army. Moral integrity is a characteristic of successful leaders" (p. 56).

The use of the words *rewards* and *punishments* come directly from the literature, words that capture one key aspect of sternness as described by the Sun Tzu, as translated by Cleary (2000). However, the use of rewards and punishments today has been questioned. Kohn (1993) argued that a person should never use rewards and punishments. He contended that rewards and punishments change the relationship between people. They also change the focus from internal motivation for the completion of a task to an external motivation where a person is working only for the reward or fear of punishment. Kohn raised an important issue when thinking about rewards and punishments as a part of the behaviors of sternness. However, rewards and punishments are a means to establishing obedience and are not the focus of the behavior. The focus is on obedience, unity, and discipline. Rewards and punishments are one way to achieve that end. This distinction allows for a broader definition of rewards and punishments than one may assume. Kohn offered some suggestions on minimizing the external motivational nature of rewards: get rewards out of people's faces; offer rewards after the fact, as a surprise; never turn the quest for rewards into a contest; make rewards as similar as possible to the task; give people as much choice as possible about how rewards are used; and try to immunize individuals against the motivation-killing effects of rewards. One of the best ways to keep a focus on internal motivation instead of external motivation is the use of choice. Kohn explained the importance of choice in the workplace:

The loss of autonomy entailed by the use of rewards or punishments helps explain why they sap our motivation. But managers must do more than avoid these tactics; they need to take affirmative steps to make sure employees have real choices about how they do their jobs. (p. 192)

Choice is an important part of helping a person move from an external motivation to an internal motivation as they find value in their choices. In a way, sternness is offering a new definition of rewards and punishments that focuses on using external motivation to increase a person's internal motivations.

Marshall (2007) agreed with Kohn (1993) that rewards and punishments do not work in

education for many of the same reasons Kohn listed. However, Marshall distinguished between education and business. His focus was that schools are different than business and should not be run like a business. One cannot equally compare the school and business because they have a different focus: "Business produces products. The product may be tangible or intangible and in the form of information, services or goods. Learning is a process, not a product" (Marshall, p. 249). Marshall argued that "money is a *satisfier*—not a motivator" (p. 251), and the use of money as a reward is an example of external motivation which does not work. However, a person can be fired from a job, which is a form of punishment. Marshall offers a different way of creating internal motivations, which involves choice and reflections.

Bandura (1986) offered a different view of external and internal motivations than Kohn (1993) and Marshall (2007):

Self-motivation and self-directedness require certain basic tools of personal agency that are developed, in part, through the aid of external incentives. Many activities through which competencies are built are initially tiresome and uninteresting. . . It is not until some proficiency is acquired that the activity becomes rewarding, potentialities are likely to remain undeveloped. . . Distinctions are often drawn between extrinsic and intrinsic motivators as though they were antithetical. What is commonly referred to as intrinsic motivation includes several types of contingencies between actions and their effects. (p. 240)

It is not easy to separate internal and external motivations because both play a role in the development of personal agency. External motivations are often needed at the start of a task until internal motivation takes over. Bandura (1986) explained this process: "In social cognitive theory, interest grows from satisfactions derived from fulfilling challenging standards and from self-percepts of efficacy gained through accomplishments and other sources of efficacy" (p. 243). He illustrated how rewards can be a positive external motivator: "In Deci's (1975) theory, rewards diminish intrinsic motivation when they appear controlling but increase when they convey information about competency" (p. 244). Podsakoff, Bommer, Podsakoff, and MacKenzie's (2006) research supported the work of Bandura with a thorough examination of rewards and punishments in business. The researchers conducted a meta-analysis of the relationship "between leader rewards and punishment behaviors and employee attitudes, perceptions, and performance" (p. 113). The researchers concluded:

Our meta-analysis suggests that leader reward and punishment behaviors have significant unique effects on a variety of important employee attitudes, perceptions and behaviors, and that the manner in which the leaders administer rewards and punishments is a critical determinant of the effectiveness of these leader behaviors. In addition, perceptions of justice and role ambiguity were identified as potentially important mediators of the effects of these leaders' behaviors on employee criterion variables. Generally speaking, the results confirm the importance of leader reward and punishment behaviors and the central role they have been given in theories of leadership. (p. 138)

The results of this study suggest that employees did not mind the use of reward and punishment behaviors as long as the rewards and punishments were administered contingently. Contingent-based rewards are based on external issues such as job performance or clearly stated expectations. Bandura (1986) supported this assertion that employees will support contingent-based rewards and punishments more than noncontingent rewards and punishments due to the role of personal agency. Bandura (1986) wrote, "Extrinsic incentives and other situational influences affect actions in large part through the exercise of personal agency. So even incentive influences, commonly regarded as purely external, depend on self-regulatory influ-

ence for their impact" (p. 261). A person still has to find importance in the rewards and punishments for them to be meaningful to that person.

Pink (2009) studied motivation and proposed a new paradigm focused on autonomy, mastery and purpose called Motivation 3.0. Motivation 3.0 is a call for more intrinsic motivation and less external motivation. Pink (2009) concludes, "The science shows that the secret to high performance isn't our biological drive or our reward-and-punishment drive, but our third drive—our deep-seated desire to direct our own lives, to extend and expand our abilities, and to make a contribution" (p. 144-145). Pink's challenge is consistent with the case made in the research of leadership sternness. A leader with sternness needs to consider the role that rewards and punishments can play in a person's life, increasing internal motivation while recognizing the role external motivation has in the relationship. It is not an easy tightrope to walk when using rewards and punishments, but a stern leader will try to use rewards and punishments appropriately as a motivation.

Reliability

The ILS has been found to be very reliable, achieving a Cronbach's alpha reliability score of .94 for the 45 items. A modified version of the ILS with 41 items has a Cronbach's alpha reliability score of .95. Cronbach's alpha was performed on each behavior subgroup and was found to be satisfactory for "internal consistency with establish obedience ($\alpha = .87$), consistency in actions ($\alpha = .94$) and difficulty in tasks ($\alpha = .76$)" (Winner, 2008, p. 72).

Validity

Winner (2008) found the ILS to have both face and construct validity. Principle component analysis found, "The behavior subgroups within sternness did load on a single latent factor (leader sternness) with factor loadings of .913 (establish obedience), .946 (consistency in actions), and .866 (difficult tasks)" (p. 68).

RESULTS

The ILS uses a ratio measure to capture the respondent's behavioral intention of sternness. The scores range from 0 (*never*) to 10 (*always*) for each of the 45 questions. In order to yield ratio data, the subject can respond by marking a response along a continuum from 0 to 10 in .5 increments. At this time, a respondent taking the ILS would receive an overall sternness score between 0 and 450 with commentary. Winner (2008) suggested that the ILS can be used for individual interventions with the respondent to identify ways to strengthen the respondents' overall use of sternness specifically within the three co-occurring behaviors. The first co-occurring behavior, a willingness to establish obedience through rewards and punishments within limits, has a range of 0 to 250. For individual interventions, this behavior can be broken down into three subbehaviors, (a) a willingness to establish rewards, (b) a willingness to enforce punishments, and (c) an understanding of the limits of too many rewards and punishments. The second co-occurring behavior is a consistency in actions to ensure good behavior through rituals and respect, which has a range of 0 to 130. This behavior can be broken down into two subbehaviors, (a) consistency in actions and (b) proper use of rituals to enhance respect. The third co-occurring behavior is a determination to do the difficult tasks of leadership and it has a range of 0 to 70. Intervention or coaching strategies can be created to strengthen a person who has low scores within the six subbehaviors. A respondent may score too high in each of the six subbehaviors and would need to learn how to moderate his or her specific behavior. In addition, a respondent may have a mix of high and low scores for the six subbehaviors. Interventions using the six subbehaviors would increase the person's self-directed leadership and effectiveness within an organization.

The online instrument was created and published through Survey Monkey, located at www.surveymonkey.com. There is a basic version of the survey tool, but for the more robust features, a monthly or annual fee is required.

The self-reported instrument takes about 10 minutes to complete. Participation is anonymous. All results are confidential.

COMMENTARY

A practitioner can use this knowledge of the three co-occurring behaviors of sternness to increase the effectives of the leaders within her or his organization. Whether it is through individual or group training, the aspects of sternness can be used to facilitate the growth of leadership within a person or team. Additionally, the instrument may be used to reveal congruence among team members regarding core organizational values, thus facilitating a greater degree of cooperation among the leadership team. The key value of the ILS is helping leaders discover their own propensity towards (a) using rewards and punishments as motivation (b) evaluating if their actions and words are congruent and (c) appraising their commitment to difficult leadership tasks.

The ILS was designed to measure the three co-occurring behaviors of sternness. These co-occurring behaviors have specific individual and organizational implications. The first co-occurring behavior of sternness is a willingness to establish obedience through rewards and punishments. The focus is not on specific rewards and punishments; rather, rewards and punishments are only a means to establish cooperation within the group. The focus is on the ability to establish unity or discipline within a team or person, by using rewards and punishments. The goal is to help a person increase his or her internal motivation by using the external motivation of rewards and punishment. Bandura (1986) supports the view that internal motivations are often aided by external motivations, i.e. rewards and punishments. The work of Bandura was sustained by Podsakoff, Bommer, Podsakoff, and MacKenzie, (2006). Podsakoff, et al. researched an analysis of the relationship "between leader rewards and punishment behaviors and employee attitudes, perceptions, and performance" (p. 113). The researchers concluded, "Generally speaking, the results confirm the importance of leader reward and punishment behaviors and the central role they have been given in theories of leadership" (p. 138). As previously stated, a practitioner could use this information to increase the effectiveness of an organization by increasing the internal motivation of the members of that organization by offering choice as a reward for participants within the work group. As the group develops a greater sense of unity, discipline for the work, and cooperation among group members, the leader is able to "reward" the group with greater degrees of choice while simultaneously increasing individual and group intrinsic motivation.

The second co-occurring behavior is a consistency in actions to ensure good behavior through rituals and respect. The focus is on helping a leader be more consistent and dependable. A leader deliberately using consistent rituals to create a life worthy of respect is the goal of this second behavior. Kouzes and Posner (2002) emphasized the importance of modeling the way of consistency: "Leaders take every opportunity to show others by their own example that they're deeply committed to the values and aspirations they espouse" (p. 77). A stern leader understands the importance of a consistent lifestyle that earns the respect of followers. Additionally, rituals can be used by the stern leader as a means to embed the values of the leader within the organizational culture (Schein, 2000) through consistent actions and practices. The stern leader is also able to evidence congruence with the organization's core values while setting an example of behavior for others to follow. Practitioners can use the ILS to increase the integrity and consistency of the leaders while at the same time respecting the role of followers within the organization (Ricketson, 2009).

The third co-occurring behavior is a determination to do the difficult tasks of leadership.

The thrust of this behavior is a steel resolve to do what is just and right, even when it is tough. Winner (2008) declared the importance of this co-occurring behavior for a leader:

A leader with sternness allows his or her own intellect to guide her or his behavior. He or she is not easily guided by emotions. This leader has a strong moral core, which helps interpret her or his emotions in light of what is the right thing to do. Then, the leader chooses the right course of action even if it is difficult. (p. 77)

A stern leader will face the challenges of leadership with clear values and a commitment to do the right thing, even at the leader's own detriment.

Practitioners will find the instrument easily accessible and useable. Its utility centers primarily on assessing degrees of sternness in individuals within a leadership context. By defining sternness in a way that promotes leader effectiveness, rather than the common understanding of sternness as a negative attribute, practitioners can focus on developing effective ways of directing this leadership attribute within the leader-follower relationship. Additionally, those leaders who score high degrees of sternness can gain a greater degree of self-efficacy in their leadership style. In fact, the organization at large can gain a greater appreciation for those who have this leadership quality and the benefits they bring to the organization.

The instrument may be further used as a means to bring about conflict resolution within the organization by indicating the degrees of sternness among conflicting parties. As each person in conflict assesses himself or herself, an understanding can be gained and a dialogue begun that moves toward greater understanding of self and others. As Herrington, Bonem and Furr (2000): noted:

In dialogue, an individual offers his or her perspective or assumptions for examination by the group. The object of dialogue is to allow others to see what you see and why you see it, not to convince them. Dialogue can create a rich understanding if information is shared openly and if all participants listen deeply. (p. 140)

This understanding can then be used as a bridge toward resolution of the conflict.

Researchers may want to compare leadership sternness with other leadership theories that incorporate rewards and punishments. Podsakoff, et al, (2006) identified path-goal theory, Sim's reinforcement contingency and transactional leadership. Additional research is needed to understand how leadership sternness interacts with other leadership theories dealing with motivation, rewards and punishments.

The study of sternness is essential to a complete understanding of leadership. Winston and Patterson (2005) conducted a very thorough review of leadership literature that included "160 documents containing 1 to 25 constructs, or statements, describing or defining leadership we compiled 1,000-plus constructs/statements that we categorized into 92 discrete dimensions with the last category labeled as miscellaneous" (p. 4). However, sternness was not a part of their integrated definition of leadership. In addition, no instrument existed to measure sternness in an adult leader. Furthermore, the study of leader sternness is required to complete the understanding of the conative factors important to self-directed leadership (Carr et al., 2007).

The importance of leader sternness is not limited to the field of leadership but expands to include self-directed learning. Vaill (1996) suggested the term *leaderly learning* to describe the overlap of leadership and learning:

I have given the form of learning as a way of being a special name: leaderly learning. The word learning is not used here as a noun, meaning, "knowledge attained." Rather it is to be taken as a gerund—thus, it describes on an ongoing process of action. The ongoing process of learning is occurring all the time in executive life. The

word leaderly is an adjective modifying learning. Thus, leaderly learning is the kind of learning that a managerial leader needs to engage in as an ongoing process in the job. (p. 127)

Vaill asserted that self-directed learning is essential to leadership: "The relevance of self-directed learning to leadership is this: the behavior we call leadership is, being it is anything else, an initiative from within oneself" (p. 61). Bandura (1997) discussed the importance of being self-directed:

Development of capabilities for self-directedness enables individuals not only to continue their intellectual growth beyond their formal education but advance to the nature and quality of their life pursuits. Changing realities are placing a premium on the capability for self-directed learning throughout the life span. The rapid pace of technological change and the accelerated growth of knowledge require continual upgrading of competencies if people are to survive and prosper under increasing competitive conditions. (p. 227)

Self-directed people are more able to adapt to the changes of society. A key aspect of being self-directed is human agency. Bandura (2006) described agency succinctly:

To be an agent is to influence intentionally one's functioning and life circumstances. In this view, personal influence is part of the casual structure. People are self-organizing, proactive, self-regulating and self-reflecting. They are not simply onlookers of their behavior. They are contributors to their life circumstances, not just products of them. (p. 164)

Bandura (2006) offered a challenge with this understanding of agency: "At a broader social level, the challenges center on how to enlist these agentic human capabilities in ways that shape a better and sustainable world" (p. 177). The result of this study produced an instrument that allows for a greater understanding of sternness intentions of an adult leader and, ultimately, fosters the leader to acquire self-directed leadership.

The ILS is based in theory, which allows for a new understanding of leader sternness in a self-directed leader. Normative statistics would elevate the potential of this leadership construct. The ILS flowed out of the autonomous learning literature. Self-efficacy theory (Bandura, 1997) has been shown to influence autonomous learning (Ponton, Derrick, et al., 2005). The relationship between self-efficacy and sternness, as described by Sun Tzu, should be explored to see how a leader's sternness might be influenced by self-efficacy.

The ILS is available for anyone to use. In order to use the instrument for research or in an organization, those interested are advised to contact the ILS author, who will provide a research code necessary for participants to gain access to the ILS. The resulting data will be gathered by the ILS author and returned in Excel spreadsheet form or SPSS form depending on the desire of the person conducting the research. Contact information is available at the survey site. The ILS has not been used in research beyond its reliability and validity study. Further research is needed to develop normative statistics for the total score and for each co-occurring behavior subgroup. This effort would make available a better estimate of the normative statistics.

Cost

The ILS is a fee-based survey, the cost of which can be negotiated with the ILS author. There is also a database fee for extracting the data from the ILS and converting it to Excel or SPSS.

Location

The ILS is located at: http://leadershipsternness.blogspot.com/

REFERENCES

Adams, J. S. (1963). Towards an understanding of inequity. *Journal of Abnormal and Social Psychology, 67*(5), 422–436. doi:10.1037/h0040968

Ajzen, I., & Fishbein, M. (1980). *Understanding attitudes and predicting social behavior*. Upper Saddle River, NJ: Prentice-Hall.

Alves, J. C., Manz, C. C., & Butterfield, D. A. (2004). Developing leadership theory in Asia: The role of Chinese philosophy. *International Journal of Leadership Studies, 1*(1), 3–27.

Ames, R. T. (2000). Sun Tzu: The art of war. In Carr, C. (Ed.), *The book of war* (pp. 7–65). New York, NY: Modern Library.

Bandura, A. (1986). *Social foundations of thought and action: A social cognitive theory*. Upper Saddle River, NJ: Prentice Hall.

Bandura, A. (1997). *Self-efficacy: The exercise of control*. New York, NY: W. H. Freeman.

Bandura, A. (2006). Toward a psychology of human agency. *Perspectives on Psychological Science, 1*(2), 164–180. doi:10.1111/j.1745-6916.2006.00011.x

Carr, P., Coe, J., Derrick, G., & Ponton, M. (2007). *Leadership and self-directed learning: Implications from the art of war*. PowerPoint presentation at the International Self-Directed Learning Symposium, Orlando, FL.

Carr, P. B. (1999). The measurement of resourcefulness intentions in the adult autonomous learner (George Washington University). *Dissertation Abstracts International, 60*(11), 3849. (Publication No. AAT 9949341)

Chen, M. (1994). Sun Tzu's strategic thinking and contemporary business. *Business Horizons, 37*(2), 42–48. doi:10.1016/0007-6813(94)90031-0

Chene, A. (1983). The concept of autonomy in adult education: A philosophical discussion. *Adult Education Quarterly, 34*(1), 38–47. doi:10.1177/0001848183034001004

Cleary, T. (1989). The art of war and the I Ching: Strategy and change. In Cleary, T. (Trans. Ed.) *Mastering the art of war* (pp. 1–29). Boston, MA: Shambhala.

Cleary, T. (Trans. Ed.). (2000). *The art of war: Complete texts and commentaries*. Boston, MA: Shambhala.

Confessore, G. J. (1992). An introduction to the study of self-directed learning. In G. J. Confessore & S. J. Confessore, S. J. (Eds.), *Guideposts to self-directed learning* (pp. 1-6). King of Prussia, PA: Organizational Design and Development.

Confessore, G. J., & Park, E. (2004). Factor validation of the learner autonomy profile, version 3.0 and extraction of the short form. *International Journal of Self-Directed Learning, 1*(1), 39–58.

Derrick, M. G. (2001). The measurement of an adult's intention to exhibit persistence in autonomous learning (George Washington University). *Dissertation Abstracts International, 62*(05), 2533. (Publication No. AAT 3006915)

Fishbein, M., & Ajzen, I. (1975). *Belief, attitude, intention, and behavior: An introduction to theory and research*. Reading, MA: Addison-Wesley. Retrieved from http://www.people.umass.edu/aizen/f&a1975.html

Gagliardi, G. (2002). *Sun Tzu's the art of war & the art of career building*. Seattle, WA: Clearbridge.

Gagliardi, G. (2004a). *The art of war plus its amazing secrets*. Seattle, WA: Clearbridge.

Gagliardi, G. (2004b). *The art of war plus the warrior class: 306 lessons in modern competition*. Seattle, WA: Clearbridge.

Herrington, J., Bonem, M., & Furr, J. H. (2000). *Leading congregational change: A practical guide for the transformational journey*. San Francisco, CA: Jossey-Bass.

Kohn, A. (1993). *Punished by rewards: The trouble with gold stars, incentive plans, A's, praise and other bribes*. New York: Houghton Mifflin.

Kouzes, J. M., & Posner, B. Z. (2002). *The leadership challenge* (3rd ed.). San Francisco, CA: Jossey-Bass.

Krause, D. G. (2005). *The art of war for executives*. New York, NY: Perigee.

Li, D. H. (2000). *The art of leadership by Sun Tzu: A new-millennium translation of Sun Tzu's art of war*. Bethesda, MD: Premier.

Long, H. B. (1998). Theoretical and practical implications of selecting paradigms of self-directed learning. In Long, H. B. (Eds.), *Developing paradigms for self-directed learning* (pp. 1–14). Norman, OK: University of Oklahoma.

Marshall, M. (2007). *Discipline without stress, punishment or reward* (2nd ed.). Los Alamitos, CA: Piper Press.

McNeilly, M. (1996). *Sun Tzu and the art of business: Six strategic principles for managers*. New York, NY: Oxford Press.

Merriam, S. B., & Caffarella, R. S. (1999). *Learning in adulthood: A comprehensive guide* (2nd ed.). San Francisco, CA: Jossey-Bass.

Meyer, D. T. (2001). The measurement of intentional behavior as a prerequisite to autonomous learning (George Washington University). *Dissertation Abstracts International, 61*(12), 4697. (Publication No. AAT 9999882)

Michaelson, G., & Michaelson, S. (2003). *Sun Tzu for success*. Avon, MA: Adam Media.

Michaelson, G. A. (2001). *Sun Tzu: The art of war for managers*. Avon, MA: Adams Media Corporation.

Northouse, P. G. (2010). *Leadership: Theory and practice* (5th ed.). Thousand Oaks, CA: Sage Publications, Inc.

Pink, D. H. (2009). *Drive: The surprising truth about what motivates us*. New York, NY: Riverhead.

Podsakoff, P. M., Bommer, W. H., Podsakoff, N. P., & MacKenzie, S. B. (2006). Relationships between leader reward and punishment behavior and subordinate attitudes, perceptions, and behaviors: A meta-analytic review of existing and new research. *Organizational Behavior and Human Decision Processes*, *99*(2), 113. doi:10.1016/j.obhdp.2005.09.002

Ponton, M., Carr, P., & Derrick, G. (2004). A path analysis of the conative factors associated with autonomous learning. *International Journal of Self-Directed Learning*, *1*(1), 59–69.

Ponton, M., Derrick, G., Hall, J. M., Rhea, N., & Carr, P. (2005). The relationship between self-efficacy and autonomous learning: The development of new instrumentation. *International Journal of Self-directed Learning*, *2*(1), 50–61.

Ponton, M. K. (1999). The measurement of an adult's intention to exhibit personal initiative in autonomous learning (George Washington University). *Dissertation Abstracts International*, *60*(11), 3933. (Publication No. AAT 9949350)

Ponton, M. K., & Carr, P. B. (1999). *A quasi-linear behavioral model and an application to self-directed learning*. Hampton, VA: NASA Langley Research Center. (NTIS NASA/TM-1999-209094)

Ricketson, R. (2009). *Followerfirst: Rethinking leading in the church*. Cumming, GA: Heartworks Publications.

Schein, E. H. (2010). *Organizational culture and leadership* (4th ed.). San Francisco, CA: John Wiley & Sons, Inc.

Vaill, P. B. (1996). *Learning as a way of being: Strategies for survival in a world of permanent white water*. San Francisco: Jossey-Bass.

Walsh, W. M., & McGraw, J. A. (2002). *Essentials of family therapy: A structured summary of nine approaches* (2nd ed.). Denver, CO: Love.

Winner, W. D. (2008). *The measurement of sternness in an adult self-directed leader* (Regent University). In publication.

Winston, B. E., & Patterson, K. (2005). *An integrative definition of leadership*. Retrieved May 31, 2009, from http://www.regent.edu/acad/global/publications/working/integrativedefinition.pdf

Wong, Y. Y., Maher, T. E., & Lee, G. (1998). The strategy of an ancient warrior: An inspiration for international managers. *Multinational Business Review*, *6*(1), 83.

Wu, W.-Y., Chou, C. H., & Wu, Y.-J. (2004). A study of strategy implementation as expressed through Sun Tzu's principles of war. *Industrial Management + Data Systems*, *104*(5/6), 396.

KEY TERMS AND DEFINITIONS

Affect: A feeling towards an object.

Agency: Refers to actions done intentionally; behaviors done because of conation.

Autonomous Learner: A person who has the characteristic of learner autonomy.

Autonomous Learning: An agentive learning process in which the conative factors of desire, initiative, resourcefulness and persistence are manifest.

Autonomy: The characteristic of the person who independently exhibits agency.

Behavior: An observable and measurable act.

Behavior Syndrome: A set of co-occurring behaviors.

Cognition: One's knowledge or opinion about an object.

Conation: An intention developed independently.

Intention: A determination to engage in a behavior with respect to an object or to reach a desired state.

Punishments: A punishment can be any negative feedback, economic or psychological consequence, given to an employee, subordinate, follower or person.

Rewards: A reward can be any positive feedback, economic or psychological, given to an employee, subordinate, follower or person.

Ritual: A practice or pattern of behavior regularly performed in a set manner.

Self-efficacy: A self-assessment of perceived capability.

Sternness: Three co-occurring behavioral intentions including a willingness to establish obedience through rewards and punishments within limits, consistency in actions to ensure good behavior through rituals and respect, and a determination to do the difficult tasks of leadership.

Chapter 12
The Shepherd Leadership Inventory (SLI)

Jamie Swalm
Regent University, USA

ABSTRACT

Because shepherding is one of the oldest occupations of humanity, the metaphor of the shepherd as leader dates back thousands of years and is a universal image. Therefore, the shepherd leader metaphor is an ideal vehicle through which to study leadership. The Shepherd Leadership Inventory (SLI) measures the degree to which individual leaders are leading as shepherd leadership in the workplace. Through the initial study of the shepherd leader metaphor beginning with the Scriptures and continuing through modern authors, it was determined shepherd leaders are leaders who insure the wellbeing of their followers through the three primary leader behaviors of guiding, providing, and protecting. The Shepherd Leadership Inventory (SLI) incorporates items to assess these behaviors and was validated through the use of principal component factor analysis. This chapter discusses the background and development of the SLI including reporting on the reliability and validity of the instrument. The results of the inventory are discussed along with commentary on the SLI's relevance to researchers and practitioners. Information regarding cost and location, as well as additional reading recommendations, is included.

THE SHEPHERD LEADERSHIP INVENTORY: INTRODUCTION

The Shepherd Leader Metaphor

The basis for shepherd leadership is the metaphorical usage of shepherding imagery which the Scriptures us to describe leadership. From the beginning of the Bible to the end, the shepherd as leader metaphor occurs often suggesting God relates to his people and leaders relate to their followers as shepherds (Donelson, 2004). Overall the shepherd leader metaphor occurs more than five hundred times in the Old and New Testaments and is the primary biblical metaphor for spiritual leadership (Anderson, 1997). Since Morgan (1997) suggests metaphors aid the ability to understand leadership by providing a framework through which to view leadership concepts, it follows the shepherd leader metaphor provides a lens through which

DOI: 10.4018/978-1-4666-2172-5.ch012

to understand leadership. The metaphor is easier to understand than the leadership construct so by progressing from the metaphor to the construct the student of leadership is able to more clearly understand leadership. In short, the metaphor of the shepherd as leader is a lens through which leadership is more easily understood. Therefore the shepherd leadership metaphor provides a lens through which the people of God understand God's leadership and what is required of them as leaders to lead according to God's desire. It also provides a framework for people to understand their relationship with God and their responsibility as leaders to leader their followers as shepherds.

Throughout history the metaphor of the shepherd leader developed over thousands of years because the occupation of shepherding is one of the oldest known occupations of humanity (Leman & Pentak, 2004). As one of humanities earliest occupations, shepherding represented a viable means of economic prosperity in early agrarian societies (Elwell & Beitzel, 1998). Therefore shepherding became widely known throughout the world. As an example, the domestication of sheep dates back to as early as 9000 BC (Achtemeier, Harper, & Row, 1985). Because shepherding was important to early agrarian societies and because shepherding wise widespread, a large and complex set of shepherd imagery developed over the course of thousands of years. This imagery became linked to leadership. For example, in ancient times good and just leaders were pictured as shepherds of their people (Tappy, 1995). This connected leadership actions or behaviors with the metaphor of the shepherd. Usually the shepherd leader was pictured as a benevolent leader interested in caring for the people. Freedman (1992/1996) suggests the widespread development of shepherd leader imagery resulted in the shepherd's crook becoming a common ancient symbol of the leader's power and authority which continues to this day.

The shepherd leader metaphor is also spiritual in nature because the basic underlying framework for the metaphor develops significantly throughout the historical context of the Scriptures. Since the imagery of the shepherd leader occurred often throughout history, the Biblical writers often use shepherding imagery to describe leadership, placing the shepherd leadership metaphor squarely in a spiritual framework. Ultimately, the use of the shepherd leader imagery in the Scriptures suggests God as he reveals himself through the Scriptures describes himself as a shepherd leader. This suggests there is something inherently consistent about the leadership of a shepherd and God's leadership of His people. As a result, the largest body of literature describing the development of shepherd leadership imagery is contained in the Scriptures of the Old and New Testaments. The vast majority of authors writing about shepherd leadership today use the Scriptures as the basis of their work. For example, in their book "Like a Shepherd Lead Us", Fleer & Siburt (2006) edit a work composed of seven chapters written by seven different authors on the subject of leading like a shepherd. Each author uses the Scriptures as their theoretical framework for leading like a shepherd. Wagner (1999) suggests because of the prominence of the shepherd leaders metaphor, spiritual leadership should model their ministries after it. McCormic & Davenport (2003) use the Biblical framework of Psalm 23 to suggest shepherd leaders are leaders concerned with the whole person. They are suggesting that shepherd leadership is more about being a certain type of leader instead of applying an external leadership strategy to the decision making process. Their point is well made and echoed by the shepherd leadership inventory. On the surface a shepherd leader can appear as a leader who performs certain behavioral tasks associated with shepherd leadership. It would follow that anyone could be a shepherd leader by engaging in these tasks. Yet being a shepherd leader is primarily about being as opposed to doing. In other words, the doing of the shepherd leader flows from the being of the shepherd leader. Shepherd leaders perform certain behavioral tasks because they are shepherd leaders as opposed to being shepherd leaders because they perform those tasks. The behaviors do not make a shepherd leader a shepherd leader. Instead, they demonstrate that a leader is a shepherd leader. Perhaps this is best seen in the example of Jesus. In the New Testament, Jesus is the great shepherd leader. The Apostle Paul describes the heart of his shepherd leadership in Philippians 2:4-11 by indicating Jesus did not look only to his own interests but also to humanities interests through the crucifixion. As a result god exalted him to the highest place and gave him the name that is above every name. So Jesus is a shepherd leader not because of the behavior of allowing himself to be crucified, but rather because he looked to the interests of others and therefore allowed himself to be crucified. In other words, it is looking to the interests of others that made Jesus a shepherd leader, not the behavior of being crucified. Ultimately this demonstrates shepherd leadership cannot be separated from the motivational component. Shepherd leaders are shepherd leaders because they truly desire the wellbeing of their followers. Jesus captured the essence of this idea when he said, "I am the good shepherd. The good shepherd lays his life down for the sheep." (John 10:11). Following these words Jesus contrasts the good shepherd with the hired hand who runs away when he sees the wolf coming. The hired hands runs away because he cares nothing for the sheep while the good shepherd lays down his life for the sheep because he cares for the sheep. The very essence of a shepherd leader is a leader who cares about their followers and works toward their wellbeing. This principle is seen in the Old Testament, the New Testament, and in contemporary shepherd leadership material both scholarly and popular.

Shepherd Leadership in the Old Testament

Throughout the Old Testament, the writers often use shepherding imagery as a metaphor for leadership. This is not surprising given shepherding was a very important occupation in the agrarian economics of Palestine most likely contributing to its widespread use (Balz & Schneider 1993; Bromiley, 1991). Sheep in ancient times were important for their wool (Leviticus 13:47-48), for their milk (Deuteronomy 32:14), for their meat (1 Samuel 14:32), for their hides (Exodus 25:5), and for their horns (1 Samuel 16:10). Often, a person's economic wealth in Palestine was described by how many sheep they owned (Psalm 144:13) suggesting sheep represented economic prosperity in Palestine during Old Testament times (Elwell & Beitzel, 1988). Confirming the economic importance of sheep, the Biblical writers mention sheep more than 500 times, often in connection with their economic importance. Because of the economic importance of sheep in Palestine along with the widespread use of the shepherding occupation, shepherding language became common to the Old Testament writers (Bromiley, 1991) both in literal and metaphorical usage (Wood, 1996). For the same reasons, the shepherd metaphor formed an ideal image for God to describe himself as a leader through and communicate what a leader is or should be. As a result, Old Testament writers use shepherd language metaphorically to describe the relationship of God to his people and the relationship between rulers and their subjects (Easton, 1996).

A careful examination of the shepherd leadership metaphor in the Old Testament reveals because God is a good shepherd he raises up good shepherd leaders to lead his people. Since God's primary purpose as a shepherd leader is to insure the wellbeing of his people, the primary purpose of shepherd leaders is to insure the wellbeing of their followers (Psalm 28:9; Psalm 78:71; Isaiah 56:11; Jeremiah 3:14-15; Jeremiah 23:1-4; Zechariah 10:2; Zechariah 11:4-17; Ezekiel 34:1-6; Ezekiel 34:11-12; Micah 5:4). Additionally, the Old Testament writers indicate the shepherd leader uses three broad behaviors to insure the wellbeing of their followers. These include guiding in Genesis 48:15-16; Genesis 49:24; Numbers 27:15-17; Psalm 23; Psalm 80:1-2; Isaiah 40:11; Ezekiel 34:1-6; Zechariah 11:4-17), providing in Psalm 23; Ezekiel 34:1-6; Ezekiel 34:11-16; Ezekiel 34:26-27; Zechariah 11:4-17, and protecting in Genesis 48:15-16a; Genesis 49:24; Psalm 23; Psalm 80:1-2; Isaiah 13:14; Ezekiel 34:1-6; Ezekiel 34:25; Ezekiel 34:28).

Therefore, the model of shepherd leadership emerging from the Old Testament writers suggests God as a shepherd leader insures the wellbeing of his people. Therefore it is the role of human shepherd leaders to insure the wellbeing of their followers. Samuel (1996) suggests the Hebrew word for shepherd is a cognate cousin of the Hebrew word for neighbor and friend signifying love and companionship. This suggests shepherd leaders lead as shepherds because they care for their followers. As God shepherds his people, so the shepherd leader leads his followers. As God cares for his people, so the shepherd leader cares for his followers. As God desires the wellbeing of his people, so the shepherd leader desires the wellbeing of his followers. As God guides, provides, and protects his people, so the shepherd leader guides, provides, and protects his followers.

Shepherd Leadership in the New Testament

The writers of the New Testament pick up on the shepherd leadership metaphor developed by the writers of the Old Testament and continue to unpack its meaning. Whereas in the Old Testament the emphasis of the metaphor was on God the Father as a shepherd leader and human leaders emulating his shepherd leadership, in the New Testament the emphasis switches to Jesus as the Son of God. For the New Testament writers, Jesus becomes the primary shepherd leader of God's people and the leaders of the various New Testament churches become the human shepherd leaders of God's people.

The most detailed passage in the New Testament describing Jesus as a shepherd leader is contained in John 10:11-18. From this passage two key characteristics of shepherd leaders emerge. First, shepherd leaders are good in the same way Jesus is the good shepherd. The word translated good in John 10:11 is the Greek word "Kalos." It means to be of excellent or virtuous character with the associated thoughts, feelings, and actions (Zohaides, 2000). This suggests Kalos describes an intrinsically good character for others to emulate (Wiersbe, 1989). Jesus uses the word to describe his actions in contrast to the actions of the hired hand who runs when wolves attack. The reason the hired hand runs is he more interested in his own wellbeing than the wellbeing of the sheep. The good shepherd however cares for the sheep out of a genuine desire for their wellbeing. Whereas the motivation of the hired hand is self-interest, the motivation of the good shepherd is love for the sheep and his desire for their wellbeing. It appears in this passage this selflessness is built upon the shepherd leader knowing the sheep by name. Real shepherds had very personal relationships with their sheep where they knew each by name (Keller, 1970). For shepherd leadership, this is more than the shepherd leader knowing each of his followers by name. It indicates a personal, caring relationship between the leader and follower. The personal relationship is not position oriented but rather relationally oriented. Through this personal and caring relationship the shepherd leader leads his followers to insure their wellbeing.

The second key characteristic of shepherd leaders indicated by Jesus in John 10:11-18 is shepherd leaders lay down their lives for the sheep. This is a picture of the shepherd protecting the sheep, one of the chief jobs of the shepherd. Donelson (1996) sees the self-sacrifice aspect of shepherd leadership as paramount in the ministry of Jesus. In general, sheep are defenseless animals unable to protect themselves from predators outside and other sheep inside. Outside the flock, natural predators include wolves, coyotes, and stray dogs

(Lucado, 2003). While protecting the sheep the shepherd could become seriously injured or die in the process. The good shepherd, because he cares for the sheep, will protect the sheep at all costs because he cares more for the sheep even than his own life. Therefore in John 10 Jesus is speaking about his own willingness to lay down his life for his sheep which are a metaphor for his followers. This willingness to lay his life down stems from the character and love of the shepherd, not the worthiness of the sheep. Applied to shepherd leadership, this suggests shepherd leaders also protect their followers not because their followers are worthy, but because it is the right thing to do. The true shepherd leader is willing to sacrifice himself for the protection of his followers.

Through passages like John 10, the New Testament writers create a continuity of shepherd leadership imagery throughout the Scriptures. Specifically in the New Testament the purpose of shepherd leaders continues to be insuring the wellbeing of their followers. This is seen in Matthew 9:36, John 18:11, Hebrews 13:20-21, 1 Peter 5:1-5, and Jude 12. Additionally the primary behaviors shepherd leaders use to insure the wellbeing of their followers continues to be guiding, providing, and protecting as seen in Matthew 26:21, John 10:11, Jude 12, and Revelation 7:17.

Shepherd Leadership in Contemporary Literature

Building upon the shepherd leadership framework developed by the Old and New Testament writers, several contemporary authors have developed the idea of shepherd leadership. Each of these contemporary authors takes the framework developed by the Biblical authors and applies shepherd leadership principles to leadership in a contemporary setting. For example, Donelson (2004), in his dissertation on shepherd leadership, explores shepherd leadership as a possible model for leadership in the church today. For Donelson, modern shepherd leader research is discovering

and developing what the Biblical writers have already provided, particularly in the relational are of leadership. Another author, Huntzinger (1999), suggests the biblical metaphor of the shepherd is the primary way God's people sought to understand their relationship with him and they used this imagery because of their familiarity with shepherding as a profession. Anderson, (1997), in his book Spiritual Leadership for the 21st Century, They Smell Like Sheep, agrees. He suggests shepherding is the primary Biblical model for spiritual leadership and suggests all leaders return to shepherd leadership and the primary leadership paradigm. Rardin (2001) agrees with him however argues for a practical theology of leadership from the Old and New Testaments called servant shepherd leadership.

Because of the Biblical foundations of shepherd leadership, many contemporary authors approach shepherd leadership from a spiritual perspective. For example, in their book entitled Like a Shepherd Lead Us, Freer & Siebert, (2006) edit a collection of essays each on the topic of shepherd leadership. Although several of the essays apply shepherd leadership principals to a secular work environment, none approach the topic of shepherd leadership from outside a Biblical paradigm. Therefore even in current shepherd leadership scholarship, the foundation of shepherd leadership continues to be the Biblical texts of the Old and New Testament. As a result, contemporary shepherd leadership literature also suggests shepherd leaders insure the wellbeing of the followers through the primary behaviors of guiding, providing, and protecting.

Many contemporary authors suggest the primary purpose of shepherd leaders is to insure the wellbeing of their followers. For example, Stowe (1976), in his book entitled The Ministry of Shepherding, suggests the role of the shepherd leader is serving others by caring for them. For Stowe, Jesus is the primary example of a shepherd leader. As Jesus demonstrated compassionate love for his followers, so shepherd leaders demonstrate compassionate love for their followers. In the Song of the Shepherd, Horsfall (2004) agrees. In looking at Psalm 23 in the Old Testament he sees the relationship between the shepherd and the sheep as a picture of each person's relationship with God. As God cares for his people as a shepherd, so shepherd leaders care for their followers. Anderson (1997) agrees by applying the same principle to God the Father in the Old Testament suggesting God the Father's relationship with his people is the model for shepherd leadership today. Building on the spiritual component of shepherd leadership, Anderson suggests the purpose of shepherd leaders insuring the wellbeing of their followers flows directly from the shepherd leader's relationship with God. The result is for Anderson is the shepherd leader always places the wellbeing of those they lead first. Also in similar fashion, Wray (2006), in his chapter entitled Soul Care and the Heart of a Shepherd, suggests the primary role of shepherd leaders is to care for the souls of those God entrusts to them. He unpacks the principle practically by suggesting five behaviors shepherd leaders engage in. These include identifying and supporting the weak, participating in the healing process for the sick and injured, searching for those who go astray, reaching out to the lost, and ministering with kindness and gentleness. In the current work, each of these may be considered aspects of guiding, providing, and protecting as elements of shepherd leaders insuring the wellbeing of their followers. In addition to Wray (2006), several authors after addressing the purpose for shepherd leadership suggests various behaviors the shepherd leader may utilize to accomplish their primary purpose of insuring the wellbeing of their followers. For example, (Harris, 2006) suggests guarding against becoming busy, frantic, and overwhelmed with ministry responsibilities. As a practical way of accomplishing this he suggests the shepherd leader model his or her life after the pattern of Jesus in Luke 5:15-16 by engaging in extended times of prayer. In a similar vein Childers (2006) takes this principle beyond prayer

and challenges shepherd leaders to take up their cross and follow Jesus. His point is as Jesus died for his followers, so the shepherd leader is to die, metaphorically, for his or her followers. Death is not a physical death, but a death to self-interest, self-centeredness, the pursuit of the shepherd leader's agenda which is replaced by the agenda of insuring the wellbeing of followers. Horsfall (2004) takes a unique approach by suggesting the selflessness of the shepherd leader flows from the relationship between the shepherd leader and follower. For Horsfall, shepherd leaders invest in their followers by building relationships with them and it is then through the quality of these relationships the shepherd leader is able to overcome self interest and lead for the wellbeing of their followers. Leman & Pentak (2004) in The Way of the Shepherd make a similar point by suggesting shepherd leaders make a significant commitment to their followers demonstrated by their investment of personal energy and involvement with their followers. For them, shepherd leadership is a lifestyle which places great value of the worth of followers. In this way shepherd leaders are distinguished by their heart of love for their followers. Young (2006) agrees, seeing shepherd leaders as individuals who build relationships with people, exercise influence by setting the example, focus on building others up, and serving people sacrificially. Each of these behaviors flows from the heart of the shepherd leader authentically desiring the wellbeing of his or her followers.

In addition to suggesting the primary purpose of shepherd leaders is to insure the wellbeing of followers, many contemporary authors also suggest one of the primary behaviors shepherd leaders utilize to accomplish this is guiding. For example, Harris (2006) discusses the tension spiritual leader's face as they guide followers in a way that leaves room for the active presence of Christ. He recommends while guiding, shepherd leaders maintain an appropriate distance allowing the follower to focus on the presence of God and not focus on the spiritual leader. For Harris, the shepherd leader then guides on behalf of God, leading followers where God desires them to go. Leman & Pentak (2004) agree, suggesting the imagery of the staff of direction the shepherd carried symbolizes the guiding role of shepherd leaders. They go as far as to suggest the staff of direction or guiding was the shepherd's most important tool. Similarly they suggest guiding is one of the most important roles of the shepherd leader. Behaviorally they suggest to guide effectively the shepherd leader must know where he or she is leading, be out in front of followers, and keep followers moving forward in a coordinated manner for goal accomplishment. Stowe (1976) takes this same guiding aspect of shepherd leadership and applies it behaviorally to pastoral ministry. For Stowe, the pastor as shepherd leader guides a church ministry through decision making, delegation, leading the board, congregational meetings, and utilizing sound financial processes. In this manner the spiritual shepherd leader fulfills the guiding responsibility. Horsfall (2004) agrees the guiding function of the shepherd leader is important suggesting that sheep, as a metaphor for followers, without guidance, are incapable of guiding themselves.

Contemporary authors also suggest providing is a key behavior of shepherd leadership. Several authors focus primarily on this aspect of shepherd leadership, particularly providing for people who are sick. For example, Shelly (2006), focuses on the compassion and care Jesus as a shepherd leader showed to people who were sick, such as the paralyzed man (Mark 2:1-12), and the blind man (John 9:1-12). From this she suggests human suffering deserves the attention of the shepherd leader and is therefore a part of the shepherd leader's role helping or providing for those who are in need. Horsfall (2004) sees providing as one of the primary aspects of shepherd leadership according to Psalm 23. The provision

aspect of Psalm 23 is a common theme among authors writing about Psalm 23 (Roper, 1994; Slemming, 1942; Keller, 1970). Leman & Pentak (2004) apply this principle to the followers of shepherd leaders suggesting it is the responsibility of shepherd leaders to provide for their followers as one means of insuring the wellbeing of their followers. This includes providing behaviors such as providing people with information, new job opportunities, staying visible, and dealing with problems when they occur. Stowe (1976), applies these providing principles to a ministry context suggesting the spiritual shepherd leader provides spiritual nourishment to followers. He suggests the pastor's study is a symbol of the calling to be the shepherd leader of the flock indicating for Stowe the importance of the responsibility of the shepherd leader to spiritually provide for the flock. Although the specific behavioral applications of what it means to provide for followers in various settings changes, the larger underlying principle is shepherd leaders provide for their followers.

Contemporary authors also suggest shepherd leaders protect their followers. For example, Lowry (2006) suggests it is the role of the shepherd leader to protect the sheep by mediating conflict in the church. Practically he suggests five strategies for mediating conflict including think like you are Chinese, focus on the process, go below the line, use the satisfaction triangle, and remember God's promise. Through these strategies Lowry correctly suggests conflict hurts followers and therefore one means of the shepherd leader protecting followers is to reduce conflict among them. Additionally, Horsfall (2004) suggests the protecting aspect of shepherd leadership is one of the most important. In Psalm 23 he sees David's expression of how God protected him as shepherd leader and how he in turn protects the people as their shepherd leader. Keller (1970) suggests that when the shepherd arrives to protect the sheep, they sense his protection and visibly relax. The corollary to leadership is the capacity of shepherd leaders to place their followers at rest through behaviors that protect them. Leman & Pentak (2004) agree that one of the primary roles of the shepherd leader is to protect the sheep. They suggest two ways shepherd leaders specifically protect their followers from conflict in the workplace. The first is by eliminating the influence of troublesome followers and the second by addressing conflict immediately when it occurs. More specifically Leman & Pentak suggest shepherd leaders can protect their followers by setting boundaries, providing proper discipline for improper conduct, defending followers from others who would hurt them, and regularly inspecting their progress to insure they are performing effectively. Young (2006) suggests shepherd leaders protect their people even when it requires personal sacrifice to do so.

Stevenson (2006) also sees the shepherd leader as a protector of the sheep.

Overall the review of the literature regarding shepherd leadership suggests most of the authors writing on shepherd leadership use the Biblical paradigm of shepherd leadership to apply shepherd leadership principles in a spiritual leadership context. Several make behavioral shepherd leadership applications to the secular work environment. An analysis of these authors suggests in accordance with the Biblical paradigm the purpose of shepherd leadership is to insure the wellbeing of followers. (Stowe, 1976; Horsfall, 2004; Anderson, 1997; Wray, 2006; Harris, 2006; Childers, 2006; Leman & Pentak, 2004; Young, 2006). Also consistent with the Biblical Paradigm, the primary means through which shepherd leaders insure the wellbeing of followers includes guiding them (Harris, 2006; Leman & Pentak, 2004; Stowe, 1976; Horsfall, 2004), providing for them (Shelly, 2006; Leman & Pentak, 2004; Stowe, 1976), and protecting them (Lowry, 2006; Horsfall, 2004; Keller, 1970; Leman & Pentak, 2006; Young, 2006; Stevenson, 2006). This suggests shepherd leaders lead for the wellbeing of their followers through the behaviors of guiding, providing, and protecting.

Development of the Shepherd Leadership Inventory (SLI)

For the development of the SLI, a validated inventory was created to both enable the further study of shepherd leadership and provide a framework for the practical application of shepherd leadership principles to the practice of leadership. The SLI was based upon theory developed from the existing shepherd leadership information to include guiding, providing, and protecting items together representing the behaviors shepherd leaders use to insure the wellbeing of their followers. Items in the SLI were randomized according to a Kerlinger and Lee (2000) table of random numbers.

The development of the SLI involved the following steps: (a) a comprehensive literature review of shepherd leadership including the Old Testament, New Testament, and current shepherd leadership popular press and academic literature; (b) the initial development of draft SLI items reviewed by the author's dissertation committee chair for face validity and revised using her feedback into the SLIv1. Two criteria were considered when generating the initial items used in the SLI. First, the respondent score for each item should accurately reflect the behavior of the respondent. Second, the respondent score for each item should be a ratio measure. To accomplish this, the behavioral items were scored from never (score 1) to always (score 5) in 1.0 increments thus yielding ratio data representative of shepherd leader behaviors; (c) the review of the SLIv1 for face validity by two pilot groups and one focus group then revised using their feedback into the SLIv2. The first pilot group consisted of 7 members of the New Castle County Evangelical Ministers Fellowship. The second pilot group consisted of 6 staff members of the Red Lion Evangelical Free Church. The focus group consisted of a smaller group of 3 staff members of the Red Lion Evangelical Free Church who had participated in the second pilot group. Together these groups constituted a mixed group of pastors, parachurch leaders, and ministry staff members who generally understand both leadership and shepherding through the nature of their positions and training. This insight into shepherd leadership made these individuals ideal for assessing the face validity of the SLIv1 item pool; (d) the readability of the SLIv2 was calculated at a 9th grade level using the Flesch-Kincaid tool in Microsoft Office 2009 and revised to obtain a 6th grade reading level; (e) Following the author's dissertation proposal defense, one question was added to the SLIv2 through feedback from the committee resulting in the SLIv3 consisting of 26 items randomized accordingly to a Kerlinger and Lee (2000) table of random numbers; (f) the SLIv3 was administered to the regular attendees of the Red Lion Evangelical Free Church through an online survey utilizing Survey Monkey. The survey link was delivered via email which resulted in 199 individuals completing the survey. The sample data indicated that the majority of the sample were female (65.5%) and either 25-44 years of age (43.7%) or 45-64 years of age (45.4%). Additionally the majority of respondents were Caucasian (89.9%). A Kruskal-Wallis independent samples test was performed on the demographics of gender, age, and educational level. The purpose was to test for significant relationships between the behavior subgroups and sample demography. The Kruskal-Wallace was chosen because the dependent variables are categorical rather than continuous. The Kruskal-Wallis test revealed a significant difference in gender only in the providing subgroup suggesting in general men and women view the providing aspect of shepherd leadership differently. The data suggest the sample demography does not affect the guiding or protecting subgroups of shepherd leadership and only gender affects the providing subgroup of shepherd leadership; (g) approximately 3 weeks later the SLIv3 was again administered to those who had completed the SLIv3 during the first administration through an online survey utilizing Survey Monkey. The survey link was again delivered via email; (h) test retest survey results

were analyzed using principal component factor analysis to determine the reliability and validity of the SLIv3 around the three primary shepherd leadership behaviors of guiding, providing, and protecting.

RELIABILITY

To assess the reliability of the SLIv3, principal component factor analysis was performed on the SLIv3 item pool and the Cronbach's alpha determined. The Cronbach's alpha for the 26 item SLIv3 was calculated as a measure of internal consistency to be 0.93 indicating a very high internal consistency for the SLIv3. Principal component factor analysis determined all items loaded above the 0.3 level which is the minimum bivariate correlation level suggested by Kline (2000). The Cronbach's alpha of the guiding subgroup was calculated at 0.89. The Cronbach's alpha for the providing subgroup was 0.84, and for the protecting subgroup, 0.79. Principal component factor analysis indicates the SLIv3 is a reliable instrument.

Additionally, ninety-four individuals completed the test-retest study with approximately to 4 weeks between tests. For the 26 item SLIv3, a Pearson product-moment correlation was calculated for the test-retest total scores. The test-retest reliability correlation for all 26 items was calculated at 0.79 for the transformed data and 0.78 for the raw data. Kline (2000) recommends the test-retest correlations score a minimum of 0.8 suggesting the test-retest correlation as just reliable. The behavioral subgroup of guiding had a correlation of 0.74 for the transformed scores and 0.72 for the raw scores. The behavioral subgroup of providing had a correlation of 0.77 for the transformed scores and 0.77 for the raw scores. The behavioral subgroup of protecting had a correlation of 0.7 for the transformed scores and 0.69 for the raw scores. Therefore the test retest data suggests the SLIv3 is reliable.

Upon closer examination of the retest data, it was noted that 19 of the 94 individuals who completed the retest had scores significantly different from the first time they completed the inventory, contributing negatively to the test-retest reliability date. It is hypothesized given the magnitude of the discrepancy of the scores these individuals did not take the retest with much thought, meaning they may have filled in responses quickly or randomly. When these 19 responses are removed and the retest reliability recalculated with the remaining 75 retest responses, the retest reliability for the 26 items is 0.90 for both the transformed and raw scores, further suggesting the SLI is very reliable according to Kline (2000).

VALIDITY

To assess the content validity of the SLIv3, principal component factor analysis was performed on the SLIv3 item pool to determine how effectively each item contributes to measuring its corresponding shepherd leadership behavior. The primary shepherd leadership behaviors of guiding, providing, and protecting, constitute the three factor structure. Each factor is composed of a set of underlying items measuring each shepherd leader behavior.

Because principal component factor analysis is often used as an objective basis for creating validated scales (Hair, Anderson, Tatham, & Black, 1998), it was the ideal statistical tool to use in this study. The approach sought to explain the variables through their common underlying factors or dimensions by analyzing the interrelationships among the variables. This allowed the researcher to assess the correlations of each item on the SLIv3 to each other and each item's contribution to its corresponding primary behavior factor. Hence principal component factor analysis of the SLIv3 item pool indicated which items measure the same behavior and the degree to which they measure it (Kerlinger & Lee, 2000).

Specifically, factor analysis was performed after transforming the item responses through ranking and standardizing (i.e., raw scores to ranked scores to z-scores). This resulted in distributions of zero mean, standard deviations of unity, and skewness levels of absolute value less than 0.03. This process is important because although mild to moderate kurtosis does not significantly affect a product-moment computation, it is possible for skewed distributions to affect it (Cureton & D'Agostino, 1983). Additionally, the Kaiser-Meyer-Olkin Measure of Sampling Adequacy (MSA) and Bartlett's test of Sphericity were performed and confirmed the correlation matrices were suitable for factor analysis. All items loaded positively on the principal component. The first principal component was used because the first principal component represented the best grouping of items that correspond to each behavior (Gorsuch, 1983).

For the guiding subgroup, the first principal component extracted from the transformed scores accounted for 53.4% of the variance while the second component accounts for 11.2%. The raw scores of the first principal component account for 49.7% of the variance while the second component accounts for 11.0%. The first principal component extracted from the transformed scores of the providing subgroup accounts for 50.5% of the variance with no second component detected. The raw scores of the first principal component account for 49.6% of the variance with no second component detected. The first principal component extracted from the transformed scores of the protecting subgroup accounts for 37.3% of the variance with no second component detected. The raw scores of the first principal component account for 34.6% of the variance while the second component detected for the raw scores accounts for 11.9% of the variance.

Additionally, the bivariate correlations for the transformed data of each item showed that all items correlated positively and significantly at the 0.01 level (two-tailed test), and therefore should be included in the instrument (Kline, 1994)

The data from the principle component factor analysis indicate the SLI is a valid instrument.

RESULTS

An individual who completes the SLI receives individual item scores, providing, guiding, and protecting subgroup scores, and a total score. The individual item scores represent the degree to which a leader is functioning in a particular behavior associated with shepherd leadership. The subgroup score represents the average degree to which a leader is functioning behaviorally in one of the shepherd leader subgroups of guiding, providing, or protecting. The total score represents the degree to which an individual is behaviorally functioning as a shepherd leader.

COMMENTARY

The information gained from the SLI is of great value to both the practitioner of shepherd leadership and the shepherd leadership researcher. For the practitioner of shepherd leadership, presenting the results in the manner described allows the shepherd leader to determine their shepherd leadership behavior at the level of their individual behaviors, their larger guiding, providing, and protecting subgroup behaviors, or their overall effectiveness as a shepherd leader. As a result an individual completing the survey is able to assess specific areas of shepherd leadership strength and shepherd leadership behaviors which may need strengthening. From this information an individual is able to develop specific strategies to improve specific areas of their shepherd leadership and thereby become a more effective shepherd leader.

For the shepherd leadership researcher, the information gained from the survey allows for additional research into shepherd leadership through further statistical analysis. For example, the information gained from the survey allows the researcher to analyze survey data at the individual item level, at the guiding, providing, and protecting subgroup level, or the overall shepherd leader level. In this manner the SLI provides the researcher with a wealth of information necessary for further research into shepherd leadership.

Additionally, one of the more important values of the SLI development process was the development of the emerging leadership theory of shepherd leadership. In attempting to operationalize the theory of shepherd leadership into a behavioral construct the development of the SLI suggests shepherd leadership is more about being than about doing. The SLI revealed the primary purpose of the shepherd leader is to insure the wellbeing of their followers. This is accomplished through the three primary behaviors of guiding, providing, and protecting. Each behavior in turn may be broken down into a series of specific behaviors the shepherd leadership demonbstrates to accomplish insuring the wellbeing of their followers in that particular area. On the surface this creates the perception that a shepherd leader is a leader who performs certain behavioral tasks associated with shepherd leadership. It would follow then that anyone could become a shepherd leader by engaging in these taks. Yet the development of the SLI revealed that shepherd leadership is primarily about being, not doing. The doing flows from the being, not the being from the doing. In other words shepherd leaders perform certain behavioral tasks becuase they are sheperd leaders, they are not shepherd leaders because they perform these behavioral tasks. The tasks demonstrate a leader is a shepherd leader. The taks do not make a person into a shepherd leader. Therefore shepherd leadership is about primarily who a leader is, not what a leader does.

For example, in the New Testament Jesus is the great shepherd leader. The Apostle Paul describes the heart of his shepherd leadership in Philippians 2:4-11. In this passage Paul describes how

Jesus did not look only to his own interests, but through the crucifixion looked to our interests as well. As a result God exalted him to the highest place and gave him the name that is above every name. So Jeuss is a shepherd leader not becuase he allowed himself to be crucified, but becuase he looked to our interests and therefore allowed himself to be crucified. The behavior of allowing himself to be crucified flowed from him looking to the interests of others. It is because he looked to the interests of others that he is a shepherd leader. The crucifixion is simply the behavioral outcome that demonstrates he is a shepherd leader. In other words it is looking to the interests of others that makes him a shepherd leader, not the behavior of being crucified. If for example Jesus would have allowed himself to be crucified only to receive the exaltation from God the Father, Jesus would not then be a shepherd leader becuase at its core he would have allowed himself to be crucified because of self interest, not looking to the interests of others. The outward behavior of the crucifixion would have been the same, but the internal motivation would have been selfish as opposed to selfless. Jesus captured the essence of this idea when he said, "I am the good shepherd. The good shepherd lays his life down for the sheep." (John 10:11). Following these words, Jesus then contrasts the good shepherd with the hired hand who runs away when he sees the wolf coming. In verse 13 Jesus gives the reason the hired hand runs away. He says, "The man runs away becuase he is a hired hand and cares nothing for the sheep." (John 10:13). So the good shepherd lays down his life for the sheep becuase he cares for the sheep while the hired hand runs away becuase he cares nothing for the sheep. The good shepherd is the good shepherd then becuase he cares for the sheep. The hired hand is not the good shepherd becuase he does not care for the sheep. So in the words of Jesus, it is the value of caring for the sheep which makes the good shepherd the good shepherd. The corresponding behaviors simply demonstrate the core motivation of the shepherd's heart.

In these words of Jesus the sheep represent followers and the shepherd or the hired hand represent leaders. Therefore true shepherd leaders are shepherd leaders because they are sincerely motivated by a desire to insure the wellbeing of their followers. This desire results in certain behaviors which insure the wellbeing of their followers in the areas of guiding, providing, and protecting. It is however not the behaviors which make the leader a shepherd leader, it is the motivatioin of the shepherd leader. Shepherd leaders are leaders who lead for the wellbeing of their followers.

The development of the SLI also identified several areas where future research is needed. First, the Kruskal-Wallis independent samples test performed on the demography of age, gender, and education level indicated gender affects the shepherd leader subgroup of providing. This may indicate men and women view the shepherd leader behavior of providing differently and raises the larger question of how gender affects shepherd leader behavior. Therefore it is recommended that further study be conducted on the relationship between gender and the providing subgroup to determine if gender is truly a significant factor in how respondents view the providing shepherd leader behaviors. This can be accomplished by administering the SLI to a larger sample and further analyzing the impact of gender on providing. If further research confirms gender impacts the providing subgroup, additional research should also be conducted to determine the reasons for that impact. This can be accomplished by developing an additional inventory to further explore the relationship between gender and the providing subgroup within the SLIv3 and administering the inventory to a large sample.

Second, additional analysis of the reliability of the SLI is warranted. Although the test-retest data for the 26 item SLIv3 suggests the inventory is reliable with a correlation of 0.79 for the transformed data, the test-retest data with 19 respondents removed indicated a correlation of 0.90 for the transformed data. Although reliable, this raises the question of just how reliable of an instrument is the SLI. Although it is hypothesized these 19 individuals did not take the retest with much thought, possibly filling in responses quickly or randomly, further research is necessary to confirm this hypothesis. Administering a test-retest of the SLI to a large sample with further analysis is necessary to accomplish this goal.

Cost

Cost for use of the SLI is determined based on the purposes for which the SLI will be used. Please contact the author at www.JamieSwalm.com. for further information.

Location

The SLI is located at www.JamieSwalm.com

REFERENCES

Achtemeier, P. (1985). *Harper's bible dictionary*. San Francisco, CA: Harper & Row.

Anderson, L. (1990). *They smell like sheep (Vol. 1)*. New York, NY: Howard Books.

Balz, R., & Schneider, G. (1993). *The exegetical dictionary of the New Testament*. Grand Rapids, MI: Eerdmans.

Bromiley, G. (Ed.). (1991). *The international standard Bible encyclopedia*. Grand Rapids, MI: William B. Eerdmans Publishing Company.

Childers, J. (2006). Moving to the rhythms of Christian life: Baptism for children raised in the church. In Fleer, D., & Sibert, C. (Eds.), *Like a shepherd lead us* (pp. 95–122). Abilene, TX: Leafwood Publishers.

Cureton, E., & D'Agostino, R. (1983). *Factor analysis: An applied approach*. Hillsdale, NJ: Lawrence Erlbaum Associates.

Donelson, W. (2004). *Shepherd leadership*. Unpublished dissertation, Regent University, Virginia Beach, VA.

Elwell, W., & Beitzel, B. (Eds.). (1988). *Baker encyclopedia of the Bible*. Grand Rapids, MI: Baker Book House.

Fleer, D., & Siburt, C. (Eds.). (2006). *Like a shepherd lead us*. Abilene, TX: Leafwood Publishers.

Freedman, D. (Ed.). (1996). *The anchor Bible dictionary*. New York, NY: Doubleday. (Original work published 1992)

Gorsuch, R. L. (1983). *Factor analysis* (2nd ed.). Hillsdale, NJ: Lawrence Erlbaum Associates.

Hair, J. F., Anderson, R. E., Tatham, R. L., & Black, W. C. (1998). *Multivariate data analysis*. Upper Saddle River, NJ: Prentice Hall.

Harris, R. (2006). Spirituality for the busy, frantic, and overwhelmed. In Fleer, D., & Charles, S. (Eds.), *Like a shepherd lead us: Guidance for the gentle art of pastoring* (pp. 15–31). Abilene, TX: Leafwood Publishers.

Horsfall, T. (2004). *Song of the shepherd: Meeting the God of grace in Psalm 23*. Cambridge, MA: Cowley Publications.

Huntzinger, J. (1999). *The end of exile: A short commentary on the shepherd/sheep metaphor in exilic and post-exilic prophetic and synoptic gospel literature*. Unpublished Master's thesis, Fuller Theological Seminary, Pasadena, CA.

Keller, P. (1970). *A shepherd looks at Psalm 23*. Grand Rapids, MI: Zondervan.

Kerlinger, F. N., & Lee, H. B. (2000). *Foundations of behavioral research* (4th ed.). Stamford, CT: Wadsworth Thompson.

Kline, P. (1994). *An easy guide to factor analysis*. New York, NY: Routledge.

Leman, K., & Pentak, W. (2004). *The way of the shepherd, 7 ancient secrets to managing productive people*. Grand Rapids, MI: Zondervan.

Lowry, R. (2006). Before we split: Mediating conflict in the church. In Fleer, D., & Siburt, C. (Eds.), *Like a shepherd lead us* (pp. 123–138). Abilene, TX: Leafwood Publishers.

McCormick, B., & Davenport, D. (2003). *Shepherd leadership*. San Francisco, CA: Jossey-Bass.

Morgan, G. (1997). *Images of organization*. Thousand Oaks, CA: Sage Publications Inc.

Rardin, R. (2004). *The servant's guide to leadership*. Newtown, CT: Selah Publishing.

Roper, D. (1994). *Psalm 23: The song of a passionate heart*. Grand Rapids, MI: Discovery House Publishers.

Samuel, M. (1996). *The Lord is my shepherd: The theology of a caring god*. Northvale, NJ: Jason Aronson, Inc.

Shelly, R. (2006). I was sick, and you looked after me: Pastoral leadership in ministering to the sick. In *Like a shepherd lead us* (pp. 71–94). Abilene, TX: Leafwood Publishers.

Slemming, C. (1942). *He leadeth me: Shepherd life in Palestine, Psalm 23*. Fort Washington, PA: CLC Publications.

Stevenson, G. (2006). The church goes to the movies: Standing at the intersection of the church and popular culture. In *Like a shepherd lead us* (pp. 139–161). Abilene, TX: Leafwood Publishers.

Tappy, R. (1995). Psalm 23: Symbolism and structure. *Catholic Biblical Quarterly, 57*(2), 255–280.

Wagner, G. (1999). *Escape from church, Inc.: The return of the pastor-shepherd*. Grand Rapids, MI: Zondervan.

Wood, D. (1996). Shepherd. In *The new Bible dictionary* (3rd ed., *Vol. 3*). Grand Rapids, MI: Intervarsity Press.

Wray, D. (2006). Soul care and the heart of a shepherd. In *Like a shepherd lead us* (pp. 51–70). Abilene, TX: Leafwood Publishers.

Young, S. (2006, Winter). Jesus as shepherd leader. *Denver Seminary Magazine, 2*(4), 5–6.

ADDITIONAL READING

Anderson, L. (1990). *They smell like sheep (Vol. 1)*. New York, NY: Howard Books.

Childers, J. (2006). Moving to the rhythms of Christian life: Baptism for children raised in the church. In Fleer, D., & Sibert, C. (Eds.), *Like a shepherd lead us* (pp. 95–122). Abilene, TX: Leafwood Publishers.

Donelson, W. (2004). *Shepherd leadership*. Unpublished dissertation, Regent University, Virginia Beach, VA.

Fleer, D., & Siburt, C. (Eds.). (2006). *Like a shepherd lead us*. Abilene, TX: Leafwood Publishers.

Harris, R. (2006). Spirituality for the busy, frantic, and overwhelmed. In Fleer, D., & Charles, S. (Eds.), *Like a shepherd lead us: Guidance for the gentle art of pastoring* (pp. 15–31). Abilene, TX: Leafwood Publishers.

Horsfall, T. (2004). *Song of the shepherd: Meeting the God of grace in Psalm 23*. Cambridge, MA: Cowley Publications.

Huntzinger, J. (1999). *The end of exile: A short commentary on the shepherd/sheep metaphor in exilic and post-exilic prophetic and synoptic gospel literature*. Unpublished Master's thesis, Fuller Theological Seminary, Pasadena, CA.

Keller, P. (1970). *A shepherd looks at Psalm 23*. Grand Rapids, MI: Zondervan.

Lowry, R. (2006). Before we split: Mediating conflict in the church. In Fleer, D., & Siburt, C. (Eds.), *Like a shepherd lead us* (pp. 123–138). Abilene, TX: Leafwood Publishers.

Lucado, M. (2003). *Safe in the shepherd's arms: Hope and encouragement from Psalm 23*. Nashville, TN: J. Countryman.

McCormick, B., & Davenport, D. (2003). *Shepherd leadership*. San Francisco, CA: Jossey-Bass.

Morgan, G. (1997). *Images of organization*. Thousand Oaks, CA: Sage Publications Inc.

Rardin, R. (2004). *The servant's guide to leadership*. Newtown, CT: Selah Publishing.

Roper, D. (1994). *Psalm 23: The song of a passionate heart*. Grand Rapids, MI: Discovery House Publishers.

Shelly, R. (2006). I was sick, and you looked after me: Pastoral leadership in ministering to the sick. In *Like a shepherd lead us* (pp. 71–94). Abilene, TX: Leafwood Publishers.

Slemming, C. (1942). *He leadeth me: Shepherd life in Palestine, Psalm 23*. Fort Washington, PA: CLC Publications.

Stevenson, G. (2006). The church goes to the movies: Standing at the intersection of the church and popular culture. In *Like a shepherd lead us* (pp. 139–161). Abilene, TX: Leafwood Publishers.

Wagner, G. (1999). *Escape from church, inc.: The return of the pastor-shepherd*. Grand Rapids, MI: Zondervan.

Wiersbe, W. (1996). *Be comforted*. Wheaton, IL: Victor Books.

Wood, D. (1996). Shepherd. In *The new Bible dictionary* (3rd ed., *Vol. 3*). Grand Rapids, MI: Intervarsity Press.

Wray, D. (2006). Soul care and the heart of a shepherd. In *Like a shepherd lead us* (pp. 51–70). Abilene, TX: Leafwood Publishers.

Young, S. (2006, Winter). Jesus as shepherd leader. *Denver Seminary Magazine, 2*(4), 5–6.

Zodhiates, S. (2000). *The complete word study dictionary: New Testament*. Chattanooga, TN: AMG Publishers.

KEY TERMS AND DEFINITIONS

Guiding: Assisting another through giving direction, advice, or counsel.

Leader: A person giving direction to followers.

Metaphor: A figure of speech used to represent something else.

Protecting: To defend or guard from harm.

Providing: To make available or furnish something another needs.

Shepherd Leader: A person who leads for the wellbeing of his or her followers.

Shepherd Leader Inventory (SLI): A validated scale measuring shepherd leadership.

Chapter 13
Development of the Leader Integrity Assessment

J. Alan Marshall
United States Air Force, USA

ABSTRACT

The purpose of this research is to develop a direct and concise perceived leader integrity instrument that is posed from a positive perspective. The integrity construct in this study is developed from the tradition of moral philosophy and virtue ethics. The integrity construct in this study incorporates two aspects of integrity found in the literature, namely value-behavior congruence and a requirement that this congruence be grounded in morality. The moral philosophy used in this study to ground the integrity construct is virtue ethics as proposed by ancient philosophy and later maintained by Christian virtue ethics in the middle ages. An expert panel was used to establish content validity and construct validity/reliability was established via analysis of three samples of Air Force personnel associated with the U-2 pilot community. Nomological validity is established by leveraging the resultant Leader Integrity Assessment 15 to investigate the hypothesized moderating effects on the relationship between leader prototypicality and follower trust in the leader as proposed in the Kalshoven and Den Hartog (2009) Ethical Leadership Model. Overall, the Leader Integrity Assessment 15 was found valid and reliable and the integrity construct was found unidimensional as hypothesized.

INTEGRITY

Integrity is a term used in management and leadership research as a "normative descriptor" (Palanski & Yammarino, 2007, p. 171). However, in common usage, the term has a "myriad of meanings" (Dunn, 2009, p. 102). Palanski and Yammarino, (2007) stated that integrity research has suffered from "too many definitions and too little theory" (p. 171). The lack of a consistent use of integrity as a normative descriptor and the varied usage in common language, have led to narrow construct definitions that have thwarted broader theoreti-

DOI: 10.4018/978-1-4666-2172-5.ch013

cal development (Dunn, 2009). However, Audi and Murphy (2006) recognized that "integrity is widely considered a moral virtue" (p. 3). Accordingly, Palanski and Yammarino (2007) proposed that a formulation of integrity as a moral virtue "enables scholars to draw upon thousands of years of philosophical reflection to build a sound theoretical framework that provides an explanation of both the concept of integrity and its relationship to closely related terms" (p. 172). Due to the critical role that integrity plays in several emerging leadership theories such as ethical leadership (Brown, et al., 2005), transformational leadership (Bass, 1985), authentic leadership (Luthans & Avolio, 2003), spiritual leadership (Fry, 2003), and servant leadership (Greenleaf, 1977), a theoretical development of an integrity measurement scale based in virtue ethics and moral philosophy is in order.

Although functional, formulations of integrity in management and leadership research lack a common theoretical thread (Dunn, 2009). Harcourt (1998) identified integrity as "a person sticking by what that person regards as ethically necessary or worthwhile" (p. 189). Northouse (2007) defined integrity as "the quality of honesty and trustworthiness" (p. 20). Furrow (2005) described integrity as "the extent to which our various commitments form a harmonious, intact whole" (p. 136). Solomon (1999) defined integrity as "that sense of cohesion such that one is not torn apart by conflicts" (p. 38). Schlenker (2008) described integrity as "a steadfast commitment to one's principles" (p. 1079). Yukl and Van Fleet (1990) proposed an integrated definition of integrity such that integrity "means that a person's behavior is consistent with espoused values, and is honest and trustworthy" (p. 155). Addressing criticisms of integrity definitions allowing for immoral yet consistent behaviors, Yukl (2006) updated his definition of integrity to mean that a "person's behavior is consistent with a set of justifiable moral principles" (p. 421). Fields (2007) similarly defined integrity as "having personal values grounded in morality" (p. 196). Although many of these definitions are quite different, there seems to

be a baseline consensus among researchers that integrity involves congruence between one's values and one's behaviors. Musschenga (2001) labeled this aspect of integrity as "personal integrity" and also proposed the complimentary concept of "moral integrity" which is the result of "socially shared, moral identity-conferring commitments" (p. 222). Accordingly, although lacking a common theoretical thread, many leadership researchers seem to agree in that as a minimum, integrity involves a wholeness or consistency of behavior that is simultaneously grounded in morality. However, this conceptual dualism is missing in the development of prominent perceived integrity instruments routinely used in leadership research.

Existing Integrity Instruments

In constructing one of the two prominent integrity instruments used in much leadership research, Simons (2002) defined "behavioral integrity" (BI) as "the perceived pattern of alignment between an actor's words and deeds" (p. 19). Although this formulation captures one of the two common themes in the leadership literature (congruence between values and behaviors), it completely ignores the accompanying consensus amongst many leadership researchers that the integrity construct must be linked with morality (Fields, 2007). The BI approach implies that a clearly immoral person could be viewed as possessing integrity as long as their immoral behavior was consistent with their immoral values. In such a formulation, a genocidal Nazi or a lone wolf killer could possess integrity as long as their behavior was consistent with their sociopathic or psychopathic values. BI researchers addressed this critique by saying that although "one might not support [an immoral] colleague's actions or seek vulnerability to him, at least one knows that he means what he says" (Simons, 2002, p. 19). This rebuttal is unsatisfying for researchers looking for an integrity instrument that addresses both value-behavior congruence and morality as seemingly identified in leadership literature (Palanski & Yammarino, 2007).

Craig and Gustafson (1998) developed a 31-item Perceived Leader Integrity Scale (PLIS) for assessing follower perceptions of leader integrity. Along with the previously discussed BI scale, the PLIS is the other widely used perceived integrity instrument in leadership research (Palanski & Yammarino, 2007). The PLIS investigates seven behavioral domains associated with ethical and unethical leadership namely "follower development, workload allocation, truth telling, unlawful discrimination, rule compliance, maliciousness, and self-protection" (Craig & Gustafson, 1998, p. 130). Although PLIS researchers recognized the existence of "several competing ethical theories," theoretical development of the PLIS domains was exclusively grounded in rule-based utilitarianism which drove an attempt to identify the absence of a long list of rule based negative behaviors (Craig and Gustafson, 1998). As a result, the PLIS is relatively long for a single personality trait instrument. The PLIS has also been criticized for being indirect, posed from a negative perspective, and more appropriately measures any lack of leader integrity rather than the presence of integrity (Perry, 2002). Additionally, according to Palanski and Yammarino, the PLIS "does not appear to compliment the various conceptualizations in the management and leadership literature" (2007, p. 172). For these reasons, a more direct, concise and positive perspective integrity instrument grounded in virtue ethics and moral philosophy was developed in this study. The integrity instrument in this study is direct in that it directly investigates the presence of integrity as a moral component of character as opposed to the PLIS approach of investigating the lack of integrity in a leader. The integrity instrument in this study is concise in that this direct approach allows for a fewer number of items on the instrument than the PLIS and the length is more in line with other single personality trait instruments. The integrity instrument in this study is posed from a positive perspective in that it investigates the presence of positive traits versus the absence of negative traits as in the PLIS.

INTEGRITY CONSTRUCT THEORETICAL DEVELOPMENT

The primary moral question for ancient moral philosophers was "which virtues make a good character?" (Palanski & Yammarino, 2007, p. 175). Plato proposed that the cardinal virtues of prudence, justice, temperance and courage were central to the perfection of human character (Cooper & Hutchinson, 1997). In his *Nicomachean Ethics*, Aristotle proposed that the "human good turns out to be activity of the soul in accordance with virtue" (McKeon, 2001, p. 943). Aristotle argued that virtue was moderation between extremes, and in the case of "truthfulness," virtue was found in the moderation between the extremes of boastfulness and false modesty (McKeon, 2001. p. 961). With this said, the ultimate goal of identifying moral virtues was to establish "what type of persons ought we to be?" (Palanski & Yammarino, 2007, p. 176). This is in sharp contrast to modern and post-modern rule based ethics, which seek to establish "what is the right thing to do?" (Palanski & Yammarino, 2007, p. 176). This distinction is important in that theoretical development of an integrity construct based in virtue ethics and moral philosophy should focus more on identifying a component of good character, rather than strictly focusing on identifying specific behaviors (Palanski & Yammarino, 2007, 2009). Indeed, Aristotle said that if "the virtues are neither passions or faculties, all that remains is that they should be states of character" (McKeon, 2001, p. 957). This is in line with Dewey's (1960) proposal that to be considered as ethical, "it is never enough to simply do the right thing" (Ciulla, 2004, p. 28). Although the manifestation of specific behaviors can expose the lack of an integrating character trait such as integrity, no one, or definitive list of behaviors alone can establish the presence of integrity. In the same way, the absence of negative behaviors alone cannot be judged as proof of the presence of integrity. For example, with the previously mentioned virtue of truthfulness, the presence of false modesty could uncover a lack of truthfulness, but a lack of false modesty alone could not establish the presence of the virtue of truthfulness, or the presence of good character in general (Solomon, 1999). Logically speaking, the integrity related behaviors associated with the virtue of truthfulness are necessary, but are not sufficient evidence of good character (Palanski & Yammarino, 2007).

Even with the fading of the influence of the ancient cardinal virtues, the rise of the influence of the Christian virtues of faith, hope, love and obedience in the middle ages maintained philosophical emphasis on character development and virtue ethics in Western thought (Rachels, 2003). However, in an effort to construct a moral philosophy based solely in reason, as opposed to "virtues from a transcendental source" (Palanski & Yammarino, 2007, p. 176), thinkers in the Renaissance moved exclusively to rule based ethics that attempted to answer the question "what is the right thing to do?" (Palanski & Yammarino, 2007, p. 176). Terms such as integrity (derived from the Latin term integer or wholeness), which were developed with precise meanings in ancient and medieval moral philosophy, became ambiguous when applied to a different a question with a different goal (Lowe, Cordery & Morrison, 2004). Integrity took on different meanings such as honesty and trustworthiness which overlapped with other concepts that were more related to what one should do, versus what type of person one should strive to be (Palanski & Yammarino, 2007, 2009). This approach led modern efforts to define integrity in terms of what is the right thing to do versus what is the right type of person to be. The concerns of the ancient and Judeo-Christian philosophers that moral action required humans to overcome self-centered action gave way to an emphasis on reason applied to situations and a case-by-case rule based evaluation of the right thing to do (MacIntyre, 1984). Social contract theory proposed by theorist such as Hobbes (1651/1968), Locke (1689/1967), Rousseau (1762/1967), Rawls (1971) and Smith (1776/1986), attempted to estab-

lish "the rules of the game" for ethical behavior in a reason-based society (Palanski & Yammarino, 2007, p. 176). However, due to widely held perceptions that modern rule based ethics have failed to produce reliable moral behavior in society, many post-modern philosophers have pointed to a need to return to a consideration of virtue ethics and character development based in moral philosophy (Anscombe, 1958; Bennett, 1993; Dunn, 2009; Kotva, 1996; MacIntyre, 1984; Mooney, 2000; Palanski & Yammarino, 2007; Wilson, 1998).

For, ancient and medieval philosophers, virtue was a character component that enabled a man to move from the man he was, to the kind of man he ought to be (MacIntyre, 1984). Furthermore, MacIntyre proposed "there is at least one virtue recognized by the tradition which cannot be specified at all except with reference to the wholeness of human life – the virtue of integrity" (1984, p. 203). This aspect of both ancient and medieval moral philosophy overtly captures one conceptualization of integrity evident in the leadership literature (value-behavior congruence), but the ancient and medieval traditions also covertly capture the moral conceptualization hinted at in leadership literature. Plato, Aristotle and others in the tradition, argued "one cannot posses any of the virtues of character in a developed form without possessing all of the others" (MacIntyre, 1984, p. 155). This fundamental Aristotelian argument captures the integrating moral conceptualization of integrity in that both the ancient cardinal virtues of prudence, justice, temperance and courage, and the medieval Christian virtues of faith, hope, love and obedience, clearly link the congruence between values and behaviors to morality (Musschenga, 2001). With Aristotle, for a person to have the virtue of integrity, not only would his or her values and actions require consistency in a unified life, these values and actions would have to be consistent with the cardinal virtues as well as the aforementioned virtue of "truthfulness" (McKeon, 2001, p. 961). Similarly, for the medieval Judeo-Christian philosopher, not only would a virtuous person of integrity display value-behavior congruence, he or she would also need to display the virtues of faith, hope, love and obedience (MacIntyre, 1984). Under either formulation, it is clear that no immoral person could be assessed as having integrity despite displaying value-behavior congruence. This formulation of integrity based in virtue ethics and moral philosophy theoretically binds together the two conceptualizations common in the leadership literature namely value-behavior congruence, and a requirement for values and behaviors to be linked to morality (Dunn, 2009).

Although this discussion might seem to lead integrity researchers to focus exclusively on virtue ethics and character development, both ancient and medieval moral philosophers recognized the importance of behaviors. The Aristotelian view of integrity was summarized by Puka (2005) as "the spring of excellence in living" (p. 24). The previously discussed Aristotelian virtue of truthfulness is a prime example that doing the right thing was important to Aristotle. Similarly, Judeo-Christian philosophers of the middle ages would no doubt quote Jesus in saying "you will know them by their fruit" (Matthew, 7:16). Accordingly, the value-behavior congruence implied in virtue ethics confirms that good behaviors are the fruit of good character, facilitated by the virtues. The virtue of integrity appears to be especially relevant to this concept and according to McFall (1987), "if integrity is a moral virtue, then it is a special sort of virtue" and it appears that the formulation of integrity as a virtue "adds a moral requirement to personal integrity" (p. 14). With a solid theoretical base for a philosophical link between values, actions and morality, the task now turns to the theoretical development of an instrument to measure the integrity construct in this study.

To accomplish this task, it is necessary to recognize that "agents can act with integrity to a greater or lesser degree" (Williston, 2006, p. 566). This concept is important for researchers wanting to develop a valid and reliable integrity instrument and is in contrast to the view that integrity

is something that is either lacked or possessed. Dunn (2009) proposed that "unsophisticated conceptions of integrity imagine that you either have integrity or you do not" (p. 104). Williston characterized this dichotomous view of integrity by two possibilities where at one extreme an agent "will act unfailingly in accordance with [his/]her core commitments, at the other [he/]she will unfailingly violate them" (p. 566). However, as Williston posits, "these two possibilities are equally improbable" and "most agents, most of the time, find themselves between them" (Williston, 2006, p. 566).

Having established that integrity should be a continuous construct, it is important to clearly define the construct to be measured. This study incorporates the philosophically grounded definition proposed by Dunn (2009) such that integrity is a "coherence among a set of moral values, with this set of moral values having consistency with a set of social values, and that integrity further requires congruence between an agent's behavior and this set of moral/social values over time and across social context's" (p. 110). This definition begs a brief discussion of value origins before proceeding. Weber (1947) believed that we value, believe and act in a rational manner. Weber developed a rational model for explaining reasons for human beliefs, values and moral feelings. This primarily instrumental approach proposed that people make rational value choices based on risks versus rewards. A person believes and behaves in a manner that is primarily based on "instrumental rationality," however Weber also recognized the possibility of non-instrumental reasons for action (as cited in Boudon, 2001, p. 93). For example, if a belief or value is in line with cultural norms there is great instrumental value or reward in that belief or value. On the other hand, a belief or value contrary to cultural norms could pose great risks or costs and may be based on non-instrumental reasons. Weber labeled possible non-instrumental reasons for action as being based on "axiological rationality" (as cited in Boudon, 2001, p. 93). Similarly, Joas (2000) concluded that we choose values and hold beliefs in an effort to satisfy either "the good," or "the right" (p. 145). In some instances, values might be based on an instrumental approach in an effort to ensure a "good" outcome. In other cases, values might be based on an axiological approach in an effort to ensure "right" actions (Joas, 2000, p. 145). However, recognizing that "right acts do not always flow from good will," Joas argued that a universal theory of values must incorporate a balancing of the good and the right (p.172). According to Joas, "there is no primacy of the good or the right, [there] is a relationship of neither super-ordination nor subordination, but rather one of complementariness" (2000, p. 173). Accordingly, Joas furthered Weber's partition for the origins of values by categorizing Weber's view of instrumental values as being oriented toward the accomplishment of the good, and Weber's view of axiological values as being oriented towards accomplishment of the right. However, Joas hinted at more of a balancing between instrumental and axiological origins for values in that "there can only be a reflective equilibrium between the good and the right" (2000, p. 175).

Boudon (2001) proposed a more general cogni-tivist model of value origins that also broke value choices down into two major types; those that are of the consequential, instrumental type (the good) and those that are of the non-consequential, axi-ological type (the right). However, for Boudon, some of our values, beliefs and behaviors are more instrumental and some are more axiological. In some instances people value, believe and behave because the rewards outweigh the costs. In other instances people believe and behave irrespective of instrumental factors because they deeply be-lieve that those values, beliefs and actions are the right ways to think and to act. Axiological values and beliefs operate because the actor believes they are the right things to value and to believe. Although Hall (1976) recognized that such deeply held beliefs can be heavily influenced by culture,

Boudon argued that we primarily hold axiological beliefs "because we have strong reasons for doing so" (2001, p. 142). Tithing, fidelity and military service in a time of war are just a few examples of behaviors heavily influenced by axiological reasons that may not seem rational when viewed from a purely instrumental perspective.

With this said, McFall (1987) suggested that personal integrity "requires that a person "subscribe to some consistent set of principles or commitments" (p. 8). Additionally, although observers might not approve of these principles or commitments, an impartial observer "must at least recognize them as ones a reasonable person might take to be of great importance" (McFall, 1987, p. 11). Becker (1998) further refined this concept by proposing that integrity "involves acting in accordance not with any value system, but with a morally justifiable one" (p. 157). Similarly, Yukl (2006) declared that values must be "consistent with a set of justifiable moral principles" (p. 421). Finally, Audi and Murphy (2006) conceptualized an integrity construct that included "a will to do what one reasonably believes (but does not know) is right" (p. 6). However, Audi and Murphy also cautioned that by "leaving people too free to decide for themselves what counts as conduct that expresses integrity, we can also make it too easy to pay lip service to moral commitment" (2006, p. 10).

All of these approaches to capturing the moral aspect of integrity are in line with the Aristotelian requirement for "practical wisdom" in the applica-tion of the moral virtues (McKeon, 2001, p. 1036). For both Plato and Aristotle, it does not seem a stretch to imagine their tolerance of a value system that is recognizable and justifiable to a reasonable man, even if that reasonable man might not agree with all aspects of the value system (Plato, 1997, Aristotle, 2009). Indeed, Rugeley and Van Wart (2006) proposed that the Aristotelian focus was an argument that one who uses reason well "does so with community and society firmly in mind" (p. 382). This is also true with respect to Plato's argument that excellence in life was grounded in excellence in citizenship, as judged (or justified) by the community of citizens (Cooper & Hutchinson, 1997). It follows then that in the arena of morality, the ancient philosophers would place some weight to values justifiable to a reasonable man of the community. For this reason, this study defines integrity by refining the Dunn definition to "a coherence among a set of [*reasonably justifiable*] moral values, with this set of moral values having consistency with a set of social values, and that integrity further requires congruence between an agent's behavior and this set of moral/social values over time and across social context's" (Dunn, 2009, p. 110, as amended). This modification of the Dunn integrity definition is in keeping with Audi and Murphy's (2006) argument that moral values should be reasonable, Becker (1998) and Yukl's (2006) proposal that moral values should be justifiable, and McFall's (1987) stipulation that moral values should be both recognizable and reasonable. Although this definition does not completely resolve relativistic criticisms of previous integrity formulations, it does address the Nazi dilemma in that within an acceptably broad enough community, reasonable citizens would not justifiably label a genocidal Nazi as having integrity. Although critics may argue that German societal norms may have supported Nazism in the 1930s and 1940s, much of this support was established through iron-fisted totalitarianism rather than through a consensus generated by German ethical thinkers (Kershaw, 2001; Mason & Caplan, 1995). Kershaw took this argument further in that the "national community, much trumpeted by Nazi propaganda, amounted to a myth; that beneath the surface veneer of a nation pulling together behind its Fuhrer, socio-economic realities affecting the daily lives of ordinary Germans, revealed a remarkably disunited and discontented society" (2001, p. *xv*). Additionally, the adopted definition undermines the lone wolf argument for an individualized basis for integrity in that a larger community of moral citizens must be able to judge personal values as reasonably

justifiable to qualify the person in question as possessing integrity.

Following this formulation of the integrity construct, a person could be judged as possessing integrity as long as their behaviors are congruent with a set of reasonably justifiable moral values, even if the observer might not agree with all aspects of those values. This would be comparable to a person being recognized as "devout" such as a devout catholic, or a devout protestant, even though the observer might not follow in the same religious tradition. In such a case, the observed devout person is credited with adhering to (behaving in accordance with) a reasonably justifiable moral code that is recognized by a larger community. This formulation should restrict either the sociopath (Nazi) or psychopath (lone wolf) from being judged as possessing integrity, even though they might exhibit value-behavior congruence. This approach is also consistent with Audi and Murphy's proposal that integrity "need not be formulated on the basis of any particular theory of morality" (2006, p. 11). Kantianism (Kant, 1785/2002), Utilitarianism (Bentham, 1789/2010), Objectivism (Rand, 1961), and Christian virtue ethics all incorporate concepts such as honesty, truth telling, justice and temperance even if they "interconnect them in different ways" while demonstrating the "demands of a sound morality" (Audi & Murphy, 2006, p.11).

The definition of integrity leveraged in this study thus sets forth five potential construct requirements or facets namely: value-behavior congruence, temporal stability, consistency across roles, external coherence, and internal coherence (Dunn, 2009). The first three of these facets (value-behavior congruence, temporal stability and consistency across roles) incorporate the consistency component of integrity salient in leadership literature, and the last two facets (external and internal coherence) philosophically ground the integrity construct in morality. Each of these facets emerges and is further developed with an eye toward the leadership literature, as well as the tradition of virtue ethics and moral philosophy.

Value-Behavior Congruence

As previously stated, a common theme for integrity in the leadership literature is the requirement for "consistency of an acting entity's words and actions" (Palanski & Yammarino, 2007, p. 111). Simons (2002) formulated "behavioral integrity" identifying two theoretical components; one component was "consistency between espoused and actual displayed values" (p. 174). The other aspect of behavioral integrity was explicit promise keeping (Simons, 2002). Value-behavior congruence in this study is consistent with the behavioral integrity construct developed by Simons (2002).

Temporal Stability

Kohlberg (1984) proposed that humans progress in moral reasoning capability beginning with a morality based on ethical egotism, followed by a morality based on social expectations and culminating in a morality based in ethical altruism. Following the literature moving away from the proposition that a person's moral-reasoning capability is a sufficient measure of personal morality (Gibbs, 1995; Krebs & Denton, 2005; Schlenker, 2008), this study adopts the position that moral identity, "which is relatively constant over time" is a better measure of morality than moral reasoning capability (Dunn, 2009, p. 113). Furthermore, it is proposed that "stability over time is an essential aspect of integrity" (Dunn, 2009, p. 113). Similarly, Kotva (1996) stated "the virtues are not a matter of whim or caprice, but of stability; they are relatively stable aspects of one's character" (p. 24). MacIntyre (1984) proposed that the virtue of integrity or "constancy" is a "virtue the possession of which is a prerequisite for the possession of other virtues" (p. 183). All of these propositions support the position that the formulation of integrity as a virtue requires stability of the construct over time (Dunn, 2009).

Consistency across Roles

The value-behavior coherence evident in the behavioral integrity construct (Simons, 2002) has an associated requirement for consistency across roles such that there is no "splitting of oneself into different selves" or more simply put, a "lack of integrity" (Dunn, 2009, p. 115). Discussing related virtues, MacIntyre stated, "we cannot be genuinely courageous or truthful and be so only on occasion" (1984, p. 198). Furrow (2005) described roles as "identity-conferring commitments" (p. 139), and such commitments must be "unconditional in that to violate them would be to lose the sense that one has a stable sense of self" (p. 137). Dobel (1990) recognized that inconsistencies across roles as well as discontinuities between roles and values "disturb all aspects of the weave of one's life and raise most of the serious issues of personal integrity" (p. 355). Again, the unity of the virtues and value-behavior congruence require consistency across roles and contexts (MacIntyre, 1984).

External Coherence

Palanski and Yammarino (2007) reviewed the literature and found "the terms 'ethics/ethical' and 'morality/moral' generally refer to actions which are in accordance with socially acceptable behavior" (p. 174). This finding moves the discussion from personal integrity to moral integrity (Musschenga, 2001). According to Dunn (2009), "integrity requires consistency between organizational values and personal values" (p. 111). Requiring a consistency between organizational and personal values ensures the grounding of personal values in morally and socially acceptable behavior (Dunn, 2009). External coherence is directly relatable to Weber's (1947) instrumental rationality in that values that generate external coherence are generally consequential in nature and result in either great costs for resisting, or great benefits for aligning with organizational values. Further developing "strong reasons" for an actor to display external coherence (Boudon, 2001, p.142), MacIntyre, described the term "practice" as the social space where a community defines the attainment of human excellence (1984, p. 187). This is important since Plato identified excellence in citizenship as the only way to be an excellent man (Plato, 1997). Following this thought, as a citizen of the moral community, the excellence of man should be defined within the practice or social space of morality (Cooper & Hutchinson, 1997). This understanding establishes the requirement for personal values to be linked with the values (and thus morals) of the community at large, or the organization at large if applicable (Rachels, 2003). However, central to this study, Dunn (2009) argued that values are "ordered preferences of moral goods" (p. 111). External coherence not only demands a "consistency between organizational values and personal integrity" (p. 111), but further demands that "this consistency is not merely measured by the inclusion of the same or similar values within the value set of the group and the values set of the individual, but more particularly, the same or similar ordering of these values" (Dunn, 2009, p. 111).

Finally, fundamental to the linkage between personal values and community values, is the seemingly universal requirement that persons of integrity must hold an unfailing commitment to honesty. Schlenker, Pontari and Christopher (2001) proposed that "deceit is universally condemned because it undermines the ability of members of society to rely on one another" (p. 9). Yukl and Van Fleet (1990) hinted at this integrity requirement by proposing that "integrity means that a person's behavior is consistent with espoused values and that the person is honest" (as cited in Becker, 1998, p. 155). Even though the integrity construct is broader than honesty alone (a point already established), this study considers honesty as a component of the integrity construct as dictated by the requirements of external coherence with organizational values or societal values at large.

Internal Coherence

According to Kotva (1996), in virtue ethics "being precedes doing, but doing shapes being" (p. 30). This concept is in line with Bandura's (1986) triadic reciprocal causation model as proposed in social cognitive theory. In social cognitive theory, the person, behavior and environment interact to shape both motivation and behavior (Bandura, 2000). Furthermore, "right action, right judgment, and rightly ordered character are intimately linked; indeed, the ability to determine and do the right thing is premised on one's having the requisite states of character" (Kotva, 1996, p. 30). Formulations of internal coherence lead to the proposition that there is a requirement for a "consistency between various convictions" (Dunn, 2009, p. 115). Internal coherence is directly relatable to Weberian axiological rationality in that values that generate internal coherence are non-consequential to the extent that they are primarily based in beliefs about what is the right way to be, demonstrated by the thing to do. Strong reasons for an actor displaying internal coherence are based in the belief that a particular value or behavior is right, irrespective of instrumental concerns (Boudon, 2001). McFall (1987) laid out three salient aspects of internal coherence: authenticity, coherence between principles and action, and coherence between principles and motivation.

Shakespeare's (1600/2007) admonition "to thine own self be true" in *Hamlet* might best fit in the authenticity aspect of internal coherence (as cited in Palanski & Yammarino, 2007, Act I, scene iii). Accordingly, authenticity is "this private sense [that] deals with the alignment of one's words, actions and internalized values" (Palanski & Yammarino, 2007, p. 174). Avolio and Gardner (2005) defined authenticity as " owning one's personal experiences, be they thoughts, emotions, needs, wants, preferences, or beliefs" (p.320). Harter (2002) associated authenticity with the injunction to "know oneself" (p. 382). This conceptualization philosophically links authenticity with Plato's use of the phrase "know thyself" as inscribed on the

Temple of Apollo at Delphi (Scholtz, 2006, p. 1). However, as McFall proposed, the problem with viewing internal coherence strictly as authenticity is that "being true to oneself, may involve being false to others" (1987, p. 5). On the other hand, Bass (2008) found that leaders "may deceive others by not being true to themselves" (p. 223). This observation moves the discussion from authenticity to coherence between principles and action.

An example of internal coherence between principles and action would be a refusal to rearrange priorities or principles to accommodate external pressures such as pressure to maximize profits at the expense of vulnerable employees, or the refusal to yield to immoral temptations to maximize personal gain. The concept of internal coherence has been recognized by moral writers for millennia represented by the belief that "a double minded man is unstable in all his ways" (James 1:8). As proposed by Dunn (2009) all types of rationalization, "redescription" and lying to oneself would fit into this category (McFall, 1987, p. 7). In this context, rationalization is a process where a person acts or believes contrary to their values and then justifies the actions and beliefs with morally acceptable reasons or excuses (Freud, 1937). Rorty and Williams (1979) framed redescription as a process through which novel and attractive depictions of current and future social situations are presented (Calder, 2007). Although the definition might seem obvious, Martin (1979) operationally defined the phrase "lying to oneself" as "intentional self-deception involving persuading oneself into holding unwarranted beliefs or keeping oneself ignorant" (p. 441).

The final aspect of internal coherence, coherence between principles and motivation, can be violated if a person is "doing the right thing (for what he takes to be) the wrong reason" (McFall, 1987, p. 7). For example, if a person is unduly proud about being honest and even garners pleasure from being brutally honest to others needlessly, then perhaps the person is not motivated from a principled devotion to honesty, but rather a motivation to satisfy self through self-righteousness. Such a person would most likely not display internal coherence between moral principles and motivation (McFall, 1987).

LEADER INTEGRITY ASSESSMENT

In this study, the Leader Integrity Assessment (LIA) was developed following the DeVellis (2003) "Guidelines in Scale Development" (p. 60). The Devellis' guidelines steps include:

1. Determine clearly what is to be measured
2. Generate item pool
3. Determine format
4. Have items reviewed by expert panel
5. Consider inclusion of validated items
6. Administer items to administrative sample
7. Evaluate items
8. Optimize scale length

Item Pool

The item pool was created incorporating suggestions from an expert panel of judges with expertise in leadership studies or a related field. The panel was asked to provide recommendations for a minimum of five to a maximum of ten items per facet of leader integrity. Items were arranged in a Likert-style presentation (Likert, 1967), and scale designations ranged from "strongly disagree" to "strongly agree." Other possible designations were, "neutral," "disagree" and "agree." Items were posed from a positive perspective such that items incorporate positive character traits rather than negative character traits. For the LIA, a representative item states: "my leader is honest," as opposed to "my leader is dishonest." Comparing the integrity instrument in this study with other instruments of potentially similar lengths, such as the Servant Leader Assessment, it was found that it takes respondents approximately five minutes to complete the LIA instrument for this study (Dennis & Bocarnea, 2005, p. 605). After recommendations from the expert panel were included into the item pool, the items were given to an administrative sample of respondents. This process began with the submission of proposed items to a small focus group of six participants that were similar to the target population to collect feedback on time required as well as identification of any confusing items. Focus group results were tested for reliability using Cronbach's alpha (Cronbach, 1951) and variance was analyzed amongst respondents. Focus group results were then used to refine items and prepare the item pool for the pre-test (Devellis, 2003).

A pre-test was administered to a sample group of participants that were similar to the target population (DeVellis, 2003). Due to the initial instrument length of 20 items, the number of participants of the pre-test sample allowed for a minimum of n > 100 to ensure valid exploratory factor analysis and reliability testing using Cronbach's alpha (Hair, et al., 2006). Descriptive statistics were analyzed to test for any kurtosis (peakness/flatness) or skewness (left/right skew) of the data. This analysis included analysis of histograms and normal probability plots (Hair, et al., 2006). According to Hair, et al. (2006), exploratory factor analysis "explores the data and provides the researcher with information about how many factors are needed to best represent the data" (p. 773). Minimum factor loadings for exploratory factor analysis were set at (.4) and factors were identified using the latent root criteria (eigenvalues > 1), complemented by scree plot analysis (Hair, et al., 2006). It was desired that each integrity facet retain a minimum of three items, however all item pool items were theoretically evaluated for inclusion in the instrument (Hair, et al., 2006, p. 780).

Face and Content Validity

Face validity is not validity in a technical sense; it is a judgment that a scale "measures what it appears to measure" (Kerlinger & Lee, 1992, p. 668). However, the judgment that the LIA has sufficient face validity started with an evaluation of whether or not the chosen items represent valid representations of the leader integrity construct as operationalized in the study. Further discussion of face validity occurred in consultation with an expert panel once the item pool was established. A panel of expert judges were asked to evaluate each item in the item pool and Cohen's Kappa was calculated as the ratio of the proportion of actual agreement between the judges minus the chance agreement, divided by one minus the agreement (Cohen, 1960, p. 40). Each judge held a Ph.D. in a social science field and a minimum of $k = .60$ was used to establish sufficient content validity. Since sufficient content validity was not established after the first round of consultations, further recommendations from the judges were incorporated into the instrument and the procedure was repeated. This process was continued until sufficient content validity of $k = .90$ was established.

Reliability

Reliability is the "proportion of variance attributable to the true score of the latent variable" (Devellis, 2003, p. 27). For the instrument developed in this study, the latent variable represent's the perceived leader integrity construct. The primary method of assessing reliability in this study was the calculation of Cronbach's alpha. However, the initial method of evaluating the reliability of this instrument was to calculate the item-to-total correlation and the inter-item correlations for each item. Hair, et al., (2006) provided a rule of thumb for the item-to-total correlation to be .5 or higher and the inter-item correlations to be .30 or higher (p. 137). These calculations were used to identify individual items that were suspected of reducing reliability of the integrity instrument. SPSS (2009) was used to calculate Cronbach's Alpha (with a generally accepted value of alpha = .7 set as minimum (Hair, et al., 2006, p. 137). The minimum Cronbach's Alpha was attained for each scale facet in the analysis, however the previously calculated inter-item and item-to-total calculations were used to identify the item with the lowest internal consistency. The lowest rated item was considered for removal from the item pool. Finally, exploratory/confirmatory factor analysis was conducted to test "how well the measured variables represent the constructs" (Hair, et al., 2006, p. 770). However, in the expected case of a unidimensional construct, exploratory and confirmatory factor analysis will produce similar if not exactly the same results.

Construct Validity

Construct validity is the "extent to which a set of measured variables actually represents the theoretical latent construct those variables are designed to measure" (Hair, et al., 2006, p. 771). Construct validity is assessed by investigating three primary aspects of validity namely: convergent validity, discriminant validity and nomological validity. Convergent validity assesses if a particular scale correlates with other like scales or if high factor loadings or communalities "indicate that they converge on some common point" (Hair, et al., 2006, p. 777). Discriminant validity assesses if a scale is sufficiently different from other similar scales. Nomological validity assesses whether or not a scale predicts as theorized (Hair, et al., 2006). In this study, sufficient convergent validity was judged achieved if the LIA and a similar scale such as the Ethical Leadership Scale converge and were found to be sufficiently correlated (.5 or greater desired). In this study, discriminant validity was deemed established if the LIA was found to be distinct from a similar scale such as the Cook and Wall (1980) leader prototypicality scale. A determination of discriminant validity in this study was accomplished by an investigation of average variance extracted. The average variance extracted (AVE) was estimated as the average correlation between the individual items of the two applicable scales. If the average variance extracted is greater than the shared variance for any similar

construct, then discriminant validity is supported. This condition would imply that more variance is due to distinctness between constructs than variance due to measurement error (Campbell & Fiske; 1959, Farrell, 2010). In this study, nomological validity was judged established if results that flow from the data collected via the LIA predicted construct relationships such as predictions that follower perceptions of leader integrity moderate the relationship between leader prototypicality and follower trust in the leader as hypothesized in a larger model such as the Kalshoven and Den Hartog (2009) Ethical Leadership Model. Regression analysis, an investigation of significance, and exploratory/confirmatory factor analysis were used to assess nomological validity in this study.

LIA CONSTRUCT OPERATIONALIZATIONS

To complete the development of a direct, concise and positive perspective leader integrity assessment, thorough operationalizations of the integrity construct were accomplished. From these operationalizations, specific items were developed in consultations with the expert panel. Operationalizations spring directly from the philosophically based integrity facet descriptions provided in the integrity construct section of this paper. Potential items from each operationalization were used to create the item pool for the Leader Integrity Assessment. The items listed in the item pool were the products of two rounds of consultation with the expert panel.

Value-Behavior Congruence Operationalization

Following Simons' (2002) formulation of behavioral integrity, in this study value-behavior congruence is operationally defined as a consistency between espoused and actual values as displayed in one's actions, including explicit promise keeping

(Palanski & Yammarino, 2007). This definition implies that scale items should address three main issues: one's espoused values should be consistent with actual values, one's actual values should be consistent with one's actions, and the leader keeps promises.

Temporal Stability Operationalization

Before defining temporal stability, a discussion of time horizon is required. Recognizing the undeniable development of moral reasoning highlighted by Kolberg (1984), it is understood that over a long time horizon, the moral reasoning capability of a child develops into the moral reasoning capability of an adult. On such a long time horizon, ones' integrity would obviously change. Even on a shorter time frame, young adults tend to have differing values from their own selves only decades later. However, for the purposes of this study, it seems reasonable to view temporal stability on a time horizon consistent with an average employee's time spent working for a single organization. According to the U. S. Bureau of Labor Statistics, the average tenure of U. S. employees in companies for 2010 was 4.4 years (United States Department of Labor, 2011). This time frame is in line with the average three to four year tour of duty with a single organization for current United States Air Force members. Thus, the time horizon used to evaluate temporal stability in this study should be on the order of months and years and thus should be short enough to avoid the confounding effects of long-term moral development on follower evaluations of temporal stability. Therefore, for the purposes of this study, temporal stability of a leader's integrity is defined as consistency of a leader's integrity over time with respect to the time the observer has spent under the supervision of the leader. This definition implies that the integrity of the leader is generally set or well established and that stability is referenced in terms of months and years as opposed to decades or a lifetime.

Consistency across Roles Operationalization

According to Dunn (2009), integrity precludes a "splitting of oneself into different selves" (p. 115). For the purposes of this study, consistency across roles is defined as a consistency of values and actions across roles and contexts. This definition implies that a person of integrity: espouses the same vales regardless of setting, acts in accordance with espoused values regardless of who is present, and acts consistently regardless of the role they are filling.

External Coherence Operationalization

Following Dunn's development of the integrity construct, external coherence "requires a consistency between organizational values and personal values" (2009, p. 111). The requirement for external coherence ensures that personal morality is linked to the morality of the larger community and precludes an individualistic basis for morality. However, since a formulation of integrity which requires a consistency between organizational values and personal values is only recognized "to the extent to which such integrity is in evidence" (Dunn, 2009, p. 110), the concept of external coherence must include enacted behaviors that demonstrate the consistency of organizational and personal values. For this reason, both personal values and personal behaviors must conform to the espoused vales of the organization. Since values are defined as ordered preferences of moral goods (Dunn, 2009), this conformity between organizational values and personal values must not only include the existence of the same values, but also the same ordering of those values. One explicitly identified requirement for external coherence in this study involves the recognition that most communities and organizations that operate in a western cultural environment greatly value the nearly universal requirement for honesty (Schlenker, et al., 2001). Recognizing the implicit relationship between honesty and value-behavior coherence, honesty is explicitly included in the operationalization of external coherence. Thus, for the purposes of this study, external coherence is defined as a consistency between organizational values and personal values and behaviors, including an explicit requirement for honesty. This definition implies that a person of integrity: acts in accordance with organizational values, prioritorizes personal values in a similar fashion as the organization, and is committed to honesty.

Internal Coherence Operationalization

Dunn (2009) defined internal coherence as a "consistent set of principles or commitments" (p. 115). McFall (1987) established three aspects of internal consistency namely: authenticity, coherence between principles and action, and coherence between principles and motivation. External coherence, as previously outlined, is more related to a consistency between self and the external world whereas internal coherence is more related to a consistency between self and an internal world of internal values. Rationalization, redescription and lying to oneself would all violate the concept of internal coherence. This formulation of internal consistency demands that one's internal value set does not conflict with itself. For the purposes of this study, internal coherence is operationally defined as authentic consistency between principles, actions and motivations. This definition implies that a person of integrity: is authentic, refuses to rearrange priorities or change principles due to pressure, does not rationalize or make excuses so that inconsistent personal actions appear to match internal values, and does the right things, for the right reasons.

SAMPLE 1

Sample 1 in this research was dedicated to establishing sufficient validity and reliability for the Leader Integrity Assessment. Sample 1a was collected for initial validity and reliability testing and to winnow the number of items in the Leader Integrity Assessment item pool. Sample 1b was collected for validity and reliability testing of the finalized Leader Integrity Assessment (LIA 15).

Sample 1a Participants

The targeted organization in this study was the 9th Reconnaissance Wing located at Beale Air Force Base, California where the venerable U-2 reconnaissance aircraft is based. The U-2 reconnaissance aircraft is a single piloted, high altitude, single engine aircraft well known as the most difficult military aircraft to fly in the U. S. inventory. Since its first flight in 1955, it has flown in almost every military conflict that the United States has been engaged. Due to the extremely difficult nature of the mission, the selection process for U-2 pilots is very rigorous. Each pilot must have significant experience as a combat aviator to apply for the program and only those with the strongest flight records are accepted for an interview. Each interviewee completes a two-week interview including psychological testing, an in-depth medical exam and three flights in a two-seat model of the aircraft to determine if the pilot has the aptitude to fly and land the challenging aircraft. Once accepted into the U-2 program, each pilot undergoes an additional yearlong training process to prepare them for their first mission and to initiate them into a very exclusive club of military pilots. The dedication of these pilots to their mission requires them to fly the most challenging aircraft in the world, for well over 10 hours at a time, while wearing a space suit, all alone and often hundreds of miles behind hostile lines. Even before May 1, 1960 when legendary pilot Francis Gary Powers was shot down in a U-2 over the Soviet Union during the Cold War, the community of U-2 pilots was known as the brotherhood (Pocock, 2005). This non-gender specific label describes a community of pilots that cherishes tradition and symbolism such as the U-2 solo patch they proudly wear on their shoulder. Many U-2 pilots say "more people can wear a Super Bowl ring than can wear the U-2 patch" (Wallace, 2009, p. 45). This saying springs from the fact that since 1955, only about 900 pilots have ever flown the aircraft and only approximately 90 U-2 pilots are active at any one time with another 90 to 100 pilots serving in various staff and headquarters positions (Wallace, 2009). The community of U-2 pilots was specifically selected for this study due to their highly developed sense of honor and integrity, which is central to this research endeavor.

Sample 1a Response Rates

Initial participants of Sample 1a in this research were taken from this small community of existing and recent U-2 pilots. The total population solicited for Sample 1a numbered approximately 219 people. A convenience sample of 108 respondents was collected via personal contacts in organizations within the community. Persons of contact in each organization solicited pilots via e-mail and face-to-face contact. An on-line survey instrument was used to collect responses over a one-month period with respondents remotely accessing the instrument through the Internet. At 49.3%, the response rate in this study was slightly higher than reported institutional web based response rates of 25 to 35 percent for college student surveys. The higher Internet response rate for this study is most likely related to the close knit nature of the community sampled and another reason may be that personal relationships have been shown to aid in establishing higher response rates (Bruce, 2008).

Although the online survey received 108 responses, only 101 of the responses were complete, valid responses. Seven responses in this sample were removed for missing, incomplete or erroneous data. Due to requirements for being an

officer, all U-2 pilot respondents held a minimum of a bachelor's degree and many held advanced degrees. All respondents were U. S. citizens with high security clearances. Of the 101 complete responses, 9.9% (10) of the respondents attained the rank of a company grade officer, and 90.1% (91) attained the rank of a field grade officer. This corresponds to the elevated rank associated with the high experience levels required of U-2 pilots. With the requirement for U-2 pilot applicants to have approximately 5 to 7 years of military pilot experience prior to training in the U-2, comes the demographic reality that most of these pilots had attained the higher rank of a field grade officer and reached this rank at an older age. All but two of the respondents were male (99 of 101) which is reasonable due to the extremely low number of females that have been members of the U-2 pilot community. Only six female pilots were currently or recently active in the U-2 community and the female response rate of 33% (two of six) was somewhat lower than the male response rate (48.8%). However this response rate is in line with recently reported Internet response rates of 25 to 35% (Bruce, 2008). This point is particularly important considering the phenomenon where the difference of a single respondent could change the calculated female response rate by a large amount. For example, the increase of a single female respondent in this study would have increased the female response rate from 33% to 50%, which would have been higher than the male response rate, whereas the absence of that single respondent dropped the female response rate below the male response rate. As defined by the respondents, 88.1% reported having served in combat and 11.9% reported not having served in combat. This was reasonable considering the job description for a U-2 pilot includes the high potential for combat participation. As a summary, the U-2 pilot sample was predominantly comprised of middle aged, male, field grade officers with combat experience and was considered by the researcher as a limitation to the generalization of the results.

Sample 1a Scale Content Validity, Reliability, and Data Distribution

Face and content validity was built into the scale with the Cohen's kappa of expert judge agreement reaching $k = .90$ (.60 minimum). Cronbach's alpha for the initial 20 item scale was calculated at $\alpha = .97$ (.70 minimum). Histograms of the Leader Integrity Assessment Instrument item pool response scores were visually judged normally distributed and all skew and kurtosis values were between +1.96 and -1.96. Skew and kurtosis values between +1.96 and -1.96 have been found to support the assumption of normal distribution (Hair, et al., 2006). This analysis led the researcher to judge the data in Sample 1a to be sufficiently close to normally distributed to proceed with further analysis.

Sample 1a Factor Analysis

After judging Sample 1a data to be distributed sufficiently close to a normal distribution, the data were tested for the appropriateness for factor analysis. The Kaiser-Meyer-Olkin Measure of Sampling Adequacy (KMO) and Bartlett's test of spheriocity were used for this analysis. In Sample 1a, the KMO value was found to be .94 with a Bartlett's significance level of less than .001. KMO tests whether or not partial correlations between items are excessively small such that higher KMO values (on a 0 to 1.0 scale) indicate that factor analysis is appropriate. KMO values above .80 have been deemed "meritorious" for appropriateness of factor analysis (Hair, et al., 2006, p. 114). Bartlett's test of spheriocity tests the hypothesis that "at least some" of the items are "significantly correlated" indicating the absence of an identity matrix (Hair, et al., 2006, p. 114). The high KMO value and the low Bartlett's significance level led the researcher to judge that no identity matrix existed in Sample 1a data and exploratory factor analysis was appropriate (Hair, et al., 2006). Exploratory factor analysis was completed on the data using principal component

analysis. Principal component analysis may be more appropriate for initial scale development than common factor analysis because the principal component method leverages a simple "linear transformation of the original variables" whereas common factor analysis "yields one or more composite variables" that represent estimates of "hypothetical variables" (Devellis, 2003, p. 148). Factors in this study were initially identified as those components represented by an eigenvalue greater than 1.0 or "latent root criterion" (Hair, et al., p. 119). In Sample 1a, principal component factor analysis initially extracted two factors with factor 1 responsible for over 70% of variance and an eigenvalue of 14.02, and factor 2 responsible for only 5.31% of variance with an eigenvalue of 1.06. All other components had eigenvalues well below 1.0 and were immediately ignored. All 20 items loaded at or above .7 on factor 1 whereas only 2 items loaded on factor 2, albeit only at .49 for one and .53 for the other. The other 18 items loaded below .4 for factor 2. Examining the factor loadings of the data led the researcher to remove factor 2 from the descriptive structure of the data since the factor loadings on factor 2 were well below the recommended minimum of .70 for factor retention (Hair, et al., 2006). A single factor structure was in line with the theoretical development of the integrity construct in this study as a single construct with five facets. Scree plot analysis also supported the retention of only a single factor in that the vertical portion of the scree plot was entirely captured by the inclusion of only the factor 1 eigenvalue.

Sample 1a LIA Item Pool Convergent Validity

To establish convergent validity for the LIA item pool, factor loadings and communalities were analyzed for an indication that items were converging toward the latent variable. The LIA item pool was highly correlated with inter-item correlations well above .5. Factor loadings and communalities above .5 indicated sufficient convergence with .7 desired (Hair, et al., 2006). Analysis of the inter-item correlation matrix showed all items were highly correlated (above .6) which was also indicative of a single factor structure. Although the 20 x 20 correlation matrix proved too cumbersome for display in this forum, several high inter-item correlations (above .65) led the researcher to drop five nearly redundant items and finalize the Leader Integrity Assessment with 15 items. Cronbach's alpha for the remaining 15 items in the LIA was calculated at $\alpha = .97$. A link to the finalized LIA 15 is provided in Appendix A. Due to this action, as well as a concern for the small number of females in the Sample 1a sample, a second sample labeled Sample 1b was collected for additional validation of the finalized LIA 15.

Sample 1b Response Rates

Participants for Sample 1b were taken from a group of intelligence officers that routinely support intelligence platforms such the U-2 reconnaissance aircraft. Out of a group of approximately 135 intelligence officers, 82 responses were captured for a 60.7% response rate. All of the respondents were officers who held a minimum of a bachelor's degree, all were U.S citizens, and all held high security clearances. Of the 82 responses, 4 were removed for missing, incomplete or erroneous data. Of the 78 complete responses (n > 75 minimum), 75.6% (59) were male and 24.4% (19) were female. The female response rate in this sample is slightly above the 18.9% of officers who are female in the United States Air Force (U.S. Dept. of Labor, 2011). Of the respondents in Sample 1b, 16.7% (13) held the rank of company grade officer, and 83% (65) held the rank of field grade officer. The median age for the respondents was between 41 and 45 years of age and 76.9% reported having served in combat.

Sample 1b LIA 15 Reliability and Data Distribution

Cronbach's alpha for the LIA 15 in Sample 1b was calculated at $\alpha = .98$. The histogram of the sum of the LIA 15 response scores as well as the histograms of the individual items of the LIA 15 were plotted and visually assessed to be normally distributed. Skew and kurtosis values were between -1.96 and +1.96, which is an indication of normality (Hair, et al., 2006). This analysis led the researcher to judge that the data in the Sample 1b sample were normally distributed and sufficiently reliable to proceed with further analysis.

Sample 1b Factor Analysis

Before proceeding, the data were tested for the appropriateness of factor analysis. Again the KMO Measure of Sampling Adequacy and Bartlett's test of spheriocity were used for this analysis. In Sample 1b, the KMO value was found to be .91 with a Bartlett's significance level of less than .001. The high KMO value and the low Bartlett's significance level led the researcher to judge that no identity matrix existed in Sample 1b data and exploratory factor analysis was judged appropriate (Hair, et al., 2006). In Sample 1b, principal component factor analysis extracted one factor with factor 1 responsible for over 77% of variance and an eigenvalue of 11.61. All other components had eigenvalues well below 1.0 and were immediately ignored. All Sample 1b LIA 15 items loaded well above .7 on factor 1 with the minimum factor loading of .82 (Table 1). Scree plot analysis of Sample 1b factor analysis supported the retention of a single factor in that the vertical portion of the scree plot was entirely captured by the inclusion of only factor 1.

Table 1. Sample 1b LIA 15 principal component factor analysis factor loadings

Component	Eigenvalue	Var	Communalities	Item	Factor 1
1	11.61*	77.40	.83	1	.92
2	.64	4.24	.85	2	.92
3	.52	3.48	.75	3	.87
4	.43	2.86	.68	4	.82
5	.32	2.12	.67	5	.82
6	.31	2.07	.81	6	.90
7	.27	1.82	.77	7	.88
8	.20	1.31	.86	8	.93
9	.19	1.25	.85	9	.92
10	.16	1.04	.77	10	.85
11	.11	.75	.70	11	.84
12	.09	.59	.79	12	.89
13	.07	.49	.82	13	.90
14	.06	.40	.77	14	.88
15	.03	.20	.72	15	.85 ___

Note. *Eigenvalue above 1.0.

Sample 1b LIA 15 Convergent Validity

To establish convergent validity for the LIA 15, factor loadings and communalities were analyzed for an indication that items were converging toward the latent variable. The Sample 1b LIA 15 was highly correlated with inter-item correlations well above .5. Factor loadings and communalities above .5 indicated sufficient convergence with .7 desired with only two items below .7 (.67 and .68 respectively). The Sample 1b LIA 15 communalities also indicated sufficient convergence (Table 1). The results for Sample 1b confirmed the preliminary results from Sample 1a and progression to Sample 2 with a sufficiently valid and reliable leader integrity instrument was warranted.

SAMPLE 2

The purpose of Sample 2 was to provide nomological validity for the LIA 15 as well as to provide additional validity, reliability and factor analysis. Nomological validity was established with respect to the hypothesis that perceived leader integrity moderates the relationship between leader prototypicality and follower trust in the leader as proposed in the Kalshoven and Den Hartog (2009) Ethical Leadership Model (Marshall, 2012).

Sample 2 Participants

Sample 2 participants were associated with the U-2 community, which is based in the 9th Reconnaissance Wing, Beale Air Force Base, California. The sample population was taken from seven organizations whose primary mission is associated with the operation and intelligence exploitation of the U-2 reconnaissance aircraft. The population is comprised of approximately 650 officer and enlisted personnel that work in administration, personnel, intelligence, operations, logistics/maintenance, communications, and equipment. The membership of this group comprises male and female members, as well as a demographic representation consistent with the demographic representation for the Air Force population at large.

Sample 2 Response Rates

A convenience sample of 245 respondents was collected via personal contacts in seven organizations within the U-2 community. Persons of contact in each organization solicited members via e-mail and face-to-face contact. An on-line survey instrument was used to collect responses over a one-month period with respondents remotely accessing the instrument through the Internet. At 34.2%, the response rate in this study was in line reported with institutional web based response rates of 25 to 35 percent for college student surveys (Bruce, 2008). Although the online survey received 245 responses, only 222 of the responses were complete, valid responses. Twenty-three responses in the sample were removed for missing, incomplete or erroneous data. All respondents were U. S. citizens with high security clearances. Of the 222 complete responses, 83.3% (185) were male and 16.7% (37) were female. The female response rate in Sample 2 is slightly less than the overall distribution of 20.3% for females in the Air Force at large. However, a smaller distribution of females is reasonable in the traditionally male environment that exists in many combat organizations. With this said, approximately 68.9% of the sample reported having served in combat and 31.1% reported not having served in combat. The age distribution of the respondents was in line with the age distribution of the Air Force at large. Of the 222 respondents, 37.4% (65) were enlisted and 70.6% (157) were officer personnel. The enlisted distribution broke down to 66.2% (43) junior enlisted personnel (E1-6), and 33.8% (22) senior enlisted personnel (E7-9).

Sample 2 Missing Data and Response Bias

Of the 245 responses, 23 complete responses were removed from the data due to either missing scores for more than 50% of any one variable, or missing any individual item scores from an applicable dependent variable. Of the retained responses, only .12% of individual item scores were missing (12 out of 9990 item scores). These missing item scores were imputed by mean replacement. Due to the extremely small percentage of missing individual item scores (far less than 10%), and the researcher's assessment that the missing data represented data missing completely at random (MCAR), the use of mean replacement seemed reasonable and was assumed to have negligible effect on Sample 2 results (Hair, et al., 2006). The results of wave analysis as well as analysis of responses collected after the close of study data collection led the researcher to conclude that response bias with respect to late or non-respondents was not a significant concern for Sample 2.

Sample 2 LIA Reliability, Data Distribution, Homoscedasticity, and Linearity

Cronbach's alpha for the data from LIA 15 in Sample 2 was calculated as $\alpha = .98$. The histograms for the LIA 15 in Sample 2 were visually assessed to be normally distributed and skew and kurtosis values were between -1.96 and +1.96 (Hair, et al., 2006). This analysis led the researcher to judge that the data in the Sample 2 were reliable and distributed sufficiently close to a normal distribution to proceed with further analysis. After judging that Sample 2 data were distributed sufficiently close to a normal distribution, the data were checked for homoscedasticity and linearity. Both homoscedasticity and linearity were confirmed by analyzing scatter plots for integrity and the dependent variable. In this study, the overall dependent variable was follower trust in the leader as proposed in the Kalshoven and Den Hartog (2009) study. To confirm homoscedasticity, data were expected and confirmed as scattered in an "elliptical distribution of points" around a linear diagonal line with respect to the dependent variable (Hair, et al., 2006, p. 83). Similarly, to confirm linearity, data should follow along this same diagonal line. All data in Sample 2 were judged to be linear from scatter plot analysis.

Sample 2 LIA 15 Construct Validity

Construct validity consists of convergent validity, discriminant validity and nomological validity (Hair, et al., 2006). To establish convergent validity for the LIA 15, correlation with a similar scale, the Ethical Leadership Scale, and the factor loadings and communalities were analyzed for an indication that items were converging toward the latent variable. The LIA 15 was highly correlated with the Ethical leadership Scale with $r = .91$. Factor loadings and communalities above .5 indicated sufficient convergence with .7 desired (Hair, et al., 2006). The LIA 15 communalities

indicated sufficient convergence with .7 desired (Table 2). Discriminant validity for the LIA 15 was established by comparing the average correlation between items of the Cook and Wall (1980) leader prototypicality scale with the LIA 15 scale. The average variance extracted (AVE) was estimated as the average correlation between the individual prototypicality items and the LIA 15 items. The estimated $AVE = .64$ was higher than the squared shared correlation between the LIA 15 and prototypicality scales (squared correlation = .47). With estimated AVE higher than the shared correlation squared, sufficient discriminant validity was judged established (Hair, et al., 2006).

Sample 2 LIA 15 Factor Analysis

Before proceeding, LIA 15 data were tested for the appropriateness for factor analysis. In Sample 2, the LIA 15 KMO value was found to be .96 with a Bartlett's significance level of less than .001. The high KMO value and the low Bartlett's significance level led the researcher to judge that

Table 2. Sample 2 principal component factor analysis factor loadings

Component	Eigenvalue	%Var	Communalities	Item	Factor 1
1	11.37*	75.70	.75	1	.92
2	.62	4.15	.81	2	.92
3	.46	3.07	.73	3	.87
4	.41	2.72	.72	4	.82
5	.40	2.65	.69	5	.82
6	.34	2.25	.82	6	.90
7	.28	1.85	.79	7	.88
8	.21	1.36	.82	8	.93
9	.20	1.30	.84	9	.92
10	.18	1.17	.68	10	.85
11	.14	.96	.63	11	.84
12	.13	.84	.77	12	.89
13	.12	.78	.83	13	.90
14	.10	.64	.68	14	.88
15	.08	.54	.80	15	.85

Note. *Eigenvalue above 1.0.

no identity matrix existed in Sample 2 LIA 15 data and exploratory factor analysis was appropriate (Hair, et al., 2006). In Sample 2, principal component factor analysis extracted one factor with factor 1 responsible for over 75.7% of variance and an eigenvalue of 11.37 (Table 2). All other components had eigenvalues well below 1.0 and were immediately ignored. All LIA 15 items loaded well above .7 on factor 1 with the minimum factor loading of .82. Factor loadings and communalities from the principal component extraction for Sample 2 LIA showed a unidimensional structure with sufficient convergence.

Sample 2 Nomological Validity

To establish nomological validity for the LIA 15, hierarchical regression was used to investigate the effects of perceived leader integrity on the relationship between leader prototypicality and follower trust in the leader as proposed in the Kalshoven and Den Hartog (2009) ethical leadership model. In this analysis, it was hypothesized that leader integrity moderated the relationship between leader prototypicality and follower trust in the leader. Indeed, integrity was found to moderate the relationship between leader prototypicality and follower trust in the leader and support for the research hypothesis provided evidence of nomological validity for the LIA 15 instrument (Marshall, 2012). Nomological validity, included with the established convergent and discriminant validity, complete the elements of construct validity as previously required for the LIA 15.

NOTE

The opinions and conclusions presented in this research are my own and do not constitute an endorsement by or opinion of the United States Air Force or the Department of Defense.

REFERENCES

Anscombe, E. (1958). Modern moral philosophy. *Philosophy (London, England)*, *33*, 1–19. doi:10.1017/S0031819100037943

Aristotle. (2009). *Nicomachean ethics*. As cited in Ross (2009). Greensboro, NC: WLC Books.

Audi, R., & Murphy, P. E. (2006). The many faces of integrity. *Business Ethics Quarterly*, *16*, 3–21.

Avolio, B. J., & Gardner, W. (2005). Authentic leadership development: Getting to the root of positive forms of leadership. *The Leadership Quarterly*, *16*, 315–338. doi:10.1016/j.leaqua.2005.03.001

Bandura, A. (1986). As cited in Bandura, A. (2001). *Social foundations of thought and action: A social cognitive theory*. Englewood Cliffs, NJ: prentice-Hall.

Bandura, A. (2000). Exercise of human agency through collective efficacy. *American Psychological Society*, *9*(3), 75–78.

Bass, B. M. (1985). *Leadership and performance beyond expectations*. New York, NY: Free Press.

Bass, B. M. (2008). *The Bass handbook of leadership*. New York, NY: Free Press.

Becker, T. E. (1998). Integrity in organizations: beyond honesty and conscientiousness. *Academy of Management Review*, *23*(1), 154–161.

Bennett, R. (1993). *The book of virtues*. New York, NY: Simon & Shuster.

Bentham, J. (2010). *An introduction to the principles of morals and legislation*. Oxford, UK: Clarendon Press. (Original work published 1789) doi:10.1002/9780470776018.ch1

Boudon, R. (2001). *The origin of values*. London, UK: Transaction Publishers.

Brown, M. E., Trevino, L. K., & Harrison, D. A. (2005). Ethical leadership: A social learning perspective for construct development and testing. *Organizational Behavior and Human Decision Processes, 97*, 117–134. doi:10.1016/j.obhdp.2005.03.002

Bruce, S. (2008). *Experience based suggestions for achieving a high survey response rate.* Retrieved from http://www.virginia.edu/case/education/documents/surveyresponseratesummarypaper-final.pdf

Calder, G. (2007). *Rorty's politics of redescriptions.* Cardiff, UK: University of Wales Press.

Campbell, D., & Fiske, D. (1959). Convergent and discriminant validation by the multi-trait/multi-method matrix. *Psychological Bulletin, 56*, 81–105. doi:10.1037/h0046016

Ciulla, J. B. (2004). *Ethics: The heart of leadership.* London, UK: Praeger Publishers.

Cohen, J. (1960). A coefficient of agreement for nominal scales. *Educational and Psychological Measurement, 20*(1), 37–46. doi:10.1177/001316446002000104

Cook, J., & Wall, T. (1980). New work attitude measures of trust, organizational commitment and personal need non-fulfillment. *Journal of Occupational Psychology, 53*, 39–52. doi:10.1111/j.2044-8325.1980.tb00005.x

Cooper, J. M., & Hutchinson, D. S. (Eds.). (1997). *Plato: Complete works.* Indianapolis, IN: Hackett Publishing.

Craig, S., & Gustafson, S. (1998). Perceived leader integrity scale: An instrument for assessing employee perceptions of leader integrity. *The Leadership Quarterly, 9*(2), 127–145. doi:10.1016/S1048-9843(98)90001-7

Cronbach, L. J. (1951). Coefficient alpha and the internal structure tests. *Psychometrika, 16*(3), 297–334. doi:10.1007/BF02310555

Dennis, R., & Bocarnea, M. (2005). Development of the servant leadership assessment instrument. *Leadership and Organization Development Journal, 65*(5), 1857.

DeVellis, R. (2003). *Scale development: Theory and applications.* London, UK: Sage Publications.

Dewey, J. (1960). *Theory of the moral life.* New York, NY: Holt Rinehart and Winston.

Dobel, J. P. (1990). Integrity n the public service. *Public Administration Review, 50*(3), 354–366. doi:10.2307/976617

Dunn, C. P. (2009). Integrity matters. *International Journal of Leadership Studies, 5*(2), 102–125.

Farrell, A. M. (2010). Insufficient discriminant validity: A comment on Bove, Pervan, Beatty and Shiu (2009). *Journal of Business Research, 63*(3), 324–327. doi:10.1016/j.jbusres.2009.05.003

Fields, D. (2007). Determinants of follower perceptions of a leader's authenticity and integrity.

Freud, A. (1937). *The ego and mechanisms of defense.* London, UK: Hogarth Press.

Fry, L. W. (2003). Toward a theory of spiritual leadership. *The Leadership Quarterly, 14*, 693–727. doi:10.1016/j.leaqua.2003.09.001

Furrow, D. (2005). As cited in Dunn (2005). *Ethics: Key concepts in philosophy.* New York, NY: Continuum International Publishing Group.

Gibbs, J. C. (1995). The cognitive development perspective. In Kurtines, W. M., & Gewirtz, J. L. (Eds.), *Moral development: An introduction* (pp. 27–48). Boston, MA: Allyn & Bacon.

Gove, P. B. (Ed.). (1976). *Webster's third new international dictionary.* Springfield, MA: Merriam Company.

Greenleaf, R. K. (1977). *Servant leadership.* New York, NY: Paulist Press.

Hair, J., Black, W., Babin, B., Anderson, R., & Tatham, R. (2006). *Multivariate data analysis* (6th ed.). Upper Saddle River, NJ: Pearson.

Hall, E. T. (1976). *Beyond culture*. New York, NY: Anchor Books.

Harcourt, E. (1998). As cited in Dunn (2009). Integrity practical deliberation and utilitarianism. *The Philosophical Quarterly, 48*(191), 189-198.

Harter, S. (2002). Authenticity. In Snyder, C. R., & Lopez, S. (Eds.), *Handbook of positive psychology*. Oxford, UK: University Press.

Hobbes, T. (1651, 1968). *Leviathan* (C. MacPherson, Ed.). London, UK: Penguin Books.

Joas, H. (2000). *The genesis of values*. Chicago, IL: University Press.

Kalshoven, K., & Den Hartog, D. N. (2009). Ethical leader behavior and leader effectiveness: The role of prototypicality and trust. *International Journal of Leadership Studies, 5*(2).

Kant, I. (2002). *The groundwork of the metaphysics of morals (A. Zweig* (Hill, T., Trans. Ed.). Oxford, UK: Oxford University Press. (Original work published 1785)

Kerlinger, F., & Lee, H. (2000). *Foundations of behavioral research*. Northridge, CA: Wadsworth.

Kershaw, I. (2001). *Backing Hitler: Consent and coercion in Nazi Germany*. Oxford, UK: Oxford University Press.

Kohlberg, L. (1984). *Essays in moral development: The psychology of moral development*. New York, UK: Harper & Row.

Kotva, J. (1996). *The case for Christian virtue ethics*. Washington, DC: Georgetown University Press.

Krebs, D. L., & Denton, K. (2005). Toward a more pragmatic approach to morality: A critical evaluation of Kohlberg's Model. *Psychological Review, 112*(3), 629–649. doi:10.1037/0033-295X.112.3.629

Likert, R. (1967). A technique for the measurement of attitudes. *Archives de Psychologie, 140*, 1–55.

Locke, J. (1967). An essay concerning the true origin, extent and end of civil government. In Burtt, E. (Ed.), *The English philosophers from Bacon to Mills*. New York, NY: The Modern Library. (Original work published 1689)

Lowe, K. B., Cordery, J., & Morrison, D. (2004). *A model for the attribution of leader integrity: Peeking inside the black box of authentic leadership*. Paper presented at the 2004 Gallup Leadership Institute Conference, Lincoln, NE.

Luthans, F., & Avolio, B. (2003). Authentic leadership development. In Cameron, K., Dutton, J., & Quinn, R. (Eds.), *Positive organizational scholarship: Foundations for a new discipline*. San Francisco, CA: Berrett-Koehler Publishers.

MacIntyre, A. (1984). *After virtue*. Notre Dame, IN: University of Notre Dame Press.

Marshall, J. A. (2012). *Ethical leadership, prototypicality, integrity, trust and leader effectiveness*. Dissertation, Regent University, Virginia Beach, VA.

Martin, M. W. (1979). Self-deception, self-pretence, and emotional detachment. *Mind, 88*(1), 441–446. doi:10.1093/mind/LXXXVIII.1.441

Mason, T., & Caplan, J. (1995). *Nazism, Fascism and the working class*. New York, NY: Cambridge University Press. doi:10.1017/CBO9780511622328

McFall, L. (1987). Integrity. *Ethics, 98*, 5–20. doi:10.1086/292912

McKeon, R. (2001). *The basic works of Aristotle.* New York, NY: Random House.

Mooney, V. (Ed.). (2000). *When no one sees.* Colorado Springs, CO: NavPress.

Musschenga, A. (2001). Education for moral integrity. *Journal of Philosophy of Education, 35*(2), 219–235. doi:10.1111/1467-9752.00222

Northouse, P. G. (2007). *Leadership: Theory and practice.* London, UK: Sage Publications.

Palanski, M. E., & Yammarino, F. J. (2007). Integrity and leadership: Clearing the conceptual confusion. *European Management Journal, 25*(3), 171–184. doi:10.1016/j.emj.2007.04.006

Palanski, M. E., & Yammarino, F. J. (2009). Integrity and leadership: A multi-level conceptual framework. *The Leadership Quarterly, 20*, 405–420. doi:10.1016/j.leaqua.2009.03.008

Plato,. (1997). The republic. In Cooper, J. (Ed.), *Plato: Complete works.* Cambridge, MA: Hackett Publishing Company.

Pocock, C. (2005). *50 years of the U-2.* Atglen, PA: Schiffer Military History.

Puka, B. (2005). Teaching ethical excellence: Artful response-ability, creative integrity, character opus. *Liberal Education*, 22–25.

Rachels, J. (2003). *The elements of moral philosophy* (4th ed.). New York, NY: McGraw Hill.

Rand, A. (1961). *For the new intellectual.* New York, NY: Signet.

Rawls, J. (1971). *A theory of justice.* Cambridge, MA: Harvard University Press.

Rorty, R., & Williams, M. (1979). *Philosophy and the mirror of Nature.* Princeton, NJ: Princeton University Press.

Rousseau, J. J. (1967). *The social contract and discourse on the origin of inequality* (Crocker, L., Ed.). New York, NY: Pocket Books. (Original work published 1762)

Rugeley, C., & Van Wart, M. (2006). As cited in Dunn (2009, p. 117). Everyday moral exemplars: The case of Judge Sam Medina. *Public Integrity, 8*(4), 381-394.

Schlenker, B. R. (2008). Integrity and character: Implications of principled and expedient ethical ideologies. *Journal of Social and Clinical Psychology, 27*(10), 1078–1125. doi:10.1521/jscp.2008.27.10.1078

Schlenker, B. R., Pontari, B. A., & Christopher, A. N. (2001). Excuses and character: Personal and social implications of excuses. *Personality and Social Psychology Review, 5*, 15–32. doi:10.1207/S15327957PSPR0501_2

Scholtz, A. (2006). *Know thyself.* Retrieved from http://classics.binghamton.edu/greek.htm

Shakespeare, W. (2007). Hamlet. In Bates, J. (Ed.), *Complete works: By William Shakespeare.* New York, NY: Modern Library. (Original work published 1600)

Simons, T. (2002). Behavioral integrity: The perceived alignment between managers' words and deeds as a research focus. *Organization Science, 13*(1), 18–35.

Smith, A. (1986). The wealth of nations. In Heilbroner, R. L. (Ed.), *The essential Adam Smith.* New York, NY: W. W. Norton & Company. (Original work published 1776)

Solomon, R. (1999). As cited by Dunn (2009, p. 105). *A better way to think about business: How personal integrity leads to corporate success.* New York, NY: Oxford University Press.

SPSS. (2009). *SPSS graduate student (version 18.0).* Nikiski, AK: Polar Consulting.

Starratt, R. J. (2004). *Ethical leadership*. San Francisco, CA: Jossey-Bass.

United States Department of Labor. (2011). *U. S. Bureau of Labor Statistics*. Retrieved from http://www.bls.gov/news.release/tenure.nr0.htm

Wallace, L. (2009). Dragon hearts. *Flying,* March 2009, 40-47.

Weber, M. (1947). As cited in Yukl (2006). *The theory of social and economic organizations.*

Williston, B. (2006). Blaming agents in moral dilemmas. *Ethical Theory and Moral Practice, 9,* 536–576. doi:10.1007/s10677-006-9036-4

Wilson, J. R. (1998). *Gospel virtues*. Downers Grove, IL: Inter-Varsity Press.

Yukl, G. (2006). *Leadership in organizations*. Upper Saddle River, NJ: Pearson Prentice Hall.

Yukl, G. A., & Van Fleet, D. D. (1990). Theory and research on leadership in organizations. In Dunnette, M. D., & Hough, L. M. (Eds.), *Handbook of industrial and organizational psychology*. Palo Alto, CA: Consulting Psychologists Press.

KEY TERMS AND DEFINITIONS

Ethics: "Norms and virtues by which members of a community bind themselves to a moral way of living" (Starratt, 2004, p. 6).

Integrity: The operational definition for integrity in this study was specifically used to develop the facets of the integrity construct in the leader integrity assessment and may contain aspects not required for a practical conceptualization of integrity. Thus, for clarity, integrity is practically defined as *a congruence between behavior and a reasonably justifiable set of coherent moral values.* This practical definition assumes a social component in the requirement for values to be reasonably justifiable, as well as the temporal and contextual aspects of social interaction.

Leader: Considering the adopted definition of the term leadership, in this study a leader is defined as someone engaged in leadership. This intentionally broad definition, and the seemingly circular justification, is chosen to leverage the definition of leadership such that a leader need not be formally identified nor permanently assigned.

Leadership: A process of influencing people to achieve a common goal.

Moral and Ethical: This study adopts the definitions provided by Gove (1976) who defined "moral" as "relating to principles or considerations of right and wrong" (p. 1468), and defined the term "ethical" as "involving questions of right and wrong" (p. 780).

Values: In this study values are defined in accordance with Dunn (2009), as "ordered preferences of moral goods," be they for instrumental or axiological reasons (p. 110). This definition allows for either instrumental or axiological reasons for values and is neutral in that people come to believe in specific values through similar processes based on rationality, either for instrumental or axiological reasons.

APPENDIX

Cost of Leader Integrity Assessment (LIA 15)

The LIA 15 is available for a nominal fee.

Location

The scale is available in electronic form at http://www.leaderintegrityresearch.com

Chapter 14
Measuring Followership

Paul Kaak
Azusa Pacific University, USA

Rodney A. Reynolds
California Lutheran University, USA

Michael Whyte
Azusa Pacific University, USA

ABSTRACT

The focus in this chapter is a proposal for a measure of followership with three dimensions: resistant follower, compliant follower, and mature follower. The chapter contains an internet link to specific items and a format for the measure. The rationale centers on various theoretic views about followership. The chapter provides suggestions for use of the measure within organizations. The conclusion centers on a program for future research.

A HISTORY OF FOLLOWERSHIP RESEARCH

The question of good leadership has not always concerned itself with its necessary corollary, good followership (see Baker, 2007; Collinson, 2006; Dvir & Shamir, 2003; Goffee & Jones, 2006; Haslam & Platow, 2001; Russell, 2003). James MacGregor Burns (1978), the renowned "father of leadership studies," launched the conversation in noting, "One of the most serious failures in the study of leadership has been the bifurcation between the literature on leadership and the literature on followership" (p.3). Hollander (1978)

notes "...the followers as well as the leader are vital to understanding leadership as a process. Followers support the leadership activities and the leader's position" (p.16). While Hollander has made a career of studying this process (1992a, 1992b, 1995, 2008), it was Kelley (1988; 1992) who provided the most extensive critique that our obsession with leadership was missing the associative emphasis on followership.

Although the bell had been rung by these scholars, those focusing on leaders continued to fill the space sparsely inhabited by researchers interested in followers. But among them, there have been those who suggested leaders would do well to consider the motivations and develop-

DOI: 10.4018/978-1-4666-2172-5.ch014

mental readiness of their followers. Hersey (1984) suggests that the key to successful leadership is in choosing a style appropriately based on the "situation" of the follower (p. 58). In reflecting back on the legacy of the Path-Goal theory, House (1996) points out that working with followers to achieve their goals would have "powerful effects on follower motivation and work unit performance" (p. 343). Although followers are instrumental for these theorists, the focus is still on what leaders can do to strategically influence follower effectiveness.

As the conversation has continued, there has been increasing acknowledgement that leadership is highly dependent on relationships of mutual trust (Brower, Schoorman, & Tan, 2000; Uhl-Bien, 2006; Uhl-Bien & Maslyn, 2003; Golden & Veiga 2008.). The Leader-Member Exchange (LMX) theory made this "vertical dyadic linkage" between leaders and followers the hub of its analysis (Dansereau, Graen, & Haga, 1975; Graen & Cashman, 1975; Graen & Uhl-Bien, 1995). LMX is a means of recognizing relationships based on in-groups and out-groups, with reference to leader-follower proximity. The model submits to the reality of hierarchical relationships in which loyalty is fundamental to successful relationships while betrayal is a deal-breaker. The LMX is helpful for followers who want to negotiate their place in the leader-follower relationship through maneuvers that are designed to please their particular leader.

One wonders, however, if this kind of followership is mutually transformational in the same way as Burns (1978) understood leadership as transformational for both the leader and follower. Furthermore, in keeping with recent conceptualizing in leadership studies, how can followers be more "authentic" (Shamir & Eliam, 2005)? Perhaps, as Rost (2008) points out, the word followership has too much baggage and needs to be traded in for "collaborator."

In practice, successful followership appears to have some similarity to emotional intelligence. Since followers typically don't choose their leader, there may be another set of choices for which they have agency. Because leaders themselves arrive at their roles in the organization with various degrees of emotional maturity, followers who are emotionally intelligent themselves will be more capable of making either a bad situation tolerable or fair, or a good situation great.

Researchers have applied emotional intelligence to the subject of leadership (Goleman, 1998a; Goleman, 1998b; Ashkanasy & Tse, 2000; Ashkanasy & Daus 2002; Goleman, Boyatzis, & McKee, 2002; Boyatzis, & McKee, 2005; McKee, Boyatzis, & Johnston, 2008) and those interested in good followership will find this literature to be helpful. Gardner, et. al (2005) present a conceptual framework showing that as leaders model what is today being called authentic leadership *vis a vis* the emotional intelligence behaviors of self-awareness and self-regulation, followers are more likely to respond in kind, also showing emotional intelligence, resulting in positive follower outcomes and performance. Might the reverse also be true?

The work that follows emerged because the qualities in the literature of emotional intelligence are similar in practice to the inclinations of good followers. In part, this is an intuitively simple process because defining a bad follower is commonly understood. A bad follower is rebellious, disrespectful, negative, sabotaging, etc. But does that mean an exemplary follower is simply defined as the opposite of each of these?

TAXONOMIES FOR FOLLOWERSHIP

Kelly (1992) provided early recognition of this definitional challenge. Just as there are different approaches to leadership, Kelly's taxonomy shows that there are different types of followers. For him, the four styles are illustrated in this figure 1.

Blackshear (2004) offers a Followership Continuum that looks at employees through the stages of their development within an organizational context. The five stages of dynamic and changing followership performance are explained by Blackshear as follows:

Figure 1. Followership styles (Kelley, 1992, p. 97)

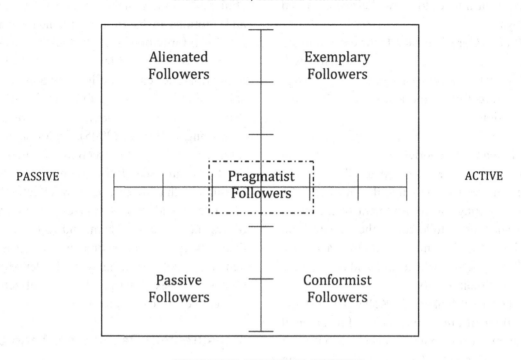

INDEPENDENT, CRITICAL THINKING

Alienated Followers

Exemplary Followers

PASSIVE

Pragmatist Followers

ACTIVE

Passive Followers

Conformist Followers

DEPENDENT, UNCRITICAL THINKING

Stage 1 Employee: The first stage of followership in the workplace begins by becoming an employee, providing work in return for some form of pay.

Stage 2 Committed Follower: At the committed followership stage the employee is bound to the mission, idea, organization, or has an internal pledge to an effort or person.

Stage 3 Engaged Follower: At the engaged followership stage, the follower is an active supporter, willing to go above and beyond the routine.

Stage 4 Effective Follower: The effective follower is capable and dependable.

Stage 5 Exemplary: The exemplary follower could easily be the leader. Instead, the exemplary follower sets ego aside and works to support the leader. They lead themselves. (p. 5)

Blackshear suggests that Stage 5 followers are extraordinary (p. 7). Her research interest involves the questions of what intrapersonal, organizational and leadership dynamics encourage or hinder movement along the continuum.

Kellerman (2008) added to the conversation by providing a classification of her own. Her types, she suggests, are significantly influenced by the style of leader the follower happens to be working under. Her five types are defined here:

1. *Isolates* don't want to be bothered by leaders and show little to no concern for having a good relationship with those whom they follow.

2. *Bystanders* are willing to be led but are not engaged.

3. *Participants* are glad to accommodate but only when they agree with the leader. Otherwise they may be a source of conflict.

4. *Activists* have a deep commitment to both the organization and the leader. They will do what it takes to show their support and loyalty

5. *Diehards* are dedicated to the cause and the leader who embodies that cause. They will follow the leader passionately or challenge her forcefully if the leader veers from the mission.

Kellerman's categories are less clean than Kelley's and less sequential than Blackshear's. She recognizes the challenge that leaders have in differentiating the commitment of followers to the leader versus followers to the organization. Sometimes this becomes conflictual and thus the follower needs to determine and manage the direction of their loyalty.

Furthermore, thinkers like Kelley, Blackshear, and Kellerman are getting at the fundamental and somewhat problematic concern about what is meant by "good"? One should query about followership in the same way that Ciulla queries about leadership: "The ultimate question is not 'What is leadership?' but 'What is good leadership?' The word good refers to both ethics and competence" (Ciulla, 1995, p.5). In the same way that followers want leaders who are both, so too leaders and teams value followers who are both ethical and competent. The assessment being proposed here is concerned about followership that is both morally good and effective.

Authentic Followership

Our premise is that the similarities between emotional intelligence and good followership can aid followers in navigating their responses to good and bad leaders in circumstantially appropriate ways. The bias of this chapter is that good followership is not merely unthinking compliance but instead requires a mature level of self-awareness, self-management, social awareness, and relationship management (Boyatzis & McKee, 2005, p. 29). It

is, therefore, not just – as Kelley (1992) emphasizes – "critical thinking" that is important but also the ability to "monitor one's own and others' feelings and emotions, to discriminate among them and to use this information to guide one's thinking and actions" (Salovey & Mayer, 1990, p. 189). The hope is that such emotionally intelligent followership will result in a kind of mature followership that can also be called *authentic* and *exemplary*. According to Bar-On (2005), "emotional-social intelligence is a cross-section of interrelated emotional and social competencies, skills and facilitators that determine how effectively we understand and express ourselves, understand others and relate with them, and cope with daily demands" (p. 3). For our concerns here, these daily demands involve working with a leader who may be perceived as either good or bad, effective or ineffective, ethical or unethical.

Measurement Development and Use

The items found in this assessment are not intended to be a precise correlation to the marks found in the research on emotional intelligence. Although links can be perceived, these items evolved via intuitive connections between the observed behavior of followers and the tacit understanding of emotional intelligence on the part of the assessment designers. The basis for the construction of the items was to allow honest respondents to perform self-assessments and locate their own development as a follower.

To approach assessment in this way removes the leader from the sole responsibility for defining good followership. Leaders ought not to think of defining followership as only their prevue of judgment. The attempt by leaders to control the definition of followership likely skews – perhaps inappropriately – to their self-motivations. A controlling-type leadership style may define good followership as unquestioned obedience. A laisse faire leader may define a good follower as someone to leave alone – trusting them to complete their work without supervision. A leader with questionable ethics probably thinks a good follower is the one who keeps their mouth shut; the proverbial "whistle-blower" is – for this leader – the worst kind of follower. A self-assessment, based on behaviors in real leader-follower relationships, can provide followers a chance to name their level of maturity as a follower. In so doing, they can be more mindful about choosing the kind of follower they would like to become.

Due to the fact that the vast majority of research in the area of leadership is focused almost exclusively on the role of the leader/supervisor, more research and reliable assessment instruments directed at followers/collaborators is desperately needed. Countless books and journal articles look down, rather than up, the chain of command. Gordon's (2003) compilation of "Successful Leadership Development Tools" is an excellent example of a resource for leaders that contains assessment techniques that are aimed almost exclusively at leaders rather than subordinates or followers. As Gordon so aptly states, however, "the one indispensable factor defining effective leaders is credibility in the eyes of followers" (p. xv). We propose that the credibility of the follower could also be enhanced through use of followership assessments that would benefit all organizational collaborators.

Below are some ways the followership assessment can be used:

1. It can provide 2-way initial expectations between employers and employees. Literally thousands of current USAF officers have been trained using the "positive motivation model". The USAF Academy (USAFA) Leadership Development Manual (Abeyta, 1992) outlines the five essential elements of their model of mutual respect: expectations, skills, feedback, consequences and growth. Clear, distinct expectations from both the supervisor and subordinate can lead to significantly enhanced mutual understanding and a more productive work and/or learning environment (pp. 11-21). The measurement of followership can help identify and clarify how individuals can contribute to the organization in positive ways.

2. It can help identify both potential future supervisors or individuals who would benefit from additional training or education. Just as leaders should have a succession plan, followers should be offered the skill-training necessary to do well, along with prospects for personal and career growth (USAFA, 1992, pp. 23-27). Learning about one's own followership style can possibly increase future leadership opportunities and abilities.

3. Use of this assessment may enable employees to serve as change agents. Knowing one's followership disposition can aid in attempts to have influence. According to Bass and Stogdill (1990), subordinates can impact their organizations and provide an often necessary "upward influence" (p. 347) on their bosses and, consequently, have a positive impact on the workplace. This is particularly instructive for those that may not have supervised anyone in the past or received any formal leadership training. Academic researchers should be particularly interested in how followership affects influence within the organization.

4. Information from the followership measure can enhance 360-degree feedback for both employees and employers. Chappelow (1998) outlines three distinct benefits of 360-degree feedback. It can be used for "developmental processes for individual managers and leaders", to "determine group strengths and developmental needs", and to "broaden employee awareness of valued behaviors" (pp. 39-40). In fact, feedback on how they follow is not just for individuals down the hierarchy. It can also provide significant self-awareness for the individuals at the top of the infamous organizational pyramid. Even leaders are occasionally followers.

The kinds of followers anticipated here are:

1. *The Resistant Follower*. This person generally doesn't like being a follower. Living in submission to any kind of leader – even a good one – is not their inclination. They may believe they could do better than those who lead them or not. But that isn't the issue. They may be easily threatened, or they may simply have unresolved anger or sadness. These followers simply do not want to be directed by someone up-the-hierarchy. The resistant follower is similar to Kellerman's "isolate", has no corollary in Blackshear, and resembles the "alienated" follower in Kelley's typology.

2. *The Compliant Follower* is the person that most leaders would be glad to have working for them. Their attitude as followers is neither enthusiastic nor dour. They have simply resigned themselves to do what needs doing in the role they have been placed. The compliant follower can be seen developmentally in Blackshear's Stage 1-4, is similar to Kelley's "conformist" and Kellerman's "bystander."

3. Idealized here, is *the Mature Follower*. They fulfill their role with a high level of emotional intelligence because they have come to realize that these behaviors are key factors for the maintenance of good leader-follower relationships. While holding high ethical standards and retaining a commitment to the organization, they allow for human error on the part of the leader and respond to it with courage and grace. In some cases, they may be "better" than their leader in that they have a healthy sense of self, order, as well as a good understanding of relational processes. The mature follower is an "exemplary" follower, to use labels found in Blackshear and Kelley and can be seen in various stages of commitment as described in Kellerman's "participant," "activist," and "diehard."

The proposed measure is located at, http://www.callutheran.edu/assessment/resources/research.php.

FUTURE RESEARCH

The followership instrument requires testing for data reduction, reliability, and validity. There are many possible 'known groups' (self or other-nominated) for possible validation tests. The hope here is that this initial effort will generate an upswing in followership research and theorizing.

Followers – like leaders – are more made, than born. Understanding exemplary followership is an opportunity for developmental intentionality. This is an important area for those looking for personal well-being, organizational health, and a positive contribution to pursue. Individuals intent on being good followers will take on this challenge.

REFERENCES

Abeyta, D. A. (1992). *United States Air Force Academy leadership development manual*. Colorado Springs, CO: Forbes.

Ashkanasy, N. M., & Daus, C. S. (2002). Emotion in the workplace: The new challenge for managers. *The Academy of Management Executive*, *16*(1), 76–86. doi:10.5465/AME.2002.6640191

Ashkanasy, N. M., & Tse, B. (2000). Transformational leadership as management of emotion: A conceptual review. In Hartel, C. E. J., & Zerbe, W. J. (Eds.), *Emotions in the workplace: Research, theory and practice*. Westport, CT: Quorom Books.

Baker, S. D. (2007). Followership: The theoretical foundation of a contemporary construct. *Journal of Leadership & Organizational Studies*, *4*(1), 50–60. doi:10.1177/0002831207304343

Bar-On, R. (2005). The Bar-On model of emotional-social intelligence. In Fernández-Berrocal, P., & Extremera, N. (Eds.), *Special Issue on Emotional Intelligence, Psicothema, 17.*

Bass, B. M. (Ed.). (1990). *Bass & Stogdill's handbook of leadership: Theory, research and managerial applications* (3rd ed.). New York, NY: The Free Press.

Blackshear, P. B. (2003, Summer). The followership continuum: A model for fine tuning the workforce. *Public Management, 32*(2), 25–29.

Boyatzis, R., & McKee, A. (2005). *Resonant leadership.* Boston, MA: Harvard Business School Press.

Brower, H. H., Schoorman, F. D., & Tan, H. H. (2000). A model of relational leadership: The integration of trust and leader-member exchange. *The Leadership Quarterly, 11*(2), 227–250. doi:10.1016/S1048-9843(00)00040-0

Burns, J. M. (1978). *Leadership.* New York, NY: Harper & Row.

Chappelow, C. T. (1998). 360-degree feedback. In McCauley, C. D., Moxley, R. S., & Van Velsor, E. (Eds.), *The Center for Creative Leadership handbook of leadership development* (pp. 39–41). San Francisco, CA: Jossey-Bass.

Ciulla, J. B. (1995). Leadership ethics: Mapping the territory. *Business Ethics Quarterly, 5,* 5–24. doi:10.2307/3857269

Collinson, D. (2006). Rethinking followership: A post-structuralist analysis of follower identities. *The Leadership Quarterly, 17,* 179–189. doi:10.1016/j.leaqua.2005.12.005

Dansereau, F. Jr, Graen, G., & Haga, W. J. (1975). A vertical dyad linkage approach to leadership within formal organizations: A longitudinal investigation of the role making process. *Organizational Behavior and Human Performance, 13,* 46–78. doi:10.1016/0030-5073(75)90005-7

Dvir, T., & Shamir, B. (2003). Follower developmental characteristics as predicting transformational leadership: a longitudinal field study. *The Leadership Quarterly, 14,* 327–344. doi:10.1016/S1048-9843(03)00018-3

Goffee, R., & Jones, G. (2006). The art of followership. *European Business Forum, 25,* 22–26.

Golden, T. D., & Veiga, J. F. (2008). The impact of superior-subordinate relationships on the commitment, job satisfaction, and performance of virtual workers. *The Leadership Quarterly, 19,* 77–88. doi:10.1016/j.leaqua.2007.12.009

Goleman, D. (1998a). What makes a leader? *Harvard Business Review, 76*(6), 92–102.

Goleman, D. (1998b). *Working with emotional intelligence.* New York, NY: Bantam.

Goleman, D., Boyatzis, R., & McKee, A. (2002). *Primal leadership: Realizing the power of emotional intelligence.* Boston, MA: Harvard Business School Press.

Gordon, J. (Ed.). (2003). *The Pfeiffer book of successful leadership development tools.* San Francisco, CA: Pfeiffer.

Graen, G., & Cashman, J. F. (1975). A role making model of leadership in formal organizations: A developmental approach. In Hunt, J. G., & Larson, L. L. (Eds.), *Leadership frontiers* (pp. 143–165). Kent, OH: Kent State University Press.

Graen, G. B., & Uhl-Bien, M. (1995). Relationship-based approach to leadership: Development of leader-member exchange (LMX) theory of leadership over 25 years: Applying a multi-level multi-domain perspective. *The Leadership Quarterly, 6*(2), 219–247. doi:10.1016/1048-9843(95)90036-5

Haslam, S.A., & Platow, M.J. (2001). The link between leadership and followership: How affirming social identity translates vision into action. *Personality and Social Psychology Bulletin, 27*(11), 1469–1479. doi:10.1177/01461672012711008

Hersey, P. (1984). *The situational leader*. New York, NY: Warner Books.

Hollander, E. P. (1978). *Leadership dynamics: A practical guide to effective relationships*. New York, NY: The Free Press.

Hollander, E. P. (1992a). The essential interdependence of leadership and followership. *Current Directions in Psychological Science, 1*(2), 71–75. doi:10.1111/1467-8721.ep11509752

Hollander, E. P. (1992b). Leadership, followership, self, and others. *The Leadership Quarterly, 3*(1), 43–54. doi:10.1016/1048-9843(92)90005-Z

Hollander, E. P. (1995). Ethical challenges in the leader-follower relationship. *Business Ethics Quarterly, 5*(1), 55–65. doi:10.2307/3857272

Hollander, E. P. (2008). *Inclusive leadership: The essential leader-follower relationship*. New York, NY: Routledge.

House, R. J. (1996). Path-goal theory of leadership: Lessons, legacy and a reformulated theory. *The Leadership Quarterly, 7*(3), 323–352. doi:10.1016/S1048-9843(96)90024-7

Kellerman, B. (2008). *Followership: How followers are creating change and changing leaders*. Boston, MA: Harvard Business School Press.

Kelley, R. E. (1988). In praise of followers. *Harvard Business Review, 66*(6), 142–148.

Kelley, R. E. (1992). *The power of followership: How to create leaders people want to follow, and followers who lead themselves*. New York, NY: Doubleday.

McKee, A., Boyatzis, R., & Johnston, F. (2008). *Becoming a resonant leader: Develop your emotional intelligence, renew your relationships, sustain your effectiveness*. Boston, MA: Harvard Business School.

Riggio, R. E., Chaleff, I., & Lipman-Blumen, J. (Eds.). (2008). *The art of followership: How great followers create great leaders and organizations*. San Francisco, CA: Jossey-Bass.

Rost, J. (2008). Followership: An outmoded concept. In Riggio, R. E., Chaleff, I., & Lipman-Blumen, J. (Eds.), *The art of followership: How great followers create great leaders and organizations*. San Francisco, CA: Jossey-Bass.

Russell, M. (2003). Leadership and followership as a relational process. *Educational Management and Administration, 31*(2), 145–157. doi:10.1177/0263211X0303102103

Salovey, P., & Mayer, J. (1990). Emotional intelligence. *Imagination, Cognition and Personality, 9*(3), 185–211.

Shamir, B., & Eilam, G. (2005). "What's your story?" A life-stories approach to authentic leadership development. *The Leadership Quarterly, 16*(3), 395–417. doi:10.1016/j.leaqua.2005.03.005

Uhl-Bien, M. (2006). Relational leadership theory: Exploring the social processes of leadership and organizing. *The Leadership Quarterly, 17*, 654–676. doi:10.1016/j.leaqua.2006.10.007

Uhl-Bien, M., & Maslyn, J. (2003). Reciprocity in manager-subordinate relationships: Components, configurations, and outcomes. *Journal of Management, 29*(4), 511–532.

KEY TERMS AND DEFINITIONS

Compliant Follower: The person that has accepted that their role is to consistently do what they have been assigned to do.

Emotional-Social Intelligence: "…a cross-section of interrelated emotional and social competencies, skills and facilitators that determine how effectively we understand and express ourselves, understand others and relate with them, and cope with daily demands" (Bar-On, 2005, p. 3).

Mature Follower: This person fulfills their role with emotional-social intelligence and ethical standards. They are committed to the maintenance of a good leader-follower relationship, as long as this is possible. They allow for error on the part of the leader and respond properly.

Resistant Followership: This person doesn't like being cast as a follower. Living in submission is not their inclination. These followers do not want to be directed by someone up-the-hierarchy.

Chapter 15
An Online Measure of Discernment

Hazel C. V. Traüffer
Grand Canyon University, USA

Corné L. Bekker
Regent University, USA

Mihai C. Bocarnea
Regent University, USA

Bruce E. Winston
Regent University, USA

ABSTRACT

The Discernment Practices Indicator (DPI) reports three-factors: (a) Courage, (b) Intuition, and (c) Faith with Cronbach alpha values of (a) .85, (b) .89, and (c) .85, respectively. The Courage factor addresses the leader's mental and moral courage; willingness to accept uncertainty; use of common sense; ability to seek new ways to look at old things; see a future full of possibilities, believing in the equality of all people; and to be firm, but loving, in addressing issues. The Intuition factor addresses the leader's understanding of his or her emotions; willingness to make decisions, based on a hunch; as well as paying attention to body cues or thoughts that may flash across the mind. The Faith factor addresses the leader's use of quiet time (to include prayer and meditation) to reflect and find meaning; use of principles of faith as guidance; as well as incorporating religious beliefs in professional undertakings.

DISCERNMENT PRACTICES INDICATOR: AN ONLINE MEASURE OF DISCERNMENT

Bass (1990) contended that decision-making is the most critical of the leader's responsibilities, and a measure of the leader's effectiveness lies in the quality of these decisions. Traüffer's (2008) dissertation sought to determine if there was a role for discernment in the leader-decision process and using in-depth interviews, a literature review on *discernment* and related topics, as well as feedback from an expert panel determined that discernment had a role in understanding how leaders make decisions. Traüffer pointed out the paucity of research on the topic of discernment, thus making

DOI: 10.4018/978-1-4666-2172-5.ch015

her study of discernment a foundational piece for the stream of research.

Leadership and organizational decision-making have been largely addressed from a classical, reductionist approach, but the set of challenges leaders face can seldom be successful with traditional methods of decision-making. These methods are variations of the behavior model of rational choice, whereby leaders arrive at decisions based on a reflection of experiences (Simon, 1955). Current leadership challenges suggest that we cannot always approach decision-making from this perspective, because several factors in the experience may not duplicate, or may differ from those in the present issue. Thus, the experience becomes either irrelevant or insufficient, and this requires leaders who desire to keep their organizations viable in emerging contexts to develop and master a new way of thinking. Therefore, it is necessary to reform current decision-making paradigms to meet the social realities of our times. A study of discernment contributes to the literature through the introduction of a new paradigm and cognitive ability that places the divine centre stage and integrates the leaders' self-perception and identity into the organizational context for optimal performance, instead of the leader relying on best practices of past experiences.

The attempt to further the understanding of the discernment concept is not simply about philosophy or theology; rather, it is about uncovering truths whose "applicability is not bound to any one time or culture" (Plaut, 1961, p. 7). In other words, though revealed in one context, it is possible that the truths underlying the concept of discernment are relevant to our current times and issues, and may provide an explanation for leadership, as well as organizational behavior. Still, to discover these truths and present a coherent and comprehensive rendition of the construct, it is necessary to explicate the meaning of discernment, as well as what it entails. At present, there is no simple definition of, or scholarly consensus about, what discernment means. However, the *Merriam-Webster Online*

Dictionary (p.89) likens the concept to "wisdom," the Hebrew word transliterated as chokmo, which Whybray (1972) deemed "not only a practical guide to the successful life but a characteristic of God himself, from whom alone it can be obtained" (p. 14). Therefore, any definition or understanding of discernment requires an understanding of the concept wisdom.

The issue of decision quality and its effect on organizational life is not confined within any specific geographic boundary. Furthermore, the nature of being human affords no one an immunity from moral and ethical lapses. News headlines of the corporate implosions that result from unethical decisions (Colvin, 2003; Mehta, 2003), as well as the moral failures of renown and high-profile executives, whose extraordinary influence had the potential to mobilize vast arrays of resources, including human and financial, towards impressive achievements (Allen & Klenke, 2009), lead to the stark realization that the viability of organizations depends on the quality of the decisions their leaders make; yet, there has been little to no work that examines the role of discernment in the process. Two basic theories speculate that leaders in organizations make decisions either by rational choice or intuition. Simon (1955) presented a perspective which implies that theorists of rational choice adopt the schematized model of economic man that suggests that humans are rational beings. As such, humans have the capacity to engage in what Simon describes as

A well-organized and stable system of preferences, and a skill in computation that enables him to calculate, for the alternative courses of action that are available to him, which of these will permit him to reach the highest attainable point on his preference scale. (p. 99)

Based on this perspective, our present practice relies on a paradigm that reduces decision-making to a simple cause-effect and analytical process, where leaders seek and find "the best alternative, the one that emerges from thorough information search and careful deliberation" (Janis, 1989, p.13). Simon (1957) outlined the process as the practice of (a) generating several options, (b) comparing all options, (c) identifying the best option, and (d) taking that decision. Implicit in the rational choice approach is the idea that a comparison of options leads to optimal decision-making. The mere fact that vast amounts of information can surround any given situation makes this approach, though logical and definitive, very slow and time-consuming (Gladwell, 2005), requiring exhaustive information search and careful reflection (Janis, 1989), and cannot be deemed completely rational, given our human cognitive limitations (Simon, 1976). Janis noted that the "chronic limitations on the human mind in dealing with complexity" (p. 132) make it highly possible for unsuccessful outcomes to occur, despite the care taken in carrying out the steps that Simon (1957) outlined. Furthermore, it is impossible for any leader to know everything there is to know about all the variables that influence a situation, in order to make the best judgment. Thus, a leader can never be sure of anything and must make decisions using partial or incomplete information. Moreover, the context in which today's leaders must make decisions bear little resemblance to those of yesteryear, making the best option of yesterday little more than a passing idea.

The other theory, called intuitive decision-making, rejects the scientifically analytical approach, and relies on the leader's intuitive ability to recognize the key elements in a given situation and then use those key elements to make his or her decisions. Gladwell (2005), in his controversial work, depicted the power of trusting one's intuition rather than relying on analysis. Gladwell related how the J. Paul Getty Museum purchased a marble sculpture, known as a kouros, dating from the sixth century B.C.E., after subjecting it to a rigorous and scientific testing by a geologist from the University of California. The scientist used several tools, including an electron micro-scope, electron micro-probe, mass spectrometry, X-ray diffraction, and X-ray fluorescence to analyze a small sample taken from the statue. Before paying the US$10 million asking price, the museum had every piece of data pertaining to the kouros scrutinized and checked against all known records, and all analyses pointed to an authentic piece of work. With great pride and confidence, the museum marked its unveiling with a front-page story in the *New York Times*. Nevertheless, something was amiss. The kouros, it turns out, was a fake. How could that be; had not the museum used an analytical and scientific method to arrive at their decision? However, not everyone fell for it. Other art experts, who saw the kouros, had reactions that prompted one of them to respond, "I'm sorry to hear that," upon learning that, indeed, The Getty had purchased the statue. Another had suggested that the museum try to get its money back. Gladwell believed that biases and self-interest can hide the truth. He quoted the Getty's curator of antiquities, Marion True, as saying, "I always considered scientific opinion more objective than esthetic judgments ... Now I realize I was wrong" (Gladwell, p. 17), when the truth about the kouros was revealed. With an acquisition such as the kouros, the museum stood to gain international recognition. Therefore, it is understandable that the curator would have wanted the statue to be real. More than that, though, Gladwell exposed our tendency to employ a social science research reductionist approach to understanding phenomena, whereby making sense of our world results from tearing things apart and analyzing the parts rather than the whole. Then, given our understanding of a part, we assume a "one size fits all" attitude. However, such an attitude can lead to bad decisions, as the museum personnel later found out. Gladwell wrote that the curator and other museum personnel "were so focused on the mechanics and the process that they never looked at the problem holistically. In the act of tearing something apart, you lose its meaning" (p. 125). Could Marion True have failed to analyze a particular part for added information, or did True fail to consider the information in the decision-making process because its source would not have been considered 'scientifically objective'?

Gladwell (2005) asserted that an individual receives information in two ways. The first is through the facilitation of the conscious strategy, whereby the individual thinks about what he or she has learnt and, eventually, derives insight. This strategy supports the rational choice approach, which, while logical and definitive, can be time-consuming. The second strategy evokes the subconscious that is "entirely below the surface of consciousness. It sends its messages through weirdly indirect channels, such as the sweat glands in the palm of the hands. It's a system in which our brain reaches conclusions without immediately telling us that it's reaching conclusions" (Gladwell, p. 10). It was by means of the second strategy that the art experts in Gladwell's account received information that alerted them to the in-authenticity of the kouros; one experienced sweaty palms, one had the feeling as if there was something separating him from the statue, and a third heard the word "fresh." If such a strategy can provide the kind of information that can keep us from failing, why are not leaders in organizations mindful? Morgan (1997) purported that "based on pattern recognition rather than formal logic or analysis … intuitive managers learn to recognize clusters or chunks of information and act accordingly [but] are unable to give formal accounts or justifications of why a particular decision has been made" (p. 80). Gladwell maintained that, although human beings have developed a "decision-making apparatus that's capable of making very quick judgements based on very little information" (p. 12), there is very little, if any, conviction that one's snap judgments and first impressions can be educated and controlled. It could be that leaders are more likely to disregard information that is "not scientifically tested" because "we live in a world that assumes that the quality of a decision is directly related to the time and effort that went

into making it" (Gladwell, p. 13). Gladwell went on to say that "the task of making sense of ourselves and our behavior requires that we acknowledge there can be as much value in the blink of an eye as in months of rational analysis" (p. 17).

On the one hand, it is clear that leaders cannot rely on experiences to direct the future or even the present; on the other, it is totally naïve for leaders to make decisions solely on gut-feelings and sweaty palms. To do either is to risk trivializing situations that could become major disasters. If rational analysis and intuition are conceptually independent, is *cross-pollination* possible? In other words, is it possible for rational analysis and intuition to co-exist, to infuse each other? Gladwell (2005) thought so. Although there is no mention of the word *intuition* in Gladwell's book Gladwell asserted that it is a rational approach in which thin-slicing minimizes the timing by cutting to the core of what really matters which, for Burns (1978), is whether society ultimately benefits from the leader's decisions; while for Bass (1985), it is whether the leader's decisions result in transformation of followers' attitudes and behaviors. Gladwell suggested that "when we have a hunch, our consciousness … sift[s] through the situation in front of us, throwing out all that is irrelevant while we zero in on what really matters" (pp. 33-34). Underlying this coexistence is an intertwining of our left-brain bias and linear approach to understanding phenomena with the more intuitive, non-linear right-brain orientation. Morgan (1997) subscribed to such co-existence, noting that instead of an either/or, "A more fully developed decision-making perspective would balance and integrate right and left brain capacities" (p. 80), allowing leaders to consider confronting and flowing with the uncertainty inherent in today's environments, rather than making decisions that seek to eliminate or reduce uncertainty.

The lack of research on discernment could very well be the result of our merely taking a social science research reductionist approach to understanding phenomena, by making sense of parts rather than the whole and, given our understanding of a part, we assume a "one size fits all" attitude. Thus, our present practice relies on a paradigm that reduces decision-making to a simple cause-effect process, whereby we make choices based on a set of alternatives and estimates of the consequences of all possible outcomes (Simon, 1957). By contrast, Vroom and Yetton (1973) moved us toward a more holistic approach toward decision-making suggesting that both "cognitive and social" (p. 4) processes regulate the choices we make. Furthermore, they noted that from the moment the leader recognizes the need for a decision to the time he or she makes the decision, activities that are both intrapersonal and interpersonal become involved. However, Vroom and Yetton contended that the interpersonal or social aspects offer a more direct relevance to the processes of leadership. They took the posture that a "leader not only makes decisions but also designs, regulates, and selects social systems that make decisions" (Vroom & Yetton, p. 5). These social systems determine the extent to which a leader may or may not involve subordinates in the decision-making process. Vroom's and Yetton's examination of how leaders approach decision-making led them to conclude that several processes exist by which leaders make decisions. Notwithstanding, there are certain processes they should use but which process they would actually use is another matter. Vroom and Yetton suggested that situational conditions should guide the chosen process because situational factors often affect the choices leaders make. In essence, the method or roadmap that guides decision-making should be a systematic one that shows leaders "what to do and when to do it, what information he should use and how he should use it" (Kepner & Tregoe, 1965, p. 41). Popular press author Gladwell (2005) referred to the art of *blinking* by which a leader knows what to do, but nothing systematic has been done in the academic research field to examine this. The blink concept appears analogous to discernment in its implication that the leader knows "what information" he or she should use; however, the concepts diverge as blink fails to indicate that the leader knows "what to do," "when to do it," or "how" to use the information he or she has. If Gladwell is correct, the concept of blinking may move us toward an understanding of discernment, which has a dearth of information in the scientific literature.

The Discernment Concept

Rost (1991) pointed out that theory development usually occurs with paradigm shifts, which, according to Wheatley (1999), organizations are now experiencing. Drawing attention to behaviors that leaders today engage, Wheatley argued that these behaviors are embedded in a worldview anchored in seventeenth century physics and Newtonian mechanics that see the world as predictable; albeit, "the science has changed ... we need to ... ground our work in the science of our times ... [and] include what is presently known about how the world organizes" (p. 8). If, indeed, organizational paradigms are shifting, leaders need to embrace new attitudes toward decision-making by developing some kind of behavioral strategy that enables them to "toggle back and forth between [their] conscious and unconscious modes of thinking, depending on the situation" (Gladwell, 2005, p. 12). Discernment, as a model for optimum decision-making, offers this advancement. The focus of discernment stands in marked contrast to the rational choice paradigm. Rational choice relies totally on conscious modes of thinking and on experience and knowledge that "anything real has visible and tangible physical form" (Wheatley, 1999, p. 10). Discernment, on the other hand, goes beyond the physical form and embraces the leader's holistic system of body, mind, and spirit, allowing the leader to think contextually and allegorically, to reach into the future to grasp potential and possibilities, and to act upon them. Thus, leaders who practice discernment are likely to develop entrepreneurial attitudes towards decision-making, instead of being satisfied with best practices or benchmarking.

Definition of Discernment

The English word discernment comes from the combination of two Latin words: *dis*, meaning "apart" and *cernere*, meaning "to sift"". *Merriam-Webster's Online Dictionary* interprets discernment in terms of concepts such as perception, penetration, and insight; defines it as "the quality of being able to grasp and comprehend what is obscure"; and equates it to "wisdom," noting that wisdom comes with age and experience. WordNet 2.0 renders it as "the cognitive condition of someone who understands" that gives an individual the "ability to make good judgments" (http://dictionary.reference.com/search?q=discernment). These definitions imply that discernment represents a multidimensional concept of decision-making by logic and reason, by empathy gained through understanding, and by moral ethics. Although the dictionary offers some insight into the meaning of discernment from a literary standpoint, its academic quality must be considered, if the concept is to garner the attention necessary to appropriate it in contemporary organizational contexts. From an academic perspective, discernment falls within the discipline of spirituality, which *Merriam-Webster's Online Dictionary* defines as the sensitivity or attachment to religious values and the quality or state of being spiritual. Moreover, *Merriam-Webster's Online Dictionary* defines "spiritual" as affecting the spirit, as well as relating to sacred matters. Beazley (1997) defined spirituality as a faith relationship in which an individual aligns him or herself to an image of power and acts in ways that reveals trust and loyalty to this image, to survive in an uncertain world. Beazley contended that this faith relationship influences how an individual thinks, feels, and behaves, which are terms that reflect Bass' (1985) transformational leadership paradigm. Autry (2001) concurred that spirituality involves a relationship with the Transcendent; but, a distinction exists between "spirituality at work" and the "personal spirituality that comes from your relationship with the sacred, with God, with a higher power" (Autry, p. 8). For Autry, a relationship with the divine manifests itself in one's attitude, motivation, and behavior expressed in service to others. What is not clear, however, is the distinction between spirituality expressed at work and that in one's personal and everyday life. Yet, the postures presented here seem to conform to the historical, religious literature (1 Kings 3:3-14) in which the writer links spirituality, self-awareness and concern for others, self-efficacy, knowledge, and wisdom which, when applied together, results in just, right, and fair decisions.

DePree (1992) asserted that while "you cannot buy discernment; you can find it" (p. 221), a testament that suggests that discernment does not just happen, a searching takes place. DePree disclosed that the search must take place "somewhere between wisdom and judgment" (p. 221), if one must find discernment.

The nature of the Solomonic discourse causes its reader to think about certain basic elements that might be useful in understanding discernment and to persuade one to adopt similar attitudes. For example, by acknowledging that he is "only a child" and "do [es] not know how…" (1 Kings 3:7 NIV), Solomon proved to be in tune with his abilities and honest about his human limitations. This may describe an attitude of teachability, as well as the value or acts of self-awareness: humility, vulnerability, and integrity, whereby a leader acknowledges that he or she does not have all the answers. In addition, it may refer to a leader's belief in his or her ability to accomplish a task. Bandura (1997) referred to this belief in one's ability as self-efficacy. Acknowledging the present place and time, "here among the people …" (v. 8), describes sensitivity to the context in which the leader makes the decision. It is to adopt a situational approach, since no one-size fits all and, therefore, may refer to a leader's willingness to consider individuality. Further, verses 8-9 highlight the notion of stewardship and the need to enlist the help of others. The fact that Solomon declared himself God's servant and requested a skill to aid his governance is indicative of an attitude of service and of knowledge-sharing with the recognition that others, whether superiors or subordinates, may hold valuable pieces of information that may promote optimum decision-making. This type of declaration is indicative of the leader's level of emotional intelligence. It may refer to the leader's courage in asking help from others who may have a more intimate knowledge of a given situation and might further refer to the value or act of a willingness to learn, as well as a reliance on God. Still, to acknowledge the role of steward may describe the value or act of seeing the sacred in all things, the inherent spiritual truth that all things and all people belong to God, and of seeing things whole. In essence, it is to acknowledge that the leader's service is to God and that one's relationship to the divine manifests in one's relationship to his or her fellowman. This value engenders love and may describe a decision-making approach that acknowledges corporate social responsibility, expressing concern for others by considering the needs, wants, and desires of all stakeholders. Furthermore, the question, "Who is able to govern this great people of yours?" (1 Kings 3:9b), initially suggests a questioning of one's ability. The global platform and dynamics of organizational operation provide a backdrop against which to interpret the explanation for "who is able." In Proverbs 8:14, personified wisdom makes explicit what is implicit—God provides the force, the ability, the understanding, and the power that makes all things possible. This illustrates the apostle Paul's expression that he can do all things through Christ who gives him strength (cf. Philippians 4:13) and Jesus' promise to his disciples that they will receive power, when the Holy Spirit comes upon them (cf. Acts 1:8a). Black, Morrison, and Gregersen (1999) contended that leaders who are inquisitive enough to learn and understand, who engage the many differing worldviews and exhibit integrity of character, and who have a clear

sense of knowing what needs to be done and when will be able to govern successfully.

Finally, the discourse considers the motives behind Solomon's attitude and behavior and gives us a peek into that which underscores discernment. Solomon's motivation was one of morality, to be able "to distinguish between right and wrong" (1Kings 3:9). In other words, Solomon desired to know and act on the truth. In terms of leadership behavior, this may describe the value or acts of ethical and moral conduct and a willingness to stand up for what is right, regardless of the opposition or threat to one's person, a testament to high levels of integrity and character. The latter part of the discourse (vs. 10-14) informs readers that Solomon's request pleased the LORD so much so that the LORD not only gave Solomon the skill of "a wise and discerning heart," Solomon also received what he did not ask for (vs.10-14). It seems that when elements of honesty, truthfulness, humility, integrity, vulnerability, consideration of others, willingness to learn, spirituality, and ethical and moral conduct cohere, the result is discernment. If this is so, a model of discernment should reflect these elements.

Literature Review and Pool of Items

A review of the literature led to the following 40 statements about discernment (Table 1).

Qualitative Interviews with a Panel of Experts

In the initial phase, the study drew on the qualitative phenomenological tradition for data collection and analysis, characterized by open-ended interviews that aimed to capture the participants' "specific language and voices" (Creswell, 2003, p. 22) about the discernment concept through interviewing eight leaders to access their perspectives and to reveal some of the things that even direct observation cannot reveal about discernment, assuming that their perspectives were "meaningful,

Table 1. Pool of items from the literature[1]

Item Number	Item	Concept	Source
1	Before considering an action, I actively evaluate the situational conditions surrounding the issue now.	Contextual factors	Vroom and Yetton (1973)
2	I may choose a course of action from several options, but I keep other options open in case I need to change my mind.	Commitment to truth	Simon (1957)
3	I am receptive to different thoughts and perspectives.	Seek counsel	Vroom and Yetton (1973)
4	I rely on my own experiences to inform my decisions.	Self-knowledge	Vroom and Yetton (1973)
5	I am quick to tap into the insights of others.	Seek counsel	Vroom and Yetton (1973)
6	My judgment of the situation determines how I make a decision.	Judgment	Vroom and Yetton (1973)
7	My view of a situation always influences my decisions.	Contextual factors	Vroom and Yetton (1973)
8	I am quick to tap into the insights of others whenever a decision affects them.	Concern for others	Vroom and Yetton (1973)
9	I often question whether my knowledge of a situation is substantial.	Seek counsel	Kepner and Tregoe (1965)
10	I take time to assess the information available to me.	Commitment to truth	Kepner and Tregoe (1965)
11	I anticipate how my decision will affect others.	Concern for others	Vroom and Yetton (1973)
12	I filter all the information to focus only on what matters at the time.	Commitment to truth	Gladwell (2005)
13	I use quiet time (prayer, meditation, etc.) as a gateway to find meaning for my life.	Spirituality	Conlin (1999)
14	When I am in doubt, I seek answers from religious writings.	Spirituality	Conlin (1999)
15	I incorporate my religious beliefs in my professional undertakings.	Spirituality	Conlin (1999)
16	I have the mental courage to pursue the goals I set.	Courage	Csikszentmihalyi (1990)
17	I have the moral courage to pursue the goals I set.	Courage	Csikszentmihalyi (1990)
18	I seek out new ways to look at old things.	Continuous learning	Csikszentmihalyi (1990)
19	I see a future that is full of possibilities.	Visionary	Senge, et al (2005)
20	I do not give in to the feelings of frustrations.	Perseverance	Senge, et al (2005)
21	I am not afraid to take risks.	Risk-taking	Senge, et al (2005)
22	I am committed to the truth.	Integrity	Senge, et al (2005)
23	I always seek to do the right thing.	Righteousness	Senge, et al (2005)
24	I am open about my doubts and fears.	Humility	Autry (2001)
25	I consider my job a call to serve.	Service	Autry (2001)
26	I solicit information to fill the gaps I identify in my knowledge base.	Continuous learning	Csikszentmihalyi (1990)
27	I believe in the created equality of all people.	Justice	Patterson (2003)
28	I am not afraid to use tough love.	Love	Patterson (2003)
29	I let my walk mirror my talk.	Integrity	Hamel (2000)
30	I allow common sense to override policy, when it is the right thing to do.	Prudence	Hamel (2000)
31	I am willing to accept uncertainty.	Risk-taking	Hamel (2000)
32	I never arrive; I am continually becoming.	Continuous learning	Scharmer (2002)
33	I pay attention to the biases I bring to a situation.	Continuous learning	Scharmer (2002)
34	I am content to learn "on-the-fly."	Learning	Black, et. al (1999)
35	I understand my emotions.	Self-awareness	Scott (1971)
36	I can control my emotions.	Self-control	Scott (1971)

continued on following page

Table 1. Continued

Item Number	Item	Concept	Source
37	I am able to express myself to others.	Self-confidence	Scott (1971)
38	I always look for ways to develop my leadership skills.	Learning	Blenkinsopp (1995)
39	I believe honesty is the best policy.	Integrity	Whybray (1965, 1972)
40	I care about what happen to others.	Love	Berry (1995)

knowable, and able to be made explicit" (Patton, 1980, p. 196).

The intent was to explore and capture the participants' experiences as "fully and as fairly as possible" (Patton, 2002, p. 380). Therefore, the researchers captured the feelings, thoughts, and intentions of the interviewees. The researchers gained an understanding of how these leaders organize their world and the meanings they attach to what goes on in their world (Patton, 1980). The researchers used a design that combined the general interview guide, or protocol, and the standardized open-ended interview. The guide, or protocol, is a checklist that provided a framework of the issues—questions, sequence of the questions, and opportunity to make decisions about what information to explore further—before the interview began. Its purpose was to free up the interviewer to explore, probe, and ask questions to illuminate a particular subject in a conversational manner and to help ensure that the interviewer optimized the allocated time. The guide also enabled the interviewer to present a systematic, yet comprehensive approach, by delimiting the issues for discussion, but keeping the interaction focused, "allowing individual perspectives and experiences to emerge" (Patton, p. 201).

The participants comprised five men and three women; and, per the sample frame, had at least five direct reports and had been in their positions for five or more years. The time spent in a leadership role for these eight leaders spans 39 years—from 1968 to current day. The interviewees possessed a minimum of an undergraduate degree, but the majority holds, or is pursuing, post-graduate degrees. As it pertains to their ideology, just over 50% of those interviewed referred to themselves as "Christians" or "Believers"; 25% did not claim an ideology but are affiliated with institutions that strongly support a Judeo-Christian worldview; and one person neither made a claim nor gave any indication as to their worldview. Of those interviewed, 50% strongly stated how they include their ideology in their decision-making processes. They each viewed prayer and a relationship with the Divine as integral and paramount to success. All the interviewees articulated that they use some sort of a formula to guide their decision-making; although, one interviewee stated that doing so was not a conscious effort. Moreover, 50% considered their work an act of "service" or, as one leader put it, "a calling." Table 2 shows the additional ten items added to the item pool, based on the interviews.

Building the DPI Instrument

A snowball sample method resulted in a sample of 240 that represented 78.8% (189) male and 21.3% (51) female organizational leaders, with ages ranging from 26 to 73 ($M = 51.8$, $Mdn = 52.0$, and $SD = 7.5$). Regarding ethnicity, 78.8% (189) were Caucasian; 10.4% (25) Black (African-American, Caribbean etc.); 5.8% (14) were Asian/Pacific Islander; 3.8% (9) Hispanic; and 1.3% (3) represented other ethnicities. All but four of the 240 leaders (1.7%) held academic accomplishments beyond a high school level. Approximately

Table 2. Items added as a result of the interviews²

Item Number	Item
1	I allow common sense to inform my decisions.
2	I leave my mind open to change, given new information.
3	I am willing to make/have made decisions, based on a hunch.
4	I pay attention to whatever thoughts flash across my mind and whatever cues my body gives me.
5	Principles of my faith guide me.
6	My decisions reflect my values.
7	I do not let my ego get in the way of serving the greater good.
8	I am considerate of the feelings of others.
9	I am truthful.
10	I am open to learning new things.

19 (8%) of the leaders had taken some college courses but not completed a degree program; one leader held an Associate degree; and 30% (72) held Bachelor's degrees, or first degrees. Beyond that, 9.2% (22) had pursued some graduate studies but had not earned a graduate degree; 45.4% (109) held second degrees, including those of Master's and Juris Doctor; and 5.4% (13) pursued post-graduate studies and held doctoral degrees.

Demographic data regarding religious affiliation, current leadership position, primary area of leadership responsibility, and work status among the 240 leaders showed marked diversity. The data showed 5 leaders (2.1%) having a religious affiliation with Buddhism, 7 (2.9%) with Hinduism, 4 (1.7%) with Islam, 23 (9.6%) with Judaism, and 5 (2.1%) sharing no affiliation. A vast majority, 196 (81.7%), showed a religious affiliation to Christianity. Regarding their respective leadership positions, the data revealed 13.3% (32) were chief executive officers or presidents of their organizations; 42.9% (103) held senior leadership roles, such as chief officers and vice presidents; 17.5% (42) were executive directors or department directors; 1.3% (3) were pastors; 23.3% (56) were managers or leaders of leaders; and 1.7% (4) reflected other leadership positions. The data also revealed that the leaders held re-

sponsibilities in the following areas: 39.2% (94) in administration, 0.8% (2) in counseling, 0.4% in discipleship, 13.3% (32) in some aspect of human resources, 23.3% (56) in strategy development, 1.3% (3) in pastoral care, 1.3% (3) in teaching, and 20.4% (49) in other marked areas of responsibility. Further analysis of the 49 leaders showed 10.2% (5) having responsibilities in the legal arena, 32.5% (16) in the area of finance and planning, 6.1% (3) in healthcare, and 18.3% (9) in information technology. The remaining 32.9% were involved in the areas of health and beauty, marketing, sales, internal governance, media and entertainment, and security. Two leaders reported their primary area of responsibility included all the given options. The work status data revealed that 96.3% (231) held positions that were full-time paid, 1.3% (3) were part-time paid, 1.7% (4) were full-time unpaid, and 0.8% (2) were part-time unpaid. The data also revealed that the organizational affiliations of the leaders spanned both profit and non-profit organizations with 5.5% (13) in religion, 10% (24) in education, 8.3% (20) in government, 72.5% (174) in business, 2.1% (5) in non-profit organizations, and 1.3% (3) in healthcare. One respondent (0.4%) stated affiliation with "Other" organizational networks.

Further demographic data gave insight into the number of individuals who report directly to the 240 leaders, tenure of the leaders in their positions, and the total number of years each has held a leadership position. In addition, analysis of the demographic data exposes the geographic regions in which these leaders carry out their responsibilities. The data showed 57.1% (137) of the leaders having at least five but less than 11 direct reports, 27.9% (67) having somewhere between 11 and 15, 10% (24) having a range of 16 to 20, and 5% (12) having a number of direct reports in excess of 21. The study was designed to include only those leaders with five or more years in their positions; the data revealed the current job tenure, ranging from 5 to 33 years (M = 7.6, Mdn = 6.5, SD = 3.87, variance = 14.99, range = 28). The time spent in a leadership role for the 240 leaders was a minimum of 6 years (M = 18.2, Mdn = 16.0, SD = 7.8, variance = 61.0, range = 36). The geographic regions represented included 5% (12) Asia, 2.1% (5) Australia, 2.1% (5) Caribbean, 9.6% (23) Europe, 78.3% (188) North America, and 2.9% (7) South America. The demographic profile of survey participants is presented in Table 3.

Data Analysis

Data were submitted to a correlation analysis that showed significant correlations between the variables with inter-item correlation (p= .63; N=240) at the 0.01 level (1-tailed), as well as at the 0.05 level (2-tailed). Correlated variables imply that an oblique rotation solution is appropriate (Hair et. al., 1998); hence, the data were submitted to principal components analysis in an exploratory factor analysis with a direct oblimin rotation.

The results of the principal components analysis using an oblique rotation returned a component analysis showing several items cross-loading on more than one factor. The researchers removed the cross-loading items and continued to submit the remaining items to the same principal component analysis, until no cross-loading occurred.

Discernment Practices Indicator (DPI) Scale

The final version of the Discernment Practices Indicator contains 14 items that reflect three underlying dimensions of a leader's discernment. The items on the Discernment Practices Indicator,

Table 3. Demographic profile of participants

Demographics (N = 240)	Number	Percentage
Gender		
Male	189	78.8
Female	51	21.3
Ethnicity		
Caucasian	189	78.8
Black (e.g., African-American, Caribbean, etc.)	25	10.4
Asian/Pacific Islander	14	5.8
Hispanic	9	3.8
Other	3	1.3
Academic accomplishment		
High School	4	1.7
Associates degree	1	0.4
Some college; no degree	19	7.9
College degree (e.g., Bachelor's)	72	30.0
Some graduate school; no degree	22	9.2
Graduate degree (e.g., Master's, J.D.)	109	45.4
Doctorate (e.g., M.D., Ed.D., Ph.D., D.S.L.)	13	5.4

continued on following page

Table 3. Continued

Demographics (*N* = 240)	Number	Percentage
Religious affiliation		
Buddhism	5	2.1
Christianity	196	81.7
Hinduism	7	2.9
Islam	4	1.7
Judaism	23	9.6
None	5	2.1
Leadership position		
CEO/president	32	13.3
Senior leader (CFO, vice president, etc.)	103	42.9
Executive director	42	17.5
Pastor	3	1.3
Manager	56	23.3
Other	4	1.7
Primary leadership responsibility		
Administration	94	39.2
Counseling	2	0.8
Discipleship/small group ministry	1	0.4
Human resources	32	13.3
Strategy development	56	23.3
Pastoral care	3	1.3
Teaching	3	1.3
Other	49	20.4
Industry/network affiliation		
Business	174	72.5
Education	24	10.0
Government	20	8.3
Healthcare	3	1.3
Religion	13	5.5
Non-profit	5	2.1
Other	1	0.4
Work designation		
Full-time paid	231	96.3
Part-time paid	3	1.3
Full-time unpaid	4	1.7
Part-time unpaid	2	0.8
Geographic location		
Asia	12	5.0
Australia	5	2.1
Caribbean	5	2.1
Europe	23	9.6
North America (United States & Canada)	188	78.3
South America (incl. Central America)	7	2.9

with corresponding factor loadings, are presented in Table 4. Eigenvalues were 5.34, 2.16, and 1.82, respectively.

The first factor accounted for 35.6% of the variance. The eight items on this factor addressed the leader's mental and moral courage; willingness to accept uncertainty; use of common sense; ability to seek new ways to look at old things; see a future full of possibilities, believing in the equality of all people; and to be firm, but loving, in addressing issues. With "mental courage" having the highest loading (.81) on the factor, *Courage* appeared an appropriate label. Three items loaded on the second factor, which accounted for

Table 4. 3-factor DPI scale

Item	Factor		
	1	**2**	**3**
Mental courage to pursue goals.	.81		
Moral courage to pursue goals.	.75		
Seek new ways to look at old things.	.75		
See future full of possibilities.	.79		
Believe in equality of all people.	.58		
Common sense overrides policy, when it is the right thing to do.	.65		
Willing to accept uncertainty.	.67		
Be firm, but loving, in addressing issues.	.64		
Understand my emotions.		.80	
Willing to make/have made decisions on hunch.		.92	
Pay attention to thoughts and body cues.		.93	
Use quiet time (prayer, etc.) to reflect and find meaning.			.80
Incorporate religious beliefs in professional undertakings.			.88
Principles of faith guide me.			.90

14.4% of the variance. These items addressed the leader's understanding of his or her emotions; willingness to make decisions, based on a hunch; as well as paying attention to body cues or thoughts that may flash across the mind. The item that focused on "paying attention to body cues and thoughts that flash across the mind" had the highest loading (.93) on the second factor; thus, to label it *Intuition* seemed appropriate. The third factor, also with three items, accounted for 12.2% of the variance. The three items addressed the leader's use of quiet time (to include prayer and meditation) to reflect and find meaning, use of principles of faith as guidance, as well as incorporating religious beliefs in professional undertakings. The item that focused on the use of faith principles as guide had the highest loading (.90) on the factor. As such, *Faith* seemed an appropriate label.

RELIABILITY

Reliability analysis (Cronbach's alpha) for Factor 1, Courage, with eight items, returned a score of .85, with no improvement if items were deleted. An alpha value in the high .80s is an acceptable bound for a scale designed for individual diagnostic (DeVellis, 2003; Nunnally, 1978). Factor 2, Intuition, with three items, returned a score of .89, and Factor 3, Faith, with three items, returned a score of .85. Removing the item, "I use quiet time to reflect and find meaning," from the Faith factor would have raised its alpha to .89. However, removing the item would result in a 2-item factor, generally considered "weak and unstable" (Costello & Osborne, 2005, p. 5) and would necessitate ignoring the factor in further analysis. The scale mean was 105.26 with a standard deviation of 13.66. Means and standard deviation for the sub-scales are presented in Table 5.

Table 5. Sub-scales' means and standard deviations

Sub-scale	*M*	*SD*	Variance	*N* of Variables
Courage	68.25	5.64	31.76	8
Intuition	16.51	7.17	51.36	3
Faith	20.50	5.46	29.87	3

Validity

The three factors show face validity and content validity with the literature review data. No additional validation studies have been done to date.

RESULTS

The participant, who completes the online instrument, receives a summary report stating the percent of possible score on each of the three factors and a brief description of each factor, as shown in Figure 1.

COMMENTARY

The significant findings associated with the 14 variables of the DPI scale are important for scholars, researchers, and practitioners alike. For scholars and researchers, especially those studying the decision-making of leaders and organizations, as well as those studying the role of spirituality on leader behavior, the significant findings provide strong statistical support for affirming that discernment has expression within the lives of contemporary organizations. Today, the scientific literature is void of information for the role of discernment in contemporary organizational life. While the concept first spoke to a

Figure 1. Result's screen after completing the online DPI

Discernment Practices Indicator

Of the three factors of the DPI you scored:

XX% of the maximum possible for Courage

The eight items (items 2, 3, 5, 6, 8, 9, 11, and 12) address the leader's mental and moral courage; willingness to accept uncertainty; use of common sense; as well as ability to seek new ways to look at old things; see a future full of possibilities, believing in the equality of all people; and to be firm, but loving, in addressing issues.

XX% of the maximum possible for Intuition

The three items (items 7, 10, and 13) address the leader's understanding of his or her emotions; willingness to make decisions, based on a hunch; as well as paying attention to body cues, or thoughts that may flash across the mind.

XX% of the maximum possible for Faith

The three items (items 1, 4, and 14) address the leader's use of quiet time (to include prayer and meditation) to reflect and find meaning; use of principles of faith as guidance; as well as incorporating religious beliefs in professional undertakings.

For the research/statistical folk:

The three factors of Courage, Intuition, and Faith have Eigenvalues of 5.34, 2.16, and 1.82 respectfully. In addition the three factors of Courage, Intuition, and Faith have Cronbach Alpha scores of .86, .89, and .84, respectively.

first century society, as rendered in the Hebrew Book of Proverbs, this empirical study translated the scriptural text for contemporary application and demonstrated that discernment has value in contemporary leadership and organizational praxis and is, therefore, worthy of scholarly investigation. This study contributes to the on-going challenge of applying scriptural texts in contemporary performance contexts. Researchers can utilize this study as a base upon which to conduct further investigations about phenomenon. Furthermore, the research utilized the "still-evolving" blended approach of mixed methods research, which was ideal for a study about a phenomenon that, in true form, has ideological underpinnings; is open to exploration from multiple worldviews; and is an impetus for creating a bridge between systematic, objective opinions and the intuitive, subjective judgments. The study used both qualitative and quantitative data collection and analysis to explore the existence of discernment and presented the findings as a blend. Therefore, this study advances the mixed methods research design.

For practitioners, the DPI addressed the issue of instrumentation concerning determining or assessing the presence of discernment in leader behavior. This study focused, in part, on a psychometric evaluation of survey items, based upon the theoretical insights regarding decision-making strategies (Gladwell, 2005; Kepner & Tregoe, 1965; Simon, 1957; Vroom & Yetton, 1973) and spirituality and effective leadership (Autry, 2001; Beazley, 1997; Conlin, 1999; Csikszentmihalyi, 1990; Senge, 1990; Hartsfield, 2003; Klenke, 2003; Patterson, 2003; Winston, 2002). The results of this study are promising; the outcome is an instrument comprised of a tailored questionnaire that measures attitudes, motivations, and behaviors that directly affect the performance of individuals.

Cost

The DPI is free and available for anyone to use it.

Location

The DPI may be found at the following URL: http://www.regent.edu/acad/global/discernment/home.cfm

REFERENCES

Allen, V. L., & Klenke, K. (2009). Failed moral decision making in high-profile leaders: A social cognitive study of William Jefferson Clinton's political leadership. *International Leadership Journal, 2*(1), 5–26.

Autry, J. A. (2001). *The servant leader: How to build a creative team, develop great morale, and improve bottom-line performance.* New York, NY: Three Rivers Press.

Bandura, A. (1997). *Self-efficacy: The exercise of control.* New York, NY: W.H. Freeman and Company.

Bass, B. M. (1985). *Leadership and performance beyond expectations.* New York, NY: Free Press.

Bass, B. M. (1990). *Bass and Stogdill's handbook of leadership.* New York, NY: Free Press.

Beazley, H. (1997). *Meaning and measurement of spirituality in organizational settings: development of a spirituality assessment scale.* (Dissertations and Theses database AAT 9820619)

Berry, D. K. (1995). *An introduction to wisdom and poetry of the Old Testament.* Nashville, TN: Broadman & Holman Publishers.

Black, J. S., Morrison, A. J., & Gregersen, H. B. (1999). *Global explorers: The next generation of leaders.* New York, NY: Routledge.

Blenkinsopp, J. (1995). *Wisdom and law in the Old Testament: The ordering of life in Israel and early Judaism* (Revised ed.). New York, NY: Oxford University Press. doi:10.1093/acprof:oso/9780198755036.001.0001

Colvin, G. (2003, October 27). Corporate crooks are not all created equal. *Fortune*, 64.

Conlin, M. (1999, November 1). Religion in the workplace: The growing presence of spirituality in corporate America. *Business Week*, 150-161.

Costello, A. B., & Osborne, J. W. (2005). Best practices in exploratory factor analysis: Four recommendations for getting the most from your analysis. *Practical Assessment, Research & Evaluation, 10*(7). Retrieved on November 14, 2007 from http://pareonline.net/pdf/v10n7.pdf

Creswell, J. W. (2003). *Research design: Qualitative, quantitative, and mixed methods approaches* (2nd ed.). Thousand Oaks, CA: Sage Publications, Inc.

Csikszentmihaly, M. (1990). *Flow: The psychology of optimal experience* (1st ed.). New York, NY: HarperCollins Publishers.

DePree, M. (1992). *Leadership jazz*. New York, NY: Doubleday.

DeVellis, R. F. (2003). *Scale development: Theory and applications*. Thousand Oaks, CA: Sage Publications, Inc.

Gladwell, M. (2005). *Blink: The power of thinking without thinking*. New York, NY: Little, Brown and Company.

Hair, J. F. Jr, Anderson, R. E., Tatham, R. L., & Black, W. C. (1998). *Multivariate data analysis* (5th ed.). Upper Saddle River, NJ: Prentice Hall International.

Hamel, G. (2000). *Leading the revolution*. Boston, MA: Harvard Business School Press.

Hartsfield, M. (2003). *The internal dynamics of transformational leadership: Effects of spirituality, emotional intelligence, and self-efficacy*. (Dissertations and Theses database, AAT 3090425).

Janis, I. L. (1989). *Crucial decisions: Leadership in policymaking and crisis management*. New York, NY: The Free Press.

Kepner, C. H., & Tregoe, B. B. (1965). *The rational manager: A systematic approach to problem-solving and decision-making*. New York, NY: McGraw-Hill.

Klenke, K. (2003). The "S" factor in leadership education, practice, and research. *Journal of Education for Business*, *79*(1), 56–60. doi:10.1080/08832320309599089

Mehta, S. (2003, October 27). MCI: Is being good good enough? *Fortune*, 117–124.

Morgan, G. (1997). *Images of organization* (2nd ed.). Thousand Oaks, CA: Sage Publications, Inc.

Nunnally, J. (1978). *Psychometric theory* (2nd ed.). New York, NY: McGraw-Hill.

Patterson, K. A. (2003). *Servant leadership: A theoretical model*. Dissertation, School of Leadership Studies, Regent University, Virginia Beach, VA. (Dissertation Abstracts International, UMI No. 3082719).

Patton, M. Q. (1980). *Qualitative evaluation methods*. Beverly Hills, CA: Sage Publications, Inc.

Patton, M. Q. (2002). *Qualitative research & evaluation methods* (3rd ed.). Thousand Oaks, CA: Sage Publications, Inc.

Plaut, W. G. (1961). *The Book of Proverbs: A commentary*. New York, NY: Union of American Hebrew Congregations.

Rost, J. C. (1991). *Leadership for the twenty-first century*. New York, NY: Praeger Publishers.

Scharmer, C. O. (2002). *Presencing: Illuminating the blind spot of leadership* (working title). Retrieved on June 7, 2004 from www.dialogonleadership.org

Scott, R. B. (1971). *The way of wisdom in the Old Testament.* New York, NY: Macmillan Publishing Co., Inc.

Senge, P., Scharmer, C. O., Jaworski, J., & Flowers, B. S. (2005). *Presence: An exploration of profound change in people, organizations, and society.* New York, NY: Currency, Doubleday.

Simon, H. A. (1955). A behavioral model of rational choice: Cowles Foundation Paper 98. *The Quarterly Journal of Economics, 69,* 99–118. doi:10.2307/1884852

Simon, H. A. (1957). *Administrative behavior: A study of decision making processes in administrative organizations* (2nd ed.). New York, NY: Free Press.

Traüffer, H. (2008). *Towards an understanding of discernment: A twenty-first century model of decision-making.* (Dissertations and Theses database AAT 3325539).

Vroom, V. H., & Yetton, P. W. (1973). *Leadership and decision-making.* Pittsburg, PA: University of Pittsburg Press.

Wheatley, M. (1999). *Leadership and the new science: Discovering order in a chaotic world.* San Francisco, CA: Berrett-Koehler Publishers, Inc.

Whybray, R. N. (1965). *Wisdom in Proverbs.* London, UK: SCM Press Ltd.

Whybray, R. N. (1972). *The book of Proverbs: The Cambridge Bible commentary.* New York, NY: Cambridge University Press.

Winston, B. E. (2002). *Be a leader for God's sake: From values to behaviors.* Virginia Beach, VA: School of Leadership Studies, Regent University.

KEY TERMS AND DEFINITIONS

Blinking: The art of *blinking* by which a leader knows what to do.

Courage: Willingness to act on convictions.

Decision-Making: The process through which an individual determines what action to take or whether to make a conscious effort to take no action.

Discernment: The acquisition and application of knowledge to make decisions that are right, fair, and just.

Faith: Use of quiet time (to include prayer and meditation) to reflect and find meaning.

Intuition: Paying attention to body cues and thoughts that flash across the mind.

Qualitative Phenomenological Tradition for Data Collection and Analysis: This methodology is characterized by open-ended interviews that aimed to capture the participants' "specific language and voices" (Creswell, 2003, p. 22) about the discernment concept and to reveal some of the things that even direct observation cannot reveal about discernment.

ENDNOTE

[1] For a more detailed literature review please see "Towards an Understanding of Discernment: A Twenty-First Century Model of Decision-Making" (Doctoral dissertation Regent University, 2008) by H. Traüffer, 2008, *ProQuest Dissertations Abstracts International-A, 69* (08). (Publication No. AAT 3325539)

Chapter 16
The Inventory of Learner Persistence

M. Gail Derrick
Regent University, USA

ABSTRACT

The Inventory of Learner Persistence (ILP) was designed to assess persistence in learning and specifically within the context of autonomous learning. Autonomous learning is defined as the manifestation of persistence along with desire, resourcefulness, and initiative in learning; learner autonomy is defined as the characteristic or personal attribute of the individual to exhibit agency or intentional behavior. Thus, persistence in learning is the exhibition of volition, goal directedness and self-regulation. The development of items for the ILP provides a theoretical framework for defining persistence from a cognitive and psychological perspective and provides a mechanism for understanding persistence from other than a post hoc behavioral standpoint. The implications of such assessments can provide an analysis of where a learner may be in terms of their development and readiness for learning that will require persistent skills for success.

INTRODUCTION

Much of the research into persistence in learning has been viewed as an outcome or result such as the completion of a program or degree. In education, particularly in higher education, persistence rates are reported in terms of graduation attainment and program completion. As an outcome measure of student success, persistence for degree completion provides useful data for the evaluation of programs. In this type of analysis, persistence is seen as the end result and does not provide any understanding into the individual differences or any understanding of why an in-

DOI: 10.4018/978-1-4666-2172-5.ch016

dividual has the ability, capacity, drive, or will to complete a learning endeavor as encompassing as a degree program or as specific as a course. These types of descriptors are usually described in the psychological literature and while their importance is understood, little research had been done to quantify and articulate exactly what the behaviors are and how they are manifested. This aspect of persistence resides in the cognitive and psychological behaviors of an individual that are manifested in persistent-like behaviors. This dimension requires some understanding of what the individual is cognitively doing prior to the demonstration of the persistent behaviors. It would be expected that the display of any intentional behaviors would require some cognitive processing. After all, one does not arbitrarily react or respond; we are thinking organisms and have the capacity to deliberately select and chose a course of action. Thus, before one can exhibit any behavioral control one must be able to cognitively exhibit control in thinking processes. Intentional and deliberate behavior requires forethought, planning, assessment of capability and resources both internal and external. Thus, understanding persistence in learning is grounded in intentions, beliefs, and attitudes to persist in learning.

The Inventory of Learner Persistence (ILP) was designed to assess persistence in learning and specifically within the context of autonomous learning. Autonomous learning has been defined as the manifestation of persistence along with desire, resourcefulness, and initiative in learning; and, learner autonomy is the characteristic of the individual to exhibit agency –that is intentional behaviors.

The research and subsequent development of the ILP provides a conceptual model and theoretical foundation for understanding the behaviors associated with intentions to exhibit persistence in adult learners. Intentions are grounded in the research of Fishbein and Ajzen (1975) and Ajzen (1985, 1988, 1991). Ajzen asserts that an intention is an indication of an individual's attitude toward the behavior, social pressure (subjective norm) and control (perceived behavioral control). By changing or influencing any one of the three facets, the likelihood of increasing the intention to perform the actual behavior will likely increase the chance of the actual behavior being performed. The Theory of Planned Behavior (TPB; Ajzen, 1988, 1991) proposes a model about how human action is guided in that intentions are the precursors of behavior. The ILP is not concerned therefore with the actual behaviors in as much as the intention to perform the behavior; in this instance, persistence in learning.

The behaviors identified as important to persistence in autonomous learning are: volition, self-regulation, and goal-directedness. Much of the persistence in learning literature and research has focused on quantitative outcomes such as retention and attrition in programs. However, the ILP is concerned with the level of intentions that an individual manifests prior to the actual performance of the behavior. From this perspective, the ILP serves as both a model and measurement of the cognitive and motivational aspects associated with persistence in learning. This model provided the theoretical foundation for the development of a self-assessment instrument, the Inventory of Learner Persistence, which identified and quantified an individual's intention to persist in autonomous endeavors. The construct of persistence in autonomous learning is presented in terms of attitudes to engage in specific learning behaviors, but measured in terms of behavioral intentions.

A distinction is to be noted with respect to the term self-directed and autonomous. While the terms are used interchangeably, self-directed learning implies a behavior while autonomous learning implies intentions to exhibit a behavior such as persistence in learning. The intention and behavior correlation is a robust relationship since we do form intentions for behaviors that we do not plan to do nor do we exhibit deliberate behaviors for which there was no intention.

The Inventory of Learner Persistence evaluates specific behavioral attributes that can be measured and used to assess an individual's intention to persist in autonomous learning. Construct, face, and content validity were assessed in addition to reliability via Cronbach's alpha measure of internal consistency and a test-retest reliability study. Principal component factor analysis was used to assess the three-factor construct. Based upon the results, the constellation of items assessed provides a valid and reliable measure of the intention to persist in autonomous learning.

Background

The early research in lifelong learning examined the external conditions and settings under which the learning occurred. During the 1960's, research focused on how and why adults engage in learning activities. Houle (1961) prepared a series of lectures on what kinds of men and women retain alert and inquiring minds throughout their lifespan. He classified learners into three subgroups; goal-oriented--those that were engaged in the learning due to an external requirement or need; activity-oriented--those that were engaged in the learning because of the social aspects associated with the endeavor; and learning-oriented--those that were curious and enjoyed learning. This work was followed by a nationwide study, undertaken by Johnstone and Rivera (1965), who determined that "self-learning" activities comprised a major part of the learning that was being undertaken by adults in the United States.

Tough (1979) built on Houle's earlier work by focusing on the behavior of adults while planning their learning projects. He found that 20 percent of adult learning was planned and organized by someone other than the learner, while 80 percent was self-planned and self-guided. Tough's research became the basis for numerous studies that verified the existence of self-learning, and exposed the prevalence and pervasiveness of self-planned and executed learning activities.

Houle (1961) writes, "Effort to explore the reasons why some people become continuing learners has made it clear that there is no simple answer to this complex question. Each person is unique and his [or her] actions spring from a highly individualized and complex interaction of personal and social factors" (p. 80). According to Houle (1961) behind any decision to learn something new lies a complex network of motives, interests, and values, and behind them, yet another layer of complex inter-linked factors; "a cataract of consequences" (p. 29). If the goal is to produce lifelong learners, then we must provide opportunities that foster autonomous learning endeavors—that is, facilitate the development of resourcefulness, initiative, and persistence in any learning, formal or other learning. We learn due to a gap of where we are and where we want to be. The key is to make the learning the intrinsic motivator despite external requirements or conditions.

SELF-DIRECTED AND AUTONOMOUS LEARNING

Guglielmino (1978) conducted a Delphi survey of experts in the field of self-directed learning to ascertain the characteristics of a self-directed learner. The results of the survey found that " A highly self-directed learner, is one who exhibits initiative, independence, and persistence in learning; one who accepts responsibility for his or her own learning and views problems as challenges, not obstacles; one who is capable of self-discipline and has a high degree of curiosity; one who has a strong desire to learn or change and is self-confident; one who is able to use basic study skills, organize his or her time and set an appropriate pace for learning, and to develop a plan for completing work; one who enjoys learning and has a tendency to be goal-oriented" (p. 93). Guglielmino's work has become the cornerstone and foundation of much of the research into self-directed learning and she continues to be a leader in the field.

Confessore (1992) extended Guglielmino's work and established that notion that "self-directed [autonomous] learning manifests itself in people who feel a need to learn something" (p. 3) and that success is ultimately dependent upon the individual's personal desire, initiative, resourcefulness, and persistence. Further research was conducted to develop and validate an instrument to not only explain the construct of persistence but also to measure the individual factors from a cognitive perspective.

Autonomous learning refers to the conative manifestations of desire in learning while learner autonomy refers to the behavioral manifestation of resourcefulness, initiative, and persistence in learning. The term "conative" is used with aspects of autonomous learning because "conation refers to behavioral intentions" (Fishbein & Ajzen, 1975, p. 12) and subsequent intentional action.

Persistence in Autonomous Learning

The behavior of persistence in learning was explained by Skager (1979) who stated that the "essential feature of [autonomous learners'] behavior is a willingness to initiate and maintain systematic learning on their own" (p. 519). Initiative does not imply the capacity to maintain motivation or to sustain goal-oriented activity in the face of frustration, competing goals, or obstacles. It is the sustained maintenance of persistent behavior that enables the individual to attain the goal. The study of the behaviors associated with persistence is critical to the understanding of why some individuals are successful and why other individuals are not successful in their learning endeavors.

According to Schunk and Zimmerman (1994) "educators have moved away from explanations of learning and performance that stress learner's abilities and responses to environmental stimuli …to concern with student's attempts to manage their achievement efforts through activities that influence the instigation, direction and persistence of those efforts" (p.ix). Persistence in a learning

activity is encouraged by a sense of progress in closing the gap between current and desired competence and in redefining and sometimes extending the reference point of desired competence. Scholars and practitioners agree that commitment and, in particular, its behavioral concomitant of persistence as a course of action--is desirable in work organizations (Sandelands, Brockner, & Glynn, 1988).

The construct of persistence in learning has foundations in behavioral intentions (Fishbein & Ajzen, 1975), goal theory (Bandura, 1997, 1986; Heckhausen & Kuhl, 1985; volition (Corno, 1989, 1993, 1994; Heckhausen & Kuhl, 1985) and self-regulation (Corno, 1989, 1993, 1994; Schunk & Zimmerman, 1994; Garcia & Pintrich, 1994). Volition is the mediating force between intentions to learn and the behaviors [the strength of the desire or reason for and against acting upon that desire] to learn. Persistence in a learning endeavor is predicated upon the volitional control that enables the individual to self-regulate the behavior necessary for success in an autonomous learning situation. The volitional behavior enables the individual to sustain the effort and perseverance necessary to remain focused on the achievement of a goal, despite obstacles, distractions, and competing goals. The factors associated with persistence in autonomous learning are volition, self-regulation, and goal-maintenance.

Volition is the strength of the desire or reason for and against acting upon the desire to learn. Volitional control is the commitment to a goal and is attained by the regulation of self. Self-regulation of those enduring behaviors necessary for goal attainment is contingent upon volition. The strength of the desire for acting in a particular way influence the level of volition required to self-regulate the behavior. Individuals persist with learning that is challenging through regulation of cognitive and behavioral processes. Volitional control is commitment to a goal and attained by the regulation of the self. Self-regulation of those enduring behaviors necessary for goal attainment is contingent upon volition. The strength of the desire for acting in a particular way influences the level of volition required to self-regulate the behavior. In other words, persistence in a learning endeavor is the volitional behavior that enables the individual to sustain the effort and perseverance necessary to remain focused on the achievement of a goal, despite obstacles, distractions and competing goals.

Item Development

Self-assessment items for the Inventory of Learner Persistence were developed within each of the three persistent-related behaviors of volition, self-regulation, and goal-directness. Each of the behaviors associated with persistence in autonomous learning has specific characteristics associated with that behavior. The characteristic behaviors of persistence in autonomous learning endeavors are identified through research that identifies persistence as a behavior syndrome described by the presence of the co-occurring behaviors of volition, self-regulation, and goal-directedness.

The field of self-directed learning has been plagued by lack of a clear definition, and conflicting conceptualizations (Oddi, 1987). According to Oddi (1987) and Merriam and Cafarella (1999), self-directed learning research can be characterized into two perspectives: a process or a personality characteristic. The process perspective of self-directed learning is focused on the activities that the learner engages in such as planning, goal setting, assessing progress, and acquiring resources (Knowles, 1975; Oddi, 1987). For example, Knowles (1980) states:

Learning is described psychologically as a process of need meeting and goal-striving by the learners. This is to say, individuals are motivated to engage in learning to the extent that they feel a need to learn and perceive a personal goal that learning will help to achieve; and they will invest their energy in making use of available resources (including teachers and readings) to the extent that they perceive them as being relevant to their needs and goals. (p. 56)

The psychological perspective focuses on the mental, cognitive, and attitudinal characteristics of the learner necessary for learning to occur. Aspects of this dimension include the learner identifying the needs that serve as motivational factors for learning goals and the learner's personal attributes or characteristics. Long (1989) asserts that a model for thinking about self-directed learning without the psychological and cognitive domain is focused on teaching, not learning. He goes on to say that learning is not restricted to a narrow process of acquiring knowledge; rather, it is concerned with motivation and personal growth in the cognitive, affective, ethical and aesthetic domains.

Long (1989) states:

The psychological conceptualization implies that fundamentally learning is self-initiated, self-directed, and self-regulated cognitive process whereby the learner can choose to ignore instruction, to merely absorb it by causal attention, to carefully memorize without critical reflection, or to seek to change or create an understanding information (p. 9).

An examination of factors that contribute to successful learning and independent learning is more than pure cognitive ability. Learning is a complex and multifaceted process in which many components contribute to the achievement of learning goals. Understanding those cognitive and motivational aspects associated with persistence will add to the understanding and research.

INVENTORY OF LEARNER PERSISTENCE SELF-ASSESSMENT ITEMS

Volilion (16 Questions)

Questions 1, 14, 2, and 10 on the ILP

Volition is the tendency to maintain focus and effort towards goals despite potential distractions, obstacles, or competing goals. Volition promotes the intent to learn, and protects that commitment from competing goals and distractions by controlling the individual's effort and environment (e.g. Corno, 1993; Kuhl, 1985). In everyday language, the term denotes "willfulness or dogged perseverance in pursuit of difficult goals" (Corno, 1994, p. 229).

Q1: I will remain committed to my learning goal although there are obstacles.
Q14: I will work towards my learning goal despite distractions.
Q2: I will maintain my determination to accomplish difficult learning goals.
Q10: I will persist with my primary learning goal although I have other learning goals to achieve.

Questions 3 and 4 on the ILP

The predictive validity of volition found that "productive follow-through" is an essential factor for college success (e.g. Willingham, 1985). Productive follow-through is defined as "a pattern of persistent and successful striving over time" (Corno, 1994, p. 235).

Q3: I will exert whatever effort is necessary over an extended time if I intend to learn something.
Q4: I will consistently work towards achievement of my learning goal no matter how long it may take to accomplish that goal.

Questions 27 and 6 on the ILP

Action control theorists Heckhausen and Kuhl (1985) define volition as a psychological state characterized by thoughts about the implementation of goals into action.

Q27: I will think of creative ways to achieve my learning goal.
Q6: I will devise a plan to achieve my learning goal.

Questions 7, 8, 12, 13, 9, and 11 on the ILP

Heckhausen and Kuhl's (1985) theory of volition emphasizes the use of available resources, whatever the sources. Effort is defined as trying to enlist all resources in the pursuit of a goal. Corno (1994) asserts that volition involves internal goal-maintenance--noticing the erosion of effort and "nipping it in the bud" (p.232).

Q7: I will seek out resources when I am intent upon achieving a learning goal.
Q8: I will not let a temporary lack of effort towards achieving my learning goal become permanent.
Q12: I will put little effort into the accomplishment of a learning goal. [Reverse-Code]
Q13: I will use all of the internal resources that are available to me in order to accomplish my learning goal.
Q9: I will monitor my other activities in order to remain focused on my learning goal.
Q11: I will use all of the external resources that are available to me to accomplish a learning goal.

Questions 15 and 16 on the ILP

According to Corno (1994), volition picks up where motivation leaves off. Motivation denotes commitment, and volition denotes follow-through.

Task motivation, the effort required to stay on task and persist, is allied with volition. Volition is defined as maintaining intentional effort and diligence, which influence persistence and task performance (e.g. Corno, 1994; Pintrich & DeGroot, 1990). Corno (1993) asserts that volition is an essential aptitude for educational success. Its function is meta-motivational in directing and sustaining effort toward learning goals.

Q15: I will remain intent on achieving my learning goal although the value of the learning goal has decreased.

Q16: I will maintain the effort needed to accomplish additional tasks related to my learning goal.

Self-Regulation (16 Questions)

Questions 17, 28, and 18 on the ILP

Self-regulation is viewed as the integration of "skill" and "will" (Garcia & Pintrich, 1994). Skill is viewed as the use of various learning strategies (e.g. rehearsal and elaboration, planning and monitoring). Will refers to the motivation and goals for learning. This juxtaposition of self with cognitive, metacognitive, and volitional control strategies is the essence of self-regulation. Action control theorists assert that when individuals move from planning and goal setting to the implementation of plans, goals tend to be protected and fostered by self-regulatory activity rather than reconsidered or changed (Heckhausen & Kuhl, 1985; Corno, 1994). According to self-regulation theory, students who can control their cognition, motivation and volition can influence their independent learning (Garcia & Pintrich, 1994). Corno (1989) states that wanting to self-regulate one's learning is not enough; one must be able to protect his/her primary intention from distracting or competing intentions.

Q17: I will let other activities interfere with the accomplishment of my learning goal. [Reverse-Code]

Q28: I will postpone doing activities that are more interesting in order to accomplish my learning goal.

Q18: I will keep my learning goal my top priority although I may have other important things to do.

Questions 19, 20, and 21 on the ILP

According to Huitt (1997), self-regulation is: a style of engaging with tasks in which [individuals] exercise a suite of powerful skills: setting goals for upgrading knowledge, deliberating about strategies to select those that balance progress towards goals against unwanted costs, and as steps are taken and the task evolves, monitoring the accumulating effects of their engagement. As these events unfold seriatim, obstacles may be encountered. It may become necessary for self-regulating people to adjust or even abandon initial goals, to manage motivation and to adapt and occasionally invent tactics for making progress (p. 245).

Q19: I will assess my progress towards my learning goal by determining the value of the learning.

Q20: I will change my original learning goal if I am not making suitable progress.

Q21: I will be flexible when assessing how to achieve my learning goal.

Question 24, 25, 26, 23, and 29 on the ILP

Self-regulation refers to the self-generated thoughts, feelings, and actions, which are systematically oriented toward attainment of a goal. Self-regulation refers to the degree that individuals are metacognitively, motivationally, and behaviorally active participants in their own learning; the individual's ability to understand and control their learning (Schunk & Zimmerman, 1994; Winne, 1995; Zimmerman, 1994). According to Butler and Winne (1995) effective learners are self-regulating; a style of engaging in tasks such as goal setting, deliberation in the strategies to select, monitoring the effects of their engagement. Individuals, who can self-regulate, adjust or even abandon initial goals if obstacles are encountered, manage motivation to adapt and invent tactics for making progress.

Self-regulated learners are aware of the qualities of their own knowledge, beliefs, motivation and cognitive processing. This provides grounds on which the students judge how well unfolding cognitive engagement matches the standards they set for successful learning (e.g. Corno, 1993; Zimmerman, 1994).Schunk and Zimmerman (1994) have shown that characteristics of self-regulated learners include behaviors such as "extraordinary persistence on learning tasks, confident, strategic, resourceful in overcoming problems, and display continued effort" (p. 5).

Q24: I will maintain my desire to learn.

Q25: I will remain confident in my abilities to achieve my learning goal although my progress is slow.

Q26: I will do fun activities rather than find time for my learning. [Reverse-Code]

Q23: I will manage my time to achieve my learning goal when I have other deadlines.

Q29: I will lose focus on my learning goal when pressured to achieve other goals. [Reverse-Code]

Questions 22 and 38 on the ILP

McCombs (1997) views the self-determining aspect at the center of understanding why some students want to self-regulate their own learning and others do not. She views the motivation to learn as a function of a personal assessment of the meaningfulness of particular learning experiences or activities and the process of self-initiating,

determining, choosing and controlling learning goals, processes, and outcomes. The major condition necessary for self-regulation is choice and control. Zimmerman (1994) asserts that regulation of thinking and processes by the self are achieved by choice and control over the learning situation.

Q22: I will choose when I want to learn.

Q38: I will have little control over what I want to learn. [Reverse-Code]

Questions 30 and 31 on the ILP

Self-regulation is constituted as a series of volitional episodes (Kuhl & Goschke, 1994). As self-regulated learners engage in learning tasks, they draw on knowledge and beliefs to construct an interpretation of a task's properties and requirements. Based on that interpretation they construct a goal. Goals are approached by applying tactics and strategies that generate products that are both mental and behavioral. By monitoring these processes of engagement, internal feedback is created. The individual may reinterpret and redirect future engagement (set new goals) or adjust (select strategies that are more appropriate, skills or procedures). This may alter the knowledge and beliefs and influence future self-regulation.

Q30: I will control my learning efforts by controlling my life activities.

Q31: I will be successful in my learning endeavors because I assess my progress.

Question 32 on the ILP

It appears that self-regulative strategies predict academic performance better than cognitive strategies (Pintrich & DeGroot, 1990; Schunk & Zimmerman, 1994). As students achieve a high level of mastery, cognitive functioning becomes automated. Additionally, it appears that accuracy of one's self-monitoring directly influences one's capability to self-regulate performance outcomes (Schunk & Zimmerman, 1994).

Motivation to self-regulate learning is also related to attribution processes. Feedback provides information that improvement is contingent upon perseverance. Knowing that can instill confidence for success and motivation to persist (Borkowski & Thorpe, 1994). Effective self-regulation requires that one have goals and the motivation to attain them (Bandura, 1986; Schunk, 1991; Zimmerman, 1994 ;).

Q32: I will be successful in my learning endeavors because success is important to me.

Goal Directedness (20 Questions)

Questions 34, 35, 5, and 36 on the ILP

Proximal goals result in greater motivation than distal goals because it is easier to determine progress, and the perception of progress raises self-efficacy. Goal-setting literature has shown that distant goals have less effect on performance than do goals that are more proximal. Short-term performance goals focus on the process needed for successful behavior and enhances performance (Harackiewicz, Abrahams, & Wagerman, 1987). The successful attainment of a proximal goal may lead a subject to experience a sense of success, to revise beliefs about self-efficacy, and to develop intrinsic interest in instrumental activities that will serve to accomplish additional proximal goals, and will in turn increase the likelihood of accomplishment of an ultimate goal (Brody, 1983). Self-efficacy is validated as progress is made toward the goal. Anticipated consequences of behavior rather than the consequences themselves boost motivation (Bandura, 1986).

Bandura's (1986) view of self-judgement implies the comparison of present performance with one's goal. Self-judgement is affected by the importance of goal attainment. Comparing one's performance indicated information about goal progress. Goal properties include specificity, proximity, and level of difficulty (e.g. Bandura, 1986; Schunk & Zimmerman. 1994).

Q34: I will set a very specific learning goal to achieve.

Q35: I will set learning goals that are not very difficult. [Reverse-code]

Q5: I will measure progress towards achieving my learning goal in small increments.

Q36: I will keep focused on the final learning goal although I have other learning goals to accomplish.

Questions 33 and 37 on the ILP

The autonomy of personal goals predicts goal attainment (e.g. Sheldon & Elliot, 1997). Goals that are undertaken with a full sense of willingness and choice are better attained than goals compelled by internal or external forces or pressures.

Q33: I will work much harder to accomplish learning goals that I determine for myself.

Q37: I will feel pressured to learn something if I am in control of the learning. [Reverse-Code]

Question 40 on the ILP

Elliott and Dweck (1988) and Ames (1992) support the notion that goals guide thinking, feeling and behavior. These two studies document two primary goal-orientations in learning environments; mastery goals (process, learning, or task-involvement goals) and performance goals (ego-involvement goals).

The focus of the individual with mastery goals is an understanding the work environment and on improving levels of competence. The attribution of success is the internal attribute of the amount of personal effort expended. An individual with performance goals will focus on determining one's ability or self-worth. The attribution of success is either the internal attribute of ability or the external attributes of luck or task difficulty. In a learning situation, learners with mastery goals are more likely to focus on developing competence while learners with performance goals are more likely to focus either on the end result in terms of grade or other external standards of success or on not embarrassing oneself because of failure.

Q40: I will learn because I value learning.

Question 41 on the ILP

Orientation towards different types of goals is based on perceived ability perceptions. Individuals who develop and maintain persistent perceptions of their abilities report higher performance expectations, greater control over learning, and greater interest on learning for intrinsic reasons. (e.g. Covington, 1992; Eccles et al., 1983; Harter & Connell, 1984).

Q41: I will learn only when I need to learn.

Question 42 on the ILP

Individuals are more likely to have a learning orientation when they believe they can improve ability by investing more effort (e.g. Dweck & Bempechet, 1983; Dweck & Leggett, 1988; Nicholls & Miller, 1984). Dweck and Elliot (1983) report that individuals who have this incremental conception of ability prefer tasks that are hard, new and challenging; for these individuals, feelings of competence are maximized by high effort.

Q42: I will measure progress towards my learning goal by assessing new skills that I learn.

Question 43 and 44 on the ILP

Individuals faced with extensive task usually break them down in to manageable segments (e.g. Heads, 1989; Batterill, 1977; Syer & Connolly, 1984; Wiggers, Anderson, Whitaker & Harmon, 1980).

Q43: I will form a long-term plan for a learning goal by establishing short -term goals.
Q44: I will learn because I expect to learn.

Questions 45 and 46 on the ILP

There are remarkable examples of students who have achieved success despite overwhelming obstacles and barriers. The ongoing and salient feature of these successful students was their commitment to succeed and their strong sense of personal self-efficacy to achieve their goal (Schunk & Zimmerman, 1994). Personal attributes of time management, practice, mastery of learning methods, goal-directedness, and sense of self-efficacy have been identified as characteristics for success.

Thompson (1992) found seven common themes for participation or perceived barriers (nurse participation in continuing education); finding the right time, maintaining a balance, re-slicing the pie, juggling, support and non-support. Finding the right time focuses on the initial decision to participate. Two components of finding the right time were commitment and re-slicing the pie. Commitment is necessary for finding the right time. Reasons, beliefs, and doubts about the ability to succeed affect the development of commitment. Commitment was the coming together of attitudes, feelings and goals in such a way that made the individual really want to participate.

Cross's (1981) chain of response model describes the individual and external conditions and forces leading to participation in adult education. Individual variables are self-evaluation, attitudes towards education, and importance of goal/expectations that participation will meet the goal. External conditions include life transition, opportunities and barriers, and information. Forces begin with the individual and lead to external conditions. Cross (1981) speculates that the strongly motivated work around barriers. Carver and Scheier (1990) state that if obstacles are encountered one must reassess the goal. The individual can invest more effort or modify the plan.

Q45: I will find the right time to achieve my learning goal.

Q46: I will be challenged to work if the learning goal is difficult.

Question 39 on the ILP

Weiner (1972) reported that changes in motivational tendencies result from the attainment of a goal or the failure to achieve a goal. Weiner's subjects either encountered success at an easy task or failure at a difficult task (e.g. digit-symbol substitution-writing a particular symbol for each digit appearing on a card). Subjects could perform as much as they liked as a measure of persistence. Success at the initial task decreases motivational tendencies.

Q39: I will not be challenged to work if the learning goal is too easy.

Question 47 on the ILP

The degree of acceptance of set goals affects performance-who sets the goal is important-the higher the degree of self-efficacy the greater the performance. We are influenced by external rewards and penalties but only motivated by these external factors when they are internalized. Triandis, Dunnette, and Hough (1994) assert that every new goal leads to another set of actions because new discrepancies between the world and the goals.

People do not respond passively to environmental stimuli-rather, according to action theory, people influence and shape their environment as well. Goals are changed according to one's accomplishments, usually in the direction of higher efficiency on the environment. Thus, most people will proceed to develop new goals even when a certain goal has been achieved.

Goals anticipate future results; therefore goals should be considered anticipative of cognitive structures (e.g. Hacker, 1986a) that guide the action process. While the actual behavior guiding goals is usually conscious, it does not have to be in the focus of attention all the time (e.g. life goals like honesty).

Q47: I will keep my learning goal in mind when I am actively working toward that learning goal. [Reverse-Code]

Question 48 on the ILP

Heckhausen and Kuhl (1985) state the process of goal behavior begins with a wish. This wish is translated to a want. When there are potential opportunities, the time is right, and there is some urgency and importance, wants may translate into an intention and then act as action-guiding goals. Motivation plays a significant role in initiation and maintenance of effort toward learning and the achievement of cognitive goals (Corno, 1994; Pintrich & DeGroot, 1990). Motivation is a process whereby goal-directed effort is initiated and sustained; (self-efficacy (Bandura, 1986); attributions theory (Weiner, 1972); goal orientations (Dweck & Elliot, 1983); perceived control (Deci & Ryan, 1985).

Motivation is the force that energizes behavior, giving it direction and underlying the tendency to persist. Behavior is determined by a combination of forces in the individual and the environment. Individuals have different needs, desires, and goals. People make choices from alternative plans of behavior based upon their perceptions of the extent to which a given behavior will lead to desired outcomes. Expectancy is the probability that effort will lead to high performance, instrumentality is the probability that performance will lead to a particular outcome, and valence is the value placed on that outcome (Vroom, 1964).

The outcomes of motivation (effort, performance, reward, and need satisfaction) affect the individual's level of motivation on a continuous basis. Successful performance in a learning situation results in increased learner satisfaction, setting up a cycle of reinforcement that becomes stronger over time.

Learners high in achievement motivation feel more pride in successful accomplishment and will strive to follow this success with more effort on increasingly difficult tasks. That is causal attribution of self-responsibility for success, which augments positive achievement. Pride for success is postulated to mediate the observed relationship between achievement related needs and volitional achievement striving (Weiner, 1972).

Q48: I will apply effort towards my learning goal because I know that I am responsible for my learning.

Question 49 on the ILP

Motivation is the "commitment-the coming together of attitudes, feelings and goals" (Thompson, 1992, p.103). The process for deciding to participate (entering motivation) and the effort required to stay on task and persist (task motivation) establish the entering motivational state. Effort and persistence will be greatly influenced by the entering motivational state. Entering motivation influences effort expended on a learning task. It is important to appreciate how entering motivational states are established. It requires a commitment to a particular goal(s) and the intent to act. Corno (1989) asserts that motivational factors .shape intentions and fuel task involvement.

Valence reflects the attraction to a particular learning goal. Factors that determine valence are personal need (values) and affective states (preferences). Needs and values reflect the reasons for persisting in a task.

Expectancy is the belief that a desired outcome can be achieved. This factor composed of personal and contextual characteristics that influence goal achievement (i.e. competency, skills, ability and knowledge of the individual) while assessing goals. Perceptions of ability or self-efficacy affect the decision to participate as well as goals and learning environments. Control by the learner influences persistence. Anticipated control reflects the perceived ability and opportunity to exercise control over the learning process.

Q49: I will participate in learning difficult things because I believe that learning will improve my ability to learn other difficult things.

Question 50 on the ILP

Heider's (1958) analysis of action theory identified basic features of goal-related action and outcomes that may influence social perceptions in interpersonal judgments. Heider's concept of trying has two aspects; intentions and exertion or effort. Intention, what a person tries to do, refers to the direction of motivation or the goal itself. Effort expenditure, the quantitative aspect of trying, refers to the strength of motivation to reach the goal. Heider (1958) asserts that if one chooses only one action to reach a goal, then the individual does not really want to attain the goal. Variability of action to attain goal may convey more goal desire and effort to reach a goal. Heider (1958) asserts "if we know that a person has tried many different possibilities in attempting to solve a problem we conclude that he has worked hard at it" (p. 117).

Q50: I will seek alternate solutions to any problem that I encounter in my learning endeavors.

Question 51 on the ILP

McCombs (1997) states that learners of all ages are naturally quiet adept at being self-motivated and at directing and managing their own learning on tasks that they perceive as interesting, fun, personally meaningful, or relevant in some ways. Cross (1981) asserts that adults must experience choice and willingness along with success for motivation to be sustained.

Q51: I will learn when the learning is personally useful to me.

Question 52 on the ILP

A learner with internal locus of control would be more likely to value and expend effort intrinsic rather than extrinsic rewards. Initial motivation is based in the individual subjective prediction of the probability of performance, reward and need satisfaction. Initial motivation results in actual effort.

Motivation directly influences only the amount of effort a person will expend towards performing required behaviors (i.e. learning tasks). Learners who believe the learning goals are achievable and will result in personal rewards to meet their individual needs, will be more motivated than those who are not. The learner's perception is what counts.

Q52: I will learn when I value the reward I will get.

VALIDITY AND RELIABILITY

The original study used a data set of (N=257). Descriptive analysis of the data (N=257) found that the mean for each item response generally exceeds 7.00, and may be indicative of an adult's desire to engage in autonomous learning. An item analysis was performed for each factor on ILP to determine if all items constructed within the framework of a specific persistence-related behavior would correlate with a single latent factor. Items should meet the 0.3 standard for selection according to Kline (1993). Kline (1993) states that factors with loadings less than 0.3 are considered weakly correlated and should be rejected.

Following the criterion for rejection suggested by Kline (1993), item analysis would reject items 20, 28, 29, 36, 37, 40, 44, 47, and 48. The criterion consists of a product-moment correlation less than 0.3 between an item and the total behavior subscore. Bivariate correlations indicate that these items generally do not have a significant positive correlation with other items in their behavior. Of the nine items, whose correlation is less than 0.3, items 20, 28, 29 were borderline (correlation between 2.5 and 2.9). These items warrant close scrutiny.

A factor analysis performed on the data indicates that the majority of items load positively on the first principal component. Gorsuch (1983) states that the first principal component best represents the variables. Results of the data for the ILP indicate that a variance of 54 is accounted for in Factor 1; variance of 41 for Factor 2; and 38 for Factor 3.

The data suggest that of the 52 items on the Inventory of Learner Persistence, suggests that 17, 20, 26, 28, 29, 38 (Factor 2 Self-Regulation) and items 35, 36, 37, 41, 45, 46, 47, 48, and 52 (Factor 3 Goal-Directedness) may be candidates for removal. Items 17, 29, 37, 41, 45, 46, 48 had negative factor loadings. Of these items, items 17, 29, 37 were reverse code items. Each subgroup of items associated with volition, self-regulation, and goal-directedness should load on their first principal component.

Reliability of the Inventory of Learner Persistence

The internal consistency of the ILP is high despite items whose correlation and factor loadings were less than the established standard of 0.3. Items that were weakly correlated and with low factor loadings were reviewed with the foundation research in mind. The interpretation of the items and the scoring of the reverse-code items were reviewed in terms of clarity and specificity.

Test-Retest Reliability

The test-retest reliability of 0.846 for the Inventory of Learner Persistence indicates that the instrument is reliable and valid despite items whose correlation and factor loadings are low. Revision of the suspect items and additional testing should improve the reliability and validity although it is currently within an acceptable range of 0.8 as established by Kline (1993). Additional testing with a diverse population sample should indicate the items that are redundant or not appropriate.

Item Review

Because each item on the Inventory of Learner Persistence was initially considered construct and face valid, an examination of each suspect item is necessary. There are no items in Factor 1- Volition that are suspect. Items for Factor 2 Self-Regulation that are suspect are listed below. Because each item on the ILP is considered to be construct and face valid, a closer inspection of each item is necessary to discover conceptual difficulties with the item.

Range of Scores for the ILP

It should be noted that the range of scores in this study revealed a narrow range. The minimum single item score in this study was 0.00 on 21 of the 52 items. The maximum single item score was 10.00 on all 52 items of the ILP. There were two items that had a minimum single score of 5.00 (items 13 and 24). The remaining items had minimum single scores that ranged from 0.00 to 4.50. The mean scores appear to be high with means ranging from 3.0264 to 8.7424.

Use of the Zero to Ten Point Scale

The zero to ten-point scale was to differentiate with accurate precision the intentions to perform that behavior. The ILP scale delivered the precise data that allowed for the extensive interpretation and statistical analysis.

Summary

The data suggests that items 17, 20, 26, 28, 29 and 38 for Factor 2 (Self-regulation) and items 34, 36, 37, 41, 45, 46, 47, 48, 52 for Factor 3

(Goal-directedness) not be used as they currently exist. The data suggests that items 17, 28, and 18 for Factor 2-Self-Regulation may warrant additional investigation. Item 17 is reverse-coded and should be reviewed for context of meaning. Items that are borderline acceptance should be reviewed with other items within that domain to determine what items best assess the domain. Factor 3- Goal-Directedness should be carefully analyzed to determine what items best assess the intended behavior. Again, items that are reverse-code should be assessed as to the context of intended meaning.

The internal consistency of the ILP is high for each behavior subscore and the total battery of items. The test-retest is computed to be 0.846. The instrument is considered valid and reliable in the current version despite the low score of some items in factor 3. The ILP is a valid and reliable instrument in its current version although removing the suspect items may increase the internal consistency.

IMPLICATIONS FOR TEACHING AND LEARNING

The future world of work will require a shift in the way and manner that organizations view learning and human capital. A RAND study (Karoly & Panis, 2004) identified three major trends that will impact the future workplace environment:

1. **Demographic Changes:** The U.S. workforce will continue to grow but at a much slower pace. The workforce has become more homogeneous in that age, gender, and ethnicity have become more evenly distributed.

2. **Technology Changes:** The continued technology escalation will further advance the need for a skilled worker, increase productivity, and change the nature of the way business and employee recruitment is conducted in a global marketplace.

3. **Global Economic Change:** The changes in economies are inextricably linked through global trade and capital. As technology streamlines processes, the global economic exchanges are no longer insulated from the stress and strain of one nation. The interaction of the indentified trends requires changes in the practices, training, and education of the global workforce; and, how human resource professional adapt and transform to meet changing conditions will need to be examined as well.

RAND (Karoly & Panis, 2004) also reports that implications of these trends will mean a decentralized approach in organizational hierarchy and employee/employer relationships will be individualized. Organizations will need to adopt hiring practices that encourage the participation of women, elderly, and those with disabilities to offset the slowing growth in the labor force. And, most importantly, is the emphasis on retraining and lifelong learning for maintaining the competitive edge in the global workforce. The emphasis on specialized training to quickly adapt to changing technology requires learners who know how to learn and are able to set learning goals, self-regulate their actions both cognitive and behaviorally, and exhibit personal control in the learning. Employees must exhibit the self-direction needed for the new work environment that will be changing with technology innovation and competitive outsourcing. The ILP can provide both employee and employer an assessment that will enable training and education to be more effective through diagnostic results.

The current global economic crisis and global downsizing of businesses indicates a movement to more efficient and operative models of human resource management. The availability of information obtainable through technology and the worldwide web continues to have profound implications for teaching and learning. Knowledge is no longer a finite constant to be transmitted in an incremental and hierarchal method but an exploding evolution. Information and knowledge are growing an exponential rate with new information generated more rapidly than ever and even more quickly becoming obsolete. The implications for human resource development suggest we rethink what knowledge is essential and what requisite skills and attributes for learning are needed for today and the future. The focus of human development requires an emphasis on *knowing how to learn.* The generation of knowledge information available to anyone with internet access requires learners who know who to access the *right* information in order to get the task or job completed. The teaching and learning (development) focus must change from less emphasis on the answer to more emphasis on learners who are able to work independently and in a self-directed manner. A greater emphasis on the learner, and the structures and mechanisms that sustain and develop the qualities and attitudes required for learning are necessary. The shift in thinking has focused on the internal conditions (attitudes and beliefs) that are necessary for sustained and enduring learning rather than the external surroundings and settings.

ADDITIONAL INFORMATION

The ILP is located on Survey Monkey (see link below) http://www.surveymonkey.com/s.aspx?sm=wb_2fmuFGRgdzaeJ6tjyP0VQ_3d_3d)

and can be used in most any context such as persistence with dissertation completion, persistence to stay in teaching, and persistence to exercise. The factors of volition, self-regulation, and goal directed behaviors form the foundation for persistence from a cognitive and motivation perspective. A researcher would need to change the items accordingly for contexts other than learning and conduct a factor analysis for item review. Permission from the author and developer of the ILP is required prior to making any modifications or for use; there is no charge for a one time use for research such as for a dissertation. Please contact Dr. M. Gail Derrick at gailder@regent.edu for access to the instrument.

REFERENCES

Ames, C. (1992). Classroom goals, structure, and student motivation. *Journal of Educational Psychology*, *84*, 261–271. doi:10.1037/0022-0663.84.3.261

Ajzen, I. (1985). From intentions to actions: A theory of planned behavior. In Kuhl, J., & Beckman, J. (Eds.), *Action control: From cognition to behaviour* (pp. 11–39). New York, NY: Springer. doi:10.1007/978-3-642-69746-3_2

Ajzen, I. (1988). *Attitudes, personality and behaviour*. Milton Keynes, UK: Oxford University Press.

Ajzen, I. (1991). The theory of planned behaviour. *Organizational Behavior and Human Decision Processes*, *50*, 179–211. doi:10.1016/0749-5978(91)90020-T

Bandura, A. (1997). *Self-efficacy: The exercise of control*. New York, NY: W. H. Freeman and Company.

Bandura, A. (1986). *Social foundations of thought and action: A social cognitive theory*. Englewood Cliffs, NJ: Prentice-Hall.

Borkowski, J. G., & Thorpe, P. K. (1994). Self-regulation and motivation: A life–span perspective. In Schunk, D. H., & Zimmerman, B. J. (Eds.), *Self-regulation of learning and performance*. Hillsdale, NJ: Lawrence Erlbaum Associates, Publishers.

Brody, N. (1983). *Human motivation*. New York, NY: Academic Press.

Butler, D. L., & Winne, P. H. (1995). Feedback and self-regulated learning: A theoretical synthesis. *Review of Educational Research*, *65*, 245–281.

Carver, C. S., & Scheier, M. F. (1990). Origins and functions of positive and negative affect: A control-process view. *Psychological Review*, *97*, 19–35. doi:10.1037/0033-295X.97.1.19

Confessore, G. J. (1992). An introduction to the study of self-directed learning. In G. J. Confessore & S. J. Confessore (Eds.), *Guideposts to self-directed learning: Expert commentary on essential concepts* (pp. 1-6). King of Prussia, PA: Organization Design and Development, Inc.

Corno, L. (1989). Self-regulated learning: A volitional analysis. In B. Zimmerman & D. Schunk (Eds.), *Self-regulated learning and academic achievement* (pgs. 111-142). New York, NY: Springer-Verlag.

Corno, L. (1993). The best laid plans: Modern conceptions of volition and educational research. *Educational Researcher*, *22*(2), 14–22.

Corno, L. (1994). Student volition and education: outcomes, influences, and practices. In Schunk, D. H., & Zimmerman, B. J. (Eds.), *Self-regulation of learning and performance*. Hillsdale, NJ: Lawrence Erlbaum Associates, Publishers.

Cross, K. P. (1981). *Adult learners*. San Francisco, CA: Jossey-Bass Publishers.

Deci, E. L., & Ryan, R. M. (1985). *Intrinsic motivation and self-determination in human behavior*. New York, NY: Plenum Press.

Dweck, C. S., & Elliot, E. S. (1983). *Achievement motivation* (Mussen, P. H., Ed.). 4th ed.). Handbook of child psychology New York, NY: Wiley.

Elliott, E., & Dweck, C. (1988). Goals: An approach to motivation and achievement. *Journal of Personality and Social Psychology*, *54*, 5–12. doi:10.1037/0022-3514.54.1.5

Fishbein, M., & Ajzen, I. (1975). *Belief, attitude, intention, and behavior: An introduction to theory and research*. Reading, MA: Addison-Wesley publishing Company.

Garcia, T., & Pintrich, P. R. (1994). Regulating motivation and cognition in the classroom: The role of self-schemas and self-regulatory strategies. In Schunk, D. H., & Zimmerman, B. J. (Eds.), *Self-regulation of learning and performance. (1994)*. Hillsdale, NJ: Lawrence Erlbaum Associates, Publishers.

Gorsuch, R. L. (1983). *Factor analysis*. Hillsdale, NJ: Lawrence Erlbaum Associates.

Guglielmino, L. M. (1978). Development of the self-directed learning readiness scale. Doctoral dissertation, University of Georgia, 1977. *Dissertation Abstracts International, 38,* 6467A.

Harackiewicz, J. M., Abrahams, S., & Wagerman, R. (1987). Performance evaluation and intrinsic motivation: The effects of evaluative focus, rewards, and achievement orientation. *Journal of Personality and Social Psychology, 53,* 1015–1023. doi:10.1037/0022-3514.53.6.1015

Heckhausen, H., & Kuhl, J. (1985). From wishes to action: The dead ends and short cuts on the long way to action. In Frese, M., & Sabini, J. (Eds.), *Goal directed behavior: The concept of action in psychology* (pp. 134–157). Hillsdale, NJ: Lawrence Erlbaum Associates.

Heider, F. (1958). *The psychology of interpersonal relations*. New York, NY: Wiley. doi:10.1037/10628-000

Houle, C. O. (1961). *The inquiring mind: A study of the adult learner who continues to participate to learn*. Madison, WI: University of Wisconsin Press.

Huitt, W. (1997). *The SCAN report revisited*. Paper delivered at the Fifth Annual Gulf South Business and Vocational Education Conference, Valdosta State University, Valdosta, GA, April 18.

Johnstone, J. W. C., & Rivera, R. J. (1965). *Volunteers for learning*. Chicago, IL: Aldine Publishing Company.

Karoly, L., & Panis, C. (2004). *The 21st century at work: Forces shaping the future workforce and workplace in the United States*. Santa Monica, CA: RAND Corporation.

Kline, P. (1993). *The handbook of psychological testing*. New York, NY: Routledge.

Knowles, M. (1975). *Self-directed learning*. Chicago, IL: Follett.

Knowles, M. (1980). *Modern practice of adult, education: From pedagogy to andragogy*. San Francisco, CA: Jossey-Bass Publishers.

Kuhl, J. (1985). Volitional mediators of cognition-behavior consistency: Self-regulation processes and action verses state orientation. In Kuhl, J., & Beckman, J. (Eds.), *Action control: From cognition to behavior* (pp. 101–128). New York, NY: Springer-Verlag.

Kuhl, J., & Goschke, T. (1994). A theory of action control: Mental subsystems, modes of control, and volitional conflict-resolution strategies. In Kuhl, J., & Beckmann, J. (Eds.), *Volition and personality: Action verses state orientation* (pp. 93–124). Seattle, WA: Hogrefe & Huber.

Long, H. B. (1989). *Self-directed learning: Emerging theory and practice*. Oklahoma Research Center for Continuing Professional and Higher Education of the University of Oklahoma.

Merriam, S. B., & Cafarella, R. S. (1999). *Learning in adulthood*. San Francisco, CA: Jossey-Bass Publishers.

McCombs, B. L. (1997). *Understanding the keys to learning*. Retrieved from www.mcrel.org/products/noteworth/html

Oddi, L. F. (1987). Perspectives on self-directed learning. *Adult Education Quarterly, 38*(1), 21–31. doi:10.1177/0001848187038001003

Pintrich, P. R., & DeGroot, E. (1990). Motivational and self-regulated learning components of classroom academic performance. *Journal of Educational Psychology, 82*, 33–40. doi:10.1037/0022-0663.82.1.33

Sandelands, L. E., Brockner, J., & Glynn, M. A. (1988). If at first you don't succeed, try, try again: Effects of persistence-performance contingencies, ego involvement, and self-esteem on task performance. *The Journal of Applied Psychology, 73*(2), 208–216. doi:10.1037/0021-9010.73.2.208

Schunk, D. H. (1991). Self-efficacy and academic motivation. *Educational Psychologist, 26*(3 & 4), 207–231.

Schunk, D. H., & Zimmerman, B. J. (1994). *Self-regulation of learning and performance*. Hillsdale, NJ: Lawrence Erlbaum Associates, Publishers.

Skager, R. (1979). Self-directed learning and schooling: Identifying pertinent theories and illustrative research. *International Review of Education, 25*, 517–543. doi:10.1007/BF00598508

Thompson, D. (1992). Beyond motivation: Nurse's participation and persistence in Baccalaureate programs. *Adult Education Quarterly, 42*, 94–105. doi:10.1177/0001848192042002003

Tough, A. (1979). *The adult's learning project*. San Diego, CA: University Associates.

Triandis, H. C., Dunnette, M. D., & Hough, L. M. (1994). *Handbook of industrial and organizational psychology*. Palo Alto, CA: Consulting Psychologists Press.

Vroom, V. (1964). *Work and motivation*. New York, NY: John Wiley.

Weiner, R. (1972). Attribution theory, achievement motivation, and the educational process. *Review of Educational Research, 42*, 203–215.

Winne, P. H. (1995). Inherent details in self-regulated learning. *Educational Psychologist, 30*(4), 173–187. doi:10.1207/s15326985ep3004_2

Zimmerman, B. J. (1994). Dimensions of academic self-regulation: A conceptual framework for education. In Schunk, D. H., & Zimmerman, B. J. (Eds.), *Self-regulation of learning and performance: Issues and educational application.* Mahwah, NJ: Erlbaum.

ADDITIONAL READING

Carr, P. B., & Derrick, M. G. (March 2009). Managing troubled times or leading: The role of leadership for the effective executive. *Effective Executive, 90.* The ICFAI University Press.

Derrick, M. G. (2000). The measurement of the intentions to exhibit persistence in the adult autonomous learner. Doctoral dissertation, The George Washington University, 2001. *Dissertation Abstracts International, 62*(5), 2533.

Derrick, M. G. (2001). Persistence, a conative factor of the adult autonomous learner. In Long, H. B. (Eds.), *New ideas about self-directed learning.* Schaumburg, IL: Motorola University Press.

Derrick, M. G. (2002). Persistence and the adult autonomous learner. In Long, H. B. (Eds.), *Twenty-first century advances in self-directed learning.* Schaumburg, IL: Motorola University Press. Book Chapter.

Derrick, M. G. (2003). Understanding learner autonomy and autonomous learning as it relates to self-directed learning. In Long, H. B. (Eds.), *Current developments in e-learning and self-directed learning.* Schaumburg, IL: Motorola University Press. Book Chapter.

Derrick, M. G. (2004). Supporting learners for e-learning: Creating a culture of lifelong learning. In Aragon, S. R. (Ed.), *Facilitating learning in online environments*. Jossey-Bass.

Derrick, M. G. (2009). Curiosity and adult learners. In Derrick, M. G., & Ponton, M. K. (Eds.), *Emerging directions in self-directed learning*. Chicago, IL: Discovery Association Publishing House.

Derrick, M. G. (June 2009). Self-directed leadership in turbulent times. *MBA Review*. The ICFAI University Press.

Derrick, M. G., & Carr, P. B. (May 2009). Human resource development: Challenges of the 21st century. *HRM Review*. The ICFAI University Press.

Derrick, M. G., & Jordan, H. M. (2007). Organizational strategies for success. In Rovai, A. P., Gallien, L. B. Jr, & Stiff-Williams, H. R. (Eds.), *Closing the African American achievement gap in higher education*. New York, NY: Teachers College Press.

Derrick, M. G., & Pilling-Cormick, J. (2003). Foundations for lifelong learning: building successful self-directed e-learning approaches from k-12 to higher education. *2003 E-Learn Conference Proceedings*. Retrieved from http://dl.aace.org/13973

Derrick, M. G., & Ponton, M. K. (2008). *Emerging directions in self-directed learning*. Discovery Association Publications.

Derrick, M. G., Carr, P. B., & Ponton, M. K. (2003). Facilitating and understanding autonomy in adult learners. *New Horizons in Adult Education, 17*(2). Retrieved from http://www.nova.edu/~aed/newhorizons.html

Derrick, M. G., Carr, P. B., & Ponton, M. K. (2006). Enhancing and facilitating self-efficacious behaviors in distance learning environments. *New Horizons in Adult Education, 19*(3).

Derrick, M. G., Ponton, M. K., & Carr, P. B. (2004). A preliminary analysis of learner autonomy in online and face-to-face settings. *International Journal of Self-Directed Learning, 2*(1), 62–70.

Derrick, M. G., Ponton, M. K., Rhea, N. E., & Kohns, J. W. (2005). Differences in learner autonomy in online and face-to-face environments. *World Conference on E-Learning in Corporate, Government, Healthcare, &. Higher Education, 2005*, 1992–1997.

Derrick, M. G., Rovai, A. P., Ponton, M. K., Confessore, G. J., & Carr, P. B. (2007). An examination of the relationship of gender, marital status, and prior educational attainment and learner autonomy. *Educational Research Review, 2*(1), 1–8.

Ponton, M. K., Carr, P. B., & Derrick, M. G. (2004). A path analysis of the conative factors associated with autonomous learning. *International Journal of Self-Directed Learning, 1*(1), 59–69.

Ponton, M. K., Derrick, M. B., & Carr, P. B. (2005). The relationship between resourcefulness and persistence in adult autonomous learning. *Adult Education Quarterly, 55*(2), 116–128. doi:10.1177/0741713604271848

Ponton, M. K., Derrick, M. G., Confessore, G. J., & Rhea, N. E. (2005). The role of self-efficacy in autonomous learning. *International Journal of Self-Directed Learning, 2*(2), 81–90. Retrieved from http://www.sdlglobal.com/docs/2.2IJSDLfinal.pdf

Ponton, M. K., Derrick, M. G., Hall, J. M., Rhea, N. E., & Carr, P. B. (2005). The relationship between self-efficacy and autonomous learning: The development of new instrumentation. *International Journal of Self-Directed Learning, 2*(1), 50–61.

Ruelland, D., Gabrielle, D., Derrick, M. G., Pilling-Cormick, J., & Piskurich, G. (2002). Supporting learners for e-learning. *2002 E-Learn Conference Proceedings*. Retrieved from http://dl.aace.org/9487

KEY TERMS AND DEFINITIONS

Autonomous Learner: An individual who exhibits the characteristics of volition, goal-directedness, and self-regulation in persistence in learning.

Autonomous Learning: An intentional learning process in which the conative factors of persistence are evident.

Autonomy: The characteristic of the individual who can independently exhibit intentional behavior, a personal attribute or quality.

Conation: A self-motivated behavior or behavioral intention.

Goal-Directed: The establishment of goals that serves as motivators for action.

Intention: The goal to engage in a behavior.

Persistence: The behavior of sustained action in spite of the presence of obstacles or competing goals.

Self-Regulation: Processes that exercise control over thinking, affect, and behavior.

Volition: The maintenance of intentional focus and effort towards goals despite distractions.

Section 4
Uses and Comparisons

Chapter 17
The Mutual Influence of Technology and Leadership Behaviors

Tobias Heilmann
University of Zurich, Switzerland

Ulf-Dietrich Reips
Universidad de Deusto, & IKERBASQUE, Basque Foundation for Science, Spain

ABSTRACT

The present book chapter focuses on e-leadership, reviewing and discussing the latest developments in new (e-)leadership conceptions, such as transformational leadership and others. The authors propose alternative, albeit well-proven measures (e.g., MLQ 5X Short, Bass & Avolio, 1990) and an e-leadership tool called Virtual Team Trainer (VTT; Reips & Ito, 2007). The VTT uses the Online Leader Behavior Description Questionnaire (OLBDQ; Reips & Heilmann, 2009), assessing the Ohio State Leadership styles consideration and initiating structure. Alongside personality tests and group process development units that were built from the Existential Mapping Process (EMP; Horowitz, 1985), the tool contains modules that help leaders and team members to identify their Ohio State leadership styles. The VTT relates the results of the self- and other-questionnaires regarding team structure, development, and modifications and improvement of leadership skills. The VTT is available free for use via the iScience Server portal at http://iscience.eu.

DOI: 10.4018/978-1-4666-2172-5.ch017

E-LEADERSHIP: WHEN INFORMATION TECHNOLOGY SYSTEMS INFLUENCE AND ARE INFLUENCED BY LEADERSHIP BEHAVIORS, PROCESSES, AND OUTCOMES

Over the last decade, a new branch of leadership research, e-leadership, has significantly gained in importance (e.g., Avolio, Walumbwa, & Weber, 2009). The fundamental issue for leadership researchers and practitioners around the world regarding this subject is: how do information technology systems transform leadership styles, the processes of leadership, and the outcomes, at an individual and collective level – and vice versa – how are information technology systems influenced by leadership processes? Unfortunately, e-leaders often make extensive use of information technology systems without fully realizing their impact on organizational dynamics. The changes in information technology systems happen too fast for leadership research to keep up with, thus causing the understanding of e-leadership styles and their processes to lag behind new technological advancements. Furthermore, within leadership research and application, a number of new leadership theories have recently emerged: the so-called *new leadership paradigms* (Bryman, 1993). The current chapter defines this two-fold gap between theoretical and technological advancements and proposes solutions to close it.

According to Bass (1990), leadership is about the development and maintenance of relationships, the structuring or restructuring of situations and the perceptions and expectations of the members. Leadership is about affecting others and modifying the motivation or competence of team members. Indeed, information technology systems enable leaders to interact with individuals or teams from different departments or even from remote continents (e.g., Avolio & Kahai, 2003). However, in order to be a successful e-leader, it is important to understand that certain leadership behaviors may need to be modified to fit the mode of communication, as a virtual team member's perception of the leadership may be different, as compared to the traditional face-to-face setting.. E-leaders may need to use procedures that differ from traditional leadership processes.

The first section of this chapter reviews and discusses the most recent leadership conceptions. We will provide a review of so-called *new leadership theories* (Bryman, 1993), such as *transformational leadership* (Bass, 1985), *authentic leadership* (Avolio, Gardner, Walumbwa, Luthans, & May, 2004), *charismatic leadership* (e.g., Conger & Kanungo, 1998), and *ethical leadership* (Brown, Treviño, & Harrison, 2005).

In the second section we will then apply the new leadership conceptions – in particular transformational leadership – to virtual environments. The section refers to common questions in transformational e-leadership, while reporting the latest research studies on specificities of transformational e-leadership and differences between face-to-face- and transformational e-leadership-interaction. Particular attention is paid to possible pitfalls – for example, how do information technology systems impact individual outcomes, such as objective performance, in a transformational e-leadership process? Is trust of special relevance in the e-leadership process? Does anonymity influence the e-leadership process? Further, we will report on remaining methodological issues in the measurement of transformational e-leadership.

The third section of this chapter deals with technological developments that can be used to build and maintain virtual teams and to measure virtual team processes and outcomes. As a specific example of an applied e-leadership tool, we will present the Virtual Team Trainer (Reips et al., 2007), which is available via the *iScience Server* portal at http://iscience.eu. We will show that the assessment of transformational leadership produces a number of methodological restrictions. We decided that our e-leadership tool should assess the Ohio State Leadership (OSL) conceptions.

These conceptions are well-proven alternatives to the new leadership paradigms such as transformational leadership. Integrating the theoretical and technological developments as well as the methodological restrictions in sections 1 and 2, we outline a set of features that seem essential e-leadership tools.

The concluding fourth section presents a summary and an overall discussion as well as an outlook for further research.

NEW LEADERSHIP THEORIES

New leadership theories (Bryman, 1993) place a greater emphasis on "vision/mission articulation, … motivating and inspiring, … creating change and innovation, … the empowerment of others, … [and] stimulating extra effort" (Bryman, 1993, p. 111). In contrast, "old leadership" theories, such as behavior approaches – for example the Ohio State Leadership Studies led by the researchers Stogdill, Shartle, and Hemphill (Stogdill, 1950) – and situational approaches, such as Fiedlers's contingency model (1967), the decision-making model by Vroom and Yetton (1973), or the path-goal theory of leadership by House (1971, 1996), mainly focus on planning, allocating responsibility, controlling, problem-solving or creating routines (Bryman, 1993).

Several new leadership theories have emerged which share the "new view" and thus share strong conceptual overlaps, as will be described further below. Because transformational leadership theory is the new leadership theory that best integrates the other approaches, and is the most studied new leadership conception, we will focus on and explain the paradigm of transformational leadership by comparing it with the new approaches.

Transformational Leadership

Research regarding the theory of transformational and transactional leadership has been conducted for over 24 years. Based on the work of Burns (1978) and House (1977), Bass (1985) proposed a distinction between transformational and transactional leadership. According to Bass (1985), transformational leaders transform – that is, they motivate followers to do more than they were originally expected to do by widening employees' scope and creating acceptance for the group mission, which results in extra effort. Transformational leader behaviors have an effect on followers' effort, performance, and satisfaction by raising followers' self-efficacy, self-esteem (Kark, Shamir, & Chen, 2003; Kirkpatrick & Locke, 1996) and locus of control (Bass, 1985) through expressing high expectations of followers and belief in followers' abilities. Bass (1985) proposes that *transformational leadership* is accomplished through four dimensions: *Idealized influence* refers to the leader's serving as a role model for followers. Transformational leaders have high standards of moral and ethic conduct, and provide followers with a vision and a sense of mission. *Inspirational motivation* refers to leaders providing a strong vision for the future based on values and ideals. Transformational leaders use emotional appeals to focus followers' efforts to achieve more than they would in their own interest. *Intellectual stimulation* refers to a leader's ability to stimulate followers' creativity by questioning and challenging them. An example of this would be a leader who promotes IT-specialists' efforts to develop unique ways to solve problems that have caused slowdowns in the IT landscape. *Individual consideration* refers to a leader paying attention to the individual needs of her or his followers, and developing followers as a coach or consultant. A transformational leader might spend time treating every follower in a caring and unique manner. E.g., for some followers, the transformational leader may provide more consideration or mentoring, for others he or she might give more specific directives for solving tasks.

In contrast, transactional leadership – another leadership style related to transformational leadership proposed by Bass (1985) – aims at monitoring and controlling employees through rational or economic means, by operating within existing structures and systems. Transactional leadership is comparable to the so-called "old" leadership theories mentioned above.

Transformational leadership is consistently related to several outcomes across study settings such as business, college, military, and the public sector (Judge & Piccolo, 2004), and across cultures (Den Hartog et al., 1999). The list of studies on transformational leadership outcomes is long. In essence, on an organizational level, transformational leadership is positively linked to organization and business unit performance (Whittington, Goodwin, & Murray, 2004) such as economic criteria (Geyer & Steyrer, 1998; Howell & Avolio, 1993), as well as group performance (Sosik, Avolio, & Kahai, 1997). On an individual level, transformational leadership is a valid predictor for psychological criteria such as commitment (e.g., Meyer, Stanley, Herscovitch, & Topolnytsky, 2002), creativity (e.g., Jung, Chow, & Wu, 2003), follower job performance and job satisfaction (e.g., Fuller, Patterson, Hester, & Stringer, 1996; Lowe, Kroeck, & Sivasubramaniam, 1996), motivation (e.g., Bass, Avolio, Jung, & Berson, 2003), and many others.

Authentic Leadership

According to Avolio, Gardner, Walumbwa, Luthans, and May (2004), authentic leaders are "those who are deeply aware of how they think and behave and are perceived by others as being aware of their own and others' values/moral perspectives, knowledge, and strengths; aware of the context in which they operate; and who are confident, hopeful, optimistic, resilient, and of high moral character" (p. 802). What distinguishes transformational leadership and authentic leadership conceptually? Avolio and Gardner (2005) argue that transformational leadership

may be immoral if transformational leaders project an image of good leadership, yet act in a way that serves their own interests at the cost of their followers. Avolio et al. (2004) and Avolio and Gardner (2005) reason that the concept of transformational leadership only pretends to be "universally positive" (Judge, Woolf, Hurst, & Livingston, 2006, p. 211). Avolio et al. (2004) find support for their reasoning in a statement by Bass (1985), who assumed that "transformational leadership is not necessarily beneficial" (p. 21). Indeed, this is somewhat inconsistent with the predominant conceptual assumption by Bass (1997), who stated that "transformational leaders move their followers to transcend their own self-interests for the good of the group, [and for the] organization" (p. 133).

Paradoxically, although Avolio and Gardner (2005) argue that transformational leadership and authentic leadership are distinct from each other, they believe that authentic leadership "could incorporate … transformational … leadership" (p. 329). Due to the lack of research, it is not possible to tell whether transformational leadership is less moral than authentic leadership. It is not even clear whether transformational leadership is a necessary condition for authentic leadership or vice versa (Judge et al., 2006, p. 211). However, what is missing is research showing that authentic leadership has the same impact on individual and organizational outcomes as transformational leadership. At the moment, transformational leadership seems preferable over authentic leadership in theory and application.

Charismatic Leadership

The terms *charismatic leadership* and *transformational leadership* are often used interchangeably (Hunt & Conger, 1999) – even by leadership researchers. However, we believe one should differentiate between them on a conceptual level. House (1977), who is credited with advancing charismatic leadership research, further developed Weber's conception (1947) of charismatic leadership. The word "charisma" is etymologically Greek and means "gift". According to Weber (1947), a person with charisma is "set apart from ordinary people and treated as endowed with supernatural, superhuman, or at least specifically exceptional powers or qualities [...] regarded as of divine origin or as exemplary, and on the basis of them the individual concerned is treated as a leader" (p. 358). Conger and Kanungo (1998) argue that charisma "is not some magical ability limited to a handful" (p. 161). They report widely accepted, typically charismatic characteristics such as possessing and articulating a vision, willing to take risks to achieve a vision, exhibiting sensitivity to followers' needs, and demonstrating novel behavior. According to Kirkpatrick and Locke (1996), charismatic leadership focuses clearly on communication styles. However, even if their framework of charismatic leadership has similarities to transformational leadership, and the differences between both concepts seem to be "minor" or "fine tuning" (House & Podsakoff, 1994, p. 71), there is an important hierarchical distinction. Bass (1985) suggests that "charisma is a necessary ingredient of transformational leadership, but by itself is not sufficient to account for the transformational process" (p. 31).

Ethical Leadership

Brown et al. (2005) defined ethical leadership as "the demonstration of normatively appropriate conduct through personal actions and interpersonal relationships, and the promotion of such conduct to followers through two-way communication, reinforcement, and decision-making" (p. 120). In brief, an ethical leader is an ethical role model. Some researchers saw a need to closer examine the ethics of leadership due to ethical scandals in business (Brown & Treviño, 2006). Is there any difference between ethical leadership and transformational leadership? Transformational leader-

ship is defined as having an ethical component, whereby transformational leaders demonstrate "high standards of ethical and moral conduct" (Avolio, 1999, p. 43) that are applied through idealized influence. Furthermore, research shows that followers perceive leaders with higher moral reasoning to be more transformational. The sticking point for ethical leadership researchers is that Bass (1985) argued that transformational leaders could be ethical or unethical, depending on their motivation. Generally, ethical leadership researchers would agree that transformational leadership and ethical leadership overlap. "Transformational and ethical leaders care about others, act consistently with their moral principles (i.e., integrity), … and are ethical role models for others" (Brown & Treviño, 2006, p. 599). However, Brown et al. (2005) suggested that ethical leadership and transformational leadership are distinct constructs and set out to prove their point empirically. In fact, to their surprise, the results of their study did not show "distinctiveness" (p. 129). A closer look at their study reveals that their ethical leadership scale is highly correlated with the examined transformational dimension *idealized influence* behavior, a transformational subdimension that refers to the actions of the leader (e.g., Antonakis, Avolio, & Sivasubramaniam, 2003). Furthermore, the data from confirmatory factor analyses indicate that the ethical leadership scale by Brown et al. (2005) and idealized influence behavior do overlap. Regardless, Brown et al. (2005) make a case for a "construct valid measure" (p. 132). We do not think that these results are sufficiently compelling to justify the "distinctiveness" of ethical leadership at this point.

ADDING THE "E": TRANSFORMATIONAL E-LEADERSHIP

The (new) leadership theories mentioned above – unlike old leadership approaches – were implicitly conceptualized for face-to-face interactions. However, e-leadership, that is the leadership of virtual teams, is defined as "a social influence process mediated by advanced information technologies to produce changes in attitudes, feelings, thinking, behavior, and/or performance of individuals, groups, and/or organizations" (Avolio, Kahai, & Dodge, 2001, p. 617). Communication in virtual teams is thus mainly information-based, i.e., communication technologies. And communication is certainly the main aspect of the so-called new leadership approaches described above (e.g., Avolio & Kahai, 2003). Communication "holds the group structure together... without communication, groups could not exist; without communication, people could not interact" (Applbaum et al., 1974, p. 9).

To help understand how leadership works in teams that communicate mainly via Internet, we turn to the young and recently evolved field of Internet Psychology (e.g. Joinson, McKenna, Postmes, & Reips, 2007; Reips & Bosnjak, 2001; Sassenberg, Postmes, Boos, & Reips, 2003). E-leadership relies on communication processes that are influenced by interacting psychological and technological factors. To the same degree that Internet-based communication follows different rules than offline communication, the traditional conceptions of leadership are affected in e-leadership. On the Internet, teams may be formed and cooperate much more frequently than offline teams, and under conditions of high anonymity. There is evidence that such conditions can be very beneficial under certain circumstances, and thus moving to the "e" (or rather "i" – however, for reasons of convention we will stick to "e") provides new opportunities for leaders. For example, indispensability effects support motivation gains among inferior group members even during sequential group work under highly anonymous (i.e. Internet) conditions (Wittchen, Schlereth, & Hertel, 2007).

The question is, whether new leadership communication-centered behaviors have the same effect on individuals or organizational criteria in virtual teams as they do in traditional teams. As a general statement, one can say that there is more opportunity for misinterpretations when using electronic communication such as e-mail. The relatively low potential for building trust online when using text-only communication (Riegelsberger, Sasse, & McCarthy, 2007) may be partly due to such misunderstandings (Reips, 2008). Having said this, we must admit that research in this area is somewhat lagging behind. To our knowledge, no research on new leadership paradigms exists in the setting of virtual teams, except on transformational leadership. This significant research will be summarized next.

Transformational E-Leadership: Outcomes of and Conditions in Different Information Technology Systems Settings

Transformational E-Leadership through E-Mails

In two experimental studies, Kelloway et al. (2003) showed that individuals can detect and respond to transformational leadership behaviors expressed through *e-mails*. Furthermore, performance in group tasks was higher for those who experienced transformational e-leadership behaviors. For example, participants who read intellectually stimulating e-mails rated their leader as being more intellectually stimulating than participants who read a non-intellectually stimulating e-mail. Furthermore, participants who received an e-mail with a transformational leadership message as opposed to a non-transformational message reported higher job satisfaction or perceived interpersonal justice. Next, participants who had to perform in a virtual group task showed higher motivation and higher performance.

Transformational E-Leadership in Group Decision Support Systems

Sosik, Avolio, and Kahai (1997) were the first to study transformational leadership in virtual (experimental) settings. They found that transformational leadership affected the effectiveness of virtual teams working on creativity tasks within *a group decision support system*. High transformational leadership led to solutions of higher quality, i.e. original solutions or questions about solutions, than conditions with low transformational leadership. Furthermore, groups that were led with a highly transformational leadership style reported higher perceived performance, extra effort, and increased satisfaction with the leadership.

Similar to Sosik et al. (1997), Sosik, Avolio, Kahai and Jung (1998) provided evidence that transformational leadership behaviors affect the collective belief of group members that the group can be effective (i.e., group potency), as well as the actual effectiveness in *brainstorming* sessions in *anonymous* group decision support systems. According to Sosik et al. (1998), the effectiveness of those groups may be a function of the interaction between leadership style and *anonymity*. The explanation lies in the fact that transformational leaders influence group members' beliefs about their ability to perform cooperatively for the "good of the group" (Bass & Avolio, 1994).

Kahai, Sosik and Avolio (2003) replicated the effect of transformational leadership in anonymous virtual teams within the frame of creativity tasks. Under transformational e-leadership and anonymous conditions, study participants generated more solutions to an assigned problem and helped the leader to determine the group's most appropriate solutions. Furthermore, transformational leadership limited *social loafing*, which may occur when group members are not identified, by getting all members to work for the good of the group.

Why is anonymity so important in transformational e-leadership? An explanation by Kahai et al. (2003) is that transformational e-leaders may challenge virtual team members in a positive way to exert effort instead of threatening them. That is, if (virtual) team members feel more anonymous, they might accept comments by their virtual leader more likely as being constructive and less personal.

Transformational E-Leadership in an Avatar Environment

In an experimental study, Hoyt and Blascovich (2003) showed that transformational leadership was associated with higher qualitative performance in creativity tests within avatar settings when compared with a low transformational leadership condition. Furthermore, groups that were led with a highly transformational leadership style reported higher perceived performance, extra effort, or satisfaction with leadership. On the other hand, the quantitative performance was not better than in low transformational leadership conditions. Trust appeared to play an important role, mediating the relationships between transformational e-leadership and outcomes. According to Hoyt and Blascovitch, trust is more likely to form if a relationship is built between the leader and the follower – such as happens in transformational leadership.

Transformational E-Leadership in Desktop Videoconference and Text-Based Chat

Hambley, O'Neill and Kline (2007) conducted an experiment examining the impact of transformational behaviors in *desktop videoconference* and *text-based chat* on team interaction styles and outcomes. They found that transformational leadership – along with transactional leadership – had a positive impact on teams' problem solving tasks across communication media. However, transformational e-leadership did not provide an add-on effect. That is, its impact was not higher than that of transactional leadership. But this lack of an effect may be due to validity issues when measuring transformational leadership, as will be described in the next section.

Limitations of Transformational E-Leadership Research

Overall, research suggests that information technology systems do not constrain transformational leadership. However, transformational e-leadership research faces some challenges. First of all, researchers may want to further explore the effectiveness of transformational e-leadership. It seems that studying transformational leadership may also represent the other new leadership theories within e-leadership research, due to its high explanations of variance in various criteria.

Nevertheless, a crucial issue is the assessment of transformational e-leadership. The assessment of transformational leadership behaviors in traditional settings faces some problems, namely the validity of the most extensively validated and used measure of transformational leadership (Felfe, 2006; Judge et al., 2006); the Multifactor Leadership Questionnaire (MLQ) by Bass and Avolio (1990). This measure also assesses transactional leadership. There are many controversies and criticisms concerning the relatively high levels of multicolinearity reported among the transformational leadership scales (Avolio, Bass, & Jung, 1999; Felfe, 2006; Heinitz, Liepmann, & Felfe, 2005; Judge & Piccolo, 2004). Some authors even suggested that the transformational scales do not measure different or unique underlying constructs (Bycio, Hackett, & Allen, 1995; Carless, 1998). A large number of studies failed to confirm the proposed factorial model. The number of factors range from two (e.g., Tepper & Percy, 1990), to three (e.g., Hinkin, Tracey, & Enz, 1997), four (e.g., Lievens, Van Geit, & Coetsier, 1997), five (e.g., Bycio et al., 1995; Koh, Steers, & Terborg, 2005; Yammarino, Spangler, & Bass, 1995) or six factors (e.g., Avolio, Bass, & Jung, 1999; Hater & Bass, 1988). From the authors' point of view, this situation is unsatisfactory. Also from a practitioner's point of view, the lack of validity is clearly a disadvantage: One would not be able to provide reliable information feedback concerning leadership behavior in an online development tool, as will be presented further below.

ALTERNATIVES: THE OHIO STATE LEADERSHIP BEHAVIORS

Due to the methodological restrictions in traditional and transformational e-leadership research, we propose going back to the Ohio State Leadership (OSL) research (Stogdill, 1950) when doing research for practitioners. The Ohio State Leadership group identified two valid factors (Fleishman, 1953; Hemphill & Coons, 1957; Halpin & Winer, 1957): *consideration* and *initiating structure*. Consideration behaviors are essentially relationship behaviors, such as being friendly and supportive and building respect, trust and liking between leaders and followers. Initiating structure implies behaviors such as organizing work, giving structure to the work context, defining roles and responsibilities, and scheduling work activities. Specifically, consideration seems to be the conceptual progenitor of transformational leadership, as they share basic conceptual similarities (Judge, Piccolo, Ilies, 2004; Seltzer & Bass, 1990). In fact, until the introduction of transformational leadership, the topics of consideration and initiating structure dominated leadership research. According to Fleishman (1995), "consideration and initiating structure have proven to be among the most robust of leadership concepts." (p. 51). For example, the two leadership factors have been used as operationalizations for autocratic vs. democratic, directive vs. participative, and task-oriented vs. relation-oriented leadership styles (e.g. Seltzer & Bass, 1990). We further argue for the OSL because a recent meta-analysis by Judge et al. (2004) clearly shows that both OSL concepts have important main effects on various indicators of effective leadership, such as job satisfaction,

Figure 1. Welcome screen to the Virtual Team Trainer

motivation or leader effectiveness. Furthermore, we assume that the two-factorial structure has good face validity and is widely accepted by practitioners. In addition, the scales for OSL are short and reliable (e.g. Seltzer & Bass, 1990).

In the next section, we will present an e-leadership tool that integrates consideration (high overlap with transformational leadership) and initiating structure, as well as some of the implications derived through experiments with transformational e-leadership, and technological developments.

THE VIRTUAL TEAM TRAINER

The Virtual Team Trainer (VTT, see Figure 1) was developed as a general team development tool that runs on the Internet (Reips & Ito, 2007). The tool contains personality tests, group process development units and modules which help leaders and team members identify their OSL leadership style, relate it to team structure and development, and subsequently modify and improve on their leadership skills. The VTT is available free for use via the *iScience Server* portal at http://iscience.eu.

Within the VTT, the leadership modules are embedded within a broader set of tools for self-evaluation, team analysis and development. For example, the module "Rate" offers team ratings by using three sets of categories taken from the Existential Mapping Process (EMP, Horowitz, 1985; Tucker, 1987; Reips, 1992): Roles, Scripts and Stage Directions. In any given moment of a group interaction, each individual can be perceived as "performing" one of six Roles, in combination with one of the five Scripts. The individual stages her/his behavior in a certain "Direction" (Vector), with a certain "Energy" (Valence), and with a more spontaneous or more delayed "Timing" (Velocity). For a given scene from a team session, a user of the VTT thus may rate some or all team members on one or several of the EMP categories. Ratings of the same scene by different team members are automatically combined to a set of team statistics by the VTT. Ratings of several scenes and/or sessions of the same team by several of its members are suited to reveal team processes as they unfold over time.

For research purposes, and for more comprehensive support in team development, the combination of data from several submodules is suited

Figure 2. Items with rating options from the OLBDQ in VTT's leadership test submodule.

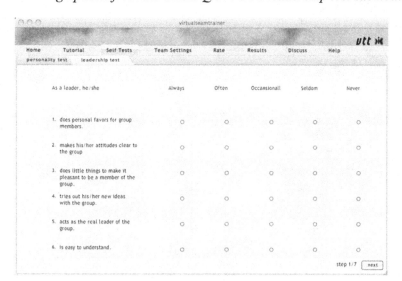

to reveal an in-depth analysis of the processes underlying leadership functions. For example, via the VTT, leadership can be linked to personality characteristics and team dynamics as rated in the Existential Mapping Process. These processes can be followed over time, and via comparison of different teams, the individual components can be separated from team components, leadership components, and from interactions between these factors.

Diagnosing the Ohio State Leadership Style within VTT

Figure 2 shows the Online Leader Behavior Description Questionnaire (OLBDQ; Reips & Heilmann, 2009) test tab that is part of the leadership module within the VTT. Upon entering the module, the instructions, adapted from Stogdill (1950), read "On the following pages, a list of items that may be used to describe the behavior of the chosen team member is presented. This is not a test of ability. It simply asks you to describe as accurately as you can, how the chosen team member behaves as a leader of the group that she/he supervises. Note: The term 'group,' as employed

in the following items, refers to a department, division, or other unit of organization that she/he supervises. The term "members," refers to all the people in the unit that she/he supervises. 1. READ each item carefully. 2. THINK about how frequently she/he engages in the behavior described by the item. 3. DECIDE whether she/he 'always', 'often', 'occasionally', 'seldom' or 'never' acts as described by the item. 4. CHOOSE one of the 5 radio buttons following the item to show the answer you selected."

Once all ratings have been made, VTT will display a graphical visualization of the results upon request. The two dimensions *consideration* ("people orientation") and *initiating structure* ("task orientation") are crossed to make up a leadership behavior space (see Figure 3). The target person's leadership style resulting from her/his answers to the questionnaire is marked as a red dot. Two dotted lines that intersect the leadership behavior space currently represent the averages from the LBDQ test manual, but in the future they will mark the average scores from all users who have taken the test in VTT. These lines will then dynamically adjust through the use of the VTT. Thus, the underlying user database, i.e.,

Figure 3. Results screen showing one's individual result in the consideration-initiation leadership space

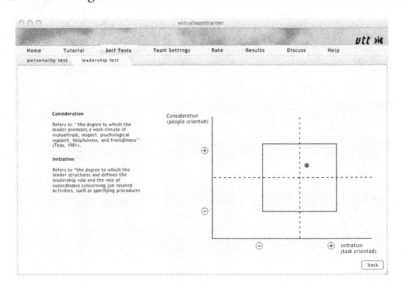

sample, is growing steadily. The lines result in four simplifying quadrants that are useful to communicate leadership style easily, for example in training sessions.

Before actually filling in the questionnaire, a user needs to decide on the target person and state. One can either rate oneself or anonymously rate a different person from one of one's teams, and

the test can be taken for *actual* leadership behavior or for one's *ideal* leadership behavior. If one intends to rate someone else, VTT first asks for the team (via a list of all teams it knows one is a member of), then for the team member to be rated (see Figure 4).

A user may come back and repeatedly take the test, thus documenting changes over time (Figure

Figure 4. Options for team and member selection in other-ratings

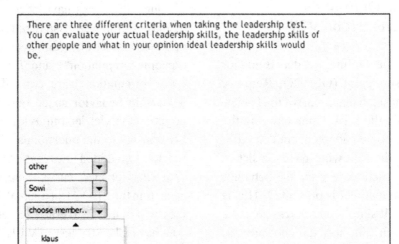

Figure 5. A VTT screen illustrating time series of sessions, thus the longitudinal aspect of leadership and team data can be analyzed

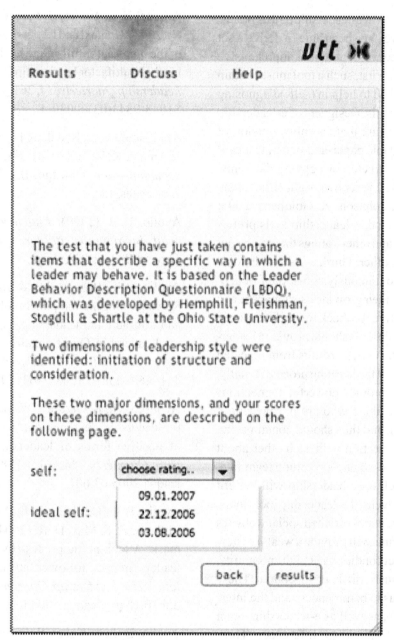

5). Accordingly, with frequent use, the OLBDQ module in VTT works as a leadership diagnosis and management tool. Also, self-evaluations can be compared to those by others, and those of leaders can be compared to those of regular team members. With wide use of the VTT in perhaps thousands of real teams, we will be able to derive many factors and combinations of factors that distinguish more successful from less successful e-leadership.

CONCLUSION

From the conception of e-leadership and its practical application, we have been able to derive a set of features that seem essential in comprehensive e-leadership tools. First, such a tool must contain validated tests suited to help in (self-)diagnosing one's leadership skills. Designers of e-leadership tools need to be aware that an online version of a previously available paper-and-pencil test cannot simply be constructed by copying the items; it must be validated in its own right (Buchanan, 2001; Buchanan, Johnson, & Goldberg, 2005; Reips, 2006). Second, e-leadership tools preferably contain self- and other-ratings that can be put in relation to each other. Third, e-leadership tools can and should continuously adjust their benchmarks, i.e., utilize their growing user database as a reference for relative feedback for each new user. Fourth, e-leadership tools should provide a leadership memory to the user, so results from repeated sessions can support the learning process. Finally, e-leadership tools provide powerful connections between team members who are not present at the same location, and thus should contain some means of communication with each other about the results in regards to one's common team fate.

Future research on e-leadership will benefit highly from the advent of e-leadership tools in the style of communication-enriched social websites and tools. Real teams will provide a wealth of new data under Internet conditions of high anonymity, that were previously difficult to obtain. These results will help us to better understand the interplay of leadership, as well as e-leadership, team constellation, and individual differences. Thus, we will be able to develop more finely grained (e-)leadership theories.

REFERENCES

Antonakis, J., Avolio, B. J., & Sivasubramaniam, N. (2003). Context and leadership: An examination of the nine-factor full-range leadership theory using the Multifactor Leadership Questionnaire. *The Leadership Quarterly, 14*, 261–295. doi:10.1016/S1048-9843(03)00030-4

Applbaum, R. L., Bodaken, E. M., Sereno, K. K., & Anatol, K. W. E. (1974). *The process of group communication*. Chicago, IL: Science Research Associates, Inc.

Avolio, B. J. (1999). *Full leadership development: Building the vital forces in organizations*. Thousand Oaks, CA: Sage.

Avolio, B. J., Bass, B. M., & Jung, D. I. (1999). Re-examining the components of transformational and transactional leadership using the Multifactor Leadership Questionnaire. *Journal of Occupational and Organizational Psychology, 72*, 441–462. doi:10.1348/096317999166789

Avolio, B. J., & Gardner, W. L. (2005). Authentic leadership development: Getting to the root of positive forms of leadership. *The Leadership Quarterly, 16*, 315–338. doi:10.1016/j.leaqua.2005.03.001

Avolio, B. J., Gardner, W. L., Walumbwa, F. O., Luthans, F., & May, D. R. (2004). Unlocking the mask: A look at the process by which authentic leaders impact follower attitudes and behaviors. *The Leadership Quarterly, 15*, 801–823. doi:10.1016/j.leaqua.2004.09.003

Avolio, B. J., & Kahai, S. S. (2003). Adding the "e" to e-leadership: How it may impact your leadership. *Organizational Dynamics, 31*, 325–338. doi:10.1016/S0090-2616(02)00133-X

Avolio, B. J., Kahai, S. S., & Dodge, G. E. (2001). E-leadership: Implications for theory, research, and practice. *The Leadership Quarterly, 11*, 615–668. doi:10.1016/S1048-9843(00)00062-X

Avolio, B. J., Walumbwa, F. O., & Weber, T. J. (2009). Leadership: Current theories, research, and future directions. *Annual Review of Psychology, 60*, 421–449. doi:10.1146/annurev.psych.60.110707.163621

Bass, B. M. (1985). *Leadership and performance beyond expectations*. New York, NY: Free Press.

Bass, B. M. (1990). *Bass & Stogdill's handbook of leadership: Theory, research, and managerial applications*. New York, NY: Free Press.

Bass, B. M. (1997). Does the transactional-transformational leadership paradigm transcend organizational and national boundaries? *The American Psychologist, 52*, 130–139. doi:10.1037/0003-066X.52.2.130

Bass, B. M., & Avolio, B. J. (1990). *Transformational leadership development: Manual for the Multifactor Leadership Questionnaire*. Palo Alto, CA: Consulting Psychologists Press.

Bass, B. M., & Avolio, B. J. (1994). *Improving organizational effectiveness through transformational leadership*. Thousand Oaks, CA: Sage.

Bass, B. M., Avolio, B. J., Jung, D. I., & Berson, Y. (2003). Predicting unit performance by assessing transformational and transactional leadership. *The Journal of Applied Psychology, 88*, 207–218. doi:10.1037/0021-9010.88.2.207

Brown, M. E., & Treviño, L. K. (2006). Ethical leadership: A review and future directions. *The Leadership Quarterly, 17*, 595–616. doi:10.1016/j.leaqua.2006.10.004

Brown, M. E., Treviño, L. K., & Harrison, D. A. (2005). Ethical leadership: A social learning perspective for construct development and testing. *Organizational Behavior and Human Decision Processes, 97*, 117–134. doi:10.1016/j.obhdp.2005.03.002

Bryman, A. (1993). *Charisma and leadership in organizations*. Newbury Park, CA: Sage.

Buchanan, T. (2001). Online Personality Assessment. In Reips, U.-D., & Bosnjak, M. (Eds.), *Dimensions of Internet science* (pp. 57–74). Lengerich, Germany: Pabst Science.

Buchanan, T., Johnson, J. A., & Goldberg, L. (2005). Implementing a Five-Factor personality inventory for use on the Internet. *European Journal of Psychological Assessment, 21*, 115–127. doi:10.1027/1015-5759.21.2.115

Burns, J. M. (1978). *Leadership*. New York, NY: Harper & Row.

Bycio, P., Hackett, R. D., & Allen, J. S. (1995). Further assessments of Bass's (1985) conceptualization of transactional and transformational leadership. *The Journal of Applied Psychology, 80*, 468–478. doi:10.1037/0021-9010.80.4.468

Carless, S. A. (1998). Assessing the discriminant validity of transformational leadership behavior as measured by the MLQ. *Journal of Occupational and Organizational Psychology, 71*, 353–358. doi:10.1111/j.2044-8325.1998.tb00681.x

Conger, J. A., & Kanungo, R. N. (1998). *Charismatic leadership in organizations*. Thousand Oaks, CA: Sage.

Den Hartog, D., House, R. J., Hanges, P. J., Ruiz-Quintanilla, S. A., & Dorfman, P. W. (1999). Culture specific and cross culturally generalizable implicit leadership theories: Are attributes of charismatic/transformational leadership universally endorsed? *The Leadership Quarterly, 10*, 219–256. doi:10.1016/S1048-9843(99)00018-1

Felfe, J. (2006). Transformationale und charismatische Führung - Stand der Forschung und aktuelle Entwicklungen [Transformational and charismatic leadership: State of research and recent developments]. *Zeitschrift für Personalpsychologie, 5*, 163–176. doi:10.1026/1617-6391.5.4.163

Fiedler, F. E. (1967). *A theory of leadership effectiveness*. New York, NY: McGraw-Hill.

Fleishman, E. A. (1953). The description of supervisory behavior. *The Journal of Applied Psychology, 37*, 1–6. doi:10.1037/h0056314

Fleishman, E. A. (1995). Consideration and structure: Another look at their role in leadership research. In Dansereau, F., & Yammarino, F. J. (Eds.), *Leadership: The multiple-level approaches: Classical and new wave* (pp. 51–60). Stamford, CT: JAI Press.

Fuller, J. B., Patterson, C. E. P., Hester, K., & Stringer, D. Y. (1996). A quantitative review of research on charismatic leadership. *Psychological Reports, 78*, 271–287. doi:10.2466/pr0.1996.78.1.271

Geyer, A. L., & Steyrer, J. M. (1998). Transformational leadership and objective performance in banks. *Applied Psychology: An International Review, 47*, 397–420. doi:doi:10.1111/j.1464-0597.1998.tb00035.x

Halpin, A. W., & Winer, B. J. (1957). A factorial study of the leader behavior descriptions. In Stogdill, R. M., & Coons, A. E. (Eds.), *Leaders behavior: Its description and measurement* (pp. 39–51). Columbus, OH: The Bureau of Business Research College of Commerce and Administration, Ohio State University.

Hambley, L. A., O'Neill, T. A., & Kline, T. J. B. (2007). Virtual team leadership: The effects of leadership style and communication medium on team interaction styles and outcomes. *Organizational Behavior and Human Decision Processes, 103*, 1–20. doi:10.1016/j.obhdp.2006.09.004

Hater, J. J., & Bass, B. M. (1988). Superiors' evaluations and subordinates' perceptions of transformational and transactional leadership. *The Journal of Applied Psychology, 73*, 695–702. doi:10.1037/0021-9010.73.4.695

Heinitz, K., Liepmann, D., & Felfe, J. (2005). Examining the factor structure of the MLQ: Recommendation for a reduced set of factors. *European Journal of Psychological Assessment, 21*, 182–190. doi:10.1027/1015-5759.21.3.182

Hemphill, J. K., & Coons, A. E. (1957). Development of the leader behavior description questionnaire. In Stogdill, R. M., & Coons, A. E. (Eds.), *Leaders behavior: Its description and measurement* (pp. 6–38). Columbus, OH: The Bureau of Business Research College of Commerce and Administration, Ohio State University.

Hinkin, T. R., Tracey, J. B., & Enz, C. A. (1997). Scale construction: developing reliable and valid measurement instruments. *Journal of Hospitality & Tourism Research (Washington, D.C.), 21*, 100–120. doi:doi:10.1177/109634809702100108

Horowitz, L. J. (1985). *The existential mapping process*. Unpublished manuscript, Sonoma State University.

House, R. J. (1971). A path-goal theory of leader effectiveness. *Administrative Science Quarterly, 16*, 321–339. doi:10.2307/2391905

House, R. J. (1977). A 1976 theory of charismatic leadership. In Hunt, J. G., & Larson, L. L. (Eds.), *Leadership: The cutting edge* (pp. 189–207). Carbondale, IL: Southern Illinois University Press.

House, R. J. (1996). Path-goal theory of leadership: Lessons, legacy, and a reformulated theory. *The Leadership Quarterly, 7*, 323–352. doi:10.1016/S1048-9843(96)90024-7

House, R. J., & Podsakoff, P. M. (1994). Leadership effectiveness: Past perspectives and future directions for research. In Greenberg, J. (Ed.), *Organizational behavior: The state of the science* (pp. 45–82). Hillsdale, NJ: Erlbaum.

Howell, J. M., & Avolio, B. J. (1993). Transformational leadership, transactional leadership, locus of control, and support for innovation: Key predictors of consolidated-business-unit performance. *The Journal of Applied Psychology*, *78*, 891–902. doi:10.1037/0021-9010.78.6.891

Hoyt, C. L., & Blascovich, J. (2003). Transformational and transactional leadership in virtual and physical environments. *Small Group Research*, *34*, 678–715. doi:10.1177/1046496403257527

Hunt, J. G., & Conger, J. A. (1999). From where we sit: An assessment of transformational and charismatic leadership research. *The Leadership Quarterly*, *10*, 335–343. doi:10.1016/S1048-9843(99)00039-9

Judge, T. A., & Piccolo, R. F. (2004). Transformational and transactional leadership: A meta-analytic test of their relative validity. *The Journal of Applied Psychology*, *89*, 755–768. doi:10.1037/0021-9010.89.5.755

Judge, T. A., Piccolo, R. F., & Ilies, R. (2004). The forgotten ones? The validity of consideration and initiating structure in leadership research. *The Journal of Applied Psychology*, *89*, 36–51. doi:10.1037/0021-9010.89.1.36

Judge, T. A., Woolf, E. F., Hurst, C., & Livingston, B. (2006). Charismatic and transformational leadership. A Review and an agenda for future research. *Zeitschrift für Arbeits- und Organisationspsychologie*, *50*, 203–214. doi:10.1026/0932-4089.50.4.203

Jung, D., Chow, C., & Wu, A. (2003). The role of transformational leadership in enhancing organizational innovation: Hypotheses and some preliminary findings. *The Leadership Quarterly*, *14*, 525–544. doi:10.1016/S1048-9843(03)00050-X

Kahai, S. S., Sosik, J. J., & Avolio, B. J. (2003). Effects of leadership style, anonymity, and rewards in an electronic meeting system environment. *The Leadership Quarterly*, *14*, 499–524. doi:10.1016/S1048-9843(03)00049-3

Kark, R., Shamir, B., & Chen, G. (2003). The two faces of transformational leadership: Empowerment and dependency. *The Journal of Applied Psychology*, *88*, 246–255. doi:10.1037/0021-9010.88.2.246

Kelloway, E. K., Barling, J., Kelley, E., Comtois, J., & Gatien, B. (2003). Remote transformational leadership. *Leadership and Organization Development Journal*, *24*, 163–171. doi:10.1108/01437730310469589

Kirkpatrick, S. A., & Locke, E. A. (1996). Direct and indirect effects of three core charismatic leadership components on performance and attitudes. *The Journal of Applied Psychology*, *81*, 36–51. doi:10.1037/0021-9010.81.1.36

Koh, W. L., Steers, R. M., & Terborg, J. R. (1995). The effects of transformational leadership on teacher attitudes and student performance in Singapore. *Journal of Organizational Behavior*, *16*, 319–333. doi:10.1002/job.4030160404

Lievens, F., Van Geit, P., & Coetsier, P. (1997). Identification of transformational leadership qualities: An examination of potential biases. *European Journal of Work and Organizational Psychology*, *6*, 415–530. doi:10.1080/135943297399015

Lowe, K. B., Kroeck, K. G., & Sivasubramaniam, N. (1996). Effectiveness correlates of transformational and transactional leadership: A meta-analytic review of the MLQ literature. *The Leadership Quarterly, 7,* 385–425. doi:10.1016/S1048-9843(96)90027-2

Meyer, J. P., Stanley, D. J., Herscovitch, L., & Topolnytsky, L. (2002). Affective, continuance, and normative commitment to the organization: A meta-analysis of antecedents, correlates, and consequences. *Journal of Vocational Behavior, 61,* 20–52. doi:10.1006/jvbe.2001.1842

Reips, U.-D. (1992). *The composition and systematic exploration of an observation device for the existential mapping process.* Unpublished Master's thesis, Sonoma State University.

Reips, U.-D. (2006). Web-based methods. In Eid, M., & Diener, E. (Eds.), *Handbook of multimethod measurement in psychology* (pp. 73–85). Washington, DC: American Psychological Association. doi:10.1037/11383-006

Reips, U.-D. (2008). Potenziale jenseits der Privatsphäre: Risiken und Chancen internetbasierter Kommunikation [Potentials beyond privacy: Risks and benefits of Internet-based communication]. *Psychoscope, 29,* 8–11.

Reips, U.-D., & Bosnjak, M. (Eds.). (2001). *Dimensions of internet science.* Lengerich, Germany: Pabst.

Reips, U.-D., & Heilmann, T. (2009). *The OLBDQ: An online version of the leader behavior description questionnaire.* Manuscript in preparation.

Reips, U.-D., & Ito, T. (2007, January 10). *The virtual team trainer.* Presentation in lecture series "Educational Engineering", ETH Zürich & Educational Engineering Lab, University of Zürich.

Riegelsberger, J., Sasse, A., & McCarthy, J. D. (2007). Trust in mediated interactions. In Joinson, A., McKenna, K. Y. A., Postmes, T., & Reips, U.-D. (Eds.), *The Oxford handbook of Internet psychology* (pp. 53–69). Oxford, UK: Oxford University Press.

Sassenberg, K., Postmes, T., Boos, M., & Reips, U.-D. (2003). Studying the Internet: A challenge for modern psychology. *Swiss Journal of Psychology, 62.* doi:10.1024//1421-0185.62.2.75

Seltzer, J., & Bass, B. M. (1990). Transformational leadership: Beyond initiation and consideration. *Journal of Management, 16,* 693. doi:10.1177/014920639001600403

Sosik, J. J., Avolio, B. J., & Kahai, S. S. (1997). Effects of leadership style and anonymity on group potency and effectiveness in a group decision support system environment. *The Journal of Applied Psychology, 82,* 89–103. doi:10.1037/0021-9010.82.1.89

Sosik, J. J., Avolio, B. J., Kahai, S. S., & Jung, D. I. (1998). Computer-supported work group potency and effectiveness: The role of transformational leadership, anonymity, and task interdependence. *Computers in Human Behavior, 14,* 491–511. doi:10.1016/S0747-5632(98)00019-3

Stogdill, R. M. (1950). Leadership, membership and organization. *Psychological Bulletin, 47,* 1–14. doi:10.1037/h0053857

Tepper, B. J., & Percy, P. M. (1994). Structural validity of the multifactor leadership questionnaire. *Educational and Psychological Measurement, 54,* 734–744. doi:10.1177/0013164494054003020

Vroom, V. H., & Yetton, P. W. (1973). *Leadership and decision making.* Pittsburgh, PA: University of Pittsburgh Press.

Weber, M. (1947). *The theory of social and economic organization.* New York, NY: Free Press.

Whittington, J. L., Goodwin, V. L., & Murray, B. (2004). Transformational leadership, goal difficulty, and job design: Independent and interactive effects on employee outcomes. *The Leadership Quarterly, 15*, 593–606. doi:10.1016/j. leaqua.2004.07.001

Wittchen, M., Schlereth, D., & Hertel, G. (2007). Social indispensability in spite of temporal and spatial separation: Motivation gains in a sequential task during anonymous cooperation on the Internet. *International Journal of Internet Science, 2*, 12–27.

Yammarino, F. J., Spangler, W. D., & Bass, B. M. (1993). Transformational leadership and performance: A longitudinal investigation. *The Leadership Quarterly, 4*, 81–108. doi:10.1016/1048-9843(93)90005-E

ADDITIONAL READING

Antoni, C., & Hertel, G. (Eds.). (2009). Team innovation, knowledge and performance management: Requirements for different types of teamwork. *Special issue of the European Journal of Work and Organizational Psychology, 18*, 251-379.

Balthazard, P. A., Waldman, D. A., & Atwater, L. E. (2008). The mediating effects of leadership and interaction style in face-to-face and virtual teams. In Weisband, S. (Ed.), *Leadership at a distance: Research in technologically-supported work* (pp. 127–150). New York, NY: Erlbaum.

Cascio, W. F., & Shurygailo, S. (2003). E-leadership and virtual teams. *Organizational Dynamics, 31*, 362–376. doi:10.1016/S0090-2616(02)00130-4

Clawson, V. K., Bostrom, R. P., & Anson, R. (1993). The role of the facilitator in computer-supported meetings. *Small Group Research, 24*, 547–565. doi:10.1177/1046496493244007

Hertel, G., Geister, S., & Konradt, U. (2005). Managing virtual teams: A review of current empirical research. *Human Resource Management Review, 15*, 69–95. doi:10.1016/j.hrmr.2005.01.002

Hertel, G., Konradt, U., & Orlikowski, B. (2004). Managing distance by interdependence: Goal setting, task interdependence, and team-based rewards in virtual teams. *European Journal of Work and Organizational Psychology, 13*, 1–28. doi:10.1080/13594320344000228

Jarvenpaa, S., Knoll, K., & Leidner, D. (1998). Is anybody out there? Antecedents of trust in global virtual teams. *Journal of Management Information Systems, 14*, 29–64.

Joinson, A. N., McKenna, K., Postmes, T., & Reips, U.-D. (Eds.). (2007). *The Oxford handbook of Internet psychology*. Oxford, UK: Oxford University Press.

Kozlowski, S. W. J., & Bell, B. S. (2003). Work groups and teams in organizations. In Borman, W. C., Ilgen, D. R., & Klimoski, R. J. (Eds.), *Handbook of psychology: Industrial and organizational psychology* (pp. 333–375). London, UK: Wiley.

Reips, U.-D., & Birnbaum, M. H. (2011). Behavioral research and data collection via the Internet. In Vu, K.-P. L., & Proctor, R. W. (Eds.), *The handbook of human factors in Web design* (2nd ed., pp. 563–585). Mahwah, NJ: Erlbaum. doi:10.1201/b10855-37

KEY TERMS AND DEFINITIONS

Authentic Leadership: Authentic leaders know who they are, what they believe and value, and they act upon these values and beliefs while transparently interacting with others.

Consideration: The concept of consideration goes back to the Ohio State Studies in the 1950'. It is the degree to which leaders are participative, pleasant, egalitarian, and concerned about the group members' welfare.

E-Leadership: Unlike the traditional, face-to-face leadership, e-leadership takes place in a context where work is mediated by information technology.

Ethical Leadership: Ethical leaders are ethical role models.

Existential Mapping Process (EMP): A group observation and development system developed by Horowitz (1985) and others. The system contains Roles, Scripts and Stage Directions. In any given moment of a group interaction each individual can be perceived as "performing" one of the six Roles in combination with one of the five Scripts. The individual stages her/his behavior in a certain "Direction" (Vector), with a certain "Energy" (Valence), and with a more spontaneous or more delayed "Timing" (Velocity). The Virtual Team Trainer (VTT) combines the Existential Mapping Process with the idea of a structured social Internet platform.

Initiating Structure: This concept has its roots in the Ohio State Studies in the 1950'. Initiating Structure is the degree to which a leader deals with clarifying the task requirements, providing information, and structuring tasks.

Online Leadership Behavior Description Questionnaire: The Online Leader Behavior Description Questionnaire (OLBDQ) consists of 40 statements, measuring the two factors of consideration and initiating. Typical items are as follows: "He is friendly and approachable" (consideration), or "He let group members know what is expected from them" (initiating structure).

Multifactor Leadership Questionnaire: The Multifactor Leadership Questionnaire is the mostly widely used measure of transformational leadership as well as for the other leadership factors described above. This measure contains 45 items. There are 36 items that represent the several leadership factors described above, and nine items that assess three leadership outcome scales, that is satisfaction with the leader, extra effort and (leader) effectiveness. This measure exists in two versions, the rater form (followers rate their leader) and the leader form (leader's self- rating).

Transactional Leadership: Transactional leadership aims at monitoring and controlling employees through rational or economic means, operating with existing structures and systems.

Transformational Leadership: Transformational leaders' behaviors affect followers' effort, performance, and satisfaction by raising their self-efficacy, self-esteem and locus of control through expressing high expectations of followers and belief in followers' abilities.

Virtual Team Trainer: The Virtual Team Trainer (VTT) is a general team development tool that runs on the Internet. The VTT contains modules that help leaders and any team member to test their personality, invite others, rate others' team behavior, and – most importantly in this context - identify their leadership style (consideration and initiating structure), relate it to team structure and development, and subsequently modify and improve on their leadership skills.

Chapter 18
Preferred Features of Course Management Systems in Post Secondary and Corporate Online Learning

Orly Calderon
Long Island University, USA

ABSTRACT

The instrument described in this chapter is designed for instructors of e-learning, for the purpose of giving faculty an opportunity to identify, express, and suggest features in a Course Management System (CMS) that they feel are pedagogically important. Appropriate for use in universities or corporations, this survey can provide instructors with a greater voice in the CMS decision making process, thereby giving pedagogy a greater influence on the practice of technology implementation in the learning environment. This chapter describes the construction of the survey, its psychometric properties, and preliminary data gathered at a private university in New York State. The findings differentiate among CMS' features that faculty consider important, not important, or feel neutral about. Further, the results underscore the differences between previous users and non-users of CMSs in assigning importance to types of features. The author discusses the implications of using the survey in both educational and corporate settings with the purpose of helping institutions that utilize e-learning to meet the educational standard set by current best practices.

DOI: 10.4018/978-1-4666-2172-5.ch018

POST SECONDARY AND CORPORATE ONLINE LEARNING: PREFERRED FEATURES OF COURSE MANAGEMENT SYSTEMS

Definition of E-Learning

On-line, or e-learning, refers to learning that is "facilitated and supported through the use of information and communication technologies" (Clarke, Lewis, Cole, & Ringrose, 2004, p.33). Instructors in e-learning environment use computers to deliver content, and utilize instructional technology in their teaching (Rovai, 2004). Students within the e-learning environment engage in various learning activities that feature electronically-delivered content, and allow the participants (students and instructor) to communicate with each other via the internet (Zhang & Zhou, 2003). Such activities may be synchronous (simultaneous) or asynchronous (non-simultaneous), depending on the purpose of the activity and the software or computer-based application used to carry the activity out. Garrison, & Kanuka, (2004) point out that e-learning may be utilized either fully on-line or in a blended format (i.e., combining face-to-face learning experiences in the classroom with on-line and computer-based learning experiences).

E learning, as a method of education and training, has become prevalent in post-secondary institutions as well as in the corporate world. According to the National Center of Educational Statistics (2008), 65% of all degree-granting post-secondary institutions offer college-level credit granting online education courses. Within the corporate world, the use of e-learning for training purposes is increasing rapidly (Pack, 2002). Newton & Doonga (2007) who have investigated the perceptions of training managers regarding the experience of providing E training to corporate clients, state that a universal shift towards E training is evident across companies from all areas of industry and commerce.

Pros and Cons of E-Learning in Higher Education and Corporate Training

The advantages of e-learning in educational and corporate contexts have been studied rather extensively, and with mixed results. Within post-secondary education institutions, advantages of e-learning encompass two main factors: convenience, and pedagogical value. For example, Albrecht, (2006), reports that students appreciate the convenience of e-learning in that it cuts down on commuting to class time, and affords flexible study time that better accommodates a busy daily schedule.

Other studies focused on the potential for pedagogical value of e-learning in post-secondary institutions. Neville, Heavin, & Walsh, (2005), examined how utilization of e-learning technology might contribute to the learners' experience, and to the relationship between the students and the instructor. Their findings indicate that, when e-learning environments utilize computer technology that is carefully designed to meet learning needs, such technology can provide structural flexibility that can increase learners' motivation. Moreover, well- designed e-learning methods of instruction are learner's-centered, rather than teacher's-centered, and thus are advantageous in accommodating different learning styles. Morgan (2003) notes that teaching within an e-learning environment requires pre-planning and careful re-organization of the content material, and therefore is associated with a more thoughtful teaching, increased student engagement, and increased opportunities for student-student and student-instructor interaction.

Zhang and Zhou (2003) investigated learner-content interaction within an undergraduate e-learning environment. They found that students who received E training appreciated the self-paced learning, and the collaborative learning environment (Zhang and Zhou, 2003). Moreover, students who received training via the interactive e-learning environment outperformed students who received training in the traditional face-to-face learning environment, and were as satisfied with the learning experience as the students in the face-to-face group (Zhang and Zhou, 2003).

Within the corporate world, research has pointed out the advantages of e-learning in terms of flexibility of time and location of the training. Workers who utilize E training need not lose work time and can receive what amounts to direct on-the-job-training (Newton & Doonga, 2007; Zhang and Zhou, 2003). Newton and Doonga, (2007), list seven distinct advantages of E training that have been identified by suppliers and managers of e-learning within the corporate world. The first four advantages (in ranking order of importance) are associated with better management considerations (e.g., flexibility in terms of location of training; reduction of time away from work while in training; access to large volumes of training materials and improved ability to monitor training, Newton & Doonga, 2007, p.124). The remaining advantages that have been indentified in this study are associated with pedagogical considerations, (e.g., more interesting learning experiences via the use of simulations and games; improved quality of training materials, and the ability to access learning in remote locations, Newton & Doonga, 2007, p.124). Similarly, Clarke, Lewis, Cole & Ringrose, (2005), report that companies that utilize e-learning to train employees cite savings in resources, chiefly those that are associated with cost and time of training.

On the other hand, research also indicates clear disadvantages of e-learning, both within higher education, and corporate training environments. According to Rovai, (2004), students who are educated in on-line learning environment report that they feel isolated from their peers and the instructor, that that have difficulties managing their time within the on-line course and that they experience difficulties accessing the materials on-line. Universities and corporations alike have identified administrative disadvantages of e-learning, such as increased preparation time for on-line courses, increased costs associated with updating the digitally delivered content, and the need to create and maintain proper infrastructure and support services (Newton and Doonga, 2007; Zhang & Zhou, 2003). Other disadvantages associated with corporate E training include: Low computer literacy among trainees, limited computer access in the work place, and limited staff and resources for technical support (Clarke et al., 2005; Newton & Doonga 2007).

It appears that pedagogical consideration is the key factor that differentiates successful from unsuccessful design and delivery of e-learning in both post-secondary institutions, and the corporate workforce. Clearly, the challenge involves a thoughtful linking of pedagogy with computer technology. Rovai (2004) points out that successful e-learning is partially contingent on a thoughtful shift from an instructional emphasis on didactic and face-to-face interaction, towards encouraging students to engage in guided discovery and independent inquiry via internet technology. Thus, e-learning technology must reflect a careful consideration for modifying the student-teacher and student-student relationships within the e-learning environment. Several researchers focus on specific types of technology tools that must be included within the e-learning environment in order to maximize its pedagogical efficacy, whether in post-secondary education institutions or within corporate training. Sugar et al. (2007) note that, to be effective, the on-line learning environment should be able to support content delivery as well as social and collaborative interactions among students and the instructor. Similarly, Neville et al. (2005) found that users of e-learning technology find existing commercial systems to be useful in managing content, but limited in their ability to integrate features that promote critical thinking and interactive learning. Similar conclusions were derived by other research on the use of e-learning in corporate training. For example, Lim, Lee & Nam (2007) studied variables that were relevant to effective organizational training, learning, and performance in face-to-face and e-learning environments, respectively. They identified several factors that were essential for the e-learning environment to be efficacious: First, users of the e-learning environment and its associated technology must demonstrate a high sense of computer skills self-efficacy. Second, the e-learning environment must be designed to link context and pedagogy by underscoring commonalties between the training content and the work environment. Third, the e-learning environment must allow for communication between the trainer and trainees. Finally, the e-learning environment must enjoy adequate organizational support (Lim et al., 2007).

Ong, Lai, & Wang (2004) researched features of e-learning environment that were valued within the engineering profession. They found that e-learning systems that were user-friendly and that had trustworthy mechanism for protection of content and education records were valued the most by international high-tech organizations that implemented e-learning as a training method for their employees.

Pack (2002) reviewed different e-learning platforms that were provided by different vendors, each with its own relative strengths that appeal to the needs of respective companies. Pack (2002) notes that the majorities of companies have some e-learning programs, but these represent a small component of their training protocol. According to Pack (2002), companies report that e-learning involves expensive, cumbersome, and confusing technology, and that such technology does not always provide efficacious solutions to the content and organizational needs of the company. Pack (2002) concludes that there is evident need for technology that will combine management of content with design and delivery of content, including opportunities for contextual interactive learning.

Neville et al. (2005) also note the importance of pedagogical considerations in the design of computer technology tools for delivering e-learning.

Such pedagogical considerations should include tools that encourage collaborative learning with the instructor acting as a facilitator. Newton & Doonga (2007) recommend that e-learning environments consider use of computer tools that encourage learners' control of the pace and sequencing of learning, and allow for interactive learning, utilizing chunking of the material. Lim, Lee & Nam (2007) identified the importance of pedagogy and content for effective organizational training. They found that in order for trainees to maximize knowledge and skills, the content, and the context within which it is delivered, must be as similar as possible to the working environment.

Definition of Course Management System (CMS)

Typically, e-learning courses and training programs utilize course management systems (CMS) that are designed to promote knowledge and skills. The term CMS has been defined slightly differently by various researchers, but most of the definitions currently used in the literature refer to the purpose of a CMS as well as to its computer-technology components. Levine (2008) broadly defines a CMS as a "system used to manage the content of a website" (Levine, 2008, p.4). Morgan (2003) defines CMS more specifically as a "software system specifically designed and marketed for faculty and students to use in teaching and learning…[and] include course content organization and presentation, communication tools, students assessment tools, grade book tools and functions to manage class materials and activities" (Morgan, 2003, p.9). Clarke at al., (2005) refer to a Managed Learning Environment and a Virtual Learning Environment, which they define, respectively, as " a whole range of different software and systems that interrelate, share data and contribute to learning management" and "specific piece of software that enables learners and staff to interact, and includes content delivery and tracking" (Clark et al, 2005, p.34). Hanson and Robson (2004) use the term "course management technology" to describe "course support structure… including portal-based services, whether purchased or developed locally" (Hanson and Robson, 2004, p.2). Similarly, Newton and Doonga (2007) refer to actual software that allows training via self-study, utilizing computer technology.

For the purpose of this chapter, and drawing on the above definitions of learning management systems as they appear in both higher education and corporate training literature, a CMS is defined here as a virtual learning tool that manages course content and learning activities by allowing the instructor and students to post materials, work collaboratively, and communicate online.

Challenges of Using CMSs in an E-Learning Environment

In order to maximize the efficacy of students and employees' e-learning, post-secondary institutions as well as corporations must choose a CMS that will satisfy the pedagogical requirements discussed above. As Neville et al. (2005) note: "Good pedagogy and reasonable technology will produce a successful course [but] poor pedagogy and the best technology in the world does give you failure" (p. 125). However, the task of actually finding an ideal CMS can be elusive since existing software may not necessarily fulfill the pedagogical needs of the e-learning environment. For example, Morgan, (2003) who has investigated the use of, and satisfaction with, CMS in a post-secondary educational institution, notes that faculty members are concerned about the following gaps between available features of commercial CMS software and educational needs:

- CMs are not flexible enough to allow customization and faculty control over the learning environment.
- Poor CMS measurement tools lower the institutional capabilities to monitor for upgrading and training needs.

- Available commercial CMSs may not fit certain disciplines-specific needs. This incongruity has been noted especially in regards to subjects such as "mathematics, physics, and other equation-dependent disciplines" (Morgan, 2003, p.51).
- Available commercial CMSs may not be well designed to meet pedagogical needs. Specifically, faculty members express dissatisfaction with the quiz tool for its "inadequate assessment options" beyond multiple quizzes (Morgan, 2003, p.52).

Similar gaps exist between available software and educational needs within corporate training e-learning environments. Clarke et al. (2005) report that a search for software that can accommodate the e-learning needs of the English National Health Service (NHS) has yielded no match between existing commercial software and the specified desired software features that have been identified by the NHS' workforce. Consequently, the NHS has contracted with a vendor to develop customized software that would address the gaps between the existing features, and the "desirable" features (Clarke et al., 2005, p. 35).

Generally speaking, current research about utilization of CMSs in e-learning environments, either within the educational or corporate arenas, indicates that the selection of a CMS is oftentimes based on administrative capabilities and constraints. These include: Choices among internal, open-source or commercial systems; monitoring capabilities of the material posted on the system; the level of the system's visibility outside of the institution etc. (Franklyn & van Harmelen, 2007; Katz, 2003). Furthermore, several researchers have noted the need for technology that would be pedagogically driven (Clarke et al., 2005; Lim et al., 2007; Morgan, 2003; Neville et al., 2005; Pack, 2002), and balanced against other considerations such as cost, infrastructure, integration with the institution's information management systems, instructors' training and support, students' training and support (Gallagher, 2003; Morgan 2003), and ease of the CMS's use (Lim et al., 2007; Ong, Lai, & Wang, 2004).

The Purpose of the Current Instrument

In direct response to the challenges of CMSs' selection and utilization that have been described above, the purpose of the current instrument is to survey instructors, and allow them to identify, express, and suggest features in a CMS that they believe are important for successful teaching in an e-learning environment. This survey differs from previous research along two main dimensions. First, previous studies have mostly focused on evaluation of existing CMS packages. For example, Morgan (2003) has surveyed faculty members in the University of Wisconsin in order to identify patterns of use and satisfaction with a CMS that has already been implemented within the university. Similarly, Hanson and Robson (2004) have developed an evaluative framework to assess the benefits of CMS products after these have been purchased and implemented (Hanson and Robson, 2004, p.3). The Course Management Study Group at Mount Holyoke has developed a faculty-targeted questionnaire for the purpose of comparing existing CMSs software, and making a recommendation for the best match between the university's needs and available products. An exception to research that has looked exclusively at existing CMS software, is a study conducted by Levine (2008). In addition to evaluating frequency of use and satisfaction with specific CMS packages, Levine studied specific attributes of CMS, regardless of a specific package or vendor, that were important to companies of all sizes across multiple areas of industry. However, this study targeted companies that used CMS for customer relations rather than staff training purposes. In contrast, the survey that is described in this chapter is designed to assess faculty's perception of CMS features, associated with learning and training, that are not necessarily present in any one given

system. Thus, this survey aims to assist in the proactive evaluation of CMS' features for educational purposes, rather than retroactively evaluating existing software packages. Chiefly, this survey has been developed with an eye towards providing information that is useful in the development of software that is customized to meet the specific needs of the learning environment.

Second, even when previous research did focus on proactive evaluation of computer technology in the e-learning environment (e.g., Neville at al, 2005), such research focused on evaluating perception of how isolated features might contribute to the learning experience. In contrast, the current instrument is designed to assess faculty's perceptions regarding the importance of *types* of features (i.e., pedagogical features, content management features, administrative management features, support features) in the e-learning environment. Thus, the survey is useful in understanding faculty's needs in terms of the typology of CMS's features and their relative importance in teaching within the e-learning environment.

Method

Participants

The initial administration of the survey utilized an all-inclusive sample: the survey was distributed to all full-time faculty members of a large private university in New York State with multiple campuses in urban and suburban areas. Sixty-one faculty members responded to the survey. The participants represented all of the university's campuses and most of the departments. The highest faculty representation was from the schools of nursing, library, and the psychology department, closely followed by representation from the College of Management, and programs within the liberal arts program (i.e., faculty from the departments of English, history, and the arts).

More than two-thirds of the respondents reported that they had taught using a CMS in the past. On the average, previous users have taught about seven courses using various CMSs, usually WebCT (use of which was reported by a third of the participants). Participants also reported some use of Blackboard and Moodle. On the average, participants in the study who have used CMSs in the past, reported that they were satisfied with the CMS experience and that they did not find it difficult to use CMSs in their courses.

Procedure

In order to avoid a self–selection bias by inadvertently targeting only computer-savvy participants, 652 surveys (including cover letters and consent forms) were sent by both e-mail and inter-campus mail to all full-time faculty of a large private university in New York State. Faculty members who agreed to participate could choose to complete either an on-line or a hard copy version of the survey and had the option of returning it via either e-mail or inter-campus mail to the author for scoring and analysis. Participants were given 3 weeks to complete and return the survey. Surveys that were received after that deadline were not included in the analysis. Sixty-one completed surveys were returned within the specified timetable, representing almost a 9.4% return rate.

Instrument

The Survey is comprised of two parts. Part A consists of forty-six 5-point Likert scale items, each asking the participants to rate the importance of each listed feature of a potential CMS. In accordance with other research that has investigated variables that are associated with off-line training as well as e-learning environment (see Lim et al., 2007; Morgan, 2003) the items on the survey represent features that can be utilized along a continuum of a learning environment (i.e., face-to-face, blended, and on-line courses). Each item features five response options with *1* representing *"not important at all"*, and *5* representing *"very*

important". The features included in the survey encompass several dimensions: Type of preferred computer platform, capability to support various file formats, exam processing, inclusion of pedagogical enhancement and administrative management tools, availability of technical support, and preference towards availability of one standardized CMS package vs. multiple CMS packages at a given institution. Thus, the scores on the survey convey the participants' level of relative preference for features that are associated with each of these dimensions, essentially providing a typology of preferred CMS features. Finally, the survey was designed to elicit comments from participants to ensure that the instrument captures a comprehensive view of faculty preferences, including features that may have not been listed quantitatively. Thus, Part A of the survey includes an open-ended response item that asks the participants to list any additional features that they think might be important to include in a CMS.

Part B of the scale consists of seven items designed to gage the participants' professional discipline and level of previous experience, satisfaction, and comfort in using CMSs. Findings from previous research indicate differences among faculty members who teach in different disciplines and who have various levels of experience with CMS in terms of satisfaction with CMS, and sophistication of CMS use in the learning environment (Morgan 2003; Ong et al., 2004). However, whereas previous research defined experience with the CMS in terms of number of years the faculty member has been using a CMS in his or her teaching (Morgan 2003), the current survey defines experience in terms of number of courses in which the faculty member has utilized a CMS, whether in a face-to-face format, blended format or entirely on-line. Finally, Part B features another open-ended response item that invites the participant to offer any additional comments or suggestions regarding the use of a CMS. This item differs from the open-ended response item in Part A in that it is not limited to comments about preferred features of a CMS (a deductive-content type of question). Rather, it allows the participant to express any additional thoughts about the use of CMS that might have been invoked while completing the survey, utilizing an inductive, qualitative approach to the data.

Reliability

Several steps were taken to promote the reliability of the survey: first, items that assess the target dimension (i.e., preference for pedagogical enhancement tools) were dispersed throughout the survey, rather than grouped together, in order to avoid a response bias. Second, some items on part B utilize a reverse- scoring strategy, designed to decrease a floor or ceiling effect response pattern (reverse scoring was not used in Part A of the survey so as to preserve the unity of the survey format and not jeopardize its face validity). Third, the response options feature a *"neutral"* option, also designed to decrease the potential for either a floor or ceiling effect response pattern. Finally, in order to increase participation, and in order to avoid a self-selection sampling bias, an effort was made to access participants who may not be computer-savvy. Thus, 652 surveys were sent by both e-mail and inter-campus mail to all full-time faculty of a large private university in New York State. Sixty-one completed surveys were returned, representing almost a 9.4% return rate.

Validity

In the process of constructing this survey instrument, efforts were made to promote its face validity. The survey begins with a statement that explains what a CMS is, in order to ensure that participants are able to link each item on the survey with its overall purpose of assessing preference for features of CMS. Additionally, part A utilizes a unified format for all items that assess preference for CMS' features.

The Items on the survey derive their content validity from several sources: First, the features that are listed represent existing features in several currently available commercial and open-source CMSs. Second, the survey lists features that are associated with aspects of CMSs and e-learning environment that have been identified in the literature as important to the success of the e-learning experience both in academic and corporate contexts. Examples include the CMS' ability to deliver content in several formats, i.e., visual, audio, etc., (Clark et al., 2005; Morgan 2003; Rovai, 2004), instructor -student and student-student communication enhancement(Clarke et al., 2005; Morgan 2003;Rovai, 2004), availability of technical support (Franklyn & van Harmelen, 2007; Kaleta, Skibba & Joosten, 2007; Levine, 2008; Lim et al., 2007; Morgan, 2003; Neville et al., 2005) and simplicity of use (Levine, 2008; Morgan 2003; Neville et al., 2005; Ong et al., 2004). Items on part B of the survey are based on previous research regarding the use of online course management that has been conducted in Mount Holyoke in 2005 (Course Management Study Group, 2005). In accordance with previous research on faculty use of CMSs (see Morgan, 2003), items on Part B are designed to test for differential validity of preferences for experienced vs. non-experienced users of a CMS and for instructors from various disciplines.

Finally, a pilot version of the survey was distributed to 10 faculty members (selected based on availability) at one of the university's campuses for review and feedback. These instructors provided feedback on the content and format of the survey and several items have been modified accordingly, thus enhancing both content and face validity of the survey.

Instrument Adaptability

Although the instrument was originally designed to survey faculty members in a post-secondary educational institution, it could be easily adapted to survey instructors in other e-learning environments such as corporate training. First, the features that are listed in part A are consistent with the needs of the e-learning corporate training environment as described in current literature (e.g., Clarke et al, 2005; Lim et al., 2007; Newton & Doonga, 2007; Pack, 2002). Second, items that assess importance of features that are seemingly specific to a post secondary educational institution can easily be re-formatted to fit assessment within a corporate training environment without changing the underlying variables that are measured by such items. For example, item 30 on the survey assesses the importance of the CMS' ability to "automatically update student roster from registrar's database". Essentially, this item measures the importance of the CMS' ability to successfully integrate with other institutional databases. When used within corporate training context, this item can be re-worded to reflect integration with other, domain-specific, databases. Similarly, items on part B can be easily modified to fit the assessment needs within the corporate setting. For example, item 1 on part B measures the participant's professional discipline in order to allow for differential analysis of results across academic subjects. When used in a corporate setting, this item can be re-worded to measure the area of industry the company operates within, thus allowing for differential analysis of results across industry and/ or commercial domains.

RESULTS

Data from the initial administration of the survey were analyzed to test for reliability and validity of the instrument. The results indicate that the survey features excellent reliability (Cronbach alpha *.95)*. Factor variance analysis indicates that the survey measures 8 factors that are somewhat over-lapping. Factors 6 (preference for features that support administrative management of the course) and 2 (preference for features that support

upload of different file formats) feature the highest loadings on the total score of part A. Factor 6 accounts for 58% of the variance in total score (r=.761, p<.01) and factor 2 accounts for 53% of the variance in total score (r=7.26, p<.01). Table 1 summarizes the variance (in percentage) associated with each factor.

The main purpose of this descriptive survey is to assess the degree of the instructor's preference that is associated with each feature, and ultimately, with a typology of features. Thus, the most useful method of analysis for part A of the survey is computation of measures of central tendency (mean and standard deviation) for each individual item, rather than for the total score. For that purpose, the descriptive categories of the response options were operationalized as the following mean scores: *Not important at all* = < 1.5; *not very important* = 1.6-2.5; *neutral* = 2.6-3.5; *important* = 3.6-4.5; *very important* => 4.5.

The results from the initial administration of the survey to faculty members in a large private university in New York indicated that, on the average, no item in part A of the survey was rated as "not important at all", suggesting that faculty valued, to some extent, all the listed features. Two items, assessing preference for features that allow uploading of text files and presentation files, respectively, received rating of "very important" (M= 4.77, sd=.5; M=4.68, sd=.71). Only one item, assessing the preference for a feature that supports a 3D simulation of the instructor and students, received the average rating of *not very important* (M=2.72, sd=1.18). Of the remaining 45 items listing features of a CMS, 15 items were rated, on the average, as neutral in their importance to faculty. These items are listed in Table 2. The remaining items on part A of the survey received the average rating of *important*, with faculty expressing the highest preference for an item that assesses the importance of the CMS' ability to support uploading of text files. Table 3 summarizes the items that were rated as important to faculty.

Table 1. Factor variance analysis

	Name	Items	Pearson *r* (for total score)	% variance
Factor 1	Computer Platform	1-3	.40 P<.01	16
Factor 2	Upload of different file formats	4-11	.726 P<.01	53
Factor 3	Supports virtual world technology	12	.472 P<.01	22
Factor 4	Supports processing of exams	13-18	.574 P<.01	33
Factor 5	Includes pedagogical enhancement tools	19-25; 39-41	.684 P<.01	47
Factor 6	Supports administrative management of course	26-32; 36; 37; 42-44	.761 P<.01	58
Factor 7	Availability of technical support	33-35	.437 P<.01	19
Factor 8	University policy re available selection of CMS	46-47	.269 P<.05	7

Table 2. Items rated as "neutral"

Item	N	Mean	Standard Deviation
1. Operates from a Mac computer.	56	3.23	1.51
11. Upload of instructor's and students' photos.	61	3.16	1.14
13. Instant creation of exams.	60	3.40	1.27
14. Automatic scoring of exams.	60	3.33	1.32
16. Standard exam visual format.	61	3.37	1.14
18. Submit exam with one click.	60	3.50	1.11
21. Includes a chat room.	61	3.42	1.16
22. Includes a video chat.	61	3.00	1.09
23. Includes an internal e-mail.	61	3.50	1.28
24. Includes a blog.	61	3.18	1.16
25. Includes a wiki.	59	3.25	1.04
46. University's use of one standardized CMS.	60	3.56	1.26
47. University's flexibility using multiple CMSs.	60	3.31	.98

A second purpose of the survey is to distinguish between previous users and non users of a CMS in terms of their preferences for specific CMS' features. To the extent that such differences exist, they may be indicative of the differences in users vs. no-users' understanding of how a CMS can be optimally utilized in an e-learning environment. Such differences may underscore the need for instructors' training in the pedagogical utilization of tools and applications of a CMS. Data from the preliminary administration of the survey were analyzed utilizing an Independent *t* test. The results indicated that, compared to previous users of a CMS, non users displayed a higher preference for CMS' applications that support a standard visual format of on-line exams, and that allow students to save their answers as they are progressing through an on-line exam ($t(41.5)=-3.578, p<.001$, $M=4.05>M=3.09$; $t(41.5)=2.451$, $p<.001$, $M=4.23>M=3.57$). Additionally, non-experienced users of CMSs expressed a significantly higher preference for the spell check feature compared to experienced users of CMSs ($t(37.45)=-2.035$, $p<.05$, $M=4.35>M=3.85$).

Table 3. Items rated as "important"

Item	N	Mean	Standard Deviation
2. Operates from a PC computer.	57	4.33	1.17
3. Operates from both Mac and PC.	59	4.08	1.08
4. 2-3 mouse clicks to upload course materials.	58	3.77	1.12
5. Upload of image files.	61	4.40	.88
6. Upload of video files.	61	4.22	1.02
7. Upload of audio files.	61	4.22	.93
10. Conversion into PDF.	61	3.93	1.12
15. Automatic transfer of grades to grade book.	61	3.65	1.19
17. Save answers on exams.	61	3.75	1.10
20. Includes a discussion board.	61	4.11	1.05
26. Delete feature for unwanted files.	59	4.45	.85
27. Has spell check.	60	4.00	.93
28. Tracks participation of students.	59	3.88	.98
29. Integration with other web applications.	59	3.84	1.07
30. Automatic update of roster.	60	4.21	1.04
31. Allows instructor to enter data in grade book.	59	4.20	.99
32. Preserves students' anonymity on course evaluation.	60	3.90	1.14
33. University-based support personnel.	59	4.45	.87
34. Online help tutorials.	60	4.13	.83
35. Online help-desk.	60	4.26	.75
36. Security key for course entry.	60	4.30	.72
37. Instructor can design/modify course template.	59	4.27	.82
38. Meets pedagogical needs in on-line courses.	59	4.27	.97
39. Meets pedagogical needs in blended courses.	57	4.14	1.09
40. Meets pedagogical needs in F2F courses.	57	4.35	.89
41. Organization of materials in online courses.	59	4.01	1.12
42. Organization of materials in blended courses.	58	3.93	1.10
43. Organization of materials in F2F courses.	57	4.17	1.05

Previous users of a CMS displayed a significantly higher preference for a wiki feature compared to non users ($t(36.8) = 2.283, p<.05, M=3.45>M=2.82$).

Qualitative data were analyzed for the open-ended response item. Nineteen participants, (less than a third of the sample) offered qualitative comments in response to the item: *"please tell us about any additional features that you think might be of importance in a CMS"*. Faculty who were previous users of a CMS offered most of the comments. Content analysis of these comments indicated that they addressed three main domains: Most of the comments addressed features that were associated with course management, followed by some comments regarding pedagogical utility of CMS features, and, finally, a few comments addressed the importance of support services.

Comments within the course management category features addressed several themes:

Importance of management and organization of content files; the need for management of e-mail (for example, forwarding a CMS e-mail to another account, ability to search e-mail); the importance of managing the flow of information (exporting and importing files, alert reminders for assignments); the value of management of grades; and the importance of integrating the CMS with other software or university web-based systems (e.g., integration of course roster with registrar's system; integration with various discipline-specific software).

Several faculty members offered comments regarding pedagogically-linked features such as the ability to offer simulation-based examinations, ability to allow students to peer-review each other's work and the ability to include features that are geared towards the visually impaired. Finally, some faculty discussed the importance of support and training for both faculty and students in the use of a CMS.

DISCUSSION

The findings indicate that the survey that is described here is a valid and reliable instrument that can be effectively used to give instructors a greater voice in determining specific aspects of a CMS that can enhance the e-learning experience in accordance with current best practices. This instrument can be used as a research tool to determine what applications of a CMS are considered valuable (and presumably pedagogically sound) across different contexts of e-learning (e.g., post secondary education, corporate training, various subject- based disciplines or professional areas of industry and commerce), thus enhancing our understanding of the relevant building blocks of the e-learning experience.

The survey is particularly useful in an applied, case-by case context. Post secondary education institutions and corporations can utilize this instrument to identify the specific features that are preferred in their unique e-learning environments. For example, based on the current results, it appears that, in order to meet the needs of the e-learning environment in the particular university that has been studied here, a CMS should optimally include the following features: A PC operating platform; an ability to present course content via links to relevant web sites and uploading of multiple formats of files, especially text files; include asynchronous instructor-student and student-student interaction features such as a discussion board; include features that allow faculty an easy management of the course (keep track of grades, organize material within the system) as well as integration with university-wide student support services (e.g., registrar) and include features of technical support, especially university-based support personnel. The results from the quantitative analysis are further supported by the qualitative content of faculty comments that emphasize importance of features that assist in course management and organization of content. These findings are consistent with previous research that has identified important trends in faculty's pattern of CMS use (see Morgan, 2003) with a special emphasis on CMS' features that are associated with "content management and presentation" (Morgan, 2003, p. 33), and with a need for support services (Gallagher, 2003). These results are also consistent with findings from research on E training within the corporate world, wherein the following capabilities have been identified as key to the success of E training: A seamless integration of the CMS into the company's existing web-based system (Newton & Doonga, 2007), technical and pedagogical support (Lim at al., 2007; Neville et al., 2005) and protection of content that is presented or managed by the CMS (Ong et al., 2004).

Further, the current findings indicate a differential preference for CMS' features between previous users and non-users. Non-users of a CMS seem to prefer CMSs with features that mimic a traditional face-to-face learning environment, such as the format and scoring of exams. On the other hand, experienced users indicate preference for CMSs that include more pedagogically sophisticated features, such as the wiki. These findings are consistent with previous research that notes the impact of past teaching experience in an e-learning environment on instructors' conceptualization of the nature and use of several aspects of the e-learning environment (Wittman, Morotem & Kelly, 2007). The findings indicate the importance of instructors' training in the CMS's technology and its pedagogical potential, especially in regards to engaging students in collaborative learning. This information can assist the university in making a decision on how to best utilize a CMS in order to ensure that its e-learning program follows current best practices recommendations that emphasize the importance of instructor-student and student-student interaction features, (Rovai, 2003; Sugar et al., 2007), as well as the importance of the ability to present course content in multiple formats (Rovai, 2003).

The survey is designed to be discipline-sensitive. Faculty preferences for CMS' features can be compared across professional disciplines and departments. Although this analysis has not been performed here due to the small sample size, universities and corporations can calculate the relative importance of CMS' features to faculty or instructors from various disciplines, and thus customize the CMS to fit the needs of a particular learning environment or a particular subject matter. This information can help the university or corporation to ensure that "the technology that is used should have a specific educational or pedagogical purpose, and that the bells and whistles should not be added just because they are there, but because they serve a pedagogical purpose" (Neville et al., 2005, p127).

Additionally, this survey can be useful in indicating which features of an e-learning environment are marginal in terms of their relative

pedagogical value as seen by instructors. For example, the current results indicate that faculty do not have a particular preference for either a standardized use of a specific CMS within the university (thus forcing all faculty members to use the same software), or a flexible use of multiple systems (thus requiring efforts in training and adjusting to multiple systems). While these results contradict findings from previous research (e.g., Morgan 2003), which indicates that faculty are wary of multiple platforms due to the stress and time that is associated with training and adjusting to various systems, the current findings may be explained by faculty's emphasis on the need for support services. Possibly, faculty believe that as long as they are provided with adequate support, the issue of standard or multiple CMS platforms is irrelevant to their teaching. Recognizing that, at least from a faculty point of view, a standard or a flexible platform of CMS is pedagogically irrelevant, the university can make cost effective decisions about purchasing a CMS and allocating resources for adequate training and support services without jeopardizing the educational integrity of its e-learning program.

In conclusion, based on data from this survey, universities and corporations can make decisions to purchase a specific CMS that best approximates their needs, or work with vendors of CMSs to develop the ultimate "fit" with the educational and training needs of their constituents.

ACKNOWLEDGMENT

The author wishes to acknowledge Dr. Laura Martin, Ed.D., who has been instrumental in the development of the survey described in this chapter. The author also wishes to thank Dr. John White, Director, Assessment Programs, at StudentVoice, and Melissa Wright, Senior Coordinator for Campus Support at StudentVoice (aka Campus Labs) for their assistance with this project.

REFERENCES

Albrecht, B. (2006). Enriching students' experiences through blended learning. *Educause Research Bulletin, 12*, 1–12.

Allen, I. E., & Seaman, J. (2007). Blending in: The extent and promise of blended education in the United Sates. In Picciano, A. G., & Dziuban, C. D. (Eds.), *Blended learning research perspectives* (pp. 65–80). USA: The Sloan Consortium.

Clarke, A., Lewist, D., Cole, I., & Ringrose, L. (2005). A strategic approach to developing e-learning capability for healthcare. *Health Information and Libraries Journal, 22*, 33–41. doi:10.1111/j.1470-3327.2005.00611.x

Franklin, T., & van Harmelen, M. (2007). Web 2.0 for content for learning and teaching in higher education. Retrieved from http://www.jisc.ac.ok/media/documents/programmes/digitalrepositores/web2-content-learning-and teaching.pdf

Gallagher, S. R. (2003). The new landscape for course management systems. *Research Bulletin (Sun Chiwawitthaya Thang Thale Phuket), 10*.

Garrison, D. R., & Kanuka, H. (2004). Blended learning: Uncovering its transformative potential in higher education. *The Internet and Higher Education, 7*, 95–105. doi:10.1016/j.iheduc.2004.02.001

Glackin, M., Boisselle, J. H., Burke, J., DeGrenier, A., Kass, F., Kysela, B., & Maddaline, S. (2005). Online course management at Mount Holyoke: Current use and recommendations for the future. *Report of the Course management Study Group.*

Hanson, P. B., & Robson, R. (2004). Evaluating course management technology: A pilot case study. *Educause Research Bulletin, 24.* Retrieved from www.educause.edu/ecar/

Kaleta, R., Skibba, K., & Joosten, T. (2007). Discovering, designing and delivering hybrid courses. In Picciano, A. G., & Dziuban, C. D. (Eds.), *Blended learning research perspectives* (pp. 111–143). USA: The Sloan Consortium.

Katz, R. (2003). Balancing technology and tradition: The example of course management systems. *EDUCAUSE Review, 38*, 48–56.

Levine, A. (2008). *2008 content management systems satisfaction survey.* Retrieved from http://nten.org/research

Lim, H., Lee, S. G., & Nam, K. (2007). Validating e-learning factors affecting training effectiveness. *International Journal of Information Management, 27*, 22–35. doi:10.1016/j.ijinfomgt.2006.08.002

Morgan, G. (2003). Faculty use of course management systems. *Educause Center for Applied Research, 2.*

Neville, K., Heavin, C., & Walsh, E. (2005). A case in customizing e-learning. *Journal of Information Technology, 20*, 117–129. doi:10.1057/palgrave.jit.2000041

Newton, R., & Doonga, N. (2007). Corporate e-learning: Justification for implementation and evaluation of benefits: A study examining the views of training managers and providers. *Education for Information, 25*, 111–130.

Ong, C. S., Lai, J. Y., & Wang, Y. S. (2004). Factors affecting engineers' acceptance of asynchronous e-learning systems in high-tech companies. *Information & Management, 41*, 795–804. doi:10.1016/j.im.2003.08.012

Pack, T. (2002). Corporate learning gets digital. *E-Content, 25,* 22-26. Retrieved from http://vnweb.hwwilsonweb.com

Rovai, A. P. (2007). A constructivist approach to online college learning. *The Internet and Higher Education, 7*, 79–93. doi:10.1016/j.iheduc.2003.10.002

Sugar, W., Martindale, T., & Crawley, F. E. (2007). One professor's face-to-face teaching strategies while becoming an online instructor. *The Quarterly Review of Distributed Education, 8,* 365–385.

US Department of Education, National Center for Education Statistics. (2008). *Distance education at degree-granting post secondary institutions 2006-2007.*

Wittman, H., Morote, E., & Kelly, T. (2007). Faculty conceptions and misconceptions about hybrid education. In C. Crawford (Ed.), *Proceedings* of *Society for Information Technology and Teacher Education International Conference* (pp. 1168-1173). Chesapeake, VA: AACE.

Zhang, D., & Zhou, L. (2003). Enhancing e-learning with interactive media. *Information Resources Management Journal, 16,* 1–14. doi:10.4018/irmj.2003100101

ADDITIONAL READING

Choi, H. J., & Johnson, S. D. (2007). The effect of problem-based video instruction on learner satisfaction, comprehension and retention in college courses. *British Journal of Educational Technology, 38,* 885–895. doi:10.1111/j.1467-8535.2006.00676.x

Davis, H. C., & Fill, K. (2007). Embedding blended learning in a university's teaching culture: Experiences and reflections. *British Journal of Educational Technology, 38,* 817–828. doi:10.1111/j.1467-8535.2007.00756.x

Dobbs, K. (2000). Who is in charge of e-learning? *Training (New York, N.Y.), 37,* 54–59.

Garrison, D. R., & Vaughan, N. D. (Eds.). (2008). *Blended learning in higher education.* San Francisco, CA: Jossey-Bass.

Herther, N. K. (1997). Education over the web: Distance learning and the information professional. *Online, 21,* 63-69. Retrieved from http://vnweb.hwwilson.com

Holton, E. F., Coco, M. L., Lowe, J. L., & Dutsch, J. V. (2006). Blended delivery strategies for competency- based training. *Advances in Developing Human Resources, 8,* 210–228. doi:10.1177/1523422305286153

Levine, A., & Meyer, B. (2008). *2008 donor management software satisfaction survey.* Portland, OR: NTEN.

McGee, P., Jafari, A., & Carmean, C. (Eds.). (2005). *Course management systems for learning: Beyond accidental pedagogy.* Hershey, PA: Idea Group, Inc. doi:10.4018/978-1-59140-512-2

Picciano, A. G., & Dziuban, C. D. (Eds.). (2007). *Blended learning research perspectives.* USA: The Sloan Consortium.

Piccoli, G., Ahmad, R., & Ives, B. (2001). Web-based virtual learning environments: A research framework and a preliminary assessment of effectiveness in basic skills training. *Management Information Systems Quarterly, 25,* 401–426. doi:10.2307/3250989

Scott, B. (2002). The pedagogy of on-line learning: A report from the University of the Highlands and Islands Millennium Institute. *Information Services & Use, 22,* 19–26.

Stewart, B., & Graham, R. (2008). Content management for the enterprise: CMS definition and selection. *Educause Research Bulletin, 22.* Retrieved from http://www.educause.edu/ecar

Weigel, V. (2005). From course management to curricular capabilities. *EDUCAUSE Review, 40,* Retrieved from http://www.educause.edu

Wild, R. H., Griggs, K. A., & Downing, T. (2002). A framework for e-learning as a tool for knowledge management. *Industrial Management & Data Systems*, *102*, 371–380. doi:10.1108/02635570210439463

KEY TERMS AND DEFINITIONS

Asynchronous E-Learning: A learning activity, utilizing internet and other computer-based media, wherein each participant accesses the material and/or responds to it individually within a distinct time frame, not shared by other participants. Common strategies of Asynchronous e-learning include visiting relevant web sites, and posting on discussion boards.

Blended Learning: Sometimes called hybrid or web-enhanced learning, this term refers to an integration of traditional face-to-face learning activities with internet-based and other computer-based media activities for the purpose of teaching and learning within a single course unit.

Blog: This is a web-based logging software that allows one author to create a journal-like document that can be published on line and distributed to multiple participants in a particular course or a web community. Participants typically communicate via posting comments to the author's original document.

Course Management System: A CMS is a software tool that is designed to organize and deliver the content of a particular course or unit of knowledge, and allows for synchronous and/or asynchronous communication among students and instructor. A CMS typically includes features such as discussion boards, chat, wiki, grade book, e-mail, and capabilities to organize and store learning materials (links to relevant web sites, power point presentations etc). Examples of current and commonly used commercial CMSs include Blackboard, Angel and Desire2Learn. Examples of some open source CMSs include Moodle and Sakai.

Discussion Board: An application within course management systems (see above) that allows or asynchronous communication among students and instructor within a specific course. Participants utilize this tool by posting comments, questions, and responses, and can view and respond to posts from others in a threaded manner.

E-Learning: Sometimes known as *virtual learning*, or *E training*, refers to learning activities that utilize the internet and other computer based media, such as discussion boards, u-tube, video conferencing, chat, e-mail, etc., for the purpose of disseminating and sharing knowledge in a structured, thoughtful way. e-learning can occur using digital technology exclusively, or by integrating use of the internet and computer-based media with traditional face-to-face teaching and learning activities (see blended learning, above).

Interactive E-Learning: Encompasses web-based and computer-based learning activities that allow the participants to: (a) interact with each other via web-based communication tools, and (b) interact with, or access the digitally presented material, in a non-linear, self-paced manner.

Synchronous E-Learning: A learning activity, utilizing internet and other computer-based media to deliver content to, and engage participants simultaneously. Common strategies of Synchronous e-learning include use of chat, and video-conferencing.

Web 2.0 Tools: These are computer-based applications and software that allow the participants to observe and receive information, as well as create and publish information on the internet, in an interactive modality. Examples of Web 2.0 tools include virtual environment software such as Second Life.

Wiki: This is a web-based software that allows multiple authors to collaborate on creating a single, cohesive document, that can subsequently by published online and shared by multiple participants in a particular course or a web community.

APPENDIX

Author's Notes on Instrument's Availability

Use of this instrument or its adaptation for use in related environments is cost free, but requires proper citations of the developer:

Dr. Orly Calderon, Psy.D., Long Island University

The instrument is available in a Word format from the author at: Orly.Calderon@liu.edu.

Or mail your request to:

```
Dr. Orly Calderon
Social Work Department
Long Island University, C.W. Post Campus
720 Northern Blvd, Brookville, NY, 11548
```

To preview an online version of the survey, readers may click on the link below. Readers may need to type the link into their internet browser's address bar and hit "Enter." To move through the survey, readers will need to click on responses and "take" the survey as a respondent would. This link will not collect data and is solely for previewing purposes.

http://www.studentvoice.com/p/?uuid=9cb54a39f2ed4918a72d08a28b99e4ba&p=1

The link below provides access to the survey in read-only form. Readers can type this address directly in their internet address browser and hit "Enter." Once the survey populates, readers will find every question of the survey in an outline view. This view will display coding given to each answer choice as well as any skip patterns used in the assessment.

http://www.studentvoice.com/liu/cmspreferredfeaturequestionnaire.mht

Access to the documents above is provided through StudentVoice(aka Campus Labs), a leader in assessment solutions and technology for higher education. The holistic, web-based platform provides the basic tools for successful assessment practice including example assessment plans and instruments, expert consultation to assist with assessment planning and design, and innovative technology for data collection, analysis, and reporting. To use StudentVoice to facilitate use of this CMS survey, or learn more about StudentVoice services, visit www.studentvoice.com or contact a StudentVoice representative at info@studentvoice.com.

Chapter 19
Online Survey Software

Jason D. Baker
Regent University, USA

ABSTRACT

The commonality among online instruments – regardless of discipline – is the use of online tools to administer the electronic measurements, collect participant responses, and aggregate the results for data analysis. Under the heading of software as a service (SaaS) or cloud computing, online survey software makes it possible for individuals and organizations to easily develop and administer online instruments. This chapter provides a background into SaaS and cloud computing, profiles three leading online survey software tools – SurveyMonkey, Qualtrics, and LimeSurvey – along with the PollEverywhere online and mobile polling tool. The chapter concludes with the corresponding cost and links to these online survey tools along with relevant terms and resources.

INTRODUCTION

As the Internet has grown, online surveys have emerged as commonplace, with individuals and organizations alike developing and administering surveys. A Google search for "online surveys" reveals approximately 110 million results, including hundreds of free and fee-based tools for use in market research, customer satisfaction, academic studies, and even personal surveys just for fun (Google, 2012). Facebook, the largest social net-

working site with over 845 million users, boasts numerous surveys ranging from serious medical studies to silly movie quotes.

With so many electronic surveys available, completing online surveys has become a frequent activity of online users. A 2009 study from Dennis, Osborn, and Semans found that "one in four opt-in [online] panelists had participated in 20 or more surveys in the past four weeks" (p. 5). Additionally, individuals can earn money by completing

DOI: 10.4018/978-1-4666-2172-5.ch019

online surveys through such services as Amazon Mechanical Turk (Mason & Suri, 2011).

Behind all of these online surveys are websites running various online survey software programs that make it possible to administer online instruments, electronic measurements, surveys, and polls with publishing and distribution costs essentially zero. This is a dramatic change from previous administration methods such as telephone or postal mail which had significantly higher costs associated with surveys.

These online survey platforms are a subset of a movement called software as a service (SaaS) or, more recently, cloud computing. After providing some background into SaaS and cloud computing, a number of online survey software programs will be profiled. In particular, two leading commercial software programs – SurveyMonkey and Qualtrics – are introduced, followed by a profile of the open source LimeSurvey product. Additionally, the online and mobile polling tool PollEverywhere is profiled. The chapter then concludes with the associated cost and links to these tools and relevant terms and readings.

BACKGROUND

Online survey software is an example of software as a service (SaaS) or cloud computing. The Gartner research group defines software as a service as "software that's owned, delivered and managed remotely by one or more providers" (Gartner, 2012b, para. 1). SaaS then is software that's run on remote computers but able to be accessed on local ones. As Gartner further stipulates, if a vendor has to install software locally, then it's not SaaS (para. 1).

SaaS is considered a subset of the larger concept of cloud computing. Gartner (2012a) defines cloud computing as "a style of computing in which massively scalable IT-enabled capabilities are delivered 'as a service' to external customers using Internet technologies" (para. 1). The cloud is basically the Internet but it represents a particular use of the Internet. The idea is that you can store content in the cloud (e.g., documents, music, video, files, etc.) or you can run programs in the cloud (e.g., word processing with Google Docs rather than installing Microsoft Word on your local computer) or you can even run entire virtual computers online (e.g., leased instances through Amazon Web Services).

The concept of storing materials online isn't a particularly new one; in addition to the "thin client" concept that came and went in the late 1990s where the idea was that everything important would be online and you'd not need as powerful of a computer on your desktop, the "client-server" model of mainframes (i.e., big powerful centralized computer access from dumb terminals) is a forerunner. However, the movement toward online computing and storage has been accelerating of late, due not only to good marketing and terminology (i.e., "the cloud") but also because of new tools being made available to developers and consumers alike.

The advantage of hosting surveys online (in the cloud) rather than running surveys locally are numerous. The most obvious is that the surveys themselves are accessible to anyone with Internet access. However, this could be done with a locally-installed survey program as well, just as long as the resulting survey was posted to an available web server. As with other web-based publications, the per-unit cost of an online survey is essentially zero, in contrast to print surveys which have a finite cost to print or copy each additional survey. Additionally, the distribution costs of online surveys are essentially zero, in contrast to the postal mailing or telephone call costs associated with traditional methods of survey distribution.

Beyond the low publication and distribution costs associated with online surveys, the benefit of employing online survey software (particularly SaaS or cloud-based) is that the researcher is not responsible for maintaining the software itself. Online survey software companies typically handle the development, administration, and maintenance of the software, leaving the researcher to focus complete attention on the development and delivery of the online instrument and the resulting data analysis. Users of online survey software are required to have an account login, which may be free or fee-based depending on the application, but typically do not have to run their own web server in order to employ one of these tools.

PROFILES

SurveyMonkey and Qualtrics are two of the leading commercially-supported online survey software programs. As both are administered via a web-based interface and are maintained by their respective vendors, they are examples of SaaS or cloud-computing applications. The two programs are similar in that they can be used for a variety of online surveys and instruments ranging from simple to complex and offer a variety of design options for the researcher.

LimeSurvey is a leading open source survey program that runs on a Linux web server using a MySQL database. Although it is a web-based online survey program similar to SurveyMonkey and Qualtrics, it's installed and supported by the user and not managed by the host vendor. The benefit, however, is that LimeSurvey is open source, meaning that the source code is freely available for viewing and modification.

PollEverywhere isn't nearly as sophisticated as SurveyMonkey, Qualtrics, and LimeSurvey but has become popular for simple feedback surveys and polls. It stands out because it's easily accessible not only through online connections but mobile devices via text messaging, which makes it particularly useful for real-time live feedback.

SurveyMonkey

SurveyMonkey is a commercial online survey platform that was started in 1999 and has been used to design and deliver millions of online surveys, including usage by every firm in the *Fortune* 100. As with all online survey software tools, one first creates an account on SurveyMonkey and then enters the online survey administration area. Users are then given the option to create a new survey from scratch, copy an existing survey, or use a pre-designed survey template which can then be customized.

More than 60 survey templates have been developed for a variety of disciplinary fields such as human resources, customer feedback, demographic, education, events, and political which can be adapted at employed at no additional cost. For example, the survey template for employee satisfaction includes 14 items such as "How well are you paid for the work you do?" and "How likely are you to look for another job outside the company?" which are answered via Likert-style scales.

SurveyMonkey supports 15 different question types including multiple-choice (single answer allowed), multiple-choice (multiple answers allowed), rating scales, Likert scales, semantic differential scales, numerical text boxes, standard demographic questions (e.g., name, address, email), image, and even essay (although open-ended questions cannot be tallied the same way as multiple choice and other fixed questions). Questions can also be arranged for sequential completion, all-at-once completion, or skip logic where the answer to one question determines what will come next in the survey.

Once all of the questions and answer options are entered and ordered, the user also customize the overall look and feel of the survey, including setting colors, logos, page numbers, progress bars, and other visual accoutrements. Users can test the survey before publishing and opening it up for actual data collection. Once activated, the survey administrator can send invitations via email or Facebook for users to then complete the survey via their computer or iOS mobile device. Results are then saved in the online system and survey administrators can view individual and aggregate results through the management interface, as well as exported into a number of formats including PDF, HTML, CSV, Excel, or SPSS.

Qualtrics

Qualtrics is a commercial online survey platform founded in 1997 that has powered over one hundred million surveys delivered online using their platform. Whereas SurveyMonkey's website appears targeted to individuals and organizations based on ease of use, Qualtrics' website has a decidedly research-oriented feel and appears to be targeted more to organizational use rather than casual individual use and boasts that all 30 of *BusinessWeek's* Top 30 business schools use their platform.

When creating a survey using the Qualtrics Survey Research Suite, administrators have the option to use a guided quick survey builder, copy an existing survey as the basis of a new one, or pick from over 100 survey templates in the Qualtrics library. The available templates are wide-ranging and include such topics as student course evaluation, website visitor profile, informed consent, and customer satisfaction surveys. For example, the survey template for website feedback includes items such as "What are your reasons for visiting our site today" and "Where did you hear about our website?" with corresponding categorical choices available for selection.

Qualtrics supports over 100 different question types which not only include the standard textual feedback items (e.g., Likert-scale questions, multiple-choice lists, textboxes) but also a variety of rich media question items including image selection and embedded audio and video. Each question can be edited down to the HTML and Javascript level and customized independent of the overall look and feel of the survey template. Questions can be randomized, customized for specific users, or adjusted based on answers to

previous questions within the survey itself using skip logic, branch logic, or loops.

The overall look and feel of each survey can be adjusted online via a word processor-like interface or at the HTML code level. Once completed, the survey can be viewed and tested prior to administration. Qualtrics offers the option to email survey invitations and schedule automatic reminder messages for those who haven't yet completed the survey and thank those who have. Surveys can also be exported to Microsoft Word or PDF for paper-based administration. Once administered, survey results can be viewed individually or in the aggregate via the online administration system or exported to Excel, SPSS, Word, PowerPoint, or PDF formats.

In addition to their survey suite, Qualtrics also offers additional research and analytics services including 360 Evaluations, Site Intercept, and Qualtrics Panels. 360 Evaluations offers 360-degree assessment tools to gather feedback from managers, peers, and direct reports, along with team evaluation and personal assessment tools such as personality and learning style instruments. Site Intercept is a real-time website feedback tool that provides online visitors a targeted opportunity to receive information or provide feedback while they're on the site. Qualtrics Panels is a service in which the company assembles feedback panels based on target demographic specifications.

LimeSurvey

LimeSurvey is an open source alternative to SurveyMonkey or Qualtrics. The open source software movement began as a community effort to create a free version of the Unix operating system and developed into a philosophy of volunteers developing code that's freely shared with others (Raymond, 1998). Although open source doesn't necessary mean no-cost – people in the movement often like to say that open source is free as in free speech, not necessarily free as in free beer – many open source applications are indeed no-cost. LimeSurvey is an open source survey software application that started in 2003 under the name PHP Surveyor and was renamed LimeSurvey in 2007.

LimeSurvey possesses many of the same survey features as SurveyMonkey or Qualtrics such as a web-based administration interface, a variety of question types, online data analysis, control over the survey look and feel, and import and export functions. LimeSurvey features 28 different question types including single choice, multiple choice, Likert-style scales and arrays, ranking, numbering, and free-form text entry. Surveys can include images and movies, be printed out for paper-based administration, formatted a variety of colors and styles through HTML code changes, and made conditional through skipping and branch logic. As with other programs, LimeSurvey includes basic data analysis within the online administration system and the ability to export responses to CSV, PDF, SPSS, and Microsoft Excel. Additionally, LimeSurvey is multilingual and offers over 50 different languages for both administrators and users.

LimeSurvey lacks the built-in premade survey templates that SurveyMonkey or Qualtrics offer. Additionally, being an open source application, administrator support is largely done through a community support forum. There are commercial support options for LimeSurvey that can provide hosting, training, and paid support via email, Skype, or telephone, but these are separate from the product itself. Although LimeSurvey is not the only open source survey software, it appears to be the most popular of the platforms.

PollEverywhere

PollEverywhere is different from the other software options in that it's designed not as a comprehensive online survey platform but rather as an audience response polling tool. PollEverywhere was founded in 2008 and functions as a live polling service that can receive responses online via the web or through mobile text messages or even via Twitter. Additionally, the results can be displayed in real-time online or embedded into a PowerPoint or Keynote slide presentation.

Rather than having a large number of question types, PollEverywhere is limited to multiple choice and free-form text responses. Once the poll has been created, the results are displayed and updated in real-time as users reply online or via mobile device. The poll administrator controls not only the content of the poll but the start and stop time, whether polls are open to anyone or a select group of registered users, how many times people can vote, and whether responses are graded. Polls with free-form text responses can be moderated so answers are approved before being displayed on the resulting screen.

The multiple response options and real-time updating of PollEverywhere make it more suited to live audience or classroom feedback rather than complex surveys or psychometric instruments which are better suited for more traditional online survey software platforms.

COST

SurveyMonkey has four subscriptions plans ranging from free to $65 per month. The free version is limited to 10 questions and 100 responses per survey and limits the customization and exporting options whereas the $65 per month plan offers unlimited questions, surveys, customization, and includes telephone support for its users. The two plans in-between ($17 and $25 per month respectively) offer various degrees of survey sophistication and options.

Qualtrics offers a free trial of their online survey software create, distribute, and collect online survey responses. Beyond the free trial, Qualtrics offers various pricing structures depending on the size and scope of the organizational use of their platform. Additional Qualtrics products such as the 360-degree assessment tool and their panel assembly service have separate costs associated with them.

LimeSurvey is an open source application made available online for free. The software can be downloaded and installed from the LimeSurvey website. Additionally, many web-hosting providers offer one-click installation of LimeSurvey through a menu-driven system such as Fantastico De Luxe, Plesk, or Virtualmin, but it still requires the end-user to manage the software. Commercial LimeSurvey hosting and support options are also available through third-party vendors.

PollEverywhere has a variety of business and non-profit plans that range from free to $1400 per month. The free plan permits up to 40 responses per poll while the highest plan supports up to 20,000 responses per poll and includes a variety of identification, segmentation, and moderation options not available in the free plan. There are a number of additional plans in-between (e.g., $15 per month, $65 per month, etc.) that vary in their response limits and features. Additionally, PollEverywhere offers custom plans for K-12 and higher education organizations.

LOCATION

SurveyMonkey is available at http://www.surveymonkey.com

Qualtrics is available at http://www.qualtrics.com

LimeSurvey is available at http://www.limesurvey.com

PollEverywhere is available at http://www.polleverywhere.com

REFERENCES

Dennis, J. M., Osborn, L., & Semans, K. (2009, March). *Comparison study of early adopter attitudes and online behavior in probability and non-probability web panels.* Retrieved from http://www.knowledgenetworks.com/ganp/reviewer-info.html

Gartner. (2012a). *Cloud computing.* Retrieved from http://www.gartner.com/it-glossary/cloud-computing/

Gartner. (2012b). *Software as a service.* Retrieved from http://www.gartner.com/it-glossary/software-as-a-service-saas/

Google. (2012). *Online surveys.* Retrieved from http://www.google.com/search?q=online+surveys

Mason, W., & Suri, S. (2010). Conducting behavioral research on Amazon's Mechanical Turk. *Behavioral Research Methods.* Retrieved from http://research.yahoo.com/files/mturkmethods.pdf

Raymond, E. S. (1998). The cathedral and the bazaar. *First Monday, 3*(3). Retrieved from http://www.firstmonday.org/htbin/cgiwrap/bin/ojs/index.php/fm/article/view/578/499

ADDITIONAL READING

Anderson, J., Brown, G., & Spaeth, S. (2005). Online student evaluations and response rates reconsidered. *Innovate Journal of Online Education, 2*(6). Retrieved from http://innovateonline.info/pdf/vol2_issue6/Online_Student_Evaluations_and_Response_Rates_Reconsidered.pdf

Archer, T. M. (2007). Characteristics associated with increasing the response rates of Web-based surveys. *Practical Assessment, Research & Evaluation, 12*(12). Retrieved from http://pareonline.net/pdf/v12n12.pdf

Archer, T. M. (2008). Response rates to expect from Web-based surveys and what to do about it. *Journal of Extension, 44*(1). Retrieved from http://www.joe.org/joe/2008june/rb3.php

Duda, M. D., & Nobile, J. L. (2010). The fallacy of online surveys: No data are better than bad data. *Human Dimensions of Wildlife, 15*(1), 55–64. doi:10.1080/10871200903244250

Fan, W., & Yan, Z. (2010). Factors affecting response rates of the web survey: A systematic review. *Computers in Human Behavior, 26*(2), 132–139. doi:10.1016/j.chb.2009.10.015

Hamilton, M. B. (2009). Online survey response rates and times. *Response*, 1-5. Retrieved from http://www.supersurvey.com

Kaskalis, T. H. (2004). Localizing and experiencing electronic questionnaires in an educational web site. *International Journal of Information Technology, 1*(4), 187–190.

Marra, R. M., & Bogue, B. (2006). *A critical assessment of online survey tools*. Paper presented at the WEPAN Conference, Pittsburgh, PA. Retrieved from http://citeseerx.ist.psu.edu/viewdoc/download?doi=10.1.1.94.2162&rep=rep1&type=pdf

Molasso, W. R. (2005). Ten tangible and practical tips to improve student participation in Web surveys. *Student Affairs Online, 6*(4). Retrieved from http://studentaffairs.com/ejournal/Fall_2005/StudentParticipationinWebSurveys.html

Shih, T. H., & Fan, X. (2008). Comparing response rates from Web and mail surveys: A meta-analysis. *Field Methods, 20*(3), 249–271. doi:10.1177/1525822X08317085

SurveyMonkey. (2009). *Response rates & surveying techniques: Tips to enhance survey respondent participation.* Retrieved from http://s3.amazonaws.com/SurveyMonkeyFiles/Response_Rates.pdf

Truell, A. D., Bartlett, J. E. II, & Alexander, M. W. (2002). Response rate, speed, and completeness: A comparison of Internet-based and mail surveys. *Behavior Research Methods, Instruments, & Computers, 34*(1), 46–49. doi:10.3758/BF03195422

Wright, K. B. (2005). Researching Internet-based populations: Advantages and disadvantages of online survey research, online questionnaire authoring software packages, and Web survey services. *Journal of Computer-Mediated Communication, 10*(3). Retrieved from http://jcmc.indiana.edu/vol10/issue3/wright.html

KEY TERMS AND DEFINITIONS

Branching or Branch Logic: An approach to routing participants to different subsequent survey questions based on the responses to prior questions.

Cloud Computing: Computing power (resources, software, applications, storage) delivered online as a service rather than run locally.

Open Source Software: An approach to software development where code is collaboratively written and made freely available for modification.

Skip Logic: A variation of branching where one or more survey questions are skipped based on responses to prior questions.

Software as a Service: Software administered and managed remotely on a server and accessed by a client online rather than running on a local computer.

Compilation of References

(2004).*Life Styles Inventory LSI 1 Self-Development Guide*.Plymouth, MI:Human Synergistics, Inc.(Original work published 1973)

(2004).*Life Styles Inventory LSI 2: Description by Others Self-Development Guide*.Plymouth, MI:Human Synergistics, Inc.(Original work published 1990)

A Cross-Cultural Perspective. (2005). (Original work published 1987). Retrieved from http://humansynergistics.com/news/CaseStudies.aspx

Abeyta, D. A.(1992).*United States Air Force Academy leadership development manual*.Colorado Springs, CO:Forbes.

Achtemeier, P.(1985).*Harper's bible dictionary*.San Francisco, CA:Harper & Row.

Adams, J. S.(1963).Towards an understanding of inequity. *Journal of Abnormal and Social Psychology*,*67*(5),422–436.doi:10.1037/h0040968

Agar, M.(1994).*Language shock: Understanding the culture of conversation*.New York, NY:William Morrow and Company, Inc.

Ajzen, I.(1985).From intentions to actions: A theory of planned behavior. InKuhl, J., & Beckman, J.(Eds.),*Action control: From cognition to behaviour*(pp.11–39).New York, NY:Springer.doi:10.1007/978-3-642-69746-3_2

Ajzen, I.(1988).*Attitudes, personality and behaviour*. Milton Keynes, UK:Oxford University Press.

Ajzen, I.(1991).The theory of planned behaviour. *Organizational Behavior and Human Decision Processes*,*50*,179–211.doi:10.1016/0749-5978(91)90020-T

Ajzen, I., & Fishbein, M.(1980).*Understanding attitudes and predicting social behavior*.Upper Saddle River, NJ:Prentice-Hall.

Akerlof, G. A.(1991).Procrastination and obedience. *The American Economic Review*,*81*(2),1–19.

Albrecht, B.(2006).Enriching students' experiences through blended learning. *Educause Research Bulletin*,*12*,1–12.

Allen, C. L.(1953).*God's psychiatry*.New Jersey:Fleming H. Revell Company.

Allen, I. E., & Seaman, J.(2007).Blending in: The extent and promise of blended education in the United Sates. InPicciano, A. G., & Dziuban, C. D.(Eds.),*Blended learning research perspectives*(pp.65–80).USA:The Sloan Consortium.

Allen, V. L., & Klenke, K.(2009).Failed moral decision making in high-profile leaders: A social cognitive study of William Jefferson Clinton's political leadership. *International Leadership Journal*,*2*(1),5–26.

Alper, J. S., & Beckwith, J.(1993).Genetic fatalism and social policy: The implications of behavior genetics research. *The Yale Journal of Biology and Medicine*,*66*,511–524.

Alves, J. C., Manz, C. C., & Butterfield, D. A.(2004). Developing leadership theory in Asia: The role of Chinese philosophy. *International Journal of Leadership Studies*,*1*(1),3–27.

Alvesson, M.(1987).Organizations, culture and ideology. *International Studies of Management and Organizations*,*3*,4–18.

Ames, C.(1992).Classroom goals, structure, and student motivation. *Journal of Educational Psychology,84,*261–271.doi:10.1037/0022-0663.84.3.261

Ames, R. T.(2000).Sun Tzu: The art of war. InCarr, C.(Ed.),*The book of war*(pp.7–65).New York, NY:Modern Library.

Anderson, L.(1990).*They smell like sheep*(*Vol. 1*).New York, NY:Howard Books.

Anderson, L. R.(1966).Leader behavior, member attitude, and task performance of intercultural discussion groups. *The Journal of Social Psychology,69*(2),305–319.doi:10.1080/00224545.1966.9919730

Andreescu, V., & Vito, G. F.(2010).An exploratory study of ideal leadership behaviour: The opinions of American police managers. *International Journal of Police Science and Management,12*(4),567–583.doi:10.1350/ijps.2010.12.4.207

Andrews, D., Nonnecke, B., & Preece, J.(2003).Electronic survey methodology: A case study in reaching hard-to-involve Internet users. *International Journal of Human-Computer Interaction,16*(2),185–210.doi:10.1207/S15327590IJHC1602_04

Anscombe, E.(1958).Modern moral philosophy. *Philosophy (London, England),33,*1–19.doi:10.1017/S0031819100037943

Antonakis, J., Avolio, B. J., & Sivasubramaniam, N.(2003).Context and leadership: An examination of the nine-factor full-range leadership theory using the Multifactor Leadership Questionnaire. *The Leadership Quarterly,14,*261–295.doi:10.1016/S1048-9843(03)00030-4

Appelbaum, S. H., & Steed, A. J.(2005).The critical factors in the client-consulting relationship. *Journal of Management,24*(1),68–93.

Applbaum, R. L., Bodaken, E. M., Sereno, K. K., & Anatol, K. W. E.(1974).*The process of group communication.* Chicago, IL:Science Research Associates, Inc.

Appleton, B. A., & Stanwyck, D.(1996).Teacher personality, pupil control ideology, and leadership style. *Individual Psychology,52*(2),119–129.

Argyris, C.(1977, September-October).Double-loop learning in organizations. *Harvard Business Review,*115–125.

Argyris, C.(1992).*On organizational learning.*Cambridge, MA:Blackwell.

Aristotle. (2009).*Nicomachean ethics.*As cited in Ross (2009). Greensboro, NC: WLC Books.

Ashkanasy, N. M., & Daus, C. S.(2002).Emotion in the workplace: The new challenge for managers. *The Academy of Management Executive,16*(1),76–86.doi:10.5465/AME.2002.6640191

Ashkanasy, N. M., & Tse, B.(2000).Transformational leadership as management of emotion: A conceptual review. InHartel, C. E. J., & Zerbe, W. J.(Eds.),*Emotions in the workplace: Research, theory and practice.*Westport, CT:Quorom Books.

Audi, R., & Murphy, P. E.(2006).The many faces of integrity. *Business Ethics Quarterly,16,*3–21.

Autry, J. A.(2001).*The servant leader: How to build a creative team, develop great morale, and improve bottom-line performance.*New York, NY:Three Rivers Press.

Avolio, B. J.(1999).*Full leadership development: Building the vital forces in organizations.*Thousand Oaks, CA:Sage.

Avolio, B. J., Bass, B. M., & Jung, D. I.(1999).Re-examining the components of transformational and transactional leadership using the Multifactor Leadership Questionnaire. *Journal of Occupational and Organizational Psychology,72,*441–462.doi:10.1348/096317999166789

Avolio, B. J., & Gardner, W. L.(2005).Authentic leadership development: Getting to the root of positive forms of leadership. *The Leadership Quarterly,16,*315–338.doi:10.1016/j.leaqua.2005.03.001

Avolio, B. J., Gardner, W. L., Walumbwa, F. O., Luthans, F., & May, D. R.(2004).Unlocking the mask: A look at the process by which authentic leaders impact follower attitudes and behaviors. *The Leadership Quarterly,15,*801–823.doi:10.1016/j.leaqua.2004.09.003

Avolio, B. J., & Kahai, S. S.(2003).Adding the "e" to e-leadership: How it may impact your leadership. *Organizational Dynamics,31,*325–338.doi:10.1016/S0090-2616(02)00133-X

Avolio, B. J., Kahai, S. S., & Dodge, G. E.(2001).E-leadership: Implications for theory, research, and practice. *The Leadership Quarterly,11*,615–668.doi:10.1016/S1048-9843(00)00062-X

Avolio, B. J., Walumbwa, F. O., & Weber, T. J.(2009).Leadership: Current theories, research, and future directions. *Annual Review of Psychology,60*,421–449.doi:10.1146/annurev.psych.60.110707.163621

Ayman, R., & Chemers, M. M.(1983).Relationship of supervisory behavior ratings to work group effectiveness and subordinate satisfaction among Iranian managers. *The Journal of Applied Psychology,68*(2),338–341. doi:10.1037/0021-9010.68.2.338

Baker, R. B., & McCullough, L. B.(Eds.). (2008). *The Cambridge world history of medical ethics*.New York, NY:Cambridge University Press.doi:10.1017/CHOL9780521888790

Baker, S. D.(2007).Followership: The theoretical foundation of a contemporary construct. *Journal of Leadership & Organizational Studies,4*(1),50–60. doi:10.1177/0002831207304343

Balz, R., & Schneider, G.(1993).*The exegetical dictionary of the New Testament*.Grand Rapids, MI:Eerdmans.

Bandura, A.(1986).As cited in Bandura, A.(2001).*Social foundations of thought and action: A social cognitive theory.*Englewood Cliffs, NJ: prentice-Hall.

Bandura, A.(1986).*Social foundations of thought and action: A social cognitive theory.*Englewood Cliffs, NJ:Prentice-Hall.

Bandura, A.(1986).*Social foundations of thought and action: A social cognitive theory.*Upper Saddle River, NJ:Prentice Hall.

Bandura, A.(1997).*Self-efficacy: The exercise of control.* New York, NY:Freeman.

Bandura, A.(2006).Toward a psychology of human agency. *Perspectives on Psychological Science,1*(2),164–180. doi:10.1111/j.1745-6916.2006.00011.x

Bantz, C. R.(1993).*Understanding organizations: Interpreting organizational communication culture.*Columbia, SC:University of South Carolina Press.

Barbuto, J., & Wheeler, D.(2006).Scale development and construct clarification of servant leadership. *Group & Organization Management,31*(3),300–326. doi:10.1177/1059601106287091

Bar-On, R.(2005).The Bar-On model of emotional-social intelligence. InFernández-Berrocal, P., & Extremera, N.(Eds.),*Special Issue on Emotional Intelligence, Psicothema, 17.*

Barrett, A. (2008).*The nonprofit ethics survey: A contextual approach.*Doctoral dissertation, The University of San Diego.

Bass, B. M.(1985).*Leadership and performance beyond expectations.*New York, NY:Free Press.

Bass, B. M.(1990).*Bass & Stogsdill's handbook of leadership: Theory research and managerial applications*(3rd ed.).New York, NY:Free Press.

Bass, B. M.(1997).Does the transactional-transformational leadership paradigm transcend organizational and national boundaries? *The American Psychologist,52*,130–139. doi:10.1037/0003-066X.52.2.130

Bass, B. M.(2008).*The Bass handbook of leadership.*New York, NY:Free Press.

Bass, B. M.(Ed.). (1990).*Bass & Stogdill's handbook of leadership: Theory, research and managerial applications*(3rd ed.).New York, NY:The Free Press.

Bass, B. M., & Avolio, B. J.(1990).*Transformational leadership development: Manual for the Multifactor Leadership Questionnaire.*Palo Alto, CA:Consulting Psychologists Press.

Bass, B. M., & Avolio, B. J.(1994).*Improving organizational effectiveness through transformational leadership.* Thousand Oaks, CA:Sage.

Bass, B. M., Avolio, B. J., Jung, D. I., & Berson, Y.(2003). Predicting unit performance by assessing transformational and transactional leadership. *The Journal of Applied Psychology,88*,207–218.doi:10.1037/0021-9010.88.2.207

Bass, B., & Steidlmeier, P.(1999).Ethics, character, and authentic transformational leadership behavior. *The Leadership Quarterly,10*(2),181–218.doi:10.1016/S1048-9843(99)00016-8

Bates, C. M. (2006, February).*Identity, identification, and the organization: A Burkean approach to understanding the use of electronic message boards to discourage organizational identification*. Paper resented at the convention of the Western States Communication Association meeting in Palm Spring, CA.

Beazley, H. (1997).*Meaning and measurement of spirituality in organizational settings: development of a spirituality assessment scale*. (Dissertations and Theses database AAT 9820619)

Beck, B. L., Koons, S. R., & Milgram, D. L.(2000).Correlates and consequences of behavioral procrastination: The effects of academic procrastination, self-consciousness, self-esteem and self-handicapping. *Journal of Social Behavior and Personality,15*,3–13.

Becker, T. E.(1998).Integrity in organizations: beyond honesty and conscientiousness. *Academy of Management Review,23*(1),154–161.

Behr, E. T.(1998, March).Acting from the center: Your response to today's leadership challenges must be grounded in personal values. *Management Review,51*(5).

Bennett, R.(1993).*The book of virtues*.New York, NY:Simon & Shuster.

Bentham, J.(2010).*An introduction to the principles of morals and legislation*.Oxford, UK:Clarendon Press.(Original work published 1789)doi:10.1002/9780470776018.ch1

Bentler, P. M.(1990).Comparative fit indexes in structural models. *Psychological Bulletin,107*,238–246. doi:10.1037/0033-2909.107.2.238

Berry, D. K.(1995).*An introduction to wisdom and poetry of the Old Testament*.Nashville, TN:Broadman & Holman Publishers.

Beswick, G., & Mann, L.(1994).State orientation and procrastination. In Kuhl, J., & Beckmann, J.(Eds.),*Volition and personality: Action versus state orientation*(pp.391–396). Gottingen, Germany:Hogrefe & Huber.

Birnbaum, M. H.(2001).*Introduction to behavioral research on the internet*.Upper Saddle River, NJ:Prentice-Hall.

Black, J. S., Morrison, A. J., & Gregersen, H. B.(1999). *Global explorers: The next generation of leaders*.New York, NY:Routledge.

Blackshear, P. B.(2003, Summer).The followership continuum: A model for fine tuning the workforce. *Public Management,32*(2),25–29.

Blake, R. R., & Mouton, J. S.(1964).*The managerial grid*. Houston, TX:Gulf Publishing.

Blanchard, K.(2007).*Leading at a higher level*.Upper Saddle River, NJ:Pearson.

Blanchard, K., & Hodges, P.(2005).*Lead like Jesus: Lessons from the greatest leadership role model of all times*. Nashville, TN:W Publishing Group.

Blenkinsopp, J.(1995).*Wisdom and law in the Old Testament: The ordering of life in Israel and early Judaism*(Revised ed.).New York, NY:Oxford University Press.doi:10.1093/acprof:oso/9780198755036.001.0001

Boatwright, K. J., Lopez, F. G., Sauer, E. M., VanDerWege, A., & Huber, D. M.(2010).The influence of adult attachment styles on workers' preferences for relational leadership behaviors. *The Psychologist Manager Journal,13*(1),1–14.doi:10.1080/10887150903316271

Bogg, T., & Roberts, B. W.(2004).Conscientiousness and health-related behaviors: A meta-analysis of the leading behavioral contributors to mortality. *Psychological Bulletin,130*,887–919.doi:10.1037/0033-2909.130.6.887

Boglarsky, C. A., & Kwantes, C. T. (2005, Summer). *Conflict perceptions and their role in manager's choice of resolution style*. Paper presented at the Fourth Biennial Conference on Intercultural Research, Kent, OH.

Boglarsky, C. A., & Kwantes, C. T. (2005, Summer).*Who is happy and why? Subjective well-being and associated thinking styles of US and Canadian students*. Paper presented at the 17th Annual Convention of the American Psychological Society, Los Angeles.

Bollen, K. A.(1989).*Structural equations with latent variables*.New York, NY:Wiley.

Boothkewley, S., Edwards, J. E., & Rosenfeld, P.(1992). Impression management, social desirability, and computer administration of attitude questionnaires - Does the computer make a difference? *The Journal of Applied Psychology,77*(4),562–566.doi:10.1037/0021-9010.77.4.562

Borkowski, J. G., & Thorpe, P. K.(1994).Self-regulation and motivation: A life–span perspective. InSchunk, D. H., & Zimmerman, B. J.(Eds.),*Self-regulation of learning and performance*.Hillsdale, NJ:Lawrence Erlbaum Associates, Publishers.

Boudon, R.(2001).*The origin of values*.London, UK:Transaction Publishers.

Bowling, A.(2005).Mode of questionnaire administration can have serious effects on data quality. *Journal of Public Health,27*(3),281–291.doi:10.1093/pubmed/fdi031

Boyatzis, R., & McKee, A.(2005).*Resonant leadership*. Boston, MA:Harvard Business School Press.

Brody, N.(1983).*Human motivation*.New York, NY:Academic Press.

Bromiley, G.(Ed.). (1991).*The international standard Bible encyclopedia*.Grand Rapids, MI:William B. Eerdmans Publishing Company.

Brower, H. H., Schoorman, F. D., & Tan, H. H.(2000).A model of relational leadership: The integration of trust and leader-member exchange. *The Leadership Quarterly,11*(2),227–250.doi:10.1016/S1048-9843(00)00040-0

Browne, M. W., & Cudeck, R.(1993).Alternative ways of assessing fit. InBollen, K. A., & Long, J. S.(Eds.),*Testing structural equation models*(pp.136–162).Newbury Park, CA:Sage.

Browning, L. D.(1978).A grounded theory of organizational communication. *Communication Monographs,45*,93–109.doi:10.1080/03637757809375957

Brown, J. D., & Marshall, M. A.(2001).Great expectations: Optimism and pessimism in achievement settings. InChang, E. C.(Ed.),*Optimism and pessimism: Implications for theory, research, and practice*(pp.239–255). Washington, DC:American Psychology Association. doi:10.1037/10385-011

Brown, M. E., & Treviño, L. K.(2006).Ethical leadership: A review and future directions. *The Leadership Quarterly,17*,595–616.doi:10.1016/j.leaqua.2006.10.004

Brown, M. E., Trevino, L. K., & Harrison, D. A.(2005). Ethical leadership: A social learning perspective for construct development and testing. *Organizational Behavior and Human Decision Processes,97*,117–134. doi:10.1016/j.obhdp.2005.03.002

Brown, M. E., Treviño, L. K., & Harrison, D. A.(2005). Ethical leadership: A social learning perspective for construct development and testing. *Organizational Behavior and Human Decision Processes,97*,117–134. doi:10.1016/j.obhdp.2005.03.002

Brown, S. E., & Sikes, J. V.(1978).Morale of directors of curriculum and instruction as related to perceptions of leader behavior. *Education,99*(2),121–126.

Bruce, S. (2008).*Experience based suggestions for achieving a high survey response rate*.Retrieved fromhttp://www.virginia.edu/case/education/documents/surveyresponseratesummarypaper-final.pdf

Bryman, A.(1993).*Charisma and leadership in organizations*.Newbury Park, CA:Sage.

Buchanan, T.(2001).Online Personality Assessment. InReips, U.-D., & Bosnjak, M.(Eds.),*Dimensions of Internet science*(pp.57–74).Lengerich, Germany:Pabst Science.

Buchanan, T., Johnson, J. A., & Goldberg, L.(2005). Implementing a Five-Factor personality inventory for use on the Internet. *European Journal of Psychological Assessment,21*,115–127.doi:10.1027/1015-5759.21.2.115

Buchanan, T., & Smith, J. L.(1999).Using the Internet for psychological research: Personality testing on the World Wide Web. *The British Journal of Psychology,90*,125–144. doi:10.1348/000712699161189

Buckmaster, N.(1999).Associations between outcome measurement, accountability and learning for non-profit organisations. *International Journal of Public Sector Management,12*(2),186–197. doi:10.1108/09513559910263499

Burke, R.(2006).Leadership and spirituality. *Foresight,8*(6),14–25.doi:10.1108/14636680610712504

Burns, J. M.(1978).*Leadership*.New York, NY:Harper & Row.

Butler, D. L., & Winne, P. H.(1995).Feedback and self-regulated learning: A theoretical synthesis. *Review of Educational Research,65*,245–281.

Bycio, P., Hackett, R. D., & Allen, J. S.(1995).Further assessments of Bass's (1985) conceptualization of transactional and transformational leadership. *The Journal of Applied Psychology,80*,468–478.doi:10.1037/0021-9010.80.4.468

Calder, G.(2007).*Rorty's politics of redescriptions*.Cardiff, UK:University of Wales Press.

Caldwell, R.(2003).The changing roles of personnel managers: Old ambiguities, new uncertainties. *Journal of Management Studies,40*(4),983–1004.doi:10.1111/1467-6486.00367

Cameron, K. S., & Quinn, R. E.(1999).*Diagnosing changing organizational culture: Based on the competing values framework*.Reading, MA:Addison-Wesley.

Campbell, D. T., & Fiske, D. W.(1959).Convergent and discriminant validation by the multitrait-multimethod matrix. *Psychological Bulletin,56*,81–105.doi:10.1037/h0046016

Campbell, D. T., & Russo, M. J.(2001).*Social measurement*.Thousand Oaks, CA:Sage.

Campbell, D. T., & Stanley, J. C.(1963).*Experimental and quasi-experimental designs for research*.Chicago, IL:Rand McNally & Company.

Campbell, D., & Fiske, D.(1959).Convergent and discriminant validation by the multi-trait/multi-method matrix. *Psychological Bulletin,56*,81–105.doi:10.1037/h0046016

Camrey, A. L.(1973).*A first course in factor analysis*. New York, NY:Academic Press.

Canales, M. T., Tejeda-Delgado, C., & Slate, J. R.(2008). Leadership behaviors of superintendent/principles in small, rural school districts in Texas. *Rural Educator,29*(3),1–7.

Cangemi, J.(2009).Analysis of an adversarial labor/management situation in a Latin American industrial setting. *Organization Development Journal,27*(1),37–47.

Carlbring, P., Brunt, S., Bohman, S., Austin, D., Richards, J., Ost, L., & Andersson, G.(2005).Internet vs. paper and pencil administration of questionnaires commonly used in panic/agoraphobia research. *Computers in Human Behavior,23*(3),1421–1434.doi:10.1016/j.chb.2005.05.002

Carless, S. A.(1998).Assessing the discriminant validity of transformational leadership behavior as measured by the MLQ. *Journal of Occupational and Organizational Psychology,71*,353–358.doi:10.1111/j.2044-8325.1998.tb00681.x

Carr, P. B. (1999). The measurement of resourcefulness intentions in the adult autonomous learner (George Washington University).*Dissertation Abstracts International, 60*(11), 3849. (Publication No. AAT 9949341)

Carr, P., Coe, J., Derrick, G., & Ponton, M. (2007).*Leadership and self-directed learning: Implications from the art of war*.PowerPoint presentation at the International Self-Directed Learning Symposium, Orlando, FL.

Carver, C. S., & Scheier, M. F.(1990).Origins and functions of positive and negative affect: A control-process view. *Psychological Review,97*,19–35.doi:10.1037/0033-295X.97.1.19

Cattell, R. B.(1966).The screen test for the number of factors. *Multivariate Behavioral Research,1*,140–161. doi:10.1207/s15327906mbr0102_10

Cattell, R. B.(1978).*The scientific use of factor analysis in the behavioral and life sciences*.New York, NY:Plenum. doi:10.1007/978-1-4684-2262-7

Chang, H. W., & Lin, G.(2008).Effect of personal values transformation on leadership behavior. *Total Quality Management,19*(1-2),67–77. doi:10.1080/14783360701601967

Chappelow, C. T.(1998).360-degree feedback. InMcCauley, C. D., Moxley, R. S., & Van Velsor, E.(Eds.),*The Center for Creative Leadership handbook of leadership development*(pp.39–41).San Francisco, CA:Jossey-Bass.

Chavez, L. R., Hubbell, F. A., Mishra, S. I., & Valdez, R. B.(1997).The influence of fatalism on self-reported use of Papanicolaou smears. *American Journal of Preventive Medicine,13*,418–424.

Chene, A.(1983).The concept of autonomy in adult education: A philosophical discussion. *Adult Education Quarterly,34*(1),38–47.doi:10.1177/0001848183034001004

Chen, M.(1994).Sun Tzu's strategic thinking and contemporary business. *Business Horizons,37*(2),42–48. doi:10.1016/0007-6813(94)90031-0

Child, D.(1973).*The essentials of factor analysis*.New York, NY:Holt.

Childers, J.(2006).Moving to the rhythms of Christian life: Baptism for children raised in the church. In Fleer, D., & Sibert, C.(Eds.),*Like a shepherd lead us*(pp.95–122). Abilene, TX:Leafwood Publishers.

Cho, H., & LaRose, R.(1999).Privacy issues in internet surveys. *Social Science Computer Review,17*(4),421–434. doi:10.1177/089443939901700402

Christner, C. A., & Hemphill, J. K.(1955).Leader behavior of B-29 commanders and changes in crew members' attitudes toward the crew. *Sociometry,18*(1),82–87. doi:10.2307/2785831

Church, A.(1997).Do you see what I see? An exploration of congruence in ratings from multiple perspectives. *Journal of Applied Social Psychology,27*(11),983–1020. doi:10.1111/j.1559-1816.1997.tb00283.x

Ciulla, J. B.(1995).Leadership ethics: Mapping the territory. *Business Ethics Quarterly,5*,5–24. doi:10.2307/3857269

Ciulla, J. B.(2004).*Ethics: The heart of leadership*.London, UK:Praeger Publishers.

Clarke, A., Lewist, D., Cole, I., & Ringrose, L.(2005).A strategic approach to developing e-learning capability for healthcare. *Health Information and Libraries Journal,22*,33–41.doi:10.1111/j.1470-3327.2005.00611.x

Cleary, T.(1989).The art of war and the I Ching: Strategy and change. In Cleary, T.(Trans. Ed.)*Mastering the art of war*(pp.1–29).Boston, MA:Shambhala.

Cleary, T.(Trans. Ed.). (2000).*The art of war: Complete texts and commentaries*.Boston, MA:Shambhala.

Cohen, D., & Nisbett, R.(1998).Are there differences in fatalism between rural Southerners and Midwesterners? *Journal of Applied Social Psychology,28*,2181–2195. doi:10.1111/j.1559-1816.1998.tb01366.x

Cohen, J.(1960).A coefficient of agreement for nominal scales.*Educational and Psychological Measurement,20*(1),37–46.doi:10.1177/001316446002000104

Cole, M. S., Bedeian, A. G., & Feild, H. S.(2006).The measurement equivalence of Web-based and paper-and-pencil measures of transformational leadership - A multinational test. *Organizational Research Methods,9*(3),339–368. doi:10.1177/1094428106287434

Collins Business. (2001).*Good to great: Why some companies make the leap... and others don't*.New York, NY:Author.

Collinson, D.(2006).Rethinking followership: A poststructuralist analysis of follower identities. *The Leadership Quarterly,17*,179–189.doi:10.1016/j.leaqua.2005.12.005

Colvin, G.(2003, October 27).Corporate crooks are not all created equal. *Fortune*,64.

Condit, C. M., Gronnvoll, M., Landau, J., Shen, L., Wright, L., & Harris, T. (2009).*Believing in both genetic determinism and behavioral action: A materialist framework and implications*.Public Understanding of Science, iFirst.

Confessore, G. J. (1992). An introduction to the study of self-directed learning. In G. J. Confessore & S. J. Confessore, S. J. (Eds.),*Guideposts to self-directed learning*(pp. 1-6). King of Prussia, PA: Organizational Design and Development.

Confessore, G. J., & Park, E.(2004).Factor validation of the learner autonomy profile, version 3.0 and extraction of the short form. *International Journal of Self-Directed Learning,1*(1),39–58.

Conger, J. A., & Kanungo, R. N.(1998).*Charismatic leadership in organizations*.Thousand Oaks, CA:Sage.

Conlin, M. (1999, November 1). Religion in the workplace: The growing presence of spirituality in corporate America.*Business Week*, 150-161.

Cook, C., Heath, F., & Thompson, R. L.(2000).A meta-analysis of response rates in Web- or internet-based surveys. *Educational and Psychological Measurement,60*(6),821–836.doi:10.1177/00131640021970934

Cook, C., Heath, F., Thompson, R. L., & Thompson, B.(2001).Score reliability in Web- or Internet-based surveys: Unnumbered graphic rating scales versus Likert-type scales. *Educational and Psychological Measurement,61*(4),697–706.doi:10.1177/00131640121971356

Cooke, R. A.(1983).*Organizational culture inventory.* Plymouth, MI:Human Synergistics International.

Cooke, R. A., & Lafferty, J. C.(1981).*Level I: Life style inventory - An instrument for assessing and changing the self-concept of organizational members.*Plymouth, MI:Human Synergistics, Inc.

Cooke, R. A., & Rousseau, D. M.(1983).Relationship of life events and personal orientations to symptoms of strain. *The Journal of Applied Psychology,68,*446–458. doi:10.1037/0021-9010.68.3.446

Cooke, R. A., & Rousseau, D. M.(1983).The factor structure of Level 1: Life styles inventory. *Educational and Psychological Measurement,43,*449–457. doi:10.1177/001316448304300214

Cooke, R. A., Rousseau, D. M., & Lafferty, J. C.(1987). Thinking and behavioral styles: Consistency between self-descriptions and descriptions by others. *Educational and Psychological Measurement,47,*815–823. doi:10.1177/001316448704700336

Cooke, R. A., Rousseau, D. M., & Lafferty, J. C.(1987). Thinking and behavioral styles: Consistency between self-descriptions and descriptions by others. *Educational and Psychological Measurement,47,*815–823. doi:10.1177/001316448704700336

Cook, J., & Wall, T.(1980).New work attitude measures of trust, organizational commitment and personal need non-fulfillment. *Journal of Occupational Psychology,53,*39–52.doi:10.1111/j.2044-8325.1980.tb00005.x

Cook, T. D., & Campbell, D. T.(1979).*Quasiexperimentation: Design and analysis issues for field settings.*Boston, MA:Houghton Mifflin.

Cooper, J. M., & Hutchinson, D. S.(Eds.). (1997).*Plato: Complete works.*Indianapolis, IN:Hackett Publishing.

Corno, L. (1989). Self-regulated learning: A volitional analysis. In B. Zimmerman & D. Schunk (Eds.),*Self-regulated learning and academic achievement*(pgs. 111-142). New York, NY: Springer-Verlag.

Corno, L.(1993).The best laid plans: Modern conceptions of volition and educational research. *Educational Researcher,22*(2),14–22.

Corno, L.(1994).Student volition and education: outcomes, influences, and practices. InSchunk, D. H., & Zimmerman, B. J.(Eds.),*Self-regulation of learning and performance.*Hillsdale, NJ:Lawrence Erlbaum Associates, Publishers.

Costello, A. B., & Osborne, J. W. (2005). Best practices in exploratory factor analysis: Four recommendations for getting the most from your analysis.*Practical Assessment, Research & Evaluation, 10*(7). Retrieved on November 14, 2007 fromhttp://pareonline.net/pdf/v10n7.pdf

Craig, S., & Gustafson, S.(1998).Perceived leader integrity scale: An instrument for assessing employee perceptions of leader integrity. *The Leadership Quarterly,9*(2),127–145. doi:10.1016/S1048-9843(98)90001-7

Creating a Customer-Driven Culture Using Project Teams in the Insurance Industry. (2005). (Original work published 1987). Retrieved fromhttp://humansynergistics.com/news/CaseStudies.aspx

Cresswell, J. W., Plano Clark, V. L., Gutmann, M. L., & Hanson, W. E.(2003).Advanced mixed methods research designs. InTashakkori, A., & Teddlie, C.(Eds.),*The handbook of mixed methods in social and behavioral research*(pp.209–240).Thousand Oaks, CA:Sage.

Creswell, J. W.(2003).*Research design: Qualitative, quantitative, and mixed methods approaches*(2nd ed.).Thousand Oaks, CA:Sage Publications, Inc.

Cronbach, L.(2004).My current thoughts on coefficient alpha and successor procedures. *Educational and Psychological Measurement,64*(3),391–418. doi:10.1177/0013164404266386

Cronbach, L. J.(1951).Coefficient alpha and the internal structure tests. *Psychometrika,16*(3),297–334. doi:10.1007/BF02310555

Cross, K. P.(1981).*Adult learners.*San Francisco, CA:Jossey-Bass Publishers.

Csikszentmihaly, M.(1990).*Flow: The psychology of optimal experience*(1st ed.).New York, NY:HarperCollins Publishers.

Cuellar, I., Arnold, B., & Gonzalez, G.(1995). Cognitive referents of acculturation: Assessment of cultural constructs in Mexican Americans. *Journal of Community Psychology,23*,339–356. doi:10.1002/1520-6629(199510)23:4<339::AID-JCOP2290230406>3.0.CO;2-7

Cureton, E., & D'Agostino, R.(1983).*Factor analysis: An applied approach*.Hillsdale, NJ:Lawrence Erlbaum Associates.

Dansereau, F. Jr, Graen, G., & Haga, W. J.(1975).A vertical dyad linkage approach to leadership within formal organizations: A longitudinal investigation of the role making process. *Organizational Behavior and Human Performance,13*,46–78.doi:10.1016/0030-5073(75)90005-7

Davison, C., Frankel, S., & Smith, G.(1992).The limits of lifestyle: Re-assessing fatalism in the popular culture of illness prevention. *Social Science & Medicine,34*,675–685. doi:10.1016/0277-9536(92)90195-V

Day, V., Mensink, D., & O'Sullivan, M.(2000).Patterns of academic procrastination. *Journal of College Reading and Learning,30*,120–134.

De Beuckelaer, A., & Lievens, F.(2009).Measurement equivalence of paper-and-pencil and internet organisational surveys: A large scale examination in 16 countries. *Psychologie Appliquee-Revue Internationale,58*(2),336–361. doi:10.1111/j.1464-0597.2008.00350.x

de Vries, R. E.(2008).What are we measuring? Convergence of leadership with interpersonal and non-interpersonal personality. *Leadership,4*(4),403–417. doi:10.1177/1742715008095188

DeCaro, N., & Bowen-Thompson, F. O.(2010).An examination of leadership styles of minority business entrepreneurs: A case study of public contracts. *The Journal of Business and Economic Studies,16*(2),72–79.

Deci, E. L., & Ryan, R. M.(1985).*Intrinsic motivation and self-determination in human behavior*.New York, NY:Plenum Press.

Den Hartog, D., House, R. J., Hanges, P. J., Ruiz-Quintanilla, S. A., & Dorfman, P. W.(1999).Culture specific and cross culturally generalizable implicit leadership theories: Are attributes of charismatic/transformational leadership universally endorsed? *The Leadership Quarterly,10*,219–256.doi:10.1016/S1048-9843(99)00018-1

Dennis, J. M., Osborn, L., & Semans, K. (2009, March). *Comparison study of early adopter attitudes and online behavior in probability and non-probability web panels.* Retrieved from http://www.knowledgenetworks.com/ganp/reviewer-info.html

Dennis, R. (2004).*Servant leadership theory: Development of the servant leadership assessment instrument.* Unpublished 3133544, Regent University, Virginia Beach.

Dennis, R., & Bocarnea, M.(2005).Development of the servant leadership assessment instrument. *Leadership and Organization Development Journal,65*(5),1857.

Dent, E., Higgins, M., & Wharff, D.(2005).Spirituality and leadership: An empirical review of definitions, distinctions, and embedded assumptions. *The Leadership Quarterly,16*,625–653.doi:10.1016/j.leaqua.2005.07.002

DePree, M.(1992).*Leadership jazz*.New York, NY:Doubleday.

Derrick, M. G. (2001). The measurement of an adult's intention to exhibit persistence in autonomous learning (George Washington University).*Dissertation Abstracts International, 62*(05), 2533. (Publication No. AAT 3006915)

Derue, D. S., Nahrgang, J. D., Wellman, N., & Humphrey, S. E.(2011).Trait and behavioral theories of leadership: An integration and meta-analytic test of their relative validity. *Personnel Psychology,64*(1),7–52.doi:10.1111/j.1744-6570.2010.01201.x

deVaus, D. A.(2001).*Research designs in social research*. Thousand Oaks, CA:SAGE Publications.

DeVellis, R. F.(1991).*Scale development: Theory and applications*.Newbury Park, CA:Sage.

Dewey, J.(1960).*Theory of the moral life*.New York, NY:Holt Rinehart and Winston.

Dillman, D. A.(2000).*Mail and internet surveys: The tailored design method*(2nd ed.).New York, NY:John Wiley & Sons.

Dobel, J. P.(1990).Integrity n the public service. *Public Administration Review,50*(3),354–366.doi:10.2307/976617

Donelson, W. (2004).*Shepherd leadership*. Unpublished dissertation, Regent University, Virginia Beach, VA.

Dunn, C. P.(2009).Integrity matters. *International Journal of Leadership Studies,5*(2),102–125.

Dvir, T., & Shamir, B.(2003).Follower developmental characteristics as predicting transformational leadership: a longitudinal field study. *The Leadership Quarterly,14*,327–344.doi:10.1016/S1048-9843(03)00018-3

Dweck, C. S., & Elliot, E. S.(1983).*Achievement motivation*(Mussen, P. H., Ed.).4th ed.). Handbook of child psychologyNew York, NY:Wiley.

Eaton, J., & Struthers, C. W.(2002).Using the Internet for organizational research: A study of cynicism in the workplace. *Cyberpsychology & Behavior,5*(4),305–313. doi:10.1089/109493102760275563

Edvardsson, B.(1990).Management consulting: Towards a successful relationship. *International Journal of Service Industry Management,1*(3),4–19. doi:10.1108/09564239010136902

Egede, L. E., & Bonadonna, R. J.(2003).Diabetes self-management in African Americans: An exploration of the role of fatalism. *The Diabetes Educator,29*,105–115. doi:10.1177/014572170302900115

Elliot, M., & Meltsner, S.(1993).*The perfectionist predicament: How to stop driving yourself and others crazy*.New York, NY:Berkley Books.

Elliott, E., & Dweck, C.(1988).Goals: An approach to motivation and achievement. *Journal of Personality and Social Psychology,54*,5–12.doi:10.1037/0022-3514.54.1.5

Elwell, W., & Beitzel, B.(Eds.). (1988).*Baker encyclopedia of the Bible*.Grand Rapids, MI:Baker Book House.

Emery, J.(2001).Is informed choice in genetic testing a different breed of information decision-making? A discussion paper. *Health Expectations,4*,81–86.doi:10.1046/j.1369-6513.2001.00124.x

Epstein, J., Klinkenberg, W. D., Wiley, D., & McKinley, L.(2001).Insuring sample equivalence across internet and paper-and-pencil assessments. *Computers in Human Behavior,17*(3),339–346.doi:10.1016/S0747-5632(01)00002-4

Ess, C.(2007).Internet research ethics. InJohnson, A. N., & McKenna, K.(Eds.),*The Oxford handbook of internet psychology*.New York, NY:Oxford University Press.

Ess, C., & Jones, S.(2004).Ethical decision-making and internet research: Recommendations from the AoIR ethics working committee. InBuchanan, E. A.(Ed.),*Readings in virtual research ethics: Issues and controversies*.Reading, PA:Information Science Publishing.doi:10.4018/978-1-59140-152-0.ch002

Ethics Resource Center. (2008).*National nonprofit ethics survey: An inside view on nonprofit sector ethics.*

Fabrigar, L. R., Wegener, D. T., MacCallum, R. C., & Strahan, E. J.(1999).Evaluating the use of exploratory factor analysis in psychological research. *Psychological Methods,4*(3),272–299.doi:10.1037/1082-989X.4.3.272

Falcione, R. L., Sussman, L., & Herden, R. P.(1987).Communication climate in organizations. InJablin, F. M., Putnam, L. L., Roberts, K. H., & Porter, L. W.(Eds.),*Handbook of organizational communication: An interdisciplinary perspective*(pp.195–204).Beverly Hills, CA:Sage.

Farling, M. L., Stone, A. G., & Winston, B. E.(1999). Servant leadership: Setting the stage for empirical research. *The Journal of Leadership Studies,6*(1/2),49–72. doi:10.1177/107179199900600104

Farrell, A. M.(2010).Insufficient discriminant validity: A comment on Bove, Pervan, Beatty and Shiu (2009). *Journal of Business Research,63*(3),324–327.doi:10.1016/j.jbusres.2009.05.003

Felfe, J.(2006).Transformationale und charismatische Führung - Stand der Forschung und aktuelle Entwicklungen [Transformational and charismatic leadership: State of research and recent developments].*Zeitschrift für Personalpsychologie,5*,163–176.doi:10.1026/1617-6391.5.4.163

Ferdig, M. A., & Ludema, J. D. (2005). Transformative interactions: Qualities of conversations that heighten the vitality of self-organizing change. In W. A., Pasmore, & R. W. Woodman (Eds.), *Research in organizational change and development: Vol. 15* (pp. 169-205). Stamford, CT: JAI Press.

Fiedler, F. E. (1967). *A theory of leadership effectiveness.* New York, NY: McGraw-Hill.

Field, A. (2005). *Factor analysis using SPSS.* Retrieved on March, 3, 2008, from www.sussex.ac.uk/Users/andyf/factor.pdf

Fields, D. (2007). Determinants of follower perceptions of a leader's authenticity and integrity.

Finance Industry— Leadership development. (2005). (Original work published 1987). Retrieved from http://humansynergistics.com/news/CaseStudies.aspx

Fink, A. (2003). *The survey handbook* (2nd ed.). Thousand Oaks, CA: Sage.

Fishbein, M., & Ajzen, I. (1975). *Belief, attitude, intention, and behavior: An introduction to theory and research.* Reading, MA: Addison-Wesley. Retrieved from http://www.people.umass.edu/aizen/f&a1975.html

Fishbein, M., & Ajzen, I. (1975). *Belief, attitude, intention, and behavior: An introduction to theory and research.* Reading, MA: Addison-Wesley publishing Company.

Fleer, D., & Siburt, C. (Eds.). (2006). *Like a shepherd lead us.* Abilene, TX: Leafwood Publishers.

Fleishman, E. A. (1953). The description of supervisory behavior. *The Journal of Applied Psychology, 37,* 1–6. doi:10.1037/h0056314

Fleishman, E. A. (1995). Consideration and structure: Another look at their role in leadership research. In Dansereau, F., & Yammarino, F. J. (Eds.), *Leadership: The multiple-level approaches: Classical and new wave* (pp. 51–60). Stamford, CT: JAI Press.

Frankel, M. S., & Siang, S. (1999). *Ethical and legal aspects of human subjects research on the internet: A report of a workshop June 10-11, 1999.* Retrieved from http://www.aaas.org/spp/dspp/sfrl/projects/intres/report.pdf

Franklin, T., & van Harmelen, M. (2007). Web 2.0 for content for learning and teaching in higher education. Retrieved from http://www.jisc.ac.ok/media/documents/programmes/digitalrepositores/web2-content-learning-and teaching.pdf

Freedman, D. (Ed.). (1996). *The anchor Bible dictionary.* New York, NY: Doubleday. (Original work published 1992)

Freud, A. (1937). *The ego and mechanisms of defense.* London, UK: Hogarth Press.

Fry, L. (2003). Toward a theory of spiritual leadership. *The Leadership Quarterly, 14,* 639–727. doi:10.1016/j.leaqua.2003.09.001

Fry, L. W. (2003). Toward a theory of spiritual leadership. *The Leadership Quarterly, 14,* 693–727. doi:10.1016/j.leaqua.2003.09.001

Fuller, J. B., Patterson, C. E. P., Hester, K., & Stringer, D. Y. (1996). A quantitative review of research on charismatic leadership. *Psychological Reports, 78,* 271–287. doi:10.2466/pr0.1996.78.1.271

Furrow, D. (2005). As cited in Dunn (2005). *Ethics: Key concepts in philosophy.* New York, NY: Continuum International Publishing Group.

Gagliardi, G. (2002). *Sun Tzu's the art of war & the art of career building.* Seattle, WA: Clearbridge.

Gagliardi, G. (2004a). *The art of war plus its amazing secrets.* Seattle, WA: Clearbridge.

Gagliardi, G. (2004b). *The art of war plus the warrior class: 306 lessons in modern competition.* Seattle, WA: Clearbridge.

Gallagher, S. R. (2003). The new landscape for course management systems. *Research Bulletin (Sun Chiwawitthaya Thang Thale Phuket), 10.*

Garcia, T., & Pintrich, P. R. (1994). Regulating motivation and cognition in the classroom: The role of self-schemas and self-regulatory strategies. In Schunk, D. H., & Zimmerman, B. J. (Eds.), *Self-regulation of learning and performance. (1994).* Hillsdale, NJ: Lawrence Erlbaum Associates, Publishers.

Garrison, D. R., & Kanuka, H.(2004).Blended learning: Uncovering its transformative potential in higher education. *The Internet and Higher Education,7*,95–105. doi:10.1016/j.iheduc.2004.02.001

Gartner. (2012a).*Cloud computing*. Retrieved from http://www.gartner.com/it-glossary/cloud-computing/

Gartner. (2012b).*Software as a service*. Retrieved from http://www.gartner.com/it-glossary/software-as-a-service-saas/

Gay, L. R., & Airasian, P.(2003).*Educational research competencies for analysis and applications*(7th ed.).Upper Saddle River, NJ:Merrill Prentice Hall.

Gersick, C. J. G.(1989).Making time: Predictable transitions in task groups. *Academy of Management Journal,33*,274–309.doi:10.2307/256363

Geyer, A. L., & Steyrer, J. M.(1998).Transformational leadership and objective performance in banks. *Applied Psychology: An International Review,47*,397–420. doi:doi:10.1111/j.1464-0597.1998.tb00035.x

Gibbs, J. C.(1995).The cognitive development perspective. InKurtines, W. M., & Gewirtz, J. L.(Eds.),*Moral development: An introduction*(pp.27–48).Boston, MA:Allyn & Bacon.

Giddens, A.(1984).*The constitution of society*.Berkley, CA:University of California Press.

Glackin, M., Boisselle, J. H., Burke, J., DeGrenier, A., Kass, F., Kysela, B., & Maddaline, S. (2005). Online course management at Mount Holyoke: Current use and recommendations for the future.*Report of the Course management Study Group.*

Gladwell, M.(2005).*Blink: The power of thinking without thinking*.New York, NY:Little, Brown and Company.

Glasser, J. K.(2002).Factors related to consultant credibility. *Consulting Psychology Journal: Practice and Research,54*(1),28–42.doi:10.1037/1061-4087.54.1.28

Goffee, R., & Jones, G.(2006).The art of followership. *European Business Forum,25*,22–26.

Golden, T. D., & Veiga, J. F.(2008).The impact of superior-subordinate relationships on the commitment, job satisfaction, and performance of virtual workers. *The Leadership Quarterly,19*,77–88.doi:10.1016/j.leaqua.2007.12.009

Goldhaber, G. M., & Rogers, D. P.(1979).*Auditing organizational communication systems: The ICA Communication Audit*.Dubuque, IA:Kendall/Hunt.

Goleman, D.(1998a).What makes a leader? *Harvard Business Review,76*(6),92–102.

Goleman, D.(1998b).*Working with emotional intelligence*. New York, NY:Bantam.

Goleman, D., Boyatzis, R., & McKee, A.(2002).*Primal leadership: Realizing the power of emotional intelligence*. Boston, MA:Harvard Business School Press.

Google. (2012).*Online surveys*. Retrieved from http://www.google.com/search?q=online+surveys

Gordon, J.(Ed.). (2003).*The Pfeiffer book of successful leadership development tools*.San Francisco, CA:Pfeiffer.

Gorsuch, R. L.(1983).*Factor analysis*(2nd ed.).Hillsdale, NJ:Lawrence Erlbaum Associates.

Gove, P. B.(Ed.). (1976).*Webster's third new international dictionary*.Springfield, MA:Merriam Company.

Graen, G. B., & Uhl-Bien, M.(1995).Relationship-based approach to leadership: Development of leader-member exchange (LMX) theory of leadership over 25 years: Applying a multi-level multi-domain perspective. *The Leadership Quarterly,6*(2),219–247.doi:10.1016/1048-9843(95)90036-5

Graen, G., & Cashman, J. F.(1975).A role making model of leadership in formal organizations: A developmental approach. InHunt, J. G., & Larson, L. L.(Eds.),*Leadership frontiers*(pp.143–165).Kent, OH:Kent State University Press.

Gratzinger, P. D., Warren, R. A., & Cooke, R. A.(1990). Psychological orientation and leadership: Thinking styles that differentiate between effective and ineffective managers. InClark, K. E., & Clark, M. B.(Eds.),*Measures of leadership*(pp.239–247).West Orange, NJ:Leadership Library of America.

Gratzinger, P. D., Warren, R. A., & Cooke, R. A.(1990). Psychological orientations and leadership: Thinking styles that differentiate between effective and ineffective managers. InClark, K. E., & Clark, M. B.(Eds.),*Measures of leadership*.Greensboro, NC:Center for Creative Leadership.

Greene, C. N.(1975).The reciprocal nature of influence between leader and subordinate. *The Journal of Applied Psychology*,*60*(2),187–193.doi:10.1037/h0076552

Greene, J. C., Caracelli, V. J., & Graham, W. F.(1989). Toward a conceptual framework for mixed-method evaluation designs. *Educational Evaluation and Policy Analysis*,*11*(3),255–274.

Greenleaf, R. K.(1977).*Servant leadership*.New York, NY:Paulist Press.

Gregorian, V. (2004, April). Philanthropy should have glass pockets.*The Chronicle of Philanthropy*, 43 – 44.

Greiner, L., & Metzger, R.(1983).*Consulting to management*.Englewood Cliffs, NJ:Prentice Hall.

Guglielmino, L. M. (1978). Development of the self-directed learning readiness scale. Doctoral dissertation, University of Georgia, 1977.*Dissertation Abstracts International, 38,*6467A.

Hackman, M. Z., Ellis, K., Johnson, C. E., & Staley, C.(1999).Self-construal orientation: Validation of an instrument and a study of the relationship to leadership communication style. *Communication Quarterly*,*47*(2),183–195.doi:10.1080/01463379909370133

Hair, J. F. Jr, Anderson, R. E., Tatham, R. L., & Black, W. C.(1998).*Multivariate data analysis*(5th ed.).Upper Saddle River, NJ:Prentice Hall International.

Hair, J., Black, W., Babin, B., Anderson, R., & Tatham, R.(2006).*Multivariate data analysis*(6th ed.).Upper Saddle River, NJ:Pearson.

Hale, J. R., & Fields, D. L.(2007).Exploring servant leadership across cultures: A study of followers in Ghana and the USA. *Leadership*,*3*(4),397–417. doi:10.1177/1742715007082964

Hall, E. T.(1976).*Beyond culture*.New York, NY:Anchor Books.

Halpin, A. W. (1957).*Manual for the leadership behavior description questionnaire*. Ohio State University, Fisher College of Business. Retrieved March 22, 2009, fromhttp://fisher.osu.edu/offices/fiscal/lbdq

Halpin, A. W.(1954).The leadership behavior and combat performance of airplane commanders. *Journal of Abnormal Psychology*,*49*(1),19–22.doi:10.1037/h0055910

Halpin, A. W., & Winer, B. J.(1957).A factorial study of the leader behavior descriptions. InStogdill, R. M., & Coons, A. E.(Eds.),*Leaders behavior: Its description and measurement*(pp.39–51).Columbus, OH:The Bureau of Business Research College of Commerce and Administration, Ohio State University.

Hambley, L. A., O'Neill, T. A., & Kline, T. J. B.(2007). Virtual team leadership: The effects of leadership style and communication medium on team interaction styles and outcomes. *Organizational Behavior and Human Decision Processes*,*103*,1–20.doi:10.1016/j.obhdp.2006.09.004

Hamel, G.(2000).*Leading the revolution*.Boston, MA:Harvard Business School Press.

Hammer, C. A., & Ferrari, J. R.(2002).Differential incidence of procrastination between blue- and white-collar workers. *Current Psychology (New Brunswick, N.J.)*,*21*,333–338.doi:10.1007/s12144-002-1022-y

Hanson, P. B., & Robson, R. (2004). Evaluating course management technology: A pilot case study.*Educause Research Bulletin, 24.*Retrieved fromwww.educause.edu/ecar/

Harackiewicz, J. M., Abrahams, S., & Wagerman, R.(1987).Performance evaluation and intrinsic motivation: The effects of evaluative focus, rewards, and achievement orientation. *Journal of Personality and Social Psychology*,*53*,1015–1023.doi:10.1037/0022-3514.53.6.1015

Harcourt, E. (1998). As cited in Dunn (2009). Integrity practical deliberation and utilitarianism.*The Philosophical Quarterly, 48*(191), 189-198.

Harris, N. N., & Sutton, R. I.(1983).Task procrastination in organizations: A framework for research. *Human Relations*,*36*,987–995.doi:10.1177/001872678303601102

Harris, R.(2006).Spirituality for the busy, frantic, and overwhelmed. InFleer, D., & Charles, S.(Eds.),*Like a shepherd lead us: Guidance for the gentle art of pastoring*(pp.15–31).Abilene, TX:Leafwood Publishers.

Harter, S.(2002).Authenticity. InSnyder, C. R., & Lopez, S.(Eds.),*Handbook of positive psychology*.Oxford, UK:University Press.

Hartsfield, M. (2003).*The internal dynamics of transformational leadership: Effects of spirituality, emotional intelligence, and self-efficacy.* (Dissertations and Theses database, AAT 3090425).

Haslam, S. A., & Platow, M. J.(2001).The link between leadership and followership: How affirming social identity translates vision into action. *Personality and Social Psychology Bulletin,27*(11),1469–1479. doi:10.1177/01461672012711008

Hater, J. J., & Bass, B. M.(1988).Superiors' evaluations and subordinates' perceptions of transformational and transactional leadership. *The Journal of Applied Psychology,73*,695–702.doi:10.1037/0021-9010.73.4.695

Heckhausen, H., & Kuhl, J.(1985).From wishes to action: The dead ends and short cuts on the long way to action. InFrese, M., & Sabini, J.(Eds.),*Goal directed behavior: The concept of action in psychology*(pp.134–157).Hillsdale, NJ:Lawrence Erlbaum Associates.

Heider, F.(1958).*The psychology of interpersonal relations*.New York, NY:Wiley.doi:10.1037/10628-000

Heinitz, K., Liepmann, D., & Felfe, J.(2005).Examining the factor structure of the MLQ: Recommendation for a reduced set of factors. *European Journal of Psychological Assessment,21*,182–190.doi:10.1027/1015-5759.21.3.182

Hemmelgarn, A. L., Glisson, C., & James, L. R.(2006, Spring).Organizational culture and climate: Implications for services and interventions research. *Clinical Psychology: Science and Practice,13*(1),73–89.doi:10.1111/j.1468-2850.2006.00008.x

Hemphill, J. K.(1955).Leadership behavior associated with the administrative reputation of college departments. *Journal of Educational Psychology,46*(7),385–401. doi:10.1037/h0041808

Hemphill, J. K., & Coons, A. E.(1957).Development of the leader behavior description questionnaire. InStogdill, R. M., & Coons, A. E.(Eds.),*Leaders behavior: Its description and measurement*(pp.6–38).Columbus, OH:The Bureau of Business Research College of Commerce and Administration, Ohio State University.

Hendlin, S. J.(1992).*When good enough is never enough: Escaping the perfection trap*.New York, NY:Putnam.

Heneman, H. G. III, Metzler, C. A., Roosevelt Thomas Jr, R., Donohue, T. J., & Frantzreb, R. B.(1998).Future challenges and opportunities for the HR profession. *HRMagazine,43*(3),68–72.

Herold, D., & Fields, D.(2004).Making sense of subordinate feedback for leadership development: Confounding effects of job role and organizational rewards. *Group & Organization Management,29*(6),686–701. doi:10.1177/1059601103257503

Herrington, J., Bonem, M., & Furr, J. H.(2000).*Leading congregational change: A practical guide for the transformational journey*.San Francisco, CA:Jossey-Bass.

Hersey, P.(1984).*The situational leader*.New York, NY:Warner Books.

Hills, R. J.(1963).The representative function: Neglected dimensions of leadership behavior. *Administrative Science Quarterly,8*(1),83–101.doi:10.2307/2390888

Hinkin, T. R., Tracey, J. B., & Enz, C. A.(1997).Scale construction: developing reliable and valid measurement instruments. *Journal of Hospitality & Tourism Research (Washington, D.C.),21*,100–120. doi:doi:10.1177/109634809702100108

Hinkle, D. E., Wiersma, W., & Jurs, S. G.(2003).*Applied statistics for the behavioral sciences*(5th ed.).Boston, MA:Houghton Mifflin.

Hobbes, T.(1651, 1968).*Leviathan*(C. MacPherson, Ed.). London, UK: Penguin Books.

Hofstede, G.(2001).*Culture's consequences: Comparing values, behaviors, institutions, and organizations across nations*(2nd ed.).London, UK:Sage Publications.

Holland, T. (2001). The perils of procrastination.*Far Eastern Economic Review, 164*, 66-72.

Hollander, E. P.(1978).*Leadership dynamics: A practical guide to effective relationships*.New York, NY:The Free Press.

Hollander, E. P.(1992a).The essential interdependence of leadership and followership.*Current Directions in Psychological Science*,*1*(2),71–75.doi:10.1111/1467-8721.ep11509752

Hollander, E. P.(1992b).Leadership, followership, self, and others. *The Leadership Quarterly*,*3*(1),43–54. doi:10.1016/1048-9843(92)90005-Z

Hollander, E. P.(1995).Ethical challenges in the leader-follower relationship. *Business Ethics Quarterly*,*5*(1),55–65. doi:10.2307/3857272

Hollander, E. P.(2008).*Inclusive leadership: The essential leader-follower relationship*.New York, NY:Routledge.

Horney, K.(1945).*Our inner conflicts*.New York, NY:W. W. Norton & Co.

Horowitz, L. J. (1985).*The existential mapping process*. Unpublished manuscript, Sonoma State University.

Horsfall, T. (2004).*Song of the shepherd: Meeting the God of grace in Psalm 23*. Cambridge, MA: Cowley Publications.

Houle, C. O.(1961).*The inquiring mind: A study of the adult learner who continues to participate to learn*.Madison, WI:University of Wisconsin Press.

House, R. J.(1971).A path-goal theory of leader effectiveness. *Administrative Science Quarterly*,*16*,321–339. doi:10.2307/2391905

House, R. J.(1977).A 1976 theory of charismatic leadership. InHunt, J. G., & Larson, L. L.(Eds.),*Leadership: The cutting edge*(pp.189–207).Carbondale, IL:Southern Illinois University Press.

House, R. J.(1996).Path-goal theory of leadership: Lessons, legacy, and a reformulated theory. *The Leadership Quarterly*,*7*,323–352.doi:10.1016/S1048-9843(96)90024-7

House, R. J., Filley, A. C., & Kerr, S.(1971).Relation of leader consideration and initiating structure to R and D subordinates' satisfaction. *Administrative Science Quarterly*,*16*(1),19–30.doi:10.2307/2391283

House, R. J., Hanges, P. J., Javidan, M., Dorfman, P. W., & Gupta, V.(Eds.). (2004).*Culture, leadership, and organizations: The GLOBE study of 62 cultures*.Thousand Oaks, CA:Sage Publications, Inc.

House, R. J., & Podsakoff, P. M.(1994).Leadership effectiveness: Past perspectives and future directions for research. InGreenberg, J.(Ed.),*Organizational behavior: The state of the science*(pp.45–82).Hillsdale, NJ:Erlbaum.

Howell, J. C.(2006).*The beatitudes for today*.Louisville, KY:Westminster John Knox Press.

Howell, J. M., & Avolio, B. J.(1993).Transformational leadership, transactional leadership, locus of control, and support for innovation: Key predictors of consolidated-business-unit performance. *The Journal of Applied Psychology*,*78*,891–902.doi:10.1037/0021-9010.78.6.891

Hoyt, C. L., & Blascovich, J.(2003).Transformational and transactional leadership in virtual and physical environments. *Small Group Research*,*34*,678–715. doi:10.1177/1046496403257527

Huitt, W. (1997).*The SCAN report revisited*. Paper delivered at the Fifth Annual Gulf South Business and Vocational Education Conference, Valdosta State University, Valdosta, GA, April 18.

Hu, L., & Bentler, P. M.(1999).Cutoff criteria for fit indexes in covariance structure analysis: Conventional criteria versus new alternatives. *Structural Equation Modeling*,*6*(1),1–55.doi:10.1080/10705519909540118

Human Synergistics. (1986).*Improving store management effectiveness*.Atlanta, GA:Coca Cola Retailing Research Council.

Hunter, J. E., & Gerbing, D. W.(1982).Unidimensional measurement, second order factor analysis, and causal models. InStaw, B. M., & Cummings, L. L.(Eds.),*Research in organizational behavior*(*Vol. 4*).Greenwich, CT:JAI Press.

Hunt, J. G., & Conger, J. A.(1999).From where we sit: An assessment of transformational and charismatic leadership research. *The Leadership Quarterly*,*10*,335–343. doi:10.1016/S1048-9843(99)00039-9

Huntzinger, J. (1999).*The end of exile: A short commentary on the shepherd/sheep metaphor in exilic and post-exilic prophetic and synoptic gospel literature.* Unpublished Master's thesis, Fuller Theological Seminary, Pasadena, CA.

Hutcheson, G., & Sofroniou, N.(1999).*The multivariate social scientist: Introductory statistics using generalized liner models.*Thousand Oaks, CA:Sage.

Inderlied, S. D., & Powell, G.(1979).Sex-role identity and leadership style: Different labels of the same concept? *Sex Roles,5*(5),613–625.doi:10.1007/BF00287664

Janis, I.(1972).*Victims of groupthink.*Boston, MA:Houghton Mifflin.

Janis, I.(1982).*Groupthink: Psychological studies of policy decisions and fiascos*(2nd ed.).Boston, MA:Houghton Mifflin.doi:10.1177/000271627340700115

Janis, I. L.(1989).*Crucial decisions: Leadership in policymaking and crisis management.*New York, NY:The Free Press.

Janz, N., & Becker, M.(1984).The health belief model: A decade later. *Health Education & Behavior,11*,1–47. doi:10.1177/109019818401100101

Joas, H.(2000).*The genesis of values.*Chicago, IL:University Press.

Johns, E. F.(1989).*The reliability of the life styles inventory (LSI 1).*Plymouth, MI:Human Synergistics, Inc.

Johnstone, J. W. C., & Rivera, R. J.(1965).*Volunteers for learning.*Chicago, IL:Aldine Publishing Company.

Jones, M. D., Chen, S.-L. S., & Hall, G. J.(Eds.). (2004). *Online social research: Methods, issues & ethics.*New York, NY:Peter Lang.

Jones, R. A.(1994).The ethics of research in cyberspace. *Internet Research,4*(3),30–35. doi:10.1108/10662249410798894

Judge, T. A., & Bono, J. E.(2001).Relationship of core self-evaluations traits self-esteem, generalized self-efficacy, locus of control, and emotional stability-with job satisfaction and job performance: A meta-analysis. *The Journal of Applied Psychology,86*,80–92.doi:10.1037/0021-9010.86.1.80

Judge, T. A., & Piccolo, R. F.(2004).Transformational and transactional leadership: A meta-analytic test of their relative validity. *The Journal of Applied Psychology,89*,755–768.doi:10.1037/0021-9010.89.5.755

Judge, T. A., Piccolo, R. F., & Ilies, R.(2004).The forgotten ones? The validity of consideration and initiating structure in leadership research. *The Journal of Applied Psychology,89*,36–51.doi:10.1037/0021-9010.89.1.36

Judge, T. A., Woolf, E. F., Hurst, C., & Livingston, B.(2006).Charismatic and transformational leadership. A Review and an agenda for future research. *Zeitschrift für Arbeits- und Organisationspsychologie,50*,203–214. doi:10.1026/0932-4089.50.4.203

Jung, D., Chow, C., & Wu, A.(2003).The role of transformational leadership in enhancing organizational innovation: Hypotheses and some preliminary findings. *The Leadership Quarterly,14*,525–544.doi:10.1016/S1048-9843(03)00050-X

Kahai, S. S., Sosik, J. J., & Avolio, B. J.(2003).Effects of leadership style, anonymity, and rewards in an electronic meeting system environment. *The Leadership Quarterly,14*,499–524.doi:10.1016/S1048-9843(03)00049-3

Kaleta, R., Skibba, K., & Joosten, T.(2007).Discovering, designing and delivering hybrid courses. InPicciano, A. G., & Dziuban, C. D.(Eds.),*Blended learning research perspectives*(pp.111–143).USA:The Sloan Consortium.

Kalichman, S., Kelly, J., Morgan, M., & Rompa, D.(1997). Fatalism, current life satisfaction, and risk for HIV infection among gay and bisexual men. *Journal of Consulting and Clinical Psychology,65*,542–546.doi:10.1037/0022-006X.65.4.542

Kalshoven, K., & Den Hartog, D. N.(2009).Ethical leader behavior and leader effectiveness: The role of prototypicality and trust. *International Journal of Leadership Studies,5*(2).

Kant, I.(2002).*The groundwork of the metaphysics of morals*(A. Zweig(Hill, T., Trans. Ed.).Oxford, UK:Oxford University Press.(Original work published 1785)

Kaptein, M., Huberts, L., Avelino, S., & Lasthuizen, K.(2005, Fall).Demonstrating ethical leadership by measuring ethics: A survey of U.S. public servants. *Public Integrity,7*(4),299–311.

Kark, R., Shamir, B., & Chen, G.(2003).The two faces of transformational leadership: Empowerment and dependency. *The Journal of Applied Psychology,88*,246–255. doi:10.1037/0021-9010.88.2.246

Karoly, L., & Panis, C.(2004).*The 21st century at work: Forces shaping the future workforce and workplace in the United States*.Santa Monica, CA:RAND Corporation.

Katerber, R., & Hom, P. W.(1981).Effects of within-group and between-groups variation in leadership. *The Journal of Applied Psychology,66*(2),218–223.doi:10.1037/0021-9010.66.2.218

Katz, D., Maccoby, N., & Morse, N. C.(1959).*Productivity, supervision, and morale in an office situation*.Ann Arbor, MI:Institute for Social Research, The University of Michigan.

Katz, R.(2003).Balancing technology and tradition: The example of course management systems. *EDUCAUSE Review,38*,48–56.

Kellerman, B.(2008).*Followership: How followers are creating change and changing leaders*.Boston, MA:Harvard Business School Press.

Keller, P.(1970).*A shepherd looks at Psalm 23*.Grand Rapids, MI:Zondervan.

Keller, R. T.(2006).Transformational leadership, initiating structure, and substitutes for leadership: A longitudinal study of research and development project team performance. *The Journal of Applied Psychology,91*(1),202–210. doi:10.1037/0021-9010.91.1.202

Kelley, R. E.(1988).In praise of followers. *Harvard Business Review,66*(6),142–148.

Kelley, R. E.(1992).*The power of followership: How to create leaders people want to follow, and followers who lead themselves*.New York, NY:Doubleday.

Kelloway, E. K., Barling, J., Kelley, E., Comtois, J., & Gatien, B.(2003).Remote transformational leadership. *Leadership and Organization Development Journal,24*,163–171.doi:10.1108/01437730310469589

Kenis, I.(1977).A cross-cultural study of personality and leadership. *Group & Organization Studies,2*(1),49–60. doi:10.1177/105960117700200107

Kenis, I.(1978).Leadership behavior, subordinate personality, and satisfaction with supervision. *The Journal of Psychology,98*(1),99–107.doi:10.1080/00223980.1978.9915952

Kepner, C. H., & Tregoe, B. B.(1965).*The rational manager: A systematic approach to problem-solving and decision-making*.New York, NY:McGraw-Hill.

Kerlinger, F. N., & Lee, H. B.(2000).*Foundations of behavioral research*(4th ed.).Stamford, CT:Wadsworth Thompson.

Kershaw, I.(2001).*Backing Hitler: Consent and coercion in Nazi Germany*.Oxford, UK:Oxford University Press.

Kilroy, J. J. (2008).*Development of seven leadership behavior scales based upon the seven leadership values inspired by the beatitudes*(Doctoral dissertation). Available from ProQuest Dissertation and Theses database, 149 pages; AAT 3340922. Retrieved from http://proquest.umi.com/pqdlink?did=1654488921&Fmt=7&clientId=79356&RQT=309&VName=PQD

Kim, M. S., & Hunter, J. E.(1993).Relationships among attitudes, behavioral intentions, and behavior: A meta-analysis of past research, Part 2. *Communication Research,20*,331–364.doi:10.1177/009365093020003001

Kirk, J., & Miller, M. L.(1986).*Reliability and validity in qualitative research*.Beverly Hills, CA:Sage.

Kirkpatrick, S. A., & Locke, E. A.(1996).Direct and indirect effects of three core charismatic leadership components on performance and attitudes. *The Journal of Applied Psychology,81*,36–51.doi:10.1037/0021-9010.81.1.36

Klassen, R. M., Ang, R. P., Chong, W. H., Krawchuk, L. L., Huan, V. S., Wong, I. Y. F., & Yeo, L. S.(2010). Academic procrastination in two settings: Motivation correlates, behavioural patterns, and negative impact of procrastination in Canada and Singapore. *Applied Psychology: An International Review,59*,1–19.

Klenke, K.(2003).The "S" factor in leadership education, practice, and research. *Journal of Education for Business,79*(1),56–60.doi:10.1080/08832320309599089

Klenke, K.(2005).Corporate values as multi-level, multi-domain antecedents of leader behaviors. *International Journal of Management,26*(1),50–66.

Kline, P.(1993).*The handbook of psychological testing.* New York, NY:Routledge.

Kline, P.(1994).*An easy guide to factor analysis.*New York, NY:Routledge.

Knowles, M.(1975).*Self-directed learning.*Chicago, IL:Follett.

Knowles, M.(1980).*Modern practice of adult, education: From pedagogy to andragogy.*San Francisco, CA:Jossey-Bass Publishers.

Kohlberg, L.(1984).*Essays in moral development: The psychology of moral development.*New York, UK:Harper & Row.

Kohn, A.(1993).*Punished by rewards: The trouble with gold stars, incentive plans, A's, praise and other bribes.* New York:Houghton Mifflin.

Kohn, M. L., & Schooler, C.(1983).*Work and personality: An inquiry into the impact of social stratification.* Norwood, NJ:Ablex Pub. Corp.

Koh, W. L., Steers, R. M., & Terborg, J. R.(1995).The effects of transformational leadership on teacher attitudes and student performance in Singapore. *Journal of Organizational Behavior,16,*319–333.doi:10.1002/job.4030160404

Kolbell, E.(2003).*What Jesus meant: The beatitudes and a meaningful life.*Louisville, KY:Westminster John Knox Press.

Kotva, J.(1996).*The case for Christian virtue ethics.* Washington, DC:Georgetown University Press.

Kouzes, J. M., & Posner, B. Z.(2002).*The leadership challenge*(3rd ed.).San Francisco, CA:Jossey-Bass.

Kouzes, J., & Posner, B.(2001).Bringing leadership lessons from the past into the future. InBennis, W., Spreitzer, G., & Cummings, T.(Eds.),*The future of leadership*(pp.81–90).San Francisco, CA:Josey-Bass.

Kouzes, J., & Posner, B.(2006).*A leader's legacy.*San Francisco, CA:Josey-Bass.

Krantz, J. H., & Dalal, R.(2000).Validity of Web-based psychological research. InBirnbaum, M. H.(Ed.),*Psychological experiments on the internet.* San Diego, CA:Academic Press.doi:10.1016/B978-012099980-4/50003-4

Krause, D. G.(2005).*The art of war for executives.*New York, NY:Perigee.

Kraut, A. I., & Saari, L. M.(1999).Organizational surveys: Coming of age for a new era. InKraut, A. I., & Korman, A. K.(Eds.),*Evolving practices in human resource management*(pp.302–327).San Francisco, CA:Jossey-Bass.

Krebs, D. L., & Denton, K.(2005).Toward a more pragmatic approach to morality: A critical evaluation of Kohlberg's Model. *Psychological Review,112*(3),629–649. doi:10.1037/0033-295X.112.3.629

Kriegbaum, R.(1998).*Leadership prayers.*Wheaton, IL:Tyndale House Publishers.

Kriger, M., & Seng, Y.(2005).Leadership with inner meaning: a contingency theory of leadership based on the worldviews of five religions. *The Leadership Quarterly,16*(5),771–806.doi:10.1016/j.leaqua.2005.07.007

Kubr, M.(1996).*Management consulting: A guide to the profession*(3rd ed.).Geneva, Switzerland:International Labour Office.

Kuhl, J.(1985).Volitional mediators of cognition-behavior consistency: Self-regulation processes and action verses state orientation. InKuhl, J., & Beckman, J.(Eds.),*Action control: From cognition to behavior*(pp.101–128).New York, NY:Springer-Verlag.

Kuhl, J., & Goschke, T.(1994).A theory of action control: Mental subsystems, modes of control, and volitional conflict-resolution strategies. InKuhl, J., & Beckmann, J.(Eds.),*Volition and personality: Action verses state orientation*(pp.93–124).Seattle, WA:Hogrefe & Huber.

Kvale, S.(1996).*Interviews: An introduction to qualitative research interviewing.*Thousand Oaks, CA:Sage.

Lafferty, J. C.(1973).*Level I: Life styles inventory (self description)*.Plymouth, MI:Human Synergistics, Inc.

Lafferty, J. C.(1980).*Item frequency and distribution – Level 1 life styles inventory*.Plymouth, MI:Human Synergistics, Inc.

Lafferty, J. C.(1989).*Life styles inventory LSI 1: Inventory*. Plymouth, MI:Human Synergistics, Inc.

Langan, J.(1977).Beatitude and moral law in St Thomas. *The Journal of Religious Ethics,5*,183–195.

Lautenschlager, G. J., & Flaherty, V. L.(1990).Computer administration of questions - More desirable or more social desirability. *The Journal of Applied Psychology,75*(3),310–314.doi:10.1037/0021-9010.75.3.310

Lay, C. H., & Silverman, S.(1996).Trait procrastination, anxiety, and dilatory behavior. *Personality and Individual Differences,21*,61–67.doi:10.1016/0191-8869(96)00038-4

Leary, T.(1955).The theory and measurement of interpersonal communication. *Psychiatry,18*,147–161.

Leary, T.(1957).*Interpersonal diagnosis of personality*. New York, NY:Ronald Press.

Leman, K., & Pentak, W.(2004).*The way of the shepherd, 7 ancient secrets to managing productive people*.Grand Rapids, MI:Zondervan.

Leslie, J. B., & Fleenor, J. W.(1998).*Feedback to managers: A review and comparison of multi-rater instruments for management development*(3rd ed.).Greensboro, NC:Center for Creative Leadership.

Levine, A. (2008).*2008 content management systems satisfaction survey*. Retrieved from http://nten.org/research

Li, D. H.(2000).*The art of leadership by Sun Tzu: A new-millennium translation of Sun Tzu's art of war*.Bethesda, MD:Premier.

Liden, R. C., Wayne, S. J., Zhao, H., & Henderson, D. (2005, November).*Development of a multidimensional measure of servant leadership*. Paper presented at the Annual Meeting of the Southern Management Association, Charleston, SC.

Lievens, F., Van Geit, P., & Coetsier, P.(1997).Identification of transformational leadership qualities: An examination of potential biases. *European Journal of Work and Organizational Psychology,6*,415–530. doi:10.1080/135943297399015

Likert, R.(1967).A technique for the measurement of attitudes. *Archives de Psychologie,140*,1–55.

Lim, H., Lee, S. G., & Nam, K.(2007).Validating e-learning factors affecting training effectiveness. *International Journal of Information Management,27*,22–35.doi:10.1016/j.ijinfomgt.2006.08.002

Lincoln, Y. S., & Guba, E. G.(1985).*Naturalistic inquiry*. Newbury Park, CA:Sage.

Littrell, R. F.(2002).Desirable leadership behaviors of multicultural managers in China. *Journal of Management Development,21*(1),5–74.doi:10.1108/02621710210413190

Littrell, R. F., & Nkomo, S. M.(2005).Gender and race differences in leader behavior preferences in South Africa. *Women in Management Review,20*(8),562–580. doi:10.1108/09649420510635204

Littrell, R. F., & Valentin, L. N.(2005).Preferred leadership behaviors: Exploratory results from Romania, Germany, and the UK. *Journal of Management Development,24*(5),421–442.doi:10.1108/02621710510598445

Litwin, G., & Stringer, R.(1968).*Motivation and organizational climate*.Cambridge, MA:Harvard University Press.

Locke, J.(1967).An essay concerning the true origin, extent and end of civil government. InBurtt, E.(Ed.),*The English philosophers from Bacon to Mills*.New York, NY:The Modern Library.(Original work published 1689)

Loewenstein, G.(1992).The fall and rise of psychological explanations in the economics of intertemporal choice. InLoewenstein, G., & Elster, J.(Eds.),*Choice over time*(pp.3–34).New York, NY:Russell Sage Foundation.

Lohmann, R. A.(2007, May/June).Charity, philanthropy, public service, or enterprise: What are the big questions of nonprofit management today? *Public Administration Review,67*(3),437–444.doi:10.1111/j.1540-6210.2007.00727.x

Long, H. B.(1989).*Self-directed learning: Emerging theory and practice*.Oklahoma Research Center for Continuing Professional and Higher Education of the University of Oklahoma.

Long, H. B.(1998).Theoretical and practical implications of selecting paradigms of self-directed learning. InLong, H. B.(Eds.),*Developing paradigms for self-directed learning*(pp.1–14).Norman, OK:University of Oklahoma.

Lord, R., & Brown, D.(2001).Leadership, values, and subordinate self-concepts. *The Leadership Quarterly*,*12*,133–152.doi:10.1016/S1048-9843(01)00072-8

Lowe, K. B., Cordery, J., & Morrison, D. (2004).*A model for the attribution of leader integrity: Peeking inside the black box of authentic leadership*. Paper presented at the 2004 Gallup Leadership Institute Conference, Lincoln, NE.

Lowe, K. B., Kroeck, K. G., & Sivasubramaniam, N.(1996).Effectiveness correlates of transformational and transactional leadership: A meta-analytic review of the MLQ literature. *The Leadership Quarterly*,*7*,385–425. doi:10.1016/S1048-9843(96)90027-2

Lowin, A., Hrapchak, W. J., & Kavanagh, M. J.(1969). Consideration and initiation of structure: An experimental investigation of leadership traits. *Administrative Science Quarterly*,*14*(2),238–253.doi:10.2307/2391102

Lowry, R.(2006).Before we split: Mediating conflict in the church. InFleer, D., & Siburt, C.(Eds.),*Like a shepherd lead us*(pp.123–138).Abilene, TX:Leafwood Publishers.

Luthans, F., & Avolio, B.(2003).Authentic leadership development. InCameron, K., Dutton, J., & Quinn, R.(Eds.),*Positive organizational scholarship: Foundations for a new discipline*.San Francisco, CA:Berrett-Koehler Publishers.

MacIntyre, A.(1984).*After virtue*.Notre Dame, IN:University of Notre Dame Press.

Manewitz, M.(1997).When should you call a consultant? *HRMagazine*,*42*,84–88.

Marshall, J. A. (2012).*Ethical leadership, prototypicality, integrity, trust and leader effectiveness*.Dissertation, Regent University, Virginia Beach, VA.

Marshall, M.(2007).*Discipline without stress, punishment or reward*(2nd ed.).Los Alamitos, CA:Piper Press.

Martin, M. W.(1979).Self-deception, self-pretence, and emotional detachment.*Mind*,*88*(1),441–446.doi:10.1093/mind/LXXXVIII.1.441

Masi, R. J. (1993).*Impact of the transformational leader style, empowering culture, and individual empowerment on productivity and commitment to quality: An empirical investigation of the behavioral aspects of these two outcomes*.Unpublished doctoral dissertation, University of Illinois at Chicago, Chicago.

Masi, R. J., & Cooke, R. A.(2000).Effects of transformational leadership on subordinate motivation, empowering norms, and organizational productivity. *The International Journal of Organizational Analysis*,*8*,16–47.doi:10.1108/eb028909

Maslow, A. H.(1954).*Motivation and personality*.New York, NY:Harper and Row.

Mason, W., & Suri, S. (2010). Conducting behavioral research on Amazon's Mechanical Turk.*Behavioral Research Methods*.Retrieved fromhttp://research.yahoo.com/files/mturkmethods.pdf

Mason, T., & Caplan, J.(1995).*Nazism, Fascism and the working class*.New York, NY:Cambridge University Press. doi:10.1017/CBO9780511622328

Maxcy, S. J.(2003).Pragmatic threads in mixed methods research in the social sciences: The search for multiple methods of inquiry and the end of the philosophy of formalism. InTashakkori, A., & Teddlie, C.(Eds.),*The handbook of mixed methods in social and behavioral research*(pp.51–89).Thousand Oaks, CA:Sage.

Mayo, R., Ureda, J., & Parker, V.(2001).Importance of fatalism in understanding mammography screening in rural elderly women.*Journal of Women & Aging*,*13*,57–72. doi:10.1300/J074v13n01_05

McClellan, D. C.(1985).*Human motivation*.Glenview, IL:Scott, Foresman.

McCombs, B. L. (1997).*Understanding the keys to learning*. Retrieved fromwww.mcrel.org/products/noteworth/html

McCormick, B., & Davenport, D.(2003).*Shepherd leadership*.San Francisco, CA:Jossey-Bass.

McFall, L.(1987).Integrity. *Ethics*,*98*,5–20. doi:10.1086/292912

McKee, A., Boyatzis, R., & Johnston, F.(2008).*Becoming a resonant leader: Develop your emotional intelligence, renew your relationships, sustain your effectiveness.* Boston, MA:Harvard Business School.

McKeon, R.(2001).*The basic works of Aristotle*.New York, NY:Random House.

McLachlin, D. R.(1999).Factors for consulting engagement success. *Management Decision*,394–402. doi:10.1108/00251749910274162

McNeilly, M.(1996).*Sun Tzu and the art of business: Six strategic principles for managers*.New York, NY:Oxford Press.

Mehta, S.(2003, October 27).MCI: Is being good good enough? *Fortune*,117–124.

Merriam, S. B., & Caffarella, R. S.(1999).*Learning in adulthood: A comprehensive guide*(2nd ed.).San Francisco, CA:Jossey-Bass.

Mertler, C. A., & Vannatta, R. A.(2005).*Advanced and multivariate statistical methods: Practical application and interpretation*(3rd ed.).Glendale, CA:Pyrczak.

Meyer, D. T. (2001). The measurement of intentional behavior as a prerequisite to autonomous learning (George Washington University).*Dissertation Abstracts International, 61*(12), 4697. (Publication No. AAT 9999882)

Meyer, A. D., Goes, J. B., & Brooks, G. R.(1995).Organizations reacting to hyperturbulence. InHuber, G. P., & Van de Ven, A. H.(Eds.),*Longitudinal field research methods: Studying processes in organizational change*(pp.66–111). Thousand Oaks, CA:Sage.

Meyer, J. P., Stanley, D. J., Herscovitch, L., & Topolnytsky, L.(2002).Affective, continuance, and normative commitment to the organization: A meta-analysis of antecedents, correlates, and consequences. *Journal of Vocational Behavior*,*61*,20–52.doi:10.1006/jvbe.2001.1842

Meyers, L. S., Gamst, G., & Guarino, A. J.(2006).*Applied multivariate research: Design and interpretation.* Thousand Oaks, CA:Sage.

Michaelson, G. A.(2001).*Sun Tzu: The art of war for managers*.Avon, MA:Adams Media Corporation.

Michaelson, G., & Michaelson, S.(2003).*Sun Tzu for success*.Avon, MA:Adam Media.

Miles, M. B., & Huberman, A. M.(1994).*Qualitative data analysis: An expanded sourcebook*(2nd ed.).Thousand Oaks, CA:Sage.

Milgram, N. A.(1991).Procrastination. InDulbecco, R.(Ed.),*Encyclopaedia of human biology*(*Vol. 6*, pp.149–155).New York, NY:Academic Press.

Milgram, N. A., Sroloff, B., & Rosenbaum, M.(1988). The procrastination of everyday life. *Journal of Research in Personality*,*22*,197–212.doi:10.1016/0092-6566(88)90015-3

Milgram, S.(1974).*The individual in a social world: Essays and experiments*.New York, NY:McGraw Hill.

Miller, G. R., & Nicholson, H. E.(1976).*Communication inquiry: A perspective on a process*.Reading, MA:Addison-Wesley.

Mitroff, I., & Denton, E.(1999).*A spiritual audit of corporate America*.San Francisco, CA:Jossey-Bass.

Mooney, V.(Ed.). (2000).*When no one sees*.Colorado Springs, CO:NavPress.

Morgan, G. (2003). Faculty use of course management systems.*Educause Center for Applied Research, 2.*

Morgan, G.(1997).*Images of organization*.Thousand Oaks, CA:Sage Publications Inc.

Morse, J. M.(1991).Approaches to qualitative-quantitative methodological triangulation. *Nursing Research*,*40*(2),120–123.doi:10.1097/00006199-199103000-00014

Moving toward franchising in the retail industry: Building a strong sales culture. (2005). (Original work published 1987). Retrieved fromhttp://humansynergistics.com/news/CaseStudies.aspx

Mulaik, S. A., James, L. R., Van Alstine, J., Bennett, N., Lind, S., & Stilwell, C. D.(1989).Evaluation of goodness-of-fit indices for structural equation models. *Psychological Bulletin,105*,430–445.doi:10.1037/0033-2909.105.3.430

Mulligan, L. N.(2007, June).What's good for the goose is not good for the gander: Sarbanes-Oxley-style nonprofit reforms. *Michigan Law Review,105*(8),1981–1999.

Musschenga, A.(2001).Education for moral integrity. *Journal of Philosophy of Education,35*(2),219–235. doi:10.1111/1467-9752.00222

Nadler, D. A., Shaw, R. B., & Walton, A. E.(1995).*Discontinuous change: Leading organizational transformation.* San Francisco, CA:Jossey-Bass.

Nediger, W. G., & Chelladurai, P.(1989).Life Styles Inventory: Its application in the Canadian context. *Educational and Psychological Measurement,49*,901–909. doi:10.1177/001316448904900413

Neff, J. A., & Hoppe, S. K.(1993).Race/ethnicity, acculturation, and psychological distress: Fatalism and religiosity as cultural resources. *Journal of Community Psychology,21*(1),3–20. doi:10.1002/1520-6629(199301)21:1<3::AID-JCOP2290210102>3.0.CO;2-9

Neville, K., Heavin, C., & Walsh, E.(2005).A case in customizing e-learning. *Journal of Information Technology,20*,117–129.doi:10.1057/palgrave.jit.2000041

Newton, R., & Doonga, N.(2007).Corporate e-learning: Justification for implementation and evaluation of benefits: A study examining the views of training managers and providers. *Education for Information,25*,111–130.

Niederdeppe, J., & Levy, A. G.(2007).Fatalistic beliefs about cancer prevention and three preventive behaviors. *Cancer Epidemiology, Biomarkers & Prevention,16*,998–1003.doi:10.1158/1055-9965.EPI-06-0608

Northouse, P.(2007).*Leadership theories and practice*(4th ed.).Thousand Oaks, CA:Sage Publishing.

Northouse, P. G.(2007).*Leadership: Theory and practice.* London, UK:Sage Publications.

Nunnally, J.(1978).*Psychometric theory*(2nd ed.).New York, NY:McGraw-Hill.

Oddi, L. F.(1987).Perspectives on self-directed learning. *Adult Education Quarterly,38*(1),21–31. doi:10.1177/0001848187038001003

O'Donoghue, T., & Rabin, M.(1999).Incentives for procrastinators. *The Quarterly Journal of Economics,114*,769–816.doi:10.1162/003355399556142

Olympic Gold — Achievement or Competitive?(2005). (Original work published 1987). Retrieved fromhttp://humansynergistics.com/news/CaseStudies.aspx

Ong, C. S., Lai, J. Y., & Wang, Y. S.(2004).Factors affecting engineers' acceptance of asynchronous e-learning systems in high-tech companies. *Information & Management,41*,795–804.doi:10.1016/j.im.2003.08.012

Onwuegbuzie, A. J.(2000).Academic procrastinators and perfectionistic tendencies among graduate students. *Journal of Social Behavior and Personality,15*,103–109.

Pacanowsky, M. E., & O'Donnell-Trujillo. (1982). Communication and organizational cultures. *Western Journal of Speech Communication,46*,115–130. doi:10.1080/10570318209374072

Pack, T.(2002).Corporate learning gets digital.*E-Content, 25*,22-26.Retrieved fromhttp://vnweb.hwwilsonweb.com

Palanski, M. E., & Yammarino, F. J.(2007).Integrity and leadership: Clearing the conceptual confusion. *European Management Journal,25*(3),171–184.doi:10.1016/j.emj.2007.04.006

Palanski, M. E., & Yammarino, F. J.(2009).Integrity and leadership: A multi-level conceptual framework. *The Leadership Quarterly,20*,405–420.doi:10.1016/j.leaqua.2009.03.008

Parrott, R., Silk, K., Weiner, J., Condit, C., Harris, T., & Bernhardt, J.(2004).Deriving lay models of uncertainty about genes' role in illness causation to guide communication about human genetics. *The Journal of Communication,54*,105–122.doi:10.1111/j.1460-2466.2004.tb02616.x

Patterson, K. A.(2003).*Servant leadership: A theoretical model. Unpublished UMI 3082719.* Virginia Beach: Regent University.

Patterson, K. A., Russell, R. F., & Stone, A. G.(2004). Transformational versus servant leadership - A difference in leader focus. *Leadership and Organization Development Journal,25*(4).

Patton, M. Q.(1980).*Qualitative evaluation methods.* Beverly Hills, CA: Sage Publications, Inc.

Patton, M. Q.(2002).*Qualitative research & evaluation methods*(3rd ed.).Thousand Oaks, CA: Sage Publications, Inc.

Perrow, C.(1979).*Complex organizations: A critical essay.* New York, NY: Random House.

Perry, N. W., & Ware, M. E.(1987).Facilitating growth in a personal development course. *Psychological Reports,60*,491–500.doi:10.2466/pr0.1987.60.2.491

Peters, T.(2002).*Playing God? Genetic determinism and human freedom.* New York, NY: Routledge.

Peters, T. J., & Waterman, R. A. Jr. (1982).*In search of excellence: Lessons from America's best-run companies.* New York, NY: Warner Books.

Pfeffer, J.(1982).*Organizations and organization theory.* Boston, MA: Pittman.

Phelps, E. A.(2006).Emotion and cognition: Insights from studies of the human amygdala. *Annual Review of Psychology,57*,27–53.doi:10.1146/annurev. psych.56.091103.070234

Pink, D. H.(2009).*Drive: The surprising truth about what motivates us.* New York, NY: Riverhead.

Pintrich, P. R., & DeGroot, E.(1990).Motivational and self-regulated learning components of classroom academic performance. *Journal of Educational Psychology,82*,33–40.doi:10.1037/0022-0663.82.1.33

Plato,. (1997).The republic. InCooper, J.(Ed.),*Plato: Complete works.* Cambridge, MA: Hackett Publishing Company.

Plaut, W. G.(1961).*The Book of Proverbs: A commentary.* New York, NY: Union of American Hebrew Congregations.

Pocock, C.(2005).*50 years of the U-2.* Atglen, PA: Schiffer Military History.

Podsakoff, P. M., Bommer, W. H., Podsakoff, N. P., & MacKenzie, S. B.(2006).Relationships between leader reward and punishment behavior and subordinate attitudes, perceptions, and behaviors: A meta-analytic review of existing and new research. *Organizational Behavior and Human Decision Processes,99*(2),113.doi:10.1016/j. obhdp.2005.09.002

Ponton, M. K. (1999). The measurement of an adult's intention to exhibit personal initiative in autonomous learning (George Washington University).*Dissertation Abstracts International, 60*(11), 3933. (Publication No. AAT 9949350)

Ponton, M. K., & Carr, P. B. (1999).*A quasi-linear behavioral model and an application to self-directed learning.* Hampton, VA: NASA Langley Research Center. (NTIS NASA/TM-1999-209094)

Ponton, M., Carr, P., & Derrick, G.(2004).A path analysis of the conative factors associated with autonomous learning. *International Journal of Self-Directed Learning,1*(1),59–69.

Ponton, M., Derrick, G., Hall, J. M., Rhea, N., & Carr, P.(2005).The relationship between self-efficacy and autonomous learning: The development of new instrumentation. *International Journal of Self-directed Learning,2*(1),50–61.

Poulfelt, F.(1997).Ethics for management consultants. *Business Ethics (Oxford, England),6*(2),65–70. doi:10.1111/1467-8608.00050

Powe, B. D.(1995).Fatalism among elderly African Americans: Effects on colorectal screening. *Cancer Nursing,18*,385–392.doi:10.1097/00002820-199510000-00008

Powe, B. D.(1997).Cancer fatalism: Spiritual perspectives. *Journal of Religion and Health,36*,135–144. doi:10.1023/A:1027440520268

Powe, B. D.(2001).Cancer fatalism among elderly African American women: Predictors of the intensity of the perceptions.*Journal of Psychosocial Oncology,19*,85–96. doi:10.1300/J077v19n03_07

Powe, B. D., Daniels, E. C., & Finnie, R.(2005).Comparing perceptions of cancer fatalism among African American patients. *Journal of the American Academy of Nurse Practitioners,17*,318–324.doi:10.1111/j.1745-7599.2005.0049.x

Powe, B. D., & Finnie, R.(2003).Cancer fatalism: The state of the science. *Cancer Nursing,26*,454–465.

Powe, B. D., & Johnson, A.(1995).Fatalism as a barrier to cancer screening among African-Americans: Philosophical perspectives. *Journal of Religion and Health,34*(2),119–126.doi:10.1007/BF02248767

Powe, B. D., & Weinrich, S.(1999).An intervention to decrease cancer fatalism among rural elders. *Oncology Nursing Forum,26*,583–588.

Preston, C.(2007).Nonprofit leaders' debate: Whether or not all philanthropy is equal?*The Chronicle of Philanthropy, 20*(2), Prewitt, K. (2006). Foundations. InPowell, W., & Steinberg, R.(Eds.),*The nonprofit sector: A research handbook*(1st ed., pp.355–377).New Haven, CT:Yale University Press.

Puka, B.(2005).Teaching ethical excellence: Artful response-ability, creative integrity, character opus. *Liberal Education,22*–25.

Putnam, L. L., & Cheney, G.(1985).Organizational communication: Historical developments and future directions. InBenson, T. W.(Ed.),*Speech communication in the twentieth century*(pp.130–156).Carbondale, IL:Southern Illinois University Press.

Putti, J. M.(1985).Leader behavior and group characteristics in work improvement teams – The Asian context. *Public Personnel Management,14*(3),301–306.

Putti, J. M., & Tong, A. C.(1992).Effects of leader behavior on subordinate satisfaction in a civil service-Asian context. *Public Personnel Management,21*(1),53–63.

Quinn, R. E., & Rohrbaugh, J.(1983).A spatial model of effectiveness criteria: Towards a competing values approach to organizational analysis. *Management Science,29*,363–377.doi:10.1287/mnsc.29.3.363

Rachels, J.(2003).*The elements of moral philosophy*(4th ed.).New York, NY:McGraw Hill.

Raftery, A. E.(1995).Bayesian model selection in social research. InMarsden, P. V.(Ed.),*Sociological methodology*(pp.111–163).Cambridge, UK:Basil Blackwell.

Rand, A.(1961).*For the new intellectual*.New York, NY:Signet.

Rardin, R.(2004).*The servant's guide to leadership*. Newtown, CT:Selah Publishing.

Rawls, J.(1971).*A theory of justice*.Cambridge, MA:Harvard University Press.

Raymond, E. S.(1998).The cathedral and the bazaar. *First Monday,3*(3). Retrieved from http://www.firstmonday.org/htbin/cgiwrap/bin/ojs/index.php/fm/article/view/578/499

Reips, U.-D. (1992).*The composition and systematic exploration of an observation device for the existential mapping process*. Unpublished Master's thesis, Sonoma State University.

Reips, U.-D., & Heilmann, T. (2009).*The OLBDQ: An online version of the leader behavior description questionnaire*. Manuscript in preparation.

Reips, U.-D., & Ito, T. (2007, January 10).*The virtual team trainer*. Presentation in lecture series "Educational Engineering", ETH Zürich & Educational Engineering Lab, University of Zürich.

Reips, U. D.(2000).The web experiment method: Advantages, disadvantages and solutions. InBirnbaum, M. H.(Ed.),*Psychological experiments on the internet*(pp.89–117).San Diego, CA:Academic Press. doi:10.1016/B978-012099980-4/50005-8

Reips, U.-D.(2006).Web-based methods. InEid, M., & Diener, E.(Eds.),*Handbook of multimethod measurement in psychology*(pp.73–85).Washington, DC:American Psychological Association.doi:10.1037/11383-006

Reips, U.-D.(2008).Potenziale jenseits der Privatsphäre: Risiken und Chancen internetbasierter Kommunikation [Potentials beyond privacy: Risks and benefits of Internet-based communication].*Psychoscope,29*,8–11.

Reips, U.-D., & Bosnjak, M.(Eds.). (2001).*Dimensions of internet science*.Lengerich, Germany:Pabst.

Ricketson, R.(2009).*Followerfirst: Rethinking leading in the church.*Cumming, GA:Heartworks Publications.

Riegelsberger, J., Sasse, A., & McCarthy, J. D.(2007). Trust in mediated interactions. InJoinson, A., McKenna, K. Y. A., Postmes, T., & Reips, U.-D.(Eds.),*The Oxford handbook of Internet psychology*(pp.53–69).Oxford, UK:Oxford University Press.

Riggio, R. E., Chaleff, I., & Lipman-Blumen, J.(Eds.). (2008).*The art of followership: How great followers create great leaders and organizations.*San Francisco, CA:Jossey-Bass.

Riordan, C., & Vandenberg, R.(1994).A central question in cross-cultural research: Do employees of different cultures interpret work-related measures in an equivalent manner? *Journal of Management,20,*642–571.

Robbins, H., & Finely, M.(1996).*Why change doesn't work: Why initiatives go wrong and how to try again – and succeed.*Princeton, NJ:Peterson's.

Roberts, L. L., Konczak, L. J., & Macan, T. H.(2004).Effects of data collection method on organizational climate survey results. *Applied H.R.M. Research,9*(1),13–26.

Rogers, R. W.(1983).Cognitive and physiological processes in fear appeals and attitude change: A revised theory of protection motivation. InCacioppo, J. T., & Petty, R. E.(Eds.),*Social psychophysiology: A source book*(pp.153–176).New York, NY:The Guilford Press.

Roper, D.(1994).*Psalm 23: The song of a passionate heart.*Grand Rapids, MI:Discovery House Publishers.

Rorty, R., & Williams, M.(1979).*Philosophy and the mirror of Nature.*Princeton, NJ:Princeton University Press.

Rossi, P. H., Wright, J. D., & Anderson, A. B.(Eds.). (1983). *Handbook of survey research.*San Diego, CA:Academic Press.

Rost, J.(2008).Followership: An outmoded concept. InRiggio, R. E., Chaleff, I., & Lipman-Blumen, J.(Eds.),*The art offollowership: How great followers create great leaders and organizations.*San Francisco, CA:Jossey-Bass.

Rost, J. C.(1991).*Leadership for the twenty-first century.*New York, NY:Praeger Publishers.

Rousseau, J. J.(1967).*The social contract and discourse on the origin of inequality*(Crocker, L., Ed.).New York, NY:Pocket Books.(Original work published 1762)

Rovai, A. P.(2007).A constructivist approach to online college learning. *The Internet and Higher Education,7,*79–93. doi:10.1016/j.iheduc.2003.10.002

Rubin, H. J., & Rubin, I. S.(1995).*Qualitative interviewing.*Thousand Oaks, CA:Sage.

Rugeley, C., & Van Wart, M. (2006). As cited in Dunn (2009, p. 117). Everyday moral exemplars: The case of Judge Sam Medina.*Public Integrity, 8*(4), 381-394.

Rummel, R. J.(1970).*Applied factor analysis.*Evanston, IL:Northwestern University Press.

Rush, M. C., Phillips, J. S., & Lord, R. G.(1981).Effects of a temporal delay in rating on leader behavior descriptions: A laboratory investigation. *The Journal of Applied Psychology,66*(4),442–450.doi:10.1037/0021-9010.66.4.442

Russell, M.(2003).Leadership and followership as a relational process. *Educational Management and Administration,31*(2),145–157.doi:10.1177/0263211X0303102103

Salem, P. J. (2004b, May).*A longitudinal study of organizational communicational communication climate.*Paper presented at the Annual Meeting of the International Communication Association meeting in New Orleans, LA.

Salem, P. J., Barclay, F., & Hoffman, M. (2003, May). *Organizational culture at the edge: A case study of organizational change.* Paper presented at the Annual Meeting of the International Communication Association meeting in San Diego, CA.

Salem, P.(1999).The changes and challenges for organizational communication in the next century. InSalem, P.(Ed.),*Organizational communication and change*(pp.3–27).Cresskill, NJ:Hampton Press.

Salem, P. J.(1994).Learning to learn: The challenges in Russia. *Intercultural Communication Studies,4*(2),17–41.

Salem, P. J.(2004a).Mead on management. *Review of Communication,4*(1),97–105. doi:10.1080/1535859042000250344

Salem, P. J.(2008).The seven communication reasons organizations do not change. *Corporate Communications,13*(3),333–348.doi:10.1108/13563280810893698

Salem, P. J.(2009).*The complexity of human communication*.Cresskill, NJ:Hampton Press.

Salovey, P., & Mayer, J.(1990).Emotional intelligence. *Imagination, Cognition and Personality,9*(3),185–211.

Samuel, M.(1996).*The Lord is my shepherd: The theology of a caring god*.Northvale, NJ:Jason Aronson, Inc.

Sandelands, L. E., Brockner, J., & Glynn, M. A.(1988). If at first you don't succeed, try, try again: Effects of persistence-performance contingencies, ego involvement, and self-esteem on task performance. *The Journal of Applied Psychology,73*(2),208–216.doi:10.1037/0021-9010.73.2.208

Santos, J. R.(1999, April).Cronbach's alpha: A tool for assessing the reliability of scales. *Journal of Extension,37*(2),1–5.

Sashkin, M. (1979). Instrumentation: A review of Ralph M. Stogdill's leadership behavior description questionnaire – Form XII.*Group & Organizational Studies (pre-1986), 4*(2), 247-250.

Sassenberg, K., Postmes, T., Boos, M., & Reips, U.-D.(2003).Studying the Internet: A challenge for modern psychology. *Swiss Journal of Psychology,62*. doi:10.1024//1421-0185.62.2.75

Schaefer, D. R., & Dillman, D. A.(1998).Development of a standard E-mail methodology - Results of an experiment. *Public Opinion Quarterly,62*(3),378–397. doi:10.1086/297851

Scharmer, C. O. (2002).*Presencing: Illuminating the blind spot of leadership*(working title). Retrieved on June 7, 2004 from www.dialogonleadership.org

Scheier, M., & Bridges, M.(1995).Person variables and health: Personality predispositions and acute psychological states as shared determinants for disease. *Psychosomatic Medicine,57*,255–268.

Schein, E. H.(1992).*Organizational culture and leadership*(2nd ed.).San Francisco, CA:Jossey-Bass.

Schein, E. H.(2010).*Organizational culture and leadership*(4th ed.).San Francisco, CA:John Wiley & Sons, Inc.

Schlenker, B. R.(2008).Integrity and character: Implications of principled and expedient ethical ideologies.*Journal of Social and Clinical Psychology,27*(10),1078–1125. doi:10.1521/jscp.2008.27.10.1078

Schlenker, B. R., Pontari, B. A., & Christopher, A. N.(2001).Excuses and character: Personal and social implications of excuses. *Personality and Social Psychology Review,5*,15–32.doi:10.1207/S15327957PSPR0501_2

Schmidt, W. C.(1997).World-Wide Web survey research: Benefits, potential problems, and solutions. *Behavior Research Methods, Instruments, & Computers,29*(2),274–279.doi:10.3758/BF03204826

Schneider, B.(Ed.). (1990).*Organizational climate and culture*.San Francisco, CA:Jossey-Bass.

Schneider, B., Ashworth, S. D., Higgs, A. C., & Carr, L.(1996).Design, validity, and use of strategically focused employee attitude surveys. *Personnel Psychology,49*(3),695–705.doi:10.1111/j.1744-6570.1996. tb01591.x

Scholtz, A. (2006).*Know thyself*. Retrieved from http://classics.binghamton.edu/greek.htm

Schriesheim, C. A.(1982).The great high consideration – High initiation on structure leadership myth: Evidence on its generalizability. *The Journal of Social Psychology,116*,221–228.doi:10.1080/00224545.1982.9922774

Schriesheim, C. A., House, R. J., & Kerr, S.(1976). Leader initiating structure: A reconciliation of discrepant research results and some empirical tests. *Organizational Behavior and Human Performance,15*(2),297–321. doi:10.1016/0030-5073(76)90043-X

Schriesheim, C. A., & Kerr, S.(1974).Psychometric properties of the Ohio State leadership scales. *Psychological Bulletin,81*(11),756–765.doi:10.1037/h0037277

Schriesheim, C. A., Kinicki, A. J., & Schriesheim, J. F.(1979).The effect of leniency on leader behavior descriptions. *Organizational Behavior and Human Performance,23*(1),1–29.doi:10.1016/0030-5073(79)90042-4

Schriesheim, C. A., & Murphy, C. J. (1976). Relationships between leader behavior and subordinate satisfaction and performance: A test of some situational moderators. *The Journal of Applied Psychology, 61*(5), 634–641. doi:10.1037/0021-9010.61.5.634

Schunk, D. H. (1991). Self-efficacy and academic motivation. *Educational Psychologist, 26*(3 & 4), 207–231.

Schunk, D. H., & Zimmerman, B. J. (1994). *Self-regulation of learning and performance.* Hillsdale, NJ: Lawrence Erlbaum Associates, Publishers.

Scott, R. B. (1971). *The way of wisdom in the Old Testament.* New York, NY: Macmillan Publishing Co., Inc.

Scott, S. G., & Lane, V. R. (2000). A stakeholder approach to organizational identity. *Academy of Management Review, 25*(1), 46–62.

Seligson, A. L., & Choi, L. (2006). *Critical elements of an organizational ethical culture.* Washington, DC: Ethics Resource Center.

Seltzer, J., & Bass, B. M. (1990). Transformational leadership: Beyond initiation and consideration. *Journal of Management, 16*(4), 693–703. doi:10.1177/014920639001600403

Seltzer, J., & Bass, B. M. (1990). Transformational leadership: Beyond initiation and consideration. *Journal of Management, 16*, 693. doi:10.1177/014920639001600403

Senge, P. (1990). *The fifth discipline.* New York, NY: Currency Doubleday.

Senge, P. M. (1990). *The fifth discipline: The art and practice of the learning organization.* New York, NY: Doubleday Currency. doi:10.1002/pfi.4170300510

Senge, P., Scharmer, C. O., Jaworski, J., & Flowers, B. S. (2005). *Presence: An exploration of profound change in people, organizations, and society.* New York, NY: Currency, Doubleday.

Senior, V., Marteau, T., & Peters, T. J. (1998). Will genetic testing for predisposition for disease result in fatalism? A qualitative study of parents' responses to neonatal screening for familial hypercholesterolaemia. *Social Science & Medicine, 48*, 1857–1860. doi:10.1016/S0277-9536(99)00099-4

Senjaya, S. (2003, August). *Development and validation of servant leadership behavior scale.* Paper presented at the Servant Leadership Research Roundtable, Regent University, Virginia Beach, VA.

Shakespeare, W. (2007). Hamlet. In Bates, J. (Ed.), *Complete works: By William Shakespeare.* New York, NY: Modern Library. (Original work published 1600)

Shamir, B., & Eilam, G. (2005). "What's your story?" A life-stories approach to authentic leadership development. *The Leadership Quarterly, 16*(3), 395–417. doi:10.1016/j.leaqua.2005.03.005

Sheeran, P. (2002). Intention-behavior relations: A conceptual and empirical review. *European Review of Social Psychology, 12*, 1–36. doi:10.1080/14792772143000003

Shelly, R. (2006). I was sick, and you looked after me: Pastoral leadership in ministering to the sick. In *Like a shepherd lead us* (pp. 71–94). Abilene, TX: Leafwood Publishers.

Shen, L., Wright, L., Flannery, D., Harris, T., & Condit, C. (2009). *Teaching the concept of gene-environment interaction to the lay public: Challenges, rewards, and limitations.* Unpublished manuscript, The University of Georgia.

Shen, L., Condit, C., & Wright, L. (2009). The psychometric property and validation of a fatalism scale. *Psychology & Health, 24*, 597–613. doi:10.1080/08870440801902535

Simon, H. A. (1955). A behavioral model of rational choice: Cowles Foundation Paper 98. *The Quarterly Journal of Economics, 69*, 99–118. doi:10.2307/1884852

Simon, H. A. (1957). *Administrative behavior: A study of decision making processes in administrative organizations* (2nd ed.). New York, NY: Free Press.

Simons, T. (2002). Behavioral integrity: The perceived alignment between managers' words and deeds as a research focus. *Organization Science, 13*(1), 18–35.

Simsek, Z., & Veiga, J. F. (2001). A primer on Internet organizational surveys. *Organizational Research Methods, 4*(3), 218–235. doi:10.1177/109442810143003

Skager, R.(1979).Self-directed learning and schooling: Identifying pertinent theories and illustrative research. *International Review of Education,25*,517–543.doi:10.1007/BF00598508

Skenes, R. E., & Honig, C. A.(2004).Pretest/posttest use of the life styles inventory for outcomes assessment of a professional master's in managerial leadership program. *Group & Organization Management,29*(2),171–200. doi:10.1177/1059601103262043

Skenes, R. E., & Honing, C. A.(2004).Pretest/posttest use of the life styles inventory for outcomes assessment of a professional master's in managerial leadership program. *Group & Organization Management,29*(2),171–200. doi:10.1177/1059601103262043

Slemming, C.(1942).*He leadeth me: Shepherd life in Palestine, Psalm 23*.Fort Washington, PA:CLC Publications.

Smith, A.(1986).The wealth of nations. InHeilbroner, R. L.(Ed.),*The essential Adam Smith*.New York, NY:W. W. Norton & Company.(Original work published 1776)

Smith, M. A., & Leigh, B.(1997).Virtual subjects: Using the Internet as an alternative source of subjects and research environment. *Behavior Research Methods, Instruments, & Computers,29*(4),496–505.doi:10.3758/BF03210601

Smith, M. E.(2002).Success rates for different types of organizational change. *Performance Improvement,41*(1),26–33.doi:10.1002/pfi.4140410107

Solomon, R. (1999). As cited by Dunn (2009, p. 105).*A better way to think about business: How personal integrity leads to corporate success*. New York, NY: Oxford University Press.

Sosik, J. J., Avolio, B. J., & Kahai, S. S.(1997).Effects of leadership style and anonymity on group potency and effectiveness in a group decision support system environment. *The Journal of Applied Psychology,82*,89–103. doi:10.1037/0021-9010.82.1.89

Sosik, J. J., Avolio, B. J., Kahai, S. S., & Jung, D. I.(1998). Computer-supported work group potency and effectiveness: The role of transformational leadership, anonymity, and task interdependence. *Computers in Human Behavior,14*,491–511.doi:10.1016/S0747-5632(98)00019-3

Spradley, J.(1979).*The ethnographic interview*.New York, NY:Holt, Rinehart & Winston.

Sproull, L. S.(1986).Using electronic mail for data-collection in organizational research. *Academy of Management Journal,29*(1),159–169.doi:10.2307/255867

SPSS. (2009).*SPSS graduate student(version 18.0)*. Nikiski, AK:Polar Consulting.

Stacey, R. D. (2003).*Strategic management and organizational dynamics: The challenge of complexity*. New York, NY: Prentice-Hall/Financial Times.

Stacey, R. D.(2001).*Complex responsive processes in organizations: Learning and knowledge creation*.London, UK:Routledge.

Stanton, J. M.(1998).An empirical assessment of data collection using the Internet. *Personnel Psychology,51*(3),709–725.doi:10.1111/j.1744-6570.1998.tb00259.x

Stanton, J. M., & Rogelberg, S. G.(2001).Using Internet/intranet web pages to collect organizational research data. *Organizational Research Methods,4*(3),200–217. doi:10.1177/109442810143002

Starratt, R. J.(2004).*Ethical leadership*.San Francisco, CA:Jossey-Bass.

Steel, P.(2007).The nature of procrastination: A meta-analytic and theoretical review of quintessential self-regulatory failure. *Psychological Bulletin,133*,65–94. doi:10.1037/0033-2909.133.1.65

Steel, P., Brothen, T., & Wambach, C.(2001).Procrastination and personality, performance, and mood. *Personality and Individual Differences,30*,95–106.doi:10.1016/S0191-8869(00)00013-1

Steel, P., & Konig, C. J.(2006).Integrating theories of motivation. *Academy of Management Review,31*,889–913. doi:10.5465/AMR.2006.22527462

Steinberg, R.(2006).Economic theories of nonprofit organizations. InPowell, W., & Steinberg, R.(Eds.),*The nonprofit sector: A research handbook*(1st ed., pp.117–139). New Haven, CT:Yale University Press.

Stevenson, G.(2006).The church goes to the movies: Standing at the intersection of the church and popular culture. In*Like a shepherd lead us*(pp.139–161).Abilene, TX:Leafwood Publishers.

Stoddard, A.(1995).*The art of possible: The path from perfectionism to balance and freedom*.New York, NY:William Morrow.

Stogdill, R. M. (1963).*Manual for the leadership behavior description questionnaire – Form XII*. Ohio State University, Fisher College of Business. Retrieved March 22, 2009, fromhttp://fisher.osu.edu/offices/fiscal/lbdq

Stogdill, R. M.(1950).Leadership, membership and organization. *Psychological Bulletin,47*,1–14.doi:10.1037/h0053857

Stogdill, R. M.(1963).*Manual for the leader behavior description questionnaire - Form XII*.Columbus, OH:Bureau of Business Research, Ohio State University.

Stogdill, R. M.(1965).*Managers, employees, organizations*.Columbus, OH:Ohio State University, Bureau of Business Research.

Stogdill, R. M.(1969).Validity of leader behavior descriptions. *Personnel Psychology,22*(2),153–158. doi:10.1111/j.1744-6570.1969.tb02298.x

Stogdill, R. M.(1974).*Handbook of leadership: A survey of theory and research*.New York, NY:The Free Press.

Stogdill, R. M., Goode, O. S., & Day, D. R.(1962).New leader behavior description subscales. *Journal of Psychology: Interdisciplinary and Applied,54*(2),259–269.doi:10.1080/00223980.1962.9713117

Stogdill, R. M., Goode, O. S., & Day, D. R.(1963a).The leader behavior of corporation presidents. *Personnel Psychology,16*(2),127–132.doi:10.1111/j.1744-6570.1963.tb01261.x

Stogdill, R. M., Goode, O. S., & Day, D. R.(1963b).The leader behavior of United States Senators. *Journal of Psychology: Interdisciplinary and Applied,56*(1),3–8.doi:10.1080/00223980.1963.9923691

Stogdill, R. M., Goode, O. S., & Day, D. R.(1964).The leader behavior of labor unions. *Personnel Psychology,17*(1),49–57.doi:10.1111/j.1744-6570.1964.tb00050.x

Stone, G., Russell, R., & Patterson, K.(2004).Transformational versus servant leadership: A difference in leader focus. *Leadership and Organization Development Journal,25*(4),349–361. Retrieved fromwww.emeraldinsight.com/0143-7739.htmdoi:10.1108/01437730410538671

Straughan, P. T., & Seow, A.(1998).Fatalism reconceptualized: A concept to predict health screening behavior. *Journal of Gender, Culture, and Health,3*,85–100. doi:10.1023/A:1023278230797

Strauss, A., & Corbin, J.(1998).*Basics of qualitative research: Techniques and procedures for developing grounded theory*(2nd ed.).Thousand Oaks, CA:Sage.

Streufert, S., Streufert, S., & Castore, C. H.(1968).Leadership in negotiations and the complexity of conceptual structure. *The Journal of Applied Psychology,52*(3),218–223. doi:10.1037/h0025852

Sugar, W., Martindale, T., & Crawley, F. E.(2007). One professor's face-to-face teaching strategies while becoming an online instructor. *The Quarterly Review of Distributed Education,8*,365–385.

Sullivan, H. S.(1953).*The interpersonal theory of psychiatry*.New York, NY:Norton.

Szumal, J. L., & Cooke, R. A.(2004).Increasing personal success and effectiveness: Thinking and behavioral styles at work. In Silberman, M., & Philips, P.(Eds.),*The 2004 training and performance sourcebook*.Princeton, NJ:Active Training.

Tappy, R.(1995).Psalm 23: Symbolism and structure. *Catholic Biblical Quarterly,57*(2),255–280.

Tashakkori, A., & Teddlie, C.(1998).*Mixed methodology: Combining quantitative and qualitative approaches*. Thousand Oaks, CA:Sage.

Tashakkori, A., & Teddlie, C.(2003b).The past and future of mixed methods research: From data triangulation to mixed model designs. InTashakkori, A., & Teddlie, C.(Eds.),*The handbook of mixed methods in social and behavioral research*(pp.671–701).Thousand Oaks, CA:Sage.

Tashakkori, A., & Teddlie, C.(Eds.). (2003a).*The handbook of mixed methods in social and behavioral research*. Thousand Oaks, CA:Sage.

Taylor, M., Crook, R., & Dropkin, S.(1961).Assessing emerging leadership behavior in small discussion groups. *Journal of Educational Psychology,52*(1),12–18. doi:10.1037/h0045144

Teddlie, C., & Tashakkori, A.(2003).Major issues and controversies in the use of mixed methods in the social and behavioral sciences. InTashakkori, A., & Teddlie, C.(Eds.),*The handbook of mixed methods in social and behavioral research*(pp.3–50).Thousand Oaks, CA:Sage.

Tepper, B. J., & Percy, P. M.(1994).Structural validity of the multifactor leadership questionnaire. *Educational and Psychological Measurement,54,*734–744. doi:10.1177/0013164494054003020

Thompson, B.(2004).*Exploratory and confirmatory facto analysis: Understanding concepts and applications.* Washington, DC:Sage.doi:10.1037/10694-000

Thompson, D.(1992).Beyond motivation: Nurse's participation and persistence in Baccalaureate programs. *Adult Education Quarterly,42,*94–105. doi:10.1177/0001848192042002003

Thompson, L. F., & Surface, E. A.(2007).Employee surveys administered online - Attitudes toward the medium, nonresponse, and data representativeness. *Organizational Research Methods,10*(2),241–261. doi:10.1177/1094428106/294696

Thompson, L. F., Surface, E. A., Martin, D. L., & Sanders, M. G.(2003).From paper to pixels: Moving personnel surveys to the Web. *Personnel Psychology,56*(1),197–227. doi:10.1111/j.1744-6570.2003.tb00149.x

Tice, D. M., & Baumeister, R. F.(1997).Longitudinal study of procrastination, performance, stress, and health: The cost and benefits of dawdling. *Psychological Science,8,*454–458.doi:10.1111/j.1467-9280.1997. tb00460.x

Tough, A.(1979).*The adult's learning project.*San Diego, CA:University Associates.

Tracy, L.(1987).Consideration and initiating structure: Are they basic dimensions of leader behavior? *Social Behavior and Personality,15*(1),21–33.doi:10.2224/ sbp.1987.15.1.21

Traüffer, H.(2008).*Towards an understanding of discernment: A twenty-first century model of decision-making.* (Dissertations and Theses database AAT 3325539).

Trevino, L. K., Butterfield, K. D., & McCabe, D. L.(1998).The ethical context in organizations: Influences on employee attitudes and behaviors. *Business Ethics Quarterly,8*(3),447–476.doi:10.2307/3857431

Triandis, H. C., Dunnette, M. D., & Hough, L. M.(1994). *Handbook of industrial and organizational psychology.* Palo Alto, CA:Consulting Psychologists Press.

Trice, H. M., & Beyer, J. M.(1993).*The cultures of work organizations.*Englewood Cliffs, NJ:Prentice Hall.

Tse, R. (2006). The leadership files: Dr. Bruce Winston of Regent University.*The Christian Post.* Retrieved July 2006, fromhttp://www.christianpost.com/article/20060110/13937.htm

Tucker, L. R.(1951).*A method of synthesis of factor analysis studies.*Princeton, NJ:ETS.

Turner, A. N.(1982).Consulting is more than giving advice. *Harvard Business Review,60*(5),120–129.

Uhl-Bien, M.(2006).Relational leadership theory: Exploring the social processes of leadership and organizing. *The Leadership Quarterly,17,*654–676.doi:10.1016/j. leaqua.2006.10.007

Uhl-Bien, M., & Maslyn, J.(2003).Reciprocity in manager-subordinate relationships: Components, configurations, and outcomes. *Journal of Management,29*(4),511–532.

United States Department of Labor. (2011).*U. S. Bureau of Labor Statistics.*Retrieved fromhttp://www.bls.gov/ news.release/tenure.nro.htm

US Department of Education, National Center for Education Statistics. (2008).*Distance education at degree-granting post secondary institutions 2006-2007.*

Vaill, P. B.(1996).*Learning as a way of being: Strategies for survival in a world of permanent white water.*San Francisco:Jossey-Bass.

Vehovar, V., Manfreda, K. L., & Batagelj, Z.(2001). Sensitivity of electronic commerce measurement to the survey instrument. *International Journal of Electronic Commerce,6*(1),31–51.

Verbeke, W., Volgering, M., & Hessells, M.(1998).Exploring the conceptual expansion within the field of organizational behavior: Organizational culture and organizational climate. *Journal of Management Studies,35*(3),303–330. doi:10.1111/1467-6486.00095

Vetter, N., Lewis, P., & Charny, M.(1991).Health, fatalism, and age in relation to lifestyle. *Health Visitor,64,*191–194.

Vroom, V.(1964).*Work and motivation.*New York, NY:John Wiley.

Vroom, V. H., & Yetton, P. W.(1973).*Leadership and decision making.*Pittsburgh, PA:University of Pittsburgh Press.

Wade, T. J.(1996).An examination of locus of control/ fatalism for black, whites, boys, and girls over a two year period of adolescence. *Social Behavior and Personality,24,*239–248.doi:10.2224/sbp.1996.24.3.239

Wagner, G.(1999).*Escape from church, Inc.: The return of the pastor-shepherd.*Grand Rapids, MI:Zondervan.

Wallace, L. (2009). Dragon hearts.*Flying,*March 2009, 40-47.

Walsh, W. M., & McGraw, J. A.(2002).*Essentials of family therapy: A structured summary of nine approaches*(2nd ed.).Denver, CO:Love.

Walther, J. P.(2002).Research ethics in internet-enabled research: Human subjects issues and methodological myopia. *Ethics and Information Technology,4*(3),205–216. doi:10.1023/A:1021368426115

Ware, M. E., Leak, G. K., & Perry, N. W.(1985).Life styles inventory: Evidence for its factorial validity. *Psychological Reports,56,*963–968.doi:10.2466/pr0.1985.56.3.963

Warshaw, P. R., & Davis, F. D.(1985).Disentangling behavioral intention and behavioral expectation. *Journal of Experimental Social Psychology,21,*213–218. doi:10.1016/0022-1031(85)90017-4

Watzlawick, P., Weakland, J., & Fisch, R.(1974).*Change: Principles of problem formation and problem resolution.* New York, NY:Norton.

Weber, M. (1947). As cited in Yukl (2006).*The theory of social and economic organizations.*

Weber, M.(1947).*The theory of social and economic organization.*New York, NY:Free Press.

Weick, K. E.(1969).*The social psychology of organizing.* Reading, MA:Addison-Wesley.

Weick, K. E.(1979).*The social psychology of organizing*(2nd ed.).Reading, MA:Addison-Wesley.

Weick, K. E., & Quinn, R. E.(1999).Organizational change and development. *Annual Review of Psychology,50,*361–386.doi:10.1146/annurev.psych.50.1.361

Weiner, R.(1972).Attribution theory, achievement motivation, and the educational process. *Review of Educational Research,42,*203–215.

Weinstein, N. D.(1982).Unrealistic optimism about susceptibility to health problems. *Journal of Behavioral Medicine,5,*441–460.doi:10.1007/BF00845372

West, G. R. B. (2009).*Expert, coercive, legitimate, referent, and reward power bases as moderating variables upon the relationships between service, humility, and shared vision with affective organizational commitment, and job satisfaction among members of the U.S. Navy.* Unpublished Doctoral dissertation, Regent University, Virginia Beach, VA.

Wheatley, M.(1999).*Leadership and the new science: Discovering order in a chaotic world.*San Francisco, CA:Berrett-Koehler Publishers, Inc.

Whittington, J. L., Goodwin, V. L., & Murray, B.(2004). Transformational leadership, goal difficulty, and job design: Independent and interactive effects on employee outcomes. *The Leadership Quarterly,15,*593–606. doi:10.1016/j.leaqua.2004.07.001

Whybray, R. N.(1965).*Wisdom in Proverbs.*London, UK:SCM Press Ltd.

Whybray, R. N.(1972).*The book of Proverbs: The Cambridge Bible commentary.*New York, NY:Cambridge University Press.

Williston, B.(2006).Blaming agents in moral dilemmas. *Ethical Theory and Moral Practice,9,*536–576. doi:10.1007/s10677-006-9036-4

Wilson, J. R.(1998).*Gospel virtues*.Downers Grove, IL:Inter-Varsity Press.

Winne, P. H.(1995).Inherent details in self-regulated learning. *Educational Psychologist,30*(4),173–187. doi:10.1207/s15326985ep3004_2

Winner, W. D. (2008).*The measurement of sternness in an adult self-directed leader*(Regent University). In publication.

Winston, B. E., & Patterson, K. (2005).*An integrative definition of leadership*.Retrieved May 31, 2009, fromhttp://www.regent.edu/acad/global/publications/working/integrativedefinition.pdf

Winston, B.(2002).*Be a leader for god's sake*.Virginia Beach, VA:Regent University.

Winston, B. E.(2002).*Be a leader for God's sake: From values to behaviors*.Virginia Beach, VA:School of Leadership Studies, Regent University.

Winston, B., & Patterson, K.(2006).An integrative definition of leadership. *International Journal of Leadership Studies,1*(2),6–66.

Witta, E. L., & Gupton, S. L. (1999).*Crossvalidation and confirmatory factor analysis of the 30-item leadership behavior description questionnaire: Implications for use by graduate students*. Paper presented at the Annual Meeting of the American Educational Research Association 1999 Conference, 19-23 April, 1999.

Wittchen, M., Schlereth, D., & Hertel, G.(2007).Social indispensability in spite of temporal and spatial separation: Motivation gains in a sequential task during anonymous cooperation on the Internet. *International Journal of Internet Science,2*,12–27.

Wittman, H., Morote, E., & Kelly, T. (2007). Faculty conceptions and misconceptions about hybrid education. In C. Crawford (Ed.),*Proceedings of Society for Information Technology and Teacher Education International Conference*(pp. 1168-1173). Chesapeake, VA: AACE.

Wong, Y. Y., Maher, T. E., & Lee, G.(1998).The strategy of an ancient warrior: An inspiration for international managers. *Multinational Business Review,6*(1),83.

Wood, D.(1996).Shepherd. In*The new Bible dictionary*(3rd ed.,*Vol. 3*).Grand Rapids, MI:Intervarsity Press.

Wray, D.(2006).Soul care and the heart of a shepherd. In*Like a shepherd lead us*(pp.51–70).Abilene, TX:Leafwood Publishers.

Wu, W.-Y., Chou, C. H., & Wu, Y.-J. (2004). A study of strategy implementation as expressed through Sun Tzu's principles of war.*Industrial Management + Data Systems, 104*(5/6), 396.

Yammarino, F. J., Spangler, W. D., & Bass, B. M.(1993). Transformational leadership and performance: A longitudinal investigation. *The Leadership Quarterly,4*,81–108. doi:10.1016/1048-9843(93)90005-E

Young, S.(2006, Winter).Jesus as shepherd leader. *Denver Seminary Magazine,2*(4),5–6.

Yukl, G.(2002).*Leadership in organizations*(5th ed.).New Jersey:Prentice Hall.

Yukl, G.(2006).*Leadership in organizations*.Upper Saddle River, NJ:Pearson Prentice Hall.

Yukl, G. A., & Van Fleet, D. D.(1990).Theory and research on leadership in organizations. In Dunnette, M. D., & Hough, L. M.(Eds.),*Handbook of industrial and organizational psychology*.Palo Alto, CA:Consulting Psychologists Press.

Yun, G. W., & Trumbo, C. W.(2000).Comparative response to a survey executed by post, e-mail, & web form.*Journal of Computer-Mediated Communication,6*(1).

Zhang, D., & Zhou, L.(2003).Enhancing e-learning with interactive media. *Information Resources Management Journal,16*,1–14.doi:10.4018/irmj.2003100101

Zhang, Y.(2000).Using the Internet for survey research: A case study. *Journal of the American Society for Information Science American Society for Information Science,51*(1),57–68.doi:10.1002/(SICI)1097-4571(2000)51:1<57::AID-ASI9>3.0.CO;2-W

Zimbardo, P.(2007).*The Lucifer effect: Understanding how good people turn evil*.New York, NY:Random House.

Zimmerman, B. J.(1994).Dimensions of academic self-regulation: A conceptual framework for education. In Schunk, D. H., & Zimmerman, B. J.(Eds.),*Self-regulation of learning and performance: Issues and educational application*.Mahwah, NJ:Erlbaum.

About the Contributors

Mihai C. Bocarnea, Ph.D., joined Regent University in 1995 and currently serves as an Associate Professor in the School of Global Leadership & Entrepreneurship. He is an expert in the areas of communication, research methods, quantitative analysis, and statistics. His research interests include organizational communication, cross-cultural leadership, servant leadership, organizational change and pedagogy of online learning. Dr. Bocarnea has also served as research consultant for various organizations in the U.S. and overseas.

Jason D. Baker is a Professor of Education at Regent University where he serves as the advisor of the distance education cognate in the Doctor of Education program. His research interests include faculty and student perspectives toward online learning, social dynamics in the online classroom, and models of effective online learning. He has authored and edited multiple books, chapters, and articles in the area of online learning and educational technology. In addition, he has consulted with numerous organizations regarding the development and management of developing online learning programs. He holds a Ph.D. in Communication from Regent University, an M.A. in Educational Technology Leadership from The George Washington University, and a B.S. in Electrical Engineering from Bucknell University.

Rodney A. Reynolds is Director of Educational Effectiveness and Institutional Research at California Lutheran University. He received his Ph.D. degree in Communication from Michigan State University. He has held tenured/senior positions at a number of universities. When possible, Dr. Reynolds teaches courses on Research Methods, Persuasion, and Interpersonal Relationships. His research interests include measurement, social influence, message processing, and ending conversations.

* * *

Audrey Barrett received her degree in Leadership Studies with a special emphasis on Nonprofit Organizational Management from the University of San Diego in May 2008. She was nominated for and received the William P. Foster Outstanding Dissertation Award for her work to develop the Nonprofit Ethics Survey. Dr. Barrett worked as a Doctoral Research Assistant for the Institute for Nonprofit Education and Research while completing her degree and represents one of the first graduates nationally with a doctoral degree focusing on Third Sector studies. Dr. Barrett currently serves as part-time faculty at various institutions of higher education and maintains a private practice as a licensed clinical social worker. Dr. Barrett is married to her husband Kevin and together they have two sons.

Benjamin J. Bates (PhD, Michigan) is a Professor in the School of Journalism & Electronic Media and Adjunct Professor in the School of Information Sciences at the University of Tennessee, Knoxville. His research focuses on the development of media and information systems, media and information economics and policy, and the changing nature of media markets and values. This includes more than 25 years of research on Internet issues and topics. He's taught research methods at the undergraduate, Master's and Doctoral levels, was a founding board member of the Association of Internet Researchers, and has served on IRBs at two universities.

Corné J. Bekker, D. Litt. et Phil joined Regent University in 2005. He previously served as the Associate Dean for Academics for a Bible College in Johannesburg, South Africa and now as a Professor of Biblical and Ecclesial Leadership for the School of Global Leadership & Entrepreneurship and as chair of the Department of Biblical Studies and Christian Ministry in the School of Undergraduate Studies at Regent University. He is the editor of the Journal of Biblical Perspectives in Leadership (JBPL) and the co-editor of Inner Resources for Leaders (IRL).

Ben Birch is a Ph.D. student in the School of Information Sciences at the University of Tennessee, Knoxville, and a Research Assistant in the NSF-funded DataONE (www.dataone.org) project. His current research interest focuses on the emerging role of the data manager in the world of data-intensive science. He holds a Bachelor's degree in Mechanical Engineering from the Georgia Institute of Technology, and worked for a number of years as a Licensed Professional Engineer (Virginia). Returning to school, he then earned a Master's degree in Computer Science and a Master's degree in Information Sciences, both from the University of Tennessee, Knoxville.

Yael Brender-Ilan is a Professor of Management at Ariel University Center. She specializes in OB and Human Resource Management. Her research focuses on personnel selection, HR procedural and distributive justice, employee compensation and alienation, and the ethics of HR practices and procedures. She is currently the Chair of the Department of Economics and Business Administration at Ariel University Center.

Orly Calderon, Psy.D., is a full time faculty member at Long Island University, teaching courses in research design, assessment and evaluation, and psychopathology. Dr. Calderon earned her B.A. in Psychology and Education from Long Island University, her M.A. in Developmental Psychology from Teachers College, Columbia University and her Psy.D. in school and Community Psychology from Hofstra University. Dr. Calderon specializes in program evaluation and outcome assessment, and her work has been presented and published in various peer-reviewed forums and journals. She has been an active member of the Long Island University Web Learning Project from its inception, and has been involved in the design and implementation of the outcome assessment program of blended learning at the university. In 2010, she has been appointed the university's Coordinator of Blended and Online Learning Outcome Assessment.

Celeste Condit (Ph.D., University of Iowa, 1982) is a Distinguished Research Professor at University of Georgia. She is currently exploring the relationship of biological and symbolic facets of human being in producing human experience and human social structures. She has recently studied public understanding of genetics and public communication about genetics, with emphasis in gene-environment interaction and "race." She uses the "Reacting to the Past" role-playing approach in teaching Communication in Government and Communication and Social Movements. She is currently working on a book manuscript on pathos.

Gail Derrick received her Doctor of Education Degree in Higher Education Administration in May 2001 from The George Washington University, Washington, D.C. She earned her Master's of Arts in Education and Human Development with an endorsement in Secondary Administration also from The George Washington University, and a Bachelor of Arts in Secondary Education with an endorsement in General Science and Pre-Algebra from Virginia Wesleyan College, Norfolk, Virginia in 1982. Dr. Derrick's previous employment was with Troy State University, Atlantic Region, as the Associate Regional Director for Academic Affairs. Most of her career was with the Virginia Beach City Public Schools including positions as the Administrative Coordinator in the Department of Curriculum and Instruction, Science Instructional Coordinator for the middle school science program, and Mathematics/Science Teacher at Independence Middle School. In addition, she has served as an Academic Reviewer for the Virginia Department of Education for public schools accredited with warning since 1999, and a freelance item writer for the development of assessments in the area of science. Dr. Derrick is a Senior Associate for Human Resource Development Enterprises, Washington D.C., a professional services firm that helps organizations leverage learning and development activities by focusing on the autonomous learning that occurs naturally within organizations.

Dail Fields (Ph.D., Georgia Institute of Technology, 1994) serves as a Professor in the Regent University PhD program in Organizational Leadership. He served as founding Editor of the *International Journal of Leadership Studies*, a peer-reviewed research journal from 2005-2011. He was a Fulbright Scholar in Lithuania 2006-2007. Dr. Fields is the author of "Taking the Measure of Work," a reference guide to measurement in organizations published by Sage Publications in English and Chinese. He has published research studies in the *Academy of Management Journal, Journal of Management, Health Services Research, Group and Organization Studies, Journal of Occupational and Organizational Psychology*, and *Leadership*. Dr. Fields continuing research interests include leadership assessment within and across cultures, management and leadership in healthcare, and leadership development.

Fred J. Galloway is currently Associate Professor in the School of Leadership and Education Sciences at the Education at the University of San Diego, where he has also served as Associate Dean and Director of strategic programs. Prior to joining the university faculty, he was Project Director for the national Direct Student Loan Evaluation project at Macro International, as well as the director of federal policy analysis at the American Council on Education, where he represented the interests of the higher education community before the executive and legislative branches of the federal government. Dr. Galloway received his Bachelor's and Master's degrees from the University of California, San Diego in Economics, and his Doctoral degree in the Economics of Education from Harvard University. His research interests include higher education policy, the economics of education, and econometrics, and he has published numerous articles, book chapters, and policy reports in these areas.

Jeff Hale (Ph.D., Regent University, 2010) is co-owner of WellSpirit Consulting Group, Inc. in the Greater Chicago Area. Dr. Hale has 19 years of cross-cultural leadership experience including living and working for 13 years in French-speaking West Africa. He has published research studies in *Leadership* and the *International Journal of Organizational Theory and Behavior*. Dr. Hale's continuing research interests include servant leadership within and across cultures, measures of transformational ministry outcomes, and applications of hermeneutic phenomenological philosophy to organizational behavior.

Tobias Heilmann is an Assistant Professor at the Division of Social and Business Psychology at the University of Zurich, Switzerland. He leads the corporate image and corporate leadership group at the University of Zurich. He is also a Military Academy at ETH Zurich faculty, Switzerland. He holds a PhD from the University of Zurich, Switzerland. His expertise is in leadership with a focus on transformational and transaction leadership as well as on laissez-faire leadership with topics related to followers' personality, leadership processes, and outcomes.

Paul Kaak teaches numerous courses in leadership for both the MA in Leadership and the Leadership Minor at Azusa Pacific University. From 2006-2010 he was Assistant Director of the Noel Academy for Strength-Based Leadership and Education. Dr. Kaak now serves the University as a Faculty Development Fellow in the Office of Faith Integration.

John Kilroy, PhD, serves as Dean and Associate Professor at Fresno Pacific University School of Business in Fresno, California. Dr. Kilroy received his Doctorate in Organizational Leadership from Regent University School of Global Leadership and Entrepreneurship. Prior to entering Higher Education his previous experience includes the Aerospace industry, where served as Program Manager within the Advance Research and Design Technology for commercial and government research programs, and the Finance Industry as Training Director. His research interest includes the effects of mergers on surviving employees, the impact of leaders' values on employee commitment to the leader, employee performance, and organizations success. He serves as a consultant on team development, strategic planning including succession planning, and organizational change.

Dan Lawson holds multiple advanced degrees, including a Ph.D. in Organizational Leadership. As a noted author with publications in the field of leadership and ethics, he has identified a "Global Leadership Ethic" for application in corporate and non-profit organizations. He has also developed a new construct for identifying authentic leader integrity. He is recognized as a motivational speaker and well known for his seminars on leadership, assessment, ethics, integrity, and leadership development. Dr. Lawson is a Dean at Ashland University where he teaches classes on the undergraduate, Masters, and Doctoral level on such subjects as leadership, management, business ethics, organizational theory, and organizational behavior. He also oversees the Leadership Development Academy and serves as a consultant for leadership development, leadership assessment, team building, and ethics training. Dan has been married to Lynne for more than 32 years. They have two adult children, Alesia and David.

J. Alan Marshall is a Colonel in the United States Air Force. He graduated from the United States Air Force Academy in 1987 with Honors and a double major in Astronautical Engineering and Mathematics. He holds a Ph.D. in Organizational Leadership from Regent University, a Master of Science Degree in Applied Mathematics from the University of Washington, and a Master of Aeronautical Science Degree from Embry-Riddle Aeronautical University. He served in various Air Force assignments, including serving as a U-2 pilot and commander of a combat flying squadron supporting Operations Iraqi Freedom and Enduring Freedom. Colonel Marshall's major awards include: U-2 Pilot Distinguished Graduate, 8th Air Force Chief of Safety of the Year, 8th Air Force Individual Safety Award, and 380th Air Expeditionary Wing, Daedalian Exceptional Pilot of the Year Award. Colonel Marshall is married to Kendra, his wife of 22 years, and they have two boys: Nolan and Joshua.

Sharon E. Norris is an Assistant Professor of Business and Director of Graduate Studies, MBA Programs with the Gainey School of Business at Spring Arbor University. She holds a Ph.D. in Organizational Leadership with a major in Human Resource Development from Regent University's School of Global Leadership and Entrepreneurship. Her recent publications include those on topics of human resource development, leadership development, and impression management.

Tracy H. Porter is a member of the faculty of Cleveland State University where she holds the position of College Lecturer within the Department of Management and Labor Relations. Dr. Porter has extensive experience in the higher education field and has taught numerous management courses. Prior to becoming a Professor, she was a health care administrator and a management consultant. Dr. Porter received her PhD in Organizational Leadership from Regent University with a concentration in human resource development. Her current research interests are in leadership, individual differences in the leader-follower relationship, and spirituality in the workplace.

Ulf-Dietrich Reips is a tenured IKERBASQUE Research Professor at University of Deusto in Bilbao, Spain, where he leads the iScience group (http://iscience.deusto.es/). He holds a PhD and the *venia legendi* from the University of Tübingen, Germany. Prior to taking his current position in Spain, he worked for the University of Zurich, Switzerland. His main research is on Internet-based research methodologies and the psychology of the Internet. In 1994 Reips founded the Web Experimental Psychology Lab, the first laboratory for conducting real experiments on the World Wide Web, and provides many Web services for researchers and students via his iScience Server at http://iscience.eu. He has taught in several European countries as well as in the US (e.g. for the National Science Foundation and the American Psychological Association). Reips was elected the first non-US American President of the Society for Computers in Psychology and is founding editor of the *International Journal of Internet Science* (http://ijis.net). Many of his ca. 100 publications (in English, German, and Spanish, see http://personalwebpages.deusto.es/reips/pubs/publications.html) are widely cited in the field.

Rushton (Rusty) S. Ricketson is currently Associate Professor of Leadership and Chair of the Leadership Department at Luther Rice Seminary & University. He also serves as the President of Foundation of the Faith, Inc., a ministry committed to developing followers of Christ and embedding follower-first organizational cultures in organizations throughout the United States and developing countries. Dr. Ricketson has a BS in Education from the University of Georgia, a MDIV from Southwestern Baptist

Theological Seminary, a DMIN from Reformed Theological Seminary, and a PhD in Organizational Leadership with a major in Human Resource Development from Regent University. He is the author of two books, *Forgive and... Forgive Again*, and *Follower-first: Rethinking Leading in the Church.* He is married to Sharon and has two adult children.

Rody Rodriguez M.A. is currently a Doctoral student at the University of Utah. His academic career has taking him all over the Western United States. Rody received his B.A. in Communication with an emphasis on Mass Communication from California State University San Bernardino. Afterwards, Rody and his wife wisped off to the Hawaiian Islands for graduate school where he completed his M.A. in Communication from Hawaii Pacific University. His Master's thesis focused on examining the apocalypse in popular art. His present studies focus on New Media. In particular, his research has examined how culture pertains to video games, mainly MMOs.

Philip Salem (Ph. D., University of Denver) is Professor of Communication Studies at Texas State University. His publications include work on organizational communication, interpersonal communication, communication and technology, research methods, and communication theory. He has been investigating communication networks since the 1970s. He has received awards for Mahis work on communication and technology, and he was the third person to receive the Outstanding Member Award from the Organizational Communication Division of the International Communication Association. He wrote *The Complexity of Human Communication*, a book about nonlinear communication processes published by Hampton Press. He received a Fulbright Senior Specialist fellowship funding collaborative international scholarship through 2012.

Lijiang Shen (Ph.D., University of Wisconsin-Madison, 2005) is an Associate Professor in the Department of Communication Studies at the University of Georgia. His primary area of research considers the impact of message features and audience characteristics in persuasive health communication, message processing and the process of persuasion/resistance to persuasion; and quantitative research methods in communication. His research has been published in major communication and related journals.

Jamie Swalm was born and raised in New Jersey. He holds a Bachelor's of Business Administration Degree from the University of Delaware, a Master's of Divinity Degree from Westminster Theological Seminary in Philadelphia, Pennsylvania, and a Ph.D. in Organizational Leadership from Regent University in Virginia Beach, Virginia. Jamie started his career in the financial world at a large bank in Baltimore, Maryland. Following his time in the banking field, Jamie pursued theological training and entered the ministry. His ministry experience includes being a Youth Pastor, an Associate Pastor, a Senior Pastor, and a church planter. Currently Jamie serves as the Senior Pastor of the Red Lion Evangelical Free Church in Delaware. Jamie is married to his college sweetheart, Cathy. Together they have four children and live in Delaware.

Hazel Traüffer, Ph.D., currently an Organizational and Leadership consultant, brings over 10 years of operational and consulting experience in the Learning and Development field, helping clients, in both the private and public sectors, create environments conducive to autonomous learning, change implementation, and improved performance. In academia, Dr. Traüffer serves as Academic Quality Reviewer for doctoral dissertations, as well as a Professor in areas of Management in a Global Economy, Leadership Development, and Research Methodology. Her research interest includes leadership and organizational decision-making, women & leadership, spirituality & leadership, and cultural intelligence & leadership and has published articles in peer-reviewed journals. Dr. Traüffer holds a Ph.D. in Organizational Leadership, from Regent University, Virginia Beach, VA.

Gideon Vinitzky (Oct. 23, 1964 - Oct. 30, 2010) was a professor of Marketing at Ariel University Center. He specialized in interactive marketing, specifically focusing on internet marketing, virtual shopping, on-line interfaces, on-line decision making and on-line consumer experience. He developed and managed on-line web-survey software for the use of researchers who choose to put their questionnaires on-line and collect data via the internet.

Michael M. Whyte, Ph.D., is currently the Provost Emeritus and a Professor at Azusa Pacific University. As Provost from 2002 to 2010, Whyte led six schools, one college, and 400 fulltime and 700 adjunct faculty; supervised enrollment management, academic services, and seven regional campuses. With over 12 years of accreditation experience, he has also served as a Western Association of Schools and Colleges (WASC) Commissioner since 2006. Whyte's experience also includes: a B.S. in International Affairs/American Politics at the USAF Academy, Colorado Springs, Colorado in 1978, and a M.S. and Ph.D. in Education from the University of Southern California in 1982 and 1990. Whyte was Senior Associate Professor (Tenure) at the USAF Academy from1986-1995. In 1995, he was a National Defense Fellow and Visiting Professor at Howard University, and was a Professor at Northern Arizona University from 1996-1999.

W. David Winner currently teaches at Azusa Pacific Online University, Liberty Seminary, Northampton Community College and Regent University, School of Undergraduate Studies. As a former pastor with 20 years of experience serving in three churches working with teenage students, college students, young adults, and families, Dr. Winner brings a depth of practical application and real world experiences to his teaching. Dr. Winner has a BA in Youth Ministry from Eastern University, a MDIV from Palmer Theological Seminary and a PhD in Organizational Leadership with a major in Human Resource Development from Regent University. He is married to Dena and has three great kids.

Bruce E. Winston, PhD, serves as both Dean and Associate Professor of Leadership at Regent University's School of Global Leadership and Entrepreneurship in Virginia Beach, Virginia. Dr. Winston teaches, trains, and consults in the areas of leadership and organizational development as well as university administration and strategic foresight. In addition, he has 13 years of experience leading organizations in the commercial printing industry and 19 years of experience leading academic units at Regent University. Dr. Winston has lectured and consulted in the United States as well as Canada, Europe, and South Africa. He also speaks and teaches in other areas including communication, quality improvement, and marketing.

Index